D1523401

Euripides and the Tragic Tradition

WISCONSIN STUDIES IN CLASSICS
General Editors
BARBARA HUGHES FOWLER *and* WARREN G. MOON

E. A. THOMPSON
Romans and Barbarians: The Decline of the Western Empire

JENNIFER TOLBERT ROBERTS
Accountability in Athenian Government

H. I. MARROU
A History of Education in Antiquity
Histoire de l'Education dans l'Antiquité, translated by George Lamb
(originally published in English by Sheed and Ward, 1956)

ERIKA SIMON
Festivals of Attica: An Archaeological Commentary

G. MICHAEL WOLOCH
Roman Cities: Les villes romaines by Pierre Grimal, translated
and edited by G. Michael Woloch, together with
A Descriptive Catalogue of Roman Cities
by G. Michael Woloch

WARREN G. MOON, *editor*
Ancient Greek Art and Iconography

KATHERINE DOHAN MORROW
Greek Footwear and the Dating of Sculpture

JOHN KEVIN NEWMAN
The Classical Epic Tradition

JEANNY VORYS CANBY, EDITH PORADA, BRUNILDE SISMONDO RIDGWAY,
and TAMARA STECH, *editors*
Ancient Anatolia: Aspects of Change and Cultural Development

Euripides
and the
Tragic Tradition

Ann Norris Michelini

The University of Wisconsin Press

Published 1987

The University of Wisconsin Press
114 North Murray Street
Madison, Wisconsin 53715

The University of Wisconsin Press, Ltd.
1 Gower Street
London WC1E 6HA, England

First printing

Printed in the United States of America

Library of Congress Cataloging-in-Publication Data
Michelini, Ann N.
Euripides and the tragic tradition.
(Wisconsin studies in classics)
Bibliography: pp. 338–373.
Includes index.
1. Euripides—Criticism and interpretation.
2. Mythology, Greek, in literature. 3. Tragic,
The, in literature. 4. Tragedy. I. Title.
II. Series.
PA3978.M5   1987   882′.01   86–40057
ISBN 0–299–10760–4

ἄνω ποταμῶν ἱερῶν χωροῦσι παγαί
καὶ δίκα καὶ πάντα πάλιν στρέφεται

Upwards go the springs of the sacred rivers,
and justice and all things are turning backward.

For K. J. G.

τὰν δ’ ἐμὰν εὔκλειαν ἔχειν βιοτὰν
στρέψουσι φᾶμαι·
ἔρχεται τιμὰ γυναικείῳ γένει

The story will turn, so that my life will have glory.
Honor is coming to the race of women.

Contents

ix

Contents   xi

Preface

This book is written for two audiences—classical scholars and nonspecialists interested in Euripides; and each group will bring very different sets of baggage to the reading. The former come first, since it is most important to me that what I have to say should enter the debate in my field and, if possible, help to change the terms of that debate. But it is also important to me that, among the many non-classicists who are fascinated by the Greek world and its literature, some few should have the tenacity to read this book. Our view of Euripides is central to our view of the Greek fifth century, as well as to the function that classical studies serve and have served in modern culture. Even the most sophisticated nonspecialists are likely to imbibe at second hand a limited and outmoded image of the classical world, unless they are placed in a position to analyze the presuppositions on which that image is based.

I begin with the postenlightenment period in Germany, showing how and why the particular view of this artist developed then remained influential and persistent for more than a century, both inside Germany and elsewhere. The positivist tendency, particularly in modern British and American classical scholarship, encourages the view that ''the history of classical scholarship'' is a separate field of study, which may be mined by the diligent in this late day, when textual criticism and other traditional disciplines are yielding diminishing returns. I do not share this view. The history of scholarship, like other history, is a means of assimilating the past and making it usable, so that the value of such a study is largely determined by its relation to current classical scholarship. In the case of Euripidean studies, an understanding of the work of the Schlegels or A. W. Verrall is prerequisite to any new approach.

The modern history of Euripidean criticism leads inevitably to Sophokles, the artist who has embodied the classic in our era; and I have tried to show that the antithesis between these two authors has roots in the Hellenic past as far back as the fifth century itself. Euripides is an artist who deals in paradox, and his critics probably cannot avoid dealing in it too. One of the simpler paradoxes underlies my approach: in order to see Euripides for himself rather than through a Sophoclean lens, Euripides must be seen in contrast to, over against his rival. This Euripidean focus necessarily produces a somewhat flattened view of Sophokles; but I do not think that these distortions either vitiate my account of Euripides or falsify his predecessor. On the one hand, a number of detailed and perceptive treatments of Sophoclean drama have been produced recently, and they will provide a sufficient corrective to any limitations of viewpoint in this book; and, on the other, seeing Sophoclean plays in the context of a rival's different approach may help to dispel some of the mystification that accumulates around works that are seen as universal, and therefore ahistorical, masterpieces.

In Chapters 2 and 3 I have tried to show how Euripides was viewed in his own era, and thus to indicate his position as adversary to social and literary norms, a position that rather neatly inverts the social role of Sophokles and the literary forms of Sophoclean drama. Chapters 4 and 5 attempt to identify the traits common to Euripidean drama as a whole. This is a particularly valuable exercise to perform for Euripides, whose use of irregular dramatic forms and whose adeptness at variation has obscured what the plays have in common and has encouraged critics to divide the oeuvre into several incommensurable classes, carrying such labels as "romances," "political plays," "melodramas," and "true tragedies."

The second half of the book puts into practice the principles developed in the first half, in analyses of four plays. I have preferred to treat a few plays at some length, rather than to attempt to say something about every play. In a day when whole books may be devoted to a single play, while the articles published in most classical periodicals are forced by requirements of length to concentrate on a single scholarly point or critical detail, it has become difficult to combine detailed analysis with a consideration of the plays as literary units, let alone with a consideration of their relation to each other. But close analysis is a tedious exercise, if it serves no broader view, while generalizations about Euripidean style are useful only if they help in the interpretation of individual plays.

I have chosen a group of plays that cover a wide range of the effects available to Euripidean theater. *Hekabe*, a neglected masterpiece of black drama, is a valuable example of the Euripidean use of perversion and shock. *Elektra*, because it invites comparison with Sophoclean and Aeschylean versions, helps to reveal the relation of Euripidean drama to its background in literary tradition. *Herakles*, a play that conforms to tragic norms more closely than do other Euripidean plays, also challenges those norms more violently than others, while offering an extreme example—though all Euripidean examples tend to extremes—of formalist technique.

Hippolytos, one of the most-loved and most-studied of Euripidean plays, contrasts in several aspects with the rest of the oeuvre. I have wanted to stress the qualities that Euripidean plays share, and perhaps the most striking of these qualities is a critical approach to tradition. A play that comes close to being acceptable on traditional terms therefore offers an excellent foil to the rest. Other famous and favored plays, such as *Medeia* and *Bakchai*, will, I hope, find a place in the general scheme of interpretation proposed here. One play, both a traditional favorite and a focus of much disputation,

Alkestis, has been relegated to an Appendix (B). Because of the play's historical role as a shibboleth of Euripidean criticism, it demands attention; but a number of excellent modern interpretations have made a full critical analysis unnecessary.

I am anxious to dodge the ultimate pitfall waiting for the Euripidean critic, the charge of fostering a secret dislike for the author. But it is unlikely that I will succeed.[1] I view Euripides as an ironist; and the assumption is easy to make that, once we take this view, we will not be able in our heart of hearts to like and accept his work. This assumption is correct: Euripidean work is designed to be unlovable and the "implied author" of these plays makes a similar impression. But I would argue that we do not have to revere or love the plays—or the imaginary figure of their author—in order to acknowledge the fascination of Euripidean theater, or its power to illuminate. For myself, as a woman and a feminist, I know enough of secondariness, of *ressentiment,* and of rebellion to appreciate the value—and the complex significance—of refusal and negation. To explore traditional categories of thought, custom, and language is a practice as constructive as it is subversive.

In the preparation of this book I must acknowledge the support of the University of Cincinnati, and the patience of The University of Wisconsin Press, which provided me with a particularly clever and conscientious editor, Susan Tarcov. I also received help from Jim Mayer at the Press. Invaluable support and advice at crucial points in the writing of this book came from Prof. Kathryn Gutzwiller, to whom this book is dedicated. Help with the manuscript has come from Katerina Weiss, Mary Lou Bradeen, Lily Philippos, Judy Mills, and Dick Michelini. Prof. Judson Harward and Michael Lennon provided guidance in using the Pixel computer system and generously contributed their time to help me with various difficulties.

---

1. As a recent example, see Hans Strohm (1981, 136), who in rejecting the critical view of Karl Reinhardt, argues that, when R. called Euripides a nihilist, he, like Nietzsche before him, was merely revealing a dislike of Euripidean art.

A NOTE ABOUT REFERENCES

References in the notes contain only author's name and the date of the work; a full bibliographical reference can be found in the Reference List at the end of the book.

The text of Euripidean plays quoted in this book derives from various editions. Except where otherwise noted, for *Hekabe,* quotations derive from the edition of S. Daitz (1973); for *Elektra* and *Herakles,* from the Oxford edition of J. Diggle (1981.2); and for *Hippolytos,* from the edition of W. S. Barrett (1964). The text used for references to all other Euripidean plays is that of the Oxford edition. Unfortunately, I was unable to use the Diggle edition of the first volume in preparing this book; the text of plays (other than *Hekabe* and *Hippolytos*) in that volume and in the third will therefore be that of the old edition of Gilbert Murray.

Abbreviations of classical works will generally be those of the *OCD,* except in the case of Euripidean plays, for which the following abbreviations will be used:

Alkestis	Alk	Iphigeneia Among	
Andromache	Andr	the Taurians	IT
Bakchai	Ba	Iphigeneia	
Elektra	El	at Aulis	IA
Hekabe	Hek	Medeia	Med
Helene	Hel	Orestes	Or
Herakleidai	Hkld	Phoinissai	Phoin
Herakles	Her	Suppliants	Suppl
Hippolytos	Hipp	Troiades	Tro
Ion	Ion		

Transliterations of Greek names follow a system that should not seem strange to Europeans, but that often makes these names look unfamiliar to English-speaking readers. To clear up any confusion, names listed in the index are accompanied by a traditional English version. Most Greek words in the body of the text are transliterated, for the benefit of those who do not read Greek; and these words are also glossed in the index.

Part I

Toward Interpretation

1

A History of
Euripidean Interpretation

I. Euripides Dethroned and Rehabilitated: The First Stage

I.A. CLASSICISM AND THE NINETEENTH-CENTURY VIEW OF EURIPIDES

Many contradictory views on Euripides have been expressed in the past. It seems to me necessary to treat these previous views in some greater detail, if only to avoid adding another to an endless series of antinomical positions. An understanding of the central points of controversy and their history is a precondition, both to any effective analysis of contemporary views on this author and to any progress beyond the old controversies. In the two centuries that followed the first modern criticism and analysis of Euripides, scholarly progress on some fronts was offset by a circular tendency in the general view of this artist. Decade after decade, scholars who intended to avoid the errors of their predecessors ended by repeating not only the methods but even the catchwords of the traditional approach. It is not by accident that the single most influential scholar to write on Euripides was one whose thesis had a strong flavor of absurdity and paradox. Such an anomaly cannot be dismissed; it must be understood.

The rediscovery of classical literature at the turn of the nineteenth century was associated with the popularizing work of such figures as Winckelmann in fine art and the Schlegels in literature. Their work was significant, not only because of its impact on the general public who were to be the consumers of classical education, but also because of its enduring effect on the scholars who would interpret Greek culture to generations of students. The classical exemplars were also intended to inspire modern literary work that would possess the same vitality and the same importance as the Greek masterpieces.[1] While the poet Schiller argued for a distinction between ancient and modern styles, with the implication that modern poetry possessed its own special qualities,[2] in Friedrich Schlegel's opposing Classicist view,[3] modern work was the result of a steady degeneration. Both Friedrich and his brother, A. W. Schlegel,[4] argued that Greek poetry was the standard against which modern poets should measure their work.[5] Winckelmann's famous catchword for the classic quality of Greek art, "noble simplicity and quiet greatness,"[6] is reflected in the Schlegels' emphasis on the work of art as an organic whole, in which each part is subordinated to a central conception that lends meaning to every aspect of the work. F. Schlegel claimed that classical literature possesses an "inner agreement and completion" that produces a sensation of "peace and satisfaction" in its audience,[7] while modern art confuses genre barriers and strives constantly to express the new, piquant, and

1. See Behler (1983). At the December 1983 meeting of the American Philological Assn. a panel chaired by W. F. Calder 3rd discussed the history of Euripidean studies. Prof. Behler's lecture dealt with the Schlegels and their influence.

2. See *Über naive und sentimentalische Dichtung* (1795–96): Schiller identifies work of the "classic" German author, Goethe, with the *naiv* and direct poetry of the Greeks, and his own poetry with that of the modern period. Euripides marks a beginning of the degeneration (*Verderbnis*) that produced sentimental poetry ([1795–96] 1962, 432). See Gerhard (1919, 78): Schiller found Euripides lacking in the artistic richness of the classical Greek authors, while in the more intellectual style of poetry he felt that he himself could surpass Euripides. The digest of Schiller's views by Franke (1929, 39) has obvious similarities to the literary terminology of the Schlegels; but cf. A. W. Schlegel's criticism of Schiller's terms (1884, 375–76).

3. On F. Schlegel's opposition to Schiller, see Eichner (1970, 28ff.). E. points out that Schlegel later came about to a view of modern poetry that was much closer to that of Schiller (49ff.).

4. See Behler (1983), who also comments on the relation of the Schlegel brothers to each other. A. W. seems to have devoted himself to disseminating the ideas of his brother, largely unpublished during the latter's lifetime. A. W.'s *Vorlesungen über dramatische Kunst und Literatur* appeared in four editions between 1809 and 1846, including an English translation by J. Black in 1815 (American edition, 1833).

5. See F. Schlegel, "Über das Studium der griechischen Poesie," ([1795–97] 1979, 217–367).

6. "Edle Einfalt und stille Grösse"; the phrase became a byword—see the reference by Steiger to the absence of these qualities in Euripides (1912, 40). For an instance of Winckelmann's use of the expression ([1755] 1925, 81): "Das allgemeine vorzügliche Kennzeichen der griechischen Meisterstücke ist endlich eine edle Einfalt und eine stille Grösse.... So wie die Tiefe des Meeres allezeit ruhig bleibt, die Oberfläche mag noch so wüten, ebenso zeigt der Ausdruck in den Figuren der Griechen bei allen Leidenschaften eine grosse und gesetzte Seele." A. W. Schlegel saw Winckelmann's work as a model for his own (1884, 90).

7. See "Über das Studium" ([1795–97] 1979, 217ff.), where F. Schlegel praises the "*Übereinstimmung* und *Vollendung, und die Ruhe und Befriedigung*" that derive from these qualities. See Besenbeck (1930, 91).

striking, the "interessante Individualität" of its author.[8] But only beauty (*das Schöne*) can satisfy our "feverish longing" for great art.[9]

Among ancient artists one figure seemed to embody the classic, as characterized by the Schlegels, and this figure was Sophokles: the "harmony of the whole" was complete in Sophokles, and in him Greek poetic art "reached the utmost limit of its powers."[10] The art of Sophokles exemplified the Classicist standard, since it was "harmonious," observant of proper generic boundaries (*Gränze*), and had the desired quality of completion (*Vollkommenheit*).[11] Opposed to this figure was a strongly contrasting one that had more in common with the restless and individualistic modern poet. Between Sophokles and Euripides the step down from perfection was indeed an abrupt one, into a progressive degeneration, at once moral, social, and aesthetic.[12]

Far from giving the reader a sensation of peace ("Ruhe und Befriedigung"), the work of Euripides seemed to lack proportion.[13] Euripides' fondness for inappropriate embellishment led, the Schlegels claimed, to a virtual "insurrection of the individual parts against the unity of the whole."[14] Far from practicing restraint and tact, this artist emphasized passion as a means of stirring the emotions of his audience. Passion (*Leidenschaft*)[15] is used by the Schlegels to suggest an emotionalism inappropriate to males, linking the moral unfitness of Euripidean work to its emphasis on female roles and erotic

8. F. Schlegel ([1795 – 97] 1979, 222, cf. 228).

9. Ibid., p. 253: "heisse Sehnsucht." F. Schlegel suggested that Goethe might be capable of work that would produce the appropriate satisfactions (260ff.) Cf. Besenbeck (1930, 24): both Schiller and the Schlegels saw Goethe's work as marking the beginning of a new epoch in art.

10. "In der Harmonie des Ganzen ist Sophokles durchaus vollkommen" ("Über die weiblichen Charaktere in den griechischen Dichtern," F. Schlegel [1794] 1979, 57 – 58). For A. W. Schlegel (1884, 343) Sophokles exceeded Aischylos in the "innere harmonische Vollendung seines Gemüths." (Cf. 1846, 116.)

11. "Über die weiblichen Charaktere" (F. Schlegel [1794] 1979, 57 – 58); cf. also "Über das Studium," ([1795 – 97] 1979, 296 – 99). A. W. Schlegel (1884, 343ff.)

12. "Nicht lange erhielt sich der griechische Geist auf dieser Höhe." Owing to the collapse of public morality, "der Übergang von der Vollkommenheit zur äussersten Zügellosigkeit, zu der üppigsten Schwelgerei der Seele geschah nicht allmählich und stufenweise, sondern mit einem Male und plötzlich." (Echoed in Bernhardy's literary history; [(1845) 1872, 2:576].) In politics this was typified by Alkibiades; in poetry, by the "ästhetischer Luxus" of Euripides (F. Schlegel [1794] 1979, 45ff.). F. S. concludes that Euripides was at least right in pointing out that the moral decline of Athens began with the female sex (64).

13. F. Schlegel ([1794] 1979, 61): "Übereinstimmung, Gesetzmässigkeit fehlt."

14. This last is by A. W. Schlegel (1884, 358). For an earlier formulation, 1846, 137. But cf. F. Schlegel ([1794] 1979, 61). Similar views in Leeuwen (1876, 43).

15. The German word still conveys the element of weakness and susceptibility in *passio* that is lost to the English derivative.

themes.[16] The sudden fall from perfection into decadence (*Verfall*) is at one and the same time an artistic and a moral failure. It is because of Euripides' moral insufficiencies that his art lacks unity; and it was because of the moral corruption of the Athenian public that his art found favor.[17]

The antimodernist or Classicist stance that was associated with the educational mission of ancient or "classical" studies made it difficult to assimilate an artist who was perceived as similar to the moderns. In fact it was only in comparison with modern poetry like that of Racine that Euripidean art was likely to appear at all admirable.[18] This negative view of Euripides was pervasive and powerful throughout almost all the nineteenth century.[19] I would argue that, far from wondering at the literary naiveté of a generation that assumed a complete congruency between artistic form and social morality, we should carefully examine the history of this view of Euripides. It will prove to have been persistently influential at every stage in the development of Euripidean criticism, up to the present day.

While certain major figures like the Schlegels profoundly affected the modern approach to Euripides, modern work also owes much to attitudes and methods that antedated the nineteenth century. The religious and philosophical beliefs of late antiquity and the early modern period had marked Euripides as an author of particular merit whose views had been in advance of his

16. See F. Schlegel's remark in an unpublished lecture (1958, 81): "Die Leidenden des Euripides betragen sich leidenschaftlich im gemeinen Sinn, unedel und ohne Würde." Cf. ([1794] 1979, 61 and 63): "Charakter enthält er weniger als Leidenschaft; nur in leidenschaftlichen Charakteren gefällt er sich." Cf. A. W. Schlegel (1884, 376). There are many later repetitions of this notion, which became one of the basic clichés of Euripidean scholarship. In the following examples, *Leidenschaft* and female portrayals are linked or closely juxtaposed: Steiger (1912, 102–3); Friedländer (1926, 81); Howald (1930, 140–42); Pohlenz ([1930] 1954, 251); Zürcher (1947, 64, 73).

17. F. Schlegel (1979, 60). These views were at least partially motivated by the polemic of the Schlegels against modern, romantic poetic styles; see Besenbeck (1930, 18–20).

18. A. W. Schlegel made an extended comparison of Euripides and Racine (in French, 1807), to the disadvantage of the latter; cf. his apology for the apparent contradiction (1846, 132). Schlegel's influence in France is discussed by Nagavajara (1966, 350ff.); his work was quoted extensively in French translation in the literary history of Schoell (1824, 2:47–50). More traditional French attitudes to Euripides tended to emphasize the resemblances to French "tragédie classique"—see Patin ([1841–43] 1873, 1:42)—an approach that inhibited the development of a historical view of the fifth century (see Nagavajara [1966, 14]).

19. The literary history of K. O. Müller (1841, 2:146) repeats F. Schlegel's association of Euripides with female *Leidenschaft*. For A. W. Schlegel's influence on Schelling, Hegel, and Nietzsche, see Behler (1983). Nietzsche's estimate repeats conventional accusations: Euripides was a "Grübler" ([1872] 1968, 71; see discussion of this term in a note, below); he caused the death—or rather the suicide—of the tragic art form (66–67); his work derives from the popularity of weak and degenerate taste in music and art (93–94). For the extent to which Nietzsche's views parallel those of other critics of Euripides, see Silk & Stern (1981, 258–62). British views, which were not dissimilar, are discussed below, Section I.B.

time. Since the "philosopher of the stage" was esteemed for his wisdom, it made sense to continue the work of the ancients in collecting and interpreting his doctrines.[20] The pre-Christian ancient commentators had indicated the dependency of Euripides' work on the philosophy of Anaxagoras and Sokrates, and these influences were later used to explain the poet's ability to anticipate Christian doctrines.[21] Euripides' embrace of the doctrine of monotheism had placed him at odds with the culture of his time; and since his plays were produced for public performance in Athens, it was obviously impossible for the playwright to express his unorthodox views clearly. A wide field was therefore left open to interpretation and exegesis.[22] This trend in Euripidean studies persisted, although the Schlegelian emphasis on the value of aesthetic unity, combined with a renewed appreciation for fifth-century Greek culture, made it impossible for Euripides' reputation to rest on a "wisdom" that was valued for its similarity to modern ideas.[23] For most nineteenth-century readers, the qualities that had made Euripides valuable to earlier scholars and educators now became indicative of decadence in art and in culture.

The close union between moral and aesthetic standards in the new Classicism was supported by an understanding of the poet's work as an expression of the poet's personality. This unity between producer and product was antithetical to the cold objectivity of the philosopher or scientist.[24] But the

20. For *ho skênikos philosophos,* see Schmid-Stählin 3:318 n.5, 685 n.4. Cf. the influential treatise of Valckenaer, the *Diatribe in Euripidis perditorum dramatum reliquias,* published in 1767. Valckenaer points to the interest of Christian writers in Euripides and uses the affinity of Euripides for Christian thought to indicate the potential moral value of classical education (*Praefatio*).

21. Valckenaer (1767, 25 – 57) devotes a major part of the *Diatribe* to a collection of fragments thought to be Anaxagorean in flavor.

22. Valckenaer (1767, 37): Euripides believed in one god, and "dii, quales a primis Theologis Poëtis confictos vulgus Graecorum venerabatur, omnibus vitiis, quae in hominem cadunt, deformes, huic in scena Philosopho probari certe non poterant: de illis quid sentiret saepenumero neque illud obscure significavit." Note that this suspicion of hidden meaning behind the Euripidean text fits not only the course of later Euripidean criticism but also a traditional approach to biblical texts. Cf. the discussion of allegorizing and rationalizing exegesis in J. E. Ford's dissertation on Verrall (1981, 122ff., 153 – 54).

23. For this displacement of Euripides by Sophokles in nineteenth-century Classicist criticism, see U. v. Wilamowitz (1906.1, 6; 1922, 324). Franke (1929, 47 – 56) points out that many criticisms of Euripidean work were already to be found scattered through eighteenth-century evaluations. Euripides, Franke argues, was preferred largely because of his connections with the familiar Seneca (5) and because of his early availability in translation (10). But she does point to the crucial importance of the view taken of Euripides' "philosophy" (47 – 48), and she adds that the Schlegels were unique in questioning Euripides' moral and philosophical aims (58).

24. See the formulation of A. W. Schlegel (1884, 47): philosophy and poetry constitute the independent bases of culture—with religion and morality added. "Um ihr Wesen gründlich zu erforschen, muss man sie sorgfältig aus einander halten . . ." Each can remain true to itself only while it remains entirely in its own sphere. "Die Verwirrung der Gränzen hat von jeher grosses

work of Euripides, which combined some very beautiful poetry with material
that smacked strongly of philosophical, political, and moral speculation,
raised problems: if an artist's work was expressive of his inner nature, such a
mixture of irreconcilables must express a very uneven and divided nature.
Beside "Euripides the Philosopher" there must also exist, and on no very
friendly terms, "Euripides the Poet." Such an inner division would go far to
explain the quality of discontinuity and incongruity noted in his poetry.[25]

The next step in understanding Euripides' work for scholars who had
imbibed the Schlegelian view was the investigation of the poet's personality,
to search out the causes of this split. For some defenders of Euripides a
sufficient cause was to be found in the cultural atmosphere of his day, either
in the Peloponnesian War itself, or in the decadence that accompanied it.[26]
To those for whom the aesthetic quality of poetry was of central importance,
however, these excuses missed the point. The failure lay in Euripides, whose
nature lacked the strength of true poetic genius.[27]

Following the guidelines laid down by antiquity, it was easy to associate
this weakness with other unevennesses, and especially with the tendency to
insert what appeared to be extraneous material into the plays: when distracted

---

Unheil angerichtet." Our modern age, according to S., is characterized by overconcern with
antipoetic matters (78 – 79).

25. As usual, this appears first in A. W. Schlegel (1846, 139): "Man kann in ihm eine dop-
pelte Person unterscheiden"; Euripides combines the roles of poet and Sophist. Cf. H. Weil
(1879, xiii) on this inner battle: "À la fois penseur et poëte, il proteste contre les fables qu'il fait
revivre; et ce qu'il créé d'une main, il le détruit de l'autre." Cf. Leeuwen (1876, 25 – 27).
Nietzsche's formulation is especially violent ([1872] 1968, 70 – 71): Euripides was his own critic
and his own intended spectator, "Euripides as thinker [Denker] not as poet [Dichter]." The
division has become so extreme that the two halves of the divided Euripides even take different
roles in the theater, one behind the scenes and the other in the audience. As late as 1893
Decharme concludes that Euripides might have become, "en suivant la pente naturelle de son
génie, l'un des plus grands, sinon le premier, d'entre les sophistes" (58).

26. See F. Schlegel ([1794] 1979, 60) and Queck (1844, 60), who expands on these views:
Euripides' work reflected the "effrenata popularis libido atque . . . licentia" of the time.
Q. concludes that Euripidean poetry is so closely connected with its times that it cannot be
judged apart from them. Cf. the passionate defense of Euripides by Hartung (1843), whose book,
Euripides Restitutus, was intended to restore Euripides "in pristinam dignitatem" (v). Hartung
defended the injection of political material, arguing that Euripides, "quum careret animi aequi-
tate, qua in partium populorumque studiis pensandis veritas cognoscitur, quum ad dirigendam
civium voluntatem . . . aptiora, quam ad otiosam veri pulcrique cognitionem carmina componere
vellet, . . . nata sunt illa, quae a lentioribus languidioribusque hominibus in vitiis ponuntur"
(286).

27. See Bernhardy ([1845] 1872, 410): Euripides was "ein denkender Kopf," but his work
never shows him as an inspired poet. Leeuwen (1876, 34): "Euripidi non inerat vis divina
poesis."

by any passing fancy, Euripides was unable to control himself.[28] For this almost morbid susceptibility to outside influences, the biographical tradition inherited from antiquity provided a persuasive explanation in Euripides' depressive personality.[29] Unable to withstand the influences crowding in upon him in the tumultuous last years of the fifth century, he expressed in his work a variety of overmastering temporary states. This would also explain the tendency deprecated by the Schlegels for heroic and lofty tones to be transposed in Euripides into the mood of the everyday.[30] Euripides' susceptible temperament made it impossible for him to keep the low morals that he saw about him from seeping into his plays.[31] These explanations, however, save Euripides as an interesting and sympathetic personality, at the cost of making his work virtually irrelevant as art. The artistic polemic leveled at Euripides by the Schlegels stands largely confirmed, in spite of the ever-recurring defenses by his advocates.[32]

The possibility remained open that Euripides was aiming not at poetry, but at instruction. Poetry that serves as the vehicle of an argument can presumably be discarded when its meaning has been extracted: Euripidean plays could not therefore have much interest in themselves, once the passions that generated them had been dissipated by the passage of time. Euripides would

28. Patin ([1841–43] 1873, 1:214): Euripides has been involuntarily betrayed in the Pheres scene of *Alkestis* by a passion for sophistic argumentation. Masqueray (1908, 141: "Sa fantaisie sollicitée, caressée par tous les souffles qui passent, se laisse entraîner par eux"). Steiger (1900, 363): "Warum bleibt Euripides hier so weit hinter" what his art demands; "was hat ihm die Herrschaft über seinen Stoff geraubt?" The answer is that Euripides puts poetry aside, whenever another interest moves him (368).

29. See Berlage (1888, 138), "erat enim moribus tristibus et morosis"; cf. p. 23: although he did not follow Anaxagoras' doctrines, Euripides was similar to him in personality and demeanor. See also K. O. Müller (1841, 142): Euripides was a "Grübler," a favorite and persistent description, implying obsessive and ineffectual mental activity; it was repeated again and again, e.g., by U. v. Wilamowitz (1922, 289); Lesky (1968, 18). See also Decharme (1893, 548), H. Weil (1879, vi-vii); Mahaffy remarks upon Euripides' "infinitely various, unequal, suggestive mind" (1879, 36).

30. For this trait, see Queck (1844, 42); Hartung (1843, 376–81); and Patin ([1841–43] 1871, 50–51), who saw it as a sign of decadence and the willingness to do anything to please the audience.

31. See Croiset & Croiset ([1891] 1913, 352): Euripides observes too closely for a tragic poet, who should write by intuition rather than observation; Sophokles, "dans son beau rêve héroïque et légendaire" (355) could remain unaware of contemporary mores. Almost exactly the same formulation much earlier in E. Müller (1826, 8). Masqueray (1908, 13–14): only Sophokles' serenity could resist the devastating effects of outside events, which inspired "une tristesse naturelle" in Euripides' dour temperament, "sombre, pensif, taciturne."

32. This posture of defense is common among Euripidean critics at all periods; Franke (1929, 47) associates it rightly with the overwhelming predominance of Sophokles. For an early reference, see Houben (1850, 1) on the prevalence "recentiore aetate" of "defensores laudatoresque elegantes." Hartung of course (1843) will have been the most notable of these.

be, as Decharme said, more interesting as a historical document than as a work of art.[33] Attempts to treat Euripides as a philosopher who wrote poetry were persistent and widespread; and the mannerism for introducing a discussion of Euripidean views remained relatively unchanged. After a frank admission of the difficulties of reaching any conclusions, given the nature of dramatic art, the scholar would suggest that, with suitable safeguards, a cautious and conservative attempt might still yield valuable results. Familiar criteria for the detection of special Euripidean doctrines—irrelevancy to the play, frequency of recurrence, and consistency of content—would be established and work would then proceed as usual.[34] But it proved difficult to extract any single train of thought or philosophical doctrine from the work.[35] Euripides the philosopher showed much the same inadequacy as Euripides the poet, presumably for the same reasons.[36] Like the vagaries of his poetic style, the "philosophical views" of Euripides proved valuable only as the document of an anomalous personality and its interaction with the contemporary scene.

This constellation of viewpoints on Euripides was to remain in motion for many decades, absorbing new influences, but continually renewing its paradoxical circles. The positions within differed between denunciation and defense, disappointment and advocacy depending on whether Euripides' work was valued as a document of its time or rejected as an unfit representative of the classical literary tradition. The organic literary unity demanded by the Classicist critics, however, seemed impossible to ascribe to Euripides, both because of the anomalous and uneven texture of the work, and because of the dual or multiple impulses sensed behind it, most notably in its treatment of the myths and of Greek religion.

33. Less important for its quality than for its originality (1893, 208).

34. See Göbel (1849, 4–5); Berlage (1888, 2–4); Rohde (1903, 2:252–53 n.4); Decharme (1893, 26–28); Wilhelm Nestle (1901, 7ff.); Masqueray (1908, 156–57); Steiger (1912, 14–15). Later, Grube (1940, 10); Schmid-Stählin (3:688ff.); Delebecque (1951, 28, 31–33, etc.) Cf. the scornful comments of Petersen (1915, 23–24): scholars recognize the difficulties of finding Euripides' views behind the surface of the plays, only to turn their back on scruples, "um das zu unternehmen, worauf es eben abgesehen war."

35. The supposition that Euripides followed Anaxagoras consistently had been effectively dismissed—see U. v. Wilamowitz (1875, 163–64); Leeuwen (1876, 53 n.2); Berlage (1888, 38–49); Parmentier (1893). His philosophical notions were mere decorations to adorn his poetry (Leeuwen, 59).

36. Croiset & Croiset ([1891] 1913, 327): Euripides lacked the strength of mind to adopt any single system: "C'était une intelligence vive et pénétrante plutôt que forte." Berlage (1888, 26): Euripides' "inconstantia" amounts to "animi imbecillitas"; Euripides was unable to invent a new dramatic art form for similar reasons: he seems "viribus deficientibus in difficili conatu haesisse" (37).

I.B. The First Scholarly Criticism

Early humanists had argued that the poet's true beliefs were concealed behind mythological stories that would appear differently to the *vulgus* and to the initiates into the new learning.[37] This quite early line of interpretation was revived in the last years of the nineteenth century by A. W. Verrall and made the basis of a powerful reinterpretation of the plays. At virtually the same time, U. von Wilamowitz-Möllendorff's edition of *Herakles* made the first suggestion, later to be taken up strongly by others, that Euripidean work could have poetic value in spite of its violation of Classicist standards. Both approaches, without moving away from the traditional dilemmas of Euripidean criticism, greatly increased the possibility of treating the plays as literature and of interpreting them as such.

Verrall, the first holder of a chair of English literature at Cambridge, was a powerful influence on a generation of British classicists and literary scholars, opening the door both to the treatment of Greek texts as literature and to the treatment of modern literature as an academic subject worthy of respect.[38] He was often praised by later scholars for his awareness of tragic plays, not only as literary texts, but as dramatic performances. Verrall's wit and talent for paradoxical argumentation,[39] honed by the tastes of the British university in his day, were employed with extravagance in his approach to classical authors.

Verrall's broadest statement of his approach to Euripides came in 1895, when he published *Euripides the Rationalist*. There he confronted openly the general opinion of the day, citing the abuse of Euripides' work by A. W. Schlegel and Swinburne,[40] and rejecting it. He concluded that, until we are able "to admire him heartily and wholly," the only course open is a humble effort to understand Euripides (1–2). The problem, already broached by the

37. See Valckenaer (1767, 37); and F. Lübker (1863), quoted by Janske (1866, xvi): "Die rationalisierende Neigung des Dichters lässt sich in dem Ganzen nicht verkennen." Patin ([1841–43] 1871, 45): "La foule peut s'y tromper et se payer de ce mensonge littéraire," but not the wise, who knew "qu'il lui ait donné un sens pour le vulgair ignorant, et un autre pour quelques spectateurs choisis."

38. I must here express my debt to Prof. J. E. Ford for the opportunity to see his unpublished dissertation (1981, forthcoming from Athlone Pr., London). Ford demonstrates the originality of Verrall's approach, at a time when literary analysis of classical works was hardly done at all.

39. See the Commemorative Address of J. W. Mackail in Verrall's collected essays (1913, cxii), and the remarks by Verrall himself on wit (1913, 277–79). Murray (1913.2, 120): "His wit was famous and always kindly." On V.'s love of paradox, see Leaf (1912, 13).

40. Swinburne's dislike of Euripides was famous and had been frankly expressed (Ford [1981, 16ff.]): cf. "Recollections of Professor Jowett," ([1893] 1926, 5:252): Euripides was "the dreariest of playwrights," or rather "the clumsiest of botchers." Swinburne pointed out that Jowett too had despised Euripides: the latter had written Swinburne that Euripides was "no Greek in the better sense of the term."

Schlegels, was the failure of parts to mesh with the whole. Euripides seems to show himself "at once master and tiro . . . in the lack of taste and judgment, by which the elements are so incongruously and inharmoniously combined."[41] Verrall's solution was the assumption that a satiric or ironic viewpoint lay beneath the surface of the play.[42] His example was *Alkestis,* a play in which a wife dies for her husband. Ostensibly a simple tale of virtue rewarded, the play seems designed to imperil audience sympathy for the widower, when he becomes involved in an unseemly altercation with his father, at the very funeral of Alkestis.[43] Why should the play devote so much attention to scenes of this type, if its aim were in fact identical with its apparent intent, to tell a story of virtue rewarded?[44]

In all his treatments of Euripidean plays, Verrall states the case against Euripides with considerable gusto, forcing the conclusion that only his solution to this intolerable problem will save the author from condemnation as a "botcher."[45] The solution consists of a general rule, which is then applied in various ways to particular plays. Verrall suggests that Euripides does not mean what he seems to say, that he is, in some sense, "ironical."[46] "It is not possible for us to miss the discovery that the author and we are for some reason strangely at war."[47] If this is so, it is wise to accept the fact that Euripides meant it to be so; otherwise, we are reduced to advising the author how he might better have written his play, "if he had had full control of his faculties." Verrall commends a more modest course:

Once for all, let us not flatter ourselves that we can take the lead of Euripides, and show him how he might have improved this or that, if he had only known what he was doing. His clever countrymen thought him their cleverest; the works we possess are a

41. Cf. Verrall's follower Norwood (1908), defending the method by the number of times we will otherwise be obliged to ask of elements in the plays, "'Why does he mention this? . . . Why does he express it in this odd fashion?'" (131)

42. 1895, 90 – 91: "The simpler and clearer he seems, the closer you have to watch him."

43. Verrall (1895, 7) notes that Paley had complained that Admetos and his father, Pheres, were "not well-drawn" and responds that, "regarded merely as studies from life, they are drawn only too well." But the traits given them are "*useless to the conduct of the story*" and "*repugnant to the solemnity of the topic.*" (The italics are Verrall's.)

44. Verrall noted that Browning's *Balaustion's Adventure,* a retelling of the play, goes to some lengths to obviate the difficulties in the Euripidean version (1895, 11 – 16). Cf. the later work of Fritz ([1956] 1962, 256ff.), and discussion below.

45. See on *Ion* (1895, 136 – 37); on *Andromache* 1905, 9 (Menelaos' actions are impossible, "*Incredulus odi:* it is incredible and disgusting"), p. 54 (the end of *Helene* "would be repulsive if it were not too silly"), pp. 90 – 91 (denunciation of *Iphigeneia Among the Taurians*).

46. See 1895, 90 – 91. Verrall understands Euripidean irony as simple and allegorical, a hidden pattern beneath the deceptive surface; see Ford (1981, 122ff.).

47. 1895, 115.

selection of his best; and if anywhere we suspect him of dulness, we should quietly mark that place for something which probably we do not understand.[48]

Verrall concludes that we do not understand Euripides because Euripides did not want his work to be understood. An intellectual whose ideas were at odds with those of his countrymen, he was forced to hide the real meaning of his plays. When he told the story of Alkestis, he placed throughout the play hints pointing us to a reinterpretation that makes sense of what otherwise is senseless. Part of the audience was fooled by the surface meaning of the play, while the smaller but wiser part were able to make out the real meaning hidden beneath.[49]

Verrallian assumptions work best in the case of the famous Euripidean prologues and endings, which are sharply set off from the body of the drama, and may be thought of as projecting a different sort of reality.[50] "The story is contained solely in the action proper," Verrall argued, "without the prologue and finale, which are not the story but comments on the story by 'gods,' that is to say 'liars.'"[51] The paradoxical result of this theory, however, is that the gods in Euripidean plays are both "liars" and "lies." It is one thing to disbelieve in the signals coming from a source, another to disbelieve in the existence of the source altogether; and Verrall's arguments, when they descended to specifics, suggested that large portions of dramatic reality could be consistently interpreted in a direction exactly opposite to that presented by the surface of the play. It is persuasive enough that Euripides may have wanted to present Admetos as an unsatisfactory hero; it is less persuasive that he wants us to guess that Alkestis never really died at all. Similarly, we may be able to accept that Apollon in *Ion* is an unsatisfactory god; it is more difficult to imagine that he is not there at all and to reconstruct the play as it would have to be reconstructed if Apollon were erased from it.[52]

48. 1895, 119. This critical canon represents Verrall at his best. I will suggest later that its sincerity is suspect, but this should not bother anyone who can appreciate irony.

49. 1895, 101ff. I have argued elsewhere (1982, 151–52) and will attempt to demonstrate in later chapters that such a split audience is an impossibility under normal conditions of dramatic performance.

50. Verrall points to the air of unreality of these moments, with their "singular stiffness, formality, frigidity, and general artlessness" (1895, 166). See discussion in Chap. 4, below.

51. 1895, 160.

52. See 1895, 232: such a skeptical audience member would have "simply to reject the pretended solution . . . and interpret the significance of the facts in themselves either by his own wits or by such help as, in the relations of Athenian society, he could obtain without any difficulty." For an indication of the literary genre that may have inspired Verrall's ratiocination see the *Ion* edn. of 1890, where, in a dramatized postscript to the play, an Athenian stranger reveals the hidden plot in a reconstruction worthy of Sherlock Holmes. "*Where is the necklace of Erichthonius?*" thunders the sleuth at the climax of his inquiries, to be answered by "a shriek" and the escape of various malefactors. He continues, "I will tell you where it is now. In the

This procedure of erasing, tailoring, and reassembling the play's reality is at the center of Verrall's method. At the end, we are to come up with a play that, unlike the surface play we have rejected, will inspire respect. This respect, presumably, will be due to the intellectual complexity of the work and to its wit; whether the play will then be coherent as a work of art is unclear. Verrall's later development of his theory (1905) suggests that the original versions had been revised to produce the surviving plays. He performs a fairly straightforward analysis of *Helene*'s playful tone but argues that we may deduce from Aristophanes that a superior version of the play was originally performed for a private and female audience on the occasion of the Thesmophoria.[53] The concluding pages suggest that at these first performances not only were the appearances of the gods absent, but the choral odes were also omitted.[54] This addition to the theory is a great help to the problem of the dual audience; a play like *Ion* could be understood correctly by that part of the audience which had seen it earlier and would be remembering, not the public version before them, but the private and only genuine version.[55] But Verrall abandons his previous attempt to demonstrate that Euripides' work is explicable as unified and coherent poetry. Instead, we must understand that the plays have indeed been cobbled together, as Euripides' detractors charged; but this bad workmanship will have been excused by the de facto censorship exercised upon plays designed for a general audience.[56]

Typical of Verrall's critical work on Euripides is an insouciance that tolerates large amounts of absurdity and that has made his work a scandal to many. His explanations have an air of improvisation. Some plays, e.g., *Orestes,* are interpreted in a straightforwardly ironic sense; we are merely to ignore the appearance of divinities and all will work out.[57] Others, such as *Ion, Alkestis,* or *Iphigeneia Among the Taurians* require that events in the ostensible plot be understood as not having taken place. *Andromache* can be understood only by assuming that it is an incomplete play: that is, the extra material necessary for the Verrallian interpretation of the plot has to be

---

possession of . . . the Lady Creusa. And I will tell you where it was. . . . Let me trace it for you." (And so on, in great detail [xl–xli]. See Petersen [1915, 28] on Verrall's "Detektivspürsinn.")

53. Pp. 62–64.

54. P. 126ff.

55. See 1905, 130–31.

56. Verrall imagines for purposes of analogy a modern theater "in which stories of the Bible were presented" in a spirit of "acceptation and reverence" (1895, 85). The unhistorical assumptions implied here have dogged the treatments of divine roles in Euripides; cf. the similar exaggerations of Athenian orthodoxy in Murray (1913.1, 60–67).

57. 1905, 199ff.

extended to a whole separate drama.[58] The interpretation of *Herakles* seems to put the patient reader's sense of humor to the greatest test, with the aged chorus literally dreaming up the apparition of a goddess ("They just drop, as people say, where they stand") and Herakles showing his humane qualities by having "sympathy to spare for a neglected animal."[59]

The slapdash quality of the Verrallian explications encourages, even demands, a Verrallian analysis of Verrall: the critic, himself a man of wit examining the work of an ironic artist, offers textual explications that have a strong aroma of pious absurdity.[60] Verrall claims to refute the condemnation of Euripides' work that was prevalent in his day, by turning the interpretation of Euripides upside down.[61] His methods amount almost to parodies of traditional scholarship. Verrall's editions of Aeschylean plays set the standard for his later work on Euripides. Like the early textual critics, Verrall ingeniously ferreted out "absurdities" in the texts; but, instead of athetizing or emending difficult passages, he introduced fanciful interpretations that were intended to eliminate the difficulties and preserve the text.[62] We may not be able to accept the Verrallian explications of Euripides; indeed it is hard to believe that the author himself puts them forward in an entirely serious spirit. What, then, should our conclusion be? The ironist leaves it open to us to resume the traditional viewpoint that Euripides is indeed an incompetent poet. There is, however, another way available; and this implication has been the true contribution of Verrall to discussions of Euripides. Verrall's paradoxical argument had begun with the assumption that Euripides cannot be a great artist unless we can "admire him heartily and wholly" in traditional terms. In traditional terms, Euripidean plays are "bad," as Verrall demonstrated, in that they seem to undercut their own effects. Those who agree with Verrall's analysis of the problems in appreciating Euripides, but cannot accept his drastic

58. 1905, 20–23.

59. 1905, 193–94: Kerberos, reading ἀθλίου κυνός at line 1386, becomes an ordinary dog, as the trip to Hades becomes a mine disaster (185–86). For the chorus, see p. 171.

60. Satire directed at Verrallian technique tends to cut both ways. See the amusing essay of Dobson (1908), who imagines a dialogue between Sophokles and Euripides in which the latter complains that his work has always been mis- or overinterpreted. But Dobson's Euripides has a most ironic tone as he protests that he is a perfectly orthodox and traditional artist. Lesky perceptively remarked that Verrall's book is full of "geistvoller Schrulligkeit" (1956, 207).

61. Verrall was precise about this (1895, ix): the effect of current error in neglecting the unique principles of Euripidean criticism is equivalent to "that of changing, in a mathematical expression, the positive sign for the negative." Verrall went on to say that such critics resemble someone who would turn a statue upside down and then complain that its feet were in the air. Verrall's opponents, of course, would argue that it was Verrall who had upended the plays.

62. See the biographical sketch by Murray (1913.2, 118): V. "became in textual matters an ultra conservative. . . . In England at any rate the reaction against slovenly and reckless emendation in Aeschylus is largely due to Verrall."

solutions, may be driven to see Euripides as an artist whose work is ironic in form and thus cannot be assimilated to traditional critical categories.

It was this suggestion in Verrall's work that made it fruitful and that encouraged some scholars to turn to contemporary theatrical art for clues to the interpretation of Euripides. Verrall's other lasting contributions to scholarship have been less benign. Since Euripidean plays avoid homogeneity of tone and organic structural subordination, partial interpretations are very tempting; and, if a part of the play can be ignored, the critic's work is greatly simplified. The theory of the dual audience, although even Verrall himself felt obliged to moderate it, has also endured, because it provides an appealing support for the attempt to strike out a part of the play or to understand it in a way directly opposed to the surface meaning.[63]

At virtually the same time that Verrall was reopening the question of the meaning of Euripides' work, another approach to Euripides was being developed by scholars closer to the main stream of philology in Germany and in Britain. These scholars were not without respect for Verrall's contributions; and their work and his were linked by a common tendency to accept Euripidean plays as art, rather than as a quarry for other material.[64] U. von Wilamowitz' monumental edition of *Herakles* appeared in 1889; and, although he eschewed a general analysis of Euripidean technique in favor of the reconstruction of a Euripidean biography, and analysis of the single play in question, the traces of a new attitude toward the work are clearly visible. Without completely discarding the picture of this artist as experiencing a conflict between private convictions and the public requirements of his art, Wilamowitz was clearly willing to consider the peculiar qualities of the Euripidean oeuvre as valuable traits, rather than as aesthetic flaws. Euripides' struggle was heroic in itself:

A feverish urgency, a comfortless, restless . . . mood, and with it a creative power and boldness, a tireless straining after new problems and new solutions, an ever-youthful

63. For recent examples of these techniques outside Euripidean studies, see Gagarin on Dareios in Aischylos' *Persai* (1976, 51 – 52); or Calder (1971) on Neoptolemos' role in the *Philoktetes* of Sophokles.

64. Note, however, that the most extreme example of the latter tendency, the work of Wilhelm Nestle (1901), also derived strength from Verrall's suggestions of a hidden doctrine "ironically" concealed beneath the surface of the plays. See pp. 71ff., 96. Nestle's approach to Euripides, essentially that of Valckenaer, enabled him to note that Verrall's more modern stance derived from the desire to create unity and harmony in Euripidean plays (Review [1906, 623] of Verrall [1905]). Nestle, like other scholars who saw Euripides as a philosopher, was not concerned about aesthetic disharmony, which he saw as a natural result of the playwright's advanced views.

receptivity to all that is new—one cannot adequately describe the human soul that was capable of producing this series of contradictory works.[65]

From this viewpoint, it is possible to appreciate Euripides' work as something more than a collection of disjointed momentary beauties, and even to see contradiction as basic to his work. The acceptance of Euripides' mixture of seriousness with humor and political or philosophical rhetoric with dramatic form was made easier by his similarity to two modern dramatists, Ibsen and Shaw, figures who like him had been and continued to be controversial but whose work was at last beginning to attract a great deal of admiration.[66]   .

Where the early Classicists had been unable to accept the work of an artist who reminded them too much of tendencies they condemned in their contemporaries, by the end of the century it was possible to admire an artist whose work was at odds with his tradition. But the split between ideas and poetry in Euripidean work remained potentially strong: Hugo Steiger used the parallel between Ibsen and Euripides to argue, as Decharme and others had, that the plays are best understood as representing an intellectual tendency rather than as aesthetic expressions.[67] Gilbert Murray, whose approach to Euripides

---

65. "Eine fieberhafte Hast, eine trostlose, friedlose . . . Stimmung und daneben eine Schaffenskraft und Kühnheit, ein unermüdliches Haschen nach neuen Aufgaben und neuen Lösungen, eine immer junge Empfänglichkeit für all das Neue . . . —man kann sich nicht genugtun, um die Menschenseele zu schildern, der es möglich war, die Reihe widerspruchsvoller Werke zu schaffen" (1895, 1:133). Cf. (1907, 15) Euripides "rüttelt an den Gesetzen seiner Kunst wie an Ketten," and his earlier analysis of *Elektra* (1883, 226), where a note of reproach creeps in, as W. concludes that only "pious submission" to the "Majestät der Sage" can produce perfect beauty.

66. Ibsen was mentioned rather tentatively by U. v. Wilamowitz in the first edition of his *Literaturgeschichte* (1905, 50): Euripides was moving toward a kind of serious drama that could not be correctly termed either comedy or tragedy, "man könnte sagen, auf Ibsen." Steiger was the major exponent of the parallel with Ibsen; see *Euripides: Seine Dichtung und seine Persönlichkeit*, 1912. See also Hanne (1914), Howald (1914, 1ff.). For Shaw, see Norwood, a disciple of Verrall's (1921, 1–48). Wilamowitz later dismissed attempts to draw direct parallels with Ibsen as "silly" (albern) (1922, 368), provoking a pained reply from Steiger (1925, 118–19). Reviews pointed out that in assuming that Euripides, like Ibsen, was a "lecturer" or "preacher" of moral or social doctrines (Steiger 1912, 8ff.) Steiger ignored evidence in his own text of Ibsen's protests against this way of interpreting his plays (14–15): Kranz (Review [1913, 478] of Steiger [1912]); Petersen (1915, 25).

67. See 1912, 40–41: Steiger defends Euripides against the charge of pandering to public taste by showing that the artistic form of the plays has been spoiled by political, moral, and philosophical tendencies (see also p. 48). For an earlier formulation, see Steiger on *Orestes* (1897–98, 51): anachronism is motivated by a moral "Polemik" against Aischylos and Sophokles. "Diese Zerstörung des Mythos ist freilich unpoetisch, aber doch nicht unsittlich."

derived from that of Wilamowitz and Verrall,[68] combined a fine appreciation for the interaction between Euripides and his tradition[69] with a willingness to state that "Euripides is not essentially an artist."[70] Murray does seem to describe the conflict inside the work as one between two modes of literary expression, rather than between literary quality and nonliterary aims.[71] But he seems uncertain whether the conflict has been successfully resolved, and Euripides' art, appealing as it is, may still be questionable on the point of quality.[72] Like Wilamowitz, Murray often seems to cover critical difficulties with sarcasm aimed at the Philistine audience.[73] Both critics were moved by and admiring of the continual, restless cycles of renewal and change in the work; and both remained doubtful that this quality itself was wholly consonant with poetic greatness.[74]

Perhaps the greatest contribution of this new vision of Euripides was its suggestion that the lack of homogeneity in Euripidean art could be something more than a defect. In spite of, or perhaps even because of, the penumbra of critical uncertainty that surrounded the plays, Euripides could no longer be dismissed as a nonpoet or a figure of merely historical interest. If it seemed impossible to reach a dependable critical verdict on the plays, that verdict was uncertain too for the modern writers with whom he was compared and associated. Further, if Euripidean work did have aesthetic worth, it might be that the assumption of a sudden decline within the fifth century could also be

68. Murray formed a link between U. v. Wilamowitz and Verrall. For Murray's deep regard for the latter, see 1913.2, 8. Wilamowitz had overseen the proofs of Murray's Euripides text (see Murray 1954, 9–10), and the two scholars had a warm and longstanding relationship.

69. See 1913, 14–18. Murray makes clear that, since the tradition is a necessary basis of communication in literature, it cannot be disregarded, even by a bold innovator like Euripides.

70. In *A History of Ancient Greek Literature* ([1897] 1917, 273).

71. Euripides is certainly an artist first, and a thinker only second (1912, 590); cf. Wilamowitz (1922, 393).

72. In *Euripides and His Age* note the ambiguous conclusion: "To many readers it seems that his powers failed him; his mixture of real life and supernatural atmosphere . . . remains a discord, a mere jar of over wrought conventions and violent realism. To others it is because of this very quality that he has earned the tremendous rank accorded him by Goethe . . ." (1913.1, 242–43). See also the conclusion of the entry in the *Encyclopedia of Religion and Ethics* (1912, 590–91) "Euripides' distinction as a poet lies partly in a sincerity which often makes him spoil the harmony of his work rather than be content with mere make-believe . . ."

73. Pointing to "a certain unintelligible note of discord" evident in the earlier plays, Murray ends his chapter by remarking that the "ordinary public" probably felt that "It was a pity; and, as the man was now forty-six, he ought surely to have learnt how to smooth it out!" (1913.1, 78) Murray's rather exaggerated picture of the backwardness and ignorance of Euripides' public (1913.1, 46ff.) also seems aimed at creating sympathy for the progressivism in Euripides' work. For a similar ploy in Wilamowitz, see 1895, 1:121: on the caviling of the critics at Euripides' disunited structures.

74. See Wilamowitz, in text above; and 1922, 144: "Er war nie fertig geworden. Darin liegt eine Schwäche; aber Grösse liegt auch darin."

set aside,[75] raising at least the possibility that, along with Euripides, other areas of fifth-century culture were ready for rehabilitation and serious study.

II. The Beginnings of Modern Euripidean Criticism: New Trends and Old Methods

II.A. STRUCTURAL STUDIES AND THE TRADITIONAL VIEW OF EURIPIDES

The years preceding and following the Second World War were marked by the introduction of new approaches to literature whose effect on Euripidean studies was profound, if somewhat oblique. The difficulties felt by Murray and U. von Wilamowitz remained; and new techniques did little to disperse them. A further bar to progress was the isolation of scholarly communities before and during the war. Critics who wrote in English or in German tended to show little awareness of other scholarly traditions, while French-speaking scholars largely explored a tradition of their own. Because the work in German made progress on a variety of fronts, German postwar scholarship will be discussed separately later. The English-speaking tradition founded by Verrall and developed by Kitto, like the historicist approach originated by French-speaking scholars, tended to follow more circular courses and was thus less capable of serving as a foundation for new approaches. Works primarily derived from these traditions will therefore be treated as a unit in the present section.

A new period in the study of tragedy began in 1926, with the publication of W. Schadewaldt's *Monolog und Selbstgespräch*. The book dealt with the soliloquy or self-referent utterance in both lyric and lineverse, focusing on the poetic forms in which such utterances appeared and on the development and change in these formal structures over time and in the hands of different artists.[76] Schadewaldt's work revealed the stylistic techniques and the structural changes that made it possible for Euripidean drama to become what critics had always called it, a theater of intimate and strong emotion, passion,

75. Murray complained of the tendency to assume that "the great spiritual effort which created fifth-century Hellenism was a mass of foolish chatter and intellectual trickery and personal self-indulgence" (1913.1, 48).

76. Although somewhat confused and repetitive in plan and abstruse in language, the book was soon recognized as an important work. On the structure of *Monolog* itself, see the reviews by U. v. Wilamowitz ([1926] 1935, 464–65) and Sheppard (1927, 178); on Schadewaldt's style, see Körte (Review [1927, 7]) and remarks by Sheppard (ibid.). For the importance of the work, see Körte (1), Lesky (1931, 350). Schadewaldt's work had been preceded, as Lesky pointed out (346), by a series of dissertations and at least one major study of structural features in the plays: J. Schmitt (1921) had traced the development and change of the motif of self-sacrificial death (*freiwilliger Opfertod*) often restricted to a short episode in Euripidean plays, from *Alkestis* to *Iphigeneia at Aulis*.

Leidenschaft. He was also able to trace in the later plays a gradual diminution in some characteristic Euripidean features: criticism of the gods and of
traditional morality became less direct and less emotional, along with a general damping down of the entire range of emotional expression in favor of a
new poetic style.[77] Schadewaldt had developed an influential new methodology and had set the traditional perplexities about Euripidean style in an
illuminating and suggestive chronological perspective.

Even before the work of Schadewaldt a new approach to Euripides was
heralded in broader and more far-reaching terms by Tycho von Wilamowitz-
Möllendorff, whose exploration of Sophoclean dramatic technique suggested
new avenues for the literary study of tragedy.[78] T. von Wilamowitz' work
made plain that a tragic play could be understood as an aesthetic unit,
designed to present a particular impression to its audience, and that within it
the shape of actual events might be considerably deformed for the purpose of
conveying this "dramatic effect."[79] An attempt to enunciate critical principles based on this work, and on the broader demand that literary works
should be analyzed in aesthetic rather than moral or political terms, followed
more than a decade later in the work of E. Howald. In his *Die griechische
Tragödie,* Howald shared with T. Wilamowitz a denial of the relevance of
psychological and moralizing interpretations of tragedy, and with
Schadewaldt a preoccupation with literary structure as a key to valid interpretation.[80] Howald's work indicated the limitations of structural analysis.
Disregarding other factors, he traced only the generation of tension or
suspense through plot events and audience sympathy (13) with unimpressive
results.[81]

77. 1926, 127ff.: the rhetorical terms of the invective change from *Medeia* to *Herakles* and
Orestes; the corresponding effect in lyric outbursts, in the monody (162ff.); general summarizing
remarks on Euripidean development (246–59). Cf. comments of Körte (Review [1927, 6]).

78. 1917. For the effect of T. v. Wilamowitz' work, see Schadewaldt (Review [1932, 1] of
Howald [1930]); Howald (1930, 14); Lesky (Review [1931, 352] of Howald [1930]; cf. his article [1931, 350]); Lloyd-Jones (1972).

79. See Schadewaldt, previous citation.

80. 1930. For the importance of the structure see Howald (1930, 8): the structure is the hidden "second body" or skeletal frame underlying the work of art. See also Howald's earlier
Habilitationsschrift (1914), which shows him already using the same techniques as in his later
work.

81. Howald dourly reported that his method produced about the same results for each of the
plays treated: "Ungefähr dieselben technischen Beobachtungen . . . bei jedem einzelnen Werk"
(1930, 8). Cf. the remark of Lesky (1931), who points out that the less rigid procedures of
Schadewaldt and others had been more fruitful (349). Schadewaldt (Review [1932, 5] of Howald
[1930]) remarks that the tragedians are treated as accomplished hacks who handled their material
according to a very uniform formula. In the case of Euripides Howald was left with the self-
evident observation that Sophoclean drama is "unified" and "regular" and Euripidean drama—
is not. In his analysis of *Elektra*—always a difficult play—Howald finds himself generally in
agreement with none other than A. W. Schlegel (1930, 166).

Another work with the same title appeared in the same year. M. Pohlenz' book was better received than that of Howald and was to remain influential into the next generation, through a second edition in 1954. Repeating essentially the methods of U. von Wilamowitz and Murray, it treated the artistic work as the product of an interaction between history and personality.[82] But, since Pohlenz dealt with all three of the major playwrights, his use of this method led to a replication of the traditional nineteenth-century picture of Euripides.[83] Unlike his predecessors, Pohlenz concluded, the third great tragedian had been unable to fulfill his social role as instructor of his people and had left behind a flawed and disappointing body of work.[84] In the absence of other general approaches to Euripides, Pohlenz' view held the field, especially in Germany, during the succeeding decades.[85]

The period around 1930 produced a number of important works that were to affect the course of Euripidean studies. Walter Nestle's study of the entrance scenes of tragedy followed the model of Schadewaldt and once again indicated that close and comparative structural study made it possible to break away from critical perspectives that were based on unexamined presuppositions.[86] Walther Kranz's study of Euripidean lyric built upon Schadewaldt in setting out a clearer and more accurate picture of development in the poet's work, as well as of the general quality of Euripidean style and its relation to that of Aischylos.[87] Kranz was particularly interested in the late period, which he described as a time not of decadence for Euripides but of great creative fertility:

82. *Die griechische Tragödie* (1930). Pohlenz will be cited in the 1954 edn., useful as a means of showing how little his views changed in that whole period; see Lattimore (Review [1956, 197]). For Pohlenz' preoccupation with *Zeitgeist* and *Weltanschauung,* see the highly favorable reviews of Körte (1931, 37) and Pickard-Cambridge (1931, 62), and the doubts of Linforth (1931): "The desire to explain tragedy . . . by means of the historical environment sometimes leads to the fallacy of creating the environment out of the play."

83. Pohlenz ([1930] 1954): Sophokles was able to hold to a positive outlook in spite of his environment (159); "Von Weltangst wusste er nichts" (160). Euripides had a nervous temperament that made him susceptible to outside influence (421) and a prey to melancholy and distraction (353).

84. Ibid., pp. 163, 431, 439. At times, however, Pohlenz seems to grope toward the idea that Euripidean poetry does indeed express something of social value: Euripides has become the spokesman (*Dolmetsch*) for the meaning of the whole war experience for his people (382).

85. A major influence in maintaining the status quo was A. Lesky, whose preoccupation with *Alkestis* is discussed in App. B.

86. For Nestle's work on Aischylos, which led him to question the very early dating then current for *Suppliants,* see Michelini (1982, 4–5).

87. 1933, 233–35. See also the massive work of Breitenbach, which appeared at almost the same time, 1934. Breitenbach, however, adhered to a traditional picture of Euripides: his language is "der Ausdruck lebhafter Unruhe und nervöser Erregtheit, ein getreues Bild seiner zerrissenen, von Leidenschaft durchwühlten Zeit und Persönlichkeit" (291).

We are in a period of overall change in the form of Euripidean tragedy. The scope and the number of characters are increasing, as is the number of scenes. Individual parts that before had been fixed as organic elements in the whole . . . have developed independent significance and are subject to their own artistic laws. A new tragedy is taking shape; it is the product of a new view of life, one that tends more to resignation than to heroic struggle and resistance. . . . The great new choral lyric corresponds to the changed form of the whole work of art.[88]

Kranz's work was profoundly influential on later research, particularly in its focus on late Euripidean style. The reference to a new "view of life" (*Lebensgefühl*) still left a path open to familiar interpretations that saw this poetry as a reflection of the times and of the poet's changed mood.[89] Again, a concentration on careful study of certain aspects of Euripidean art, aspects that recurred in several different plays, made it possible to sidestep the paradoxes and *aporiai* that had bedeviled more general approaches. Also important during this period was the work of F. Solmsen, whose explorations of the recognition or *anagnôrisis* motif followed the lead of structural study and further concentrated critical attention on the phenomenon of late Euripidean style and its peculiar characteristics.[90]

II.B. ENGLISH - SPEAKING SCHOLARS: KITTO AND AFTER
In England and America the new approach to Euripidean studies was slow to make itself felt; scholars continued in the paths of interpretation marked out by Verrall and Murray, without much reference to work on the Continent.[91] The opening of the war in 1939, however, coincided with the

88. "Wir sind in der Zeit einer Umgestaltung der euripideischen Tragödie überhaupt. Der Umfang und die Personenzahl ist im Wachsen, die Szenenzahl steigt. Die früher im Gesamtkörper organisch ruhenden Einzelteile . . . haben sich zu selbständiger Bedeutung entwickelt und unterliegen eigenen künstlerischen Gesetzen. Eine neue Tragik verkörpert sich; sie ist die Frucht eines neuen Lebensgefühls, das mehr zur Resignation neigt als zu heroischem Kampf und Widerstand. . . . Das neue grosse Lied entspricht der veränderten Gestalt des gesamten Kunstwerks" (1933, 232). Note that this forms a contrast with the assumption of Schadewaldt that Euripides' work ended in a bankrupt and sterile formalism (1926, 107 – 8).

89. See Pohlenz ([1930] 1954, 431). Its offspring are to be found in such widely divergent studies of Euripidean style as the historicist work of Benedetto (1971.1 and 1971.2) and the different structural approaches of Ludwig (1957), Strohm (1957), and others.

90. 1932, 1934.1; cf. his essay "Όνομα and Πρᾶγμα in Euripides' *Helen*" (1934.2), which anticipated later studies of this play. Also relevant is the early work of W. Friedrich, whose detailed analysis of *Iphigeneia at Aulis* showed the derivation of the character traits of Achilleus out of his dramaturgical function in the play (1935, 73 – 81).

91. Pre-Verrallian in its impulse was D. Page's *Actors' Interpolations in Greek Tragedy* (1934). Page attempted to pick passages in *Iphigeneia at Aulis* for excision on the basis of their odd, or "melodramatic," effect (157, 158, 177, 186, etc.). See App. A on "melodrama"; Kitto was to use the same catchword in a different way. For criticisms of Page's narrow and outmoded approach, see reviews by Morel (1935, 402) and Hölzle (1937). Given the lack of consensus on

appearance of the first, and best, of several books in English dealing with the work of Euripides. This was H. D. F. Kitto's *Greek Tragedy: A Literary Study*.[92] Kitto's subtitle gave evidence of his intention, in contrast with the work of scholars like Pohlenz, to treat the plays as literary rather than historical phenomena.[93] His approach to Euripides was complicated by the problems of genre definition that arose inevitably out of his attempt to find common ground for all three tragedians. For Sophokles and Aischylos, Kitto was convinced that a tragic idea or theme could be isolated in each play;[94] it was the tendency of a given play to serve this theme that made it, in a generic sense, tragic. Lacking this essential quality, the play would lapse into another category, that of melodrama.[95] Kitto divided Euripidean plays into three categories: true tragedies, tragicomedies, and melodramas. The melodramas have a "grimness" or seriousness similar to that of tragedy, but lack the support of a "tragic idea."[96] Kitto's promise to consider tragedy on a purely literary basis had not been carried through completely; the moral categories that Pohlenz had seen as basic to tragedy were moved to the status of genre determiners, where they were not entirely at home.

Kitto's treatment of individual plays ranged in value largely according to

---

Euripidean style, excisions based on stylistic grounds were to say the least premature; but cf. the later attempt on *Phoinissai* by E. Fraenkel (1963).

92. This was the first of three editions. The treatment of Euripides, however, underwent only minor modifications. References will be to the third edition (1961). The second edition will be cited only for passages that did not appear in the third.

93. In the preface to the first edition ([1939] 1950, p. v): "I make one basic assumption. . . . it is that the Greek dramatist was first and last an artist, and must be criticized as such. Many Greeks, like many moderns, thought he was a moral teacher. No doubt he was, incidentally. Many English school-masters assert that cricket inculcates all sorts of moral virtues. No doubt it does, incidentally; but the writer on cricket does well to leave this aspect of his subject to the historian of the British Empire." These remarks are typical of K.'s determinedly breezy style, and they may also smooth over some difficulties. Cricket makes no direct reference to moral values, but tragic dramas do. Kitto's emphasis on tragedy as literature may seem self-evident to some, but cf. Lesky's strictures on Grube ([1948–67] nr.1 [1948] p. 35).

94. See (1939) 1961, 35 (on Aischylos, *Persai*); Sophokles' aim was "to express as directly as his medium allowed certain tragic ideas which sprang out of a certain apprehension about human life" (118). In *Aias* (125) and *Antigone* (131) the "idea" is that one should be humane and observe the laws; in *Elektra*, that a terrible judgment (*dikê*) will follow a terrible injustice (*adikia*, 137).

95. See (1939) 1961, 138–39: in *Medeia*, "if the wider tragic reference is not apprehended," the play and its heroine will appear to be "not far from melodrama, the making of drama for the sake only of dramatic excitement." For Melodrama, see App. A.

96. (1939) 1961, 332. See also p. 253 (characters in melodrama, like those in Euripides, are one-sidedly good or wicked); p. 346 (in his later plays, Euripides plays on "our nerves and sensations rather than . . . our minds," a characteristic of melodrama); p. 314 (in melodramatic plays the resources of art are exploited "for their own sake, not for the sake of something bigger. . . . It is when the poet has nothing in particular to say that he must be most elegant and attractive").

his own rating of the plays. In the case of *Medeia* or *Hekabe,* Kitto was able
to point effectively to a quality of deliberate contrivance and emotional
"aloofness" of the author from his creations, showing how this stylistic trait
complemented the essentially intellectual stance of the plays.[97] In the case of
the "non-tragic" plays, however, Kitto's approach is dismissive; and the
psychologizing interpretations that he had deprecated for *Medeia* and
Andromache return in full force.[98] Kitto rejected the attempt to define Euripidean "periods," arguing cogently that the reappearance of various types of
dramas in both early and late stages of Euripides' career "shows the absurdity of trying to treat dramatic style as something that develops and can be
studied separately, independently of dramatic content."[99]

At about the same time (1941), G. M. A. Grube produced his analysis of
Euripidean drama. Like Kitto, Grube did not subscribe to Verrall's attempt
to rationalize Euripidean plays and intended to focus on Euripides as a
literary artist; but Grube ignored the formalism that had been revealed by
Murray and Kitto and preferred to treat Euripides as a truthful portrayer of
reality. He did not hesitate to proclaim that "Euripides has many faults, but
artificiality and insincerity at least are not among them."[100] A comparison of
his treatment of *Elektra* with that of Kitto indicates that Grube's naive
assumption of Euripidean "realism" at times permitted him to avoid the mistakes of more sophisticated critics.

In the same period R. P. Winnington-Ingram's book on *Bakchai* (1948)
and the remarkable edition of that play by E. R. Dodds (1944) indicated the
quality of literary work possible in the English tradition. Both Dodds and
Winnington-Ingram were strongly influenced by the Verrallian view, as
mediated through Murray, of Euripides as an artist at odds with his mytho-

97. On contrivance in *Medeia,* see (1939) 1961, 201; on "aloofness" and "irony" in the
treatment of Euripidean characters, see the excellent remarks on p. 254. The whole discussion in
pp. 255–76 contains many acute observations on individual plays; Kitto finishes by comparing
the schematic quality of Euripidean tragedy to math problems in which A, B, and C plow fields
of certain relative dimensions, whereas "Sophocles gives us the real ploughman" (275).

98. Kitto argues that the formalization and distortion of character occur only in the "tragic"
plays, at the service of the tragic idea (257–58), a notion that requires him to downplay rhetoric
in *Ion* or to assert that the sole purpose of the *Elektra* is the depiction of Elektra's unfortunate
personality (334). In *Orestes,* the hero's behavior is "plain lunacy" (349). *Iphigeneia at Aulis* is
dismissed as "a thoroughly second-rate play," designed only to provide momentary excitement
for the audience (362ff.).

99. P. 371, on *Bakchai;* cf. p. 314 n.1.

100. 1941, 7. For Grube's polemic against Verrall, see pp. 11, 59. The "faults" could be
stretched to cover most of the phenomena that had disturbed other critics, e.g., the *deus ex
machina* (79) or the rhetorical and philosophical digressions of *Hekabe* (95ff.).

logical tradition.[101] Dodds's early views on Euripides as an "irrationalist" did not mark much of an advance on the vulgate approach;[102] but, by the time of his *Bakchai* edition, he was able to say that "there never was a writer who more conspicuously lacked the propagandist's faith in easy and complete solutions."[103] Winnington-Ingram was also able to see an aesthetic function in Euripidean indeterminacy; he used modern critical techniques to trace the ambiguities of key metaphors and themes through *Bakchai* (1948). The juxtaposition of tranquil and violent moods in the odes, he argued, revealed the contradictions inherent in Dionysiac religion; and this demonstration of unity in contradiction paralleled Kitto's analysis of the union between tragic significance and artifice in other plays.[104] For Winnington-Ingram the Euripidean critical view of religion, a view inherent but not stated in the play, was itself not without an element of ironic self-contradiction.[105]

English-speaking scholars in the postwar period continued to explore Euripides largely along lines that had been laid down by Verrall and Murray, Kitto and Grube.[106] L. H. G. Greenwood attempted to rationalize Verrall by exploring the aesthetic implications of plays in which the gods could represent the artist's "concealed unbelief";[107] but Greenwood's formulation of the problem was too closely involved with confusions between poetry and

101. For the influence of Verrall, see the article of Spranger (1927.1, 18), who aligns himself with a school of Verrallian rationalist critics at Cambridge. Winnington-Ingram's debt to Verrall appears on pp. 5–9 of his book (1948). He points out, however, that the rationalist approach deprives the action of the play of any significance.

102. The 1929 article is a treasury of traditional critical views on Euripides, including instructions for separating Euripides' personal views out of the plays, the distinction between Euripides the dramatist and Euripides the philosopher (98), the statement that gods are "dramatic fictions" or "satire" (101–2), the association of Euripides with Shaw (97 and 102–3), and ending with the attribution of the decline of Greek culture to attacks of "systematic irrationalism" (103) parallel to the effects of the modern theories of Freud and Jung (104). The only new element in all this is the addition of psychoanalysis as characteristic of degenerate modernity.

103. 1944, xliii = 1960, xlvi. See also his Sather Lectures (1951, 186–88): Euripides presented views both for and against the intellectual "enlightenment."

104. 1948, 116.

105. Pp. 163ff. Reviewers were split between associating Winnington-Ingram with Dodds against Verrall and Norwood (Davison [1947]); lauding him as the successor of Verrall, who had started Euripidean criticism moving again (Norwood [1949]); and condemning him for being "haunted by Verrall's ghost" (Grube [1950, 115]). All were to a degree correct.

106. Blaiklock's study of male characters in Euripides (1952) followed Grube's vision of the poet as a "realist," concerned largely with the portrayal of character. Euripides aimed at "a truthful expression of actuality as it appears to the normal observer" (x, see also p. xv). For the influence of Verrall, see p. 122ff. (*Herakles* depicts the hero as a violently insane "epileptic"; cf. Verrall [1905, 140ff.]).

107. 1953, 4. Greenwood first proposed this notion in 1930. His book (1953) carried on the attempt to develop the concept that the gods are a "fantasy" (18), without taking the further step of expunging them from the plays altogether.

philosophy and between Greek and Christian views of divinity to yield useful results.[108] It was a thoroughgoing follower of Verrall, Gilbert Norwood, who explored the most ominous possibilities of Euripidean interpretation.[109] Both Verrall and Kitto had left the possibility open that, if the plays were not to receive the kind of interpretation they recommended, Euripides' work must be condemned as "botched," "melodramatic," and generally second-rate. If Euripides did not after all have a hidden plan to justify all his anomalies, then we must resign ourselves to exploring the "blunders" of a very awkward and unsatisfying artist.[110] Norwood, having once accepted this unpleasant but stimulating thesis, was able to give the tradition of the uncertain and frivolous Euripides a vigorous and final reformulation.[111] The major problem with Norwood's analysis is that the faults and virtues proposed for Euripides seem to be so mutually contradictory as to confirm the impossibility of ever grasping the artist.[112] While the apologetic posture traditional in Euripidean studies imposed severe limitations, Norwood's negative assumptions led to nothing more coherent.

The influence of Verrall continued to lure English-speaking scholars into circular arguments, while at the same time providing them with a degree of prophylaxis against the tendency, more evident on the Continent, to ignore or explain away the peculiar characteristics of Euripidean style. Fresh evidence of this dual effect was provided as late as 1967 by Desmond Conacher's *Euripidean Drama: Myth, Theme and Structure,* the first general treatment of

108. Greenwood attempts to trace Euripides' "beliefs" through the plays (1953, 21ff.). See p. 36 for assumptions about "belief" in myth. For reviews, see Norwood (1954), who attacked G. from a Verrallian standpoint; and Griffith (1954), who regretted to see "the old Verrallian hobbyhorse at its cavortings again" and deplored the waste of ingenuity.

109. In his Sather Lectures, 1954. For early work in the mold of Verrall, see *The Riddle of the Bacchae* (1908).

110. The germ of Norwood's new approach is already present in his review of Owen's *Ion* edition (1942). For condemnation of Euripides, see 1954, 60: Euripides is "capable of astonishing freakishness and . . . of sad blunders too." For "melodrama" see 1954, 43: Euripides "had no sound reason for not displaying his tragic ideas in perfectly constructed dramas." We are confronted with "thrilling situations into which violent characters are pushed"; situations are created by "means insufficient, absurd, or incredible" (24); such techniques "produce a momentary, if powerful, effect and lead to nothing further" (25).

111. "With him intellectual control of imagination was apt to fail abruptly. . . . When this irresponsible mood lays hold on Euripides he chases every hare that shows its scut" (1954, 48). "If in the course of composition a quaint fancy struck him, down it went into the play, and a fig for consistency!" (103).

112. Euripides deforms character to suit plot (42–43); yet "his characters are better than his plays" (51). Euripides' "artistic conscience [was] at odds with what to us appears his artistic duty." This was part of Euripides' "unusual conception of dramatic art" (15), which was intended "to instruct and brace his hearers" (17). Yet at the same time, the accomplished melodramatist is a "man of the theatre," a "highly skilled technician" (29).

Euripidean drama since Grube.[113] The plays were to be ranked, in much the same way as Kitto had ranked them, according to their treatment of "myth," Conacher's term for the old problem of Euripides' apparent lack of belief in the traditional stories and the traditional gods that appear in his plays.[114] Only a few of the plays reach the level of true tragedy, while most fall into other categories.[115] This method of arranging the plays combines the familiar assumption of a fatal dissonance between Euripides' unbelief and the traditional system of myth with the equally old notion that tragic quality is inversely proportional to the presence of irony in the plays. But, if the theoretical basis for Conacher's analysis was unexamined and outworn, his approach to the plays was not.[116] From his analyses of individual plays emerges a view of Euripides that is comprehensive and sensitive. Perhaps because of his theoretical weaknesses, Conacher was not hampered by a format that favored the plays most susceptible to a conventional analysis and was often at his best with the more intractable and problematic plays.[117] The legacy of Verrall remained in Conacher's treatment of the *deus ex machina*

113. Cf. the not dissimilar quality of A. Garzya's study of "salvation" (*sôtêria*) in Euripides (1962). Euripidean protagonists, Garzya argued, show a predilection for survival and struggle persistently toward a happy resolution (15ff., 154ff.). But his attempt to connect this with Greek religion was uncertain at best (143–62), since G. failed to make a clear distinction between modern and ancient understandings of the term *salvazione*. G. frequently invokes the Verrallian dual audience to explain ironic moments, e.g., p. 17 (Admetos); p. 44 (Iason); p. 68 (Hermione). The two classes of spectators will have differing views of the attitude to war taken in *Suppliants* (61).

114. In dealing with these problems Conacher becomes entangled in the contrast between the "real" and the "fantastic" in Euripidean plays (27ff.): presumably, when the myth becomes "fantastic," then the play itself becomes less "mythical" (14–15), since the mythical material now makes an impression of unreality. For criticism of these confusions, see the reviews of W. D. Smith (1969), Wilson (1968–69, 80), and Seeck (1969, 18, and esp. 19–20 n.1). For a further attempt to explain which plays contain "a serious tragic action" and which do not, see p. 80ff., where C. discusses the thesis of Greenwood. Most of these same confusions had appeared in the talk of Kamerbeek "Mythe et réalité" (*Entretiens* [1958]).

115. "Near-mythical" and presumably "near-tragic" plays are *Herakles,* which in fact "makes use of and abuses" the world of myth (14), the political and social plays, and character tragedies such as *Elektra, Orestes,* and *Medeia.* Most plays in the late period, except for *Bakchai,* are nontragic and present mythical situations that "lack . . . credibility" (15).

116. Cf. W. D. Smith (Review [1969, 395] of Conacher [1967]): "He appears to go forth to battle . . . armed with no critical theory at all, but only with taste and tact, which he has in abundance." Smith, like other reviewers (Wilson [1968]; Petroff [1968]), saw the book as a valuable collection of articles rather than a synoptic treatment. Several of the chapters had appeared earlier. See Conacher ([1955] *Herakles,* 1956 [*Suppliants*], 1959 [*Ion*], 1961 [*Hekabe*]).

117. For praise of Conacher, see the admiring remarks of Strohm ([1968–77] nr. 10 [1973] p. 6). C. has many good things to say, whenever the problem of "myth" does not move to the fore: in *Herakles* Euripides flouts the laws of dramatic consistency "with the deliberate glee of the virtuoso" (78). *Andromache* has a "carefully contrived design" (172) that matches its "intellectual theme" (173) of a contrast between two women and two families.

and other ending portions of the plays: he repeatedly stated that these are not really part of the play and may safely be ignored.[118]

II.C. THE HISTORICIST SCHOOL

Another approach to Euripides owed little to Verrall or U. von Wilamowitz and instead built directly upon the pre-Classicist assumption that Euripidean plays were repositories for information rather than literary artifacts. Attempts to discover a philosophical viewpoint behind the plays were early called into question, but since the late nineteenth century scholars primarily from France and Belgium had been seeking to use Euripidean plays as source material for the moods and events of the fifth century. This technique was not dependent on the assumption that Euripides had consistently and consciously espoused any particular viewpoints, and it was rendered more rather than less plausible by the temperament traditionally assigned to the poet.[119] The method was taken up vigorously by scholars in the thirties, who hoped to derive from the plays information about the effect of the events of the Peloponnesian War on the Athenian populace, as well as to pinpoint the dating of individual plays by the historical allusions contained in them— on the face of it, a rather circular process.[120] The method of determining which parts of the plays conveyed political or military allusions was a familiar one: passages were selected for their lack of relevance to the play as a whole.[121]

118. 1967, 197: at the end of *Medeia* such "macabre touches" as the sun chariot are "permissible when the tragic meaning has already been expressed." In *Elektra* the Dioskouroi "have little bearing on the action of the play itself" (210). The end of *Orestes* "need not, I think, seriously affect our view of the dramatic action" (224).

119. Parmentier's analysis of Anaxagoras' influence on Euripides (1893) shows the genesis of this viewpoint out of the earlier criticism. Euripides' work does not present coherent philosophical doctrine (65); it is instead "en quelque sorte un miroir où viennent se refléter ... toutes les choses contemporaines" (13). The next step was taken by Oeri (1905), whose work had been marked by a number of extreme positions (see Schwinge [1968.1, 12 n.3] on Oeri's earlier work on *Responsionstheorie*). Oeri argued that references to the Thureatis in *Elektra* represented a kind of theatrical diplomatic proposal to Sparta (10–12).

120. For early versions, see Parmentier and Grégoire (P. [1923, 12–15] on *Herakles;* G. [1923, 92–98] on *Suppliants*); in a more extreme form, the article of Grégoire and Goossens (1940) in which the appearance of Teukros in *Helene* is interpreted as an allusion to Euagoras; the book of Delebecque (*Euripide et la guerre du Péloponnèse,* 1951); and the enormous posthumous volume derived from the papers of Goossens (1962). Note the replication of the terms of Croiset or Decharme by Delebecque (1951, 17): Euripides was not necessarily reclusive and melancholy, but he lacked inner "sérénité" and was thus more prone than other artists to reflect contemporary influences.

121. See Grégoire & Goossens (1940, 216–20), where the Teukros episode, characterized as an artistic excrescence, is used to revise the traditional dates of Euagoras' reign. Delebecque (1951) uses the same method of isolating historical allusions, see 28, 31–33, 250–51 (Sicilian allusions in the *Troiades* parodos). But cf. his more random associations: e.g., Menelaos' harsh words to Helene (*Tro* 905) may recall the wording of the Melian debates (256).

These methods, which in their extreme form compounded bad literary criticism and worse historical method, were effectively demolished by Günther Zuntz, a scholar at home in both the English and the German traditions.[122] Zuntz in turn attempted to find a better way to connect the form of the plays with contemporary events (1955); but his methods indicated that skillful literary analysis did not provide a more dependable basis for dating plays than inept criticism did.[123] Zuntz' work was most valuable for his impassioned defense of the literary integrity of the plays. He urged against the fragmentation of the work into a series of disparate voices: "It is always the poet speaking, always and never."[124] Such an analysis suggests that the mixed and multiple quality of the plays must therefore be a part of their system of literary meaning, rather than an accidental result of Euripides' personality.

Along with Zuntz, other critics have presented what may be called a modified historicist position. Like Zuntz, these critics have not tried to extract valid historical data from the plays but have used the plays to suggest the relation between Euripides' work and the spirit and mood of his times. Again, such a mode of interpretation owes much to the assumption that Euripidean plays reflect the world around them more directly than other art; but it does not imply that they are therefore less valuable than other work. J. de Romilly's study of Thukydides lent some authority to her approach to this question.[125] In Romilly's analysis Euripides has a familiar role as the poet of decline; events at the end of the war signal a collapse in the political world

122. 1958.2, 159: "Wherever the critic is blind to the context—there the poet has committed an allusion." Criticism of Grégoire's historical conclusions: "to me it seems frankly untenable" (157). See also the discussion of political allusions in Zuntz (1955.1, 60ff.).

123. Zuntz's conclusion (1955.1, 81) that, because *Suppliants* reflects a more negative attitude to war than *Herakleidai,* it is therefore later than the latter makes two unprovable assumptions: first, that we can trace fine variations in the city's mood from year to year and from month to month, and second that there would be a direct and unambiguous connection between this mood and the sort of play that Euripides chose to write. The reply of Delebecque (Review [1956] of Zuntz [1955.1]) was relatively mild: why should Zuntz's methods lead to any more precise results than his own? See reviews by Italie (1956) and Boulter (1956, 426–27): Zuntz's rejection of all external criteria is too severe, while his own dating method yields uncertain results.

124. 1958.2, 161. See 1958.1, 158: "Es ist immer Euripides, der spricht. . . . Was Euripides uns gibt, ist immer eine ganze Welt . . ." and we cannot separate out some pieces of this world as having more validity than other pieces. See also 1955.1, 20ff.

125. 1965, 1967, on *Phoinissai* (both articles include criticism of extreme historicist methods); 1972, on *Orestes.* In an earlier book, *L'évolution du pathétique* (1961), Romilly was more judicious in assuming purely historical reasons for what is also a literary phenomenon (123).

that matches the end of tragedy as an art form,[126] and the moral decline documented by Thukydides is revealed in the selfishness and amorality of the world of the late plays.[127]

There is a degree of tautology in these discoveries, however, given the close parallelisms of theme and tone between the historian and the dramatist. Since Thukydides may very well have formed his view of human actions partly through Euripides' work, and very largely through the same sources that Euripides drew upon in his plays, it should not surprise us to find the same patterns recurring in the work of both.[128] On the other hand, Thukydides views the war from the perspective of an Athenian failure that Euripides did not live to witness. The work of the historian is therefore both fascinatingly allusive to the atmosphere of late Euripides and rather poorly suited to act as a source of independent data on the public background of individual plays. Attempts to understand the plays by linking them to historical phenomena must therefore come second to understanding the plays as aesthetic units. The reversed procedure leads into a familiar circular argument that associates Euripides' work with a process of aesthetic "decline" that is identified with the assumed "decline" of Athenian democracy or with the social degeneration induced by the Peloponnesian War.[129]

III. The More Recent Work

III.A. STRUCTURAL CRITICISM

Continental scholarship of the postwar period continued to develop on two fronts. On the one hand a traditional and conservative view of Euripides as somehow combining the contradictory roles of poet and thinker ("Dichter und Denker") continued to dominate the general view of the plays, whether

126. See Romilly's article on *Bakchai* (1963): Euripidean pessimism (371) is linked to a loss of faith in the gods and the end of tragedy (380).

127. 1965, 36–38; 1967, 118. The *Orestes* article (1972) is more effective, since Romilly is able to show convincingly that one of the subthemes of the play is the corruption of the popular assembly. On the theme of moral decline during the war years, see the early and influential article of Solmsen on *Ion* (1934.1).

128. See the article of Finley, documenting parallel vocabulary and themes in Thukydides and Euripides ([1938] 1967).

129. See also the quite recent analysis of V. di Benedetto (1971.1), who attempts to prove that Euripides changed gradually from confident support of Periclean policy to a despairing retreat from the contemporary scene (151ff., 228). Strohm ([1968–77] nr. 10 [1973] p. 9) pointed out that Benedetto (see his article 1971.2) heavily overweights the evidence of the lyrics for the late plays, so that the stylistic phenomenon analyzed by Kranz becomes the key to a political or philosophical tendency. For the quality of B.'s arguments, see 1971.1, 152–53, 204–5: Euripides' use of Solon's ideas associating wealth with instability is evidence of a conservative political tendency. Cf. the comments of Burian (1976, 98).

in Schmid-Stählin's monumental literary history (1940), the work of the French scholar André Rivier (1944), or the *Entretiens* of the Fondation Hardt in 1958.[130] At the same time, other scholars were employing the structural methods begun by T. von Wilamowitz, Schadewaldt, and others to study the development of dramatic form in late Euripidean work.

A major influence, both positive and negative, was exerted on the new scholarship by Walter Zürcher, whose analysis of dramatic character in Euripides was carried out in strict accordance with the principles of T. von Wilamowitz. As Wilamowitz had for Sophokles, Zürcher denied the existence of a unified concept of character in Euripidean plays. Zürcher's view of Euripidean psychology rested on a definition of individuality and character change that placed an extreme emphasis on unity,[131] and thus conflicted with the tendency, already recognized by the Schlegels, for individual parts of Euripidean works to acquire separate validity. Although Zürcher's question about character in Euripides would seem to be answered at the start by the way in which it is stated, his service lay in emphasizing the close relation of human behavior in drama to dramatic situation; he also created an extreme position against which critics who wished to argue for the coherency or at least the significance of human action in Euripides had to measure their work.[132]

W. H. Friedrich's work on Euripides and his other studies in comparative drama had been well known since the 1930s;[133] in *Euripides und Diphilos,* published in 1953, he traced the development of dramatic structures out of the artistic process of variation, as each successive version makes use of the tradition for its own effects.[134] While the method often illuminates dramatic

130. For Schmid-Stählin see the collection of Euripides' philosophical views, 3:315 (a favorable citation of Wilhelm Nestle [1901]), 698. Rivier (his book will be cited in the more widely noticed second edition of 1975) attempted to separate the ''poet'' from his other avatars and concluded that the fitful visitations of inspiration must have puzzled the poet by their sudden accessions and departures (155, 167). Such a disjointed process could produce no lines of connection between the different plays (88–89). For the *Entretiens,* see discussion in App. B, on the work of Albin Lesky.

131. 1947, 11: ''Was verstehen wir denn unter 'Charakter'? Doch wohl das Ganze und Einheitliche einer einmaligen menschlichen Existenz. Man spricht von Lebenseinheit, Einheitsform, Ganzheitsgepräge.''

132. See Garton (1957, 249); Michelini (1979); and Winnington-Ingram (Review [1949, 15] of Zürcher [1947]), who points out that Zürcher's method permits him to deny character portrayal to simple, unified figures on the ground that this is mere Sophoclean fixed *êthos,* while arguing at the same time that more complex figures are determined solely by the dramatic effect of individual scenes.

133. See his article on *Iphigeneia at Aulis,* mentioned above (1935).

134. The application to later comedy, which makes up the second part of the book, is more problematic: as in the case of Zielinski's earlier work, attempting to reconstruct lost plays from the variants in later literature proved problematic. For criticism of that part of Friedrich's technique, see Webster (Review [1954] of Friedrich [1953]).

structure, as in Friedrich's discussion of the two versions of *Hippolytos*,[135] it
does not always lead to a persuasive interpretation of the play as a whole; and
Friedrich occasionally resorted to older methods of explaining away
uncongenial elements in the plays.[136] Most valuable was his isolation of certain characteristic features of the Euripidean stage, such as the tendency to
present forestalled or hindered actions.[137]

A second book entirely dedicated to the analysis of formal structure
appeared a few years later. W. Ludwig's dissertation, entitled *Sapheneia*,
demonstrated in precise detail the deeply ingrained tendency in Euripides
toward an orderly and formal style, with discrete elements of the work
clearly distinguished and the underlying logical architecture—whether of
grammar, motivation, or plot—in plain view.[138] Ludwig demonstrates the
importance of self-consciousness to such a style, which makes a positive virtue of avoiding naturalism and emphasizes the border that marks off art from
reality.[139] Ludwig made virtually no attempt to explain the significance or
uses of Euripidean "clarity." His argument that it is a principle of beauty is
both self-evident and insufficient.[140] If Euripides' sole aesthetic aim had been
order and symmetry, he would indeed have missed his calling, since these
qualities are more central to dialectic or mathematics than to poetry. As a
proof of Euripidean formalism, Ludwig's work was convincing and valuable,
although its refusal to interpret created a somewhat sterile approach to the
plays.[141]

135. 1953, 6 and 110ff.

136. *Tro* 647–56 is one of those places where Euripides "mehr selber spricht als seine Per-
sonen sprechen lässt" (1953, 66). See also pp. 69–70, where various features of the plays produced in 415 are associated with Euripides' presumed political or personal attitudes. It is unclear
whether or not F. wishes to treat the bitter overtones surrounding the end of *Iphigeneia at Aulis*
(1953, 108–9) as an unintentional flaw in Euripides' treatment.

137. 1953, 58–60.

138. 1957, 6–11. The Euripidean Elektra's plaint is like "ein abgezirkelter französischer
Garten" and shows an "überschauendes Disponieren und ein klares Begreifen der Gedanken in
ihren logischen Bezügen" (8).

139. 1957, 34 (of such devices as the prologue): "Sie wollen gerade nicht den Eindruck
erwecken als ob der Dichter plötzlich gleichsam den Vorhang von einer realen Wirklichkeit
zurückziehe, die schon vorher bestanden hat, und als ob der Hörer einen heimlichen Einblick in
einen scheinbar zufälligen Ausschnitt der Wirklichkeit nehmen dürfte."

140. "Die Schönheit ihrer Form liegt in ihrer Klarheit" (139). Other, subsidiary weaknesses
are due to overapplication of Ludwig's methodology: e.g., he attempts, with relatively poor success, to demonstrate the same rigid structures in Euripidean lyric (82ff.), where they run directly
counter to the tendency to formlessness analyzed by Kranz (1933, 240: on Aristophanes' parody
in *Frogs*) and particularly by Heitsch (1955, 145).

141. Ludwig's methodology differed from the structural work of Schadewaldt, and later
Strohm, in that it took relatively little account of the content of the play itself. See the criticisms
of Schwinge (1968.1, 21–22). Although Ludwig (1957, 9) warns that a drama is a structure perceived sequentially in time, his method often presents little more than a schematic outline (e.g.,
of the relative lengths of parallel speeches).

Of considerably more importance was the subtle and opaque book of H. Strohm (1957), which appeared in the same year. Strohm combined the description of repeated formal elements such as suppliancy and recognition with a developmental analysis that revealed the chronological changes in these forms as well as their successive adaptations to differing dramatic situations.[142] It is this aspect of Strohm's work that distinguishes it from other structural studies, in which often a rigidly defined form is used as a standard, e.g., to determine the chronological priority of a simpler and therefore presumably earlier version. Strohm suggests that boldness and spontaneity may be better tokens of an artist's developing command of form.[143] In Strohm's view the formalism of Euripidean poetry emerges as alive and lively, constantly replicating and developing in an endless play of alternatives, each significant and appropriate to the dramatic context of which it is a part.[144] Far from falling apart into a series of unconnected and inharmonious moments and separate formal entities, Euripidean dramatic style differentiates the parts only for the purpose of weaving them into a pattern.[145] As the style develops in the later years, it becomes richer; and the individual elements of dramatic form, such as the *anagnôrisis* or the act of self-sacrifice, expand, differentiate, and increase in complexity, often filling out the frame of an entire dramatic action.[146]

Strohm's work did much to break down the sterile opposition of well-worn positions in Euripidean scholarship, making it possible to see Euripidean formality as a part of poetic style rather than as the sign of essentially unpoetic qualities or of collapse and degeneration in the development of the art form. His book did not attempt an overview of Euripidean work, or even a comprehensive view of any single play; and Strohm himself states that a return from the consideration of parts to a consideration of the whole is a necessary precondition to further study of Euripides.[147] In his analysis of the

142. Strohm's treatment of the *agôn* is typical. His stated aim is to use a formal analysis to demonstrate the vitality and artistic validity of Euripides' work (1 – 2). His analysis shows that the *agôn*, although clearly distinguishable as a form, varies in each artistic incarnation: e.g., in *Elektra* the fact that Elektra must lure her mother into the house necessarily determines the shape of the encounter between them (14).

143. 1957, 61 – 62. It seems likely, however, that these qualities are too dynamic and variable to help much with problems over dating.

144. See p. 63: instead of "starrer Typik" we find "geisterfüllter Form." *Helene*, reviled as a parody of serious plays, is rich and colorful (77). Like Kranz (1933) Strohm wanted to move beyond the position of Schadewaldt, who had argued that the study of development in Greek tragedy shows a gradually increasing rigidity and lifelessness (1926, 107 – 8).

145. 1957, 79 – 80, on *Elektra*.

146. Pp. 85 – 86; see also pp. 91 – 92.

147. 1957, 2; see Zuntz's review (1959, 411): Strohm is right to feel that his work is a necessary contribution to "'the most urgent task' of an adequate exposition of the main works of Euripides."

plays Strohm makes little allowance for dissonance or irony, so that he often
seems to imply that, with the insights gained from structural analysis, the
work will prove to be acceptable in a relatively conventional sense.[148] His
style, often difficult and obscure, seems to acquire a special opacity in the
second half of the book, where study of the "forward movement" of the plot
makes it more necessary to deal with the knottier problems presented by individual plays.[149] It would not be unfair to say that, like Friedrich and Ludwig,
Strohm worked in an area where literary criticism could be performed
without direct dealings with the central problems of style and meaning and
without involvement in the cycle of paradoxes that had trapped Euripidean
studies in the past. In this sense, the work of these scholars represented a
substantial advance in some areas, at the cost of avoiding problems in other
ones.

III.B. NEW PERSPECTIVES

The 1960s, particularly in the latter part of the decade, produced an astonishing burst of Euripidean scholarship.[150] The separate scholarly traditions

148. In his treatment of *Orestes,* for instance, he argues that the necessity for Helene's assas-
sination and Hermione's kidnapping is "klar und unproblematisch" since these acts are
motivated by the noble *philia* of the protagonists (1957, 88 n.2; cf. 1981, 154). Dale complains
of the "monotonous award of highest distinction to every play in turn" (Review [1959, 166]).
Strohm (1957, 15 n.3) supports Zürcher's analysis, probably because it counters attempts to show
unpleasant elements in Euripidean characterizations. Strohm himself treats the Phrygian in
Orestes only as a plot element, without dealing with the peculiar effect of Orestes' confrontation
with such an opponent (125).

149. For the style, see the complaints of Dale (Review [1959, 166]), who also expresses
doubt about the results of the second part. Zuntz (Review [1959, 406–7]) suggested that Strohm
could have delineated his formal principles with greater clarity and simplicity. For opacity, see
the comments of (English-speaking) reviewers, Dale (1959) and Boulter (1958, 435).

150. See significant work on the textual tradition by such scholars as Zuntz (1965) and
Tuilier (1968), a remarkable edition of *Hippolytos* by Barrett (1964), as well as the valuable com-
mentaries of Benedetto (on *Orestes,* 1965) and Kannicht (on *Helene,* 1969). Jouan (1966) inves-
tigated the use of themes from the lost *Kypria* in the surviving and fragmentary Euripidean plays,
a somewhat problematic enterprise. Webster performed an important service in summarizing and
making accessible a wide range of information about the fragmentary plays (1967). E.-R.
Schwinge studied the Euripidean stichomythy (1968.1) in a lengthy book that showed much perceptive critical ability, as well as a sense of the history of Euripidean criticism. The arrangement
of the book, however, around an elaborate classificatory system did not produce a clear overview
(see review by Calder [1969]). Barlow (1971) sketched Euripidean poetic style, suggesting the
variety and subtlety of figurative technique in a writer whose work had been described as flatly
prosaic. Matthiessen (1964) attempted to put structural techniques at the disposal of dating problems; more valuable was his close formal analysis of recognition technique, in which he
advanced work begun by Solmsen and Strohm; see also Vögler (1967). See also in this same
period Garzya (1962), Conacher (1967), and Benedetto (1971.1), who are discussed above, as
well as the books discussed in the next section, e.g., Spira (1960), Rohdich (1968), Paduano
(1968), and Burnett (1971).

were beginning to merge to some extent, and this enhanced the vitality of research. But the persistence of old unresolved problems continued to hamper the development of a general approach; and the best results of the period are to be found in peripheral or minor works that suggested new approaches to Euripidean drama. The isolated but important pronouncements of Günther Zuntz on Euripidean irony, along with his defense of the plays as unified and significant, had hinted that the old approaches could be abandoned.[151] Further steps were taken by two prominent German scholars in articles published in the nineteen-fifties that reappeared in book form several years later.

K. von Fritz like the best of the structural critics found a means of testing and comparing dramatic structures that made it possible to overcome the complex of contradictions in Euripidean criticism.[152] By examining a whole series of treatments of the Alkestis story by dramatists who followed Euripides, Fritz was able to show that precisely those elements of the story that had been depreciated as unimportant by apologists for the play were what set the Euripidean treatment apart from all subsequent versions. His examination of the dramas derived from *Medeia* showed the same pattern.[153] Fritz had redirected critical notice to the central question of Euripidean interpretation: are the anomalous effects of Euripidean plays to be overlooked and excused, or are we to understand these effects as part of the aesthetic whole? Analysis of the way in which differing dramatists had treated the same dramatic situation strongly suggested that the Euripidean anomalies were part of a deliberately chosen aesthetic pattern.

In an attempt to reach a basis for deciding what kinds of meaning can be conveyed by dramatic form, K. von Fritz drew upon his wide acquaintance

151. Zuntz's remarks were evoked largely by his opposition to historicist criticism, discussed above. For irony, see 1955.1, 20, although Z. argues that *Suppliants* itself lacks irony. His article on *Helene* at the 1958 *Entretiens* also combines fine general insights (223–27) with rather maladroit attempts to explicate the text by emending it (206–8). Again, in that session he was at his best in his polemic against Lesky and Kamerbeek; see App. B.

152. A collection of essays on tragedy appeared in 1962. Fritz's examination of *Alkestis*, which originally appeared in 1956, had begun to influence scholarly opinion earlier, to judge by Lesky's reevaluation of his own position (1964). But the significance of Fritz's approach to Euripidean studies must have been much clearer after his essays were published together, with a preface that summarized the elements of that approach. Of the major essays, ''Tragische Schuld und poetische Gerechtigkeit'' had appeared in 1955; the article on the Medeia saga and its development in drama, in 1959. The introduction (i-xxix) and an essay on the Orestes saga (113–59) appear to have been new.

153. On *Alkestis* (1956, 66–67): the reaction of later playwrights and critics to Euripides shows that ''die Dissonanz, wie Euripides es wollte, auch von denen gehört worden ist, die das Rätsel, warum sie so tief aufgestört wurden, nicht lösen konnten.'' On *Medeia* (1959, 68ff.). Fritz influenced the work of at least one important scholar: Schwinge's interest in human psychology and interaction recalled Fritz (see 1968.1, 24 nn.25, 28).

with modern European drama. A comparison with the works of Brecht, who is known to have written with the intent of putting across specific political meanings, demonstrated the limited ability of the poet to deliver moral or political messages with any accuracy.[154] Fritz suggested that in serious drama the mimesis of interaction is paradigmatic of certain problems and truths relating to human relations. This broader allusiveness is not entirely controlled by the poet, who must design his play to enhance and complement what is already inherent in the situation that he is dramatizing.[155] This is especially significant for a play like *Alkestis,* in which, as Fritz showed, the knotty question of Admetos' acceptance of his wife's sacrifice is inextricable from the substance of the story itself. The playwright can attempt by various dramatic devices to mitigate the effects intrinsic in the relation between the married couple; but it is not possible to reverse or eliminate the underlying logic of the situation. The essay on the various versions of the Orestes saga gives a further demonstration of the way in which the verities of human situations override even the viewpoints of individual poets.[156] This perception is important to Euripidean criticism, because it helps to bring attention back from the hidden and inaccessible ''personal views'' of the poet to the content of the poetry itself.[157]

Another major impulse to the general study of Euripides was an article by K. Reinhardt, whose work on Sophokles had done much to advance a developmental view of that poet's work.[158] In ''Die Sinneskrise bei Euripides''[159] Reinhardt boldly juxtaposed the ''crisis of meaning'' in modern work that he characterized as nihilistic with the intellectual crisis in Athens at the time of the Sophists.[160] Euripidean drama, he suggested, presents a more

154. 1962, xxiv.

155. 1962, xxii-xxv. Unfortunately, modern confusions over terms like ''morality'' are so great that Fritz (see xxvi-xxvii) has often been misunderstood, or oversimplified. E.g., Lloyd-Jones (Review [1962] of Fritz [1962]), who concludes that Fritz merely means that ''moral values do not vary according to the poet's caprice'' (738).

156. 1962, 154–59.

157. See much earlier an article of clairvoyant brilliance by Zielinski (1902), who pointed out that such concepts as the ''personality'' and ''opinions'' of the author ignore both the general lability of both in most persons—and especially in artists—while also depreciating the artist's ability to touch on themes of general significance (649–51).

158. On Reinhardt's book on Sophokles (1933, and reedited without major changes in 1941 and 1947), see the introduction by Lloyd-Jones to the English translation (1979).

159. The original article appeared in 1957 and will be used for citation. It achieved wider circulation by being reprinted in a collection of Reinhardt's essays (1960) and in Schwinge's collection of essays in the *Wege der Forschung* volume (1968.2, 507–42).

160. The word ''juxtaposed'' is used advisedly: Reinhardt did not commit himself as to how far the parallel might be carried. He saw the source of the Greek ''crisis'' in a loss of religious belief (''Wanken die Götter, wankt der Sinn'' [619]), a notion derived more from modern than from ancient religion.

disturbing picture of the loss of sense and meaning in the world than does the work even of modern artists.[161] *Orestes* is used to illustrate the workings of this absurdist ethic in detail. Reinhardt saw the play as proceeding straightforwardly toward the doom of the protagonists until line 1097, at which point the plot takes a bizarre turn into a distorted and almost parodic reenactment of *Choephoroi*.[162] The sudden resolution engineered by Apollon was, Reinhardt felt, an ironic absurdity that could not be accepted "seriously." With this last stroke, the play seemed to cross itself out.[163]

Because the old question raised by Verrall had been opened again by a greatly respected German scholar, the problem of irony in Euripides became harder to ignore than it had been. Reinhardt supplied a suggestive parallel with modern work and hinted at the connections between a mannered style and absurdist or ironic art.[164] But Reinhardt's article left unexamined the nature of Euripides' "absurdist" art. Critics could still account for apparent errors and dissonances by falling back on the notion that Euripides was peculiarly susceptible to contemporary stresses, although Reinhardt had made it more difficult to reconstruct an orthodox Euripides by ignoring these dissonances altogether. Like U. von Wilamowitz, Reinhardt concluded that Euripides' greatness lay in the raising of questions and the posing of riddles that he could not or would not solve.[165]

The insights of K. Reinhardt and K. von Fritz did not stem the tide of Euripidean criticism, which was moving in another direction. Rather, their work stood almost alone, admired but not assimilated by the scholars who produced the abundant work of the following decade. Both appeared in the collection of essays in the Wege der Forschung series edited by E.-R. Schwinge. Schwinge, a skilled literary scholar who had performed a detailed

161. 1957, 625. Reinhardt goes on to argue that the combination of humanity and monstrosity in Medeia leads to an absurdity that is underlined by the bizarre effect of her last appearance, on the chariot of Helios: "Da sie menschlich wird, sinkt sie ins Absurde" (626).

162. On line 1097: "Damit könnte das Drama schliessen" (640). On the concept of parody, see p. 643. The entrance of the Phrygian slave parallels the slave who emerges to warn Klytaimestra in *Choephoroi* (644). For a further analysis of the reworking of old motifs in *Orestes*, see Zeitlin (1980, 72).

163. ". . . so wird es uns schwergemacht, die Lösung ernstzunehmen. . . . Verbeugt sich der Dichter ironisch vor der Theaterkonvention? Ist die Heilung darum so absurd, damit sich das Theater selbst durchstreiche?" (646). Cf. discussion in Chap. 8, below. For the parallel with the concept, proposed by Heidegger and Derrida, of meaning that can be present "sous rature," see Norris (1982, 69).

164. In the analysis of *Orestes* described above, esp. p. 644 on the Phrygian: "Ohne Reminiszenzen keine Manier." Cf. p. 630 on lyric. For "mannerism" as one of the aesthetic charges against Euripides, see A. W. Schlegel (1807, 10–11) and the discussion in Schwinge (1968.1, 15–19).

165. Reinhardt (1957, 646): "Zur Grösse des Euripides gehört, dass er die Frage stellen, aber nicht hat lösen mögen."

study of the Euripidean stichomythy (1968.1), produced in his introduction (1968.2) a valuable summary of the misprision of this artist's work from the beginnings of modern Classicism. He also traced the minor tradition of critics such as Murray, Dodds, Fritz, and Zuntz who were able to appreciate Euripidean poetry without amending it to fit the Classicist canon.[166] That Schwinge's own work did not deal with the central problems of meaning in Euripides may be traceable to the tendency in contemporary Euripidean studies to seek out other problems that would produce fewer quandaries.

III.C. EURIPIDES REHABILITATED

In the same period, scholars who held to the more traditional view of Euripides were increasingly becoming convinced that Euripidean plays could be defended by the techniques of modern criticism in such a way as to eliminate the doubts that had vitiated earlier critical methods and to obviate the stumbling blocks that had been used by Verrall and others to argue for an ironic and conflicted tone in the plays. Unlike critics who had defended Euripidean artistry but had avoided the problems of interpreting Euripidean tone and style, this group of scholars attempted a more broadly based rehabilitation of Euripides. In some cases this also involved an attempt to establish Euripides as a representative of cultural orthodoxy and religious traditionalism. The scholars in this last group had learned much from modern analysis of Euripides, but their different aim—to gain a synoptic view of the Euripidean oeuvre—was frustrated by a lack of common ground. No consensus emerged; and some scholars, like Greenwood earlier, found themselves under attack from several different positions.

The first and most straightforward attempt at Euripidean rehabilitation was that of A. Spira (1960), who boldly took up the position directly opposite to Verrall's,[167] arguing that far from being ironic or awkward the divine apparitions at the end of Euripidean plays are in fact the source of the comprehensive and harmonizing unity that critics for so long had found lacking. The effect of the god's final appearance is to create "suddenly a deep inner peace [Ruhe]." All parties on stage agree with the judgment of the god; passions

166. 1968.2. Note also Schwinge's documentation of structural work through the pieces by Solmsen, Snell, Friedrich, Schadewaldt, and Strohm. Solmsen (1932, 1934.1): studies of recognition (*anagnôrisis*) dramas and the techniques of late Euripidean tragedy. Snell (1937, 1928): the place in literary and intellectual history of the moral questions raised in Euripidean drama. Schadewaldt (1952): analysis of stylistic traits of very early Euripidean drama. W. H. Friedrich (1960): the treatment of the Medeia legend in Euripides and his imitators. Strohm (1949–50): the form of the intrigue in Euripides.

167. 1960, 34: Spira remarked that one who criticizes Verrall "laüft offene Türen ein." But S. notes that Verrall's influence remained pervasive and strong.

are quieted, as all bow in thankfulness to the divine ordinance.[168] Critical reception of Spira's thesis was not enthusiastic; his "theodicy" was unpersuasive, even to scholars who took an adverse view of the "ironic" Euripides.[169]

Interest in late Euripides had blossomed since Schadewaldt's observation that ideological polemic and the expression of passion had diminished in the plays produced during the later war years. The study of late Euripidean lyric (1933) by Kranz had confirmed the stylistic change; and already in 1934, in his seminal article on *Ion,* F. Solmsen had drawn stronger conclusions from Schadewaldt's observations. As morals broke down in the war, Solmsen supposed, people became more self-centered; and this change was reflected in later Euripidean tragedy, where the passion (*Leidenschaft*) characteristic of early Euripides is diminished, and there is less conflict over moral issues.[170] Among the later plays, those that had been labeled tragicomedies by Kitto,[171] *Ion, Iphigeneia Among the Taurians,* and *Helene,* seemed to fall together into a self-contained group, in that they were felt to project a tragic sense of the undependability of human knowledge and existence, as the protagonists

168. "In jener Dankbarkeit, die der Gerechtigkeit folgt, beugt sich jeder dem Spruch. . . . Die Wirkung auf den Zuschauer ist eine grosse innere Befriedigung" (1960, 97). The tendency to produce a sensation of "Ruhe und Befriedigung" was the test of truly classical art for F. Schlegel ([1795 – 97] 1979, 217ff.). See Spira, pp. 120 – 21: the knowledge brought by the god has a healing effect that is caused by the "restoration of order [Ordnung]." Pp. 160 – 61: the gods are representative of old religious attitudes, typical of epic. (I would agree with this last; see Chap. 4.)

169. Spira's work on developmental change in the *deus ex machina* was better received. See Looy (Review [1961]) on the structural analysis of Spira; and Lesky ([1948 – 67] nr. 5 [1961] 22 – 23).

For the "theodicy," see Lesky ([1948 – 67] nr. 5 [1961] p. 23; nr. 7 [1968] p. 5); and Strohm (Review [1962, 346] of Spira [1960]): Spira is right to say that Apollon is not humiliated at the end of *Ion,* but Athena's appearance is not a religious epiphany. Burnett (Review [1962]), whose own views are discussed below, while lauding the trend to a "positive criticism" of Euripides, found his analysis too secular, failing to show us how "the audience is being led to praise the god" (66). For a positive review, see Fauth (1961). The strongest support for Spira's views has come from Lloyd-Jones, who argues that the gods of Euripides were essentially those of Sophokles and Aischylos ([1971] 1983, 144ff.) and that the actions of the gods are in some sense just (150 – 54). On Spira: his book is "one of the most valuable contributions to Euripidean studies of the last decade" (155).

170. 1934.1, 407 – 8. On Schadewaldt and the diminution of *Leidenschaft,* 1934.1, 399 – 400; see also 1932, 9 on *anagnôrisis* and *mêchanêma.* See also Valgiglio (1957.2, 60 – 61 n.24).

171. (1939) 1961, 314ff. Conacher (1967) had isolated these three plays as specially belonging to a category of "romantic tragedy" (265, 341). Whitman (1974, 138 – 39) tentatively agreed. For older references to the "romantic" in Euripides, see A. W. Schlegel's summary of "romantisch" qualities in modern theater (1884, 25): "Mischung von Scherz und Rührung, vom Alltäglichen und Wunderbaren"; and Nicolai's literary history on Euripides (1873, 194 – 95).

become the playthings of a casually beneficent destiny.[172] If the tragic force of the drama seemed diminished, so did the qualities that in the earlier plays had presented such irreducible problems to critical theory. By concentrating on these plays, critics could avoid the questions raised by the more controversial dramas; the presumably wiser and sadder Euripides of the war years seemed a poet more amenable to conventional critical technique.[173]

Another and bolder attempt to find a new conception of Euripidean tragedy came from H. Rohdich.[174] The opening chapter of his book is a valuable summary of contradictory trends in Euripidean scholarship, pointing to the virtual counsel of despair in Lesky's literary history.[175] Rohdich, citing general studies of tragedy, argues that tragic suffering also implies a faith in the ability of the social order to transcend and heal this pain.[176] The Sophists destroyed the basis for tragedy, by putting their faith in human rationalism and threatening the stability of the social order (20). Rohdich saw Euripidean drama as a kind of tragedy of the tragic genre itself, as the poet attempted to defend tragedy against the Sophistic by incorporating the Sophistic into his poetry (21). Rohdich's formulation, while rather fanciful in its application of

172. For the diffusion of this idea about Euripides, see Solmsen (1934.1, 404–5); Diller ([1955] 1968, 471, 490]); Strohm (1957, 90, 119, 129); Vögler (1967, 50–51); Steidle (1968, 113–15); Schwinge (1968.1, 143 and 160).

The attempt to extract some philosophical content over and above the aesthetic form of the individual play is common to modern criticism of tragedy; for an analysis, see Reiss (1980, 12), who discusses the prevalence of a tendency toward the "hypostatization of some element that, since the neoclassical interpreters of Aristotle, we take as what is essentially expressed in and by tragedies." I would argue that the "human uncertainty" in late Euripides is more than balanced by the well-oiled and glossy plot mechanisms that carry the action to its predestined happy ending.

173. Work on *Ion, Iphigeneia Among the Taurians,* and *Helene* was abundant throughout this period and beyond. See Strohm's remark (Review [1962, 345] of Spira [1960]): "Die neue *Ion*-Interpretation . . . stellt sich zu den zahlreichen Analysen, die in den letzten Jahren den eur. Spätstil erschlossen haben." Examples are the article of Burnett (1962); and Imhof's monograph (1966). Imhof was grouped with Spira by Lesky ([1948–67] nr. 7 [1968] p. 18) and Radt (Review [1968]). For Imhof's favorable view of Spira, see 1966, 73 n.56. Not much work was done on *Iphigeneia Among the Taurians* separately, although see the edition of Strohm ([1949] 1968); but *Helene* had already attracted the attention of Solmsen (1934.2). For later articles on *Helene* see Zuntz (1958.2); Burnett (1960); Griffith (1953); Matthiessen (1968); and Segal (1971, 1972.2). Schwinge's study of stichomythy necessarily dealt heavily with these three plays, which make an extensive use of the form (1968.1, 117–31). Matthiessen's book (*Elektra, Taurische Iphigenie, und Helena,* 1964) made a structural comparison of three plays with recognition motifs. C. H. Whitman's major study of these plays, *Euripides and the Full Circle of Myth* (1974), is discussed below.

174. *Die euripideische Tragödie: Untersuchungen zu ihrer Tragik* (1968).

175. Pp. 13–16, Lesky (1957–58, 340).

176. P. 19. For a similar viewpoint, see Segal, *Tragedy and Civilization* (1981).

the presumed "tragic world view" to the literary form of tragedy itself, has a certain cogency.

Rohdich was almost unique in his willingness to confront the split between German- and English-speaking scholars and to ask what the observations of the rationalists might mean in literary terms.[177] But the major tendency of his work places him in the same group with advocates of Euripidean piety such as Spira and Burnett, since in Rohdich's view Euripides' work, far from supporting the iconoclastic views of the Sophists, opposed them radically and attempted to reassert a traditional tragic world view. In order to maintain that references to the Sophistic are associated with a consistent polemic against it, Rohdich was forced to adopt a tendentious and distorted view of fifth-century thought. Sophists are treated as robust optimists with a naive belief that freedom from suffering can be obtained through rational behavior.[178] In *Medeia* and *Bakchai* Rohdich treats Iason and Pentheus as Sophists, ignoring Sophistic elements in their opponents, Medeia and Tiresias.[179] Pentheus is marked as allied to the Sophistic view by his trust in his own eyes and visual evidence,[180] a particularly grotesque distortion, since it is quite likely that Gorgias' Sophistic theory of rhetoric rested on a skeptical view of sense impressions.[181] In addition, Rohdich's picture of the Euripidean tragic world view was qualified by the admission that the reestablished

177. It was this trait that apparently irritated critics against his book; reviewers dismissed it as Verrallian. (E.g., Reckford [1969]; Wilson [1969]). More mildly, Matthiessen (Review [1970, 239]): in trying to avoid the excessively harmonious view of Spira, R. "hat sich . . . am Ende in dem gleichen Dickicht der Spekulation verfangen wie vor ihm Verrall und Norwood." In fact, Rohdich never suggests ignoring divine aspects of the plays altogether, as, for instance, Conacher did. Unlike Garzya (1962), he makes no use of the two-level audience to cover irreducibly ironic or dissonant effects; and he tries to show how such effects could be a part of the technique of Euripidean theater.

178. See also p. 29: Alkestis' belief that one can make sense of life—e.g., through her sacrifice—is Sophistic in its optimism. In *Herakles,* the hero is a Sophist who sees his labors as valuable if they serve to guarantee him "Freiheit vom Leiden" (103). Ion subscribes to a Socratic version of this optimism (114–18). R. may have derived this notion in part from the article of Reinhardt (1957, 628). For criticism of this part of Rohdich's theory, see G. Müller (Review [1974, 329 and 332–33]).

179. Tiresias' belief that wine is needed to overcome human suffering shows that his true allegiance is to traditional values (145).

180. "Sehen und Sichtbarkeit ist die als fest beanspruchte Plattform, von der aus der aufgeklärte Geist die Welt bewältigt" (141). See also p. 142.

181. See *Defense of Helene* (DK 2:82 fr. 11B.15–18). Segal (1962, 105–7) discusses Gorgias' psychology of perception: Gorgias apparently argued that human beings communicate not reality, but sense impressions of reality, clothed in the form of the *logos* (109–10). On the Sophistic and Gorgianic affirmation of and trust in irrational forces, see Wehrli (1946, 16); Parry (1969, 352–53).

tragedy had itself undergone a tragic division in the struggle.[182] Somewhat simplified, this could seem to reproduce Pohlenz's picture of a Euripides eager to fulfill his traditional office of teacher of the people, but incapacitated for his vocation by cultural forces beyond his control. Once more, an attempt to synthesize and surmount opposing critical positions had foundered in the fatal "thicket" of Euripidean controversy.[183]

It remains to give an account of a book that, coming last in time, also had the effect of summarizing and bringing to an extreme the major currents of this fertile and contradictory period. Strohm's seminal book on formal structures in Euripidean plays found few adequate successors because, unlike the analyses of Ludwig, it did not lend itself to a relatively mechanical replication, but involved a study of literary variation that would show how structural elements altered and extended themselves to accommodate the needs of differing dramatic situations. Beginning in 1960 with her analysis of *Helene*, A. Pippin Burnett proved her ability to understand and to apply Strohm's techniques. Her book *Catastrophe Survived: Euripides' Plays of Mixed Reversal* appeared in 1971 and marked a close to work on the structure of Euripidean drama that had begun in the 1950s and had continued into the late sixties.

Burnett chose to analyze a sort of dramatic action that is quite typical of Euripides, in which the protagonists fall into one action, often involving danger or suffering, which undergoes a reversal, perhaps through vengeance or escape, in the second part.[184] Burnett showed the associated minor uses of reversal in Sophokles and Aischylos as well, where actions tended to be more unidirectional and simple. The great exaggeration of this technique in Euripides' work permitted the playwright to "force the spectator from his omniscient throne," since he could no longer, as in the theater of Sophokles, identify with an all-knowing and directing Power behind the dramatic events (15). Euripidean formalism could jar the audience through the use of "banal" traditional materials in a state of distortion or juxtaposed in unexpected ways (16).

182. "Sie selber tragisch entzweit" (1968, 21).

183. See also two books that attempted to eliminate dissonances in Euripides: W. Steidle's *Studien* (1968), a series of essays loosely oriented toward dramaturgy and staging, and G. Paduano's *La formazione del mondo ideologico e poetico di Euripide* (1968), a study of *Alkestis* and *Medeia*. Steidle defends the characters of such difficult figures as Elektra (63ff.); and Admetos (143ff.). He argues against Reinhardt and in favor of Solmsen's "tragedy of human weakness" (114–15). Paduano follows Lesky in treating Alkestis as a romantic figure. P.'s analysis of the previous scholarship is exhaustive and often perceptive; but, since he is convinced that an ironic interpretation of *Alkestis* "distrugge la possibilità di una interpretazione organica della tragedia" (19), his analysis is full of much extenuation and not a little sophistry; see App. B.

184. Burnett (1971, 1–5). On the reversal, see pp. 9–11.

Burnett's analysis showed how the plays could manipulate their audiences through the use of skillful theatrical technique. Probably because of Kitto's theories, she felt the possibility—as Strohm had not—that such manipulation would be devalued as typical of the "melodrama."[185] To forestall this, Burnett was prepared to find deeper meaning in all the plays by means even more violent and tendentious than those employed by Rohdich. Not only was the divine element in Euripidean drama required as Spira had suggested to resolve the turmoil generated on stage and in the audience by the dramatic conflicts, but the entire aesthetic range of each of these plays so rich in irony and artifice was to be subordinated to a religious goal, since each "depicts a divine pity and purpose that can, when it is ready, turn disaster into bliss."[186] This theodicy was supported by a severe and captious moral analysis that marked the actions of such figures as Kreousa and Megara as culpable and deserving of whatever misfortunes the plot visited on them.[187] The technique was even carried over into the treatment of formal elements: we are told that improper suppliant conduct is a sufficient justification for the horrible deaths of Herakles' wife and children.[188] The very dramatic forms that had been shown by Strohm and by Burnett herself to be notable for their dynamism now become rigid criteria determining which actions of dramatic characters must be subjected to censure.[189]

Though using an entirely different scheme from that of Rohdich, Burnett

185. For earlier introduction of this term by Kitto and others, see App. A. The "magnificent salvo of rescues" (1971, 48) ending *Iphigeneia Among the Taurians* could be viewed as "a blatant case of sensation for its own sake," if there were not some deeper meaning behind it (65); see also p. 183 on *Orestes*. For the connection with Kitto's assumption that only some extractable "meaning" can redeem Euripidean drama from the category of melodrama, see p. 127: the "permanent though unseen presence" of Apollon in *Ion* "redeems the two interruptions of Creusa's vengeance plot from the charge of melodrama or bad play-making . . ."

186. 1971, 14. In the actions of such a character as Orestes in *Andromache*, "evil and human fallibility have been explained in the only way they can be, as serving a providential purpose that mortals cannot know" (155). At the end of *Orestes* "Apollo's mere appearance can be expected to restore his servant's ailing faith, and with it his sanity, his *aidos*, and his normal pious lawfulness" (220).

187. E.g., Kreousa very nearly corrupts Ion "by telling him her lies about the god and tempting him to join her in her doubt" (123). See the wise remarks of Fritz on the curious standards of literary moral judgments (1962, 5ff.).

188. On Megara's impiety in choosing to leave the altar: "Now consider the unnatural suppliants of the *Heracles*. . . . Their decisions and their movements are in glaring violation of the rules of the suppliant plot" (160). Megara is guilty of materialism (162–63); and shows a lack of "belief in the efficacy of supernatural causes." The audience will recognize her impiety and see that the slaughter of her family is "not only necessary to heaven but freely chosen by those who have suffered it" (172).

189. See Segal (Review [1972]), and the review article by Knox (1972.1, 277): "One cannot help suspecting that these suppliants have offended not so much against the gods as against Burnett's Rules of the Drama . . ."

ended as he did in an interpretation that treated certain characters as the representatives of wrong and antitraditional views.[190] A further similarity is the tendentious and arbitrary nature of the moral criteria chosen; the sort of divinity that demonstrates the power of "its own loving internal order" (67) by rescuing the faithful or that visits severe punishment on a "lack of faith" (121) or worse yet "active unfaith" (162) cannot be developed out of any study of Hellenic culture and is an obvious importation from our own.[191] In its appeal to modern preconceptions, Burnett's treatment again resembled that of Rohdich, whose "Sophists," believing as they did in unconditional human "freedom" and stubbornly refusing any evidence but that of their own senses, resembled nothing so much as a caricature of modern rationalism.

Burnett's work exemplified, both in its excellences and in its failings, the quandary of modern Euripidean scholarship. Her structural study of the plays led her to a lively appreciation of the charms and piquancy of Euripidean style.[192] Her work marks an advance beyond Strohm's precisely in its grasp of this ironic quality in the plays. But the impulse toward the normalization of Euripidean theater has not been evaded but has merely been displaced onto a theodicy, where it regains and amplifies its distorting power. At the most strained points the study of dramatic structure itself becomes the tool of a sterile prescriptiveness. Worse, the preternaturally sensitive audience of Verrall, so useful to unlikely explication, is more than once called into play.[193]

190. Note particularly that each was forced into an especially violent analysis of *Herakles,* where the problem of divine justice comes very strongly to the fore, and that both direct a particular critique against the unfortunate Megara. Rohdich (1968, 84): Megara represents belief in "die Autarkie menschlicher Kraft und Fähigkeit."

191. Strohm (Review [1974, 346]) argues that this thesis "archaisiert" the gods; but his assumption seems to derive from another mistake, the tendency to push back on Aischylos and Sophokles notions of "piety" that provided a contrast with Euripides but that had little basis in Hellenic culture. An example would of course be Pohlenz' theory of tragic meaning; see Lattimore's review (1956, 199–200) of Pohlenz ([1930] 1954). Knox's assessment (1972.1, 278) is trenchant but just: Burnett's explanation of the plays requires moral and religious attitudes that can be found "nowhere, so far as I can see, in any writer who used the Greek language before the triumph of Christianity."

192. See her comments on the "Japanese finesse" of *Helene* (78), in which Euripides "teases his audience with a sense of imminent artistic disaster" (84).

193. P. 163: the "alert audience." At the end of *Herakles,* "the spectator begins to recall once more all that he knows about Heracles' life on Olympus. He remembers Hesiod's joyous lines, and the heavenly satyr play begins at last, though only on the inner stage of his imagination" (182). Burnett's critical approach underwent few modifications; see the 1977 article on *Troiades,* in which the Ganymede ode is used as the key to a theodicy which will prove that only through "joyful and submissive service to god" can human beings attain salvation (314).

III.D. THE LAST DECADE: A STEP FORWARD AND A STEP BACK

The decade between 1961 and 1971 had seen the appearance of at least seventeen major books on Euripides. The next decade was to present hardly more than four. Of these, the most striking was that of P. Vellacott, who made a determined attempt to return to the methodology of Verrall and at last get Euripides straight. Once again the differing reactions that may be evoked by the singular content and tone of Euripidean plays are to be divided among a dual or tripartite audience, no part of which is in communication with the other.[194] Where Burnett and Rohdich had each chosen one tendentious point around which to hang their analyses, Vellacott ranged widely, picking out some parts as instances of irony, others for allegorical explication, and others yet to be taken without any irony at all.[195] Where Verrall had used violent methods to make possible the acceptance of ironies in such plays as *Alkestis* and *Helene,* Vellacott's exegesis attempts to show that the plays, through a series of encoded references, consistently promoted a single unified doctrine that would be understood by somebody, or that was at least intended to be understood by somebody.[196]

Like Verrall and like Burnett, Vellacott argued that Euripides' work could not be worthy of acceptance as valid art without some explication that would reveal the apparently absent "deeper significance" that must be characteristic of such art. Only a very violent exegesis will restore Euripides to respectability.[197] It will be evident that some modification of this assumption lies behind most of the attempts at a broader interpretation of Euripides, from

194. 1975, 19: Euripides "presented his most telling truths in ways which carried illumination to the sympathetic instructed spirit, and roused anger in the shrewd and suspicious reactionary; but which made it easy for the average obtuse listener or reader to be unaware that anything harsh or disturbing had been said."

195. Examples of ironic interpretation: on Theseus' speech in *Suppliants,* "There is certainly nothing here which could be the intended 'message' of such a writer as Euripides" (27). We must therefore not believe the speech. Examples of allegorical interpretation: in *Suppliants,* "Athena is the contemporary Athenian Assembly" (32). *Phoinissai* "had proceeded to invite an identification of Thebes . . . with the imperiled fortunes of the Athenian Empire, and the mutual deaths of Eteocles and Polyneices with the mortal struggle between Athens and Sparta" (57). Examples of nonironic interpretation: "Theseus' leadership . . . is praised without irony" (30–31). Among the plays, *Helene* is uniquely "serious and philosophical" (150).

196. "It was unlikely that his plea would reach any ear that needed to hear it; but a prophet must unburden himself" (30). On *Helene,* "there is no record that anyone in the fifth or fourth century perceived the poet's mockery; it was too gentle" (136). In the case of *Herakleidai,* "Even if there were only one or two among the thousands in the theatre who . . . turned their thoughts to Plataea, . . . that fact is more significant than the blindness of the rest" (185).

197. See on *Orestes:* if we cannot find "a profound moral intention" in the play we will be compelled to admit that Euripides depends upon its "sordid appeal as a piece of sensational violence" (72). We must not assume that Euripides "chose [shocking] topics for their sensational value, without any deeper human or moral purpose" (94).

Kitto and Solmsen through Rohdich and Lesky. The analysis of K. von Fritz offers an escape from the quandary, in that it suggests how plays can make an aesthetic use of moral material, without the assumption that an extractable piece of moral instruction must emerge as a by-product of the drama. It is at any rate clear that many critics of Euripides have felt that demonstration of such a moral by-product justified almost any improbabilities of exegesis.

Another product of the seventies was C. H. Whitman's *Euripides and the Full Circle of Myth,* which appeared in 1974. Whitman devoted his book to those three "tragi-comedies" that had strongly engaged the attention of the literary interpreters of Euripides during the preceding decade. In his analyses of the three plays, Whitman largely paralleled the work of other scholars, who had seen these dramas as centering on a blind human struggle that is both mocked and blessed by divine concern.[198] A fourth chapter, on the place of the plays in a general assessment of Euripides, is of considerably more interest. There, Whitman attempted something that had largely been evaded by other critics who had used these plays: he tried to show their relation to the whole body of Euripides' work. What qualities marked them as separate, and what was their significance for the development of Euripidean art? Whitman's answers, while they did reproduce some of the presuppositions that had generated the quandary over Euripides, also provided some interesting suggestions for future development.

Using the categories of literary development proposed by Northrop Frye, Whitman suggested that the genius of Euripidean drama was an "ironic" one. While the work of Sophokles represented the classical "high mimetic" of Frye,[199] that of Euripides represented the next mode but one, that of the ironic, which produces "a kind of deliberate polytonality, as if tragedy were now being written in two keys at once."[200] This versatile and even self-contradictory mode fits several characteristics of Euripidean drama, including its self-conscious formalism.[201] This reconsideration of Euripides in generic terms was long overdue. The original rejection of Euripidean style by the Schlegels stemmed from a polemic against stylistic currents of the early nineteenth century, in which divergent elements of artifice, fantasy, irony,

198. E.g., on *Iphigeneia Among the Taurians,* the play is a skillful melodrama with deeper overtones, related to "the meaning of divinity as it enters the human scheme" (34). See also on *Helene,* pp. 53–54. On *Ion,* p. 102.

199. 1974, 107; see also p. 130: Sophokles' work is characterized by "a heroic, vertical axis, creating intension and unity." (Cf. pp. 143–44, on the horizontal axis of Euripidean art, which, in its circular sweep, included many different syntheses.)

200. 1974, 113. Frye (1957, 33–35) had presented a sequence of modes, in which the "low mimetic," essentially a period of realism, would follow the high. For elements of realism in Euripides, see Chap. 4 and discussion of *Herakles* in Chap. 8.

201. Euripides' work "betrays his presence" (114). Overnice definitions of tragedy that exclude Euripidean plays "miss his purposive use of conventional elements" (115).

and shock characterized the emerging literary art. A critical system that allows validity to a variety of artistic modes seems to offer an escape from the cycle of apology and rehabilitation.

Whitman's assessment of Euripidean style also incorporated some of the Classicist viewpoint. Again, the picture of a fragmented Euripides, torn in divergent directions by the currents of his day, explains the fragmented work of art.[202] The ironic double view and "reversals of moral perspective" (129) of many of the earlier plays amounted in Whitman's view to artistic flaws: the ironic style admitted "dynamic influences from any source whatever, rather favoring those that come from outer chaos, and leaving their results for the most part unassimilated" (131). Whitman's attempt to characterize Euripidean style as a valid, non-Sophoclean alternative could not be successful, since it was upon this negative view of irony that he based his separate analysis of the "tragi-comic" or "romantic" plays that he preferred. In these three plays, Whitman felt, we find that "all external irony"—that proceeding from our own relation to the play, as opposed to that generated by the circumstances of the plot—"is suppressed or assimilated," as everything "is adjusted to the larger, controlling vision"(139). In the recognitions that crown these plays, the "revelations are of inherent truth, like axioms rightly stated" (140). This group of plays thus includes the "whole tragic cycle" of redemption as well as suffering, while the others remain incomplete.[203]

Whitman did point out that whether or not one saw these plays as a climax of Euripidean art was largely a matter of taste; and he wisely treated them as part of an artistic development, refusing to characterize them as mere escapes from an unpleasant political or social environment.[204] But his analysis makes plain that, in spite of his characterization of Euripides as an ironic artist, it is precisely the muting or absence of "corrosive" irony in these plays that made them seem to Whitman "more complete" and more satisfying than the rest.[205] In order to make his analysis of these plays stick, Whitman was

202. "Euripides did not see life steadily, and his era provided him with little help in seeing it whole" (119). True myth represents a collective affirmation, but this is "in abeyance" in Euripides' day; "the age, not Euripides, was godless" (120). Conditions in the war years explain the "fitful disjointedness of Euripides' dramaturgy." The plays of this period are the "rather motley products of a lifelong attempt to see myth whole, an attempt outflanked by inherent contradictions seen all too clearly" (121).

203. Cf. a similar formulation in Rohdich (1968, 18).

204. Taste: p. 142. Euripides' ability to perceive a kind of salvation in these plays was "a perception appropriate to a phase, which had arisen inevitably out of the pursuit of his art" (137). The plays were not mere escapes (104).

205. Another critic who saw Euripides as a master of irony had also chosen to begin his analysis with that particular play from which he felt sure irony could be excluded. Zuntz (1955.1, 20): in *Suppliants* Euripides "narrowed his all-embracing vision. No ironical hint is allowed to threaten . . ."

forced to smooth over and extenuate elements that place them very much in line with other Euripidean work.[206] Further, the approach succeeds by skating over the central quality that has always been sensed in these three plays and that, along with their concentration on the *anagnôrisis* pattern, constitutes their claim to be treated as a group. Their lightness and insubstantiality, and the air of charm and faint unreality that pervades the dramatic proceedings, have in fact led some critics to argue that these plays do not belong to the tragic genre at all.[207] If it is indeed here, in these uncharacteristically playful and gentle dramas, that Euripides achieves something close to a "whole" or "rounded" effect, that achievement may be an indication that wholeness and roundedness are by no means central to Euripidean dramaturgy, or that, when present, these qualities tended to be compensated for by other stylistic changes.[208]

III.E. CONCLUSIONS

The years between the mid-seventies and the present have not produced much major work on Euripides, but the volume of periodical literature continues to grow.[209] Work on individual plays is a heartening counterpoise to the constant regeneration of old antinomies in the broader criticism, and a number of recent analyses do much to make clear the workings of the Euripidean aesthetic. Recently two books have been devoted to single plays, with illuminating results: P. Pucci (1980) has shown the ambiguity of emotion, rhetoric, and emotional rhetoric in *Medeia;* and C. Segal has treated *Bakchai*

206. In *Helene* the scene between Menelaos and the old doorkeeper is a stumbling block: Whitman argued that we cannot assume that Euripides "would tastelessly insert a scene of broad comedy" (46–47); see also p. 68: "In drawing Menelaus, Euripides may have gone too far . . . and so made him a little more ludicrous than was suitable for the generally serious tone; like every bold innovator, Euripides may stumble on occasion." Burian comments (1976, 110): "Evidently the comic elements cause him discomfort, and it is interesting to watch him attempt to divest the play of them or at least to mimimize their significance."

207. Knox in "Euripidean Comedy" ([1970] 1979.3, 250).

208. Only *Iphigeneia Among the Taurians* seems to lack what Whitman called "external irony." Whitman attempted to counter the bitter notes in the *Ion* by arguing that Ion attains true purity through suffering and knowledge (92–93). But uplift is hard to find in the sudden resolution: see the comment of Leeuwen (1876, 37): "Quis talia probet? Quis ferat tam caecum furorem repente mutatum in tam serenam laetitiam?" In *Helene* irony becomes a major theme: see the original article by Solmsen (1934.2); Segal (1971, 559 and 609ff.). See also Zuntz (1958.1, 223) on the "ironical coincidence of error and truth" in that play.

209. See the comment of Burian in his review article (1976, 113): "Today's critic has little indeed in the way of broad, general lines of interpretation on which to build." He goes on to say that most readers would probably agree that "the best work is being done in journals, in articles that deal with individual plays or aspects of individual plays."

as a microcosm of tragedy itself (1982).[210] *Alkestis*,[211] *Medeia*,[212] *Herakleidai*,[213] *Suppliants*,[214] *Herakles*,[215] *Elektra*,[216] *Orestes*,[217] and *Iphigeneia at Aulis*,[218] have all received analysès that go beyond apologetics and attempts at rehabilitation through exegesis. As a group these analyses suggest the variety and vigor of Euripidean drama and demonstrate that its variousness does not preclude design.

The critical controversies that I have traced over many decades have been much more than a series of disagreements and confusions over a difficult author. Their repetitive quality derives from a cultural attitude that lies at the root of most modern pedagogy and scholarship about the Greeks. The critical revolution that dethroned Euripides and replaced him with Sophokles was not a mistake that can or should be reversed: what it represented was nothing less than the point at which modern culture broke off from a continuous derivation out of ancient culture and—in acquiring a sense of its own separation from antiquity—also became aware of the fifth century as a distinct and significant moment in history. As I will attempt to suggest in the following chapter, the restoration of Sophokles to his throne corresponds to the historical reality of the roles of Sophokles and Euripides in fifth-century culture, the one representing that culture's own best view of itself, the other representing an antithesis to that view.

The Schlegels' view of Euripides was valid and was also determined by the limits of its purpose, which was to make the Athenian fifth century assimilable and useful for modern culture. The model of the "classic" which they constructed has retained its appeal both as a descriptive paradigm, creating the view of the Greek fifth century that all of us imbibed from our teachers and from the first books we read about the Greeks, and as a prescriptive paradigm, setting up a model against which poets and artists have posed their own, "modern" aesthetic. Euripides' work has been a casualty of this process.

A major part of the Euripidean knot has been the persistence of a split in the dramatist's vocation, between poet and thinker. As I have pointed out, this split is traceable to the assumptions of nineteenth-century criticism that

210. Very recent works by Foley (1984) and Burian (1985) probably indicate that the present book is part of a renewed cycle of interest in Euripides.

211. See App. B.

212. E. Schlesinger (1966); Reckford (1968); Burnett (1973).

213. Burian (1977.1); Burnett (1976).

214. W. D. Smith (1967.1); Gamble (1970).

215. Chalk (1962).

216. Zeitlin (1970).

217. Parry (1969); Burkert (1974); Fuqua (1976, 1978); and Zeitlin (1980).

218. Straat (1959); Lesky (1973.1); W. D. Smith (1979).

the poet, and especially the classical poet, is antithetic to the "thinker" or the scientist. According to this view, the elevated nature of poetic discourse matches the elusive nature of its subjects.[219] Euripidean poetry, which mimics the styles of rhetoric and philosophy and which retails the controversy of the day, appears in this light either as disappointingly "modern", or as unpoetic, or simply as bad. The apparently antithetical critical positions generated by this paradox all require continual qualification, if they are presented moderately; and, even when followed to logical extremes, they end in contradiction. If Euripides is wholly a poet and will be judged as such, then conventional standards of poetic decorum must be applied to his work, with the predictable necessity for much apology and twisting of the argument. If Euripides is not wholly a poet, then some other basis of explication for his work will make more sense than the poetic one. But the extracted material does not make systematic sense; and the reagents required to precipitate it out usually render the plays, not just bad, but thoroughly unintelligible.

The continual explanations and apologies required in either case create the phantasm of a strange poetic (or antipoetic) "personality," a ghost behind the plays, pushing and pulling them here and there. But, if the plays are treated as a hopeless hodgepodge of aesthetic mistakes, the ghost then does not become less elusive and may even acquire whole sets of monstrously contradictory traits. The skillful and facile theatrical technician who proceeds to spoil his plays out of moral principle is matched by the doctrinaire philosopher who cannot resist weakly pretty poetic fancies. The specialist in female emotional maladies (*Leidenschaft*) turns cold rhetorician, just as we become absorbed in his art. We break our hearts over the most harrowing and pathetic of tragedians (*tragikôtatos*), only to find ourselves in the next scene repressing a terrible urge to snigger.[220] The most violent and improbable expedients have long been tried against these anomalies, without success, and without consensus, since one such exploit merely provokes another of a different stamp.

It will not do to look aside from the history of Euripidean criticism with embarrassment or to hope that we are now beyond such aberrations. In the first place, the same patterns have been recapitulated even in very recent times. In the second, the understanding and assimilation of this history are necessarily a part of the process of getting beyond it. The tactic of Verrall would have been impossible, without the basis of undiscovered contradiction on which the scholarly approaches to Euripides had developed; and these same tactics could not have maintained their appeal as they did without the

219. For the parallel but somewhat different genre split between the comic and the tragic modes, see Chap. 7, below, on *Elektra*.

220. See discussion of Norwood (1954), above.

persisting support of that same, essentially unchanged foundation. If Euripidean drama is susceptible to any effective analysis—and it is the premise of this book that it is—then that analysis must be based on those qualities that have caused scandal and provoked defense and attack. Euripidean poetics must be able to confront an art of shock and discontinuity, artificiality and irony, an art that opposes tradition. Critical approaches to such an art lie very close at hand, precisely where we would expect to find them, in that same dissonant modern culture that the Classicist model was constructed to confront. Such a critical approach holds open a further possibility that cannot be realized within the framework of this book: it is possible that, in bringing Euripides back into the cultural tradition of the Greek fifth century, we may be working toward a new image of that tradition and of its significance.

2

Euripides and His Tradition

Once scholars began to concentrate on the Athenian fifth century as a unique and isolable peak in the tradition of the West, the existence of Sophokles' work, which seemed to embody the essence of the period, posed problems for the reception of Euripides. Because of the process of change, historical periods that are significant as watersheds between old and new appear to display contradictory qualities. The Athenian fifth century marks for us, at one and the same time, the culmination of the Greek aesthetic tradition, an end to its early development, and the starting point of a new and secondary cultural tradition. In this new tradition, the relation between poetry and speculative thought undergoes a reversal. In the second half of the fifth century, speculative thought is dominated by figures whose claim to be philosophers at all has been much questioned, in antiquity as in modern times,[1] just as, in comparison both to the titanic contemporary philosophers and to the great geniuses of the stage and of lyric in the fifth century, fourth-century poetry seems to dwindle in importance. Admittedly, these assessments are supported by the failure of much of this work to survive; but scholars have often been willing to acquiesce in the judgment of tradition, treating

1. Segal (1962, 100 and nn.16, 17) documents the attempt by Gomperz (1912, 31–35) to eliminate Gorgias from any consideration as a philosopher: "Der 'philosophische Nihilismus' des Gorgias ist aus der Geschichte der Philosophie zu streichen" (35). See Kerferd (1981, Chap. 2, p. 4ff.; "Towards a History of Interpretations of the Sophistic Movement"): in contrasting "philosophers" and "Sophists" Wilhelm Nestle "was really doing what his predecessors had done, namely restricting the term philosopher to a certain kind (the approved kind) of philosopher" (10).

the fifth-century Sophists and the fourth-century tragedians as negligible.[2] Because Euripides' work seemed to reach out both to the contemporary work in philosophy and in rhetoric and to the later development of Greek art in the Hellenistic period, it suffered something of the same depreciation.

A fascination with what was enduring and transmittable in the history of the fifth century has led to a strong focus on the tradition that was coming to an end, or to a culmination, and on whatever static elements in social or intellectual history could be isolated out of a period of radical change and violent conflict. Sophokles' work represented the development in Athens of an art form that could rival the Homeric epic in its significance for Greeks, both in his time and after, as well as for Western culture as a whole; and because of this, Sophoclean drama could be seen as the kind of lasting achievement (a "classic") that would hypostatize the significance of an important period.[3] Euripides' work, by contrast, has been seen as a kind of aesthetic chaos, the mere reflection of elements of the fifth century that had to be neglected, in order for the classic to emerge clearly in our view of the period.[4] More recent critics, however, have suggested that the tragic art form itself is a product of extreme cultural tension, representing perhaps a last titanic synthesis of what was rapidly becoming uncontainable, a last union of the disparate past and present.[5] As such, tragedy expresses both aspects of a watershed period, a dynamic that appears in different forms in the work of all three of the great tragedians.

Athens' movement in the middle fifth century toward a central position in Hellenic culture was symbolized by tragedy—a Panhellenic artistic achievement rivaling Homeric epic—and displayed concretely at the opening ceremonies in the theater, where a Panhellenic audience could watch the

2. For characteristics of the (lost) fourth-century tragedy, see Collard (1970, on Chairemon); Webster (1954); Strohm (1959, on *Rhesos*). Xanthakis-Karamanos (1979, 101) argues that the changes in the fourth century reflected the problems of the period, which made it difficult for people to face "true tragedies." This overlooks social problems in the fifth century; see discussion below.

3. See the article of Lesky ([1953] 1966.3, 213 – 19).

4. See the assumption of a (rather puzzlingly sudden) decline (*Verfall*), a notion forced on the Schlegels by their Classicist viewpoint (Chap. 1, Section I, above). This idea reappears in Lesky (1957 – 58, 340): Euripides belongs to the period of the "Hochklassik"; yet paradoxically the unity or closure (*Geschlossenheit*) of classic art, as symbolized by Sophokles and the Parthenon, gives way ("beginnt . . . aufzulösen") in the work of Euripides.

5. See Reiss (1980, 16 – 24): tragedy strives toward a normative synthesis through an internal discourse between clashing norms. Segal (1981, 8 – 12): the tragic hero expresses the polarized values of a society in conflict. See also the analysis of Kuhn (1942, 67): the bedrock of archaic social values still endures but is subject to ever-increasing challenges from the new individualism; and Vernant & Vidal-Naquet (1972, 70).

parade of the tribute monies from the empire.[6] Gloom from what we know about the Athenian defeat at the end of the war tends to color our view of the last years of the century;[7] but in spite of the plagues, invasions, and dissensions of the war years, we should not forget the abounding vitality of Athens before, during, and after that period. Neither should we discount either the intense stimulation or the intense discomfort that attended the intellectual, political, moral, and military turmoil.[8] If Sophokles and Euripides provide us with two different lenses for viewing the explosive changes of their period, it is likely that they did the same thing for their contemporaries, who, through the new perspective they were acquiring on the human past, were made aware of their own remarkable times as representing both an ending and a beginning.

An artist is always especially concerned with the problem of change and its dynamic, since art, of all elements in culture, is both entirely dependent upon sign systems worked out by a lengthy tradition, and uniquely committed to innovation, origination, and novelty.[9] Sophokles, whose work creates an impression of continuity with cultural tradition, was a great innovator as well; and Euripides was a great exploiter of tradition. In the pages that follow, I will suggest that a unifying factor in Euripidean poetry may be found in its juxtaposition with and response to the inherited form of tragedy. Partly because of our ignorance of the wider background, but largely as a reflection of the fifth century's literary history, this antithesis is best expressed by the contrast between Euripidean and Sophoclean tragic poetry. The claim of this viewpoint to consideration lies in its explanatory power: the apparently

6. See Pickard-Cambridge (1968, 64–67) for the order of festivities, which included the awarding of civic crowns; discussion of the civic significance of tragedy by Cantarella (1965, 49–50).

7. This view is the product both of Thukydides' history and of reflections from our own contemporary experience; see Chap. 1, Section II.C, above, on attempts to link the poetry of Euripides with the Peloponnesian war.

8. See Segal (1981, 6): "'Classical serenity' is a label affixed to an age characterized by the most immense disruptions of spirit and of events"; and Vernant & Vidal-Naquet (1972, 70).

9. The poet of oral epic may seem to us little conscious of the innovative element in his approach to the tradition, but cf. *Od.* 1.351–52. Post-Homeric poetry shows a strong awareness of the role of innovation; see Alkman *PMG* 14a, Pindaros *Ol.* 3.4. On the function of innovation, see Shklovskij's principle of *Verfremdung* or alienation ("Die Kunst als Verfahren" [(1916) 1969, 15ff.]). The term should not be confused with its use in Brechtian theatrical theory; it refers to artistic techniques for revivifying what is conventional and familiar in art or in everyday experience) and Tynjanov ([1924] 1969.2, 395–415). See also Rorty (1979, 360) on the "poetic" activity of what he calls "edifying discourse." Rorty argues that this kind of discourse—as opposed to "normal" discourse, in which we are all pretty much agreed upon terms and standards—is *supposed* to be abnormal, to take us out of our old selves by the power of strangeness . . ."

incongruous elements of Euripidean style acquire unity in their opposition to a Sophoclean norm.

In attempting to determine what part of the later view of Sophokles can be ascribed to the fifth century, it is necessary to analyze a poetic persona that, while it represents neither an accurate biographical reflection of the poet's life, nor a thorough critical reaction to the plays, does constitute the best expression of what the artist's work meant for his contemporary society as well as for the later ancient tradition.[10] We have already met with Euripides' public persona, since the picture of the brooding outsider, lonely and unhappy in domestic and social life, was readily adopted by modern critics. The story of the cave on Salamis, where the poet was said to compose in solitude, like the legend of Demosthenes' underground study (*katageion meletêrion*),[11] is a valuable indication of the way contemporaries viewed the work of these artists.[12] The isolation of the artificer from society marks his determination to achieve a conscious mastery over his art, as it suggests his possible alienation. The traditional persona of Sophokles is the complement to that of Euripides and, like it, is designed to express the significance of his work for his contemporaries and their posterity.

In analyzing the reaction of Euripidean art to Sophokles, I do not intend to probe the personal biography or psychology of either author. Data for such a biography are scanty, and what exist have been proved to be almost wholly fabricated. The dominant sources for most ancient biographies were the host of defamatory references preserved usually in the comic plays, but also perhaps surviving in speeches from the law courts.[13] But, even if accurate information were available, it would very likely be useless for literary purposes. The connection between the life experience and psyche of an artist and his work is hard to trace; and at the end of the process, given the fact that cultural norms are of more moment to the history of literature than individual deviation, the life is likely to be better illuminated than the work.[14] In any

10. On the value of such evidence, see Hartung (1843, 95): while not factually of any importance, stories about literary figures "ad intelligenda quidem veterum iudicia cernendasque hominum opiniones summi mihi momenti esse . . . videntur."

11. For the cave, see Satyros 39.9.6 (p. 62 Arrighetti). Demosthenes' chamber, or a facsimile, was extant even in Plutarchos' day; see *Demosth.* 7.

12. See Lesky, who remarks that the stories about Euripides mark the beginning of the modern Western stereotype of the artist ([1956] 1972.1, 278).

13. The undependability of poetic biography is beginning to be understood; see Lefkowitz (1981, 1979), Fairweather (1974, 233ff.). For the effect of court speeches, which contained all sorts of jibes and libels, see the process of one Hygiainon against Euripides (Aristoteles *Rhet.* 1416a29ff.; Dover [1976, 36]), and Dover's speculations (1976, 28 – 34) on the tendency of biographers and historians to accept such statements as evidence for actual events.

14. See the remarkable article of Zielinski (1902). Belief in the primary significance of the artist's biography, personality, and idiosyncratic traits has been an immense stumbling block to the study of Greek literature in the past century, as Homeric and Pindaric studies demonstrate in a variety of ways. See the Czech structuralist Mukařovský ([1966] 1978, 28): aesthetic theory

case, since Euripides' personality, obscured as it is by a thicket of heroic mythology and comic or forensic defamation,[15] must remain forever unknown to us, we must be satisfied to inspect his work, and to make use of the available biographical data that cast light on that work.

These data, which constitute the literary rather than the personal biography of the tragic poet, have much to tell us about the artist's relation to his public, the judges and audience of his work,[16] and to his fellow competitors. A relation of intense competitiveness is implied by the poet's status as originator; and in Greece, and especially in the tragic contests, competition was codified, formalized, and quantified. No poet could be in any doubt about his standing both currently and over his whole career.[17] Unlike the personal biographical data, this material is quite reliable, since it is based on didascalic records of competition that were preserved through the research of Aristoteles and that formed the basis for literary scholarship from the late fifth century on.[18] It is unnecessary to add speculation on Sophokles' subjective reaction to his success or Euripides' to his failures. The *didaskaliai* are a record of the relation of each to the audience, and of the status of each playwright

---

has demonstrated "the difference between an authentic document [of the psychological state of the subject] and an aesthetically intentional expression. . . . That even today studies are written which consider artistic expressions as [material for psychiatric study] is not the fault of modern aesthetics but of whoever is ignorant of its present state."

15. Lefkowitz points out the tendency of the poet's biography to assume certain forms familiar through heroic myth (1981, 86 – 87 and 97 – 98); see Nagy (1979, 301 – 8). Lefkowitz argues that comic defamation and heroic myth operate as two distinct and often conflicting forces in creating the Euripidean biography.

16. That the judges were ordinary people, representative of the audience, seems likely; see Pickard-Cambridge (1968, 95 – 99). That they were often influenced by the audience is certain—see Pickard-Cambridge (97: a reference to Platon, *Laws* 2, 659a); as well as Walcot (1976, 2 – 3).

17. On the relation of artist to audience, see Michelini (1982, 20 – 24). Competitiveness in literary life tends to be masked in modern times, but cf. Moss (1982, 2, a review of *Poets in Their Youth* by Eileen Simpson): M. is baffled by evidence for "the constant worry about 'reputation,' the endless concern of where one stood on the scale of 'greatness'" in the biographies of modern poets. See also the important essay of Tynjanov ([1921] 1969.3) on the relation of Dostoevskij to Gogol. One may also compare Bloom's *Anxiety of Influence* (1973); though marred by a gloomy phallic mystique (e.g., poets are frustrated by an inability to "harden apocalyptically" [24]), his work has interesting things to say about artistic rivalry, e.g., on the Satanic mission of the poet (32) as a disrupter of previous achievements.

18. *Didaskaliai* (the original meaning is equivalent to "production") were preserved in documentary form until the late fourth century, when they were published by Aristoteles, with the addition of at least some clarifying notes—see Reisch in *RE* s.v. *Didaskalia*; Pickard-Cambridge (1968, 70); Fairweather (1974, 253 – 54). For the attribution to Aristoteles himself, see Mensching (1964, 16), Schachermeyr (1972, 308 – 9); the latter sees this research as basic to Aristoteles' work on poetry. This work formed the basis for later listings such as the *Pinakes* of Kallimachos, as well as for inscriptional lists of victors, *didaskaliai,* and the like (Reisch; see also Pickard-Cambridge [71 – 73]).

relative to all others. This elaborately structured public record makes clear the concrete measurements of prestige that underlie the fantastic biographies of the poets.

Sophokles' life and his traditional persona are those of a man thoroughly embedded in society, who receives at every stage of his life the greatest appropriate honor. Unlike Euripides, who was constantly lampooned, Sophokles was not a butt of the comic poets.[19] The inscription that records him as *Hellênotamias* for 443/42 has been questioned,[20] but the appointment would have suited what we know of Sophokles' abilities and background;[21] and the historical validity of at least one generalship is confirmed by a fifth-century eyewitness, Ion of Chios.[22] The personality ascribed to him is a match to all this, charming, sexually attractive, graceful, easygoing, yet dignified and sedate.[23] What we know of the dramatic career of Sophokles suggests to us the corresponding dimensions of what must have been a remarkable talent. We have good reason to believe that his reputation and his influence were already strong in the middle years of the fifth century, when Euripides began to compete. It has been argued that we should not treat Sophokles as a formative influence on Euripides' art, since the two were for long decades contemporaries and rivals.[24] But, when Euripides' first tragedy was produced in 455, Sophokles had already been active in tragic theater for

19. According to the *Vita* (1, p. xvii Pearson). See also U. v. Wilamowitz (1907, 9) and Martin (1958, 245).

20. Avery [1973].

21. See Ehrenberg (1954, 117ff., 134 – 36) and Lefkowitz (1981, 76).

22. Ath. 13.603e. References to other generalships may come from the normal garbling process, whereby Sophokles the general must come into contact with, e.g., Nikias: Plut. *Nic.* 15; see Lefkowitz (1981, 80 – 81). Aristophanes, *Peace* 698, may refer to yet another generalship but may equally likely refer to an embassy, or to private business. On the several generalships, see Webster (1969, 12 – 13); and Woodbury (1970).

23. Cataudella (1969, 217): the traits given Sophokles are those of "una felicità esterna" typical of a handsome, rich, wellborn man, who has been successful in love and in artistic competition; see Schadewaldt, "Sophokles und Athen," on his amiability ([1935] 1970, 370 – 71) and his status as *Götterliebling* (387); and the contrasts detailed above in Chap. 1 between the pious and "serene" Sophokles and his melancholy and tormented rival.

In Phrynichos' *Muses,* perhaps written just after the poet's death, appeared the famous lines in which Sophokles is congratulated on his "blessedness" (31K); in another fragment (65K), perhaps also from this play, his poetry is likened to Pramnian wine. See also Kratinos' attack on an archon who gave a chorus to one Gnesippos, passing over Sophokles (15K; Pickard-Cambridge [1968, 84]. Note that Gnesippos—see the other attacks quoted in Athenaios 14.638f—was, like Euripides, accused of using modern music and sexual themes.) For Sophokles as graceful and witty (*dexios*) at dinner, see the anecdote from the memoir of Ion of Chios (Ath. 13, 603f and 604d). Ion goes on to say that in political matters Sophokles was not clever but was "like any other respectable Athenian [ὡς ἄν τις εἷς τῶν χρηστῶν Ἀθηναίων]." The Aristophanic characterization as "easygoing" (*eukolos*) is discussed below.

24. An argument made by DeCharme (1893, 208 – 9).

a thirteen-year period, during which his prestige must have been consistently and uniquely high.

It took Aischylos, competing against Phrynichos, Choirilos, and Pratinas, fifteen years to win a first victory;[25] it was to take Euripides, whose first play placed last,[26] the same amount of time. The slow start for Aischylos, an artist who later attained great prestige, may indicate conservative tendencies in an audience reluctant to dethrone old favorites in favor of young upstarts. But Sophokles' talent seemed able to overleap the audience's reserves, winning tributes that were apparently unprecedented. He began with a victory in 468; and it seems likely that, at some point in that first decade, he was able to defeat Aischylos as well.[27] The auspicious beginning was to be emblematic of Sophokles' good fortune as a competitor, since he is reported never to have placed last in any tragic competition. Before 458, when he had been competing for less than a decade, Sophokles had already acquired sufficient influence to induce the archons to permit the addition of a third actor to the Aeschylean complement of two.[28]

The malicious stories about Aischylos' "retreat" illustrate the extent to which a tradition may be significant, regardless of its basis in fact. Whatever reasons actually led Aischylos after 458, when he was past the age of sixty-five, to travel to Sicily,[29] it seemed reasonable to the contemporary public to

25. On Aischylos' first victory, in 485, see the *Marmor Parium*, 50 (Jacoby). On his competition with Choirilos and Pratinas, see the *Suda*, s.v. Pratinas (4:191 Adler).

26. This was *Peliades;* see the *Genos Euripidou* (Schwartz [1887, 2.2–3]). The year of Euripides' first victory, according to the *Mar. Par.* 60, was 442/41, and Euripides was by then forty-four years old. (Sophokles was over fifty; it had been twenty-six years since his first victory in 468.) For other chronological evidence, see the testimonia collected in Nauck's edition ([1871] 1913, xvi n.17).

27. Sophokles' first victory is known from several sources. The plays seem to have included *Triptolemos*: Plinius (*NH* 18.7) links Sophokles' first victory date with this play; see *Marmor Parium* 56 (p. 16–17 Jacoby). In Plutarchos (*Kimon* 8) we hear that the victory over Aischylos occurred at the first performance; but the circumstances seem wrong. The defeat of Aischylos by Sophokles would indeed be a momentous occasion; but the story deals with difficulties anticipated in the judging and so fits better the period after Sophokles had achieved his debut victory, when the young playwright would have acquired a reputation, and the material for a riot in the theater would be ready at hand; see the objections of Haigh (1896, 128 n.2). On disturbances in the theater, see Chap. 3, below. The date of such an event would be anywhere between 466 and 459, excluding 463, if that was the date of Aischylos' *Suppliants*.

28. Aischylos uses a third actor in each of the plays of the *Oresteia*. See Michelini (1984) for evidence that points to Sophokles as the first user of a third actor and to the *Oresteia* as Aischylos' premiere use of the new device. Lefkowitz (1981) argues that the attribution to Sophokles is another part of the biographical fiction (74, 77); but the question could have been resolved through the didascalic evidence.

29. This was after *Oresteia* in 458. Aischylos was said to have died in 456 and to have been buried there. The Geloans entombed him "lavishly, among the public monuments [πολυτελῶς ἐν τοῖς δημοσίοις μνήμασι]" (*Vita* [332, 21–23 Page]), thus providing enduring evidence of the place of his death. (I believe Lefkowitz [1981, 79 and 86] goes too far in discounting such

interpret this action as a retreat before the threatening prestige of his young rival.[30] It does not matter what Aischylos himself thought of his departure. In spite of the success of the titanic *Oresteia* in 458, it is undeniably true that at the court of his Sicilian patron he would be removed from continually repeated competitions in which he, as the senior competitor, stood to gain little and in which he would continue to lose prestige by any additional defeat.[31] It is one of the ironies of Sophokles' career that, when the aged Euripides in his turn left Athens for a foreign court, his emigration, like Aischylos', could be and doubtless was interpreted by contemporaries as a retreat before Sophokles.[32]

These remarkable signs of prestige and acceptance for the work of Sophokles are quite unmatched in the careers of either of the other two great dramatists and are tokens of a singular degree of public favor for this artist. During the crucial years when Euripides' talent was acquiring its mature shape, the domination of the tragic theater by the rising star of Sophokles was a basic given that could not be without its effect on any younger competitor. His work set the mark at which other contestants for public favor had to aim. Later in the century, but at least by the 420s, Aischylos' plays were being revived at the Dionysia.[33] This special status for one playwright marked him as someone who had entered, or rather had begun, a special canon of tragic poets whose work would be a permanent possession. In these same years, given the fact that Sophokles' ability to compete with and win against Aischylos had been proven while the latter was still alive, the implications for Sophokles' future could not have escaped his contemporaries. It was already obvious that someday the plays of Sophokles would also be revived and that Sophokles was destined to become the second member of the canon of tragic masters.

There has been a considerable amount of critical agreement on some

---

evidence altogether.) That the trip was an emigration rather than a visit may be popular fancy, but the advanced age of the poet tends to support a permanent move.

30. Aischylos' prestige in his later life and after his death was immense. See Aristophanes' treatment of him in *Frogs*; and the *Vita* (333.1 – 2 Page); Pickard-Cambridge (1968, 86); and Lefkowitz (1981, 73). It is precisely his success against such a competitor that gives the measure of Sophokles' prestige. The idea of Aischylos' resentment is persistent; see the *Vita* (332.6 – 7 Page): ἡσσηθεὶς νέῳ ὄντι Σοφοκλεῖ and the garbled account in Plut. *Kimon* 8.

31. On the advantages afforded poets by the courts of tyrants, see Woodbury (1968, 535 – 37), Podlecki (1980).

32. On Euripides' retreat, see Lefkowitz (1981, 103), who again seems rather excessively skeptical: the Athenians would certainly have known and remembered if Euripides had died there. But the fact of the retreat is less important for my purposes than what it signifies about the view taken of these competitive relationships.

33. See Pickard-Cambridge (1968, 86): in *Acharnians* 9 – 12, the hero Dikaiopolis anticipates a production of an Aeschylean play.

prevailing characteristics of Sophoclean theater. The plays move away from
the formal and frontal style of Aeschylean (or archaic) drama in which an
action is explored from a variety of contemplative and active standpoints,
through the media of dialogue, narrative, and choral and monodic lyric. In
Sophoclean plays a more unified style pulls the dramatic event into a tighter
focus; and the multiple viewpoints of Aeschylean theater are subordinated to
that of the individual protagonist.[34] A number of Sophoclean changes, such
as the rejection of trilogic form, supported this change of focus. In the single
play, besides the gains in unity and concentration, the exclusion of a broad
social and temporal context may help to enhance the timeless and universal
quality of the protagonist, thus expanding the significance of individual
experience.[35] Other changes, including freer interaction between and among
actors, and a greatly diminished choral role, tend to the same effect of
intensification.[36] As a result the mimic world of the theater gains in integrity,
persuasiveness, and urgency, thus acquiring the complex of qualities that we
are accustomed to call "dramatic."

The elegance of Sophoclean dramatic technique is such that these major
alterations did not appear to his contemporary audience as radical or excessively innovative; and it was not necessary for them to make a conscious
change in taste or to reject the past. The organic style that proved so enthralling also possessed the power to conceal artifice.[37] Significantly, Aristoteles
asserts that Sophokles is superior to Euripides in keeping his chorus more
closely involved as "one of the actors," although the amount and quality of
choral participation in the iambic scenes of both dramatists is virtually the
same, and in both cases is much less than in the work of Aischylos.[38] Similarly, the contrast between Aeschylean theater with its aim of shock and
"astonishment" (*ekplêxis*) and that of Euripides, the theater of *apatê*,

34. The point has been made by virtually every writer on Sophocles: see Lesky ([1956]
1972.1, 264); Jones (1962, 159); Knox (1964, 1–5); Gould (1978, 51). See Whitman (1974,
130), on the "organic architecture" of Sophoclean plays.

35. See Pohlenz ([1930] 1954, 228): Sophoclean heroes "tragen in sich das
Allgemeingültige, das auch die Jahrtausende überdauert."

36. Knox (1964, 7): Sophoklean drama enhances concentration on a heroic figure and the
"great crises of the hero's life."

37. The sleight of hand revealed by T. v. Wilamowitz's analysis of the plays (1917) is corro-
borating evidence for the deceptive naturalism of Sophoclean technique. On the innovations of
Sophokles and his ability to conceal them, see Winnington-Ingram (1980, 3); Fritz ([1934.1]
1962, 254), on Sophokles' deceptive "äussere Glätte"; Lefkowitz (1981, x): once concentration
on biographical data no longer blinds us, "it may appear that of the three tragedians, Sophocles
is the boldest innovator, both in technique and his vision of human experience..."

38. 1458a25–27: ἕνα δεῖ ὑπολαμβάνειν τῶν ὑποκριτῶν καὶ μόριον εἶναι τοῦ ὅλου καὶ
συναγωνίζεσθαι μὴ ὥσπερ Εὐριπίδῃ ἀλλ᾽ ὥσπερ Σοφοκλεῖ. On the role of the chorus, see
Kitto ([1939] 1961, 159ff.); Pohlenz ([1930] 1954, 221–22); Gredley (1973).

naturalistic deception, appropriately overlooks the real master of *apatê*, the first artist to teach us that art should conceal itself.[39] In *Frogs* a joke about Sophokles (80–82) points up the resulting blandness of his artistic personality. Euripides, being a rogue (*panourgos*), would readily consent to run away from Hades with Dionysos; but Sophokles does not have the temperament: "he was easygoing here and will be easygoing down there."[40] Unlike Euripides, the second tragedian is no threat to the prestige of Aischylos and does not attempt to rival him in Hades.[41]

With the establishment of a canon and the contemporary domination of Sophokles, tragedy began to acquire a sense of itself as a fixed and settled literary form. There is normally a continual and continually renewed struggle between artist and audience, the former pressed toward change and innovation through his attempts to better his rivals and his predecessors, the latter tending to conservatism because of its interest in retaining a vital and accessible literary tradition. In tragedy during the second half of the century this dynamic was muted, since, where the work of Sophokles was concerned, the members of the audience were no longer exercising to the full their usual critical and supervisory function. Sophokles took first place in a very high proportion of the tragic competitions in which he presented plays, placing second perhaps in only one of three or even one of four contests; and he never suffered the rebuke of a third-place ranking.[42]

The tragic norm, which before the middle of the fifth century could have existed only as an abstraction, derived from the whole history of the art form as constituted by the work of many different competing poets, had in the generation of Euripides become nearly identical with the work of one artist. So constituted, the norm would pose a considerable threat to the capacity of the

39. For *apatê*, see the *Vita Aeschyli* (332.5 Page). Cf. the remarks of Gorgias (DK2:82 fr. 23B), whose writings are very likely the source of the contrast in styles (see Pohlenz, 1920).

40. *Frogs* 82: ὁ δ' εὔκολος μὲν ἐνθάδ' εὔκολος δ' ἐκεῖ. On the description as "representative" of the conventional literary persona of Sophokles, see Lefkowitz (1981, 79–80).

41. *Frogs* 786–94. Pohlenz (1920, 165) remarks on this omission of Sophokles from the competition.

42. See *Vita* 8 (p. xix Pearson). The percentages of Sophokles' victories will vary according to interpretations of the (garbled but not totally incoherent) ancient sources. His victories may have numbered 18 (Diodoros 13.103.4—confirmed by inscriptional evidence for the Dionysia alone: *CIG* II.2, pt. 2. 2325.I [p. 666]), 20 (*Vita Soph.* 8, from Karystios), or 24 (the *Suda* [4:402 Adler]). The higher figures may include Lenaian victories. Lesky ([1956] 1972.1, 171) estimates 123 total plays. Pearson (1917, xv) assumes "at least nine" second places and finds little room for Lenaian victories. On his conservative estimate, Sophokles was victor in almost 2 out of 3 contests. See the figures of Russo (1960, 165–66) who assumes 6 Lenaian victories, for a total of 84 winning plays ($18 \times 4 + 6 \times 2$), or a 70 percent proportion of winning encounters (given 10 second-place rankings at the Dionysia). On the uncertainty of the total number of plays, however, see Pearson (1917, xviii-xxi).

art form to undergo change and development in the hands of new creators:[43] once tragedy had attained its full and perfect form, what more could be done, or what could any rival competitor have to offer that would surpass perfection?[44] Such questions would matter less to poets content, as many doubtless were, with a subordinate ranking behind the dead legend, Aischylos, and the living one. The problem of dealing with the Sophoclean reputation and model would become very pressing, however, for any poet who himself wished to attain a place in the canon.[45]

Sophoclean drama concentrated, not just on individuals, but on individuals who manifested a particular type of heroic personality that rather vividly evoked the Homeric epic.[46] This emphasis on the traditional cultural ideal of *aretê*[47] established for tragedy as a genre the same concerns with exemplary figures and, by implication, the same claims to prestige and cultural centrality that the Homeric poems had established for the epic genre.[48] For Aristoteles and the rest of the fourth century, tragedy has replaced epic as the archetypal art form.[49] In Aristoteles' terms, Sophokles had completed the work that

43. The Russian structuralists emphasized the dynamic nature of literature in its social context, e.g., Tynjanov ([1927] 1969.1, English version in Matejka & Pomorska [1971]).

44. The terminology of the excellent *Vita Aeschyli* emphasizes Sophokles' role as perfecter of the art form: (333.17–21 Page): "If anyone thinks that Sophokles was a more perfect (*teleôteros*) composer of tragedy than Aischylos, he thinks rightly; but he should consider that it was much more difficult, following after Thespis, Phrynichos, and Choirilos, to advance the tragic art form to such magnitude than it was, following after Aischylos, to arrive at the perfection (*teleiotêta*) of Sophokles."

45. The problem of getting Euripides included in the canon remained a knotty one; see *Frogs* 868ff., and discussion in Chap. 5, below. An obvious difficulty would be Euripides' failure to win often: it is extremely likely that he was beaten by Sophokles more often than the reverse.

46. See the fascinating demonstration of "tragic" themes in the *Ilias* by Rutherford (1982). Some of the results of this recapitulation will become more apparent in the discussions of tragic form in Chap. 9, below.

47. See the analysis of Whitman (1958, 59–61); Knox (1964). For the *aretê* (heroic prowess) and the *anêr agathos,* see Adkins (1960), and discussion below and in Chap. 7, on the challenge to traditional standards in *Elektra*.

48. On this development, see Schwinge (1981, 148–57). On tragedy (i.e., that of Sophokles and Aischylos) as the "true heir of epic" see the recent article by Rutherford (1982). On the tragic genre, see E. G. Schmidt (1976, 94): in the fifth century the question whether any art form could go beyond lyric and epic and could embody the wealth of conflict and contradiction in the new era was answered positively with the emergence of tragedy. See the ancient comment (garbled in the *Vita* 20 [xxi Pearson]) that Sophokles was *homêrikôtatos*; Kirkwood (1965, 53–70) quotes Pearson (1917, xxxi); see also Segal (1966, 475); Knox (1964, 52–53); Fairweather (1974, 263).

49. See Else (1957, 152, 203–4), *Poetics* 1449b9–20. The best article on the developing canon and the fifth-century sense of style is by Wehrli (1946, 18 n.1 and 21); see also more recently Kirsch (1982, 266ff.).

Aischylos had begun in enlarging tragedy and making it more serious (*spoudaion*).[50]

This state of affairs was already in formation when Euripides began to make his mark on the theater. The characteristics of his plays too are well known and have been frequently listed, although they have not been as easy to systematize. The social background of myth and its application to contemporary life had been somewhat muted by the Sophoclean focus on the individual, while in Euripides myth receives a more vivid and topical treatment than ever before.[51] Sophoclean dramatic naturalism, with its ability to make the action develop out of the interaction of characters,[52] is abandoned in favor of a return to archaic (or Aeschylean) formalism; and, as a result, the distance between audience and stage event is greatly increased. The theater once again becomes self-conscious.[53]

Further, Euripides introduces a new kind of protagonist. Where the plays do focus on events centering on an individual, we almost never come upon a Sophoclean heroic achiever or sufferer. The hero seems in many cases to have been displaced by persons of lower social rank and prestige, as the plays center on feeble oldsters, women, beggars and slaves, barbarians, and other riffraff.[54] Many of these seem more concerned with survival than with the assertion of heroic integrity;[55] and indeed there can be little question of integrity in the case of such a protagonist as Hekabe, a barbarian woman who appears in two plays reduced to abjection by grief and the effects of old age and slavery. Other factors also change our view of the protagonist: Orestes (in the play of that name) and Medeia are strong and vigorous in the pursuit of their vengeance, but their actions and the situation in which they act are such as to repel sympathy. Aischylos' Klytaimestra was a similar figure; but Euripidean malefactors are more likely to end in triumph, mantled in divine

50. For these terms see *Poetics* 1448b24 – 1449a6, and 1449a32 – 38 (see Else [1957, 71 – 78]). Wehrli (1946) argues most persuasively for a fifth-century origin for this terminology, very likely in the work of Gorgias.

51. See Diller (1958) on the social background in Euripidean tragedy.

52. See Kitto ([1939] 1961, 198ff.); for a radical treatment, see Gellie (1972, 200 – 222 ["Character"]), who shows that Sophoclean characters are often distorted out of naturalistic shape in an effort to motivate action convincingly. This does not break the long-noticed bond between character and action in Sophokles, but confirms it, as well as the strongly organic and unitary composition noted above.

53. See Imhof (1957, 42 – 44).

54. For the characteristics of the protagonists, see among others Mahaffy (1879, 107); Grube (1941, 7); Kitto ([1939] 1961, 251 – 53); Biffi (1961, 91); Arnott (1981.1, 180); Gellie (1981, 2).

55. See Schmid-Stählin 3:768; Carrière (1966, 24ff.); and Gellie (1972, 197), who writes of the "clear-sighted decisions to walk over the precipice" made by Sophoclean heroes, whom G. opposes to the survivor hero, who "needs . . . a capacity to suffer terribly without breaking and a preparedness to use his head" (196). Garzya (1962) has devoted a book to variations on this theme, although he defines *sôtêria* quite broadly and intangibly; see Chap. 1, above.

favor. Major figures such as these impel interest, curiosity, even fascination; but they seem designed to flout cultural norms rather than to embody them. Clearly these stylistic choices imply a strong contrast with Sophoclean drama.[56] I would not be the first to argue that Euripidean drama can be defined in virtually every aspect by the rubric "non-Sophoclean."[57] But the implications of this stylistic stance are more powerful than has been realized. A rejection of the heroic protagonist—in literary terms, a *recusatio* of the *spoudaion,* the "serious"[58]—meant the reversal of a general stylistic tendency that, according to Aristoteles, had been brought to its culmination by Sophokles.

Euripides turned for his support in many directions, especially to the earlier practitioners of tragedy whose work had been superseded. But he also went outside the established lines of the genre, finding a fruitful, abundant, and peculiarly appropriate source in the prose genres whose line of descent passed from Hesiodic epic through the elegiac poets and the early presocratic philosophers, genres that might perhaps be grouped together under the title "critical thought." By opening tragedy to material that had been for good aesthetic reasons confined to its periphery, Euripidean drama offered a considerable challenge to the integrity of the genre.[59] Most commentators on the formal qualities of Euripidean drama have concentrated on the diachronic aspect, pointing out the ways in which Euripides' work anticipates or foreshadows the comedy of the late fourth century.[60] But this is of course a

56. The relation to Sophokles that is here posited for Euripides' work is not contradicted by the apparent echoes of Euripidean style, e.g., in *Trachiniai*. The relationship between Sophokles and his younger competitors would not be the same in reverse, since an artist not seriously threatened by any living rival can borrow freely; see U. v. Wilamowitz (1883, 235): an artist like Sophokles could use Euripides' work, "denn er läuft keine Gefahr seine Individualität einzubüssen." On the relations between particular plays, see App. D.

57. Conacher (1967, 10–13); Kitto ([1939] 1961, 252): Euripidean characterization is "the dramatic antithesis to Sophokles' method." No doubt more would have been made of the antithetical nature of Euripides' art, but for the tendency of Euripides' critics to attribute all features of the plays to the personal idiosyncrasies of their author.

58. I do not propose to confuse a useful term (*recusatio*) by applying it too broadly, but I do think it worthwhile to point out the wider background of which it is a part. Without explicitly stating his refusal—and no such statement could be made in a tragic drama—Euripides like many other authors deliberately manipulates the disappointment of audience expectations. The whole structure of a play like *Herakles* is an elaborate, though tacit, *recusatio* of the heroic tragedy.

59. This exaggerates a normal trait of literary development; see Tynjanov ([1921] 1969.3): "Jede literarische Nachfolge ist doch primär ein Kampf, die Zerstörung eines alten Ganzen und der neue Aufbau aus alten Elementen" (303).

60. On Euripides and comedy, see Matthiessen, (1979, 107); Arrowsmith (1963, 42) points out the connection of comedy to the fragmented and multiple quality of Euripidean drama; see also Decharme (1906, 307ff.); Schmid-Stählin 3:853. On *Bakchai,* Harbsmeier (1968, 47–55), Seidensticker (1978); on *Helene,* Maniet (1947), Alt (1962, 9).

rather perverse way to go about understanding Euripides and his relation to his contemporary audience,[61] since neither author nor audience could have anticipated a metamorphosis of the comedy they knew into forms that owed much to Euripides; and contemporary comedy, or even satyr drama, can have offered Euripides little to draw upon. What Euripides' audience observed was a split or differentiation within the tragic genre. In fact, the distinction between Euripides' special subgenre and the main body of tragedy has some parallels with other genre distinctions and splits in Greek poetry.

In choosing the play of critical or moral ideas over immersion in the fictional world of myth, Euripides imitates Hesiodos' differentiation of his own type of epic from the Homeric type.[62] The antiheroic view, too, is present in some Hesiodic poetry (i.e. the *Works and Days*), as well as in elegiac poetry, and the lyric of Stesichoros, Pindaros, and others.[63] Finally, it is fascinating to observe the extent to which the relation of Euripidean tragedy to Sophoclean drama replicates the relation of *Odysseia* to *Ilias* within the Homeric corpus.[64] In contrast with the heroic male world of war in the *Ilias*, the *Odysseia* is concerned with moral ideas about *hybris* and *dikê*, lavishes attention on domestic scenes in which women are central, and abounds in fantasy and folktale elements. Its protagonist, always the least conventional and most dubious of heroes, plays the role of a beggar and consorts with swineherds. All these traits have direct parallels in Euripidean drama.

To make the necessary distinctions between the genre form as determined by Sophokles, and his own antithetical version, Euripides has quite naturally made use of a wide variety of modes through which such distinctions had been expressed in the earlier tradition. The multifarious nature of Euripidean drama, so frequently remarked upon, finds its best explanation in this juxtaposition with Sophokles. Not only does the new, secondary, and necessarily weaker antithetical form require many means to establish and express its differentiation from the dominant norm; but the fact that the Sophoclean norm was itself one of organic unity, and intense focus and concentration, further predetermines the various and multiple as characteristic of its proper

61. See Whitman (1974, 105).

62. It seems very likely that, whatever the other overtones of *Theog.* 27 – 28, the lines imply a generic contrast between narrative epic and the catalogue poetry that Hesiodos will compose; see Luther (1966, 41 – 42), and Pucci (1977, 36 n.11).

63. See Tyrtaios 12W, and commentary by Shey (1976); or Stesichoros, *PMG* 210.

64. This correspondence has been often noticed, although its significance has often been left vague: see Knox ([1970] 1979.3, 268 – 69) on *Ion*; Dingel on *Elektra* (1969); Paduano on *Telephos* (1967, 333 – 34); Eisner on *Helene* (1980); Zeitlin on *Orestes* (1980, 61ff.). Note that Rutherford (1982, 145; see also Knox [ibid.]), who shows that "tragic" situations in the *Ilias* parallel those in Aischylos and especially Sophokles, remarks that he omitted consideration of the *Odysseia* and of Euripides, whose work parallels Odyssean themes. See discussion below in Chap. 7 on the very Odyssean *Elektra*.

antithesis. The shift from *Ilias* to *Odysseia* to some extent parallels Northrop Frye's cycle of change from high to low mimetic,[65] but the pattern is too confining to fit either the *Odysseia* or Euripides perfectly. No Euripidean play remains consistently within the low mimetic mode, or indeed within any homogeneous mode. The keynote of Euripidean drama, as C. H. Whitman pointed out, is an irony that precludes a direct and consistent approach,[66] even to the "low" elements that are so conspicuous in the plays. Whereas, within the scheme of the *Odysseia* itself, we learn to accept Eumaios as "god-like swineherd" (*dios hyphorbos*) without any sense of dissonance, we are never given the time to feel comfortable with Elektra the housewife, or Hypsipyle the nursemaid. In fact, all of Frye's cycle, from high mimetic through romance, seems compressed into the complex reversals of Euripidean drama.

In attempting to grasp the effect of the plays it may be more useful to stay with Aristoteles' rudimentary but fertile distinction between the high-mimetic or serious genres (*spoudaion*) and the ridiculous (*geloion*). This division was stressed in the Aristotelian view of tragic development: in the course of its evolution tragedy became more "serious," as it made a closer approach to its natural form.[67] The division is particularly persistent in Greek literature and gives some stability to genre categories, which recent critical theory has tended to show as essentially fluid and mobile.[68] Because Euripidean irony opposes itself directly to Sophoclean high mimetic, it continually brings tragedy to the brink of its antithesis, its very annihilation. Such a technique is a perilous resort for any but the most adroit of artists. Since ludicrous elements are not consistently present in Euripidean drama, as they would be in a parody or burlesque of the high mimetic, there is a considerable risk that the

65. On Frye's five categories, myth, romance, high mimetic, low mimetic, and ironic, see Whitman (1974), who rejects the label of low mimetic for Euripides and proposes that of ironist (113–14). See Frye (1957, 33–34). For criticism of Frye's system as too rigid see Todorov (1970, 13–23: "like botany before Linnaeus"), and for genre development as a dynamic process, see Todorov (1978, 53) and earlier Mukaŕovský ([1966, "The Significance of Aesthetics"] 1978, 26–27).

66. See Whitman (1974, 106–15): Euripides shows "a kind of deliberate polytonality, as if tragedy were now being written in two keys at once" (113–14).

67. See *Poet.* 1449a19–21: ἐκ μικρῶν μύθων καὶ λέξεως γελοίας . . . ὄψε ἀπεσεμνύνθη.

68. For the development of literary genres, see the Russian structuralists: Shklovskij ([1925] 1969, 51); Tynjanov ([1921] 1969.3, 307 (on parody); [1924] 1969.2, 393ff.: genres are dynamic rather than static, "Das Genre verschiebt sich" [397].) See more recently Todorov (1978, 47, 53). The division between serious and comic forms has been severely challenged in modern literature, although resistance to its obliteration has been fierce and enduring. Ibsen, whose work was used by some classical scholars (U. v. Wilamowitz [1905, 50]; Steiger [1912]) to explain that of Euripides, has also received the same depreciating criticisms as being more comic than tragic, or as being "melodramatic" (See App. A, below; and Heilman, 1968). For a defense of comic elements in the work of Ibsen and others in modern drama, see Styan (1968, 261–68).

periodic breaks in tone will be perceived as mistakes and will thus fall out of the intentionality of poetic discourse.[69] A mistake of this sort in "serious" art is the worst of errors, the kind of offense against taste and fitness that Hermogenes called *to kakozêlon* and that we call bathos, the high mimetic in a loss of altitude.[70] If we are not in step with Euripidean style we may assume, as did many ancient and modern critics, that our playwright is prone to a variety of rather embarrassing aesthetic blunders.

For a critical appreciation of Euripidean theater, therefore, a careful analysis of humor and its uses is essential. In taking as its protagonist a figure that on the surface appears unsuitable for the heroic role, a tragic play might still maintain the requisite degree of audience identification, if the protagonist appeared to retain balance and dignity in spite of surrounding ignominy. But in Euripidean drama, the unsuitable protagonists, who may be ragged beggars or old women, tend to vibrate between circumstances that make us take them as genuinely heroic personages, effectual and self-aware, and other circumstances that force upon us the incongruity between their pretensions and their ability. In these moments of incongruity, the audience will not necessarily laugh, but they will be aware of comic deflation and of a consequent wave of risibility. These moments, to the explication of which many critical apologetics and polemics have been directed, are keys to the aesthetic structure of the plays; for it is around them that Euripidean style centers its patterns of reversal, balance, and variation.

The Euripidean stance of refusal toward the style and tone usually associated with the tragic genre gives to the plays a quality of daring and perversity. If, as we have suggested, the audience played an important role in the development of tragedy as guardians of the tradition, maintaining a healthy balance between the individual artist and the public who used his work, then clearly the stance of Euripidean drama must have radically changed the relation between author and public. The ramifications of the Euripidean refusal lead into almost every part of dramatic form, from language and style, to dramaturgy, and even to the most basic element of theater, the cooperation of playwright, actors, and audience to create the illusory reality of the perfor-

---

69. I use the term "intentionality" as it is employed by structuralist theorists, who point out that poetic or artistic language is an utterance that lacks the direction (a clearly designated recipient) and the intent (e.g., to persuade or to inform) of ordinary discourse; for the resultant complexities, see Mukařovský ([1942, first published 1966, "The Significance of Aesthetics"] 1978, 19–30; [1944, "Intentionality and Unintentionality in Art"] 1978, 92ff.).

70. See Hermogenes on *to kakozêlon* (*Peri heur.* 4.12): ἐὰν συμβῇ τινι μετὰ σεμνότητα εἰς αἰσχρὸν κατενεχθῆναι. See the refs. in Elsperger (1907, 86–87). For a case in *Hekabe*, see Chap. 6.

mance.[71] The perversity of Euripidean theater has a natural tendency to generate paradoxes and thus to involve critics in self-defeating exercises. A defense of Euripides' claims, for instance, to be "taken seriously" as a dramatist will necessarily founder, if maintaining them requires us to assume that some esoteric viewpoint can be found from which the plays will appear "straight," irony will dissolve, and the demands of the convention of the "*spoudaion*" will be satisfied.[72]

For Euripidean plays, even more than for other dramas, it is necessary to preserve Waldock's "innocent eye," to remain in touch with natural, human reactions to enacted events.[73] Above all, and I write this with some trepidation, it will be necessary to read Euripides with a sense of humor intact, and with confidence that if something strikes us as funny—provided always that we have not made a gross mistake in interpreting systems of meaning in another culture[74]—this reaction is as worthy of careful attention and analysis as any other that the play might call forth. A grasp of the incongruous will prove to be a valuable aid in threading the maze of the dramas; and indeed we should be wary of any critical approach that would begin by invalidating such a basic support to balance and honesty as one's sense of the absurd.

It will, on the other hand, not help to bring with us any ready-formed model of the sort of drama that should merit critical attention or admiration. There is little evidence that Euripides has become stale, irrelevant, or uninteresting in the modern period; but Euripides' artistic stature has in fact been diminished because his work seems so strangely familiar and contemporary.[75] That this sense of closeness has not led to much understanding should not surprise. On the contrary, it was precisely the apparent presence in Euripides' work of traits that seemed alarming or degenerate in contemporary literature that generated the condemnation of this dramatist in the late eighteenth century. It is likely that, in the postmodern era, Euripides has become more accessible as he has become less "our contemporary." In fact, the feeling of closeness is in part spurious, because it is induced by Euripi-

71. See Michelini (1982, 127).

72. See Chap. 1, above, for this phenomenon, evident in the work of A. Pippin Burnett, P. Vellacott, and many other commentators.

73. Waldock (1966, Chap. 2 ["The Documentary Fallacy"] and p. 35). Waldock is right to remind us that we cannot ignore the surface, though, like many adherents of the naive approach, he sometimes falls into the complementary error of not looking beyond the surface.

74. For an example of such a mistake, see Agamemnon's address to Klytaimestra (*Agamemnon* 914ff.), a passage in which misinterpretation is natural to modern readers (Michelini [1974, 526]).

75. Masqueray (1908, 399): "Quand on le lit, on a souvent la sensation de lire un contemporain." Murray (1913.1, 14): Euripides seems to be "a man who has in his mind the same problems as ourselves, the same doubts and largely the same ideals." Grube (1941, 15): his "ways of thought are much more akin to ours" than those of the other dramatists.

dean manipulation of genre norms. The remote grandeur of the heroic is a part of the decorum of the *spoudaion*, while its inversion often gains strong and disconcerting effects by the sudden introduction of material that is all too contemptibly familiar.[76]

The record of the centuries that has made Euripides very likely the most popular and the most admired playwright of all time stands without help from us.[77] It does not have to be established that work of this universal appeal merits serious attention. It may, of course, turn out that Euripides is, in spite of all this endless charm and fascination, a "bad" playwright, whom our artistic standards do not permit us to praise, a "sensationalist," a mere technician, a writer of "melodrama."[78] If that turns out to be true, then it will be our next task to reassess the artistic standards that compel us to condemn or to disregard work of such enduring power.

76. When Norwood facetiously asks (1954, 3), "Who would care to lunch with Atossa or Ajax?" his point derives from the trivialized meal ("lunch") and its fit with the low mode of Euripidean drama. Euripides' Elektra eats lunch and worries about what to serve; Sophokles' Elektra does not (see Chap. 7).

Note the paradox, remarked by Russell (1936, 105) and Kamerbeek (1958, 16), that Sophokles' poetry is remote from the world of contemporary concerns although his life is not, while in Euripides the relation is reversed.

77. On Euripides' later reputation in antiquity, see Matthiessen (1979, 107 – 8); and Murray (1913.1, 10 – 11). Also, Prato (1964, 9ff.); Looy (1964, 7 – 8).

78. For the charge of "sensationalism," see Norwood (1954, 41); Kitto ([1939] 1961, 326 – 29); and especially Burnett (1971, 13 and 65; 1962, 89); and above all Vellacott (1975, 72), who threatens us that, if we do not accept his interpretation, *Orestes* will turn out to be a sordid "piece of sensational violence" (see also pp. 94, 181, etc.). This fear that Euripides will be a sensationalist is the lever used to foist upon us the most extreme interpretations; see Chap. 1 and the acute comment of Petersen on Verrall's methods (1915, 27): "Das mutet wie eine Drohung an, wie die vorgehaltene Pistole des Räubers." For "Melodrama" see Chap. 1, above; and App. A.

3

Euripides and His Audience:
The Tactics of Shock

In order to oppose the norm of tragic drama, Euripides had to oppose his audience and affront their strongly expressed preferences. The result was an inevitable alienation of the artist from his public. Estrangement between artist and audience has become the most typical feature of contemporary literature and fine art; but strong forces in the Greek poetic tradition tended to work against any such split. The artist's role was confined and buttressed on all sides by social institutions.[1] The poet created his work for performance at contemporary civic functions or in private social groups; and the poetry that had been preserved from the past served functions that could be described as historical, aesthetic, educational, and religious.[2] A posture of alienation, however, is precisely what does characterize the new historical, philosophical, and rhetorical prose genres of the fifth century, all of which have associations with the Sophistic enlightenment; and it was these genres that Euripidean drama used as the source of its particular tone and style. The prose artist, instead of acting as a source of tradition and its preservation, is a critic who puts traditional values to the elenchus or who wishes to make his audience accept as true the "weaker *logos*," that is, the inverse of what they would normally believe and expect.[3]

1. On the relation of the ancient poet to his social group, see Rosler on Alkaios (1980, 26ff.).
2. For poetry as history, see Tyrtaios on the Messenian wars, or Mimnermos on the wars around Smyrna, as well as the use made of Archilochos' poetry in the Archilocheion on Paros; see also Lefkowitz (1981, 31). See Marrou (1948, 76) on the social function of Solon's poetry at Athens; and on the poet as educator, Vernant (1982, 54).
3. For the "weaker [ἥττων]" or "unjust *logos*," see Aristophanes *Clouds* (883 and 890 following, where the *logoi* a,e personified). Aristoteles associated these arguments with Protagoras (*Rhet.* 1402a24 – 28).

The teasing, provocative, and ironic tone, the flashy intellectual sleight of hand that often accompanies the Sophistic debate about values derives from the insincerity of that debate. The attacker may be maintaining a position that he would not be prepared to act upon, since his primary interest is in displaying his own artistry in argumentation, and he may—unlike his opponent—have no belief in either of the propositions being debated. There is a fundamental difference between a debate in which both opponents differ about the application of basic values to specific situations, and a debate in which one opponent questions the existence of values per se.[4] The alienation of the Sophist from his opponent, or victim, corresponds to the alienation of Euripidean tragedy from its audience. A tragic play that is itself an attack upon tragedy is necessarily grounded in irony and insincerity.

The persistent sense that things on stage in a Euripidean play cannot be what they seem is familiar to every reader. This sense of something concealed or held back, of insincerity, is at the root of the Verrallian interpretations that seek to decipher the plays as a code is deciphered, once for all time. The irritation and awkward feelings aroused in the audience by a deliberate violation of genre norms match the irritating and dissonant tone and subject matter of the contemporary intellectual debate that continually manifests itself in Euripidean theater.[5] Once this dissonant aesthetic has been recognized, we may discard at least one bugaboo, the specter of ''good taste'' and artistic suitability. Euripidean theater is and must be a theater of the unsuitable; and principles of taste or appropriateness are not effective touchstones when applied to this sort of work.[6] On the other hand, to ignore altogether the plain and frequently stated case against Euripidean ''excesses,'' ''melodrama,'' ''sensationalism,'' and ''bad taste,'' or to adopt a posture of defense against these allegations, is to miss an important opportunity for understanding Euripides. These awkward moments are neither errors nor meaningless blots, but elements of considerable aesthetic significance, valid parts of a system of literary meaning that derives from the Euripidean play's combative relation to its audience.

The literary biography of Euripides bears an appropriately inverse relation to that of his great rival. His first victory, in 442, came fourteen years into

4. See the exchange between Sokrates and Thrasymachos: the latter tells Sokrates not to concern himself with Thrasymachos' ''real'' opinions but to confine himself to refuting his *logos* (τί ... οὐ τὸν λόγον ἐλέγχεις [*Rep.* 349a9 – 10]).

5. See the description by Straat (1959, 139 – 40): the tone of Euripidean drama is one of acidity, abrasiveness, bitterness, and disillusion.

6. See a delightful remark by Patin ([1841 – 43] 1873, 1:215). Euripides' characters say embarrassing things (*sentiments honteux*) that, while perhaps not unnatural, nobody else would admit, even to themselves: '' qu'on ne s'avoue pas à soi-même, loin d'en faire confiance à autrui.'' See also Masqueray (1908, 50).

his career; but, although Aischylos had probably waited an equal time for success, Euripides was not to achieve the same steady flow of first prizes. Even after the barrier of the initial victory had been surmounted, only three other victories came to him in the next three decades.[7] The verdicts of the ordinary men who awarded the prizes were undoubtedly influenced not only by the mood of the audience but also by the solemn nature of a vote, taken under oath and in public, and intended to be preserved as a permanent historical record.[8] Plutarchos' story (*Kimon* 8) of the special jury empaneled to vote on Sophokles' first victory—or his first victory over Aischylos—confirms the difficulty that ordinary judges would have felt in choosing between the sides of a violently divided audience, or in weighing the opposing claims of current taste and traditional practice. The negative reaction of the juries to Euripides' work undoubtedly reflected a general feeling that, for all the appeal of this artist, he was not an appropriate winner of the first prize. In fact, given the provocative stance of the plays, the decision of the judges seems natural.

Euripides did, however, frequently produce plays, which means that his work was repeatedly chosen by the archons over that of other potential competitors. If the numbers cited are a dependable guide, he averaged slightly more than four tetralogies per decade, almost up to the mark of Sophokles, who produced five per decade, taking first with three or four of the five.[9] The reason why Euripides should have been so routinely granted choruses, yet denied prizes,[10] lies in the nature of the performance. The divide between failure and success in drama often seems more abrupt than in the other arts, probably because of the absolute necessity of maintaining intact the "dramatic illusion," the cooperative pretense between audience and performers upon which theater depends. A play that fails to maintain the integrity of the dramatic reality is a failure indeed. Once the audience, who

7. See Lesky ([1956] 1972.1, 278). Out of five total victories, we must count as one that of the final, posthumous production. The first victory was in 441, and *Hippolytos Crowned* won in 427; therefore, two other victories must be assumed, probably in the years following 427. Of Euripides' twenty-two productions (see Webster [1967, 5–6]), less than one in four was victorious. Russo (1960, 170) suggests that Euripides may have won in 412 with *Helene* and *Andromeda;* cf. the comments next year in Aristophanes (*Thes.* 850, 1060ff.).

8. For the composition of the panel of judges, see Martin (1958, 249–50). For the oaths, see Platon, *Laws* 2.659a: it is shocking that the judge, with the same mouth with which he gave his solemn oath, should pronounce a false judgment because he was "shaken by the roar of the masses [ἐκπληττόμενον ὑπὸ θορύβου τῶν πολλῶν]." (See Martin [261]). On the historical record, see Chap. 2 above.

9. Webster divides the sixty-six Euripidean plays that have survived in whole or fragmentary state into twenty-two productions, assuming that satyr plays have for the most part been lost (1967, 5); see Lesky ([1956] 1972.1, 278). Tuilier (1968, 29–30) divides the grand total of ninety-two titles into twenty-three tetralogies, in close agreement with Russo (1960, 167).

10. Lefkowitz (1981, 103) and Stevens (1956, 91–92) raise this point, arguing that Euripides' unpopularity has been exaggerated.

should be the allies of the performers in interpreting dramatic events, become hostile and disaffected, they cannot be recaptured; the play has lost its magic.[11]

Anecdotal evidence confirms that the huge audience in the Theater of Dionysos, composed as it was of a wide variety of Athenians and aliens, of every background, was particularly savage with bad plays. Theater audiences shouted, hissed, drummed their heels against the benches, and threw things at the actors.[12] We hear of plays and their players being driven out of the theater—the term, *ekpesein,* is the same as that for exile.[13] It was not common for two plays to be hissed off the stage in succession, but such debacles were recorded.[14] In the motivation of the officer who selected the plays for performance each year, desire to avoid such a catastrophic failure necessarily counted for more than a desire to select only plays that observed the moral and aesthetic proprieties.[15] Euripidean plays were and are notoriously good theater; and an archon who gave a chorus to Euripides could be certain that the audience would not be bored or disappointed.

Such a disjunction between what an audience enjoys and what they approve is more likely to persist in theater than elsewhere, simply because of the basic conditions of performance. One can imagine the audience watching

11. See the use of the word *psychros,* which refers primarily to jokes and figures of speech that fail to "come off" (e.g., Aristoteles, *Rhet.* 1406a32), but can also be applied to plays and playwrights; see *Thes.* 848. The playwright's need to accommodate the tastes of the audience has been well stated in the case of Menandros by Arnott (1981.2, 215ff.).

12. On the general mixture of the audience, see Kolb (1979, 530–33). Hissing: see Demosthenes' account of Aischines' problems during his acting career, 18.265, 19.337 (quoted, next note). Stones: Ath. 9.406f, and Demosth. 18.262, a famous passage in which D. claims that dramatic contests for Aischines' troop were like war to the death: ... ὑμεῖς περὶ ψυχῆς ἠγωνίζεσθε. ἦν γὰρ ἄσπονδος καὶ ἀκήρυκτος ὑμῖν πρὸς τοὺς θεατὰς πόλεμος. (The first part of the passage, not quoted, may mean that the audience threw fruit and olives at them; see Whiston [1859, 534] and *contra* Wankel [1976, 2:1154–55].) On the drumming of heels: Pollux 4.112. (Note that, while the other evidence originates in the fourth century, heel-drumming points to a time before the abandonment of wooden benches.) See Walcot (1976, 23–36), Ghiron-Bistagne (1976, 197–98).

13. See Ghiron-Bistagne (1976, 197 n.6). Demosth. 18.265; 19.337: ὅτε ... ἠγωνίζετο, ἐξεβάλλετ᾽ αὐτὸν καὶ ἐξεσυρίττετ᾽ ἐκ τῶν θεάτρων καὶ μόνον οὐκ κατελεύεθ᾽ οὕτως ὥστε τελευτῶντα τοῦ τριταγωνιστεῖν ἀποστῆναι. Aristoteles (*Poet.* 1456a18, 1459b31) associates the term with critical failure (*kakôs agônizesthai*).

14. See the anecdote in Pollux (4.88, p. 226 Bethe) about Hermon, a comic actor of the late fifth century (O'Connor [1908, 95]): he was outside the theater exercising his voice before the performance; "when all (the performances scheduled) before him were thrown out (τῶν δὲ πρὸ αὐτοῦ πάντων ἐκπεσόντων)," the herald called Hermon. Because he did not hear the call, he failed to appear and was fined.

15. See the severe disappointment recollected by Dikaiopolis: Theognis (a poet described as *psychros* [*Thes.* 170]) was told to lead in his chorus, when Dikaiopolis was expecting a revival of Aischylos instead. (*Ach.* 9–11: εἴσαγ᾽ ὦ Θέογνι τὸν χορὸν—at the *proagon*?).

a Euripidean play, tense and angry, restraining the urge to hiss, as they waited in fascination to see what came next. The apparently contradictory aims of Euripidean theater, to enthrall and delight, as well as to affront and irritate, stem equally from this paradoxical relation to the public.[16] In the light of these tensions, there is a most Euripidean bitterness in the prayer to Victory (Nikê) that closes three of the last plays: "May you hold sway over my life, and never cease to crown me."[17] For Euripides, victory could not be defined by the traditional marks of social approval; the nature of his art had foreclosed some possibilities, as it had opened others.

If the hostile relationship between Euripides and his audience is the source of the peculiar aesthetic of his plays, it seems odd that modern critics should have found his work hard to understand. For contemporary artists alienation is itself a tradition of some three generations' standing: the riots that at the beginning of the century met deviant exhibitions in the theater, visual arts, and music established a relation of hostility between audience and artist that has proven durable.[18] "Provocative" and "outrageous" are terms of praise in contemporary critical literature; and the artist's aim to provoke and arouse the audience is frustrated only by the fact that a weak, flaccid, and irrelevant tradition no longer responds vigorously to the attacks of a succession of inheritors, each more outrageous and alienated than the last. Euripides, however, faced no such threat of inanition: the tradition with which he struggled was alive, powerful, and—embodied in the drama of his great rival—in active competition with his own work. He wrote and produced plays in a public and civic forum, for an audience that could be expected to react to provocation with disapproval, shock, and fascination. In short, if Euripidean

16. I would agree with Stevens (1956, 94) that Euripides was "unorthodox sometimes and disconcerting, one who roused disapproval in some quarters, . . . but a dramatist whose plays everyone wanted to see." For the intense interest in dramatic productions, see Harriott (1962). For Euripides' paradoxical status, see U. v. Wilamowitz (1907, 14): he was not trusted with public office, but he was trusted "aus der Seele seines Volkes zu reden."

17.

    ὦ μέγα σεμνὴ Νίκη, τὸν ἐμὸν
    βίοτον κατέχοις
    καὶ μὴ λήγοις στεφανοῦσα.

The plays are Iphigeneia Among the Taurians, Phoinissai, and Orestes; all are likely to fall within a five-year period in Euripides' late career.

18. See the analysis of Poggioli (1968): "Novelty in an artistic accomplishment is something quite different from novelty in the artist's attitude vis-à-vis his own work, and vis-à-vis the aesthetic task imposed on him by his own era." See the discussion of "antagonism to the public," pp. 30–40: "If the avant-garde has an etiquette, it consists of perverting and wholly subverting conventional deportment, . . . 'good manners'" (31). Poggioli on "The State of Alienation," p. 103ff.: "The modern artist or writer tends to push aside the temptation of success" (114). This last expresses much that I have been trying to show about Euripides.

drama was designed to cause a "sensation," we of all critics in all eras should not find his tactics difficult to understand.

There were many contemporary themes available that could provoke shock and outrage. Violation of religious conventions, for instance, was producing an increasingly vigorous reaction in the last third of the fifth century, as the provocations became more frequent and more blatant. Sexual taboos, however, in most societies tend to lie outside the realm of rational discussion, and are more frequently enforced by shame rather than by ethical persuasion. Although Euripidean plays dealt with a number of controversial topics at all periods, it was the sexual plays that for Aristophanes, and probably for his audience as well, represented the essence of Euripidean effrontery. Yet, while on the theme of religion provocative plays appear throughout Euripides' career, the sexual plays cited against him at the late date of the *Frogs* belonged to an early period of his career. The gradual movement away from these most controversial themes parallels the findings of Schadewaldt (1926), who was able to trace a degree of modification in the early polemical and aggressive stance of Euripidean moralizing. Although there is no basic change in the tension between author and audience and although Euripides never abandoned sexual themes entirely, it does seem to make sense to distinguish two stages in the artist's career, and in the kinds of provocation offered to his public.

In his earlier career, during a period whose end may be placed roughly at 427, Euripides wrote a number of plays centering on sexual deviance and the social role of women.[19] The two themes are closely interrelated, since female sexuality, in Greek societies as in many others, stood under a number of restrictions that did not apply to male sexuality, whether homo- or heteroerotic.[20] In picking up the motif of tension between the sexes, Euripides was, as often, mining a traditional vein of tragedy: Aischylos too had found the opposition between male and female a suitable tool for the dramatization of heroic myth. As often, however, Euripides transforms traditional material, preferring to exploit rather than suppress the potential for discomfort in sexual themes.

An erotic or romantic theme could pose a strong challenge to the genre standards of the high mimetic. Just as one of the traits distinguishing the highest, Homeric, form of epic from the poems in the epic cycle was the

---

19. See *Stheneboia, Hippolytos Veiled, Aiolos,* and *Cretan Men,* all of which are discussed below. For other early plays that might have featured women guilty of sexual misconduct or wrongly presumed to be so (e.g., *Alope, Alkmene*), see Webster (1967, 77–96). The falsity of the accusation would lessen the shock, but would permit much the same language and dramatic treatment. On this early period, see Adrados (1959, 186).

20. Homosexual themes, as in Aischylos' Achilleus play (228M), or *Chrysippos,* did not provoke the same controversy.

repression of sexual and erotic themes,[21] so in the classical period the convention excluding the erotic from the most serious forms of art began to
break down only in the later years of the fifth century. Tragedy, especially in
the hands of Sophokles, observed a considerable degree of decorum in its
treatment of erotic themes. An interesting case in point is *Trachiniai*, a play
saturated with erotic motifs,[22] in which we never see the male protagonist,
Herakles, on stage with either wife or mistress, and in which Deianeira's own
erotic feelings—a hotter topic, because of the stronger taboo on female
erôs—are hinted with extreme delicacy.[23] Even more striking is the presentation of erotic themes in *Antigone*. In the second half of the play the heroine's
dramatic personality is somewhat distorted by the change of focus needed to
establish her romantic relation to Haimon,[24] although the overt expression of
erotic themes is kept wholly outside the speeches of the actors, appearing
only in a song of the chorus and in the messenger's narrative of the lovers'
deaths.[25] Haimon never speaks of the love that drives him to suicide;[26] but
Antigone, as she becomes an erotic object, the chosen bride denied to
Kreon's son, acquires a pathos and susceptibility that alter the stern and
determined personality established for her in the opening scenes.[27]

As an erotic subject, on the other hand, Antigone hardly exists. Her last
speech utterly denies the importance of the marriage relation, in comparison
with the overriding demands of her obligations to the family of birth.[28] Antigone affirms an important moral truth for women in Athenian society: by
linking males securely together from generation to generation and from

21. See Griffin (1977, 40) and discussion in Chap. 6, Section IV, below.

22. Recent scholarship on the play has dealt with this theme in detail: Segal (1977, 104–19),
Dubois (1979).

23. See the hints at lines 443–44, confirmed by 539–40 and 550–51, where Deianeira indicates that, if the sexual favors of her husband go to another woman, her life will be intolerable,
even if she is still the official spouse (i.e. Herakles is her *posis,* but not her *anêr*). On the repression of these themes, see Adrados (1959, 181ff.)

24. On the erotic, or romantic, aspect of *Antigone,* see Waldock (1951, Chap. 7; "Romantic
Tragedy: The *Antigone,*" esp. p. 125), Gellie (1972, 45); Cataudella (1969, 229).

25. The chorus in honor of *erôs* follows directly the scene between Haimon and his father.
The Messenger treats the double suicide as a substitute for marriage, lines 1240–41.

26. The suppressed sexual side that Haimon cannot offer is inversely presented through the
sneers of Kreon (648ff., 740, 748); see Lesky ([1956] 1972.1, 199). Fritz ([1934.1] 1962,
227–40) argued against this interpretation, pointing out that Haimon denies Kreon's charges and
that Sophoclean choruses are often wrong. But, once introduced, the theme is maintained by a
different treatment of Antigone.

27. See Gellie (1972, 45ff.).

28. The authenticity of the speech is of course much disputed: see Lesky ([1956] 1972.1,
206–7), Gellie (1972, 284 n.26). But, whether Sophoclean or not, it reflects authentic ancient
attitudes, as is fitting for what would be a very early interpolation (see Aristoteles, *Rhet.*
1417a28–34). For a recent discussion, see Szlezák (1981.1).

family to family, women performed a vital social role that could be threatened if they put sexual feelings above family obligations. A woman's proper quality (*aretê*) consisted in loyalty, first to the family of birth, and second to her family of marriage and the children who cemented that family. Antigone's relation to Haimon, as yet unsustained by offspring, can have none except erotic significance; and thus for Antigone it has no weight.[29]

It was not by accident that, while Aristoteles used *Oidipous Tyrannos* as a tragic model, the play of Sophokles most loved in the ancient period was *Antigone*.[30] The story that Sophokles was awarded his generalship because of *Antigone*, or the other that he died while reading off a passage from that play, reflects the position of *Antigone* in the popular memory as the peak of Sophoclean art.[31] This kind of audience appeal is a result of affection as well as admiration; and a major source of the play's charm must have been its heroine. The female as erotic subject is probably of all protagonists the least suitable to the tone of the tragic genre; but Sophokles knew how to endow Antigone with considerable erotic appeal, while remaining within the bounds of aesthetic convention. Such exercises, however, would be pointless for an artist like Euripides, who must confront and challenge convention.

Like Sophistic argumentation, erotic material was usually excluded from tragedy; and, as in the case of Sophistic themes, an area of immense interest became available to an artist willing to break taboos against inappropriate subject matter. The Euripidean drama that corresponds to *Antigone* as a romantic favorite is of course the famous *Andromeda,* a play in which Perseus, flying over the sea with his magic sandals, sights the heroine chained to the rocks below. Andromeda seems to him at first to be a statue, an erotic image of physical perfection that inspires the hero to rescue her from the sea monster on condition that she marry him.[32] Unlike *Antigone, Andromeda* is an openly romantic tale, complete with magic, monsters, and a happy ending.

29. See the remarks of MacKay (1962, 171). Women were dependent on their nuclear family for support or for remarriage, if the current union should be dissolved by divorce or death. What Antigone says therefore reflects accurately the reality for women in the classical period at Athens. Kakridis (1949, 152ff.) shows that the story has Hellenic roots. There is a parallel between Alkestis and Antigone in that both put parent-child or sibling relationships before the marriage relation (see Adrados [1959, 187]).

30. See Lefkowitz (1981, 86).

31. Lefkowitz (1981, 86) implies that the biographer's source thought that *Antigone* was the last play. But confusion about the date of the play would easily be cleared up by the didaskalic records. The two originally separate anecdotes have simply been merged here by a natural process: Sophokles dies reciting a passage from *Antigone* (his best play), or he dies with joy at the news of his last victory. Other versions of the death-at-victory anecdote do not mention *Antigone*, e.g., Diodoros 13.103.4 (others listed in Jahn [1882, 16.73]).

32. Fr. 125 N2, see the parody in *Thes.* 1115–18. For the sexual appeal of statues, see *Hek* 560ff., and commentary in Chap. 6, below. For Perseus as lover, see Webster (1965, 30).

The Euripidean treatment of this material, like all other Euripidean versions, was far from "straight"; but the nature of the story remains.[33] Even in the fifth century the play was a favorite of Euripidean enthusiasts: it was the play Dionysos was reading when a severe pang of desire for Euripides overcame him;[34] and in later antiquity it was *Andromeda* that was said to have produced a case of Euripides-mania on a civic scale.[35] In unleashing romantic eroticism on tragedy Euripides took, as always, great risks; but he stood to gain equally great rewards. We must at this point resist our own tendency to assume that certain aesthetic pleasures are to be condemned as a mark of substandard art. At some later point it will be necessary to confront this assumption more directly, but for the moment it should be noted that pleasure in Euripidean theater, like the sensation in Sokrates' leg, is never without its little jab of irritation.

The most shocking and notorious of Euripides' plays about women and sexuality dealt with adultery, traditionally an important topic of misogynist literature, and one that Aischylos had exploited to the full in the *Oresteia*.[36] The Euripidean plays, however, put the adulterous intriguer and her schemes at the center of the play, thereby introducing the most disturbing possible instance of the female as erotic subject, material that was potentially explosive in the tragic theater. The impact of the two most famous adultery plays, *Stheneboia* and *Hippolytos Veiled,* came from the bold and aggressive approach of an older woman to a younger man.[37] The erotic matron Stheneboia apparently used a go-between to reach the young Bellerophon, while Phaidra approached her quarry directly.[38] In staging such a confrontation,

33. See Webster (1967, 197): Perseus had much difficulty persuading Kepheus to surrender Andromeda, and a lengthy debate on marriage ensued.

34. *Frogs* 52: καὶ δῆτ' ... ἀναγιγνώσκοντί μοι
    τὴν Ἀνδρομέδαν πρὸς ἐμαυτὸν ἐξαίφνης πόθος
    τὴν καρδίαν ἐπάταξε πῶς οἴει σφόδρα.

35. The mania was mentioned in Lukian. *De Conscr. Hist.* 1; see comments in Nauck (1913, 392–93). That it has the sound of a humorous fiction does not affect the status of the story as evidence for the play's popularity. See Adrados (1959, 199). Note also the impromptu theatricals of Alexandros the Great at a drunken dinner party: he had *Andromeda* by heart (Ath. 12.537d-e).

36. Helene and her sister Klytaimestra are the usual focus of this concern in myth—see *Od.* 11.441–56; Semonides 7W 115–18; Alkaios 42LP, discussed in Rosler (1980, 221ff.).

37. The erotic subject par excellence is older and takes an aggressive approach to his younger object, the *erômenos;* see Dover (1978, 84ff.). The "female lovers [γυναῖκες ἐρῶσαι]" (*Frogs* 1044) imitate this pattern. They are also called *pornai* in Aristophanes; Webster (1967, 65) remarks that "The essential meaning seems to be a woman who offers herself to a younger man." The essential meaning, of course, is "prostitute"; but this insulting word is reserved for the worst of Euripides' bad women.

38. See Webster (1967, 82) on *Stheneboia;* but Webster believes that there may have been a later scene in which Stheneboia tried directly to persuade Bellerophon to elope with her. On *Hippolytos Veiled,* see Webster (64–71). Hippolytos may have eventually responded directly to

Euripides drove hard against social as well as dramatic convention: it was to avoid the possibility of adulterous relations that Athenian mores severely stigmatized a woman who moved outside the house or a man who entered her house when the husband was absent.[39]

To moderate the impact of the outrageous scene between the romantic protagonists, the first *Hippolytos* may have made use[40] of a device Aischylos had developed that permitted actors to be co-presences on stage without actual confrontation or interaction: one actor sat veiled and silent in a traditional gesture of social withdrawal, not directly acknowledging the presence of the speaker.[41] For Euripides the point would have been to permit and yet withhold the scandalous dialogue. Euripides, like Sophokles, wanted both to eat and to have his erotic cake; but the former dances much closer to the line of the permissible. On this occasion, however, Euripides seems to have gone too far and to have affronted the audience too seriously for the play to succeed.[42] There may be some truth in the view that sees in this episode a turning point in the artist's career, since the scandal of *Hippolytos Veiled* appears to have been a climax in the plays of sexual outrage. After the mid-twenties, we hear of no more plays in which sexual deviance is a prominent theme, while in the plays of the next two decades we find other, more complex and less controversial, means of carrying out the same aesthetic program.[43] The process would have been one of gradual change, paralleled by the stylistic development noted by Schadewaldt in which vigorous polemic against conventional views is replaced by a more "resigned" stance. Euripides' emotional exhaustion need not be assumed,

Phaidra; but it seems more likely that he spoke later to a go-between, denouncing women. Note that *Phoinix* and *Peleus* may possibly have had similar plots (Webster [84 – 86]).

39. For seclusion to prevent adultery see Dover (1973, 61 – 62); Pomeroy (1975, 80ff.)

40. The story is persuasive, but lacks solid support in evidence; see discussion in Chap. 9, section II.A., below.

41. See Taplin (1972, 75 – 6). Aischylos had probably used the device to get the effect of two or more speaking actors, before the actual enlargement of the tragic cast.

42. See the *hypothesis* of *Hippolytos Crowned* 2.11.5: τὸ γὰρ ἀπρεπὲς καὶ κατηγορίας ἄξιον ἐν τούτῳ διώρθωται τῷ δράματι. On the second play's unique and palinodic status, see Chap. 9, below.

43. See Zuntz (1955.1, 57); and Webster (1967, 116): "Euripides is no longer so interested in bad women . . ." after the early period. Webster puts *Aiolos* in the group of plays after 427; but in the plays of his third and latest group themes of sexual shock have disappeared altogether. See Schmid-Stählin 3:338: erotic themes appear at all periods, but there is a concentration of such themes in the early period. Erotic themes probably datable to the late period (see Webster [163ff.]) fall largely into two categories: a woman seduced or raped by a god (*Auge, Ion*) or straight romance associated with marriage (*Andromeda, Antigone, Meleagros, Helene*).

however: after a time, a stance of nonconformity itself becomes a convention and thus no longer requires an emphatic notation.[44]

Women as sexual subjects are less prominent in the later plays, but female roles and the social questions related to women remain important to Euripidean drama at all periods. The theme of the female draws on material in the nontragic genres, where a rich misogynist tradition, extending from Hesiodos through the elegiac and gnomic poets, explored the difficulties of the marriage relation from the male viewpoint.[45] These themes entered fifth-century prose through the thought of Sokrates and the writings of Antisthenes and other prose artists who took the unconventional side, debating the intellectual capacity of women, comparing Hellenic roles for women with those in other societies, and collecting legends about "wise women."[46] The arguments on either side, the conventional misogynist one and the paradoxical Sophistic praise of women, were an inexhaustible source of material for Euripidean art; and the outrageous positions of Sophistic argumentation became especially piquant in the mouth of a "wise woman" like Melanippe or Medeia.[47]

A female protagonist, intelligently and persuasively advocating unorthodox sexual behavior, was a dramatic object guaranteed to produce the Sophistic frisson in a number of interlocking ways, particularly in a society that imposed an almost unbroken public silence upon all women during the whole of their lives.[48] Both the strong heroines in surviving Sophoclean plays are mature virgins, a category of paradox in Athenian society, where few women of any status remained unmarried for any length of time during the period from puberty to menopause.[49] But Euripidean female protagonists, like most Athenian women, tend to be matrons. The transformation of the Euripidean Elektra is a notorious case in point. To strengthen the link between the familiar and the mythical, the role of the matron is constantly assimilated to contemporary social norms: Klytaimestra in *Iphigeneia at*

44. 1926, 131ff.; see discussion in Chap. 1, above.

45. See Hesiodos, *Theog.* 590–612; *WD* 373–75; Semonides; and Hipponax 68W. These themes surface much more abundantly, of course, in the later comedy: see Stob. 67, etc., on marriage (*Flor.* 3:15–22 Meineke).

46. See Dittmar (1912), Aischines fr. 15, 24, 25 on Aspasia; 18 on Rhodogyne; see Dittmar (299ff.) on Antisthenes' *Aspasia*. The *Menexenos* of Platon is a rather tongue-in-cheek reworking of these themes.

47. See Aristoteles' comment on Melanippe, *Poet.* 1454a31. Fr. 483 N2 (see also 484) is Aristophanes' (*Lys.* 1124ff.) comic version of Melanippe's self-presentation.

48. Schaps (1977) points out that Thukydides' Perikles was literally right when he said that it was a woman's *aretê* never to be mentioned in public: the names of respectable women are never mentioned in the orators except in an attempt to discredit them. On the way seclusion can work without being a true purdah, see J. P. Gould (1980, 48–49).

49. Girls married early and it was fully expected that a widow who was still young and not destitute would receive a second husband. See Savage (1907, 66–67).

Aulis is horribly embarrassed when she mistakenly begins to address a strange male on the assumption that he is to be her son-in-law, and Elektra irritably points out the scantiness of the kitchen resources to her husband.[50] Aischylos' Klytaimestra is a monster of heroic stature, resembling no woman of her time. The audience who watched the drama of male against female played out in the *Oresteia* were not likely to be moved, as Aristophanes claimed Euripides' audiences were, to check under the bed for an Aigisthos when they returned home from the performance.[51] Because Euripidean women have not been placed in a remote, heroic past world, where clashes with everyday life are muted, they generate a discomfort that is a part of the continuing Euripidean assault on the tragic norm.[52]

Sexual topics, like other topics in Euripides, are never presented "straight," though they may have been treated more conventionally in the great adultery dramas, since in those plays a reversal of the protagonist's expected downfall would be too offensive to be tolerated. In other dramas of romance or perversion, the stories are always subjected to further ironic twists. The closest parallel to this Euripidean technique can be found in some of the narratives of Herodotos. It is indicative of the different approach of the two playwrights to the genre that Sophokles uses identifiable allusions to Herodotean material,[53] while Euripides incorporates Herodotean technique and tone in his plays. The blandly amoral tone of Herodotos and his cynical amusement at human motivations have been ascribed to his presumed background in the "Ionian" merchant class, much as Euripides' style has been derived from the psychology of a fictional life experience imagined for him.[54] But this ironic cast of thought is very prevalent in the prose genres of the fifth century and is derivable in large measure from the insincerity and cynicism of the Sophistic attitude. Many of Herodotos' best stories, such as those about the funeral customs of cannibals or what the Egyptians do with

50. In *IA* 851, when Klytaimestra realizes her mistake, she is unable to look directly at Achilleus anymore (cf. *Hek* 974–75).

51. *Thes.* 395–97.

52. This treatment of women, however, did have deep roots in the tradition of misogynist literature, which suggests that women are full of intelligence, craft, and persuasive verbal skill, all aimed at the most socially destructive of goals, the furthering of women's sexual needs and the subversion of men's power; see Hesiodos *WD* 77–79. Because of their weakness, women naturally prefer deceit over direct action. These traits gave female themes a natural affinity for Euripidean poetry; see Chap. 2, above; as well as for Odyssean intellectual prowess and thus for the Sophistic, see Chap. 6, below, on *Hekabe*.

53. On Sophokles' ode to Herodotos, see Plut. *An seni gerend. r. p.* 785b. For the allusions (*Ant.* 905ff.; *OC* 337ff.), see Schmid-Stählin 2:318.

54. See the article by Howald (1923). H. saw the *Bösheit* of Herodotos (119), and he attributed it to the slack ethic of the Ionian bourgeoisie (124–26).

the heads of butchered animals, are designed to mock Greek pride, much as Euripides' eloquent barbarian hero did in *Telephos*.[55]

Herodotos' curiosity about sexual aberrations is well known, and there is a Euripidean quality in the relish with which he informs his audience that, once a Babylonian lady has completed her stint of temple prostitution, "You would not get her, no matter how much you were willing to pay."[56] Some few of the more elaborate Herodotean narratives resemble Euripidean plays in the malignancy with which chance mocks the assumptions of the protagonists.[57] It is as impossible to find a moral point d'appui in these stories as it is to find one in a Euripidean play:[58] it seems that we are meant to admire the cleverness of the twist and to suppress our personal interest in the actors of the events. The generic type of these narratives is the short story, or even the joke or anecdote, a form in which brevity is essential and audience involvement is tempered by a lively expectation of surprise or reversal. Of course this is a rather trivial genre, and we would be mistaken in identifying the Euripidean play even with the work of a master like Herodotos. But the similarity is there, and a careful examination of the evidence about some of the lost plays will clarify the function of these apparently trivializing reversals.

The subject of incest had less explosive social impact than that of adultery; but *Aiolos,* Euripides' great incest play, made a strong impression on the public and seems to have a certain paradigmatic significance for Aristophanes, who uses a taste for *Aiolos* to draw the line between the old reprobate Strepsiades and his newly sophisticated and Socratic son.[59] Far from being a straight play of doomed romance, however, *Aiolos* is an excellent example of

55. The two anecdotes cited are in Herodotos 3.38.3–4 and 2.39.2. For *Telephos,* see fr. 708–11 N2; and Murray (1913.1, 47–48); Webster (1967, 45ff.). Text and testimonia in Austin (1968, 66–82): in need of a magic cure that could come only from his enemies, the Mysian prince Telephos entered the Greek camp at Aulis disguised as a beggar. He eventually made a speech to the host that, to judge by the parody in *Acharnians,* attacked Greek chauvinism and defended barbarians.

56. Hdt. 1.199.5: καὶ τὠπὸ τούτου οὐχ οὕτω μέγα τί οἱ δώσεις ὥς μιν λάμψεαι.

57. A fine example of the long quasi-tragic story about family troubles between Periandros and his son in 3.50–53. In the ending twist, however, it turns out that the story is an *aition* for the enmity between Korkyra and Korinthos, since the citizens of the former kill Periandros' son so that the hated Periandros will not exchange thrones with him and come to Korkyra. The lengthy buildup of sympathy for the boy turns out to be incidental to the joke that the story is playing on his father.

58. See Jens (1964, 26–27).

59. *Clouds* 1371–72. The play is mentioned also in *Frogs* 1079–81, and see the scholiast to *Frogs* 850 (1:370 Rutherford). The famous line, "What's shameful, if it does not seem so to those who practice it? [τί δ' αἰσχρόν, ἢν μὴ τοῖσι χρωμένοις δοκῇ]" (fr. 19 N2) was frequently quoted—see *Frogs* 1475; the story about Antisthenes' retort (Plut. *De aud. poet.* 33c, transferred to Platon in Stob. 5.82); and the joke in Machon, Ath. 13.582d.

the Euripidean use of the ironic twist.[60] The star-crossed, incestuous lovers, like scores of clever plotters in Herodotos, concoct a bizarre scheme.[61] Their aim is to legitimize their liaison by persuading their father that incestuous marriages are preferable to the ordinary kind. Makareus' arguments in his discussion with his father included a listing of all the drawbacks to ordinary marriage.[62] This weaker *logos* must have gained plausibility, as well as considerable power to disturb, out of the well-documented Athenian preference for keeping marriage alliances inside the family, even to the extent of normalizing unions between uncle and niece.[63]

But the daring and plausible design of the protagonists misfires when Aiolos, in arranging for all his twelve offspring to intermarry, matches the incestuous pair with the wrong mates. The moral point d'appui is hard to find, when our sympathies are divided between the effrontery of the incestuous couple and a betrayed parent who in fact approves the incest. Even the sexual shock is trivialized: the lovers surmount the obstacle of incest easily, but are baffled by the vagaries of chance, when Aiolos decides to assign the marriages by lot.[64] A story like this one is, in a sense, a joke. We are invited to squander our investment in the struggles of the protagonists on our enjoyment of the unexpected twist that mocks them and our concern for them.[65]

60. Because of the preservation of a hypothesis on papyrus (Austin [1968, 88 – 89]) we are well informed about the plot of *Aiolos*—see Webster (1967, 157 – 60); Sisti (1979). Further information comes from Dionysios of Halikarnassos; see reference below. Two children of Aiolos by the same mother fell in love, and the girl Kanake became pregnant. A further source of scandal must have been a lyric monody by the pregnant heroine in the throes of labor—see Hartung (1843, 260 – 61); Schmid-Stählin 3:409. On the provocative and inherently comic qualities in the play, see Conacher (1967, 323 – 24).

61. The common Herodotean idiom for clever schemes, *mêchanasthai*, appears very appropriately in the *Aiolos* hypothesis, Austin (1968, 89.30). In Herodotos, it refers usually to ingenious devices for deceit; see the tricks of Thrasyboulos (1.21.2) and Peisistratos (1.59.3, 1.60.3).

62. For these arguments, see fr. 20 – 24 N2 (fr. 19 may have come from the same location). See the hypothesis (Austin [1968, 89.27]): ὁ δὲ νεανίσκος ἔπεισε τὸν πατέρα [τὰς θυ]γατέρας συνοικίσαι τοῖς υἱοῖς. Dion. Hal. *Rhet.* 9.11 (6.345 Radermacher) remarks that the whole speech, like that of the Wise Melanippe, is an elaborate *schêma*, in which one tries to advance one's private cause by making some disingenuous general argument; see also 9.2. See Jaekel (1977, 23 – 24).

63. See, for example, the family of Diogeiton (Lysias 32) and Savage (1907, 47 – 50): Athenians "actually preferred to marry a relative rather than go outside the family." See Schmid-Stählin 3:408. Keyes (1940) traced references to marriage with half-siblings through comedy, concluding that these alliances were tolerated though not preferred.

64. They committed suicide, but the baby was saved by a nurse. See Austin (1968, 89.34) and Lloyd-Jones (Review [1963, 443 – 44] of Turner[1962]).

65. On this quality in Euripides' work, see Norwood (1954, 21), who of course states it in personalized terms: Euripides never gives "his love or hatred unreservedly to any man or woman of his plays." Kitto ([1939] 1961, 253) remarks that Euripides shows a "disconcerting aloofness" toward his creations and that he is prone suddenly to "round upon a sympathetic character in the last act."

It is no doubt possible to imagine a serious and elevated treatment of the theme of bestiality; but to present such a piece effectively would require the gifts of a Sophokles or the daring of the most egregious Hellenistic sensationalist.[66] Euripides had both talent and daring, but his aims were different. In the papyrus fragment of *Cretan Men* we get a glimpse of how far this poet would press his material:[67] the mother of the Minotauros, with colossal impudence, berates her husband for making a fuss about the monster child and thus revealing their shame to the world.[68] She defends her own actions, as Gorgias did those of Helen, by a plea of divine impulsion:[69] was it likely or reasonable (*eikos*) that she would have felt sexual desire for such an object without having been driven to it by an outside force?[70] She is blameless and Minos is a fool who should be ashamed of himself. Such wonderful effrontery could be viewed by no audience without a few nervous titters; the theme is potentially ludicrous, and as usual the Euripidean treatment compounds the effect, driving very close to the edge of absurdity.[71]

In Euripides' first play, *Peliades,* the tragic *pathos* involves a father mistakenly boiled in a cauldron by his own daughters. How or whether Sophokles attempted to conquer the intractable material we do not know. Euripides found in the story an ideal subject for his maiden effort and first dramatic failure.[72] In a typical manner, the play is adorned with serious and weighty

66. *Cretan Men* dealt with Pasiphaë's erotic mania for a bull. Impregnated by the animal, she gave birth to the monstrous Minotauros; and this was eventually discovered by her husband Minos; see Austin (1968, 49–58).

On Sophoclean modifications of myth, see Chap. 9, below, on *Hippolytos.* For the taste of the Hellenistic poets for these themes, see Groningen (1977, 256).

67. See commentary and bibliography in Cantarella (1964, 69–80). We hear little of the play from the comic poets: apparently bestiality did not arouse their social consciences very much. For later mentions of the play, see *Frogs* 849ff., which may apply to this; the scholiast to that passage (p. 300 Dindorf); and Libanius *Decl.* 1.177 (5:116 Förster).

68. See Austin (1968, 57.27–28); Minos is the "doer" of the deed that shames Pasiphaë, not the other way around: κἄπειτ᾿ αὐτεῖς κἀπιμαρτύρη θεοὺς, / αὐτὸς τάδ᾿ ἔρξας καὶ καταισχύνας ἐμέ. She is guiltless: κἀγὼ μὲν ἡ τεκοῦσα κοὐδὲν αἰτία / ἔκρυψα πληγὴν δαίμονος θεήλατον. See Schmid-Stählin 3:412: the technique is called *antenklêma* by the rhetoric textbooks.

69. See DK 2:294 fr. 10B.10–14: ἔρως . . . ἀνθρώπινον νόσημα καὶ ψυχῆς ἀγνόημα, οὐχ ὡς ἁμάρτημα μεμπτέον ἀλλ᾿ ὡς ἀτύχημα νομιστέον.

70. The form of argument is attributed to the father of rhetoric, Korax of Sicily, who made it one of the main tricks in his *technê;* see Aristoteles, *Rhet.* 1402a18–21. See Pohlenz ([1930] 1954, 1:250, 2:102–3); Hinks (1940, 63–65).

71. In line 44 Minos' reply ἆρ᾿ ἐστόμωται may mean "Is she muzzled?" See Page (1941, 76).

72. See Schwartz (1887) in the *Genos Euripidou* 2.15–3.1: πρῶτον δὲ ἐδίδαξε τὰς Πελιάδας, ὅτε καὶ τρίτος ἐγένετο. If Sophokles' *Rhizotomoi* did really deal with the story of *Peliades,* then this would have been another triumph of Sophoclean tact; but see Webster (1967, 34). In the story likely to have been used in this play the sorceress Medeia tricked the daughters of Pelias into killing their father, her enemy. She showed them an old ram, which, cut up and

arguments about women and their fitness to take active decisions in life,[73] arguments that must have been exposed both as complacent or inadequate and as all too hideously right, by the evil plotting of Medeia on the one hand and by the awful results of the daughters' well-meaning initiative on the other.

The social and sexual controversies related to women are only a part of the Euripidean manner. When such themes are scaled down and modified in the later years, the mood of these dramas proves persistent, perpetuating itself through change after change. In a few of the late plays, the cynicism becomes more benign, and the scramblings of the protagonists are sometimes rewarded with a success that, for all their plotting and contriving, they have not completely earned.[74] The mockery to which Euripidean protagonists are subjected is of course derisory not only of them, but of the audience as well. While the Sophoclean play is able to arouse sympathy and identification for the most bizarrely situated and the most antisocially disposed protagonists,[75] the Euripidean antithesis will not permit the audience to trust its feelings about the protagonist or her situation.[76] At any point, the focus may change; indeed, the only certain truth on which the audience can depend—as it is the only certainty about a joke—is that the meaning cannot appear until the last twist has been played out. Of course the joke, once its meaning has discharged in a laugh, is found to be, in most cases, empty of content. The Euripidean play is not over at the last twist, nor—except in certain, limited

---

boiled, emerged intact and rejuvenated. With the aged Pelias, however, the treatment did not prove reversible.

73. See Webster (1967, 35): "Pelias is realistically portrayed as a fussy old king who is no match for the ruthless Medeia." See fr. 603 N2, for the "fussy" tone:

αἰνῶ· διδάξαι δ' ὧ τέκνον σε βούλομαι.
ὅταν μὲν ἧς παῖς, μὴ πλέον παιδὸς φρονεῖν,
ἐν παρθένοις δὲ παρθένου τρόπους ἔχειν,
ὅταν δ' ὑπ' ἀνδρὸς χλαῖναν εὐγενοῦς πέσῃς, <act as a wife should;>
. . . τὰ δ' ἄλλ' ἀφεῖναι μηχανήματ' ἀνδράσιν.

74. On the central role of chance (tychê), see Whitman (1974, 109); Garzya (1962, 72 – 73); Cataudella (1969, 342); Spira (1960, 132ff.); Pohlenz ([1930] 1954, 386); Busch (1937, 45 – 54).

75. See Knox (1964, Chaps. 1 – 2, passim); on the isolation of the Sophoclean hero, see also Gellie (1972, 216).

76. See Masqueray's delightful observations (1908, 81 – 82). Euripides seems to make fun of himself and we cannot be sure whether to trust him. "Notre plaisir est détruit." Euripides creates a pathetic scene, and then ruins it, tossing it aside like a fruit whose savor has been extracted: "Il y a une sorte de perversité très fine à se moquer des gens que l'on a émus." On Ion: "Il semble vouloir nous fair honte, comme à des enfants, du plaisir que nous avons pris du joli conte qu'il nous a fait" (130). See also the suspicion of Leeuwen (1876, 27) that the audience is being tricked (verba dari) by the poet.

circumstances[77]—is the "serious" introduction wiped out or negated by its derisory close.

The bizarre and grotesque in myth, the unsuitable stories that had to be expunged from the tradition, or altered before they could be usable for the high mimetic, are the meat of Euripidean drama. Often, again much in the fashion of the *Odysseia,* for instance in the Kyklops episode, a delicate and picturesque charm accompanies and mingles incongruously with the horrible and the ludicrous. *Peliades* very likely made use of such effects, contrasting the innocent and loving intent of its maiden characters with the revolting results. A strong extant example, and one that illustrates perfectly the sort of macabre humor inherent in the story of *Peliades,* is the climactic moment of *Phaethon.*[78] The hero's corpse, incinerated by a lightning bolt, is concealed by his terrified mother in the royal treasury, just as the wedding procession arrives caroling its happy song to Phaethon and his bride. The corpse, however, continues to burn with an unnatural fire; and the resulting smoke begins to create a problem.[79] Phaethon's stepfather Merops bustles off to see about the trouble, sententiously remarking that "this sort of thing, if laxly handled, tends to grow into a storm."[80] The irony of death and the wedding song may already have been used by Aischylos in the *Danaides* trilogy;[81] but the dreadful humor of a situation in which the domestic emergency that threatens to disturb a wedding turns out to be caused by the smouldering corpse of the bridegroom—that is essential Euripides.[82]

The Euripidean plot denies the audience a wholehearted participation in the pathetic circumstances of the dramatic protagonists. The children of Aiolos are, like Haimon and Antigone and like Romeo and Juliet,[83] plighted lovers who commit suicide serially when their plans to achieve a marriage miscarry; and the death of a bridegroom on his wedding day has great tragic potential in Greek culture, where the funeral rites for young men and women

77. One example of a beginning that is partially negated by the ending may be *Herakles;* see discussion in Chap. 8, below.
78. The familiar part of the story, in which Phaethon disastrously attempts to pilot the chariot of the Sun his father, was joined with a plot thread about Phaethon's marriage; but it is unclear just how the two themes were linked or whom Phaethon was to marry; see Diggle (1970, 155–60). D. dates the play on metrical grounds to "within a few years" of 420 (47–49).
79. A servant is concerned that fire not ruin the celebration: ἐν τοῖσιν ἡδίστοισι Φαέθοντος γάμοις (253–60).
80. φιλεῖ τὰ τοιάδε / ληφθέντα φαύλως ἐς μέγαν χειμῶν᾽ ἄγειν (266–67).
81. Fr. 124M; see Fritz (1936, 134–35).
82. See Calder (1972, 292): "The play is hilarious, even grotesque. Phaethon's corpse is brought on stage in the form of an over-cooked chop, still smoking (ἀτμόν, 215)." C. argues from this that the play was never produced, but such effects are not uncommon in Euripides and cannot be used to prove that there was anything odd about *Phaethon.*
83. On the resemblance to Haimon and Antigone, see Webster (1967, 159).

often mimicked the marriage ceremony that would never be accomplished.[84] But the structure of the plays that climax in these sad events would not permit the usually highly emotional and empathetic tragic audience to surrender fully to their feelings.[85]

But, while the twists of the plot prevent the audience from being "swept up" in the Euripidean play, they also tend to moderate the offensiveness of the plays, undercutting every shock in such a way that, eventually, the hard edge of outrage is also blunted. This technique serves to keep the balance referred to above between the necessary irritation of the audience's conventional expectations, and the danger of an outright rejection. The effect can be observed in a surviving example of Euripides' outrageous early plays, the *Medeia*. While Medeia is not an adulteress, she does follow her sexual desires, choosing her husband at dreadful cost to her family of birth; and in punishing Iason's sexual infidelity with an atrocious crime, she inverts the moral rule by which women must subordinate sexual impulse to family needs. When this figure defends the female sex, she is persuasive and offensive at once and in almost equal measure; but her arguments are largely false to her own circumstances, a fact which qualifies both offense and persuasion.[86] Her indignation against Iason is as understandable as her revenge is alienating; and the horror of the infanticide is both mitigated and exacerbated by Medeia's maternal regrets on the one hand and by her triumphal exit on the other.[87] In the end, the contradicting currents of sympathy and indignation are productive of tension rather than blandness, since the strong emotions that naturally attach themselves to the dramatic situation are constantly aroused anew, and the tension between Medeia's roles as suffering mother and as demonic avenger is continually increased up to the moment of her final exit.

84. For the parallelism of wedding and funeral rites, see Alexiou (1974, Index s.v. Marriage and Death); and for the prevalence of this theme in grave inscriptions see Griessmair (1966, 63–75). Tragic references would include: Sophokles *Antigone* 813ff., 867ff., 876ff.; Euripides *Hkld* 591ff. The legend of Iphigeneia's death and the false marriage turns around this (see Eisner [1979, 160–61]; Foley, [1982]), as does the *aition* in *Hipp* 1425–27.

85. On emotion as a factor in the tragic theater, see Taplin (1978, 168–71); but emotion cannot be so central to Euripidean theater. A. C. Schlesinger (1963, 18–19) remarks on Euripidean avoidance of emotional involvement by the audience: Euripides uses "mood control" in plays like *Andromache* and *Suppliants* to check sentimentality; see p. 66, "a considerable degree of judicial detachment is demanded of the audience." See also Forehand (1979, 174–75) on the ironic undercutting in *Ion* as a result of which "we can assess Ion's view of himself . . . with more detachment than we might" if pathetic aspects had been emphasized. W. D. Smith on *Alkestis*: as the ironic tone "chips away at" the heroic persona of Admetos, the audience is prodded into a more critical and alert view of him (1960.1, 129).

86. On Medeia's arguments, see Page (1938) on line 231, and pp. xvii-xviii: "sly deceitful arguments. . . . If the Chorus forgets, at least the audience should remember."

87. See Reinhardt (1957, 626).

Many Euripidean characters are, like Medeia, the first Phaidra, and Pasiphaë, ready to defend socially and morally offensive acts with brazen
impudence. Tyrants, usurers, cowards, and other villains, all shamelessly
flaunting their immorality, undoubtedly stirred up almost as much indignation
as the delinquent women.[88] It was of course not the mere appearance of such
vile figures that constituted a provocation, but rather the equivocal treatment
of their roles. In a drama of mockery, a character who mocks moral norms
will seem very much in tune with the play, just as the defender of the norm in
such a setting necessarily appears vulnerable. In Aischylos' *Agamemnon,* the
introduction at the play's end of a very vile character, Aigisthos, distinctly
lowers the tone of the last scene;[89] but the furious response of the normally
timid chorus, and the memory of Kassandra's hints earlier in the play, serve
to retain the scene in moral perspective. In Euripidean drama, a moral perspective is denied the audience; and the dance of provocation and retreat
keeps them constantly uncertain. There is a paradigmatic significance in the
anecdote that has Euripides interrupting his own production to respond to an
uproar in the theater:[90] he suggests that the audience, before losing their
tempers, should wait to see what will happen to the speaker of these shocking
lines by the end of the play. The Euripidean joke turns against the evil and
immoral figures in the plays as much as it does against the "sympathetic"
ones. The audience, whether they have been moved to fury or to tears, will
in either case find that their feelings have been betrayed by ever new twists
and changes.

The contemporary polemic against Euripides extended beyond the whole
play or the single scene even to the single line. The anecdote above was connected by Seneca to a famous passage praising gold.[91] A variety of such passages or single lines are used as cues by Aristophanes, with the evident
expectation that his audiences, on hearing them even many years after the
first production of the play in question, will recognize them and react

88. Tyrants, see Eteokles in *Phoin* 504–6; usurers, see the passage translated by Seneca (*Ep.*
115, discussed below); cowards, *Alk* 691 (cf. 722): χαίρεις ὁρῶν φῶς πατέρα δ' οὐ χαίρειν
δοκεῖς

89. See Denniston & Page (1957) on lines 1577–78: "He speaks in a style unlike that of
any character in Aeschylus, high or low.... Glib, leisurely flatness ... bombastic grandilo-
quence." Böhme (1956) attempted to excise the scene: "Es ist der äusserste Gegensatz zum
tragischen Sprachton des Aischylos wenn alles derart zerhackt ist wie hier" (19). On the change
in momentum caused by Aigisthos' "crude assertiveness," see Taplin (1977, 328–29).

90. Seneca *Ep.* 115.15: "Cum hi novissimi versus ... pronuntiati essent, totus populus ad
eiciendum et actorem et carmen consurrexit uno impetu, donec Euripides in medium ipse prosi-
livit petens ut exspectarent viderentque quem admirator auri exitum faceret."

91. Plutarchos (*De aud. poet.* 19e) tells a similar story about *Ixion* (fr. 1324 N2). The anecdotes' historical truth is, of course, quite irrelevant to their literary significance.

appropriately.[92] Clearly they were famous catch phrases, treasured and often repeated, according to the occasion of the citation, with indignation or amusement. The few of these famous lines whose context we know are rather puzzling. Hippolytos' "My tongue swore, not I," taken in context, is not indicative of any amoral attitudes: the young man does in fact keep, at the cost of his own life, the oath that he claims has been unfairly exacted.[93]

Such quotable, clever lines are, in miniature, instances of the overall effect of Euripidean technique, capturing in small compass the whole tone and mood both of the Sophistic, and of Euripidean irony. But, precisely because of the constant shifting of moral viewpoint in the plays, such passages tend to be embedded in contexts that partially or wholly negate their content. In context, what Hippolytos says is strongly mitigated by his shock and horror at the nurse's proposition; and, in context, it is easy to see that when Orestes in *Elektra* says that "It is better to let these matters go at random," he is not really promoting the rejection of moral standards for human conduct, but rather the opposite.[94] Aristophanes was not wrong, however, to see in the momentary flash of these epigrams a characteristic of Euripidean drama, nor was he or his audience mistaken in assuming their provocative intent. It was the misfortune of his moralist critics that their opponent, in the twists of his art, left so little room open for a blow. At the end of the play, there might be nothing for them to fix on except a few questionable and catchy witticisms.

I have suggested already that I agree with those who see a change in Euripidean techniques after 428. Personal motivations for Euripides' artistic development are unknowable and even unguessable, and, even if we had the extensive biographical data that we lack, might still prove irrelevant. The literary evidence shows that, if the playwright courted success by these changes, he was disappointed, since Euripides cannot have won more than

92. See quotations in *Clouds* (1415) and *Thesmophoriazousai* (193) of *Alk* 691; *Hipp* 612 is cited in *Thes.* (275–76) and *Frogs* (1471); see Leeuwen (1876, 125–55), who found a large number of Euripidean citations in Aristophanes. Not all, however, are cited as outrageous or in such a way as to indicate that they were generally known. Among the notorious lines were doubtless those from *Danaë; El* 379 (see discussion below; neither of these lines is cited by Aristophanes); the passage beginning "Who knows whether life is death or death is life ... [τίς δ' οἶδεν εἰ τὸ ζῆν μέν ἐστι κατθανεῖν ...]," from *Polyidos* (or *Phrixos* [fr. 638 N2]), cited in *Frogs* 1082, 1477–78; and of course the *Aiolos* line (fr. 19). For the memories of the Athenian audience and their response to the plays, which evidently became the subject of much talk, see the excellent article by Harriott (1962).

93. See Avery (1968). A.'s attempt to explain why the line should still have attracted attention in 411 is unsuccessful. However significant the line is in the meaning system of the play, its appeal as a snappy quotation can be based only on its ostensible meaning, when it appears out of context.

94. *El* 379; see the anecdote in Diog. Laert. 2.33, where Sokrates responds to this line; the story is a variation on the one about fr. 19 and Antisthenes.

two victories between 428, when *Hippolytos Crowned* took first place, and his retirement from the Attic theater in 408 – 7. *Hippolytos Crowned* is the only extant play known to have won the prize during the poet's lifetime; and an analysis of that play will show that it differs in a number of signal ways from the rest of the Euripidean oeuvre.[95] This new mode does not become a norm for the later plays. As their lack of success indicates, these plays recreate in other ways the Euripidean manner that had been established from the time of the first production.

The stance of aesthetic provocation remains the same; but the means have further diversified. While themes of sexual controversy have diminished, subjects relating to domestic life and misogyny persist, along with criticism of the divine and heroic in myth.[96] In place of the erotic motifs, there emerge in the 420s new themes from the social-moral genres, most notably those of patriotism and of doctrinaire moralism, topics that had to some extent been exploited by Aischylos, though in a different way. To Euripides they gave scope for an even fuller development of Sophistic-rhetorical style and for the exploitation of contemporary political concerns in a way that was anything but traditional. The devices of ironic sabotage that, in the plays of outrage, kept the audience off balance and uncertain work in these plays to undermine and qualify the lofty and idiosyncratic notions of the protagonists. A good example, and another exhibition of Euripidean malignant humor, is *Erechtheus,* where the complacent patriotism of Praxithea's often-quoted speech devolves into a horrific denouement in which she is bereft of all her children, and her husband as well.[97] Like much else in these plays, the inspiring speech that so appealed to Lykourgos has one meaning outside its context, and quite another in the context of the drama.[98]

A favorite device of the second period is to substitute for outrageous vice

95. See discussion in Chap. 9, below.

96. U. v. Wilamowitz suggested that Euripides turned from obscure and unfamiliar myths to the main lines of tradition in his later period (1875, 177); but this is uncertain because of dating problems. We do find an unfamiliar perspective on familiar myth, in *Elektra, Orestes, Iphigeneia at Aulis,* and the lost *Alexandros.* Also striking is *Oidipous* (dated late by its trochaic passage, see Webster [1967, 241ff.]), where the hero's blinding is not by his own hand and precedes the discovery of the incest. See also the sententious discussion of marital duties (by Iokaste?): the effect is a part of the ironical undercutting of rhetoric discussed above. For the plot, see Robert (1915, 305 – 31) and more recently Turner (1962, 81 – 83); Vaio (1964, 47 – 48); Dingel (1970, 93ff.).

97. For the plot of *Erechtheus,* see Austin (1968, 22 – 23). The queen offers to sacrifice one of her three daughters to save the city; but the girls had made a pact to commit suicide if one died; see Apollod. 3.15.4. Erechtheus himself was destroyed by Poseidon (Austin [1968, 37.59 – 60]). The papyrus remains include a dirge by Praxithea and the chorus (35 – 36) that is interrupted by Athena, who cut off the mourning with an aetiological close.

98. See Lykourgos *In Leocr.* 100. Cf. Tuilier (1968, 27 – 28).

an equally outrageous virtue. This trope is harder to pick out because the opinions voiced by the characters in question do not in principle conflict with cultural norms, although the speakers carry these ideals to eccentric and abnormal lengths. The effect may well have been equally disorienting for the fifth-century audience, although it would have been less likely to make them outraged and indignant. It is easy for us to miss the effect of these innovations, because, to a modern reader, what these characters say seems all too familiar. Christianity, and other scriptural religions, have given modern culture a powerful ideological tradition the like of which did not yet exist in Hellenic society, outside small and secret sects such as the Pythagoreans. Traditional cultures foster behavior that falls within conventional parameters, as expressed by vaguely defined norms (e.g., *arete* or the *agathos aner*) rather than by abstract principles.[99] Antigone, when she buries her brother in defiance of Kreon, clings to an old and traditional custom. She may enunciate principle to defend the custom, but Antigone is not moved to an aberrant act by private notions of right and wrong.[100] She has simply refused to neglect a custom that is commonly observed by everybody, but that in this case has been violated by Kreon. When Iphigeneia or Makaria offer themselves as sacrifices, however, they move far beyond what was normally expected of members of their society. A logical argument can be made to support almost any oddity of behavior, as the Sophists well knew; but there was no system of generally accepted principles at the disposal of the Euripidean self-sacrificers.[101]

A further warping factor in the modern view of Euripidean virtue is the standard of extreme and sacrificial virtue that in the nineteenth century derived ideas about women's social role from the Christian religious tradition, so that religious principles virtually became sexual norms as well.[102] But Greek women were not idealized as models of a self-abnegation impossible for males; and the Euripidean convention of a sacrificial *arete* is virtually without roots in Greek tradition. The standards of Greek society gave strikingly little support to extreme altruism; and, given the self-assertive and

99. On the *agathos* as a model, see Adkins (1960, 37ff.).

100. See Bowra (1944) on the traditional practices in which Antigone's "strictly personal and intimate . . . resolution" is based (92–93). See Gouldner (1965, 83) on the "common standards" of traditional Greek culture, and on Antigone (226).

101. See J. Schmitt (1921, 1); the closest approximation is certainly the warrior ethic of Tyrtaios—see 11W 5–6: one must hate one's *psyche* and love death. See *Phoin* 995–1002, *IA* 1387–91.

102. See Porterfield (*Feminine Spirituality in America* [1980, 78]) on the tendency to associate Christian self-abnegation with the domestic behavior considered appropriate for women.

egotistic norms of heroic morality,[103] it is not surprising that self-sacrifice is not an important feature in the myths of any of the major heroic figures.[104] In fact, the only cultural model available to the many Euripidean figures is not a mythical hero but a philosophical one: the connection that was presumed by Aristophanes between Euripides' work and Sokrates' ideas is confirmed in a general sense by the way in which the latter chose to die.[105] We should then see the rich proliferation of the themes of sacrifice and self-immolation in later Euripides as another, though certainly less volatile and dangerous, means of challenging the social and aesthetic standards of fifth-century Athens.

But as in all other instances of apparent moral advocacy in Euripides, the self-sacrificers and other purists are not allowed to shine with an untarnished light.[106] The effect on the audience of a virtue that exaggerated and therefore distorted conventional norms can be judged by a moment from *Andromache,* where the heroine is juxtaposed with the vicious bride Hermione as a standard of good marital conduct.[107] But Andromache's expression of this virtue takes a form that is extreme, and even bizarre. She boasts that, "to avoid giving [him] any annoyance," she even offered her breast to her dear Hector's bastards.[108] The audience would agree that women should not

103. On the high status of the powerful and assertive person, the *agathos anêr,* see Adkins (1960), e.g., p. 50: "If the *agathos* chooses to make use of his advantage . . . his claim to act as he pleases . . . is stronger than any claim [others] can bring against him." See also Gouldner (1965, 45 – 51) on competition in Greek culture.

104. Myths of sacrifice did of course exist, but only a few mythical sacrifices were pictured as voluntary. J. Schmitt (1921, 1) adopts the view of Busolt (1893 – 95, 1:220 n.2) that most of these legends are political and develop relatively late. We may contrast the legend of a Kodros with the story of a Diomedes or an Achilleus, a story centered wholly on the deeds and personality of the hero rather than his social role.

105. Sokrates, like Polyxene in *Hekabe,* is more concerned with the quality of life than with its extent; for his view of exile, see Menoikeus, *Phoin* 1004 – 5. On the connection, see Aristoph. *Frogs* 1491 – 95; and Telekleides fr. 2 and 3M (2:371, 372). F. Lucas (1923, 40) remarked, "Socrates . . . is persistently linked with Euripides by a tradition, which cannot be entirely discounted except by that type of scholar who refuses to believe any facts about antiquity which he has not himself invented." Martin (1958, 266 – 69) shows that the comic poets abuse both men in the same terms; see also Martinazzoli (1946, 57). Further discussion of Socratic reflections in Euripides occurs in Chap. 9.

106. See discussion of the role of Polyxene in Chap. 6; for another viewpoint see Strohm (1981, 153 – 55), who seems to see these figures as a point of positive moral reference for Euripides.

107. The Andromache of *Troiades* is a close cousin to this one: she proposed to make herself into an ideal wife (643ff.). Hermione is that figure of terror well known from later comedy, the dowered bride (147 – 53). On the erotic content of *Andromache,* see Garzya (1951, 122ff.).

108. 224 – 25:

καὶ μαστὸν ἤδη πολλάκις νόθοισι σοῖς
ἐπέσχον, ἵνα σοι μηδὲν ἐνδοίην πικρόν.

On the unrealistic quality of Andromache's boast, see Lee (1955, 14).

annoy their husbands, but Andromache puts this old saw into action in a way that is likely to surprise them. Women in Hellenic society, as in most societies, derived most of their security from their male children.[109] The conflicts that resulted from concubinage and second and third marriages where the claims of rival offspring were advanced by different mothers, and the resultant unenviable status of stepchildren, can be seen by consulting sources as diverse as *Alkestis* and the speeches of the orators.[110] The rights of legitimate wives, vis-à-vis concubines and other subordinate mates, are relatively clear, and are embedded in *Andromache* itself: the prerogatives and resources of the wife and of her children must not be infringed upon, and ideally the two women should not share the same household as sexual rivals.[111]

Given such a background, the picture of the complaisant queen suckling a concubine's baby is paradoxical; and the physical intimacy implied seems repugnant. Just as in other Euripidean dramas, the audience will be in a dilemma: societal values will chime with Andromache's principle that the wife must subordinate her wishes to those of the husband, but her socially and emotionally inappropriate boast will make the audience uneasy. In spite of Andromache's nobility, they may be tempted to agree with Hermione that barbarians are queer folk, who are prepared to take any moral enormity in stride.[112] The lack of a perspective on the characters from which a clear moral sighting could be obtained, a feature already noted for other plays, will be underlined later, when Hermione first recants all her self-assertion in a speech whose misogyny exceeds Andromache's—and a few moments later proceeds to elope with a man who has planned the murder of her husband!

Euripidean theater plays a dangerous game with its audience, luring them in with pathos and charm, but chilling their sympathy always, just at the crucial moment when the watchers would have become incapable of detaching themselves from the dramatic illusion. A biased and sentimental pity is

109. Besides the role of offspring in stabilizing the marital relationship, a grown son was a source of protection and support to his mother in her old age, when her much older husband, like her parents, might no longer be alive. On the son's duty to support his mother, see Schaps (1979, 83 – 84). The daughter, who would ideally always be married and under the control either of her husband or of her own sons, could offer little support.

110. On the stepmother, see *Alk* 309 – 16, and Kreousa in *Ion* 1024 – 25. In Isaios, note the quarrels over estates caused by concubines and half-brothers, Is. 6.21 (on Euktemon's abandonment of his legitimate family); in Lysias 32, note the confusion in Diogeiton's family: he has remarried and wants to spend the inheritance of his grandsons on his new family. Savage (1907) is unable to see the connection of this, and of the dependency of women on their sons, with the behavior of stepmothers; see pp. 113 – 14, a mere collection of commonplaces from the poets.

111. See the chorus' statements, several times repeated: 123ff., 181 – 82, 465ff.

112. 174 – 80; Hermione's accusations of incest and murder are meant to lead into a repudiation of polygamy.

deliberately evoked, only to be expunged by a wave of astringent irony. An outbreak of rage and rejection from the audience, the dreaded uproar in the theater (*thorybos*), is courted—and then allayed by a reversal that disarms resentment and seems for a time to right the moral universe. Besides the vibration between two extremes, there are also fainter overtones of dissonance built into scenes that seem to compel sympathy or repugnance, overtones that become dominant once the next variation begins to unfold. By approaching the audience in this way, Euripides guaranteed that they would never be able entirely to deny him their attention, though he would never gain their entire approval.

4

Formalism in the Style of Euripidean Drama

Euripides has been at various times labeled realist, romantic, or ideologue.[1] The descriptions are as notable for their variety as for their mutual contradictoriness, and any effective general treatment of Euripides' work will have to provide an explanation of this divergence. Why should the plays present such a dazzling variety of aspects to different viewers? Second, it will be necessary to sift the valid from the invalid among the various labels attached to this author. As a general rule, preference should be given to traits that seem to characterize the plays directly, in preference to those that attach to Euripides himself and require the support of a biographical fantasy.

Attempts to ground the character of the plays in the character of their author are ineffective for two reasons. First, the "character" of Euripides is an imaginary construct[2] that can provide no independent evidence about the work. Second, even genuine biographical data can be used in detailed literary interpretation only to explain anomalies in the aesthetic structure, since the structure itself is self-consistent and therefore lacks psychological significance; but the portrait of the artist that would emerge from such a critical process would tell us little about the aesthetic meaning of the work.[3] In

1. For these characteristics, see Chap. 1, Section III.D, as well as comments by Burian ("Euripides the Contortionist" [1976, 96]) and Thompson (1948, 156), who makes a fine collection of Euripidean paradoxes, only to conclude that Euripides must have been at war with himself. I hope to show that critics have been at war with themselves; see Merklin (1964, 38–39): Euripides has appeared to his interpreters as a veritable Proteus.

2. See the discussion of the biographical data in Chap. 2, above.

3. See the statement of Conacher (1967, 151) and the fine remark of Zuntz (1933, 254): "Ihn wird vergeblich biographische Neugier hinter seinen Gestalten suchen; unkenntlich bleibt er hinter seiner Schöpfung, wie die Gottheit jenseit der Welt."

the work of a skilled artist anomalies caused by oversight will be few; and the explanation is one that can be employed only when attempts to find aesthetic significance have been unsatisfactory. Because critics have been trying to fit Euripides into models suggested by their own notions of "serious" drama, there has been a great deal in the plays that did seem to be without significance and that therefore was attributed, more openly by the more naively philistine critics, to the vagaries of a brilliant mind whose first loyalty was not to the making of good plays.[4]

There is one trait commonly detected in Euripidean work that has hardly ever been linked to or derived from an imaginary biography. Euripides has often been described as a formalist, who neglects a variety of naturalistic effects available to him in Sophoclean theater, preferring a more frontal, less organic, and more old-fashioned style.[5] It has been often observed that the plays at times resemble the work of the only pre-Sophoclean dramatist known to us, Aischylos.[6] It is obvious why the biographical explanation has not been tried in this case. Formality in the aesthetic structure cannot be seen as an anomaly introduced out of some nonaesthetic and therefore personal motivation; nor is it easy to imagine that formalism is an expression of this artist's personality, as Sophokles' literary "regularity" was presumed to emanate from his.[7] Euripides has been seen by ancient and by modern critics as at war with tradition. Why then did this nonconforming artist conform so obsessively to outmoded artistic norms, while flouting those of the contemporary stage? The answer is to be found in the double impulse typical of this drama, to challenge accepted norms, but not to to move entirely beyond the range of acceptability. The reuse of disused and archaic forms, like the revival of any outmoded fashion, is an effective technique of innovation because older styles make a dual impression, first of novelty, deviation from

4. For this explanation, usually linked to Euripidean mental aberrations, see Chap. 1, above. The assumption that Euripides was a clumsy artist contradicts his characterization as a skillful master of theatrical technique, ready to sacrifice any other value to that of "dramatic effect." See Mahaffy (1879, 35), who notices the contradiction: Euripides sometimes refuses to conform and at other times shows "the desire to please his audience with all the arts which ordinary playwrights adopt." Perrotta (1963, 39) remarks on the same paradox: "come se ... a un eccesso seguisse l'eccesso contrario." See Norwood (1954, 5–6). In the Fondation Hardt discussion (*Entretiens* [1958, 273]), Winnington-Ingram countered Martin's explanation of Euripides' unpopularity as due to his "realism" by pointing out that much of Euripides seems expressly designed to cater to popular taste.

5. See Murray (1913.1, 17–19); Grube (1941, 26ff.); Ludwig (1957; see discussion in Chap. 1, above); Johansen (1959, 173ff.)

6. See Johansen (1959, 173ff.); Krausse (1905); and recently Aëlion (1983).

7. It is interesting to speculate on what critics could have said, had Sophokles been the formalist, rather than Euripides. On Sophoclean religious and cultural orthodoxy, see Pohlenz ([1939] 1954, 229–30); and Lesky, who attempts a moderate position ([1956] 1972.1, 272–73).

the expected, but second of appropriateness and familiarity.[8] Archaism was a device that could increase the palatability of the bitter stuff that Euripidean audiences had to assimilate, partly counteracting the estrangement between artist and audience, without changing the basic quality of Euripidean theater.

In several ways, archaic style clearly suited Euripides' work. Formalism is a mode that can keep many diverse elements in relation, while preserving the integrity of each; and the organic unity of Sophoclean theater, in which each element was reshaped to fit the whole, was not appropriate to Euripidean style.[9] Archaism could be used to evoke non-Sophoclean elements of the tragic tradition, and provided a link to a period when tragedy had been less focused on the heroic and the mode of the *spoudaion*. That early period of experimentation and innovation thus became accessible to the artist once again. The dynamic and elegant unity of Sophoclean dramatic style seems to lead nowhere but into itself, whereas the work of Aischylos, through its boldly experimental quality, offered many more paths to pursue, and suggested a variety of ways in which further development could take place. Euripides' practice of reviving the old is an instance of the power of literary forms to reconstitute themselves in spite of the centrifugal forces of change and development.[10] In one sense, Euripidean drama had pushed Sophoclean changes farther along; a return to older forms balanced some of these changes and reestablished some qualities of tragic drama that would otherwise have been lost.

Before beginning any discussion of Euripidean formalism it is necessary to consider Euripidean innovation, that is, those areas in which the artist followed trends that can be traced in Sophokles' work and that had already done much to change the nature of tragedy. Euripides, acting in this case as a literary successor to Sophokles, extended and exaggerated these changes. Sophokles had introduced the third actor; and, unlike Aischylos, he had early tended to play off two characters against each other in dialogue and balanced speeches. Just as Sophokles perfected the invention of his predecessor, so Euripides, especially in the later works, makes a bold use of three-person scenes, particularly in the *agôn* or verbal contest before a judge.[11] Other

8. This is a process analogous with that I discussed earlier (1982, 21–22), in which an innovation is directly linked to the suggestion and the rejection of an older version. See the Russian structuralist Tynjanov on genre development ([1927] 1969.1, cf. English trans. in Matejka [1971]); and, on communication through traditional form in literature, Kirsch (1982, 275–79).

9. See Schadewaldt (1926, 104); Michelini (1982, 69–70). Arrowsmith points out (1963, 40–42) the fragmentation and multiplicity typical of Euripidean style.

10. See Michelini (1982, 18–19); Tynjanov ([1927] 1969.1; [1924] 1969.2, 411).

11. See *Hekabe* and *Troiades,* where there is an almost perfectly balanced triangle with one equally weighted character at each apex; Strohm (1957, 32). E.g., *Hek* 218–443 (Odysseus, Polyxene, Hekabe) and 1109–1292 (Hekabe, Agamemnon, Polymestor); cf. *Tro* 860–1059.

instances would include the impressive increase in complexity in the late plays, to the point where in *Phoinissai* we see the story of Kreon's family mixed with that of the family of Oidipous in a mesh of episodes.[12] Aristophanes and other critics have remarked that the elaborate diction of Aischylos makes a sharp contrast with the notably simpler and more prosaic language of Euripides;[13] and a few have noted that this movement toward language more in harmony with normal speech is already traceable in Sophokles' work.[14] Finally, the Aeschylean theater of "astonishment" (*ekplêxis*), which confronts the audience with wonders and monsters that do not really resemble the things we see in our waking hours, was altered by a Sophoclean emphasis on human situations. Euripidean characters, of course, are even more easy to recognize; and their world includes many more details that could be seen as commonplace and familiar.[15]

The Euripidean mode, however, in each case of innovation represents not just an exaggeration of the Sophoclean, but a distorting exaggeration that stands Sophoclean theater on its head. The triangular plots and the complex interweaving of episodes facilitated a lessened stress on the individual protagonist and thus furthered the antiheroic tone of the plays. The changes in language and vocabulary introduced jarring echoes of nontragic diction. The low-life touches of servants sweeping the floor or carrying water from the springs went far beyond the Sophoclean humanization of tragedy and challenged the mode of the *spoudaion* itself, by daring the audience to link the remote world of myth with the commonplaces of everyday life. It was to counter the disruptive effects of this strange new sort of tragedy that the artist revived old forms from the Aeschylean era and beyond.

Euripides did not parallel Sophokles and Aischylos by leaving behind him as they did an enlarged tragic cast, though the multiple plot lines and many characters in Euripidean plays might well have been facilitated by a fourth performer. It may be that the requisite public approval for an increased

12. See Strohm (1957, 183–84), who repels the suggestion that in late Euripides plots have become rigid and the art form lacking in vitality.

13. *Frogs* 940–41: Euripides brags of dieting down Aischylos' swollen verbiage: παρέλαβον τὴν τέχνην παρὰ σοῦ ... οἰδοῦσαν.... ἴσχνανα μὲν πρώτιστον αὐτὴν καὶ τὸ βάρος ἀφεῖλον. See Stevens' work on colloquialisms in Euripides (1976); and Wehrli (1946), who shows that the terms in Aristophanes derive from fifth-century literary criticism and perpetuate themselves with few changes through the Hellenistic and Roman periods.

14. On Sophokles' language see Earp (1944) on the change away from Aeschylean heaviness toward speed and brevity (126–29).

15. Water carrying in *Elektra* (108ff.), washing in *Hippolytos* (121ff.), and draught playing in *Medeia* (68ff.) add the common touch. Bond (1963, 67) points out that sweeping is a regular motif in Euripides: *Hypsipyle* 2.15ff.(Bond), *Hek* 363, *Ion* 112ff., *Andr* 166, *Phaethon* 55–58 (Diggle). Some of these may have been accompanied by dances suggesting the motions involved.

number of actors would have been less readily granted to Euripides, because of his position as outsider and adversary to the tradition. But it is equally likely that further changes in the cast would have clashed with the archaizing and formalist style of Euripidean drama. It is a singular fact that the earliest plays we have are the most chary in their use of the third actor.[16] It seems that, while Sophokles reached for change early, Euripides in his earlier career sometimes chose to retreat from a Sophoclean innovation that was, when Euripides began producing plays, probably less than ten years old.[17] The adoption of an archaizing and formalist style, and indeed the whole anti-Sophoclean or antiheroic stance of Euripidean drama, is a mark of completion in the developmental process of tragedy. Once the art form had, as Aristoteles put it, acquired its natural form (*physis*), that is, a form that satisfied its audience as perfect, the next step could no longer be taken in a direct, forward progression.[18] The attempt to renew his art form and to reshape it in his own image, the attempt of every great artist in every period, forced upon Euripides a deviation from the established norm, and a corresponding recapitulation of the past.[19]

Formalism may be described as the tendency to give stylistic embellishment to structural detail, thus making the structure more accessible to the conscious appreciation of the audience.[20] Formal features often noted in Euripidean drama include elaborate, separable introductions and closing statements attached to long speeches;[21] the use of stichomythy in preference to more freely and naturalistically formed dialogue;[22] internal references to stage events, such as entrance and exit;[23] balance and symmetry in the arrangement of speeches;[24] the tendency to set strong boundaries between

16. Besides *Alkestis,* which uses only two actors, *Medeia* also has no scene in which three actors speak. In *Hippolytos,* three actors appear only in the last scene; in *Andromache* they appear only in the rescue scene. *Herakleidai,* on the other hand, makes a free use of such scenes.

17. For the date of this innovation, see discussion in Chap. 2, above, and Michelini (1984).

18. *Poet.* 1449a15 – 16: *physis* implies completion. (See also *Pol.* 1252b32.) See Else (1957, 153 n.96); and Diller (1939, 253).

19. Or, put in another way, Euripides seems to approach Aischylos because he shares with him a common distance (*Abstand*) from Sophokles (Friedländer [1928, 97]).

20. Ludwig (1957, 6) on the "Kanonisierung der Einzelteile."

21. See Johansen (1959, 99ff.): separable introductions, e.g., *comparatio paratactica,* have a "strong tendency to stand out as a self-sufficient unity." See also J. Gould (1978, 51).

22. Schwinge (1968.1, 339): Euripides used stichomythy "erneut mehr und mehr durchweg, . . . und zwar wiederum nahezu ausschliesslich in vollkommen strenger Form."

23. See the tendency of later Euripides to use tetrameter passages as accents marking off entrances and exits, Michelini (1982, 46 – 47 n.13). On the dramaturgical significance of entrance and exit in early drama, see Taplin (1977, 38).

24. See the pointed remarks of Iason (522) and Medeia (1351). Ludwig compares this formal elegance to a French garden; it displays "ein überschauendes Disponieren und ein klares Begreifen der Gedanken in ihren logischen Bezügen" (1957, 8).

emotional and discursive utterances;[25] and the transfer of information directly
to the audience by a speaker, e.g., in the prologue, in preference to an indirect
transfer through dialogue among the dramatic characters. Many of these
traits are present also in the plays of Aischylos.

An archaic and paratactic style correlates well with formalism and contrasts with the organic and hypotactic Sophoclean style,[26] and with plays that
tend to focus intensely on the unfolding of the dramatic event in time and on
the personalities of a few central figures. In Sophoclean style the dramatic
form in which events, action, and speeches occur appears to have an
unforced internal consistency, creating the illusion of reality, however far the
artistic conventions of the theater may be from the real, and however much
the flow of events has been distorted to make the action dramatically
comprehensible and persuasive.[27] It is this involving or enthralling effect that
Euripides generally eschews. Instead, as Kitto remarks, Euripides allows us,
"as Sophocles never does, to lean back and ask ourselves what it is all
about."[28]

Features that distinguish Sophoclean from Aeschylean style include the
avoidance of stage-oriented references, dialogue that is structured relatively
freely, and the limitation of the chorus to a relatively passive role. The
chorus and its treatment are especially significant, since the presence of a
chorus is the single least natural and most formal element in Greek tragic
theater. The chorus is neither a real person, with an individual personality,
nor a real group, a collection of different individual personalities.[29] This
quasi group performs in elaborate style, with song and music, using an
elevated and unfamiliar poetic language. But, while in naturalistic terms the
chorus is a monstrosity, in formal terms they are a rich resource. Their songs
serve to define the *epeisodia* of the actors; and the balance between speech
and song was, at least in the theater of Aischylos, a very fertile source of
dramatic effect and meaning. Euripides does not make a return to the old,
Aeschylean balance between chorus and actor; but as W. Kranz demon-

25. See Schadewaldt (1926, 105 – 7); Ludwig (1957, 71).

26. See the useful analysis of J. Gould (1978, 51ff.) of the special characteristics of Sophoclean style: "There is a clearly perceptible tendency for one structural member to run into, or
fuse with, another, for lines of structural division to be blurred or half-denied."

27. This distortion was discovered and analyzed by T. v. Wilamowitz (1917); see Gellie
(1972, 45ff. [on *Antigone*] and 189ff. [on *Aias*]). Of course Euripides uses such devices himself,
when he needs them to construct a suspenseful plot, see discussion in Chap. 9, Section I.A.,
below.

28. (1939) 1961, 274.

29. See Michelini (1982, 66) and the discussion of the formal management of this group by
Kaimio (1970).

strated, Euripides, like Aischylos and unlike Sophokles, was continually experimenting with the chorus and with lyric.[30]

Sophokles' approach to the chorus and to lyric was less inventive than that of Aischylos or Euripides, since Sophoclean dramatic naturalism entailed the relegation of this extraneous group to a minor role. If Sophokles' book *On the Chorus* dealt with the dramatic function of the group,[31] it is quite possible that Aristoteles' praise of the Sophoclean chorus contains a digest of Sophokles' own views: the poet should treat the chorus so far as possible as a character in the play.[32] If Sophokles did theorize about the chorus, part of his aim may have been to explain his methods and rationale in dealing with something that he and his contemporaries found increasingly awkward. But the Sophoclean compromise did not and could not, from the point of view of a formalist artist, meet the central problems of lyric and its place in drama.[33] The wide-ranging and remotely legendary odes of *Phoinissai,* the epic breadth of the parodos in *Iphigeneia at Aulis,* and the great expansion of monodic and amoebaeic song in the later plays indicate that Euripides continually wrestled with lyric and attempted to win back for it some of its original formal significance.

The Euripidean debt to Aischylos has been frequently discussed. In formal matters, however, it remains difficult to separate Aischylos from the background of his tradition. When Euripides avoids free dialogue in favor of stichomythy—e.g., in *Orestes*—we may think of Aischylos; and in this instance we are probably right to do so.[34] But it is not possible to be certain that any such formal features are really ''Aeschylean'' as opposed to merely archaic. More dependable signs of a specifically Aeschylean influence are the bold Euripidean treatment of lyric, and perhaps also the use of misogynist and patriotic themes. But it was in fact Aischylos' predecessor, Phrynichos, who introduced women's roles, and we know that Phrynichos also produced a number of dramas dealing with historical and patriotic subjects.[35]

While the innovative and challenging stance of Aischylos resembles that of Euripides in a general way, Euripides, with the whole range of previous

30. See Kranz (1933, Chap. 4.3, passim); Benedetto (1971.2).

31. *Peri tou chorou*: on the possible significance of the title, see Webster (1969, 7–8), who cites Aly (1929, 93 n.95a).

32. *Poet.* 1456a25–27.

33. See the analysis of Kaimio, who in studying the way the tragic chorus is addressed in the first and second person concludes that in Sophoclean drama the concept of the choral group is almost entirely neglected (1970, 178–79).

34. Note the indications that rigid symmetry in trimeter dialogue, and the use of the stichomythy, is a phenomenon of later Aeschylean style, correlating with and compensating for the disuse of tetrameter dialogue, Michelini (1982, 37–38).

35. *TGF* 1.3 T1 (women's roles); *TGF* 1.3 T2, 5 (political themes).

tragedy to choose from, would hardly have stopped at the work of Aischylos in his investigation of the forms of earlier tragedy. There are several apparently archaic elements in the plays that are clearly not Aeschylean. The narrative prologue, with its naive approach of speaking directly to the audience, does not really appear in Aischylos;[36] and through the tiny glimpse we have of one Phrynichan prologue there is reason to believe that Euripides was reaching back beyond Aischylos to an even earlier stage in the development of the art form.[37] Another feature of some Euripidean drama that has not, so far as I know, been recognized as archaizing, but that well may be so, is the episodic style of plays like *Suppliants* and *Andromache*. I have suggested elsewhere that episodic style, and the focus on a succession of central figures, is a necessary feature of pre-Aeschylean, single-actor tragedy, since, without the resource of a second actor who can enter to the first actor and chorus, concentration on a single central figure would require the sacrifice of almost all dramatic movement and variation.[38] The rapid shifting of focus in these two plays may have been designed to recall the shape of plays that used a single actor, or that used two actors but were composed in an older style.

A major formalizing feature of Euripidean drama has only tenuous roots in the past, although its archaic effect is undeniable: that is the *deus ex machina* or epilogue delivered by a divine speaker. We can of course point to the theodicies of the *Danaides* and *Oresteia* trilogies, or to the prophetic and magisterial role of Dareios in *Persians*.[39] But it is not possible to find in these Aeschylean instances any formal similarity that would indicate some traditional role for a divine informant in early tragedy. If the Aeschylean epiphanies are based on any such precedents, the device must go so far back into the lost history of the art form that its origin can only be guessed at.

The narrative prologue, an invariable feature of Euripidean drama,[40] and the *deus* device, which closes nine of the extant seventeen plays, are comple-

---

36. Aeschylean prologues are consistently given a rudimentary framework of dramatization, e.g., a prayer or a public speech; see the analysis of Walter Nestle (1930, 106). The speeches are also designed to set a mood or tone (*Stimmung*) for the play (see Gollwitzer [1937, 28ff.]) while Euripidean prologues contribute considerably less to atmosphere or emotional color (see Méridier [1911, 144]).

37. Walter Nestle (1930, 23): "Wir haben hier," in the Phrynichos fragment, "zweifellos das Prototyp einer euripideischen Prologrede vor uns." The reference is to *TGF* 1.3 F8, where the speaker, a Persian eunuch, appears to begin with a direct address to the audience.

38. 1982, 16–17.

39. Krausse (1905, 196) argues that we can find the "semina atque primordia" of the *deus ex machina* in Aischylos.

40. The absence of one for *Rhesos* is a good argument against Euripidean authorship. (Much more strongly indicative, however, is the play's total lack of irony.)

mentary;[41] together they reveal in several ways the effects and aims of Euripidean formalism. The Euripidean prologue can be contrasted with most Aeschylean and Sophoclean prologues mainly in the way in which it hews to its function of setting up plot situations and in the formal openness with which it approaches this task. While Sophokles' prologues are usually structured so that the speakers address themselves to an interlocutor,[42] Euripidean prologue speeches are seldom addressed to the character who will later be the speaker's partner in dialogue. In a manner typical of Euripidean formalism, the second actor's entrance is used to set off the prologue speech from the rest of the first scene, while the addition of a dialogue at the close helps to integrate the self-contained speech with the rest of the performance.[43]

Prologue speakers can also be gods, and there are few Euripidean plays that do not feature a divine intervention at either end or beginning.[44] This peculiarity of Euripidean dramaturgy—the explanations at end and beginning that link the drama to some sort of outside framework—has always interested critics. At all periods most of them have been dismayed by both prologue and *deus* scenes, complaining of the boring and flat effect of the former,[45]

41. Plays that have a divine epilogue: *Hipp*, Artemis; *Suppl*, Athena; *Andr*, Thetis; *El*, Dioskouroi; *Ion*, Athena; *IT*, Athena; *Hel*, Dioskouroi; *Or*, Apollon; *Ba*, Dionysos. On this quality of complementarity, see Spira (1960, 10), Terzaghi (1937, 304). The recognition of these elements as a frame leads some critics to suggest that they are extraneous and may safely be ignored—see Benedetto (1971.1, 149), on *Erechtheus*; Conacher (1967) on *Medeia* (197), on *Elektra* (210), on *Orestes* (224); see also Terzaghi (309).

42. *El*. (Paidagogos to Orestes); *OT* (exchange between Oidipous and a spokesman of the people); *Ph*. (Odysseus to Neoptolemos) are prologues in which a long speech is addressed to an interlocutor. Of the four other prologues three are all dialogue: *Aias* (Odysseus, Athene, Aias); *Ant*. (Antigone and Ismene); *OC* (Antigone and Oidipous).

43. On the two-stage Euripidean prologue, see Gollwitzer (1937, 73–75); Imhof (1957, 22): "Die Grundform euripideischer Prologe ist die Zweiteiligkeit." Walter Nestle (1930, 107 and 129) remarks on this division as an archaic characteristic. Méridier (1911, 13) points out that the prologue speaker may occasionally as in the suppliant dramas (*Hkld, Suppl, Her*) be on stage with a group; but the speaker never addresses the prologue to this group. On the attachment to the body of the play, see Gollwitzer (74); Imhof (1957, 24) remarks that "Der zweite Teil des Prologs zumeist mit der Parodos und dem ersten Epeisodion sich zum ersten Akt der Tragödie zusammenschliesst."

44. While only three plays feature a complete divine "frame" (*Ion, Hipp, Ba*), only six of the plays lack a divine appearance at either beginning or end. Of these, one (*Her*) has an epiphany in the middle; one (*Med*) ends with the protagonist herself delivering a prophecy from the machine; *Hekabe* is opened by an omniscient prologue figure, a ghost, and closes with a prophecy of future events (see Chap. 6, below). The lost end of *Iphigeneia at Aulis* probably included an appearance by Artemis, or a description of that appearance. Thus only *Phoinissai* and *Herakleidai* completely avoid the form.

45. Early complaints: see the remarks of the scholiast in Elsperger (1907, 6–7): ψυχρῶς διαλέγεται τῷ θεάτρῳ, and see also the remark in the *Genos Euripidou* (Schwartz [1887, p. 4]): ἐν τοῖς προλόγοις ὀχληρός. Later: U. v. Wilamowitz (1875, 202), "artis tragicae libertatem legibus perquam molestis coercuit"; Norwood (1954, 18), "His prologues bore us." Méridier (1911, 131) makes very clear the antidramatic elements: Euripides' "besoin de précision et de

and of the childish artificiality of the latter.[46] Since these unappealing usages are clearly habitual to the playwright, they must be confronted and analyzed, if it is indeed true that the appearance of "bad taste" and "bad style" in Euripides is often a clue to something of major significance.

The prologues seem out of step with the rest of Euripidean theater. Did the playwright really dare to chance boring his audience at the very start? And, if so, what did he hope to gain that would be worth the risk? A simple answer to the first query may be that the audience would not be disposed because of a few expository lines at the opening to lose interest in what might well develop into a shocking and thoroughly exciting drama, any more than the crowd at a boxing match is put off by some initial sparring. The intensity of attention may be low during the first moments, but the action is expected to begin soon. Then, too, in light of the outrageous twists that Euripides gave to his stories, and the basic unsuitability of many of the stories that he chose to tell, the prologue, however dry its tone, could be a titillating foretaste of the astonishments to come.[47]

Even if we can explain the audience's willingness to endure the prologues, we must still suggest reasons for Euripides' eagerness to inflict them on the public; and the same question arises with equal force for the *deus*, although the latter does not present quite the same danger of a loss of audience attention. The audience must by the end of the play have a considerable investment of emotion in the events, and they will be eager to hear the final resolution. In satisfying the urge of the audience to know all the details and to see into the fictional future, Euripides may be more reasonably charged with his usual sin of pandering to low desires than with the less usual one of being

---

clarté ... finit par apparaître ... comme la satisfaction d'une manie.'' On Euripides' practice in later plays, where the form only becomes more exaggerated: ''Il a cherché les cadres les plus élémentaires et, en vertu de leur simplicité, les plus commodes, et les ayant trouvés il s'en est servi à satiété, sans se préoccuper d'éviter la monotonie'' (137). Of course the picture of the demonically inventive Euripides as simply too lazy to innovate in the case of the prologue is not convincing. See also Terzaghi (1937, 312); Pohlenz ([1930] 1954, 437). Opposing this view, Strohm (1977, 121ff.) attempts to defend the *Andromache* prologue against charges of inconsequence; but, while nothing in the speech is without point, the close packing of much information does create a typically dry and didactic atmosphere.

46. Ancient opinions on the *deus* are collected by Spira (1960, 149). The device is generally seen as a resort of desperation when invention fails: (Platon *Cra.* 425d5); see Post (1964, 104). Modern: Verrall (1895, 166), both prologue and *deus* device share a ''singular stiffness, formality, frigidity and general artlessness''; Norwood (1954, 7, 18); Terzaghi (1937, 309) believed that Euripides' lack of belief in the gods forced him to resolve *Hippolytos* by an artificial means, ''un mezzo comodo e facile di concludere ... '' Note that as in the previous note Euripides is accused of the unlikely sin of taking the easy way out of a dramatic dilemma.

47. See Gollwitzer (1937, 70–71). For examples in extant plays, see *Med* 39ff. (hints of violence to come), *Hek* 45–46 (the discovery of two corpses in one day), *El* 34–35 (Elektra is a matron in this play).

lofty and tedious. The functions of the prologue and the *deus* scene are multiple; and it is appropriate that tracing a major element through various instances in separate works of art should be a complex matter. If it were not, we would be forced to conclude that the artist habitually made use of devices that could not be effectively integrated with the structure of the work.

From the perspective of formalism and formalist arrangements, the function of the scenes is to provide borders and demarcations that are clearly apparent to the audience. The fact that the prologue and *deus* can balance each other, though they do not always do so, is an indication that they form a pair, as the two markers in ring-form style do, setting off the aesthetic unit and summarizing it as well. The prologue and *deus* also function as devices for revealing matters extraneous to the body of the play, either because they lie outside the knowledge of the actors,[48] or—in the case of prologues— because they are preconditions to the dramatic action. The prologue speaker need not always be a god; actors who appear in prologues are usually central to the dramatic action to follow: they can present themselves as they fill in factual data.[49] As a result of these revelations, the whole cosmos of pre-Sophistic culture is present for our assessment, the human figures of myth, the larger mythic-historical forces that have moved them into position, the lines of aetiology and blood descent that tie myth to the reality of contemporary life, and beyond all, the gods, who preside over the convolutions of chance and fate.

Prologue and *deus* alike are facilitators of the dramatic action. Euripidean plays are given an initial impulse or head start that takes the audience a certain distance into the action, without revealing all the twists to come.[50] Another effect of the narrative prologue may be that it diminishes the need for a gradual development of the plot events out of the characters of the actors. In order to understand the events of Sophokles' *Aias,* we must first understand what sort of person Aias is; and the play devotes some time to establishing the *êthos* of its protagonist. *Oidipous Tyrannos* provides a striking example of a slow opening: we are told little about the past events leading up to the dramatic present, but in that present we are given ample

48. Nondivine characters who have special knowledge function in the same way as divine narrators, both in the prologue and at the end of the play, where prophetic knowledge makes Medeia and Polymestor able to set the action in the frame of a future. See Norwood (1954, 21), who also points to Eurystheus' prophecy in *Herakleidai* and the role of Theseus in *Herakles.*

49. See *Hkld,* Iolaos; *Suppl,* Aithra; *Her,* Amphitryon; *IT,* Iphigeneia; *Phoin,* Iokaste; *Or,* Elektra. Imhof (1957, 40), citing five plays (*Alk, Hipp, Hek, Tro, Ion*—and see *Ba*), sees the divine prologue figure as of special importance for Euripides. Unimportant figures appear only in *Medeia,* and perhaps in *Elektra,* if the Autourgos is a minor figure.

50. Gollwitzer (1937, 83ff.); Hamilton (1978). On matters omitted, see Stuart (1918, 299 – 301).

opportunity to observe Oidipous as he performs his function as monarch. Contrast the presentation of Medeia through the Nurse's prologue, and through the offstage lyrics that reveal her emotions.[51] When Medeia herself finally comes on, she is ready to begin her plotting by winning over the women of Corinth; and we, knowing the outline of her past experience and the sketch of her character, are ready to watch her with enjoyment and some understanding.

The god from the machine can similarly enhance the density of the plot and the intensity of the action. If the divine apparition stops the action, or reverses its course, forcing a denouement, then it is possible for the action of the play to proceed at top speed, without any period of slowing or dragging at the close.[52] By confining exposition of past and future to two well-defined segments at opening and close, Euripides was able to compress and enhance the dramatic excitement of the central part of the plays. The twists and reversals, the plots and counterplots, the multiple or episodic style in plays like *Suppliants, Herakleidai,* or *Andromache,* all these elements of Euripidean theater were facilitated by the device of the ordered and expository opening and close.

We might think here of the tendency for separate elements to be very clearly marked off in Euripidean style so that emotion and reasoning, for example, appear, concentrated and stylized, in separate areas. The result, as always, of this sort of arrangement is that the audience are enlisted as active rather than passive participants in the dramatic experience, since the synthesis of the parts so severed can occur only in their minds, and since they cannot trust or surrender to a dramatic event that fails to present itself as an acceptable quasi reality. In the case of the frame created by the prologue and *deus* device, the same features that help to provide an enthralling and exciting stage event also serve to set that stage event in a perspective of unreality vis-à-vis the life experience that it imitates. Sophoclean theater works always to deny the audience the distance they would require to be able to see the play in a perspective; but the Euripidean audience is encouraged to realize that the drama has arbitrarily cut a piece out of a larger fabric, beginning

51. For the Euripidean convention in which lyric precedes trimeter, see the remarks of Dale (1954, 74) on *Alk* 280ff.

52. The exciting close of *Orestes* is an example. In other plays, the effect is rather to prevent complete slackness at the ending, e.g., in *Iphigeneia Among the Taurians,* where the renewed possibility of seizing the protagonists prevents what would otherwise have been a lame close, since the people we cared about have gone and only the barbarians are left behind (cf. *Helene* as well). At the end of *Suppliants* Athena's intervention breaks the sustained mood of mourning and valedictory and reinjects the astringent tension typical of Euripides. See Ludwig (1957, 117).

always long after the first step and closing always long before the last. Instead of being absorbed in its own world, the Euripidean performance reaches out to the audience, reminding them that the neat elegance of its design was made for human minds to inhabit.[53]

The *aition* that so often closes Euripidean plays has the same effect of reminding the audience that the myth is not only a real event from the past that has been recreated for them by mimesis, but also a symbolic or significant event, different from ordinary events, and having deep roots in the religious and civic present.[54] By introducing in the prologue and often in the ending a break between the remote but highly significant "truth" of myth and the quasi-real event of the dramatic performance, Euripidean drama forces the audience to be aware of the gap between the social function of myth and its presumed historical reality; and in doing this it qualifies and ironizes both the myth's ability to signify and the apparent reality of the dramatic performance itself.[55]

A final element in the prologue/ending frame that remains to be discussed is the presence of the gods in the plays. Just as the accomplished Sophist could argue the misogynist or the modernist side with almost equal enthusiasm and insincerity, so the Euripidean style has an immense zest for the play between traditional ironies about the gods, and the new ideas that would oust the Olympians in favor of something more abstract and more moral.[56] If Euripides had been an ideologue, as some of his defenders have suggested, he would doubtless have presented no divinities at all and would have contented himself with vague allusions to high and beneficent powers directing all for the best. Instead, we are presented with the best possible arguments to show that the gods cannot exist, or that if they do they cannot be as mythology shows them—while at the same time we must absorb the countering evidence that, since they do exist and do act as in the myth,

53. See Imhof (1957, 42ff.) on "die bewusste Illusion" (44) of Euripidean theater. Whitman (1974, 114): "He constantly reminds his audience that he is making what they see before them, whereas the two earlier poets foster the illusion that the mythic tale is creating or recreating itself." See also Ludwig (1957, 34).

54. On references to aetiological myth or ritual in the *deus* device, see V. Longo (1963, 242). For the *aition* as the basic form of myth, see Dörrie (1966, 46). On the special nature of myth in tragedy, see Detienne (1977, 34–35) and Vernant (1968, 247ff.) as well as Segal (1981, 20–21) and Eisner (1979, 153ff.).

55. See Segal on *Bakchai* (1982, 266ff.); and W. Schmidt (1963, 211), who remarks on the clash between the paralogism of myth and the logical consequentiality of dramatic action.

56. Antidivine references in Euripides: see, among others, *Hipp* 120; *Her* 1307–8, 1341–46; *Ion* 442–51; *Tro* 1280–81. See Wilhelm Nestle (1901, 124–41).

the gods are even more powerful and more morally appalling than we had imagined.

A number of scholars who saw Euripidean drama as expressive of a *Zeitgeist* of irreligion were driven by the tendency of their analysis to misinterpret plain evidence about the role of divine figures. We are told that the gods in Euripidean drama are not really there, while in Sophokles their presence is always felt.[57] In fact, the use of divine figures was one aspect of Aeschylean drama generally avoided by Sophokles; and this absence seems to enhance the effect of tragic resolutions. Where the gods are least in evidence, in *Oidipous Tyrannos* and *Trachiniai* for instance, their agency acquires the most awesome power.[58] In Euripidean plays, by contrast, gods are omnipresent, continually intervening in human events, continually presenting their motivations for doing so, continually appearing with explanations and justifications of the plot resolutions, and everywhere acting as interpreters of the play to the audience.[59]

What Euripides was doing was not untraditional: the use of divinities along with humans in literary contexts has much the same effect in Euripidean theater that it does in other Greek literature. As Spira pointed out, the Euripidean treatment of the gods has obvious resemblances to that in Homeric epic.[60] In their encounters with mortals, divinities defend their power and honor according to the same ethic of *aretê* that human beings follow, with disruptive effects that are magnified by the incongruency between divine power and human vulnerability.[61] The annihilating malice of Athena in *Aias* is analogous with the motivations of the Euripidean Aphrodite,

57. Snell ([1937] 1968.2, 52]) argues that Aphrodite's role in inspiring Phaidra's love should simply be disregarded as without significance; Chapouthier (1952, 223) sees this lack of real interest as the source of Euripides' inconsistent treatment of the divine. See also Pohlenz ([1930] 1954, 428 – 29); Lesky (1958, 136 – 37); Goossens (1962, 80 – 81).

58. Conacher, who is also prone to discount the appearances of gods, sees the paradoxical role of divine agency in Sophokles: the gods are "everything and nothing," because all dramatic events fulfill divine plans by moving through the will and character of human beings (1967, 11). See Segal (1965, 157). For a Euripidean instance of this kind of motivation, see discussion of *Hippolytos* in Chap. 9, below.

59. Earlier commentators were frank: Patin ([1841 – 43] 1871, 45) remarked that the gods are like stagehands in Euripidean plays; Leeuwen (1876, 29) pointed out that, in spite of Euripidean unbelief, the gods are omnipresent in the plays.

60. 1960, 160ff. See also Strohm's comments on Aphrodite's role in Euripides and in the *Ilias* (1949 – 50, 146 – 47). See as well Matthiessen (1979, 149); and the comment of Diller (1958, 113): in Euripides' work older cultural and literary elements break through to the surface.

61. Gantz (1981, 18 – 19) has pointed out this parallel in the case of Aischylos. What Adkins has to say about the tenuousness of any obligations to social inferiors, who are by definition less able to repay *charis* or to fulfill the obligations between *philoi* (1966.1, 203 – 7), implies an almost total lack of dependability in relations between very powerful divinities and helpless human beings.

Dionysos, or Iris; and the passionate complaint of Thetis, preserved by Platon's quotation from a lost play of Aischylos, matches almost exactly the denunciations of Apollon's cruelty and perfidy in *Andromache* or *Ion*.[62]

The effects of this further revival of the archaic are various. Coming to the end of a Sophoclean play, we find ourselves confronting, as often in Aeschylean plays, the mystery of divine cruelty and kindness: "And there is nothing of this that is not Zeus." The actual presence of a divinity at such a moment would have several rather paradoxical effects. First, the presentation of divinities always runs dangerously close to bathos, because the superhuman, if it falls short of the appropriate grandeur (*semnotês*)—and how should it not fall short?—can easily provoke laughter. Aischylos, using an·almost entirely divine cast in *Eumenides,* approached this problem directly. He gave the Furies, with their doglike snufflings, a strong hint of comic quality that was suited to their grotesqueness and that suggested from the start their inadequacy as adversaries for the Olympians, Athena and Apollon.[63] For Euripidean drama the risk of bathos is, within limits, an acceptable one, since the plays in their attack on tragic seriousness continually cut close to the edge of the comic.

A second effect of the divine presence in a tragic drama is the dissipation of mystery. The complex and bitter resignation that ends *Oidipous Tyrannos, Trachiniai,* or *Aias* would be to some extent dispelled by the presence on stage of a divinity responsible for the play's action. When a god does appear, at the opening of *Aias,* we are struck by the flatness and coldness of the divine psyche; in comparison with Athena, Odysseus is weak and helpless, but he is also capable of kindness and of self-knowledge.[64] But by the end of the play we have been made aware of universal patterns in the fate of Aias that extend beyond the power of any single vengeful god. If a divine mystery is responsible for the world, then we can submit; but a humanized divinity must necessarily lack certain qualities of sympathy and fellow feeling that we expect to find in human beings. To bring a god in at the end of a play, when the action has been completed, is to risk disillusionment in several ways; but it is just this risk that is typical of Euripidean theater.

62. 284M (*Rep.* 2.383b); it may come from *Hoplôn Krisis.* See discussion by Gantz (1981, 21ff.) of this and parallel passages (e.g., the plaint of Europa, 145M); G. asks, "What *are* we to make of a playwright who encourages such stories?" (22). It is interesting to see this question being asked about another playwright than Euripides.

63. The Furies allow Orestes to escape while they dream and snort before Apollon's temple; their dignity never quite recovers from this humiliation. The aged priestess who crawls out of the temple on all fours in terror at the Furies is a figure prophetic of many in Euripides. On the comic elements, see Herington (1963, 120–25).

64. On the effect of Athena's cruelty, see Whitman (1951, 67–70). On the diminished stature of Euripidean gods, see Conacher (1967, 46).

Last, just as the direct narration of past and future events diminishes the dramatic present, so the presence of a divinity calls into question the significance of purely human experience, and reduces the apparent scope of human choice. When we see Apollon or Athena disposing of the weeping or jubilant protagonists, the human beings dwindle in this new perspective.[65] A useful exercise might be to compare the end of the *Ilias,* a resolution engineered throughout by the gods, but one from which they tactfully stay removed. If Hermes or Athena were actually in Achilleus' tent directing the reconciliation, the tragic stature of the human beings would be largely lost.[66] The presence of a divinity on stage is in itself, and quite apart from the functional effect of an omniscient player, productive of a mood that is by now familiar in Euripidean theater. Both god and human lose stature and sympathy; and the paradoxical effect of the apparent theodicy is to make the audience alert and critical of what they have been shown, aware of the unresolved tensions and dissonances in the myth.[67]

It is fair to say that the *deus ex machina* is an effect that "fails," if we think of it as designed to close off a tragic action decisively and in a way that satisfies the audience. Presumably in a successful, naive version of the divine appearance, the god would present an unquestionably valid summation of the meaning of the dramatic action, while at the same time bringing the action to a definitive conclusion. Such an effect might indeed work in a very unsophisticated dramatic milieu.[68] But an exuberant gullibility was not characteristic of the fifth century, nor could it have matched the mood of wary alertness imposed on the Euripidean audience by these intricate plays. In such a context the divine epilogue was bound to be perceived as inade-

65. W. Schmidt, however, shows that for the single Sophoclean *deus* in *Philoktetes,* the effect is not to dispose of the protagonists, but to resolve a contradiction between Philoktetes and the requirements of myth, without breaching the "charakterliche Integrität" (108) of the dramatic figure (1963, 105 – 10). The effect is thus almost the exact reverse of that in Euripides.

66. The end of *Hippolytos,* of course, shows that such a result is not inevitable; see the analysis of Knox (1952, 30 – 31).

67. My view of the *deus* scene differs greatly from that of Spira (1960, 97); see discussion of his book in Chap. 1, Section III.C. A view closer to my own was presented by the dissertation of W. Schmidt (1963).

68. See Herodotos' story of the propaganda coup scored by Peisistratos, who had himself escorted back to Athens by a young woman of unusual height masquerading as the goddess Athena; the historian comments indignantly, "The silliest thing I ever heard of [πρῆγμα εὐηθέστατον]" (1.60.3). This anecdote, among others, points to a fascination with mimesis in early Athens. At this formative period, indeed, the *deus* device would have been effective as a "straight" dramatic technique. See Masqueray's comment (1908, 46): only the naive would not laugh at these apparitions.

quate, dramatically flat, and theologically naive—in short as *psychron* in the extreme.[69]

The clumsiness of the narrative prologue, and the cheapness of the divine finale, both of which seem to revive the practices of a more naive and undeveloped dramaturgy, out of fashion in the late fifth century—these disconcerting qualities are working elements in the complex scheme of Euripidean dramaturgy. Formal rigidity can itself be an instrument of the ironic view. The more obtrusive the formality, the more difficult it will be for the audience to sink into sympathy with the Euripidean performance.[70] Along with the absurd coincidences and bizarre shifts of chance that plague the protagonists, the typical Euripidean opening and close are part of a performance that calls attention to its own artificiality with bravura gestures that are continually self-referential. The tendency to pander to audience desires, as in the case of the *deus* ending, and the tendency to regale the audience with learned embellishments that they may find difficult to absorb, as in the prologues, have a common source in the stylized design of Euripidean theater.

It would seem that failure in ordinary aesthetic terms is not failure in Euripidean terms—a fact which forces us to confront the ultimate paradox about the Euripidean dramatic aesthetic. Drama is, as we have seen, a touchy art form, where failure is experienced in a drastic and concrete way, when the audience simply refuses to tolerate the performance. Euripides is playing an aesthetic game with this most dangerous aspect of dramatic art. He dares to risk an impression of flatness, to court failure, and to compromise dramatic reality, all in the service of theatrical effect. Not only is tragedy played against itself in Euripides, but all his virtuosity is enlisted to play the dramatic illusion against itself as well.

The formalism of the plays has contradictory effects on the presentation of dramatic figures and has led to much critical confusion. Euripides has been described as a realist who presents an accurate and therefore necessarily flawed portrait of his contemporary world, the convinced enemy of heroic idealization.[71] It has been argued also that Euripides' primary dramatic concern is the accurate depiction of human character, and that most anomalies in

69. W. Schmidt (1963, 34–35) remarks that Spira's analysis of the effect of the *deus* centers too exclusively on the perspective of the actors in the play, ignoring the significance of the apparition for the audience. For them, the *deus* is a "Scheinlösung" that produces an effect of (Brechtian) alienation (*Verfremdung*) from the dramatic events.

70. See Kitto ([1939] 1961, 259).

71. See Blaiklock (1952, x): Euripides produces "a truthful statement of actuality as it appears to the normal observer." See also Grube (1941, 7). In opposition, Knox ([1970] 1979.3, 251–52).

the plays can be traced to the playwright's obsession with this single area.[72] On the other hand, it has also been pointed out that cohesive character studies are not to be found in Euripidean drama, since the playwright's fascination with one or the other special effect, including the depiction of bizarre and aberrant personalities and behavior, distorts the psychology of individuals.[73] Others have suggested that Euripidean rhetoric and an obsessive concern with ideas take precedence over the naturalistic presentation of human motivation and reaction.[74]

If we intend to treat Euripides coherently as a skilled artist whose plays have been observed to be carefully and elaborately designed, then it is time to dispose of modes of analysis that assume an artist who did not pay consistent attention to his art.[75] The rhetoric, along with the abnormal psychology and the touches of "realism," are all essential features of a coherent Euripidean style.[76] And, given that Euripides is a formalist, it seems most unlikely that his plays have any basic concern in holding a mirror up to nature. The solution once more lies in genre distinctions between tragic-heroic elements and their reverse. The incursion of antiheroic and even satiric elements into Euripidean tragedy creates the sensation of "realism" that we feel.

If we look closely at the most blatant instances, it soon becomes apparent that the realist mode is no more sustained in Euripidean drama than any other mode. And inconsistency is fatal, since the illusion necessary to realism will not survive any breach. We find in the plays a deliberate contrast between two extremes that distort the heroic into new forms: at one extreme is the trivial, the mean, the "real," while at the other is romance, the play of fancy and miracle that is equally alien to the high mimetic.[77] Euripidean "realism" is almost always balanced off by other anti-heroic features, such as romance

---

72. Blaiklock (1952, xv): "Euripides' main interest was in character and not in plot." A moderate version in Pohlenz ([1930] 1954, 422): although not uninterested in plot, Euripides is primarily concerned with character. See Gellie (1963, 250), compared with Sophokles, Euripides pays excessive attention to psychological traits.

73. See Conacher (1967, 342–43). Zürcher (1947, 64), in dissecting the uneven depiction of Medeia's character, remarks that Euripides is interested not in Medeia as an individual but in "das psychologische Phänomen der Leidenschaft." See his similar remarks on *Leidenschaft* in *Hekabe* (73ff.). Winnington-Ingram (1969, 127): Euripides has a "cavalier attitude to characterization."

74. For Euripides as a doctrinaire intellectual, see Decharme (1906, 42ff.); cf. the exaggerated portrait by Festugière (1969) of Euripides as fervently religious, "une âme contemplative" (34). Even Kitto has fallen into this trap in explaining the anomalous form of *Andromache*: because "the play means so much to Euripides, ... he cannot find the time or inclination to tinker with it and give it a false unity which would in no way assist the idea" ([1939] 1961, 232).

75. Conacher (1967, 3) and Parry (1966, 317) make this point.

76. See Barlow (1971, 123).

77. See Frye (1957, 36–37 and 186–89).

and fantasy, or by sensational coincidence and outrageous situations, or by the god from the machine. The sudden, deflating moments when the real intrudes upon the myth reflect no consistent and unswerving attention to the trivia of the everyday. The moments are significant precisely for their bathetic effect and for the way in which they puncture a heroic mood, creating another antithesis and then being swept away in their turn.

The consistency of Euripidean psychological portrayals must also be seen in the light of the very volatile quality of the Euripidean aesthetic. A number of the plays present figures of intellectual and emotional extremism, either those who, like Medeia, respond in unorthodox fashion to common situations, or those who, like Hekabe in the play of that name, are driven to extreme reactions by pressures grotesquely beyond the ordinary. That these figures were seen as an element of Euripidean realism, and that they were believed to indicate the dramatist's concern with the mysteries of the human psyche, may have something to do with the fact that many of them were female. If the feminine mentality is thought of as an abnormal variant on the male, then Euripides' bizarre women can be seen as realistic and Euripides can be credited with a special concern for this special sort of psychology.[78] We should attend instead to Kitto's suggestion that Euripidean drama is intellectualized and schematic, in a way that matches its formalist style.[79] Hekabe, Medeia, or Herakles are in a sense test cases or experimental subjects; and the extremism of their plights and their reactions permit us to examine areas of human experience that might otherwise remain hidden.

Perhaps the most striking feature of Euripidean dramatic psychology is the great emotional lability of most of the characters: violent shifts of mood and intent are brought about by changes in human relations (Kreousa in *Ion*), by the inner moods of the character (Medeia), or by bizarre coincidence (Hekabe).[80] Since dramatic character is most effectively displayed through human reaction to a social environment, it is wrong to assume that coherent dramatic character cannot exist in the absence of the self-aware consciousness of the nineteenth-century "individual," whose sharply defined personality is rather paradoxically capable of achieving change and alteration through some inner

78. Martin (1958, 265): Euripides' "realist" psychology was able to "montrer la femme dans ce qu'elle a de plus instinctif, de plus irrationnel." Cf. Bates (1930, 37–38), and the discussion of *Leidenschaft* in Chap. 1, Section I, above.

79. See Kitto ([1939] 1961, 275) on the schematic quality of Euripidean characters and dramatic situations. I do not agree with K. as to the nature of the "idea" that these arrangements are meant to convey (see Chap. 1, Section II, above), but that their appeal is and must be primarily intellectual is certainly true.

80. See Zürcher (1947, 109–14); Lesky ([1960] 1966.2, 253–59) and esp. p. 259 "eine Labilität der Reaktionsweisen."

impulsion.[81] But it is also true that, without some sense of a fixed and settled tendency in the dramatic persona, the audience will be unable to maintain a strong concern for the fate of the individual. In Euripidean plays, because of the distorting force of the violent shifts in the dramatic environment, the characters are often given no real chance to make an impression of consistency.[82] Individual volatility may also be supplemented by the tendency of the plays to shift focus from one character to another, thus building a drama out of a series of contrasting and opposing human reactions, as in *Herakleidai*, where we proceed from the sturdy but ineffectual Demophon to the absurdly heroic Iolaos, and from the supramoral altruism of ''Makaria'' to the vengeful amorality of Alkmene.

Formalism itself imposes necessary limits on consistent and homogeneous character portrayal. Well-ordered arguments, laid out along fixed rhetorical lines, can only partially reflect the impact of personality or vary to fit individual circumstance.[83] While it is difficult to prove that a given rhetorical argument is inappropriate to the user, it is fair to say that because rhetoric is a *technê*, a body of practical knowledge that can be learned, any given argument has a necessarily loose fit to the specific situation to which it is applied, and likewise to the specific psychology of the user.[84] The choice of a particular argument or trope may thus be marginally appropriate without being specially illuminating or significant for the individual's psychology.[85] More drastic yet is the effect of ironic counterpoint in the placement of arguments. Particularly strong statements are put in the mouths of characters whose situation at the time or whose fate later in the play severely alters and qualifies the impact of what they have to say.[86] Take, for instance, the arguments of the Wise Melanippe against the existence of prodigies and wonders. The theme is slightly touchy, though not as controversial as many in the

81. Vickers (1973, 53ff.) points out that dramatic character is a function of dramatic situation; see Garton (1972, 405).

82. See the comment of Lesky (1960, 17): ''Hier kommt es nun wirklich nicht mehr auf das Ethos der einzelnen Gestalt an, von dem erfüllt sie ihre Bahn mit Notwendigkeit beschreitet, hier sind die Situation und das Echo, das sie in den Herzen weckt, das eigentlich Wichtige geworden.''

83. On the domination of formality over emotion and naturalism in Euripidean rhesis and stichomythy, see Ludwig (1957, 53, 81) and Conacher (1972, 199).

84. See Garton (1957, 253); J. Gould (1978, 53 – 57).

85. See J. Gould (1978). G., however, seems to me to go too far in denying *êthos* to speeches in *Hippolytos;* see Chap. 9, below. See the recent paper of Conacher (1981): rhetoric does not exclude psychological reference.

86. On the ironic qualification of the speech from *Erechtheus*; the arguments on marriage in *Aiolos*; and the elaborate *schêma* of Makareus, see Chap. 3. A somewhat reversed effect is achieved by Herakles' moralizing speech in *Alk*, 773 – 883, which the situation leads us to take less seriously than it deserves; see Bradley (1980, 112 – 13 and 121). A final example would be Hermione's speech against female freedom; see Chap. 3, above.

plays.[87] But the meaning of the argument and the character of Melanippe are both affected by the absurd and extreme situation in which the speech takes place. Melanippe is trying to save the lives of her babies, who, after being exposed in the wilderness, were found being suckled by a cow. The babies are considered prodigious and monstrous calf/humans by the superstitious finders, who want to put them to death. Melanippe's rationalizing and heterodox speech then, as Dionysios of Halikarnassos pointed out, is an elaborate *schêma,* an argument that purports to deal with abstractions and generalities, when it is really designed to support the private biases and needs of the speaker.

Considering Melanippe's personal investment in her children, the audience will naturally withdraw some of their concern from the actual matter of the argument, investing it instead in the pathos of the hidden truth about the speaker. But that is not all: Melanippe is no ordinary woman. She has been trained in mental exercises by her prophetic mother, and as a result of her training she acquired the powers that struck Aristoteles as very unlikely in a woman (*Poetics* 1454a31). Melanippe as an intellectual and talky woman is as remote and repellent to the audience as Melanippe the suffering mother is—in terms of aesthetic convention at least—familiar and appealing. Finally, the peril that confronts Melanippe's children—that of being taken for deformed calves—has in it something essentially ludicrous. Given all these exquisitely maintained tensions, it is inevitable that, when Melanippe makes her speech, her "character," as mother or as intellectual, will be only a part of the dramatic meaning of the scene. Similarly, when Hermione in *Andromache* presents two violently contradictory arguments in succession, one against Andromache in favor of female insubordination, and a second advocating strict control over women, we are undoubtedly right if we sense that the balance in the arguments is more significant than the imbalance in Hermione's psyche, though that imbalance itself is well enough motivated.

The domination of the argumentative mode in most of the plays has its own inevitable effect on the psychological atmosphere. Not only do the individual motivations or mental states of the arguers matter less than the arguments—at least at some moments—but skilled pleaders and glib rhetoricians, like Melanippe or Medeia, are omnipresent. As Aristophanes remarked, everyone is articulate in a Euripidean play;[88] and this has its

87. Because of the potential for fraud and political manipulation in the business of oracle-mongering and prodigy-collecting, people who practiced these forms of divination were often disparaged; see Herodotos on the case of Onomakritos (7.6.3). For examples in Euripides, see Wilhelm Nestle (1901, 108–10). For the plot of the *Wise Melanippe,* see Gregorius Cor. *Rhet.* 7 (p. 1313 Walz); Dion. Hal. *Rhet.* 9.11; (6.346 Radermacher).

88. See *Frogs* 948–50. Kovacs (1980.1, 81) remarks that they argue like "seasoned barristers."

inevitable effect on the persuasiveness of psychological portrayal. At times the dominance of the rhetorical mode is signaled by one of the characters, as when Iason introduces his totally unprincipled and very effective attack on Medeia by remarking that it will take considerable talent to better his wife at this game (522–25). Because the Sophistic argument derives its effectiveness from an assault on social norms, the plays tend to abound in blatant villains and quirky idealists, all willing and able to espouse abnormal and paradoxical notions in elegant detail.[89] We are not really amazed when, as for instance in the case of Andromache against Menelaos, Euripidean characters argue better than their own interests would allow. Just as the arguments that Thukydides gives the Athenians in their debate with the Melians illuminate Athenian policy, without much resembling what Athenian negotiators are likely actually to have said on that occasion, so argumentation can be used to develop a meaning within the dramatic situation, whether or not what the character says is expressive of personal motivation. There are many more truths available to dramatic representation than those of psychological mimesis alone.

Finally, the volatile and mixed quality of the Euripidean aesthetic imposes sudden shifts in tone and focus that are inherently inimical to consistent character portrayal. We move from pathos to bathos in a moment, as characters swim in and out of tragic focus: Menelaos in *Helene* whines before an old slave woman, yet blusters heroically to Theonoe; Hekabe, prostrated with an agony of grief in *Troiades,* rouses herself suddenly to address a heterodox prayer to Zeus and to become a powerful master of rationalizing argumentation. It is not that Menelaos is unbelievable when he changes, or that Hekabe's reversal is not effective and moving. But we are not, at these moments, concentrating on subjective reactions. Instead, we are and should be conscious of the place of these utterances in a mosaic of counterpoising moments. When apparently irrelevant arguments and maxims are thrown in, diverting the current of the drama and breaking through any sustained attention to character portrayal, these are likely to be benchmarks in the shifts and stratagems of Euripidean dramaturgy. In and out of this complexity there weaves a thread of human characterization, as one of the many ligatures that bind the plays together.

89. Borecký (1955, 89) has pointed out that exaggeration rather than mediocrity is necessary to convey the typical.

5

Some Critical Principles

What earlier critics saw as gratuitous irrelevancies in Euripides' work, moments that were to be ignored in an appreciation of the whole, now appear as significant elements in the paradoxical aesthetic of a drama that sets the pattern of heroic myth against itself, while it situates antitragic elements, especially those related to critical and intellectual thought, at the heart of tragedy. It remains to ask how this kind of tragedy works and how such plays, as aesthetic wholes, can be accessible to critical understanding.

The poetry of ideas that we find in the work of Solon, Tyrtaios, or Semonides cannot be transplanted directly into tragic drama, without greatly altering the dramatic art form; and Euripides is not attempting anything of the sort. Whatever the critical hostility that over the centuries Euripidean theater has courted and has won, the plays have never been seen as other than essentially dramatic and intensely theatrical, as having their essence therefore in action rather than in discourse. Comparison with a talky, idea-ridden play like *Prometheus* reveals the distance between such a work and a Euripidean play. There are lines and speeches in *Prometheus* that are a delight to read and to recite, but one senses that the play would lack movement and even coherency on the stage. Euripidean plays invariably, in my own experience, acquire force, vigor, and persuasiveness in performance. The common cant about Euripides supports this, when Euripides, the "sensationalist," is rebuked for sacrificing consistency and seriousness to dramatic excitement.

Attempts to trace Euripides' philosophic roots have foundered on the failure to consider that Euripides is a poet. Philosophic concepts are usable in poetry in proportion to their assimilation into the culture. And at that point they are usually no longer identifiable with specific "doctrines" or specific

117

philosophical authorities. Hence, when doctrines have been sought in Euripides, those of an obscure figure such as Diogenes of Apollonia seem to
emerge (because Diogenes' doctrines were eclectic, derivative, and—for his
day—rather old-fashioned), or Euripides is claimed as a disciple of some
figure from a previous generation, such as Herakleitos or Xenophanes.[1] Less
doctrinaire interpreters have pointed out the impossibility of finding, among
the forest of Euripidean signposts, any path leading out of the play itself to
something beyond.[2] Self-contradiction is in fact essential to the Euripidean
drama of ideas. The plays use ideas and argumentation, as they use other elements in the aesthetic system, to create patterns of irony and ambivalency.[3]

A brief discussion of meanings in poetry may be necessary at this point.
Among classical scholars the assumption has tended to prevail, probably
because of its convenience as a tool of textual criticism, that aesthetic forms
can encode one and only one meaning at a time, and that it is the job of the
philologist to pick out and defend the single most likely meaning for a given
word, line, scene, or play. But the critics who pointed to ambiguity as a principle of poetic expression have been seconded since by philosophers and
linguists, who have shown that multiple, or full, or indeterminate meanings
are built into language, as they are into other systems of human communication.[4] The muddled middle, excluded by the rules of logic, cannot be
excluded from the arts of language, since poetic "play" upon words and
meanings is achieved by the repeated sacrifice of clarity and simplicity to
richness and density.[5] In Euripides, balancing contradictions in ideas, in tone,
in style, and in personalities contribute to a complex dramatic aesthetic.[6]

But in its use of ambiguity Euripidean art remains an art of paradox, taking its usual position of affirmation in denial. Ludwig's watchword for Euripidean late style is *saphêneia,* clarity (1957). But this very principle, which
is traceable everywhere, through the minutiae of language as well as the

1. See Wilhelm Nestle (1901, 47ff.); Schadewaldt (1926, 117); Rohde (1903, 256.1).

2. See Zuntz (1958.2, 160 – 61). Even Steiger, who believed in Euripides as the thoroughgoing ideologue, pointed out the tendency for dramatists of ideas to take up different ideas in different plays (1912, 30).

3. See Schuster (1954, 63), who compares the effect to that of Goethe's *Faust,* in which the
exposition of opposing views reveals the depth and complexity of its material.

4. For an analysis of ambiguity in the style of the "new criticism," see Brooks (1947),
below. For the genesis of structuralist literary criticism out of linguistic analysis, see Hawkes
(1977, 87).

5. For meaning in art, see Lotman (1967, 23; "Art as Language"): L. points to the "semantic saturation of art, a saturation impossible in any other non-artistic language. Art is the most
economical, compact method for storing and transmitting information."

6. See Friedländer's comment (1926, 112): Euripidean drama has an iridescent quality—
"Statt reinen Lichtes gibt es einen schwankenden, wenn auch farbenvollen und bezaubernden
Schein."

broader structures of discourse and dramaturgy, involves a paradox. Clarity and logic are antithetical to poetic meaning, since the techniques of logical thinking are designed to make expression unambiguous and to simplify the confusions of ordinary language.[7] The appropriate genre for *saphêneia* of expression is that of prose (*logos*), with its attention to subordination and logical consequence and its aim to induce agreement with a single, definable viewpoint. But how can such rhetorically and argumentatively formed thought be a medium for poetry?

As usual, the techniques of Euripides involve the encapsulation of contradiction and the aesthetic use of nonaesthetic materials. The complexity denied to the icy clarity of Euripidean rhetoric is reconstituted in structure, in the interplay and counterpoint of the ideas themselves, and of the speakers who present them. The "drama of ideas" uses ideas to build aesthetic, not logical, structures, in which important elements are often presented only under cancellation by other and opposing elements.[8] This can be seen most clearly in the fugal dramas, *Suppliants* and *Andromache*. In the latter the misogyny of the good woman balances the misogyny of the bad; in the former the humane optimism of Theseus balances the moving yet tarnished history of the Seven. There is no point of rest; and no position, once established, is left unchallenged. Euadne's hot heroism brings with it Iphis' sad cynicism; and the rest of *Suppliants* does not encourage a clear choice between the two.[9] The same can be said of any number of the plays, from *Alkestis* and *Medeia* through *Helene* and *Orestes*. The melody of the plays can be extracted only from a fugue of tones and moods, modes and genres, ideas and stances, which play before us, always in motion and in a rhythm that is continually renewed. We have ample scope to gauge the protean vitality of the Euripidean impulse, over four decades and seventeen plays. But its consistency in variety is perhaps most amazing; from *Peliades* through *Iphigeneia at Aulis* and *Bakchai* we find the same unity in divergence, the same readiness to define new territory by the inclusion of seemingly intolerable contradiction.

The lack of an ideological end product does not of course eliminate the

7. There are different ways of looking at this; see Brooks (1947, 9): "The tendency of science is necessarily to stabilize terms, to freeze them into strict denotations; the poet's tendency is by contrast disruptive." But cf. the analysis of Rorty, which indicates that, while poetry may contain less "normal" and more abnormal or "disruptive" discourse than scientific literature, it is only in the ideal state of scientific or logical discourse that "Everybody agrees on how to evaluate everything everybody says" (1979, 320ff.). Note also the widespread doubts of fifth-century thinkers about the dependability of proofs and *logoi*.

8. See Arrowsmith ("A Greek Theater of Ideas"; 1963, 36–37).

9. On the balance between youth and age, male and female, see Collard (1975.2, 26–27); on the ambivalent effect of Athena's concluding pronouncements, see W. D. Smith (1967.1, 166–67). Rawson found similar patterns in *Phoinissai* (1970, 118).

ideological content of the plays. To present effective arguments for and against some outrageous proposition, such as Makareus' claim that sisters and brothers should marry each other, is not to create a bland equilibrium. As the Sophists recognized, the "stronger *logos*" is so familiar that we hardly notice it, while the "weaker *logos*" has everywhere the power to disrupt and disturb. Euripides' contemporaries were right in their belief that the very injection of such *logoi* into tragedy is an ideological statement, a bold advertisement for the new thought. But the work of fifth-century thinkers, who baffled historians of philosophy by their failure to present coherent doctrines and who were masters of an art of paradoxical argumentation, may be ideally suited to aesthetic uses. Euripidean plays present no central idea and persuade to nothing; but they irritate, disturb, and disrupt, constantly recreating the intellectual and emotional experience of the Sophistic war game with arguments.[10]

The aesthetic of balance and counterpoint that I have suggested will not be able to provide certain satisfactions and harmonies that we may ordinarily expect from tragic plays. Usually absent, for instance, will be a conclusive and unifying ending: the close of a Euripidean play, rather than restating any dominant theme or harmonizing the diverging strands of the action, will more likely be playing out a last variation. As W. Schmidt pointed out, it is precisely the fallacious quality of the carefully engineered "happy ending" that constitutes its usefulness for the scheme of such a play.[11] The unity of the work lies in the pattern of the whole, not in any single resolution.[12] The same tension that pervades the whole will be present in the ending, often leaving the audience still amazed and indignant, while Medeia disappears in her sun chariot, Apollon unites Orestes and Hermione, or Herakles stumbles off on the arm of Theseus.

Also absent from Euripidean drama will usually be protagonists whose personalities are strongly unitary and whose fates deeply involve us. Instead, every figure in the drama may be sacrificed to the play of themes: the final appearance of Medeia *ex machina* (*apo mêchanês*) shows us the folly of our concern about her escape and her sufferings.[13] The Hekabe of *Troiades* who agonizes over her dead grandson was just before chopping logic like any sharp prosecutor. Hermione in *Andromache,* a hateful persecutor in one scene, becomes the focus of her own, slightly tarnished, drama of rescue in

10. For the underlying note of despair and nihilism in the Sophistic, see Adrados (1959, 183–84); Massimi (1960, 44–46); Parry (1969, 350–53). Dupréel (1948, 26) traces the taste for paradox back to the Eleatics, who set the tone of the century.

11. 1963, 26.

12. Strohm (1957, 80). Barlow (1971, 126) points out that unity in Euripidean poetry comes from the "composite view."

13. See Cunningham (1954, 159).

the next.[14] Neither can the ideas or principles espoused by Euripidean protagonists stand as an expression of their natures, as, for instance, Antigone's do for hers. We are more apt to see the least likely character expounding a given view, as when Ion argues against the principle of suppliancy at altars or Hermione lectures on the control of errant wives. The balancing play of ideas puts a sign of irony on all ideas and denies most of all the possibility of reliance on the *logos* as a source of stability.

The Euripidean aesthetic is well suited to a structural criticism based on antithesis and balance. Such an approach makes it possible to see broad ranges of coincidence even where all the items are not directly juxtaposed. An additional advantage of structuralist analysis is that it can deal effectively with resemblances that are not logically parallel and that may in fact be logically contradictory. For example, in a play like *Suppliants* or *Herakleidai* it is possible to see the repetitions and anaclastic reversals of themes relating to heroism and to youth and age, although it is not possible to extract any logical conclusion from the intersection of these themes.[15] Such techniques, however, cannot supplant the basic requirement of dramatic criticism to study an action carried out sequentially in time. The significance of the various parts of the design is greatly altered by their placement and by the way they reflect on each other. This is doubly true in Euripidean drama, where we are often forced to assimilate in sequence several contradictory views of the same person or action, making a further adjustment in our perceptions each time. Menelaos in *Helene* assumes a series of identities by turns, as conquering hero, ludicrous and pitiful beggar, reunited husband and rehabilitated hero, conscienceless trickster, cruel slaughterer of barbarians, and signal favorite of the gods. All these identities are not shuffled off in turn, but are superimposed like layers of transparency; and all of them make up what Menelaos, in this play, signifies.

The analysts of Euripidean drama have been fatally attracted by misplaced historicism. It is may be that the work of Euripides, seen in a purely diachronic light, is a falling off or declination from Sophokles' achievement. But the purely diachronic viewpoint makes a direct confrontation with an artist's work impossible: the plays become only the signpost pointing up, or down, the road to something else. Euripides' work may invite this treatment, since, in its continual gestures of declining or refusing the heroic mode, it does indeed indicate the (potential) exhaustion of the tragic art form. But the only effective approach to this artist as to any other is to confront the work

14. See Burnett (1971, 144–45).

15. For a discussion of structuralist techniques, see M. Lane's *Introduction to Structuralism* (1970, 35): "Differing structures can be brought together not despite, but in virtue of, differences, for which an order is then sought."

itself. At its worst the gaze directed backward can lead to attempts to defend Euripides by proving him a kind of botched and distorted Sophokles and thus to save him as a proper literary classic, a writer of "serious" and "important" drama as defined in Sophoclean terms.

Euripidean plays are always worth taking seriously and always worthy of respect, but only on their own terms. If we wrench our eyes away from the Sophoclean norm of the tragic and fix them on the maddening target dancing before us, we will see, with Strohm and Burnett, the variety, complexity, and vigor of Euripidean art, from the earliest period to the latest. In the diachronic aspect we are witnessing the birth of not one so much as several new kinds of drama, as in almost every turning Euripidean art casts off new and fertile dramatic devices.[16] By making the struggle against his great competitor, against the audience, and against the art form itself, Euripides was able to revivify and recreate drama in his own time and for the coming centuries, in itself an awesome triumph.

But, having praised him, we still have to turn back and contemplate the difficulties of enjoying Euripides. It is not, of course, that anybody really does not enjoy Euripidean drama. The plays are designed to be piquant, stylish, and exciting; and, unlike most art intended to have these qualities, Euripidean plays have retained a charm that has neither faded nor mellowed with the centuries, so that the Euripidean problem is as real for us as it was for the fifth-century audience. Modern critics do not aim, as the Schlegels did, at setting up a canon of ancient art, to serve as a reformist model for contemporary work; but the seductive appeal of the plays and the unabashed way in which they manipulate our responses may still cause us scandal. This artist's work does not seem to merit respect: how may we judge it fairly, without being apologetic or patronizing? The question of the poetic and dramatic value of Euripides' work must be confronted, if lurking reservations are not to reemerge, so that the critic ends after all on a note of faint praise.[17] Euripides renounces the union of tragedy with the heroic, a union that Aristoteles saw as the combined achievement of Aischylos and Sophokles.[18] His plays adumbrate through deviation and negation the shape of what the tragic

16. See Patin's comments ([1841 – 43] 1871, 43): it is a curious spectacle to see tragedy lose its old attributes and form "combinaisons imprévues, des genres qu'on ne soupçonnait point," like an empire resolving itself into a series of new kingdoms.

17. See, e.g., Conacher's struggle to come to some positive conclusion, when he considers "the invidious comparison with 'classical' tragedy." Asking himself whether Euripides' treatment of myth has harmed tragedy, he is forced to conclude that "in a strictly aesthetic context" it has (1967, 345). Cf. the similar remarks of Murray (1913.1, 242), discussed in Chap. 1.

18. Note that, in delineating the completion of tragic form, Aristoteles mentions only Sophokles and Aischylos (*Poet.* 1449a15 – 20); see the *Vita Aeschyli* (333.15 – 22 Page).

audience would like to have, and—with the partial exception of *Hippolytos* and *Bakchai*—they stubbornly withhold it.

The task of praising Euripides is made even more difficult by the details of his style. The texture of the verse is looser and less rich and fine than that of his predecessors; indeed, much of it is pure fustian. This deficit is the inevitable result of the aesthetic choices detailed above. Euripidean tragedy swings close to "normal" language, that is, to the vocabulary, grammar, and the rather flat, emotionally colorless tone of prose. Concomitantly, the remaining specifically poetic items of tragic language, often necessary to metrical composition, have been severely pruned and regularized into a narrow automaticity.[19] Many lines in Euripidean plays do not repay careful attention for their style or imagery, although there are few that do not assume some wider significance when taken in the frame of the whole. The very choice of the rhetorical mode, as I have already shown, mutes character portrayal and substitutes the dry felicities of the trope for poetic or psychological nuance. The ironic lapses into the "low" tone, with its distancing effect, also preclude elaborate beauty and dense significance. At these moments, and at others where an ironic subtext is present, the lines are meant to sound, must sound, "flat" and unresonant.[20]

The careful analysis of late Euripidean lyric by W. Kranz shows the same process at work.[21] The "weak and pretty" lyrics of late Euripides perform their role in the whole, often contrasting with flat ironies in the scenes surrounding them. The prosaic tone of the iambic scenes forces the lyric into a trivial or remote beauty, or the lyric impulse may be expressed largely in monody or the *amoibaion,* where it becomes a kind of ballet of emotion, again counterpointing the cold argumentation of the scenes to follow.[22] The same stylistic formalism that produces crisp and sententious trimeters also fosters a lyric that creates an effect of literary artifice rather than of significance and immediacy.[23] Euripides can write tense, serious lyric: we find such lyrics just where we would expect to find them, in the plays often

19. See the comments of Schmid-Stählin 3:793ff., who conclude (811–12) that, while Sophokles and Aischylos were creators of new poetic diction, Euripides regularized this diction and was the founder of the "dramatischen Κοινή der Folgezeit" (812).

20. See Austin's dismayed comment on the dry and detached style of the famous *Erechtheus* fragment (1967, 17). The style of the passage is hollow and pompous because we are receiving cues from it about what our response should be. These cues do not invalidate the message of patriotism, so much as they suggest the limitations of this sort of rhetoric, limitations that become crushingly apparent at the play's terrible denouement.

21. 1933, 243.

22. See Schadewaldt (1926, 144–45) on the violent and unordered emotional outpourings in early Euripidean lyric. On the contrast between lyric and *rhesis,* see J. Gould (1978, 50).

23. On the formal and derivative quality of much Euripidean lyric, see Delulle (1911, 26); Breitenbach (1934, 31, 60, 114–15); Heitsch (1955, 71).

singled out for their fine style, *Hippolytos* and especially *Bakchai*. But the aesthetic of the typical Euripidean play requires a different kind of lyric. The appropriate counterpoint to the glaring and garish light of *Hekabe*, for instance, is the delicate and affected pastel of the "escapist" lyric that we find in the play.[24]

Every several element in Euripidean style loses in density and significance, a process that like many others was begun by Sophokles. Structure replaces texture, as each element, especially the most trivialized or diminished, has a role to play in the whole. In many cases it is precisely the failure, the *kakozêlon* or bad taste of a particular item, that creates its significance, setting up an irony and a harmony, perhaps with something quite antithetical, but equally jarring, nearby. Deeper inconcinnities in structure, the huge flaws and reversals in plays like *Herakles* or *Hekabe*, are themselves major structural points that illumine whole dramas.

The artificiality and primitivism of the prologue/*deus* frame is another example of this technique. As an ironic stylist, Euripides emphasized, not the verisimilitude of the mimicked world of his art, but its artificiality, its secondary and intentional nature.[25] This makes an obvious contrast with the deceptive power of Sophoclean art, but the difference remains a matter of emphasis. Sophoclean art retains many formal elements, and is far from consistently naturalistic; Euripidean art is often very persuasively mimetic. That poetry presents something artificial, faked, a lie instead of truth, is a view securely rooted in the Greek poetic tradition.[26] The prose rhetoricians in Euripides' day began their speeches with an open presentation of the problems of intentionality—the *captatio benevolentiae*—that derives from a similar openness that we can trace, and have long misunderstood, in the poetry of Pindaros.[27] In choosing this self-conscious and self-presenting side of art, Euripides found excellent precedents to follow in his own tradition, quite aside from the stylistic alliance that he formed with the newly developing prose art.

Sophokles' contrasting stylistic emphasis corresponds to the special function of his poetry, to embody a dominant cultural tradition, much as the work of Homeros did at an earlier period. Euripides chose to present himself as deceiver and charlatan, the poet as liar, avoiding the equally traditional role of the poet as mouthpiece for cultural values and authentic truth, a legacy to be transmitted to future generations. Art that is recognized as having major importance in its own day becomes by definition an item in "history," as its

24. See analysis in App. C, below.
25. See Whitman (1974, 114 and 136).
26. On the poet and deception (*apatê*) see Segal (1981, 272–74 and 1978, 114–18).
27. See Bundy (1962).

contemporaries begin to view it in the perspective of an imagined future,[28] while work like that of Euripides does not recede into a historical perspective, but instead always appears "modern," linked to and limited by the time, the culture, and the personality of the artist who produced it. The traditional blandness of the Sophoclean literary persona is created by the disappearance of the artist, who so perfectly embodies cultural values, behind his work, and by the disappearance of the work itself behind the literary norm that it has helped to constitute.[29] The excoriating bitterness of Sophoclean drama has become more accessible since the work of Whitman (1958) and Knox (1964) showed us that his poetry too, rather than being an unmediated expression of moral and aesthetic norms, is built around central contradictions and tensions within Hellenic culture. Euripidean drama continues to be hagridden by the interfering ghost of its author; and the vividness of Euripides' literary personality has deflected attention from his work, just as the ideality of the Sophoclean biography has obscured the power and dynamism of Sophoclean plays.

The early Classicist critics who rejected Euripides did so because they were attempting to establish a standard of universal validity and to isolate those qualities that would invest a literary work with the authority to present an enduring vision of its culture. That these critics saw a difficulty in Euripides' work reflects their growing understanding of the fifth century, which established the canon of three tragedians that we inherited. In that canon, Aischylos is the originator; and his status is inalienable, since it is derived from his achievement in making tragedy the dominant art form and thus refounding the poetic tradition. Sophokles, who surpassed the work of the originator by bringing that work to perfection, has an equally obvious and unchallengeable rank. But what is to be done with Euripides? Later antiquity made his work the favorite, the tragedy that could be enjoyed by posterity instead of being preserved as a literary heirloom. But Aristophanes reflects the dilemma of the contemporary audience: where can Euripides fit into the developing canon? Can he too become exemplary, and thus "classic"? Or is it true, as Aristophanes' Aischylos claims, that Euripides' poetry has "died along with him" (868–71)? The conclusion in *Frogs* seems to be

28. Note that this corresponds almost exactly to the view taken of Goethe by his contemporaries, Schiller and the Schlegels (Chap. 1).

29. For an amusing example of this effect, see Ortkemper's suggestion that Sophokles stands somehow outside the theatrical development of the fifth century—as represented by Euripides and Aischylos—since he is incomparable (1969, 124). See the remark of Heitsch (1980, 38–39) on the *Ilias:* great masterworks tend to replace the background from which they developed, so that they then appear familiar and obvious to us. An example might be the formulation of Martin (1958, 247), who said of Sophokles that "Ses oeuvres, dans leur haute perfection, sont normales, commes ses idées."

that it has, since the august and rather pompous Aischylos is summoned back to Athens rather than the "favorite" Euripides.

Part of the authority that the early Classicist critics invested in the work of art accrued also to their own work, which claimed to distinguish enduring from ephemeral, worthy from unworthy art, and which established for contemporary artists a standard at which to aim. Such a criticism cannot hope to do justice to work that itself abjures cultural authority, whose products are not designed to satisfy the perceived needs of its audience, and whose relation to that audience is one of antagonism as much as of cooperation. Euripidean theater is involved with the same cultural concerns that are raised by the theater of Sophokles; but its relation to these concerns is secondary, in that it represents them almost always by a process of inversion. Euripidean poetry is a poetry of complement; and its mode is one of titanic, or diabolic, opposition or striving.[30] To say No is the function of Euripidean art, and this continual negation always looks toward something else, adumbrating that other by the play of its refusal, its irony.

By revealing the mechanisms behind his own magic, Euripides forces the audience to think about the contradictions and ambiguities of signification. The myth, as a religious and cultural force, can be treated as a significant event that illuminates religious practice or as a significant story that reveals truth about human life. The gods themselves have the same function: their agency gives significance to a reality that we would otherwise confront as a random play of events. Art and artistic tradition also shape and give meaning to culture. Euripidean drama pits these traditional systems of signification against the various critical or analytical modes that were available in its time. For artistic opposition, it uses the antiheroic or comic mode; in rhetorical or argumentative terms, it employs the antipoetic mode of the *logos*. But the achievement of Euripides' work goes far beyond a mere debunking of the heroic. For one thing, that view had always been available in Greek culture from the time of the *Margites* or, alternatively, *Works and Days*. It is the function of an artist to reveal and illuminate culture; and, by opening tragedy to the massive cultural changes that were a part of the fifth century, Euripides made his work capable of revelations that approach the prophetic level, given that much of what he shows was in his own cultural future. The best evidence that Euripides knew Sokrates and understood his work is the keen and elegant way in which the plays anatomize the workings of a new morality of altruism, whose heroes are intended to embody both justice and honor.

As Rohdich has shown, Euripides' treatment of the new—or the not-yet-

---

30. "Grossartig, titanisch war der Versuch . . ." (U. v. Wilamowitz [1883, 226]).

born—spirit of moral optimism is critical, perceptive, and acerbic.[31] The
bland, humane representatives of the new ethic appear in Euripides under the
same sign of irony as the representatives of the old.[32] The typical Euripidean
suffering and striving protagonist is often a hard-up low-life (a woman, oldster, barbarian, or beggar) whose attempts to maintain the claims of the ego
in heroic terms continually shatter against social barriers. When these
strugglers win, as they often do, the destructiveness and the vileness of their
victories indict the heroic ethic; but their suffering and striving may also call
into question the neat arrangements of the new ethic. The Socratic attempt to
harmonize the contradictory ethics of moral right (*dikê*) and heroic achievement (*aretê*) by subordinating the latter to the former led to its own contradictions. At an extreme this could mean a denial of something that had given
Hellenic traditional culture its particular vision and power, namely the
unflinching perception of human suffering and failure. By keeping the old
and the new moralities in balance, and by playing the contradictions of one
against the other, Euripides betrayed both of them and laid bare for us the full
meaning of the Greek cultural revolution.

In many cases in Euripides the ideals and the artistic forms subjected to
elenchus are not yet in being, except in his own work. If we had the works of
Antiphon and Thrasymachos intact, we would be unlikely to find better
demonstrations of the complexities of the persuasive mode than appear in
these plays.[33] Early texts on atheism, radical political change, the nature of
women, and other disruptive topics are hard to isolate, and it is likely that
such matters found their best exposition on the stage, though usually the
comic stage.[34] In Euripidean plays, and there alone, contemporary discourse
appears in its full range and complexity, driven to ideal extremes by dramatic
situation and richly elaborated in all its cultural implications. By foregoing
the writing of beautiful plays, the pleasing of his audience, and the winning
of prizes, Euripides won the ability to encompass, bring to its flowering, and
exhaust the whole second stage of the Greek cultural achievement by the

31. See Chap. 1, Section IV.1, above. I reject Rohdich's definition of this new mode as
"sophistic" pure and simple, and his assumption that Euripidean plays take a single stance
toward it.

32. One exception to this rule is *Hippolytos,* where a representative of the new ethic becomes
the central figure of the play and is assimilated to the role of tragic protagonist; see discussion in
Chap. 9, below.

33. For the priority of and influence of tragic speeches on prose rhetoric, see Finley ([1938]
1967, 74–82).

34. The case of *Sisyphos* indicates the difference in our perception of a purely fictional and
dramatic exposition of radical views: if the play is the work, not of Kritias, but of Euripides
(Dihle [1977]), or some other professional dramatist, then it ceases to express the program of the
most notorious of the intellectual radicals and becomes merely another reflection of contemporary attitudes.

prophetic exercise of his genius. Because Euripides was a true interpreter of his time, he became the stepchild of the "classic" period and won the undying plaudits of centuries that understood his work perhaps less than his distrustful contemporaries had. But the work has endured and is still there to be understood, if we are ready to begin the task of interpretation.

Part II

Four Plays

6

Hekabe: The Aesthetic of the *Aischron*

I. Structure

We know of no other parallels between *Hekabe* and the lost Sophoclean *Polyxene;* but the prologue, at any rate, seems to present a variation on the Sophoclean one. Both use a ghost as speaker,[1] and the fact that the Euripidean ghost is not esssential to the plot, along with the reminiscence of Sophoclean wording, makes likely an allusion to other, more standard treatments of the Polyxene story.[2] The gesture also draws attention to the fact that the Euripidean play deals with the deaths of two of Hekabe's children rather than one, since the ghost represents the second strand of the play, the vengeance

1. The Sophoclean fragment *TGF* 523 has the appearance of a prologue, but the message attributed to the Ghost ought to come at the play's end (Conacher [1967, 148; 1961, 4]). Calder (1966, 41–42) has argued, to me convincingly, that Achilleus appeared twice, as a winged shade in the prologue and as an armed warrior, probably in the report of a messenger. *Hekabe* also uses two prophetic appearances, the shade of Polydoros at the prologue, and Polymestor, who predicts Agamemnon's fate not out of goodwill (as Achilleus presumably did, see the *Nostoi* in Proklos [5:108 Allen]) but out of malice.

2. Both open with ''I come'' (but this may be conventional, see *Pe.* 692) and a participle of *leipô,* ''having left.'' I would argue that the apparent structural parallel is stronger evidence than verbal ones. Note that, even if we assume the temporal priority of *Polyxene,* that does not entitle us to suppose that all contrasts with Sophoclean technique in *Hekabe* are allusions to that play; see App. D.

of Hekabe for her son Polydoros. This early appearance of the second theme is virtually a necessity if the dual plot is to work and we are to transfer our concern, at some point later in the play, from one *pathos* to another.

In enlarging the story of Polyxene to include another and unrelated event, Euripides imposed a necessary change of focus, toward the single unifying link that makes the two stories into one. Hekabe is the mother bereaved of both these children; and it is in her, or rather in her experience of grief and loss, that the center of the new play must be located.[3] The role of Hekabe is in fact so dominant that there is no whole scene in which she does not take a major and active part.[4] Even during the agonized monody of Polymestor, the protagonist stands silent in the background, contemplating the success of her vengeance. The unifying force of Hekabe's role lies in her suffering. Hekabe is positioned at a convergence of events where pathos and misery are raised to an extraordinary level, not by the interaction of a peculiar ethos with a particular situation, as in some Sophoclean plays, but simply through the duplication of stresses.[5] The situation is intellectually intriguing in the same way that a scientific experiment is: carefully manufactured conditions can permit us to observe an ordinarily muddled process with clarity. Polydoros in the prologue lays considerable stress on a precise temporal convergence: for a brief time his mother will be in the Chersonnesos and able to discover her son's body; Polyxene is fated to die on this same day. "My mother will see the two corpses of her two children, me and the wretched girl."[6]

Hekabe's suffering is so remarkable as to evoke continual comment as the play progresses.[7] Polydoros ends with a word of pity.[8] Polyxene, who has no concern for her own sufferings or death (211 – 15), expresses violent sorrow at Hekabe's pain. Even the Greek herald is much struck by Hekabe and

3. Almost all the critics who do not complain of disunity make this point: Matthaei (1918, 119 – 23), resuming the original controversy between Hermann and Pflugk; Paley (1874, 513); H. Weil (1879, 203); Cataudella (1939, 127 – 28); Boella (1964, ix-x). In determining dramatic unity, Conacher has chosen a thematic rather than a structural link, arguing that such a use of Hekabe's character answers to "neither tragic, nor even dramatic, form" (1967, 152 n.16). He proposes instead the contrast between the characters of Polyxene and Hekabe (1961, 13). For a wholly negative view, see Lanza (1963, 424 – 25).

4. Medeia is the same sort of protagonist; for parallels between *Medeia* and *Hekabe,* see Steidle (1966, 141); Zürcher (1947, 73), who sees both as dramas of female *Leidenschaft.*

5. The notion that the sufferings of a protagonist must be uniquely fitted to a special "character" derives from Sophoclean models. These preconceptions have caused much difficulty with *Hekabe.* See Zürcher (1947, 84); Kirkwood (1947, 63 n.6); Abrahamson (1952, 129); Steidle (1966, 134ff.). This point is made by Conacher (1967, 83) in discussion of *Herakles.*

6. 44—there are numerous references to the day, and to one day in the play (e.g., lines 56, 317, 364, 412, 628). Such imagery is almost inevitable, given the shape of the play.

7. See Conacher (1961, 15).

8. "O mother, who from the tyrants' halls now see the day of slavery, how ill you fare—as much as once you prospered" (55 – 57).

comments on her exemplary misery in the same terms as Polydoros: she who has been so high has fallen so low.[9] After the discovery of Polydoros' body, a new theme emerges in the commiseration. Hekabe is repeatedly said to be the extreme of wretchedness, the very superlative of misery. The attendant who discovers the body calls Hekabe one who "surpasses the whole race of men and women in misery—no one will contest the crown" (660). Agamemnon, when he hears the story, exclaims, "Alas (ὦ σχετλία σύ), for your measureless sorrows! ... Ah, what woman ever was so wretched?" Hekabe replies drily, "There is none, unless you mean Fortune herself."[10] Later in her appeal, listing her blows, she calls herself "the most pitiful of mortals" (811). This echoes the earlier assessment of the chorus, who called her πολυπονωτάτη βροτῶν (721).

The main structural support of the complex plot is Hekabe's role as exemplary sufferer, the focal point of the accumulated miseries of Troy and of the final sufferings detailed in this play. The success of the play will depend upon the effective integration of this role with the other themes to create a satisfying aesthetic whole.[11] The complexity of *Hekabe* has been called a major flaw;[12] and certainly, if structure could in itself constitute a flaw, the dual plot of *Hekabe* would be a gross one indeed. But a play must stand or fall on its own terms; and basic structure, being neither accidental nor peripheral, cannot be wished away as one wishes away a fault. Complaints about the play's disunity are usually based on presuppositions that derive from the work of Sophokles. In theme at least the play is traditional: the workings of excessive and violent stress on a human nature is in no way new or alien to tragedy as Aischylos and Sophokles created it. But what happens to Hekabe on the day of the play is an arbitrary and accidental concatenation of misfortunes; this means that, while Hekabe has a fairly distinct ethos of her own, the events that she experiences are only marginally relevant to her character.

9. See Aristoteles, *Rhet.* 1386b6–7, *Poet.* 1453a5, on the role of the *anaxion pathêma* in inducing pity. See also Boella (1964, 12). Harbsmeier (1968, 59) points out that Hekabe must be seen at the same time as slave and as queen.

10. 786. The meaning of Hekabe is not in doubt, but what she says is very singular. *Tychê* in fifth-century art would have been a beautiful young woman, symbolic of good rather than bad fortune. That fortune is the embodiment of misfortune seems to express the particularly black view of this play.

11. Spranger (1927.2) took an extreme view in seeing the "problem" of the play as lying in a mechanical and inadequate expansion from an original *Polyxene.* See the comment of Abrahamson (1952, 120 n.1) "Once the meaning of the play is understood, the problem seems to disappear; and its composition . . . is seen in its uniqueness and its necessity."

12. Critics have not hesitated to depreciate the play. Matthaei (1918, 124): it "leaves much to be desired"; Norwood (1920, 216): it is "on the whole poor and uninteresting," and only one good choral ode redeems it from "crude sensationalism" (1954, 41); Bates (1930, 92): it "is not an interesting play" and "in reality it is not a great drama" (94).

The blows that Hekabe suffers are annihilating in their accumulated force, and in their incomprehensibility. Oidipous' fate in some way is the expression of Oidipous' nature, marking him out for a unique destiny, and, when he names himself the child of Luck (*tychê*), he is wrong.[13] But, when Hekabe identifies her wretched self with the deity of cosmic misrule, she does not seem to be mistaken. Oidipous' response to his catastrophe, though self-destructive, seems in some way to assert human will and choice; Hekabe's revenge, apparently self-assertive, is merely a further step in her erasure from humanity. In this play the act of decision in the face of destiny belongs to Polyxene, who, by the manner in which she accepts the inevitable, contrives to win some glory out of a vagary of Hellenic democratic realpolitik. Polyxene's role, nature, fate, and character are thus virtually the precise inversion of her mother's. It is the presence of Polyxene, the Sophoclean element, we might say, in a Euripidean drama,[14] that defines and clarifies the role of Hekabe, enabling the play to project a figure of tragic intensity and dread that is yet, in its essence, entirely antiheroic.

Hekabe packs a double plot into a very small compass; in actual length it is among the shorter of the early plays, and only *Alkestis* is much briefer.[15] Everything seems arranged for maximum speed, especially at the opening.[16] The opening song or parodos, instead of being a self-contained lyric, is an anapaestic address to Hekabe that informs her in precise and circumstantial detail of the decision about Polyxene's sacrifice and the preceding debate in the Greek assembly.[17] Little argument is required to persuade Hekabe of the approaching danger, since she has already been alarmed by a dream, one of those useful sources of foreknowledge that, like the oracles in *Trachiniai* and

13. *OT* 1080.

14. Conacher describes Polyxene as "almost Sophoclean" (1967, 158; see also 1961, 19); note the similar conclusions of Pagani (1970, 51) and Buxton (1982, 176). We have no way of knowing whether this characterization is or is not part of an extended allusion to Sophokles' *Polyxene*. Calder's reconstruction (1966) has almost nothing to tell us about the role of the protagonist; and in any case the Euripidean stance is certainly not limited to or defined by the relations between particular plays; see App. D.

15. Two other plays of the twenties that are similar to *Hekabe* in length (1295 lines) are *Andromache* (1288) and *Suppliants* (1234); both are packed, as is *Hekabe*, with incident.

16. See Garzya (1954, 209): "tutto si svolge con rapidità estrema."

17. On this parodos, see Boella (1964, 16), "non ha un carattere propriamente lirico, ma piuttosto espositivo-oratorio." In no other tragic parodos is a message brought to a character on stage, and in no other is there no nonlyric discussion of the information conveyed in lyric. The treatment of the second crisis, the discovery of Polydoros' body, is not dissimilar. There, expression of grief is subordinated to the idea of vengeance, which takes shape inside the lyric that is Hekabe's first response.

Persians, are kept vague enough to be serviceable in various ways.[18] The chorus ends by warning that Odysseus is "all but here" to carry out his dread errand; and indeed he enters at the close of the lyric *amoibaion* between mother and daughter, before the two have exchanged any trimeter dialogue. Odysseus wastes no words at his entrance, remarking that he assumes Hekabe already knows what the Greeks have decided (218–19).

The pace with which events in the play move along forces constant impromptu reactions upon Hekabe. Appalled by the vague threat of the dream, she next reacts to the clearer news of the chorus with hysteria, expressing her doubts and confusion in a flood of deliberative questions.[19] Yet, at the sudden appearance of Odysseus, she is ready to commence the struggle for her child (229–30). After an interval of calm in which Polyxene's death is reported, a second blow follows with cruel speed. Yet, when Agamemnon enters, pressing her for haste in completing the burial of Polyxene,[20] Hekabe makes ready to gain his help in her vengeance; and, once assured of cooperation, she moves to act, impatient of any delay.[21] Agamemnon closes the scene by remarking that it is only because the winds have not yet begun to blow that he can permit her this favor (900ff.). The action of the play is thus hurried along constantly by the pressures of the outside reality, and by the urgency of Hekabe's response. After the accomplishment of Hekabe's revenge, the play closes, as Agamemnon announces the rising of the winds and the imminent departure of the Greeks for their homes (1289ff.).

II. Nature and Nurture

Not only is Hekabe on stage constantly, but she is active during the whole play, and in almost every scene she must react to threats or attempt to control the movement of events. At only one point in the play does the frantic pace

18. U. v. Wilamowitz (1909, 446–49) argued that the hexameters in which Hekabe reports the dream are inauthentic; along with them he removed lines 90–97, so that references to Polyxene are absent. In support, Biehl (1966, 412 n.7; 1957, 55–62); Bremer (1971, 232–45). It is true that there is a clash between the apparition of Polydoros and the animal allegory; but the vague content supports the polyvalent use of the dream, which unites forebodings for both children. W. H. Friedrich has seen this, calling (1953, 45–46) for retention of lines 92–97 only; see Lesky ([1956] 1972.1, 331 n.81). Without the hexameters, however, it is easier to sense the awkwardness with which one incident overlies the other. For ambivalent predictive devices, see Waldock (1951, 11ff., on the "Documentary Fallacy").

19. 154–64. On these desperate deliberatives, see Schadewaldt (1926, 149), who traces the practice back to Aischylos.

20. τί μέλλεις . . . (726); σὺ δὲ σχολάζεις, ὥστε θαυμάζειν ἐμέ (730).

21. Hekabe is brusque and peremptory in her dealings both with Talthybios (σὺ δ' ἐλθέ, 604) and with Agamemnon (ἀλλ' ὡς γενέσθω· τόνδε μὲν μέθες λόγον . . . , 888).

abate; this interval of calm is the second scene, where Talthybios narrates the death of Polyxene.[22] The scene is full of great pathos, yet it contains the only good news that anyone will bring Hekabe; and the pace slows as we hear the details of an event already known and expected. Only in this scene does Hekabe receive information to which she can react at some leisure, in a contemplative mood, rather than through frantic struggle.

The structural singularity of the messenger scene is paralleled by its evocation of important themes, such as those of education (*paideia*) and nobility, that illuminate the action before and after it. Polyxene is the figure that proposes and defines these themes: her previous experience of nobility has left her reluctant to experience the humiliations of slavery.[23] In her case, learning has been a single and irreversible process that has created a fixed attitude to life: "Not to live well is a great trouble," as she remarks, in a line whose lapidary sententiousness underlines its finality.[24] Although Polyxene appears in only one scene, she has already been given scope to develop a personality of her own. Other virgins in Euripidean tragedy are at least initially obedient and retiring, whereas Polyxene shows little reticence and even reverses roles in the trimeter scene by instructing her mother in deportment. It may be merely that Polyxene's single appearance has left no room for a gradual emergence of the unmarried girl (*parthenos*). But what we hear of her death scene deepens and defines the contrast of her attitudes with those of her mother, as Hekabe reacts to and reflects upon the last act of her daughter. The pause is the more valuable because, in Hekabe's frantic efforts to save Polyxene and in her emotional reaction to that loss, there is little chance for the audience to compare and weigh the mother and the daughter.

Hekabe reacts to the messenger's account first with a rather confused admission that this news of Polyxene's noble behavior has some alleviating effect on her own measureless sorrows.[25] She then dilates upon the theme of

22. Almost all critics have been struck by the change of pace: Matthaei (1918, 139), "this pause in the very center of the play"; King (1938, 82), "This beautiful scene brings to a quiet close the first half of the play"; Lanza (1963, 429–30) refers to the contrast between the epic and solemn style of this scene and the rest of *Hekabe* with its "concitazione tragica." See also Garzya (1954, 210). Conacher (1967, 160) calls the scene a "skilful *entr'acte*."

23. The theme of slavery has received much emphasis; see Steidle (1966, 140). Daitz (1971) and Kuch (1973, 106ff.) attempt to connect the theme to the contemporary attitudes.

24. τὸ γὰρ ζῆν μὴ καλῶς μέγας πόνος (378). The similarity to Sophokles' *Aias* 479–80 is obvious, as is the resumé of Tekmessa (357 = *Aias* 489; note the similar contexts). Euripides rouses some echoes from a great debate on heroic values. See Benedetto (1971.1, 51) on Polyxene as a representative of aristocratic values; Boella (1964, 48) "Si direbbe che Euripide abbia voluto attribuire la fierezza di Aiace ad una tenera giovinetta." For the connection of these Sophoclean echoes to the issue of freedom and slavery, see Knox (1964, 41).

25. The vivid imagery of lines 585–88, in which Hekabe's sorrows distract her by pulling her first in one direction, then in another, like so many importunate children, anticipates the second half of the play, in which she will be distracted by two major griefs. The image also

nobility (*gennaiôtês*) for eleven and a half lines (592 – 603).[26] Psychological explanations for the excursus have been offered; but none has seemed plausible.[27] It does not seem likely that persons ancient or modern would express violent grief through speculative philosophical remarks. More to the point, there is little literary precedent for such a response. Other grieving Euripidean characters tend to reflect, not on questions, now rendered irrelevant by death, of upbringing and natural endowments, but on the emptiness of life and human happiness; and there is usually a gradual progression from generalities to the personal situation of the sufferer.[28] Hekabe says of her remarks that they are "a vain shot from the mind's bow," and this implies that they are to be seen as irrelevant.[29] Such an uncommon reaction, if it were supported by other traits, could serve to characterize Hekabe; but she does not react to other blows of fate with meditations on remote topics.

Hekabe's remarks at line 592 stand out, and are meant to stand out, and openly present themselves as standing out against the background of dramatic illusion. Without making the blunder of assuming that "Euripides" here takes the occasion to address the audience directly, dropping the aesthetic of drama, and aiming at some political or didactic goal, we can say that the importance of these lines is strongly emphasized by their open failure to merge with the dramatic situation, as they would do if they could be

---

resembles the actual physical motions of Hekabe during the opening, when she rushed back and forth, uncertain what to do.

26. This passage has not met with much approval. See Grube (1941, 95): "More sarcasm has been concentrated [on this] than on any other passage of Euripides." Solmsen (1975, 69 – 70) refers to it as an "outburst," leaving it unclear whether we are to blame it on Hekabe's impulsiveness or Euripides'. See also Tierney (1946, 84 – 85); and Boella (1964, 73), Euripides writes "senza curarsi della coerenza artistica"; Willem (1929, 90), "une digression froide qui fait languir le drame." The indignation of the ancients echoes faintly in the scholiast to line 603 (p. 371 Dindorf); Eustathios' *Ilias* commentary (930.39 = 3:467 Van der Valk); and the *Progymnasmata* of one Theon (1:149 Walz, the reference is in H. Weil [1879]):τὸν δὲ Εὐριπίδην καταμεμφόμεθα ὅτι παρὰ καιρὸν αὐτῷ Ἑκάβη φιλοσοφεῖ. Conacher, however, (1967, 160 n.29; 1972, 204 – 5) notes the thematic significance of the passage.

27. Schadewaldt (1926, 139) sees line 603 as an open admission that Hekabe is distracted by emotion. Conacher attributes the mental "spasm" (1961, 20) to emotional exhaustion (1967, 159). Sheppard (1924, 74) suggests that Hekabe is trying to calm herself, so as to be worthy of Polyxene.

28. See Iphis in *Suppl* 1080ff., Hekabe in *Tro,* 686ff.

29. καὶ ταῦτα μὲν δὴ νοῦς ἐτόξευσεν μάτην (603). See *Suppl* 456; Aischylos *Suppl.* 446. The most significant parallels are the great digressions in the Pindaric victory odes, where imagery of veering off course (*Py.* 11.37 – 39) alternates with metaphors from shooting and javelin throwing (*Ol.* 2.90, 13.93 – 95; *N.* 6.27, 7.71). While these moments were at one time attributed to mental aberrations of the poet, they are now recognized as transition formulae (see Bundy [1962]). In a Pindaric ode, as in a Euripidean play, disparate material is allusively juxtaposed, making for many sharp transitions. Cf. the remarks of Buxton (1982, 152 – 53) on "shifts of perspective" in Euripides.

perceived primarily as an expression of Hekabe's emotional state. As the
illusion of coherent character becomes relatively transparent, it is possible for
Hekabe, like the chorus in an Aeschylean play, to acquire a voice whose
words can extend beyond the knowledge and psychology of the mimetic
utterer. What she says is significant in direct proportion to its incongruity.[30]

Polyxene has displayed the behavior of a *gennaios*,[31] and these lines raise
the question of the nature, source, and lifespan of such qualities. The analogy, a banal one, is from vegetable life and the relation of nature (*physis*) to
planting and growth:[32] human life seems to violate a part of this traditional
analogy, however, in its tendency to retain good qualities in spite of bad
usage and nurture. Plants are dependent on nurture (*trophê*) for the production of good fruit, while by contrast the *gennaios* human being remains noble
and uncorrupted to the end. Hekabe goes on to ask herself, in a rather
meandering fashion, what the source of this incorruptible goodness might be.
In trying to choose between parentage and upbringing (*trophê*), she opines
that at least upbringing must make some contribution, through an "instruction in nobility" (*didaxis esthlou*), which, when properly learned, provides
an internal standard (κανόνι τοῦ καλοῦ μαθών) for determining what is
ignoble (*aischron*).[33]

30. This is essentially the point made by Conacher (1972).
31. 591–92:

τὸ δ' αὖ λίαν παρεῖλες ἀγγελθεῖσά μοι
γενναῖος

Tierney (1946, 84) points out the unparalleled absence of the supplementary participle; the strong
enjambment of *gennaios* should also be noted. Both have the effect of emphasizing the single
word. For its meaning, see Aristoteles, *Hist. Animal.* 488b19 (cf. *Rhet.* 1390b22):τὸ μὴ
ἐξιστάμενον ἐκ τῆς αὐτοῦ φύσεως. We might say "true to breed."
32. 592–98:

οὔκουν δεινόν, εἰ γῆ μὲν κακὴ
τυχοῦσα καιροῦ θεόθεν εὖ στάχυν φέρει,
χρηστὴ δ' ἁμαρτοῦσ' ὧν χρεὼν αὐτὴν τυχεῖν
κακὸν δίδωσι καρπόν, ἀνθρώποις δ' ἀεὶ
ὁ μὲν πονηρὸς οὐδὲν ἄλλο πλὴν κακός,
ὁ δ' ἐσθλὸς ἐσθλός, οὐδὲ συμφορᾶς ὕπο
φύσιν διέφθειρ', ἀλλὰ χρηστός ἐστ' ἀεί

See also the same analogy of the growth of the young person, used with a straightforward pathos
by Polydoros at line 20: τροφαῖσιν ὥς τις πτόρθος ηὐξόμην τάλας.
33. 599–602:

ἆρ' οἱ τεκόντες διαφέρουσιν ἢ τροφαί
ἔχει γε μέντοι καὶ τὸ θρεφθῆναι καλῶς
δίδαξιν ἐσθλοῦ· τοῦτο δ' ἤν τις εὖ μάθῃ
οἶδεν τό γ' αἰσχρόν, κανόνι τοῦ καλοῦ μαθών.

The analogical use of *kanôn* in poetry begins for us with Euripides; see fragments 303.4 N2 (*Bel-*

The passage raises a major theme in contemporary thought, that of the opposition between *physis* and *trophê;* and the confusions in the ideas Hekabe expresses have as broad a base in intellectual tradition as do the ideas themselves. Hekabe's admission that *trophê* must play some role in human excellence, a modest statement that is neither startling nor unorthodox, undermines the truth of traditional notions, already characterized by her as paradoxical and inexplicable, about the incorruptibility of human inbred virtue. If there is "instruction in nobility" (*didaxis esthlou*), then, presumably, the *aischroi* have undergone the reverse, a *didaxis aischrou,* that gives them their conflicting and inferior system of values. The possibility of this kind of bad learning is inherent in the very idea of *trophê,* and is underscored by the reference to "knowing the shameful, having learned it by the measure of the good." The problem is a familiar one, worked out in detail by Platon in the fifth book of the *Republic:* the good must be able to recognize and judge evil, without having direct knowledge of it, for that knowledge is itself corrupting.[34] Hekabe's "vain shot" is therefore a mass of fruitful contradictions, coexisting under considerable tension, and ready to spring apart under any closer analysis. What Hekabe has said furnishes themes to connect and explicate the fates of her and her daughter, and to reveal the meaning of their different paths. Above all, the question of *gennaiotês* and its reverse, of the ugly-shameful (*aischron*) and the noble-beautiful (*kalon* or *esthlon*), and of the uses and meaning of education form the thematic fiber that runs through the play from its beginning to its end.

The question that Hekabe, and through her the play *Hekabe,* is struggling with is one that is central to tragedy; and, as so often in Euripides, the nature of the genre, codified for us by the work of Sophokles, is involved in these contradictions. Earlier modern studies of psychological portrayal in Greek drama noted the relatively "primitive" rigidity of character portrayal in even such a great master of the human soul as Sophokles. Rather than showing development, Sophoclean figures tend to display a single, well-defined *êthos* that remains essentially the same under the pressures of circumstance.[35] But Sophoclean psychology represents a familiar Hellenic ethic, as much as it

lerophontes) and 376.1 N2 (*Erechtheus*). Sophokles' use of *kanôn* in a simile in *Oinomaos* (*TGF* F474.5) does not have the same significance.

34. *Rep.* 5 408d-409e: physicians must risk their bodies' health to master knowledge about disease, but jurors cannot risk the soul's health to acquire experience. ἀλλ' ἄπειρον αὐτὴν καὶ ἀκέραιον δεῖ κακῶν ἠθῶν νέαν οὖσαν γεγονέναι (409a5). The ideal dicast is old, ὀψιμαθῆ γεγονότα τῆς ἀδικίας ... ἐπιστήμῃ οὐκ ἐμπειρίᾳ οἰκείᾳ κεχρημένον (409b5). Paley (1874, 553) notes the continuing relevance of this problem in philosophy. Heberden (1901) points out the emphatic particle γε in line 602: it is the *aischron* that must be known through the *kalon.*

35. See Zürcher (1947, 14–15); and Knox (1964, 37), who documents but demurs from this view.

does an early stage of development in psychological thinking.[36] According to this ethic, *physis* is shaped somehow both by nurture and nature, so that Aias' son, if he is to become like his father and show himself a trueborn son, must also have appropriate early experiences.[37] The inherent contradiction was evident to the Sophists, and Euripides builds on it here: in spite of the importance of *trophê*, this *physis*, once shaped, becomes characteristic of the *agathos*, is by definition permanent, and cannot be erased.[38] When Euripides' play exposes the contradictions of the *physis* concept it does more than touch upon an interesting contemporary theme. Sophokles used traditional ideology about *physis* to support a rebirth of the concerns and tone of heroic epic; and this powerful synthesis created a new standard for "serious" art. In challenging this standard, Euripides was led to a different kind of tragedy, and to a different view of human psychology.

The question of *physis* was also linked to the issue of education and thus became crucial to the contemporary philosophical and rhetorical movements. Sophists, from Sokrates through Antiphon, argued that traditional *trophê* was inadequate and that new forms of training were needed, training which they often endeavored to design or to supply.[39] These curricula almost always included instruction in rhetoric, the new art of prose that was designed to short-circuit the traditional role of poetry in mediating between cultural values and political practice.[40] The fact that rhetoric was designed to be taught as a system made it relatively independent of *physis* and gave it much in common with the *technai* that the gentleman (*agathos anêr*) had in the past scorned.[41] Further, the urgency of the need for rhetoric derived from new political systems that gave more power to the citizen majority, and that

---

36. For this point, see Lesky (1972.2, 209–10).

37. *Aias* 545ff. Eurysakes will not fear blood, if he is truly Aias' son (547). His *physis* has to be made like that of his father by experience from an early age (548–49):

ἀλλ' αὐτίκ' αὐτὸν ὠμοῖς ἐν νόμοις πατρὸς
δεῖ πωλοδαμνεῖν κἀξομοιοῦσθαι φύσιν.

The contradiction is part of the traditional view of *eugeneia*.

38. See Adkins (1960, 76–77) for the fertile contradictions created by these concepts in the poetry of Theognis. Lesky (1968.2, 18) cites Antiphon (DK 2:87 fr. 60B), a passage that has most suggestive parallels with this. There the point is that *trophê* for the child, like that for the land, will produce a sound crop, which then endures (ζῇ τοῦτο καὶ θάλλει διὰ παντὸς τοῦ βίου, καὶ αὐτὸ οὔτε ὄμβρος οὔτε ἀνομβρία ἀφαιρεῖται). There *physis* doctrine blends harmoniously with *trophê*, while in our passage it becomes a paradox.

39. See Tedeschi (1978, 33–34).

40. See Johnson (1959) on the modeling of the orator's role on that of the poet.

41. On this paradox, see Turato (1974, 152).

thus promised rewards to those who could manipulate these masses.[42] The Sophistic training systems doubly challenged the traditional values based upon *physis,* first by suggesting that an art that could be learned (*mathêma*) was appropriate for the aristocrat,[43] and second by their assumption that power did not lie in the hands of the *agathos* himself, but derived from those he would have to persuade.

Hekabe's speculations about her daughter's noble or truebred *physis* suggest alternative views of human nature, and the controversy can be stated both in archaic terms—as in the contrasting figures of Achilleus and Odysseus—or in classical ones—as in the differing ethical systems of Sophoclean and Euripidean tragedy. Hekabe's musings also suggest, without actually revealing, the contradictions explored by the Sophistic debate over *trophê* and *physis.* If Polyxene's death appears to prove the truth of the unlikely proposition that aristocratic *physis* will persist through all the dyes of experience, Hekabe's life will turn out to prove the opposite, that human beings do learn and change in their learning, and that the experience of continued life often involves a *didaxis aischrou* that wipes out earlier training, as though it had never been.[44]

If we ask what *Hekabe* will prove about "Euripides' views" on the Sophistic and on rhetorical training, our answer will of course be that Euripides, like everyone else, seems to see great moral danger in such training; and we may conclude that the tenor of this play indicates the poet's essential allegiance to traditional values.[45] But the wrong answer results from the incorrectly posed question: as I have indicated above, the author's views cannot be extracted from an aesthetic construct like *Hekabe.* Euripidean drama is marked by tone, subject matter, and by theme, in this case that of rhetoric and education, as antitraditional. While it is true that rhetoric is presented in *Hekabe* in a negative and corrupt aspect, this dark side is implicit in the way the new discipline confronts the old culture. Rhetoric claimed to offer an inversion of the traditional value system; but this claim, in contrast to attempts to substitute other values, leaves the system intact, while depriving it of coherence. In portraying the tactics of rhetoric as ultimately self-destructive and self-betraying, *Hekabe* does not so much take the part of any

42. See R. Müller (1976, 21–22), on the class system and oratory; Turato (1974, 152ff.); Buxton (1982, 18–19).

43. Pindaros (using a poetic cognate *phya* instead of *physis*) depreciates learned skills as inferior to inborn ability: *Py.* 8.44, *Ol.* 2.86ff., *Ol.* 9.100: τὸ δὲ φυᾷ κράτιστον ἅπαν. πολλοὶ δὲ διδακταῖς ἀνθρώπων ἀρεταῖς . . .

44. See Luschnig (1975–76, 231).

45. This is the conclusion reached by Boella, who sees the moralizing material as simply an intrusion with no aesthetic value (1964, 136).

particular contemporary stance or view as suggest a truth that is inherent in the Sophistic movement and that it is the office of poetry to reveal.

III. Rhetoric and Persuasion

Because Euripides used the antitragic and even antipoetic themes of the Sophistic in creating his new approach to tragedy, it follows that rhetoric and rhetorical technique are a natural part of his style. But in this play rhetoric becomes a theme that has a particular and overt application to the case of Hekabe. As Conacher and Buxton have pointed out, Hekabe is faced again and again with a verbal contest (*agôn*) in which her role must be to persuade an indifferent or hostile audience to her side.[46] The old woman relies at first on the sheer pathos of her situation and on the justice of her cause to win sympathy and help. But this reliance proves worthless; and eventually, under the goad of utter desperation, Hekabe learns to adopt other techniques that lead to success.

Hekabe's first attempt at persuasion forces her to try her skill on the master of trickery himself, Odysseus; and in this she fails. Her second attempt, on an easier subject, is a success; and in the final *agôn logôn* she confutes her enemy Polymestor decisively, in a dazzling display of technique. Hekabe's progress in the techniques of persuasion parallels her steady descent on the moral plane. The theme of education, learning, and nobility that is introduced and fixed by the second episode has applications forward to the changes undergone by Hekabe, as well as backward to the refusal of Polyxene to live in a world of change and degeneration.[47]

The first mention of rhetoric occurs before the opening of the first scene, in the parodos (120–40). There, we hear of the speakers in the Greek assembly who argued for or against the death of Polyxene. Agamemnon, we learn at this early point, is on Hekabe's side, τὸ μὲν σὸν σπεύδων ἀγαθόν, because her daughter Kassandra has become his concubine (120–22). The opponents of Agamemnon, rather surprisingly, are the sons of Theseus. Although the Theseidai have some connections in the cyclic epics both with events after the fall of Troy and with Thrace, their injection here is

46. Conacher (1967, 163ff.); Buxton (1982, 170ff.). See also Tierney (1946) on lines 1132, 1187, 1240; and Sheppard (1924, 77, 84).

47. Critics are widely agreed that Hekabe degenerates from her previous noble status; see Conacher (1967, 165) on Hekabe's degradation: "only in characters such as Polyxena can *aretê* survive in splendid isolation." See also Matthaei (1918, 156), Grube (1941, 214). Hajistephanou (1975, 89–91) points out that in fact Hekabe's behavior consistently contrasts with that of Polyxene throughout. But this of course does not mean that Hekabe does not degenerate as well. It is the same chicken-egg problem of *physis:* Hekabe does not possess her daughter's inherent strength, and this makes her more prone to take bad instruction.

sufficiently gratuitous to attract some notice.[48] There might be an implication that Odysseus is in the right, since these figures of local myth are on his side. But the language used to describe Theseus' sons also pushes the audience to associate these figures with rhetoric and Sophistic debate.

Several odd usages converge, forcing us to make an association between the council of the Greeks and an Athenian assembly. First, there is the fact that the obscure sons of Theseus (called "offshoots of Athens") are mentioned here at all. Second, there is the collocation of two contemporary terms: the Theseidai are speakers (*rhêtores*) of "double arguments" (*dissoi mythoi/logoi*). *Rhêtôr,* as we see from Aristophanes, was the everyday term for the political leaders of the democracy.[49] Since the word appears nowhere else in Euripides, it is likely to represent for the audience a borrowing from nonpoetic usage and it should be understood here as it is usually understood there.[50]

The term *rhêtôr,* at least in the fourth century, could also refer to a polished and trained speaker, a master of the trade of rhetoric (*rhêtorikê technê*). In the absence of prose usage, we have no direct way of knowing whether this second meaning was already extant in the time of this play.[51] But the connection to rhetoric in any case is assured by the reference to the *dissoi mythoi* of the Theseidai. They as twins, of course, are "double"; and their arguments therefore are dual, though with a single import. But a reference in the late *Antiope* establishes the Sophistic meaning of the "double

48. Homeric epic does not mention the Theseidai, presumably Akamas and Demophon; but they did appear in the *Iliou Persis.* The Theseidai were associated with the Thracian Chersonnesos in myth, s.v. Akamas, *RE* 1144b (Reisch), Röscher 206b. I could find no evidence to support Lesky's statement ([1956] 1972.1, 330) that in the *Iliou Persis* Akamas and Demophon sacrificed Polyxene.

49. See e.g., *Ach.* 38; *Knights* 60, 358, 1350; *Thes.* 292, etc.

50. The word appears in no extant non-Euripidean tragedy; Sophokles may have used it once, with the meaning of *kritês* (*TGF* 1090). The word makes an appearance in *Peirithoos,* a play sometimes attributed to Euripides, in a strikingly anachronistic context (fr. 597.4 N2): a noble nature (*physis*) is more dependable than the law (*nomos*). The former cannot be altered by a mere *logos,* but as for the law, a *rhêtôr* can twist it at will:

ἄνω τε καὶ κάτω
ῥήτωρ σπαράσσων πολλάκις λυμαίνεται.

51. We can trace the development of meanings in the fourth century quite clearly. Platon's usage shows how *rhêtorikê* can be kept separate from *rhêtôr* to avoid confusion. In *Gorgias, rhêtôr* always can be translated as "politician" or "public speaker," while references to *rhêtorikos* and *rhêtorikê* abound; see 455a3, 457a5, 468d2. Note 520a7, where *sophistês* and *rhêtôr* are contrasting terms. It does not make sense, therefore, to assume that, because *rhêtôr* means "politician" in fifth-century usage, the cognate terms such as *rhêtorikê* were not yet in existence.

arguments" (*dissoi logoi*) for that date,[52] while the association of the "double arguments" with Protagoras and *Clouds* indicates strongly that they belong in the period of *Hekabe* as well.[53] Thus democratic leaders who are public speakers are associated with professional training in rhetoric at this early point in the play.

The characterization of Odysseus, which immediately follows, is in the same vein. Already in epic Odysseus is the master of speech, persuasion, and counsel.[54] Now his traditional wiliness (*poikilophrôn kopis*) is explicitly linked with demagoguery (*hêdulogos dêmocharistês*): the sons of Theseus have prepared the way for a dual vision of Odysseus, as mythological figure and as modern politician.[55] Odysseus is both judge and rhetorical opponent in Hekabe's first attempt at persuasion. He opens the scene briskly, advising Hekabe not to resist violently and to recognize her own powerlessness. But Hekabe is not inclined to yield. She responds, "Alas, it seems that I am presented with a great contest (*agôn megas*), full of groans and not empty of tears."[56]

She proceeds to attempt to persuade Odysseus to spare Polyxene, reminding him that he owes her *charis* for a favor in the past. The event, in which a disguised Odysseus was saved by Hekabe at Helene's intercession, is not a familiar tale;[57] but it places Odysseus in the past in a situation exactly symmetrical with that of Hekabe in the present. Odysseus, clad in rags and in the disguise of a blind cripple, was Hekabe's slave (δοῦλος ὢν ἐμὸς τότε, 249), dependent on her for his life. Blindness, the same handicap that Hekabe will later inflict on her enemy Polymestor, seems to make a strong male like Odysseus equivalent to Hekabe in weakness. Like Hekabe now, he was then "lowly" (*tapeinos*) in attitude; and he supplicated desperately for her help. Of course, if Odysseus was using the tricks of rhetoric on that occasion, then what Hekabe sees as a bond between the two was to Odysseus only part of a

52. *Antiope* was put on with *Phoinissai* in 410 (see the scholiast to *Frogs* 53 [276 Dübner]). Fr. 189 N2:

> ἐκ παντὸς ἄν τις πράγματος δισσῶν λόγων
> ἀγῶνα θεῖτ᾽ ἄν, εἰ λέγειν εἴη σοφός

53. See the comments of O'Brien (1967, 75 n.47) on *Antiope* and on Protagoras.

54. See Detienne & Vernant (1974) on Odysseus as a model of craft (217–18); on his skill at *mêtis* (227).

55. See Buxton's discussion of this passage (1982, 172). The mock history of rhetoric naturally picked Odysseus as the first practitioner; see pp.4–5, fr. 4–9 Radermacher.

56. 229ff., *agôn* is naturally susceptible to interpretation as meaning simply "suffering" or, metaphorically, "trial"; see Paley (1874, 531); but, given contexts already established in this play, the rhetorical implication cannot be suppressed.

57. In *Od.* 4.242ff., Hekabe did not appear; and Odysseus did not pretend blindness; see Abrahamson (1952, 124–25).

successful deception.[58] Hekabe, in blaming Odysseus for treachery, seems to confirm the link between her yielding and his verbal skill, since she begins by attacking the whole race of demagogues: "You who seek political honors (*dêmêgorous timas*) are a thankless breed; I would not know you, who think nothing of harming your friends, if only you speak to please the many."[59]

Hekabe's speech falls into two parts. First, she argues the merits of the case: Polyxene has done nothing to Achilleus or the Greeks for which she deserves death. The legal and moral part of the argument is carefully set off from the aspects of the plea that are intended to persuade by other means (271).[60] In the orators too the question of justice (*dikê* or *to dikaion*) is often bolstered by an appeal to the self-interest of the jurors.[61] But since it is to the speaker's advantage to confuse the motive of gain (*kerdos*) and that of *dikê* as much as possible, the kind of overt division that Hekabe makes here is unusual and has contradictory effects. In spite of the rhetorical elegance, the audience may be faintly disturbed by a division that leaves ethical issues in such a vulnerable position. Next, supplicating Odysseus as he once did her, Hekabe asks to have returned now the favor (*charis*) that she gave then, pointing to her annihilating misery and her dependence on Polyxene as her one support.

Hekabe's plea is eloquent and forceful, but it is not likely to be effective. At the opening and the close, when the speaker attempts to rise to a peak of pathos, her anger and her violent contempt for Odysseus break through her cajoling speech and rather spoil its effect.[62] She concludes with the sarcastic suggestion that he persuade the Greeks that it is "a shame [*phthonos*] to kill women that you didn't kill at first, when you dragged them away from the altars."[63] Even in her peroration, Hekabe's rage (recognized by Odysseus at

58. "What did you say then, when you were my slave?" she asks. And he responds, πολλῶν λόγων εὑρήμαθ᾽, ὥστε μὴ θανεῖν, "many verbal inventions, to avoid death" (249–50).

59. μηδὲ γιγνώσκοισθ᾽ ἐμοί (255), a somewhat unusual phrase. Tierney (1946) translates, "Would you were unknown to me!" Sheppard (1924) translates, "May I not even know you!" The latter points out that the offensive lines are phrased impersonally so as not to pose a direct affront to Odysseus. But the affront is clear enough; cf. *Il.* 9.312–13. Hekabe's reference to *philoi* is a moral standard of the aristocratic past—see Kovacs (1976, 37–39); Sheppard (1924) on line 606.

60. Noted by Buxton (1982, 175).

61. This usually occurs as part of the closing plea; see Lysias 7.30, 18.24, 19.61–62, 21.22.

62. Conacher (1961, 16–17) sees Hekabe as a "brilliant" and accomplished orator from the start. But her eloquence, like that of Medeia, is designed to sting her opponent, not to convince him (*Med* 473–74). See 251–57; Hekabe begins οὔκουν κακύνῃ, and proceeds to denounce the "thankless breed" (ἀχάριστον . . . σπέρμα) of politicians.

63. 288–90. Following H. Weil (1879, 234) editors have been content to agree with the scholiast, referring *phthonos* to "the indignation (*nemesis*) which such impious murder would excite" (Heberden [1901]; cf. Boella [1964]). I would see this as a racy colloquialism, built on the idiom οὐδεὶς φθόνος; see *Rep.* 5.476e5, *Timaios* 23d4, Aischylos *Prom.* 628. The scholiast

line 299) deforms her attempt to plead; her words are charged with a transparent and awkward malice: "Your reputation [*axiôma*], even if you speak ill, will persuade . . ."[64] Hekabe certainly does not suppose that Odysseus, whom she has repeatedly characterized as a practiced orator, will not speak well. Her sarcasm must be meant to imply that he has no reputation (*axiôma*) on which to rely.

Hekabe's inability to maintain an appropriate rhetorical mode in her appeal for pity is founded in her own sense of the falsity of that mode. In order to work, the appeal to justice and pity must assume a concern for these values in the audience, must indeed flatter the audience by presuming, and by making them believe, that they are themselves *dikaioi* and full of an *axiôma* that must be maintained by further good acts. Since Hekabe's experience of Odysseus and the Greeks indicates that he and they are lawless and cruel, her plea carries an inherent contradiction that she is not skillful enough to conceal or assimilate. Then too, Odysseus is not concerned to appear fair and just to Hekabe. Being only a slave, and an enemy slave at that, she has no leverage with a man whose value (*axiôma*) derives from his powers as a demagogue. Her appeal may be moving and effective for us, the audience; but its failure with Odysseus can hardly be surprising.

Odysseus' response we may take to be the epitome of a good and convincing argument. We have heard that he is a man of low morality and consummate verbal skill; what he says, therefore, will have less weight as showing his true thought, and more as indicating his way of arguing. And indeed his arguments are the same as those reported in the parodos. He begins with an apposite lesson in rhetorical technique: "Hekabe, be instructed (*didaskou*). Do not by being angered make one who speaks well hostile in mind."[65] When Odysseus advises Hekabe to learn, the inappropriateness of such advice to one of her years enhances its piquancy, and prepares for other, clearly thematic, references to learning and teaching. His claim to be willing

---

to Aristoph. *Ploutos* 87 (p. 329 Dübner) cites this passage as indicating that *phthonos* can mean *mempsis* (also, Eustath. *Od.* 1422.14). The οὐδεὶς φθόνος idiom, a colloquialism equivalent to "It's no problem" (see the modern Greek 'δὲν πειράζει), gives rise to its obverse, which has a tone of heavy sarcasm. The rest of what Hekabe says is certainly meant to be insulting. The implication that Greeks are in the habit of killing or dragging away refugees at altars picks up the death of Priamos (*Hek* 23 – 24) and the rape of Kassandra.

64. 293: τὸ δ' ἀξίωμα, κἂν κακῶς λέγεις, τὸ σὸν / πείσει. The text is doubtful; but the reading λέγει does not materially change the interpretation, unless (as in Sheppard [1924]) the verb is treated as a passive. Editors rather perversely translate, "Even if you seem to speak in a bad cause, " or "even if you say unpleasant things," (Boella [1964]). But the sense of the line is quite plain; cf. Ennius (fr. 84 Jocelyn and nn. 307 – 8)—haec tu etsi perverse dices; and Helene's apology, *Tro* 914.

65. 299 – 300. Τὸν εὖ λέγοντα is ambivalent, presumably between "having rhetorical talent" and "one who speaks well to you."

to save Hekabe's life is in no way indicative of his sincerity,[66] although it correlates with other offers made to Hekabe and with her own statements about her prospects. Odysseus' reason for supporting human sacrifice is public and patriotic: *charis* owed to Achilleus, unlike that owed to Hekabe, has concrete political significance, since the Greek nation cannot subsist without public confidence that public service will be rewarded.[67] The issue of whether the *charis* requested in this instance is appropriate or not never comes up in Odysseus' formulation. For him, all questions of values are to be measured only in public terms.

Having disposed of the merits of the case, Odysseus briskly passes on to Hekabe's appeal to the emotions. "If you say that your sufferings are pitiable, hear this reply. We have on our side no less wretched old gray crones,[68] even older than you—and brides bereaved of the best of grooms, whose bodies this Trojan dust hides." For Odysseus, when Greek suffering is juxtaposed with Trojan suffering, the former alone is worthy of consideration. Further, unlike all other speakers, who profess pity at Hekabe's sufferings, Odysseus is unmoved. He finds her appeal hackneyed: as his brutal language suggests, old and wretched women are nothing new.

He ends with a retort that underlines the pro-Hellenic bias of his speech: unlike Greeks, barbarians do not honor those who have died well. They deserve misfortune, therefore, as the Greeks deserve success. This is a shallow and unconvincing argument, but it cannot altogether lack appeal.[69] As in Iason's arguments against Medeia, weak rationalizing by an unsympathetic character is propped up with Hellenic chauvinism. The hearers feel a reflexive desire to agree, while at the same time they sense the rage of Hekabe and Medeia at these maddeningly unfair and frivolous exercises in

66. Abrahamson (1952, 123) points out that Odysseus is "a master at specious reasoning." For a kinder view, see Sheppard (1924), who cites line 395; and Kovacs (1976, 39ff.). But, after what we have been told about Odysseus, such perfunctory regrets are unlikely to change our view of him. When Adkins (1966.1, 198) argues that fifth-century Greeks would have had no basis for condemning a human sacrifice unless somebody could argue that it was *aischron,* he confuses complex moral issues with the limitations of moral terminology. Stylistic reasons do mute Hekabe's attack on the sacrifice; for a way in which *aischron* can be attached to such a death, see *Tro* 1191.

67. 310–11:

θανὼν ὑπὲρ γῆς Ἑλλάδος κάλλιστ' ἀνὴρ
οὔκουν τόδ' αἰσχρόν . . .

Note the contrast between the noble (*kalon*) and shameful (*aischron*), an important theme for the play.

68. 322–23: ἄθλιαι / γραῖαι γυναῖκες, suggests *graus,* a mild term of contempt in Plutarchos' anecdote about Perikles and Elpinike, *Per.* 10.

69. See the comment of Tierney (1946, 64): Odysseus shows a Sophistic "skill in representing as a token of higher civilization what was in fact a savage crime."

casuistry. In this case it cannot be easy for the audience to set aside sympathy with a character in whose suffering they will by this point have made a substantial emotional investment. One clear impression, however, must emerge: Hekabe is hopelessly far from having any effective means of persuading the Greeks or reaching a ground of common interest with them. Her case is desperate indeed.

The second *agôn* is preceded by a brief scene that presents the climactic event for the sake of which the complex plot was designed. Hekabe, who has just heard of Polyxene's death and intends to bury the body herself, sees that the maidservant is carrying a body and assumes it to be that of Polyxene (671). The woman had in fact been sent to the seashore to get water for cleansing Polyxene's body (609 – 10); but Hekabe's confusion is believable, and the audience will have corresponding difficulty in remembering where she had sent the servant. As Hekabe bends over the body and removes its covering, the grief that she has already learned to bear is replaced by a new, unforeseen, and climactic bereavement. The moment oddly resembles the tricking of Aigisthos in Sophokles' *Elektra,* and both plays are probably drawing upon the same traditional material. The Sophoclean version uses the scene type in a more natural way: Orestes in his vengeance on his enemy wants Aigisthos' experience of his *peripeteia* to be *pikron,* sharp and bitter. But the maidservant has no motivation to torture Hekabe, and the irony in what she says expresses only the bitterness of her own grief.[70] The cruelty of the *Hekabe* scene is generated by the structure of the play, which has been engineered for this moment of supreme coincidence.

Hekabe's violent reaction to this torment is appropriately expressed in lyric; and, as in the first scene, the close of the lyric finds her again confronting a verbal contest (*agôn logôn*), with a second Greek lord to persuade. She wants Agamemnon's help in revenging herself against Polymestor, the murderer of Polydoros. Because he is already connected to her through his love for Kassandra, Agamemnon is an easier subject than Odysseus; but Hekabe does not embark on this second attempt at persuasion with the vigor and impetuosity that she displayed in the first. There, in spite of Odysseus' dissuasion, she threw herself into the struggle without hesitation. Here, although Agamemnon expresses concern, she turns aside from him and debates with herself her prospects for success (736ff.). The social awkwardness of the moment emphasizes the new role of calculation and strategy in Hekabe's actions;[71] but at the end, she decides once again in favor of

70. Hekabe replies with equal irony (670); for a different interpretation, see Tierney (1946).

71. Orban (1970, 329) suggests that Hekabe "a trop souffert pour être responsable"; in support, see Sheppard (1924, 75). Boella, however, points out the coldness and clarity that Hekabe displays (1964, xiii) in the second part of the play.

activism, remarking with a determination that we now see to be characteristic, "I must dare it, whether I win or not."[72] Agamemnon is struck by Hekabe's misery and the enormity of Polymestor's crime; and indeed even the cynical Odysseus could not now dismiss her suffering as common or easily surpassed. But the sympathy of her hearer and the extremity of her plight are not themselves sufficient to win Hekabe's case. She will not persuade even Agamemnon without changing her whole approach to persuasion.

Hekabe begins in the same way as she began her original plea to Odysseus, with an argument according to moral principles.[73] She lists the various circumstances that make the crime more heinous: Polymestor was a host (*xenos*), he killed the boy deliberately, and he did not bury the body but cast it into the sea. "We may be slaves and weak," she cries, "but the gods and the law [*nomos*] that rules them are strong. For it is by custom [*nomos*] that we believe in the gods and that we distinguish just from unjust in our lives."[74] In contrast to other Euripidean plays, *Hekabe* does not make use of gods as agents in the action: no divinity will emerge at the end to set the myth into perspective. Hekabe herself seems to be a modernist in religion; and her formulation leaves it open that the gods may be, as contemporary thinkers hinted, a product of social convention.[75] But Hekabe still leans strongly on the conventional standards of right and wrong; according to these standards, Polymestor has performed an action of egregious evil that demands punishment.

The appeal to morality is followed by Hekabe's strongest appeal to pathos.

72. 751: τολμᾶν ἀνάγκη κἂν τύχω κἂν μὴ τύχω.
73. Cf. line 271.
74. 799–801:

> ἀλλ' οἱ θεοὶ σθένουσι χώ κείνων κρατῶν
> νόμος· νόμῳ γὰρ τοὺς θεοὺς ἡγούμεθα.
> καὶ ζῶμεν ἄδικα καὶ δίκαι' ὡρισμένοι.

Lanza (1963, 416–22) discusses this passage at length, showing its links to other fifth-century formulations about the concept of *nomos*. In attempting to explicate this passage, however, he assumes, as I would not, that a uniform concept of *nomos* will emerge from comparing various passages in the play.

75. The passage plays upon the phrase *hêgeisthai theous* (more commonly, *nomizein theous*, to believe in/worship gods) to imply a link between *nomos* and the gods. H. Weil (1879, 268) complains that "Euripide n'a pas assez distingué ici l'existence réelle des dieux et leur existence dans la pensée des hommes." The failure to be clear is intended. Boella (1964) suggests that the passage may mean that the idea of justice creates the necessity for gods to exist. This is somewhat persuasive, but as in the case of other glorifications of *nomos,* the implications for our belief in the gods are not good. See Massimi (1960, 46) and Tierney (1946, on line 800ff.) on these contradictions and ambiguities. Vernant, discussing the traditional value system around *dikê* and *nomos,* remarks that we confront "un univers de valeurs ambiguës, où rien jamais n'est stable ni univoque" (1968, 248).

Agamemnon is to "stand aside like an artist and contemplate the evils that I suffer."[76] In the reversal of her previous prosperity, Hekabe is truly "the most wretched of mortals" (811). Her invitation to Agamemnon to contemplate the picture she presents points to Hekabe's confidence that, just as her ethical argument (according to *to dikaion,* 271) is extremely strong, so her appeal to pity is extreme. Hekabe is virtually a test example of unjust suffering: and, if the appeal to justice and sympathy can ever work, it must be in this case. The audience, too, who have seen the arbitrarily cruel workings of Hekabe's torment, may mentally step aside at this point and contemplate Hekabe with equal degrees of pity and detachment. It is a very Euripidean moment.

But the plea does not work. Hekabe notices that Agamemnon betrays by his physical gesture, turning aside from her (812), that he is unmoved and unwon. "It seems I will accomplish nothing, poor wretch that I am," she cries. At this point occurs another of those moments of significant inconsequence that are a common device of Euripidean drama. Hekabe, contemplating her apparent failure, wonders why people are reluctant to acquire the all-important art of persuasion (*peithô*). "Why do we mortals then toil at other lessons [*mathêmata*] and practice them as we ought; but persuasion, who alone is tyrant among humans, we still do not pursue effectively, paying money [*misthous didontes*] to learn [*manthanein*] . . ." The appearance of so many terms from the contemporary debate about the new art of rhetoric suggests an explicit analogy between Hekabe's situation and contemporary life.[77] As in the previous references to *physis* and *trophê,* the anachronism enlarges the significance of what Hekabe says beyond whatever meaning it

76. 807 – 8:

οἴκτιρον ἡμᾶς, ὡς γραφεύς τ' ἀποσταθεὶς
ἰδοῦ με κἀνάθρησον οἷ' ἔχω κακά.

Murray's proposal to emend *grapheus* (painter) in line 807 to *brabeus* (judge, referee) is not persuasive. Platon's usage provides evidence for the change from the ambiguous *grapheus* (which could also mean writer) to the unambiguous *zôgraphos.* (*Grapheus* is used in *Rep.* 377e2, in conjunction with *graphein;* see 601c11. But *zôgraphos* is used just above, probably because we are not to think of a craftsman painting *on* the leather reins.) It is true that analogies with fine arts are rare, but *Hekabe* in particular is rich in them (see line 560, and perhaps 786, if we are to think of a personified figure of cosmic misrule). Hekabe's status as a typical and exemplary figure of misery has been mentioned already. The word used for gazing or contemplation (ἀναθρέω) is so rare as hardly to possess a context; it is used once in Thukydides (4.87.1) for close contemplation. It may, of course, be a technical term from painting; but we have no way of knowing.

77. Key terms such as *misthos* (pay, salary) suggest the common reproach of commercialism directed at the Sophists; see Boella (1964, 97), H. Weil (1879, 269), Avery (1982, 153). For *peithô,* see Platon, *Gorgias* 453a2. For *mathêma* (cf. *manthanein*), see Tierney (1946, on line 814) who suggests the Sophists may have been the first to use this term. For *spoudazein,* see discussion below. Further comments by Benedetto (1971.1, 88 – 89).

could hold for her own dramatic character. Ostensibly, she merely under-lines her own lack of persuasive skills; but people who are paid to teach per-suasion do not appear inside the world of myth, and therefore what Hekabe describes cannot serve to distinguish her from practiced speakers like Odys-seus. Rather, her speculations about the value of training in *peithô* can have only a vague and prophetic significance, introducing the fifth-century future as something dreamed about in the mythological past and encouraging the audience to make the connection with their contemporary world.[78]

After this preface, Hekabe describes her second attempt at persuasion with an openness typical of fifth-century rhetoric. "Perhaps it is an empty aspect of my argument to mention sex—yet still it will be said." The terms she uses to make her argument are equally frank, even vulgar: "My child sleeps against your ribs. . . . How will you show [your appreciation for] those dear nights, my lord; or what favor [*charis*] for intimate embraces in bed will my child have of you, and I of her?"[79] The role that Hekabe assumes here is quite plain: without really having done anything to deserve it, she is taking to herself the status of pimp.[80] Sexual services should win something for the daughter, and something too for the woman who bore her. Even among the tribe of "poor old women" (ἄθλιαι / γραῖαι γυναῖκες) there are few who sink to a more despised status than Hekabe does here.

Hekabe goes on to argue that "From darkness and the charms of night comes the greatest *charis* for mortals."[81] The argument suggests the *Helene* of Gorgias, where, defending the most beautiful of women against offended sexual morality, the rhetorician likened the charm of the *logos* to that of *erôs* itself, assimilating both to enchantments (*philtra*) and potions (*pharmaka*)

78. On anachronism in Euripides see Reckford (1968, 340). Boella (1964, xiv) complains that these passages disturb the coherency of Hekabe's character; and Tierney (1946, 59) cites the scholiast to line 254 (p. 281 Dindorf): καὶ ἔστι τοιοῦτος ὁ Εὐριπίδης περιάπτων τὰ καθ' ἑαυτὸν τοῖς ἥρωσι καὶ τοὺς χρόνους συγχέων. See also on *Orestes,* Fuqua (1978, 9 n.23), and Fresco (1976, 109).

79. 828 – 30:

    ποῦ τὰς φίλας δῆτ' εὐφρόνας δείξεις, ἄναξ,
    ἢ τῶν ἐν εὐνῇ φιλτάτων ἀσπασμάτων
    χάριν τίν' ἕξει παῖς ἐμή, κείνης δ' ἐγώ

For the language, see H. Weil (1879, 269), who deplores Euripides' lack of "délicatesse de senti-ment"; Casa (1962, 67 – 68) points out that the lines were amended in Ennius' version (fr. 90 Jocelyn); see also the traces of ancient critique in the scholiast to *Aias* 520 (p. 234 Elmsley), comparing Tekmessa's modesty and restraint: μαστροπικώτατα εἰσάγει τὴν Ἑκάβην λέγουσαν.

80. See Conacher (1967, 162; 1961, 23); Luschnig (1975 – 76, 232); Kirkwood (1947, 67).

81. Lines 831 – 32 have been unjustly suspected; see the note in Daitz's edn. (1973). Tierney (1946, 101) points out that the connection between *Erôs* and *Peithô* is a traditional one. See the detailed presentation of evidence from a variety of sources in Buxton (1982, 32 – 34, 38 – 39).

that intoxicate the mind and body.[82] The kind of rhetorical and erotic *charis* that Hekabe is now invoking, unlike that which she attempted to invoke earlier with Odysseus, is based not on a fair exchange of honorable service but upon the ability of sexual appeal to overmaster other considerations.[83] Immediately after, Hekabe moves to a daring and fallacious argument that will give Agamemnon a rationale, however meretricious, for assisting the dead Polydoros. "Do you see that dead man there? In helping him you will be helping a marriage relation [*kêdestês*] of yours." In no real sense is Hekabe or her son a relative by marriage (*kêdestês*) of Agamemnon's; the relation is quite another, and less honorable, one. Only the dazzling effect of erotic *charis* could make such a bizarre argument effective.[84]

Having made her most telling point, Hekabe states her intention to close, remarking, "My speech lacks one thing yet." This will presumably be the ending summary, which in conventional rhetorical style would recapitulate the speaker's arguments and conclusions. But the final plea is preceded by a formal introduction of its own that is astonishingly grotesque. "If there were a voice in my arms, hands, hair, and sole of foot, whether [contrived] by the arts of Daidalos or some god, all in unison would cling to your knees wailing and conjuring you with all sorts of arguments."[85] It might just be possible to tolerate the bizarreness of Hekabe's speaking anatomy, and to repress the picture of an eloquent foot embracing Agamemnon's knee, if the reference to Daidalos' arts did not suggest some actual grotesque realization of what otherwise could be mere wordplay.[86]

82. For these arguments in Gorgias, see Segal (1962, 104 – 05; 1982, 309ff.). On *pharmaka* and poetry, see also Pucci (1980, 25ff., etc.). The passages in Gorgias are *Helene* DK 2:82 fr. 11B 8 – 10 and 14.

83. *Charis* (variously translated as "favor," "charm," or "grace") has close attachments to sexual pleasure; see the analysis of Latacz (1966, 87), and Buxton (1982, 179).

84. For the sophistry of this argument, see Boella (1964, 99) and Conacher (1967, 162). The *kêdestês* takes part in a social relation whereby men exchange women; slaves taken in war are not given by their male relatives, who have been killed by the conquerors. Cf. the ode following this scene, and App. C.

85. 836 – 40:

εἴ μοι γένοιτο φθόγγος ἐν βραχίοσι
καὶ χερσὶ καὶ κόμαισι καὶ ποδῶν βάσει
ἢ Δαιδάλου τέχναισιν ἢ θεῶν τινος
ὡς πάνθ' ὁμαρτῇ σῶν ἔχοιντο γουνάτων
κλαίοντ', ἐπισκήπτοντα παντοίους λόγους.

Several editors mention the moving statues of Daidalos, e.g. H. Weil (1879, 270). If it is true that this particular feat of the technician would occur to the audience, we could see this passage as another oblique allusion to visual art.

86. For bathos, see comments on line 570 below. Tierney (1946, 103) remarks that "there is a certain exaggeration, not free from frigidity," in the passage.

This grossly bathetic language, in its ugliness and in its repellent flattery, provides a dissonant aesthetic effect that matches the moral bad taste of Hekabe's invocation of erotic *charis*.[87] The passage links the sometimes extravagant and forced style of early rhetoric to the moral contradictions in its methods of persuasion, and it drives both to extremes. The theme of physical decorum is raised also by the strange physicality of the image: to the conventions of moral, verbal, and physical behavior, *Hekabe* continually opposes a grotesqueness that is the appropriate expression of an inverted cultural tradition.

Hekabe closes on a moral argument, but its effect is tarnished by what preceded; and this final plea is appropriately introduced by a servile address to Agamemnon as "O master, o greatest light to all the Greeks" (841). The chorus' comment has ironic significance: they remark that laws define (*nomoi diôrisan*) necessity for mortals, so that friends become enemies and enemies, friends.[88] The phrase in Greek recalls Hekabe's earlier appeal to morality and the *nomoi,* but the ambiguities there inherent between *nomos* as humanly devised convention and *nomos* as source of dependable traditional standards have disappeared.[89] In this new formulation *nomos* has become only the arbitrary play of convention, constantly shifting and thus offering no fixed guide to morality.

Agamemnon's response lays out the problem of public and private in clear terms. It was apparent earlier that the Greeks had seen the death of Polyxene as necessary to maintain their social obligations to each other. Similarly, the vengeance of Hekabe against Polymestor will go contrary to Greek public policy, because Polydoros is an enemy (*echthros*) to them, while Polymestor is considered a friend (*philos,* 858–59). If Hekabe cares for Polydoros, that has no public significance (χωρὶς τοῦτο κοὔ κοινὸν στρατῷ); only as a private (and corrupt) *philos* can Agamemnon pursue Hekabe's interest. She responds with a general statement that again touches major themes of the play. The meaning of such concepts as "enslaved" (*doulos*) and "free" (*eleutheros*) has already been explored in the case of Polyxene, who died because she could not bear to have the name of "slave" (*doulê*), and who was concerned even in her last moments to die "free." Hekabe, by contrast,

87. It would be worth much to know whether Euripides is more directly alluding to inept use of figures of speech by early rhetors. The evidence is scanty, mostly limited to a few outré or poetic epithets; see Aristoteles, *Rhet.* 1405b35ff.

88. While line 800ff. is ambiguous, line 846ff. has been more often recognized as straightforwardly Sophistic; see Boella (1964, 100–1).

89. Kirkwood (1947) argued that Polyxene's death was an act in accordance with *nomos;* but this raises the question of the validity of *nomos* as an absolute standard all over again. On this, see Abrahamson (1952, 123–24 n.10), who points out that Odysseus' case could be presented much more powerfully than it is.

has been offered her freedom by Agamemnon (755) and has rejected it in favor of revenge. She argues here that "no mortal is free," since we are all at the disposal of one or the other outside force, whether that force is fate, or the vagaries of the mob (*ochlos*), or the ordinances of the laws (864–67).

Such a viewpoint fits the dramatic character of Hekabe, who has no experience of any middle ground between despotic power and slavery.[90] But what Hekabe says could also serve as an indictment of the kind of public policy that—in Polyxene's case—could demand, for the best of public reasons, the worst of deeds. The play, of course, takes no stand vis-à-vis democracy and the rule of the *ochlos;* instead, it uses this theme to mark a contrast between world views. Polyxene, who is the most devoted to the aristocratic standard of honor, also brings out the best in the Greek mob; Hekabe, whose view is more cynical, sees the relation between the politician (*dêmêgoros*) and the multitude (*plêthos*) as that between slave and master, manipulator and manipulated. The techniques of rhetoric that she embraces are used appropriately to manipulate Agamemnon, as Odysseus would use them to manipulate his master, the *ochlos.* This scene marks a turning point for Hekabe, just as the horrific discovery that precedes the scene marks a turning point in the plot. That the intensity of Hekabe's suffering should be reflected in a correspondingly intense drive to revenge will have been obvious to the audience through social and artistic convention,[91] and only the end point of the psychological process is permitted to appear.[92] When Hekabe firmly rejects even her freedom in favor of vengeance,[93] we realize that the play has created a situation in which a human being is given the very strongest reason imaginable to persuade and win over another; and, as Hekabe herself points out, this is what rhetorical training is made for.

The theme of the *ochlos* serves also to bridge a necessary gap in the play's structure. Rhetoric typically is exercised before *ochloi* and *plêthê;*[94] but Hekabe, because of the limitations of the drama, must exercise it on

90. See Kovacs (1976, 37ff.).

91. On revenge as a social convention, see Adkins (1960, 55); Meridor (1978, 28–32); Paley (1874, 515). As Adkins points out, the social values of the Greeks made revenge a virtual necessity for an individual who had suffered a loss of *timê*. Hekabe's need for revenge is obvious; but the audience must be reassured that, through her dream, she is able to identify Polymestor as the murderer.

92. Kirkwood (1947, 62) argued that the lack of psychological development indicates that the resolution to revenge is formed during the scene with Agamemnon. But he must ignore the significance of line 756 and make a false distinction between revenge through Agamemnon and revenge carried out by Hekabe herself.

93. She replies to Agamemnon's offer of freedom, "Not at all" (οὐ δῆτα, 756), a very firm refusal. See Boella (1964, 90).

94. For the relation of oratory to the *ochlos,* see Gorgias, *Helene* DK 2:82 fr. 11B.13, and remarks of Segal (1962, 108–9); and *Hipp* 986; *Or* 612, 871.

individuals. Emphasis on the *ochlos* reinjects into Hekabe's impromptu discovery of the arts of *peithô* the political elements that would otherwise necessarily be absent. The system of meanings that belonged to rhetoric as a cultural phenomenon is retained, with a slight realignment. Like the rhetoricians' pupils Hekabe is an aristocrat who despises the crowd. That the apprentice rhetor is a poor, widowed, and bereaved barbarian woman adds piquancy to the exercise but does not falsify it: Hekabe's plight and situation are precisely those best calculated to arouse pity in her audience and to provide an opening (*aphormê*) for the appeal to sympathy.[95] The play's design, with its arbitrary conjunction of random stresses, is on the aesthetic plane an indication of calculated artifice. The result of the experiment is a strong and convincing proof that success in rhetoric does not derive from appeals to pity, fairness, or moral standards.

Hekabe's third *agôn* is no contest at all, since the results are assured by the patronage of Agamemnon, already gained in the second. But dramatic trials, from *Eumenides* to *The Merchant of Venice,* are not less effective or significant for being rigged. It would be as impossible for Hekabe to lose her third *agôn* as it would have been impossible for her to persuade Odysseus in the first; but each scene is well suited to display respectively the components of rhetorical failure and success. This time it is Polymestor who makes an appeal for pity. His approach is naive and straightforward, since he assumes Agamemnon's goodwill. While Polymestor does explain the murder of Polydoros, much as Odysseus did Polyxene's sacrifice, on grounds of a rather farfetched realpolitik, his proclaimed motivation, that he killed the boy because he feared that a resurgent Troy would cause his people to suffer from a second Greek invasion (1138–44), is hardly calculated to flatter his audience. The rest of the speech, which relates Polymestor's sufferings at the hands of Hekabe and her friends, is couched in a tone of naive pathos.[96] The failure of such appeals in earlier scenes will lead the audience to expect his rejection, and they will not be confused by any strong sympathies for this speaker.

95. Appeals to sympathy were the specialty of one of the most innovative rhetoricians of the day, Thrasymachos of Chalkedon; see DK 2:85 fr. 6B. That he was known at the time of *Hekabe* is indicated by the reference in the *Daitaleis* of Aristophanes, in 427; see DK fr. 4A. On Thrasymachos' style, see Gotoff (1980). For Hekabe's suitability as a figure of pity, see Aristoteles, *Rhet.* 1386a6ff.: sufferings due to *tychê* provoke pity, because the sufferer is guiltless (*anaitios*). Also, 8ff., αἰκίαι σωμάτων καὶ κακώσεις καὶ γῆρας καὶ νόσοι ... ὀλιγοφιλία (διὸ καὶ τὸ διασπᾶσθαι ἀπὸ φίλων καὶ συνήθων ἐλεινόν) ...

96. Note that on the plane of dramatic economy the speech functions as the missing messenger's account of the revenge. An interesting touch is Polymestor's use of the interjection πῶς δοκεῖς (1160). H. Weil (1879, 38, on *Hipp* 446) calls it "parenthèse vive et familière"; see Tierney (1946). At this moment of supposedly pathetic reversal, it injects a jarring, faintly comic note— "And then—guess what!" See Stevens (1976, 39) on this colloquialism.

Hekabe begins her reply with another strong and highly significant piece of inconsequence. Like other references to rhetoric and persuasion, this passage acquires meaning precisely from its failure to mesh entirely with its immediate function in the play. Hekabe deplores the predominance of speech (*glôssa*) over reality (*pragmata*). To good deeds should correspond good *logoi;* to bad deeds, weak (*sathroi*) *logoi.*[97] There is no immediate application to her opponent, since Polymestor has not made any overt display of rhetorical method or any allusions to these techniques.[98] We must therefore see the reference of the passage in a broader context, in its application to Hekabe's continuing progress in the use of argument and persuasion. Introductions in which speakers state their difficulties in making an adequate presentation are a routine feature of fifth-century rhetoric and present an interesting instance of that art's propensity to self-exposure. Often the dangerous and specious skills of the adversary are deprecated, and frequently the speaker apologizes for his own lack of training.[99] What Hekabe says is founded in the paradox of a discipline that parades its skill in deception, while attempting to build arguments through the manipulation of moral themes.

Hekabe ends with a curse on learned or clever people (*sophoi*): all have ended badly and none has ever escaped. If the opening of the gnomic introduction is conventional, its close is not. The strange curse has loud reverberations of tragic irony,[100] since the speaker herself has become adept in the technique of saying bad things well.[101] Her denunciation of these professionals (οἱ τάδ' ἠκριβωκότες) exposes the self-destructive principles of contemporary rhetoric, while it reveals Hekabe's own moral vulnerability.

With her usual precision, Hekabe marks off this excursus as an introduction (*phroimion*) to her main *logos,* before passing on to the main argument. This argument is a reply to Polymestor's implied—though not really effectively presented—argument that he killed Polydoros as a service to the Greeks (1175–76). She argues that there can be no relation of *philia*

97. For the history of the very old opposition between reality and language, see Heinimann (1945, 42ff.).

98. Buxton (1982, 181) remarks that Polymestor is "not sophisticated"; cf. Tierney (1946, on lines 1132 and 1187ff.).

99. For a naive presentation of the paradox, see Antiphon 5.3–5. The speaker in Lysias 25.2 suggests that his opponents are either *adynatoi legein* or else liars. In Isaios 10.1, the opponents are bold liars who are *legein deinoi.* Lysian speakers very often apologize for inexperience, e.g., 12.3, 17.1, 19.1–2, 23.1. Cf. the opening of Polyneikes in *Phoin* 469–72, which also has a reference to rhetoric and *pharmaka.*

100. See Conacher (1967, 164; 1961, 25).

101. "To say unjust things well [τἄδικ' εὖ λέγειν]" (1191) is precisely the trick that Protagoras and others were accused of teaching; see North (1981, 243–44). The watchword of *Clouds* (882–84) is attached to Protagoras by Aristoteles, *Rhet.* 1402a24–28.

between barbarian and Greek and follows up with words that copy and distort her opponent's. "What favor [*charis*] were you pursuing in making these helpful efforts—was it that you hoped to be a marriage relation (*kêdestês*), or as a relative (*suggenês*)?"[102] The scornful questions apply with better force to the arguments of Hekabe in the second *agôn* than they do to any made by Polymestor.[103] Although she demolishes what she built then, Agamemnon's complicity has already been assured; and like any Sophist Hekabe keeps her contradicting *logoi* separate. She presents a persuasive motivation for Polymestor's acts: the argument that he killed the boy out of loyalty to the Greeks can be dismissed, since he did not act while they were still prosecuting the conflict and in need of money (1218ff.). While Hekabe denies Polymestor his attempt to make common cause with the Greeks, his allies, she herself pretends sympathy for the invaders of her country, who were "poverty-stricken and long estranged from their native land" (1220–21). Hekabe's emotions no longer prevent her, as they did in the first *agôn,* from appealing effectively to her audience; her hypocrisy is perfect.

The play has demonstrated that in the Greek view moral norms have no force as long as political goals are in question. It is thus only after her argument has cut the links of common interest between Polymestor and the Greeks that Hekabe is free to return to the question of values. Polymestor's present sufferings, she points out, are a proof that by seeking unjust gain and betraying friends one may lose everything. In closing she warns Agamemnon that if he supports Polymestor, "We will say that you enjoy vile men as being such yourself—but I won't insult my masters" (1236–37). The aposiopesis combines forcefulness with servility; but the latter is effective, while the former is otiose, since Agamemnon is already on Hekabe's side. The chorus close the *agôn* by a return to the theme of Hekabe's opening, as they piously remark that (morally) good content (*ta chrêsta pragmata*) always gives one material (*aphormas*) for *chrêstoi logoi.* Their lines stress once more the rhetorical nature of the contest between the two speakers. In relation to Hekabe's speech the significance is inverted and ironic. Good content was never enough to win Hekabe's arguments in the past; and her new techniques produce success that is independent of the quality of the material.

---

102. 1201–2: τίνα δὲ καὶ σπεύδων χάριν / πρόθυμος ἦσθα πότερα κηδεύσων τινὰ / ἢ συγγένης ὤν, ἢ τίν' αἰτίαν ἔχων Cf. line 1175, τοιάδε σπεύδων χάριν.

103. In Adkins' singular interpretation (1966.1, 203–7) Agamemnon was unaffected by Hekabe's pleas then (he "ignores this part of her speech" and thus "tacitly rejects" it) and is persuaded only now by this argument that Polymestor is not really a *philos* because he kept the gold for himself not the Greeks. Adkins admits that such a concept of *philia* as defined by or canceled by motivation does not fit his own models.

IV. Polyxene's Death Scene

The rhetorical education of Hekabe is now complete. We have yet to consider the revenge that she accomplishes and its effect on the shape and texture of the play. But first the themes and subjects developed in the series of agonal encounters must be reassessed in the light of the remarkable scene in which Polyxene's death is reported. As I stated earlier, that scene stands out as the only point of rest in an extraordinarily fast-moving and tense play. The scene sets up a model, the heroic end of Hekabe's daughter, by which we gain perspective on Hekabe's contrasting experience and sufferings.

Talthybios, who brings the news of Polyxene's death, is not brisk and hardhearted like Odysseus. He pauses first, struck with pity at the sight of Hekabe, wrapped in her robes and groveling on the ground. He then urges her to get up and to hear his story about Polyxene's death. Hekabe wonders whether the Greeks killed the girl decently (*aidoumenoi*) or dreadfully (πρὸς τὸ δεινὸν ἦλθεθ'), as killing one hated (*echthran*) (516). Talthybios partly answers the query by saying that Hekabe forces him "to gain double tears in pity at your child," since he wept to see her death and must now weep again to tell it.[104] The tale then will be not dreadful (*deinon*), but pitiful (*oiktron*); and we are prepared for the moving and even sentimental content of the speech to follow.

Polyxene's death occurred in a great assembly of all the Greeks, as of course it should have, given the reasons of state adduced by Odysseus for the sacrifice. We have noted the theme of the "crowd" (*ochlos*) in the references to oratory. Talthybios characterizes the assembled host as an *ochlos*, first in the first line of his narrative: "The whole mob of the Greek host was present in full numbers before the tomb for the sacrifice of your daughter."[105] Talthybios is told to quiet the host; and he boasts that, by bawl-

---

104. 518–19:

δiπλᾶ με χρῄζεις δάκρυα κερδᾶναι, γύναι,
σῆς παιδὸς οἴκτῳ.

Pucci (1980) used this line as the basis for an interpretation of *Medeia*. Although his work seems to me to rely too heavily on cross-references between plays, P. explores an interesting semantic vein that is also used with considerable subtlety in this play. In this case the use of the term "gain" (κερδᾶναι) is specially appropriate to the Polyxene narrative, with its invitation to indulge in a grief whose sharpness will be blurred by sentimental glamour. Our response to Hekabe herself, however, will also play upon our pleasure and lack of pleasure in contemplating her grief; cf. discussion of line 807ff., above.

105. 521. *Ochlos* is related to *plêthos* as English "mob" is to, e.g., "mass" or "multitude." See LSJ s.v. *ochlos*, I.2.

ing out, "Be quiet, silence!" several times he "made the mob still."[106] The repetition of *ochlos,* like the rather otiose detail given to the Herald's activities, has its significance, since the presence of the crowd is crucial to the death scene.

The setting of the sacrifice is familiar from the *Agamemnon* parodos: chosen youths (525) stand ready to hold up the victim, while the son of Achilleus officiates with libations to the shade of his father. But, as the sign is given to seize the victim and lift her up, Polyxene, abandoning her passive role, speaks out: "O Greeks who sacked my city, I die willingly. Let no one touch my body for I will offer my neck bravely. That I may die free, in the gods' name, let me loose before you kill me. Among the dead I am ashamed to be called slave, who am a queen."[107]

Polyxene showed in the first scene a horror of slavery; after listing its humiliations, ending with that of marriage to an inferior, the girl had said, "No! I let go this light from eyes that are free,[108] offering my body to Hades." The last ambiguous phrase suggests that Polyxene prefers to "wed death" rather than accept a low-born mate,[109] a suggestion that reflects back on her earlier statement that slavery makes her feel a longing for death (*thanein eran,* 358). Her wish to die with dignity matches her rejection of slavery and her concern that Hekabe should avoid an unseemly struggle with Odysseus (408). Just as Hekabe, by her physical gestures, shows her abjection and helplessness, as well as her desperate willingness to struggle on when hope is gone, so Polyxene's concern for physical dignity expresses her valuation of herself, her *axiôma* we might say, to use the term that Hekabe applies sarcastically to Odysseus.[110]

106. 533. "Still [Νήνεμος]" is "windless," a strong metaphor. See Boella (1964, 67): νήνεμος "presuppone 'inquietudine, agitazione.'" The multitude could, like the sea, be stirred up easily to violent action; see a reversal of this motif in *Aeneid* 1.148–53.

107. 547–52:

Ὦ τὴν ἐμὴν πέρσαντες Ἀργεῖοι πόλιν,
ἑκοῦσα θνήσκω· μή τις ἅψηται χροὸς
τοὐμοῦ· παρέξω γὰρ δέρην εὐκαρδίως.
ἐλευθέραν δέ μ', ὡς ἐλευθέρα θάνω,
πρὸς θεῶν μεθέντες κτείνατ'· ἐν νεκροῖσι γὰρ
δούλη κεκλῆσθαι βασιλὶς οὖσ' αἰσχύνομαι.

108. ἀφίημ' ὀμμάτων ἐλευθέρων φέγγος τόδε (367–68). I accept the reading of Blomfield; but reading ἐλεύθερον with the manuscripts would leave the meaning essentially unchanged.

109. Ἅιδη προστιθεῖσ' ἐμὸν δέμας. Literally, "putting my body next to Hades." The word *prostithêmi* is often used for marriage and adoption relations; see Hdt. 6.126.2. For Euripides, see *IA* 540, a similar context, and *Ion* 1545, of adoption. Hadley (1894, 60) calls Polyxene "the bride of Hades."

110. She wishes to die, "before meeting shame [that would be] unworthy [*mê kat' axian*]" (374, cf. line 408). See other references to *axion* and *axioma* (e.g., lines 293, 319, 381, 613).

Polyxene's bold speech catches the fancy of the *ochlos,* which roars its approval; and Agamemnon, working as always on behalf of the Trojan captives, orders her to be released (453 – 54). So far the scene has been conducted on a very high plane. The indignity of the manhandled *parthenos,* so pathetic and moving in the *Agamemnon* parodos, has been erased in this version.[111] The emendation of the tradition brings it into alignment with contemporary Hellenic mores, which dictated a very strict seclusion for unmarried girls.[112] The first step in modifying the picture of the sacrifice may have come in Sophokles' *Polyxene;* but we do not know how the death was described in that play.[113] What happens next, however, is quite astounding, could not and would not happen in the work of any other tragic poet, and requires the very closest attention.

Polyxene, stepping out of her captors' hands, deliberately disrobes herself, pulling down the front of her *peplos* and exposing breasts and a bosom that Talthybios informs us were "as lovely as a statue's."[114] She offers herself, kneeling, to Neoptolemos, giving him a choice of breast or neck for the stroke (563 – 65). The exact degree of Polyxene's nudity is not left to the imagination: she tears her robe down to the "midflank, by the navel,"[115] thus exposing the whole upper body along with the belly.[116] It is unclear why

111. See *Ag.* 232: the girl is hoisted like a goat over the altar; for the parallel between the two passages, see J. Schmitt (1921, 58). Fraenkel thought that Iphigeneia's robes had slipped off at line 239, κρόκου βαφὰς ἐς πέδον χέουσα (1950, 2:138); but see the objections of Lloyd-Jones (1952). Recently light has been cast on the matter by Sourvinou-Inwood (1971); see also Stinton (1976.1). Sourvinou emends Aristoph. *Lys.* 645 to read καταχέουσα, thus giving a motivation for the use of this verb in *Agamemnon,* where other words, e.g., *ataurôtos,* also suggest the rituals of Artemis. By placing hints of this gesture in a context suggesting purity and the lack of sexuality favored by Artemis, Aischylos has partly muted the incongruity involved in the implied sexuality of Iphigeneia's appeal; see discussion below. A further touch is the curious reminiscence of Iphigeneia's performances at banquets (*Ag.* 243 – 47), something that would have been unthinkable in contemporary Athenian society. It would seem that Aischylos is working to allay the discomfort caused by dissonance between heroic mores and contemporary mores; the aim of Euripides, of course, is just the opposite.

112. The *parthenos* belonged indoors and was not accustomed to see any nonfamily males; see Lysias 3.6, Xen. *Oik.* 7.6, and earlier Hes. *WD* 519 – 23, where the comfort of remaining indoors in winter is associated with the *parthenos,* whose beauty is sheltered and cared for, as she "lies deep inside the house [μυχίη καταλέξεται ἔνδοθι οἴκου]" (523).

113. See Calder's reconstruction (1966); the fragments make Agamemnon's role evident, but leave Polyxene's essentially in the dark.

114. 560 – 61: μαστούς τ' ἔδειξε στέρνα θ' ὡς ἀγάλματος κάλλιστα . . .

115. Polyxene tears her robe down from the shoulder blade (*epômis,* see Xen. *Mem.* 3.10.13), to the belly (λαγόνας ἐς μέσας παρ' ὀμφαλόν). Cf. such anatomical expressions in the *Ilias* (21.117, see 8.325) where the collarbone is referred to as παρ' αὐχένα, that is, beside and below the neck.

116. The degree of nudity is familiar in Greek art from such statues as the Venus of Arles. Paley (1874, 550) points this out, also citing Chairemon (*TGF* F14), where a maiden's dance has "freed her left flank."

Polyxene should disrobe to such an extent: she had earlier mentioned offering her neck, the usual place for the sacrificial blow.[117] She evidently hopes to win sympathy for her courage, as she does; but, as in many crucial moments in drama, when symbolic action is shown or narrated, the significance of this strange gesture is of greater import than its motivation.[118] In this brief passage, Euripides gives us in miniature some of the flavor of the great dramas of sexual shock that have been lost. Polyxene's bold action clashes with almost every context to which we can assimilate the scene, with social and literary tradition, as well as with other extant work of Euripides himself. This is Euripidean sensationalism at its most striking.

To us, who are used to the frequent detailing of female physical beauty in modern Western literature, it is hard to sense the rigidity of tragic decorum in these matters. In fact, in extant fifth-century tragedy, there is hardly a place where a woman's face or body is described as beautiful (*kalos*).[119] There is certainly no reference to breasts and their beauty anywhere else in tragedy.[120]

While nudity in informal art, such as vase painting, is not rare in the fifth century, nudity in full-size *agalmata* came later and hesitantly. On nudity, see *Encicloped. dell' arte antica,* s.v. *Nudo.* An interesting transitional example is the Niobid (datable between 440 and 430, see Ridgway [1981, 56]) who, kneeling in death, reveals a nude upper body, with the lower body draped. On this statue, see Seta (1930, 224–25). Euripides of course had his own effect on later art; see the painting (M. Schmidt [1965, 174 and pl. 59.1]) of a nude sacrificed maiden, with two wounds (one in the neck, one in the chest—an interesting iconographic reference to our passage), modestly concealing her genitalia with one hand. See also the late epigram of Pollianos (*AP* 16.150), and comment by Valgiglio (1966, 113 n.215).

117. *Sphazein* (549) properly means "to cut the throat," or "to sacrifice." See LSJ and Vermeule & Chapman (1971, 291 and n.18). The best representation remaining is the Tyrrhenian amphora *ABV* 97.27, discussed by Walters (1898).

118. See the comment of Taplin (1977, 312ff.) on the carpet scene of *Agamemnon.* Matthaei (1918, 134–35) suggests another symbolic significance, namely that Polyxene's physical perfection, like her willingness to die, marks her as the ideal sacrificial victim. This thematic significance complements the other, since the clash between the pious atmosphere pointed to by M. and the impious nature of the sacrifice parallels that between Polyxene's effect on the Greeks and the cynical view Hekabe takes of their sentiment.

119. *Kalê* or *kallistê* is not used to describe women or their bodies except here or in hymns to goddesses (e.g., *Hipp* 66). (The reference to Helene in *Tro* 772 makes a moral point; two others occur in this play [lines 636, 442] and are thus likely to be significant of the erotic atmosphere being developed in *Hekabe.*) The strong associations of *erôs* and *kalos* in everyday language apparently kept the word from being used in tragedy to describe physical appearance as readily as it had been in epic. Pagani (1970, 57) pointed out the way in which a strong enjambment emphasizes the epithet here.

120. Breasts are not mentioned at all, outside the context of nursing infants, except at *Andr* 629 (a reproach to Menelaos for being overcome by the sight of Helene's breasts and thus failing to avenge himself) and *Trach.* 925, where Deianeira denudes herself in the privacy of her own chamber, as she prepares suicide. For the changes in these conventions in the fourth century, see the valuable article by Piatkowski (1981). P. points out that physical description is largely absent from fifth-century drama, while in the fourth a code for such descriptions derived from visual art began to develop (206–8). Here, as in so much else, Euripides inaugurates cultural changes that

Descriptive language applied to female appearance tends to be conventional and is limited to brief qualifications of the neck, cheek, or foot of a woman as "white" or "well formed."[121] The dramatic situation itself is equally astonishing and anomalous. Polyxene's boldness sets her apart from every other Euripidean *parthenos*. They, without exception, show the modesty appropriate for Greek virgins, shrinking above all from contact with males in groups.[122]

If the audience's natural repugnance at seeing a young and chaste girl among a crowd of males has in this scene been ignored or lulled to sleep, we may be certain that the play will at some later point take advantage of that dissonance. We can already sense the elements of incongruity, for instance in the insistence on the presence and participation of the "mob (*ochlos*)."[123] The audience, while this conflict builds in the speech, will be torn between rejection of the scene and their natural tendency to accept what they see and hear on the stage. If the scene succeeds, the audience will be deeply moved; and the sensational and outré actions of Polyxene will be accepted as part of the abnormal and intense atmosphere of the high mimetic, where things occur that are not like everyday life.

Polyxene's action, if baffling in other ways, evokes a familiar complex of associations that has been admirably documented by W. H. Friedrich in "Medeia in Kolchis." The victim, threatened with a violent death, appeals by sexual charm to the sacrificer or avenger, who is often moved to turn aside

seem still embryonic in the late fifth century. Chairemon's seductive descriptions of females *en déshabillé* frequently allude to visual art; see *TGF* F1.5.

121. E.g., *Alk* 159; *Med* 30, 923, 1164; *Hel* 1570. There is no detail and no overt eroticism in these references; the parts of the body mentioned are those usually not covered by clothing. But even these are not entirely without sexual significance: Alkestis' blooming beauty is relevant to what she loses by choosing early death; in *Medeia* the heroine's return to a more emotional and appealing mode is signaled by the reference to her "white cheek," while the princess's innocent vanity enhances the pathos of her death. For *Ant.* 1239, a most significant reference to the "white cheek," see Chap. 3, above. Whiteness is significant simply of femininity, by artistic as well as social convention.

122. Most tragic virgins are timid about coming out, until reassured and commanded by a guardian. E.g., Antigone in *Phoinissai,* who appears jealously guarded by her *paidagôgos* and who shuns the chorus, that *ochlos gynaikôn* (196). Later, she is reluctant to face a group, until reassured by Iokaste (1264–66). In *Iphigeneia at Aulis* the heroine emerges into a nonfamily setting only at her mother's urging, and with reluctance (1338). Note especially the words of "Makaria," who also accepts a sacrificial death but who is reluctant to meet this death "in male hands [ἐν ἀρσένων . . . χερσίν]" (*Hkld* 565–66).

123. The semantic juxtaposition *parthenos/ochlos* is antithetic in Euripidean drama, and undoubtedly was so in ordinary language and thought of the day. See the note of Reckford (Review [1968, 232] of Benedetto [1965]) on the significance of *Or* 108. See also *Hkld* 44, *IA* 1030, *Phoin* 196.

his or her anger.[124] The suggestion of this motif appears in the *Agamemnon* parodos, and it would have been odd if Sophokles had not alluded to it in his lost *Polyxene*. In other versions of the Polyxene story, Polyxene's relation to Achilleus was a sexual one.[125] Since that part of the story has been suppressed in *Hekabe,* the element of sexual appeal emerges here rather suddenly, with a glaring and lurid intensity. But the conventional motivation for the appeal has been severely distorted. Polyxene uses nudity, not to enhance a plea for survival, but to win honor and respect from her captors; and there is an evident contradiction between her refusal to be touched and her provocative preparations for the sacrifice.

After signaling that the traditional seclusion of the *parthenos* has some relevance to the dramatic world of the scene, the play then flouts all such proprieties; and Polyxene's dying actions are more bizarre still. As Neoptolemos reluctantly cuts the throat of the girl, she dies with great care for decorum:

> She, though dying, still
> took great care to fall mannerly,
> hiding what must be hidden from the eyes of males.[126]

To put it bluntly, Polyxene's dignity in arranging her clothing as she falls dying is as impressive as it is improbable. Those who are charmed by Polyxene's death have good company in antiquity, as do those who are repelled and indignant.[127] The passage is "sentimental," in that its moral and

124. 1966. Suppliants come in both sexes, but in most cases a combination of sexual appeal and helplessness (which signifies sexual availability) is designed to bend the will of the attacker. Note, however, the prevalence of the typology, even in the Lykaon episode, *Il.* 21.34ff., where sexuality is not directly at issue.

125. There is no reason to assume that these stories are a late addition: the encounter of Achilleus and Polyxene at the spring where he killed Troilos was described in the *Kypria* (5:105.12 Allen) and depicted frequently in vase painting. On erotic and romantic themes in cyclic epic and their absence from Homeric epic, see Kullman (1960, 8–9); Griffin (1977, 40): "The fantastic, the miraculous, and the romantic all exceeded in the Cycle the austere limits to which the *Iliad* confines them." (See also p. 45, on Polyxene.)

126. 568–70:

ἣ δὲ καὶ θνῄσκουσ' ὅμως
πολλὴν πρόνοιαν εἶχεν εὐσχήμων πεσεῖν,
κρύπτουσ' ἃ κρύπτειν ὄμματ' ἀρσένων χρεών.

127. Favorable views: Steiger (1900, 392): "Friede und Grösse ruhen über der ganzen Darstellung"); King (1938, 84), a "vividly beautiful and imaginative narrative. It has upon Hecuba the calming effect that it must have on all its readers." Pagani (1970, 57–58): "Tutta la semplicità e la sublimità castissima di un momento estatico consumato in un clima di silenzio religioso: un trasalimento del poeta e della moltitudine nella contemplazione ammirata della bellezza e della virtu . . ." etc. See also Hartung (1843, 517); Rivier ([1944] 1975, 155). Mild discomfort is voiced by Cataudella (1939, 122): the scene is affecting, though a bit theatrical; Masqueray

aesthetic beauty is at odds with reality. Death is diminished here, where it comes second, not just to morality, but even to manners; and Polyxene's concern for appearance is correspondingly elevated to a very grandiose level. The passage was much admired in later antiquity and often quoted, and it produced a number of imitations: the chaste Lucretia and even Julius Caesar himself fell in equally good order.[128] But the long series of noble and unlikely death scenes modeled on this passage[129] reveal the gulf between Euripides and his numerous but not wholly legitimate posterity. None of the imitators produced a version as extreme as the original: a nicer observance of propriety in extremis would be hard to imagine, short of the *Mikado*.

The suggestion of the ludicrous rises very close to the surface at line 569, which emphasizes the self-conscious aspect of the girl's action: she took "great care [*pollên pronoian*] to fall in a mannerly [fashion] [*euschêmôn*]." Then, in an extra touch that pushes the passage just beyond the pale, Polyxene falls, "hiding what must be hidden from the eyes of males" (570). Hermogenes recognized and was disturbed by this line, which, with its excessive concreteness, injects many dissonant echoes.[130] But line 570 is not an anomalous mistake. It plays upon contradictions already built into the scene; and, when we are reminded of the difficulties in dying gracefully with one's clothing partly on and partly off, part of our discomfort derives directly from the earlier concrete description of Polyxene's body.

How could the audience respond to such a barrage of contradictory

---

(1908, 322–23). Cutting comments on Euripidean plays are often made glancingly, in discussions of the work of other playwrights; see Radt (1973, 122): comparing the *Agamemnon* description with *Hekabe*, "Um zu sehen, was 'an unnecessary piece of exhibitionism' ist, lese man die oft hier verglichene Szene bei Euripides *Hec.* 558ff., wo Polyxena, die sich *freiwillig* opfern lässt, sich trotzdem im letzten Augenblick ihr Kleid vom Körper reisst: der einzige Zweck den diese Gebärde dort hat, ist das Kitzeln der Sinnlichkeit, wie zum Überfluss die Aufzählung der entblössten Körperteile (559f.) und die unglaublich geschmacklose Hervorhebung des anständigen Fallens (568ff.) zeigt."

128. Later citations of the passage include Plinius, *Ep.* 4.11; Clem. Alex. *Strom.* 144.2 = 182 Stählin; Eustathios on *Il.* 2.262, 216.7 (1:328 Van der Valk) and Ps. Lukianos *Dem. Enc.* 47. Ovidius follows Euripides (*Met.* 13.479) but corrects his model: Polyxene requests that no male hands touch her in death and asks that her body be returned to Hekabe. For Lucretia, see Ov. *Fast.* 2.833; for Caesar, Suetonius 82. Seneca's Polyxene threw herself down *irato impetu* (*Tro.* 1158–59), so as to fall heavily onto the grave of her enemy. As often in Euripides, this is an amended version of the original: Polyxene now shows not mere decorousness in death but a proper resentment against her sacrificers.

129. Elegant death scenes may begin in literature, but they soon extend into literary accounts of real deaths (see the accounts of Sokrates, Theramenes, and others) and finally become a cultural norm; cf. the carefully stage-managed death of Augustus (Suetonius 99.1).

130. *De invent.* 4.12 (quoting 568–69): τοῦτο σεμνῶς εἰπὼν ἐπήνεγκεν εὐτελὲς καὶ κοινὸν καὶ κακόζηλον. See also the scholiast (p. 362 Dindorf), ἔπεσεν εἰς τὸ κακόζηλον ὅπερ κακίζουσιν οἱ ὀβελίζοντες.

signals? The scene has been promised to be pathetic, and indeed it is. Poly-xene's motivation, in so far as it has been established, is noble, brave, and decorous. Further, the picture of her nudity is appealing in the pathetic as well as the sexual sense: it imitates a familiar gesture of supplication that the audience will have recognized and enjoyed. Finally, the combination of apparent innocence and purity with sexual appeal permits us, as Talthybios does, to ogle Polyxene, even as we sympathize with her. The appeal to shameful pleasures is very satisfyingly blended with high moral tone: what audience could fail to indulge themselves? It is the same technique—here driven to harsh and glaring extremes—that Sophokles had employed so subtly in *Antigone*.[131]

The tensions built into the scene, the elements of "bad taste" and contra-diction, are delayed charges that will explode later, when the spell of the speech has passed.[132] The Euripidean trick depends upon the fact that audi-ences must trust and accept the world of the play as best they can, while the tenor of the scene maintains itself. Only when a change of mood has been signaled can a more critical viewpoint begin to emerge. If such a scene were presented without irony, then a sophisticated audience would probably experience an initial enthusiasm, followed by a sensation of uneasiness and distance that, perhaps after several more scenes of overdone and inappropri-ate pathos, might result in the failure of the play.

For the time, however, the audience will be held fast, charmed by the combination of sexual titillation and idealism, and stretching their credulity to accept the premise of the speech—that a decent girl by exposing herself before a crowd of males may win honor instead of humiliation. The same *ochlos* that roared applause at the girl's first words are now so powerfully affected by her dying gesture that they want to accord her the same honor, a public funeral rite, that is the mark of esteem for their own heroes.[133] The power of public opinion, always strong in the *ochlos,* is invoked against any Greek who fails to contribute something of his own to this best of women.[134]

Hekabe's response to this remarkable narration is the countering element that creates Euripidean irony. She begins with the striking excursus on inbred nobility (*gennaiotês*) that was discussed above. Hekabe's inconse-quence itself will serve to break the spell of emotion cast by the previous speech; and her excursus, which is a key to so many of the play's themes,

131. See Chap. 3, above.

132. See discussion of a similar technique in App. B on *Alkestis.*

133. Note that the *Kypria* reported that Neoptolemos had provided burial for Polyxene. The source is a scholiast to *Hek* 41 (pp. 229–30 Dindorf), who quotes the fifth-century Glaukos of Rhegion. On these legends see Jouan (1966, 368–71); Robertson (1970, 13); Förster (1883, 476).

134. 579–80: τῇ περίσσ᾽ εὐκαρδίῳ, ψυχήν τ᾽ ἀρίστῃ.

also has a number of applications to the contrast between herself and her daughter. It is immediately evident that the ability that enables the *gennaios* to make fine and precise estimations of the shameful (*aischron*), using the noble (*kalon*) as a standard, has been amply displayed by Polyxene in her death scene. Because of her aristocratic certainty of self, Polyxene could perform an action that would ordinarily be labeled *aischron* and make it *kalon*.

After Hekabe abruptly drops the reflective mode, she reacts to the message by rejecting the Greeks' honors to Polyxene: she will see to the funeral herself. She then passes to rather conventional reflections on the fall of the house of Priamos, which, in the wake of misfortune, appears to have been a mirage, composed rather of thoughts and words than of realities.[135] These generalities also have a direct application: the wealth and honor (*timê*) that marked Polyxene's early life made her unable to endure the world of slavery; but to Hekabe, that previous life was a mere appearance, a *schêma* (619). The difference between *kalon* and *aischron* too is a difference in appearance only, and there seems to be here a faint implied criticism of the standards for which Polyxene died.

The central portion of this speech, in which Hekabe declares her intention to perform the burial herself, contains a singular passage that virtually inverts the meaning of what Talthybios has told us. Lines 605–8 have been ignored by Euripidean apologists and detractors alike; Denys Page, however, was sufficiently struck by them to propose their excision as an actor's interpolation, although he was unable to suggest what might have inspired such an odd piece of tampering.[136] In fact the lines could not have been inserted by anyone except the artist who designed Polyxene's sublimely mawkish death scene. They are the dash of cold water that makes us aware of the incongruity and inappropriateness of all that we had accepted before. By doing so, they provide an effective transition from Hekabe's speculation that virtue may persist unchanged in adversity, a notion as idealizing and as unlikely as the death scene itself, to the end of the speech, in which we see that the transition from royalty to slavery is as swift as the awakening from a dream.

"Let no one touch her," says Hekabe. "Keep the mob (*ochlos*) from the girl, for in a numberless host the mob (*ochlos*) is licentious, and the anarchy

135. 626–27: τὰ δ' οὐδέν, ἄλλως φροντίδων βουλεύματα γλώσσης τε κόμποι.

136. 1934, 67: Page admits that sexually "indelicate" references are not usually interpolated. On the standards for determining interpolations, see the critical assessments of Page's work by Mastronarde (1978, 118, on a passage in *Phoinissai*) and Hamilton (1974, an attack on the notion that actors' interpolations were widespread in our texts).

of sailors is worse than fire—he is vile who does nothing vile."[137] In the first place, interpolation is out of the question, both because no rational motivation can be assigned, and because the passage exactly corresponds to Hekabe's first reaction to the Messenger's news. She asked there whether the Greeks treated Polyxene dreadfully, as an enemy, or not. Talthybios' reply made clear that the behavior of the Greeks was decent and modest (*aidoumenoi*); but Hekabe now returns to the second alternative, which clearly seems still the more likely to her. It is obvious what Hekabe hints at. She fears that the "mob of sailors" may violate Polyxene's body. Whereas the Herald had shown that the Greeks were vying with each other to honor Polyxene, Hekabe suspects that the power of mob conformity can work both ways;[138] and, though apparently convinced of the nobility of her daughter's gesture, Hekabe is not willing to trust the Greek reception of it. All the repressed discomfort generated by the aberrant situation in the previous speech is discharged to lend force to Hekabe's cynical and repellent suspicion. We have descended from the lofty plane of the high mimetic with a sudden and sickening movement.

For us, a reference to necrophilia at such a point in a serious drama would be a bizarre obscenity, so aberrant as to overstep entirely the boundaries of comprehensibility in a tragic context. But for the Greeks *erôs* was a disease of the eyes. Gorgias' assumption that the source of erotic attachment is the visual aspect of the beloved derives from an erotic tradition as old as Sappho.[139] In the fringes of Greek erotic lore appear a number of bizarre lovers who are seized with passion for the lifeless image of a human body—a statue, or a corpse.[140] Polyxene has already been described as offering such an image of physical perfection, when Talthybios likened her breasts to those of an *agalma,* a statue.[141] The myth of Laodameia and her statue underlines the

137. 608: κακὸς δ' ὁ μή τι δρῶν κακόν. On sailors, who were identified with the poorer class of citizens, see *IA* 914, *Frogs* 1070ff.; Platon (*Phaedr.* 243c7) depreciates the erotic habits of this group.
138. The question of mob values relates to the original decision to sacrifice Polyxene as well, since there too public policy seemed to lack a moral perspective outside its own interests; see Matthaei (1918, 137–38).
139. See Sappho 16.31, for the effect of a vision of the beloved. On the eyes, see Gorgias' theory of sense perception, in *Helene* DK 2:82 fr. 11B.15–16; see Platon *Phaedr.* 251b2, 255c6 and Sophokles *Oinomaos, TGF* F474.
140. For statues, see Lukian. *Erotes* 15–16. Pygmalion is attributable wholly to one Philostephanos (*RE* 39.109), who found the story on Cyprus. For an earlier story, see Alexis (40K) and Philemon (139K), Ath. 13.506f. See also the necrophiliac episode in Parthenius (31). The latter theme was worn out by rhetoricians; see Libanios *Prog.* 11.27 (8:435 Förster), and Philostratos, *Vit. Soph.* 261 (101K).
141. For the statue as a model of visual perfection, see also Chap. 3, above. This is one of several references to visual art in the play. Hadley (1894, 70) cites *Hipp* 631, and Platon *Charm.* 154c8, *Phaedr.* 251a, for the erotic import of the *agalma.*

logical connection between necrophilia and statue love: the lifeless statue, like the lifeless body of the beloved, can inspire a powerful *erôs,* or can assuage the pangs of loss, "cold delight though it is," as Admetos remarks.[142]

The fear of Hekabe therefore is not so far beyond the pale as to confuse the audience. Of course there is a distinction between the passion of Laodameia and what Hekabe is concerned with. She anticipates a violation, inspired by the crudest lust, in a mob of the vilest and lowest men. But, in another sense, we could say that she simply grasps the erotic element in the Greeks' admiration for Polyxene and inverts it, so that what at first seemed noble and high-minded becomes vile and crude. The *Aithiopis* seems to furnish a literary parallel: when Achilleus was apparently taken with the beauty of the dead or dying Penthesileia,[143] there Thersites, as here Hekabe, spoiled the hero's noble feeling by attributing it to mere lechery.[144] Erotic themes, perhaps more even than others, are subject to sudden switches between the *aischron* and the *kalon,* depending on whether one takes the view of the high mimetic, or that of the comic and critical. No wonder that the very highest reaches of the high mimetic excluded these dangerous themes altogether. The scene offers a number of interesting contrasts between the heroic and idealistic world of Polyxene, and the darker one of the old queen.

One reason for Hekabe's cynical viewpoint is her age, which by definition

142. *Alk* 353: ψυχρὰν μέν, οἶμαι, τέρψιν, ἀλλ' ὅμως. Admetos, like Laodameia, promises to cherish a statue of Alkestis in his bed; for the stories see Mayer (1885), and the tale in Hyg. 103–4. For the connection between *Alkestis* and the lost *Protesilaos,* see U. v. Wilamowitz (1906.1, 29 n.1); Dale (1954, 79); Paduano (1969, 75–77). Admetos is promising an obsessive and unending grief, such as Laodameia felt for Protesilaos. But note also the stylistic associations of "cold" (*psychros*), discussed in Chap. 4, above.

143. The story is in the *Aithiopis* plot summary by Proklos (5:105 Allen); see Griffin (1977, 44–45). When accused of erotic feelings for Penthesileia by the rude Thersites, Achilleus killed him, precipitating a quarrel in the army. Cf. Thersites' role in *Il.* 2.212ff. For the treatment of ugliness and the contrasting emphasis on female beauty in fourth-century visual art, see Piatkowski (1981, 201). See also Petersen (1915, 15–17) and recently Krischer (1982, 53–54, 63) on development in mimesis from type to individual. Chairemon, whose erotic descriptions of women's bodies were quoted above, probably used this myth in his *Achilleus Thersitoktonos.* For the plot, see *TGF* 71, F 1a; and Collard (1970, 26): Achilleus gave the Amazon an honorable burial, as the Greeks here wish to do for Polyxene.

144. For Thersites' role, see Eustath. 208 on *Il.* 2.219–22 (1:317 Van der Valk): "[Thersites] mocks [*skôptei*] the noble hero as a lecher [ἐπὶ λαγνείᾳ]." Proklos (1.105 Allen) uses the verbs *loidorein* and *oneidizein* for Thersites' words about Achilleus and Penthesileia. See Nagy (1979, Chap. 14) for the comic and scoptic nature of Thersites in epic. Thersites reverses the values of the heroic genre and sees the heroes perversely through the comic lens. An erotic interpretation of Achilleus' feelings for Penthesileia appears in the appropriately titled *Psogos Achilleôs* of Libanios (*Prog.* 9.1; 8:282 Förster). Some of what is said there may reflect the *Aithiopis* as ultimate source, but the theme was not uncommon. Cf. the elaborate working out of the whole *topos* of love on the battlefield in Nonnos *Dion.* 35.21–79.

removes her from the heroic ethic. In spite of the prestige of aged wisdom, the Greek worship of physical prowess and beauty dictated that, in terms of Adkins' assertive and cooperative virtues, old people would be assigned the weaker side.[145] But further, to be old is to be a survivor, to have fallen short of the best of ends, death in battle that takes the hero in his youth and beauty, endowing him with a glory that can survive him.[146] Of course Greek women had no judicial or deliberative role, and the ideal fulfillment of their social destiny did not require them to die young. But the traditional evaluation of age and youth still applies here, because Polyxene does end her life heroically by a voluntary sacrifice accepted, like that of the warrior, to avoid a charge of cowardice.[147] Talthybios sounds the theme of old age at the opening of the scene; contemplating Hekabe, he summarizes her misfortunes and concludes: "Ah, I am old; and yet may it be granted me to die before falling upon some shameful fate [πρὶν αἰσχρᾷ περιπεσεῖν τύχῃ τινί]" (498). The logic at this point is alien to us, but, in the view of a morality that is descriptive more than prescriptive, the old have already undergone the shame of losing youth and beauty. Being no longer *kaloi,* they are unlikely to have the pride required for courage and self-sacrifice.

A close thematic parallel to our passage is the poem of Tyrtaios where the death of the aged in battle is proposed as a theme of shame, contrasting with the appropriateness and beauty of the death of the young.[148] There, too, the paradox that the freshness and beauty of the young are more appealing even

145. See Vernant (1982, 57): the old are limited to *logoi* and *mythoi:* deeds (*erga*) belong to those who possess youthful vigor (*hêbê*). This division also corresponds to Adkins' hierarchy (1960, 37ff.), in which the "active" virtues, constituting *aretê* on the battlefield, supersede the "passive" ones in status.

146. This whole ethic is examined by Vernant (1982). One becomes *agathos anêr* only through the heroic death that can render *aretê* permanent (45). The aim is to escape death through immortality in song (53) and old age through meeting a *kalos thanatos* in youth (56). On this theme see also MacCary's analysis of Achilleus as a narcissistic figure (1982, Chap. II.11; "'He Whom the Gods Love Dies Young'").

147. Polyxene argues that to resist death would label her as *kakê* and cowardly (*philopsychos,* 348); cf. Makaria (*Hkld* 518, 533). Adkins (1966.1, 200) attempts to deny that Polyxene, a woman and a slave, can have anything to do with *aretê* here. But the word is one of a group of terms (e.g., *gennaios, andreios, agathos, eugenês*): that *aretê* is too indicative of power and activity to apply directly to Polyxene here is true, but without much significance.

148. Tyrtaios 10W 21–30, cf. *Il.* 22.71–76. Vernant (1982, 60–63) shows that the old risk humiliation by death in battle, a death which for them is, like other things that are decorous in younger people, *aischron.* He points to the cult of physical beauty in Sparta as a support to the cult of martial valor. I would add that, since war reverses the cultural norm according to which the old hope to be buried by the young (Hdt. 1.87.4), a major function of the heroic ethic is the commendation and explication of this contradiction in basic values.

in violent death is underlined by a hint of necrophilia.[149] The theme of sexuality makes the point perfectly, since the beauty of the young makes sexuality as *kalon* for them as it is *aischron* for the old.[150]

In this scene Euripides has contrasted two views of Polyxene's death. As often in Euripidean drama the heroic model is reduced to an episode of youthful sacrifice, while the viewpoint of others in the play intervenes to assert other and balancing ethics. To Polyxene is assigned the high morality of the high mimetic; but the morality, and the aesthetic, of heroic drama in her case are ultimately exaggerated into an unreal sentimentalization. This sentimentalized heroic is then corrected and annulled by Hekabe's comment. Her crude suspicions, and her references to sailors' habits, cause the tone of the scene to veer violently toward the vile and the ludicrous, almost to the *geloion*. But, since this play belongs to Hekabe, who dominates it from first to last, her correction of the sentimental death scene is valid for this dramatic universe. The heroic has no home here, where the human condition is seen in terms not of freedom and of will but of slavery and helplessness.

V. Revenge and Complementarity

Hekabe contains enough plot elements to make up several ordinary tragedies. First the sequence of two deaths focuses attention upon the aged heroine and the pathos of her situation. But the addition of the second death also generates a new direction in the plot, as the play changes from a drama of suffering to a drama of revenge.[151] As an avenger, Hekabe experiences a success as complete as was her previous failure. The perfect revenge demands reciprocity between the wronged and the wronger, so that exactly comparable wounds are suffered by each, and each becomes the image of the other.[152] Like Hekabe, Polymestor is reduced to powerlessness, weakness, friendlessness, and physical humiliation; and like her he loses two children in a single day.

Revenge dramas share a peculiar structural problem in that, unless steps

149. See Adkins' evaluation (1960, 163). Mutilation, as Vernant points out, is implied by an ethic that glorifies the beauty of the dead warrior's body: to destroy your enemy utterly, you must then mutilate his body (1982, 64). Of course the distinction of the Tyrtaios poem is nonlogical, since mutilation is as dreadful for the young warrior as for the old. See discussion of castration motifs in MacCary (1982, Chap. II.7; "Naked Men as Women").

150. See Harbsmeier (1968, 2): part of the Euripidean treatment of old age may have been a portrait of the aged lover (*gerôn erastês*)—see fr. 317 N2, *Danaë;* fr. 804 N2, *Phoinix*. Euripidean oldsters do not behave as they "ought," and their antics awaken what Harbsmeier suggests may be a "beklemmendes Gefühl" in the spectator (48).

151. Harbsmeier (1968, 59); Matthaei (1918, 153–54).

152. For this attempt to create an equivalency, see Burnett (1973, 2 and 22 n.50).

are taken to mute the actual event of revenge, the focus of the play must necessarily be split between the sufferings of the avengers and the sufferings that are produced by their revenge. In Sophokles' *Elektra,* the play retains its focus upon the children of Agamemnon by muting the death of Klytaimestra, who never encounters her son on stage. Aigisthos does face Orestes, but we see only the beginning of the villain's downfall;[153] and the play closes before the reversal of contemplation or remorse can be possible. Aischylos, by contrast, had stressed the suffering of Klytaimestra precisely because the reversal from revenge to responsibility is of cardinal importance to his trilogy.[154] In *Hekabe,* we are given a full-dress treatment of the revenge; and this treatment, which necessarily involves including yet another action in an already busy play, introduces a new figure in the role of victim, while it allows Hekabe to appear in the unaccustomed role of aggressor. Hekabe's status as supremely miserable is thus called into question first by her new role and second by Polymestor's suffering, which is the mirror image of her own.

Polymestor is certainly not a sympathetic figure. Unlike Eurystheus in *Herakleidai,* he does not confound us by turning out to be a less obvious villain than we had imagined. The lure that Hekabe uses, a promise of buried treasure, must satisfy the audience that Polymestor's real motivation is one of reckless greed. The presentation of his suffering is both graphic and alienating. He comes on, blinded and bereft, as a kind of parody Oidipous, singing his sorrow in lyric monody; and as we watch his mime of agony and rage, we are likely to be moved and repelled, glad of the punishment and revolted by it in almost equal measure. Polymestor goes on all fours, like an animal tracking its prey.[155] He wishes to fill himself with the flesh of his enemies, for they—like himself—are "wild beasts" (1073ff.). This theme eventually culminates in Polymestor's final prophecy that Hekabe will be transformed into a monstrous animal. Avenger and victim join in a lower realm, where the two struggle endlessly on, each seeking to achieve parity (λώβαν λύμας ἀντίποιν' ἐμᾶς, 1074–75).

The final stichomythy brings the play to a closing twist of misery, as the fates of three disparate and inimical figures mesh together. Polymestor, helpless and enraged at his betrayal, attempts a final vengeance by calling on his knowledge of certain Thracian prophecies that will open up the future and

153. See Burnett (1973, 3–4).

154. On the reversal of Klytaimestra's role, see Winnington-Ingram ([1961] 1983, 112–13); Lesky (1973, 220–221); Michelini (1979, 155).

155. In the earlier part of the play animal references, also in lyric, emphasize the pathetic loss of Hekabe's children, lines 90–91, 141–42, 205–6, 337. There is a reversal from the humanized animal as object of pity to the animalized human as object of horror.

place the events of the play in perspective. His role in this instance parallels that of the *deus ex machina,* but Polymestor has neither the moral stature of the god nor his magisterial remoteness from human suffering.[156] In attempting to strike out from a position of helplessness and dependency, he only involves himself more deeply in the darkness that spreads before the protagonists. His prediction for Hekabe holds the greatest measure of horror for the audience, since it provides concrete confirmation that Hekabe's successful revenge will not be without its effect on her. The bitch is a common epithet for an evil woman among the Greeks too: but Hekabe will be both a bitch and a monster, with eyes of fire, like Sphinx or Gorgon.[157] Her tomb will bear no trace of her human identity but will be merely "the wretched bitch's tomb [κυνὸς ταλαίνης σῆμα], a sign for sailors."[158] The utter eradication of Hekabe's name does indeed seem to be the one misfortune that she has not yet endured. But, predictably enough, having traded so much to buy her revenge, she will not renege at any cost: "I care nothing, if *you* are punished" (σοῦ γέ μοι δόντος δίκην, 1274).

Polymestor's second prophecy has more effect on the protagonists. He predicts the deaths of Kassandra and Agamemnon. Hekabe, who was unmoved before, is stung: "I spit upon it—same to you!"[159] The low insult shows her continuing vulnerability, as she is reduced to hoping that Klytaimestra may not be capable of such madness. Agamemnon too is stung, as his own death is predicted; and he orders the wretch to be marooned on an island. Polymestor's response is the same as Hekabe's to himself: "Kill me!—but a bloody bath awaits you in Argos. . . . Does it pain you to hear it?" (1281–83). All three are doomed, and all are mutually involved in ruin. Agamemnon and Hekabe, in league against Polymestor, are natural enemies, even as Polymestor was originally the friend of each. Hekabe's means of

156. Medeia's similar role at the end of her play differs, in that she is talking from the same position of invulnerability as the gods do.

157. For woman as bitch, s.v. *kyôn* LSJ II. In non-Homeric references the bitch is typified by her loud and evil language: she is like a dog who will not stop barking; see *Wasps* 1402ff., Semonides 7W 12ff., Menandros 546K and 802K: πολὺ χεῖρόν ἐστιν ἐρεθίσαι γραῦν ἤ κύνα.

158. Note the exact words of Polymestor: τύμβῳ δ' ὄνομα σῷ κεκλήσεται . . . Hekabe (1272) guesses the riddle: the name (*onoma*) will not be her own but will reflect her transformation, μορφῆς ἐπῳδόν. See the earlier remarks of Odysseus on the importance of tombs (317ff.). For *onoma,* see the chorus on Polyxene (381). Vernant (1982, 68) points to the horror of being eaten by birds and dogs as coming in part from a total loss of human identity. The only loss that could be more extreme is that suffered by Hekabe, who becomes a dog and is entombed and memorialized as a dog.

159. *Apeptysa* (1276; literally, "I spit it out"), as Boella says (1964, 145), is "espressione realistica"; cf. Sheppard (1924, 84–85). Αὐτῷ ταὐτὰ σοὶ δίδωμ' ἔχειν = "same to you"; see Tierney (1946, 133).

persuasion, the sexual relation beween her surviving child and the king, will cause the death of both; and the weakness that induced Agamemnon to betray Polymestor will also lead to the king's own betrayal by a *philos* whom he trusts.

VI. Some Central Themes

The analysis of the play's dramatic structure is now complete. It remains to assemble some major themes and show their interrelation. This is an especially important task in a play like *Hekabe,* which carries through a strong line of contemporary allusion, sometimes blending and sometimes contrasting its two modes of reference. Most important for this analysis will be a part of the play's visual aspect, its use of the ritual gesture of suppliancy. Readers of plays have a natural tendency to overlook the importance of thematic development in the visual plane:[160] a series of repeated tableaux and gestures is, like other things in the dramatic performance, cumulative in its effect. In this case, the essentially grotesque effect of vigorous activity by an aged and ungainly figure is stressed from the start.[161]

In her first scene, the urgency of Hekabe's attempt at speed (66–67) contrasts with her lameness and incapacity.[162] In the second scene, great attention is called to the suppliant gesture. Hekabe supplicates, recalling the posture of Odysseus on an earlier occasion.[163] Polyxene in her turn repudiates such gestures with equal explicitness; and she mentions Odysseus' awkward posture, as he attempts to evade her expected plea (342–44). Later, in her despair Hekabe grasps her daughter tightly ("like the ivy on the oak," 398), only to have her struggle rejected by Polyxene, who deprecates the ugly picture of an old woman dragged on the ground by a younger male.[164] But

160. On the significance of visual effect, see the important statement by Taplin (1977, 19ff.).

161. Harbsmeier (1968, 16) points out that Euripidean oldsters share a common quality of extreme infirmity combined paradoxically with great and desperate energy: p. 23 (Peleus in *Andromache*); pp. 40–49 (Iolaos in *Herakleidai*); p. 60ff. (*Hekabe.* See also Cataudella [1939, 122], who, however, overrates Hekabe's strength.)

162. When Hekabe first appears, she is being led onto the scene by her attendants, whom she exhorts to assist her (62). For her attempts at speed, see her frantic questions at line 162ff., where she debates what to do to save her daughter. At line 169, she rather grotesquely urges her own foot to "lead" her toward the tent.

163. His hand "died" (ἐνθανεῖν) in her robes (246): i.e., his tight clinging to her clothing caused the hand to become numb. Cf. her restressing of the posture at lines 273–75: ἀνθάπτομαί σου τῶνδε τῶν αὐτῶν ἐγώ.

164. 405–8:

> βούλῃ πεσεῖν πρὸς οὖδας ἑλκῶσαί τε σὸν
> γέροντα χρῶτα πρὸς βίαν ὠθουμένη,
> ἀσχημονῆσαί τ' ἐκ νέου βραχίονος
> σπασθεῖσ', ἃ πείσῃ μὴ σύ γ'· οὐ γὰρ ἄξιον.

Hekabe ultimately does not heed this advice: she ends the scene groveling on the ground, crying out to her daughter to "stretch out your hand" (438–40). Polyxene, in strong contrast, is led off veiled, concealing her emotional reaction to Hekabe's misery.[165]

In the rest of the play, Hekabe continues her odd postures. Talthybios finds her lying, "her back on the ground, locked up in her robes [ξυνκεκλημένη πέπλοις]" (487). Her scene with Agamemnon begins with Hekabe crouching, her face turned aside from the king.[166] Once Hekabe has decided upon suppliancy, the whole scene may have been played with the protagonist in the ritual posture, embracing the king's knees.[167] In an awkward moment at line 812 Agamemnon begins to turn away from Hekabe as Odysseus had from Polyxene earlier;[168] and the old woman is forced to resort to more desperate pleas, climaxing in the remarkable rhetoric in which her supplication is replicated by every part of her clamorous body, every limb a voice crying out in appeal to the master. In the final scene, it is Polymestor whose movements are helpless, clumsy, and lame, repeating the same desperate questions and reenacting the same grotesque pantomime as Hekabe did in her first scene. Like hers, his clumsy movements reflect frantic indecision as he first darts after his unseen enemies, then lurches back to the tent to protect his children's bodies.[169]

Polyxene's attitude to physical decorum is the foil for Hekabe's. Her concern for *schêma*, appearance, is extreme. The terms *euschêmôn* and *aschêmôn*, associated with Polyxene at lines 407 and 569, belong to etiquette,

165. The girl asks Odysseus to cover her head, "Since, before my death, I have melted my heart [ἐκτέτηκα καρδίαν, 433] with weeping at the mourning of my mother ..." Willem (1924) and Boella (1964, 54) point to the motivation: Polyxene wants to escape more emotional pain. For veiling of the head as emotional withdrawal, see *Hippolytos*.

166. 739, προσώπῳ νῶτον ἐγκλίνασα σόν. Note also the last scene, in which she refuses to look Polymestor in the face; this too may have been accompanied with some striking gesture (968ff.).

167. Hekabe alludes to the posture again at lines 787 and 839, so that it would appear she has never left it.

168. οἴμοι τάλαινα, ποῖ μ' ὑπεξάγεις πόδα; Porson (1851, 95) translated, "pedetentim a scena recedere conatur." But, if I suppose Hekabe is still clutching Agamemnon's knees, what we should really understand is an attempt to withdraw from the suppliant posture and relation. See the scholiast to line 812 (p. 418 Dindorf), κρατοῦσα τὰ γόνατα τοῦ Ἀγαμέμνονος ᾔσθετο τοὺς πόδας κινοῦντα. *Hupexagein* is used in epic, but not in tragedy elsewhere. In prose, it is used for a slow military retreat (Xen. *Kyr.* 3.3.60) or for any attempt to get something out of harm's way (Herodotos, of women and children in the Persian invasion, 8.40.1). It does suggest the embarrassed awkwardness of Agamemnon's attempt to reject Hekabe; cf. the corresponding maneuvers of Odysseus (342–43). The interpretation of this scene by Gould is discussed below.

169. 1056, 1081; cf. Hekabe's indecision at line 162ff. At line 1082ff. Polymestor veers back to the tent, like a ship tacking about.

where proper behavior is seen in terms of appearance.[170] *Schêma* or physical outline may be created by the stance of the person, by the way in which the body is held, or by movements in accordance with the patterns of conventional behavior, or, in other contexts, with the conventions of the dance.[171] To be graceful and mannerly is to be *euschêmôn,* as Polyxene is, when she deftly conceals her naked body in death. The thematic of gesture and appearance, of etiquette and the faux pas, is amplified, of course, by the thread of references to visual art that run through the play. The *schêma* is the outline that the artist creates; and the play continually invites us to compare the conventions and decorum of one art form with those of another.[172]

Hekabe's suppliant gestures are replicated in her attempts to cling to or be raised from a fallen position by such friendly figures as the attendants, Polyxene, and Talthybios. All these postures share the combination of violent energy and total helplessness typical of suppliancy,[173] as the suppliant attempts to plead for his life, while warding off rejection from the object of supplication—who in extreme cases may be an enemy bent on killing him.[174] The struggle for survival often noted as typical of Euripidean characters

170. On the meaning of these terms, see Tierney (1946, on line 407): *aschêmonêsai* is "evidently colloquial." Boella (1964, 51) also notes the connection of line 407 with the theme of decorum (see line 569). Most of the references to etiquette come from the fourth century, simply because we have so little fifth-century work dealing with the trivia of everyday life—see Platon *Rep.* 3.401c5; Aristoteles *EN* 1119a30; Demosth. 22.53. For a fifth-century example of advice on manners, see Bdelykleon on dining etiquette, *Wasps* 1210. Elsewhere in Euripides the meaning of *euschêmôn* is closer to "specious"; see *Med* 584, *Hipp* 490.

171. In line 619 ὦ σχήματ' οἴκων is bland and acquires its color through the other words with *schêma* that we have already discussed; see H. Weil's translation: "ô apparence imposante" (1879, 257). Here, as in *Andr* 1, the word refers to something that once looked impressive but is no longer in existence. For the emptiness of the *schêma,* see *Aiolos* fr. 25.3 N2, *Erechtheus* fr. 360.27 N2. *Schêma* typically refers to outward appearance (see *IT* 292, *Ion* 992, *Hel* 379) or to clothing and accoutrements (*Ba* 832, Aristoph. *Frogs* 463). For movements in dance, see *schêmatizein* in Aristoph. *Peace* 324. While it is possible that the rhetorical usages of *schêma* had already become current in the classical period, there seems to be no evidence for these usages until after the fourth century.

172. What the artist produces is a reproduction in lines on a flat surface, the *schêma,* not the thing itself. See Gorgias *Helene* DK2:82 fr. 11B.18: οἱ γραφεῖς ὅταν ἐκ πολλῶν χρωμάτων καὶ σωμάτων ἓν σῶμα καὶ σχῆμα τελείως ἀπεργάσωνται, τέρπουσι τὴν ὄψιν. Note the earlier reference of Hekabe to herself as a kind of artist's model of misery.

173. See the valuable article by J. Gould (1973): supplication is "symbolically aggressive, yet unhurtful" (97), because the suppliant abjures all potential for threat or competition through a humiliating self-abasement (89).

174. See the suppliancy of Lykaon, *Il.* 21.67–72. J. Gould (1973, 75, 97) sees suppliancy at the hearth as the basic ritual, emergency supplications without any altar and supplications at other types of altars being divergent offshoots. Obviously in a situation of extreme danger, suppliancy becomes more problematic but also more urgent. Suppliancy is designed (Gould [90–91]) as a preventive to acts of violence, or to establish a relationship where none would normally exist.

becomes thematically central in this play, where it is underlined by so much striking visual effect.[175]

The suppliant posture is a confession of powerlessness, and as such more appropriate to women than to men, to slaves than to free citizens.[176] Hekabe finds it easy to see herself as a slave and eventually to act as one.[177] When she argues that the slavish condition is the lot of most human beings, the norm of human existence, she touches upon a key theme of Sophistic argument, in which *nomos* is the tyrant that controls an inherently hybristic human nature.[178] This view treats human history as a process of progressive degeneration from any potential of freedom or honor, as capable individuals are subjected to the needs of the inferior majority. The Sophist, trained in the arts of verbal suppliancy, must plead with, cajole, and deceive his masters.

An important motif that has references to both suppliancy and rhetoric is that of *spoudê*.[179] *Hekabe* is a play of *spoudê*, in both the meanings of that word: there is great haste and urgency in its events and in its pace, and there is great and desperate eagerness in Hekabe's struggle to save some scrap of her humanity out of annihilation. The word and its cognates appear with striking frequency, to indicate sometimes merely the speed with which an

175. J. Gould (1973, 84–87 nn.54, 55) recognizes the importance of *hiketeia* to *Hekabe*, but his interpretation fails to allow for the aberrant stance of this play vis-à-vis the code of suppliancy. G. (85–86) traces a subtly managed crescendo of acts in *Med* 324ff., ending with the successful supplication of Kreon by Medeia. His previous account of *Hekabe* is formed on this same model: thus G. concludes that Hekabe is not really embracing Odysseus' knees, though she says that she is, and that she does not touch Agamemnon until the very end, when she is successful. As G. points out, "there is no escaping [from the embrace of a suppliant] without an act of physical violence" (86). Normally, such awkward moments would be taboo on the tragic stage; but the awkwardness of suppliant gesture is part of the system of signification in *Hekabe*.

176. See J. Gould (1973, 88): self-abasement in suppliancy fits women and children. Both the wife of the house and household slaves were welcomed to the hearth with a ritual resembling that of supplication (97–98). A number of Euripidean male characters either refuse to supplicate or refer to the inappropriateness of the action for persons like them. Adrastos (*Suppl* 164–67): ἐν μὲν αἰσχύναις ἔχω ... πόλιος ἀνὴρ τύραννος εὐδαίμων πάρος. Menelaos (*Hel* 947–49): he would shame Troy. Oidipous (*Phoin* 1622–24): τὸ γὰρ ἐμόν ποτ' εὐγενὲς οὐκ ἂν προδοίην.

177. She is *homodoulos* to her servants (60); she is a slave, Odysseus an *eleutheros* (234); same law for slave as for free (291–92); ἐν φάει δουλεύσομεν (415). Note that Hekabe rejects freedom with the same emphatic phrase (οὐ δῆτα, 756) that Polyxene used to reject slavery (367).

178. Antiphon's account of the attempt of *nomos* to hamper *physis* is not far removed: DK 2:87 fr. 44B.4: τὰ μὲν ὑπὸ τῶν νόμων κείμενα δεσμὰ τῆς φύσεώς ἐστι. *Sisyphos:* νόμους / θέσθαι κολαστάς, ἵνα δίκη τύραννος ᾖ / ... τὴν θ' ὕβριν δούλην ἔχῃ. Platon gives a similar remark to Hippias in *Prot.* 337d: *nomos* is a *tyrannos*, who "often does violence to natural self-interest [πολλὰ παρὰ τὴν φύσιν βιάζεται]."

179. For occurrences, see the following note. *Spoudê, spoudazein*, and *speudein* are all related both etymologically and in current meaning, in that all share the common linkage between an original (?) notion of haste and the idea of will and effort.

actor enters, but always with an indication of will or participation also.[180] Hekabe urges Polyxene to "put forth an effort" (*spoudazein*) in her plea to Odysseus, but Polyxene opposes to this her own counsel of good manners and restraint. The theme of etiquette correlates well with that of *nomos,* since manners and customs are sometimes called *nomoi;*[181] and, while it is uncertain whether *nomos* in its basic meaning of law is predetermined by human nature, it is evident that manners are used to control natural impulses and responses.

The cognate verb, *spoudazein,* reappears in the crucial passage about training in persuasion (*peithô,* 816). There, it means something approaching the Latin *studere,* to pursue an activity with energy and zeal.[182] Hekabe remarks that, in spite of the obvious utility of the art of *peithô,* "We yet do not pursue it (*spoudazomen*) to the end." The idea behind *eis telos* (to the end)[183] seems to be picked up in the second rhetorical excursus following line 1192, where professionals are "those who have reached precision."[184] *Telos* reappears in the second passage in a parallel phrase with different meaning: those who pursue rhetoric to professional levels (*êkribôkotes, eis telos*) are yet not able to be *sophoi* in any final sense (*dia telous*). Thematic emphasis on these phrases with *telos* recalls a familiar *topos* that is emphasized in Solon's *Hymn to the Muses,* a piece undoubtedly familiar to Euripides' audience.[185] Solon contrasts the efficacy of divine plans with the ineffectual efforts of human beings to acquire wealth and master the world. Phrases using *telos,* the "end" or "goal" which is known only to Zeus, underscore the limits of human knowledge and the tendency of human striving to fall into destruction (*atê*).[186] The theme of *spoudê* also appears in Solon: *speudein* is the key term describing human exertions in the professions, from seafaring and farming through such sophisticated *technai* as pro-

180. 66, 98, 120, 130, 216, 337, 507, 673, 817, 1175, 1201. The chorus (98) and Odysseus (216) enter *spoudêi.* Hekabe hurries on (66), and urges Talthybios on (507). The Greeks display *spoudê* in the mass (130, 673); Agamemnon and Polymestor wish (*speudein*) good things for their friends (120, 1175, 1201).

181. Shipp (1978, 6–7) argues that the notion that *nomos* (custom) precedes *nomos* (law) is a false one. He points to similar vague uses of "law" in English, usages that were prevalent before concepts of law were narrowed and fixed.

182. *Spoudazein* (see Platon, *Gorg.* 502b2), like *studere,* never quite approaches the English "study," perhaps because ancient learning and studying were usually thought of as amateur work.

183. 817: οὐδέν τι μᾶλλον εἰς τέλος σπουδάζομεν.

184. οἱ τάδ᾽ ἠκριβωκότες; for *êkribôkotes,* see Pucci (1980, 106–7); Tierney (1946, 128).

185. The same theme appears in Semonides 1W; cf. Bakchylides 1.160–84.

186. See 13W 17, 28, 58. The theme and language are traditional, as is indicated by the verbal overlaps with Semonides 1W.5 and 12.

phecy and medicine.[187] The Sophist, with his pursuit of wealth through expertise, belongs in this group; and the link between extreme rationalism and dangerous folly fits our play well. The theme of *spoudê* then serves to link gesture and etiquette, Sophistic training, and traditional moral themes into a single complex, through which we can trace to their origins the internal contradictions in the pretensions of rhetoric.

Another thematic link between gesture and rhetoric, references to signs and communication through signs (*sêmata*), is not directly tied to major themes. Most instances can be seen as a reflex of tragic diction, where "to make a sign" (*sêmainô*) often becomes a mere synonym for "to speak" (*legô*).[188] These are obvious and bland usages, but their number is rather striking.[189] Two uses of the *sêma* root seem more significant: the chorus responds to Polyxene's speech by remarking on the *charaktêr* of noble birth, which is marked (*episêmos*) among human beings;[190] and, at the play's end, Polymestor predicts that Hekabe's tomb will be *kunos ... sêma* (1273). Links with major themes are not developed, but are easy to make: gesture is a *sêma,* as is speech. Both or either can be a token of social value, the *axiôma* of a person. Polyxene seems to communicate effectively with the Greek masses through her words and gestures; but, as Hekabe's response shows us, *sêmata* are ambiguous. There seem to be no certain tokens and no fixed values. Worship of the gods themselves derives from lines of definition or boundaries (*horoi*) established by *nomos* (847), *horoi* which now prove too weak to give meaning to words and to the moral concepts they embody.[191] In the case of individuals, standards of value stamped on certain

187. 13W 43: σπεύδει δ᾽ ἄλλοθεν ἄλλος; 73: διπλάσιον σπεύδουσι.

188. Odysseus enters in haste *sêmanôn epos* (217); Hekabe blames Talthybios for *sêmanôn kaka* (512); Talthybios responds to a sign of Neoptolemos (529); Polyxene offers a *logos* as a sign, *tond' esêmênen logon* (546); Hekabe sends a message to the Argives (604); Polymestor uses the word three times to refer to the message sent him by Hekabe (983, 999, 1003). See also *sêmeion* 1009, 1125.

189. The usage *sêmainein = legein* is ubiquitous in Euripides. It appears at least four times in eight of the plays; but only three of these use it ten or more times. For two, *Phoinissai* and *Iphigeneia Among the Taurians,* thematic connections are obvious: in the latter play there is much imparting of *sêmata* by letter, while in *Phoinissai* there are the famous *sêmata* on the shields of the combatants. It seems likely, therefore, that in *Hekabe,* where usage is equivalent (twelve times), references to signing do build a significant trace in the play.

190. 379: δεινὸς χαρακτὴρ κἀπίσημος ἐν βροτοῖς. Both *charaktêr* (see LSJ, I) and *episêmos* (LSJ, II) are in ordinary language associated with coinage. While either alone would not be metaphorically striking, together they are very strong.

191. Talthybios fears that blind *tychê* may have replaced the gods as governor (488–91), while Polymestor suggests that it is the gods themselves who have mixed up (*phyrousi*) fortune and misfortune, "imposing confusion [ταραγμὸν ἐπιθέντες] so that we may worship them out of ignorance [ἀγνωσίᾳ]" (956ff.).

human beings by birth and status do not retain their *charaktêr* and are effaced by experience.[192]

The theme of the tomb, the *sêma* of an individual's life, and the measure of human worth (*axiôma*),[193] is struck throughout the piece, from the very opening, when Polydoros' ghost appears, seeking the tomb that has been denied him by Polymestor (30, 50). It was over a question of burial that Hekabe differed with the Greeks and their response to Polyxene's death. The location of the play involves a number of confusions between Sigeion and Thrace;[194] and a major motivation for alteration in the setting may have been the introduction of the myth about Kynossema.[195] We might say that Euripides has sacrificed the location of Achilleus' tomb to that of Hekabe's. In the code of burial Achilleus and Hekabe represent the exact inversion of each other: the former must receive the ultimate in honor to preserve his name forever, while Hekabe receives the ultimate in dishonor, including the obliteration of her name and nature.

It would be difficult to exaggerate the blackness of this play, or the horror of the closing scene, as the three doomed protagonists exchange hatred and predictions of death and degradation. The watchword of *Hekabe* is ugliness, *to aischron*. Tragedy traditionally deals with sufferings (*deina pathê*) such as death and pain, which are inherently *aischron,* ugly and shameful; but in Sophoclean tragedy irreducible suffering can at least be seen as a test of *aretê*. By throwing aside the heroic, this play grapples more directly with evil. Yet evil and pain in themselves are alien to poetry, since they carry with them the constant threat of grotesquerie, of the ludicrous that lies always so close to the horrible, of a lack of proportion, grace, and measure. *Hekabe* dares the audience to throw aside identification with idealized figures, and to recognize a truth about themselves in a commonplace, yet grotesque, world that falls outside the norm. Poor old women (*athliai graiai gynaikes*) were common in fifth-century Hellas, as in every time; and identification with human beings so degraded in value by age, sex, and lack of social ties was even slighter then than now. The play forces us to see in a single focus what

192. For the use of *axiôma* and *axion* in the play, see Thukydides 3.82.4, and the article of Hogan (1980) who argues that *axiôsis* there means "value."

193. For *axios* and its cognates, see discussion above, and Odysseus' remarks about honors for Achilleus' tomb (309, 319). Hekabe also uses the word for her poor burial of Polyxene: her offerings could hardly be *axia,* but they are all she can muster (613).

194. The problems are discussed by Lesky ([1956] 1972.1, 331).

195. Mentioned by F. della Corte (1962, 10). The location also makes it easy to picture Polydoros' body drifting back to the same coast from which it was thrown out. (The throwing-out is nonlogical in the first place; it serves largely to motivate the chance discovery.) For other possible motivations for the odd choice of location, see Corte (1962, 6–8); Kuch (1971, 49–50); H. Weil (1879, 207). Of course, it is not necessary to eliminate all subordinate "reasons."

the division in genres and the division between self and other serve jointly to conceal: the sense of powerlessness and insignificance that underlies all human pretensions.

Through the foil of Hekabe, Polyxene, the play sketches another model of heroism, one based on prescriptive morality rather than achievement. The perversity of Polyxene's exaggerated and improbable supplication corresponds to the perversity of a heroism that asserts the self only by annihilating the self. The erotic charm that plays over her death scene anticipates a time when *erôs* will emerge rehabilitated, purified of its physical attachments, and refined into a longing of the soul. It is typical of Euripides that here, as in *Alkestis,* the new moral theory is subjected to the same corrosive irony that attacks traditional values, a process that leads in both cases to revelation rather than advocacy.

Like the Sophistic itself, the play is both false and valid, empty and futile, yet filled with a demonic energy—*spoudê*—that is itself a celebration of the aspirations that it mocks. The ugliness of the action is matched by violations of taste and literary decorum, by anachronism and topicality, by awkward digression and equally awkward pantomime, by clashing modes of refinement and vulgarity. In the end, *Hekabe* creates its beauty, not by ennobling what is ordinarily shameful/ugly (*aischron*), but out of the very elements of the *aischron* itself. These elements, which are the inverse pattern of the cultural tradition, are juxtaposed and balanced to form a system that as a whole possesses a beauty denied by its parts.

7

Elektra: The ''Low'' Style

This first part of this chapter will concentrate upon the problems of genre raised by Elektra's personality and her sham marriage. The second will concern aspects of the play that fit better in the mainstream of its tradition, the relation between Elektra and Orestes and the vengeance plot that they jointly perpetrate. These divisions correspond roughly to two segments that can be marked off by the notorious scene of recognition, a point at which the tension between this *Elektra* and its tradition reaches a climax. The initial delay of the recognition scene permits a sustained focus on the country setting and its dominant figures, first the farmer husband of Elektra and next the old tutor, now a mountain herdsman. After the recognition, the vengeance plot proceeds relatively directly to its ends, with the focus shifting to confrontations between the siblings and their two adversaries. The fact that this analytic scheme requires me to postpone discussion of the first dialogue between Elektra and Orestes indicates that the play itself is in no real sense more bipartite than other dramas of recognition (*anagnôrisis*) and conspiracy (*mêchanêma*). The themes of the second half are already present in the first, just as the themes of the first half find their interpretation and development in the events of the second.

I. Anti-traditional Aspects

I.A. REALISM AND COMIC TONE

Elektra makes a uniquely striking use of certain techniques that appear in a more subtle and fugitive way in other plays. The concentration of these qualities apparently derives from this play's relation to previous treatments of

Oresteia motifs. In this instance the attitude of combativeness that the innovating artist takes in relation to his tradition is exaggerated, so that this conflict tends to be the major determinant of the course of the play, both in the negative and in the positive sense. The result for this play is a homogeneous stylistic quality rare in Euripides' work.

G. H. Gellie has pointed out that the matter-of-fact and circumstantial approach to dramatic events, typical of Euripidean style, is more marked than usual in this play.[1] Careful explanations provide circumstantial grounds for every event, even those that do not seem to require this support: we would readily believe that the day of Hera's festival approaches, without assurances that the message has been brought to this remote area by a milk-drinking, mountain-climbing Mykenaian.[2] Gellie has suggested that this punctiliousness reflects changing tastes in a mass audience.[3] But this same audience enjoyed work of Sophokles that lacked this trait; and other Euripidean plays presumed not to be very far in date from *Elektra* are relatively vague about details.[4] This circumstantial precision is another part of the Euripidean techniques that diminish audience credulity and absorption in dramatic reality.[5] The more circumstantial are the explanations offered by the play, the more the question of reality moves to the fore and the more the dramatic mimesis of reality becomes problematic. The "realism" of *Elektra* cannot be treated apart from the play's vigorous attack on tragic literary norms. Its untragic or antitragic stance has continued to confuse and irritate its critics up to the present day.

This play challenges the basic split between the "laughable" (*geloion*) and the "serious" (*spoudaion*), an opposition that has a strong social and

1. 1981, see p. 4, on the play's "obsession with realistic evidence," which reaches a peak in the token scene, but is evident in many other places. Against such a view of *Elektra*, see Vögler (1967, 34).

2. Gellie (1981, 3).

3. "A large popular audience will . . . use its everyday experience of the behavior of men and women to check on what the dramatist offers to its credence" (6). G. also adds that Euripides, far from "succumbing to the temptation of popular writing," is in fact "dramatising the problem" and displaying it as a "kind of game." He remarks that the play has "the flavor of the experimental" (7–8). These observations seem to me to be on the mark and to catch well the individual quality of this play.

4. E.g., *Iphigeneia Among the Taurians*. Neither the entrance of the chorus, nor the first exit and reentrance of Iphigeneia, are compellingly motivated. Sophokles' *Elektra*, referred to hereafter as *Elektra* (2), displays a similar lack of concern for precise motivation; see U. v. Wilamowitz (1883, 215).

5. Consider, e.g., the difficulty Elektra has in recognizing the messenger who brings the news of Aigisthos' death (765–66; Gellie [1981, 4]). The effect is simply to make the audience recognize that messengers bringing good or bad news are almost never questioned on the tragic stage.

psychological basis.[6] For some modern as for ancient critics, tragedy embodies the idea of literature that will be "serious," that is, literature that is worthy of study and admiration, literature that is culturally important, and literature that will engage its audience in a profound way.[7] The class component in these literary notions has frequently been deplored but seldom analyzed.[8] "Serious" literature seems to deal with persons of a very high and unquestioned social rank, even when such figures are socially obsolete, as they were in fifth-century Athens; and the serious treatment of ordinary or middle-class literary protagonists has from time to time appeared problematic even to modern sensibilities.[9] It is a paradox of human psychology that the interior view of the self seems to correspond best to a grandiose fantasy. Identification is stronger with the hero of myth, usually a very powerful person, who may be gifted as well with special physical or mental prowess, than with familiar figures more like ourselves.

The gulf between this interior world and that in which we have our social existence reproduces the basic genre distinction between the serious and the comic. In the theory of comedy developed by Henri Bergson and amplified by Arthur Koestler, the basic function of humor is to produce conformity to norms and to rebuke those who lack social awareness.[10] The comic mood is

6. *Poet.* 1449b10, 24; see Chap. 2, above. On the concept of the *spoudaion,* see Gigon (1981, 4.10), who argues that Aristoteles used this word in his writings on ethics to convey "social qualities" that come just short of the ethical, i.e., to approximate the pre-Platonic meanings of *agathos* detailed by Adkins (1960). See the discussion of Jones (1962, 56–57): in the *Poetics,* "Aristotle has in mind a generalised, aristocratic, ancient and practical ideal of human excellence . . ." The word, with its natural opposition to *geloion,* seems ideally formed, however, to convey an aesthetic concept.

7. For the German theory in this area, see Szondi ([1956] 1977, 1ff.). American critics were particularly interested in these topics in the fifties and sixties—see Myers (1956), Olson (1961), Brereton (1968), Heilman (1968), Sewall ([1959] 1980), States (1971); more recently Schwarz (1978) and Reiss (1980).

8. But see Auerbach (1946) on failed attempts to write tragedy about bourgeois characters (389ff.). French classical tragedy offers the best example of the strict definition of a "high" art form (329–32); references to any aspect of daily life are excluded (337). Cf. J. Gould (1978, 48ff.) on the discarding of everyday life in Greek tragedy.

9. Arthur Miller complains of these presuppositions in the introduction to his *Collected Plays* (1957, 31–33). See Brereton (1968, 18–19); Olson (1961, 154–55) remarks on the results when art sinks to the level of the "person of ordinary morality," and comments (245) on the incompatibility of the full range of tragedy with "ordinary" people and situations.

10. The famous treatise of H. Bergson (1912) is the locus classicus for this subject. B. was obsessed, however, with a definition of the comic that depended on "mechanistic" qualities in the comic object. Koestler (1964, Chap. I) corrected Bergson by emphasizing the viewpoint of the laugher and his attitude toward what he ridicules. Bergson had pointed out correctly that "insensibilité" is characteristic of the humorous mood and that emotive sympathy destroys the possibility of laughter: "Et il y en a un [art] aussi de décourager notre sympathie au moment précis où elle pourrait s'offrir" (143). Decharme ([1893] 1906, 257) was aware of this quality in Euripides.

thus inimical to the internal focus of the grandiose or idealizing mode; and its natural victims are often persons who have an inflated and socially inappropriate view of themselves. To avoid being the butt of the joke one must be alert to the environment and its alterations, so that the mood of humor is, by definition, discontinuous and disorienting. It is the sudden intrusion of the circumambient world of the "everyday" and of the image of the self or others, as seen from the outside and without emotive identification,[11] that creates the explosive force of laughter.

The firmness of the generic line between tears and laughter is preserved by genre etiquette, such as the tendency of "high" or "serious" art to use vocabulary and circumstances that are remote from everyday life. Bjørck has described the relation of the special language of high poetry to ordinary language as one of "prophylaxis," the purging of certain elements that must be avoided, of the language of the "everyday."[12] The association of "serious" art with exotic settings and styles helps to screen out the disruptive signals of the familiar, the everyday, the particular. The prevalence in high art of archaic customs and language, which borrow from the past a glamour lost to the diminished world of the present, is a further element in this prophylaxis of humor.[13]

Along with its circumstantiality, *Elektra* makes, of all the extant plays, the most garish contrast between the foreground of myth imagined as reality and the background of myth as unreal and undramatizable fantasy.[14] In other plays, picturesque touches of the everyday serve as ornaments, usually appended to introductory scenes or quiet interludes. But here the contrast is explicit, prolonged, and tied to the central themes of the drama, so that we cannot bridge the gulf between the heroic world, in which the protagonists are and ought to be *spoudaioi,* and the world of the play. The whole opening section (1–431) is pitched with remarkable consistency at the petit bourgeois level,[15] while issues of class and of values—precisely the issue behind artistic

11. On the lack of identification in the comic mood, see Thompson (1948, 27; 1946, 82–84), Sharpe (1959, 42), Styan (1968, 257): in ironic drama (Styan's analysis of this form is very germane to Euripides) "the detachment of comedy is not allowed us, nor the sympathy of tragedy."

12. 1952, 307–10. "Und das Übel des Unpoetischen liegt darin, dass es gemein ist und abwegige Assoziationen hervorruft . . ." (310).

13. It is of course impossible entirely to separate this model from the peculiar cultural role of Hellenic mythology. For the separation between two worlds and two chronologies, and even two realities, see Veyne (1983, 89ff. and 59, "deux programmes de vérité").

14. For the distinction between the miraculous parts of myth and those that could be translated easily into "real," i.e., contemporary events, see Segal (1982, 333–34). The division corresponds to pre-Euripidean attempts to reclaim this material by allegorizing myths or restructuring them to omit the miraculous (Veyne [1983, 62–67]).

15. See H. Weil (1879, 567): "une série de scènes dont le ton, pour ainsi dire, bourgeois contraste singulièrement avec la sombre grandeur du sujet." Friedländer (1926, 95): For the first time the world of the "armen Leute und der petits faits" is taken seriously and counterpoised to

"seriousness"—are constantly brought to the fore in talk and in action. This opening segment, which coincides with the long, functionally unmotivated delay in the recognition, is used to develop the antiheroic side of the event and of the protagonists.

I.B. THE *ELEKTRA* OF SOPHOKLES

The question of the relation of this play to the *Elektra* of Euripides' great rival cannot be solved with final certainty;[16] but the contrast between the two versions is so illuminating of this play's position in the tragic tradition that it cannot be ignored. I will argue in Section I.E., below, that the Sophoclean play is almost certainly one of the models for this *Elektra;* but, even if this should somehow be disproved, the Sophoclean version would still provide a useful and valid basis for comparison. First, each separate parallel treatment of the same material provides another view of the rich literary tradition behind the story of the house of Atreus; second, the heroic quality of the Sophoclean play makes a fascinating antithesis to what Euripides has done here.[17]

To develop the antiheroic mood of his *Elektra* in the most powerful and consistent way, Euripides turned once again to the most striking genre split in Hellenic literature, that between *Odysseia* and *Ilias.*[18] It is significant of the place of *Elektra* in the Euripidean oeuvre that this play most directly and consistently echoes the mood and setting of the *Odysseia.* The pastoral scene, in the remote and mountainous border areas, frequented by herdsmen and approached by a steep and arduous path,[19] has an obvious resemblance to the

that of the rich and noble. Pohlenz ([1930] 1954, 310): Euripides has transformed the scene until "jeder attische Kleinbürger glauben könnte, in seiner alltäglichen Umgebung zu sein."

16. This question dominated most of the early critical writing on *Elektra.* Indeed, so thorough was the dismissal of this play as a work of art (See A. W. Schlegel [1884, 366ff.]; U. v. Wilamowitz [1883, 233ff.]), that a more literary orientation for scholarship was unlikely. The problem of priority appealed as one that could be solved by careful and accurate reading. Extensive bibliography on the controversy appears in Vögler (1967, 17–51).

17. Several recent treatments, in attempting to avoid the controversy altogether, have been driven to the position that the relation between the two versions is negligible; see Steidle (1968, 82).

18. For the analogies between the *Odysseia* and the Euripidean *Elektra,* see Diller (1962, 93–94); Matthiessen (1964, 94–107); Dingel (1969); Paduano (1970, 391–92); Tarkow (1981, 145ff.). See also Chap. 2, above.

19. The area is remote (96, 168, 298) and mountainous (170, 489). The steep path is quite vividly carried through, so that, as Klytaimestra approaches in her wagon, Elektra and Orestes catch sight of her at a considerable distance (963–64). The message about the Hera festival is brought by a herdsman (to be *galaktopotas* [milk-drinking] is characteristic only of the remote herdsman—cf. Polyphemos and Alkman *PMG* 56); and the Old Man, who like Elektra lives in the border territory, works as a herdsman (412). The correlation of such a location with poverty would be plain to every citizen of Attika. On the setting, see Steiger (1912, 21); Diller (1958, 98); Albini (1962, 106); Zeitlin (1970, 649 n.20); Rivier (1975, 120), who expands Friedländer's

remote area of Ithaka where Odysseus first begins to test the prospects for his return. Like Eumaios, the peasant farmer who has married Elektra is a poor man whose high standards of loyalty put to shame the lower morals of people at court. Like Odysseus, Orestes is cautious in planning his revenge and delays long in identifying himself, even to his friends. Like Laertes, Elektra lives in the country, imposing upon herself need, labor, and physical misery as a token of her inner suffering. Like the suitors, the opponents of the protagonists are characterized by sexual corruption and by a taste for luxury that contrasts severely with the neediness of the loyalists. And, like the suitors, Klytaimestra and Aigisthos suffer a cruel revenge, plotted secretly and carried out with considerable brutality.

This parallelism between the Orestes saga and the return of Odysseus is of course derived from the epic itself, where the darker legend of Agamemnon's return serves at several key points as a model and a contrast for the roles of Odysseus, Telemachos, and Penelope.[20] By resituating the story of Orestes in a setting and mood reminiscent of the *Odysseia,* Euripides' play reasserts the domestic nature of the story; but it also introduces a strong incongruity between the somber material and the setting, which is comedic and "low" rather than heroic and "serious." The comic setting forces into prominence a generic problem of the Orestes saga, its awkward position between the heroic epics of masculine achievement and the social, moral, and family-centered world of the *Odysseia.*[21]

The incongruity was the same that had conditioned the structure of the Sophoclean *Elektra,* a play that makes a highly selective treatment of the story, so as to create maximum conformity to the norms of heroic tragedy. In arguing against Sophoclean priority G. Ronnet has remarked that *Elektra* drama was not one that had a "natural" appeal for Sophokles, since it is not the sort of situation that he usually sets up for his protagonist.[22] A good

---

point (1926, 95) about the clash between the bucolic charm of the decor and the foul deeds that take place.

20. See Dingel (1969, 107).

21. This is confirmed by the highly selective use made of the Orestes story by the Homeric epic; see Bruhn (1912, 1–4). The epics of return, centering on the reincorporation of the heroes into domestic life and characterized by recognitions, are discussed in relation to Euripidean drama by Matthiessen (1964, 106–8); Dingel (1969, 107); Tarkow (1981, 145ff.). For the epic background to the Orestes saga, see Olvieri (1897, 570–76); and Huxley (1969), who mentions Hagias of Troizen in the *Nostoi* and the anonymous author of a three-book *Return of the Atreidai* (167). For the domestic quality of the story, see also what may have been the introduction to Stesichoros' *Oresteia, PMG* 210: the themes of the long narrative lyric are being set apart from the warlike material of epic. Stesichoros also wrote a *Nostoi* (*PMG* 208); see also the work of his shadowy predecessor Xanthos (references in the Loeb *Lyra Graeca* [2:12–13 Edmonds]).

22. 1970, 316ff. and 322ff. In Sophokles' version Elektra, although subjected to every provocation that might move sympathy, is not herself the plotter or the agent of the revenge. See Vögler (1967, 26–27 and n.52); Mau (1877, 291); Kirkwood (1942, 91–93). Ronnet does seem to be accurate in saying that Sophokles was working with intractable material, although this does

argument for placing the Euripidean *Elektra* last in the series of three is supplied by the remarkable change effected in the story by Sophokles: the degree to which this Euripidean play goes beyond others in its attack upon the heroic and the "serious" may be taken as a measure of the stress brought to bear on the tradition by the Sophoclean treatment.

The question of the relation between the Sophoclean and Euripidean versions will impose itself with more force, where the secondary, or tertiary, nature of this *Elektra* becomes most apparent, in the treatment of the "tokens" of recognition. Still the emphasis of the Sophoclean play on the traditional aristocratic concept of nobility (*eugeneia*), along with its protagonist, a woman who endures the unendurable with her standards unbroken, provides the most suggestive possible antithesis to a play like this. The *Elektra* of Euripides also takes *eugeneia* as its major theme, developing a number of contrasting and conflicting meanings out of that concept, in typical Euripidean style. The play's adversary stance to its tradition is summed up in one feature that suffices to turn the traditional story of Elektra upside down. The proverbial "old maid" of mythology is presented in this play as a married woman; and, in changing her status, Elektra turns out to have changed her very nature as well.

I.C. THE PERSONALITY OF THE EURIPIDEAN ELEKTRA

Elektra and her motivations are the battleground for critics of the play.[23] The application of parts of Freudian analysis to Elektra's personality has had unfortunate effects on criticism, as has the tendency analyzed by Kurt von Fritz to use abnormal and captious standards of personal morality to evaluate

---

not imply a flaw in the play. We will discover little new about Orestes' moral dilemma, from reading *Elektra* (2); and, if we want the story of the Orestes saga, we may well find Sophokles unsatisfying. But then we will not be approaching the play on its own terms. See Reinhardt (1933, 147ff.; see also p. 173).

23. Many accounts of the play have centered on this dramatic personality and its shortcomings. U. v. Wilamowitz (1883, 229–33) and especially Steiger (1897, 573–74; 1912, 22–23), who refers to Elektra as a "Teufelin." The repetition of this characterization in Hunger (1936, 11) and Stoessl (1956.1, 61) suggests that it had enduring appeal. See Masqueray (1908, 139): "un monstre véritable." Strohm remarks on the persistency of the description (1957, 15 n.3); and see defenses by Zürcher (1947, 121–22) and Steidle (1968, 66–68). Some critics of Elektra become quite vehement: Knox ([1970] 1979.3, 254) says that she acts out of "paranoiac jealous hatred"; Conacher (1967, 205) describes her as a "bitter, self-pitying, sharp-tongued virago." Sheppard (1918, 139): "She is not indeed a monster, but she is a thwarted woman, which is often much the same thing." Grube (1941, 303): Elektra's soul is a "terrible, perverted ugly thing." Blaiklock (1952, 173): the play deals with "the warped and poisoned spirit of a girl." Kitto ([1939] 1961, 334): "This Elektra is a woman in whom it is hardly possible to find a virtue; she is implacable, self-centered, fantastic in hatred, callous to the verge of insanity." Recent strongly negative analyses of Elektra's character include Pucci (1962, 370); O'Brien (1964); Ronnet (1975, 69); Tarkow (1981, 150–52); Arnott (1981.1, 185–86).

the actions of dramatic figures.[24] Elektra has been faulted largely for emotional and social bad taste. But the unexamined use of such culture-bound criteria is very risky, and the disruptive and ironic quality of Euripidean theater makes it dangerous to rely heavily even on Hellenic norms. I would see the vehemence of the animus against Elektra as deriving from the specific generic problem of the play. The more difficult the play is to accommodate, the worse her character must become.

A psychological interpretation of Elektra that rests upon the identification of "selfishness" or "egotism" in her personality is unlikely to be valid. There are no terms available in Greek culture to translate these notions, and analysis of Greek moral values has made clear the very important role of self-aggrandizement in almost all areas of the culture.[25] Elektra has suffered a wound to her pride, and such a wound is a legitimate and honorable cause for revenge: Sophokles makes it impossible for us to doubt this in *Aias*. Euripides, in his dramas that play upon the revenge motif, makes use of the rich range of contradictions in this ethic. In losing honor or status (*timê*) the injured person has become in the descriptive moral system of Greek culture "low" (*talainos, tapeinos,* or *kakos*).[26] Failure to revenge will mean acquiescence to a lower status; and, once confined to this status, the victim will not be seen as deserving any compensation. A crucial discrepancy is therefore likely to arise between the way a revenger sees himself and the way his enemies see him, since they expect to injure him and get away with it. A woman, whose low status and traditional unfitness for aggression seem to make her a safe victim, is also the natural revenger. Between strong males, presumably, injuries, at least in a heroic setting, can and should be revenged in more immediate ways; but weak avengers must proceed, as Orestes and Odysseus do, by stealth and disguise. In such cases, the time gap between offense and revenge is most likely to be extended; and the imbalance between the desire to punish and the capacity to do so is likely to be most keenly felt.

Medeia is a good example of this gap. Iason insults Medeia most intolerably when he assumes that no relation of enmity exists between them,[27] and

24. Fritz's work is notable for its emphasis on the interplay between real and literary social judgments (1962, xxii). He points (1956, 196) to attempts to convict Antigone of a tragic "guilt" derived from her rudeness to Kreon. (On "tragic guilt" see the fuller discussion in Chap. 9, below, on *Hippolytos*.) Critics who seem ready to favor Klytaimestra over her daughter, on grounds apparently of the former's better manners, include England (1926, 103); Karsai (1979).

25. See Adkins (1960); Gouldner (1965, 41 – 77; "The Greek Contest System").

26. See Adkins (1960; e.g., pp. 63 and 161).

27. See Lesky ([1956] 1972.1, 304); Bongie (1977, 44 – 45): Iason fails to realize that Medeia shares his heroic value system, and his patronizing air is indicative of contempt.

that his wife will passively accept a devastating loss of status. Medeia's special abilities enable her to put into practice a revenge that for ordinary women would be impossible.[28] Elektra's status problems, however, are aggravated by a factor that is harder to isolate because of its confusions with the norm of the genre: Elektra falls afoul of her social status. The most startling feature of this play, Elektra's marriage,[29] has a good claim to be a Euripidean invention, seeing that this paradoxical husband turns out to be an unheroic *autourgos,* a self-employed laborer.[30] Elektra is transformed by this social translation; and the reversal of her social expectations is at the center of the Euripidean version.

Elektra has been a princess; as Polyxene remarks in *Hekabe,* such a woman lives like a god in every respect except mortality (356). Indeed Elektra had been intended as the bride of a man, her uncle Kastor, who was to become a demigod. Now she is married to a poor farmer. The Autourgos, as his conventional play name suggests, works his own land and runs his own household, with the help of a few slaves and his wife.[31] Although a respectable member of the middle ranks of society and by family status wellborn (*eugenês*),[32] the farmer, as he himself points out, has lost his claims to *eugeneia* through his poverty.[33]

The gap between Elektra's former status and her present one reflects the class divisions in fifth-century Athens between the very rich and the respectable poor, a gap much wider than any in modern industrial societies. In ancient society, the intensive use of slave labor in wealthy households and

28. Note her success at maintaining the sympathy of the chorus, and comment by Maddalena (1963, 136). U. v. Wilamowitz in the preface to his *Medeia* edition (1906.2, 31): Medeia is treated not as a barbarian but as a woman, "übermenschlich, nicht ungriechisch, d.i. unmenschlich, ist ihre Grösse. . . . Sie ist nur die potenzierte Weiblichkeit."

29. In the poetic tradition, the name Elektra is said to mean "unmarried." The etymology goes back to Xanthos, the predecessor of Stesichoros (Ael. *VH* 4.26).

30. The term is used only once in Euripides (*Or* 920), where it clearly delineates a political and economic class. See Rössler (1981, 3.198). Since this character is specifically identified with his class role throughout the play, it seems appropriate to call him by this name. His lack of a personal name is expressive both of his status and of his lack of a place in myth.

31. Our best parallel for the social reality of *Elektra* is of course the *Dyskolos* of Menandros. There, the poverty of Knemon's household is such that he has only a single elderly woman as servant. Note also his willful refusal to let anyone assist him in his farm work (328–33); and comment by Rössler (in Welskopf [1981, 3.198]), on the independence and *autonomia* of this class.

32. 35–38. The concept of *eugeneia* is a flexible one; the speaker seems only to mean that he is of citizen birth. But of course in theory every citizen family represented a *genos* that doubtless had been distinguished (*lampros*) in the distant past. On the polis as closed corporation, see Veyne (1983, 91–92).

33. This, of course, is an old and traditional problem in Greek ideas about birth and wealth; see Theognis, passim.

Electra is not married in the Soph. version, from Soph.

way Orestes sees Electra at first

Essay

Electra's character may be stronger in Eur.

the very high cost of household goods[34] meant that, whereas the very wealthy could live by a standard of comfort that we would recognize and in some aspects even envy, the respectable poor lived in relatively squalid conditions. In addition, because ancient society was a slave society, the poor (*penêtes*) suffered not only discomfort, but the greater humiliation of ambiguous status. A man who works with his hands is doing what slaves do for others.[35]

Even worse, the wife of the *penês* may have to perform tasks that take her out of the house, thus denying to her the status that accrues to secluded and inactive women.[36] When Orestes first sees his sister, he assumes that she is a slave.[37] This is partly because of her short hair, a sign of mourning that is also a sign for slave status; but his assumption derives primarily from the fact that she is carrying a water jar. The trip to the spring for water, a basic and continually repeated task, is one shared by poor women and slaves.[38] That Elektra sets herself this task over the objections of her husband, has led to a complete discounting of the problems of her social status. But these problems are severe ones, and the task Elektra chooses is precisely calculated to display them to the fullest advantage.

When she enters Elektra declares that it is not absolute need (*chreia*) that forces her to carry water, but a desire to reveal "to the gods" the *hybris* of Aigisthos (57–58). Yet she also presents to her husband a strong argument in favor of the needfulness and propriety of her activities. Elektra grounds her duty to share his labors (*ponoi*) in the cultural truism that "outside" labor belongs to the man, while it is the woman's task to fix up things inside the house.[39] The ability of the household slave staff to bring enough water

34. See A. Zimmern (1931, 215–16 and n.1) on Greek poverty and the simplicity of household arrangements.

35. See Rössler (1981, 3.198). Farming was a partial exception to the generally low status of physical labor; and thus stories about this class explore the problems of snobbery, labor, and the possible union between *eugeneia* and poverty; see—to some extent—*Clouds* and especially *Dyskolos*. Like Orestes, the gently reared Sostratos must prove that he has a good heart, while he also discovers and admires the moral qualities of the poor but wellborn rustics around him, learning that a good marriage is not based on wealth.

36. See J. Gould (1980, 48–49) on the complex ambiguities caused by the clash between economic necessity and cultural norms of female seclusion.

37. 107ff., cf. *Elektra* (2) 78–79 and *Cho.* 132ff., 915.

38. We do not have much concrete evidence for the behavior of poor women, but the fetching of water is well established as a female task even in the *Kypria*, where Polyxene goes to the spring, with her brother Troilos for protection. See J. Gould (1980, 48): although usually pictured inside the house in vase paintings, women were also depicted outdoors "fetching water and taking part in religious rituals." Cf. the "Women of Troizen," the chorus of *Hippolytos,* who heard of Phaidra's illness when they were washing clothes at the stream.

39. See Xenophon *Oik.* 7.10 and following, a lengthy elaboration of the concept of "outside" and "inside" duties for the separated sexes. For the traditionality of this concept, see Aischylos *Cho.* 921; *Seven* 201, 232. There is a logical contradiction here, since Elektra is going outside. But water is necessary for management "inside"; and this is one of the "outside" activities that is appropriate to women.

does not come up in the argument, and it should therefore be disregarded. Slaves in poor households were often under- or overaged and thus unfit for heavy labor.[40] The Autourgos must direct his own plow; and, when Elektra says that in carrying water she is sparing him trouble, we may as well believe her.

We may disapprove of Elektra's wish to bring "Aigisthos' *hybris*" to general notice, but the *hybris* is nonetheless real. Although the Autourgos wishes to spare her public humiliation, Elektra is still of course forced to weave her own clothing; and her husband himself expects her to see to the food preparation for guests.[41] While the Autourgos shows his respect for this woman's fine upbringing (πρόσθεν εὖ τεθραμμένη) by giving her a special status and foregoing his rights as husband, Elektra wishes, quite naturally, to equal his moral nobility by helping him, rather than playing the aristocrat at his expense.[42]

The relation between the oddly assorted couple is by definition anomalous and contradictory. The Autourgos at line 65, when he complains of Elektra's water carrying, assumes what we may guess to be a common husbandly tone; it is the same tone that Iason adopts when he gruffly scolds Medeia for her needless folly in packing an expensive dress off to his new bride.[43] Such interchanges make a mutually enjoyable game of marital authority: since the wife is being overconscientious rather than rebellious, the husband is not seriously angry. At other moments, when she is seen from the point of view of the myth, Elektra is infinitely her husband's superior. At these times she expresses a gratitude that is condescending yet deeply felt: the farmer is such a devoted servant that he continues to defer to Elektra, even when the situation is ripe for a reversal of roles.[44] At others, Elektra, performing in a

40. Note that at line 141, Elektra seems to address a servant, who has either accompanied her or who approaches her from the house. *Dyskolos,* which might seem to contradict the situation in *Elektra,* is in fact a help in illuminating it. When the bucket falls into the well, it is the girl and not the old servant who goes to get water from the shrine next door. This is presumably because of the decrepitude of the old woman, since otherwise it is hard to see why the *parthenos* should go on such an errand.

41. On the weaving, see lines 307–8. This reference has been wrongly associated with the offer of the chorus to lend Elektra a dress—see O'Brien (1964, 29); Arnott (1981.1, 185). On the propriety of weaving skills for women, see Xenophon *Oik.* 7.5; and *Mem.* 2.7, esp. 2.7.10: ἃ μὲν δοκεῖ κάλλιστα καὶ πρεπωδέστατα γυναικὶ εἶναι, ἐπίστανται. But, as the latter passage also indicates, respectable women no longer wove out of necessity; see Denniston (1939, on line 307). For the food preparation, see lines 421–23.

42. See Hunger (1936, 9–10).

43. *Med* 959–61. The moment is indicative of the resumption, in Iason's view, of normal relations between the married couple.

44. Note lines 67–69, which have a strong ring of sincere gratitude.

ἐγὼ σ' ἴσον θεοῖσιν ἡγοῦμαι φίλον·
ἐν τοῖς ἐμοῖς γὰρ οὐκ ἐνύβρισας κακοῖς.

Electra's refusal could also b/c of independence or pride

Electra was once high class

familiar domestic role, varies from a scrupulous observance of wifely respect, to tart domestic reprimand. Further, these tones may even chime together in an exquisite dissonance, as they do in the couple's second scene together.

The complexities of this role have a strong effect too on our perception of Elektra. It is commonly suggested that Elektra's sufferings are self-inflicted and therefore unreal. The water episode is the first piece of evidence in the indictment, and the second is the interchange in which the women of the chorus offer to lend Elektra a dress, so that she can attend the festival of Hera. Her refusal is treated as an evidence of bad faith.[45] But Elektra has more than one reason for her refusal, as we can see by her speech to Orestes: she avoids feasts because of her painfully anomalous status as a virginal matron, because of the humiliation of her diminished social status, and because she is obligated to mourn for her father.[46] Sophokles' Elektra is the model used to show the inadequacies of Euripides' heroine, but this model works both ways. Would Sophokles' Elektra have accepted the loan of a dress from a friendly chorus? Even to ask the question is to answer it: such offers do not come to the heroines of heroic tragedies.[47]

We have come here to the most diabolical part of Euripides' new setting: in a genre sense, we might say that Elektra sees herself as a conventional "serious" figure; but her circumstances thwart her, by forcing the audience to be aware of the concreteness and normality of Elektra's daily life.[48] When Elektra makes the statement that need (*chreia*) does not really force her to bear water (57), this remark, like the Autourgos' insistence that her work is unnecessary, or his complacent reflection that the springs are not, after all, very far from the house (76–77), places Elektra in the range of the everyday, and denies her the extremes of the heroic. The violence of heroic suffering compels sympathy, while at the same time the heroic victim retains the symbolic status of aristocrat that enhances identification.

"I hold you equal to the gods in love, since you have not taken advantage [*enhybrisas*] of my misfortune."

45. See Arnott (1981.1, 185).

46. See the analyses of Grube (1941, 301), Steidle (1968, 67).

47. On the borrowing of dresses, see Aristophanes *Eccl.* 446–49, *Lys.* 1189ff., and Theokritos 2.74. In a society where clothing was costly, precious dresses were kept for a long time and lent to friends, or given away as gifts or offerings, as in *Il.* 6.289–95. The theme belongs both to epic and to everyday life. The homely tone of the chorus' offer in *Elektra* is striking; note the interjection of *charisai*, "Please do!" in the chorus' offer. Denniston rejected it, remarking that, although common enough in prose, the usage here seems "curious" (1939, on line 191). But it has an authentic colloquial flavor; and, in this context, it is precisely right.

48. Friedländer's comment hits the right note (1926, 94): through the amelioration of her circumstances and her sympathetic friends Elektra's "Einsamkeit ist hier gemildert, ja aufgehoben. Gewiss, sie hat es schlecht genug."

Handwritten annotations:
Electra seemed "abandoned"
Soph. too.
Through her marriage Electra seemed to have lost her social status
could she be heroic in the Soph version?

Elektra: The "Low" Style

193

The punishment inflicted on Elektra by Aigisthos would not work with a male victim. Since marriage gives a woman her place in social existence, her marriage status is ultimately more important than is her status of birth.[49] While ordinarily the family of birth can protect a woman from humiliations in marriage by dissolving a bad marriage,[50] an abandoned child like Elektra has no recourse. It is true that Elektra's transformation into a woman of lower status is only apparent, since she remains, in secret, a marriageable virgin. But the surface of social life and its expression in human relations have a powerful reality of their own; and no art makes better use of that reality than does drama. Our Elektra thus cannot be heroic: social determinants have placed her in the wrong class. Yet what she feels is real, and it is the most obvious evidence of the unreality of much psychologizing criticism that her pain has so often been treated as nonexistent.[51] She has been characterized as "warped" or "neurotic," not inappropriate terms, since modern psychology has often had difficulty in separating personal maladjustment from social stress.[52] But anyone who is trapped in a contradiction between the habit of high status and the fact of low status will experience embarrassments similar to Elektra's. In the world of myth heroes may appear as exiles in a lower sphere. But in the real world of social interaction—the world of comedy, for instance—people like Elektra are liable to provoke either ridicule through their pretentions or annoyance through their complaints. Elektra refuses the attempt of the Autourgos to pamper her and insists on her duty to perform household tasks. But because Elektra does cling to her former identity, she must remain aware of the gulf between her past and her present. If the setting of "real" life were muted and the social ambient unnoticed, it would be easier to identify with her suffering. The miseries that Elektra recites to the disguised Orestes

---

49. See the remarks of Diller (1958, 95) on the greater dependency of women on the social world.

50. Schaps (1979, 76–77) emphasizes the protective role of the dowry in giving women economic leverage in the marriage. Cf. Medeia's remark on the difference between her own situation and that of the chorus (253–56).

51. For less condemnatory discussion of Elektra's social problem, see Elisei (1931, 153–59), Zürcher (1947, 123–31), Chromik (1967, 147), Steidle (1968, 65 n.20). Steidle points out that, when Elektra refers to her "deadly marriage" ([θανάσιμος γάμος] 247), she means "'Meine soziale Existenz ist durch die Ehe vernichtet'" (66).

52. For the tendency to interpret social problems as due to personal deficiencies, see J. B. Miller (1976, 56ff.). For Elektra's neurosis, see Conacher (1967, 204–5); Winnington-Ingram (1980, 231). U. v. Wilamowitz (1883, 229), although pre-Freudian, seems to hint at Elektra's sexual maladjustment, when he implies that, though still a virgin, she has lost her sense of modesty and with it her respect for her husband. See also Stoessl (1956.1, 89). These observations are of course not without some merit; see the less polemical comments of Albini (1962, 100–1) and Zeitlin (1970, 665–66).

[handwritten: Electra is married in Euripedes? Soph: Aegisthus threatens Punishments to lock her up in the dungeon]

are miseries, only while we remember that she is a princess. When we think of her as one of us, an ordinary person whose discomforts do not exceed the common run, then what Elektra suffers from is not misery, but simply ordinary life.

I.D. THE ROLE OF ELEKTRA'S HUSBAND

Elektra escapes the comic trap of assuming an undeserved high status, but she cannot avoid sounding continual false notes of envy or pettiness. The Autourgos, who is a comic figure, lacks her unpleasantness but often seems ludicrously out of place in his heroic pretensions. This person is given the task of delivering the prologue and is prominent in the first segment of the play, until the recognition of the principals. The Autourgos' opening speech makes clear that the marriage has been planned to "weaken" the threat posed by Elektra as a potential mother of children.[53] The Autourgos has thwarted Aigisthos' plan by refusing to benefit from marriage to a young and delicately nurtured bride. He has left Elektra untouched—"As Kypris is my witness [σύνοιδέ μοι Κύπρις]" (43). *[handwritten: → She is still a virgin]*

The little phrase carries several messages: the lowered tone and the confidential address to the audience give us just the note of the—as yet unborn—domestic comedy that will be,[54] while at the same time the touch of humor effectively turns the tables on the audience. Because his pretensions to a superior morality lead him to neglect his own evident self-interest, the Autourgos may seem to be a fool. The temptation to laugh at him would be greater for a fifth-century audience, because the Autourgos is violating the social etiquette of the tragic genre, and because his ethic would be relatively unfamiliar.[55] At the end of his speech he attacks the audience directly: people who take a cynical view are themselves fools, since they use inferior standards to determine value.[56] The Autourgos is promulgating a new standard for an *aretê* that is not based on self-assertion and self-aggrandizement, and that will be attainable by poor as well as rich.[57] But as always, Euripides

---

53. See lines 26, 39. Some have seen this theme as a borrowing from *Elektra* (2), e.g., Kaibel ([1896] 1967, 57).

54. See Moschion in the prologue of *Samia*, 19–20, 47–48.

55. See, however, an earlier Euripidean play, *Diktys*, discussed in App. D.

56. See Denniston ([1939] on lines 50–53). For the reference to *kanones* see *Hek* 602. The reference to inferiority plays upon the double meaning of *ponêros*, low in rank and low in morals.

57. See Adkins (1960, 176): "It is not until *El* that *agathos* appears in a quiet [i.e., "moral" in the modern sense] sense *used of a man*." He goes on to say that this passage is unique in Euripides' extant plays for its thoroughgoing reversal of traditional values (177–78). For the Autourgos as a new hero, expressive of new moral and social ideals, see Festugière (1957, 142); Biffi (1961, 102); and Jones (1962, 242–45). Biffi associates the Autourgos with a comic atmosphere, but all treat this character as one that Euripides sincerely and perhaps ineffectively (Jones, 244) wished to treat as *spoudaios*.

explores the contradictions of the new as well as those of the old ethic. Elektra's diminished heroic stature is balanced by the comically inflated status of the admirable plowman. ——— *Anything like this in Soph?*

The Autourgos' paradoxical "nobility" is forced into thematic prominence in a long speech by Orestes, who reflects on these perplexities. Wealth, a morally despised criterion, cannot be used to measure human worth, yet poverty does hurt people.[58] Orestes rejects any external standard of *aretê* and ends by saying that he prefers the hospitality of a poor host who is sincere to that of one who is merely wealthy (394–95). This speech is pitched in a "high" or "serious" tone, while it attacks the norms usually associated with that tone. The framing material, provided by the words and actions of the would-be host, sets off Orestes' moralizing with amusing parodic and antiheroic touches that cast a fatally comic light on the Autourgos. He makes his entry at line 341 with an exclamation of dismayed surprise (ἔα) as he sees his wife standing outside the house in conversation with two strange young men.[59] The sudden reinjection of social norms appropriately links this figure with the everyday, and hence the comic. Once appeased by his wife, the countryman, marking with a faintly ironic effect a close to Elektra's long recital of woes, cries that it is high time (πάλαι χρῆν) that "these gates be thrown open" and the guests be invited in.[60] His language is full of tragic pomp, especially the order to the "attendants" to bring the baggage into "this dwelling" (αἴρεσθ', ὀπαδοί, τῶνδ' ἔσω τεύχη δόμων). The evocation of previous scenes in which the circumstances were

58. 373–76:

πῶς οὖν τις αὐτὰ διαλαβὼν ὀρθῶς κρινεῖ
πλούτῳ πονηρῷ τἄρα χρήσεται κριτῇ.
ἢ τοῖς ἔχουσι μηδέν ἀλλ' ἔχει νόσον
πενία, διδάσκει δ' ἄνδρα τῇ χρείᾳ κακόν.

This is a rare speech, since it amounts to a moralizing excursus, with little direct connection to plot. (See Schadewaldt [1926, 139]; C. Friedrich [1955, 166].) The series of gnomic generalizations is loosely linked together by a common theme. This structure has naturally encouraged the excision of lines, sometimes amounting to a large portion of the speech: the recent edn. of Diggle (1981.2) brackets the same twelve lines as were proposed by Page (1934, 74–75). Even the more conservative scholars have opted for some cuts; e.g., U. v. Wilamowitz (1875, 191) and Schadewaldt (1926, 139 n.4) would cut lines 386–90. I suggest below a connection that would explain the apparent inconsequence of these lines too.

59. 343–44: "For a woman, it is shameful [*aischron*] to stand among young men [ἀνδρῶν νεανιῶν]."

60. The ironic quality of the Autourgos' remarks has been often noted, e.g., by O'Brien (1964, 29); cf. the farmer's suggestion at line 355 that Elektra has been telling her troubles. Misinterpretation of the way irony works in Euripides has of course led to the assumption that the Autourgos has no sympathy for Elektra's troubles; see Knox ([1970] 1979.3, 252–53).

heroic, the dwelling a king's palace, and the attendants royal lackeys[61] creates a most Euripidean tension, what we might call a suppressed urge to laugh.

A more severe test of the audience's ability to withstand the temptations of the comic follows Orestes' speech. After he and Pylades have gone in, Elektra, left alone with her husband, proceeds to rebuke him in significant terms for taking in "greater guests than yourself."[62] When he sounds the note of the previous speech, arguing that *eugeneia* must be a moral quality that will permit a man to be satisfied "in small [circumstances] and the reverse,"[63] Elektra repeats his phrase, "Well, since you have made a mistake, being [a man] in small circumstances [ἐν σμικροῖσιν ὤν], go to my father's old attendant . . . and ask for something to feed the guests." This scene has provided ready material for Elektra's critics, since her characterization as a "selfish" and "neurotic" misfit seems to them confirmed by her rudeness to her husband.[64] But the circumstances, as I have suggested above, are complicated. Shortly before, the Autourgos had implied a criticism of her behavior, calling her talk with strange men "shameful" (*aischron*), a charge that she had immediately deprecated in respectful and affectionate tones, "O my dear one, do not become mistrustful of me [ὦ φίλτατ' εἰς ὕποπτα μὴ μολῆς ἐμοί]" (345). The prompt and polite response should be an indication of Elektra's respect for her husband, where his authority really matters. It is precisely in regard to sexual propriety that Elektra must prove herself not her mother's daughter.[65] Now, however, she rebukes him, depreciating his pretensions in frank terms. As princess, Elektra is keenly aware of the squalidity of her environment, which she has just been describing to Orestes. The Autourgos, ἐν σμικροῖσιν ὤν, can have no notion of the gulf between

61. 360, the servants may be either Orestes' or those of the Autourgos, more likely the former. Cf. *Trach.* 1264, where Hyllos uses the same expression in anapaests to order the attendants to pick up Herakles' body.

62. 404 – 5:

ὦ τλῆμον, εἰδὼς δωμάτων χρείαν σέθεν
τί τούσδ' ἐδέξω μείζονας σαυτοῦ ξένους

"How could you, knowing the need (*chreia*) of our household, take in these guests who are greater than yourself?"

63. 407: οὐκ ἔν τε μικροῖς ἔν τε μὴ στέρξουσ' ὁμῶς

64. See Bond (1974, 7): Elektra is "most disrespectful to her husband"; and O'Brien (1964, 30). Solmsen (1975, 139) remarks that Elektra is "unable for any length of time to keep up an urbane tone of conversation."

65. Commentators have assumed either that the Autourgos does not trust Elektra's virtue (U. v. Wilamowitz [1883, 230]) or that Elektra's response to him is rude (Wilamowitz [ibid.] ; O'Brien [1964, 33]). Albini (1962, 101) thinks that Elektra apologizes for the Autourgos as though he were a mental defective, "mentecatto". Of course, a quasi husband may be a bit touchy on matters of propriety; see Masqueray (1908, 343).

his pretensions to a theoretical *eugeneia* and the reality of his poor[66] and ill-provisioned house.

The *Elektra* continually juxtaposes the harsh truths of experience with the sentimentality of the new ethic, which may seem to substitute for reality a fantasy that will harmonize with prescriptive moral norms. Elektra's rebuke is also appropriate to her other side; as a middle-class housewife, she reminds her husband of their real circumstances. In taking the conservative role, she acts in a way natural for women, who are trained to the exercise of *sôphrosynê,* knowledge of one's limitations, as their special virtue.[67] The two roles here overlap perfectly, thus bringing to a pitch of intensity the perceived contradiction in Elektra's situation. If she is a "bad" wife here, she is one only in comic terms—where all wives are bitchy—and not in tragic/heroic terms, where Klytaimestra and not Elektra is the model of the bad wife.

The response of the Autourgos is exactly tuned to the blend of Elektra's bad humor. He accedes meekly to the command of his social superior, the displaced princess, and yet exerts his husbandly authority over his peasant wife, ordering her back to her place supervising "inside" matters, and remarking complacently that women are wonderful at finding something or other to piece out a meal.[68] His closing reflections again stress his middling economic circumstances (*penia*): one may indeed need wealth to entertain guests and pay doctors; but as far as everyday food goes, the wealthy man can eat no more than the poor one can (427 – 31). This remark again places us in a nonheroic life, neither elevated nor deprived, but simply comfortable—or uncomfortable—in the ordinary way of human existence.

The repeated references to food are in themselves profoundly antiheroic,

66. Note line 252, it is suitable for a day laborer (σκαφεύς τις ἢ βουφορβός—see Kubo [1967, 21]), the poorest and most despised class of Hellenic society (see Dreizehnter [1981, 3:272]). We are unable to say or even to imagine what sort of scenic backdrop could have been used; see Kubo (1967, 21). However, the willingness of Euripides to add low-life touches in costume (a hallmark of a relatively early period—see Schadewaldt [1952, 64]) would presumably have extended to some corresponding "realism" in the treatment of the standard building in the background.

67. See Adkins (1960, 36 – 37). In high literature, scolding wives are not plentiful; but see the rebukes of Hekabe (*Il.* 24.201ff.), who suggests that Priamos has lost his wits, and Alkmene in *Hkld* 709 – 10.

68. 421 – 23:

χώρει δ' ἐς δόμους ὅσον τάχος
καὶ τἄνδον ἐξάρτυε. πολλά τοι γυνὴ
χρῄζουσ' ἂν εὕροι δαιτὶ προσφορήματα.

Knox ([1970] 1979.3, 253) points out that the word for additions to the menu, *prosphorêmata,* occurs nowhere else in poetry and has a distinctly everyday ring to it.

the locus classicus for this contrast being the nineteenth book of the *Ilias*.[69]
Was an echo of the disagreement between Odysseus, the patron saint of this
Elektra, and the intransigently heroic Achilleus intended to reverberate
through the first stasimon? In any case, the clash between the "real" and the
marvelous is brought to an exquisite intensity by the fanciful picture of
Achilleus' festive embarcation and decorative armor. The ode is the ideal
complement to and transition from our last experience of the Autourgos.[70]
The graceful and decorative imagery, which blends the swift and rhythmic
motions of the ships with the leaping of dolphins, the dancing of Nereids, and
even the leap of the light-footed Achilleus himself, is in striking opposition to
the meandering moralizing of the farmer.[71] The poetry of the ode is made
artificial and elaborate by strong *hyperbata* and adjectival displacement
worthy of Pindaros or Bakchylides.[72] Achilleus himself almost disappears in
the welter of mythical decor that surrounds him. The weak, circumstantial
link that ties this baroque figure to the play is simply his comradeship with
Agamemnon, whom Klytaimestra murdered; and, through the memory of
Achilleus, Agamemnon's sordid death is contrasted with the remote and
heroic first part of the Trojan cycle. The ode suggests how right Elektra was
to sense a painful and unbridgeable gulf between her original suitor, Kastor
the demigod, and her present "deadly" (*thanasimos*) marriage. After all,
Achilleus too had at one time or another been proposed as husband for a
daughter of Agamemnon.

Yet in the light of the ode, the new standard of heroism offered by the
Autourgos is persuasive in its claim to a greater realism, if not in its claim to
status. The pretty imagery, along with the artifical and affected diction,
confirm the irrelevance and illusion of the heroic pretension.[73] By juxtapos-
ing a lyric highly traditional in its verbal elaboration and decorative effect

69. See Whitman (1958, 178–79), on Achilleus' refusal of food; Knox ([1970] 1979.3, 268)
on the emphasis on food in the *Odysseia* and in Euripides.

70. On the extreme break between the lyric and this scene, see Stoessl (1956.1, 57); Walsh
(1977, 278–89); Gellie (1981, 7).

71. On the imagery, see O'Brien (1964, 16–19) and Zeitlin (1970). The remarks of the
Autourgos are marked as otiose by his apology, "While I happen to think of it [ἡνίκ' ἂν γνώμης
πέσω]" (426). On variant readings, see Denniston (1939, 101); Diggle (1981.1, 35–36).

72. τὸν τᾶς Θέτιδος κοῦφον ἅλμα ποδῶν Ἀχιλῆ (439ff.). On this style, see Kranz (1933,
229ff.); Heitsch (1955, 126); Benedetto (1971.2); Panagl (1972, 7–8). This style, traditional to
choral lyric, probably entered tragic lyric in this extreme form only in the teens of the century.
The parallels with Pindaros are more obvious, however, than are those with the new lyricists like
Timotheos.

73. See also Orestes' earlier speech (386ff.). The apparently inconsequential lines on "flesh
empty of wit" as mere decorations, *agalmat' agoras,* acquire point when Achilleus appears as
little more than an image of heroism. On the word *agalma,* see *Hekabe;* the implications of sexual appeal emphasized there may not be entirely absent here (see lines 948–51).

with lineverse scenes notable for their "low" tone, Euripides uses the original generic division between lyric and lineverse in a new way, to parallel the split in his own work between the *spoudaion* and the *geloion.*

I.E. THE TOKENS

The Paidagogos, entering in comic haste with lamb in tow at the close of the ode, resumes the fussy, everyday tone as he takes over the role of the Autourgos. The faithful servitor who nursed the hero as a child is no unfamiliar figure, although this one is notable for his great age, since he is said to have cared for Agamemnon himself. When the Old Man enters, he complains, after the manner of some Aristophanic choruses, of the uphill path and his own infirmity, his "redoubled spine and reclining knee"; his actions will likely have been a bit ungainly as an illustration of his language.[74] Later, when Orestes sees the Old Man, he asks his sister, "Of what man is this the ancient relic?" Orestes has earlier shown himself not devoid of tact, and his language here may be an indication less of rudeness[75] than of the ludicrous senility of the oldster's appearance, suggestions, and behavior.[76] In the atmosphere of most Euripidean plays, and especially in *Elektra,* bad manners are difficult to isolate, since people generally fail to behave as they "ought to," in terms of social or literary expectations.[77] With the arrival of the Old Man, the plot can at last begin to move toward its climax. Before it does so, however, the contrast between heroic treatments of the Elektra story and this Euripidean version reaches great intensity with a scene that in brusquely comic tones reexamines a famous Aeschylean moment.

It becomes necessary at this point to consider the relation of this *Elektra* to the Sophoclean play a bit more closely. The question of priority can never be answered with certainty, however, since the ambiguities of literary influence obscure any final determination. First, it is entirely possible that other

74. 492: διπλῆν ἄκανθαν καὶ παλίρροπον γόνυ. See also his action in drying his eyes with a piece of his ragged (τρύχει) robe (501–2); on this gesture, see the scorn of A. W. Schlegel (1884, 368): he "ermangelt nicht, sich mit seinen zerlumpten Kleidern die Augen zu wischen." The reference to the steepness of the path has parallels too in old comedy, e.g., *Lys.* 286ff., as does the ridicule of extreme old age. Zeitlin has shown the importance of the theme of animal sacrifice in the play (1970, 651ff.). Along with the lamb, the Old Man brings garlands and wine for a *symposion.* This with other comic echoes surrounding his entrance serves to activate the comic motif of preparation for a feast. The thematic parallel with the fabulous Golden Lamb, in the following stasimon, as undeniable as it is odd, is remarked by Kubo (1967, 19–20). The resultant false note parallels many others in this play.

75. See Denniston (1939, xxvii) and O'Brien (1964, 34).

76. His antics must be even more exaggerated in the moment of recognition, as he stares fixedly at Orestes and then shuffles around him in a circle. (Accepting Denniston's second suggestion [1939, on line 561]). On his odd behavior, see Bond (1974, 10).

77. And see Arnott, on the "double view" of these figures (1981.1, 181–82).

influences lost to us were shaping the tradition. While we have by sheer luck inherited three interrelated treatments of the theme Aischylos began in *Choephoroi,* we have not the slightest right to assume that, of the hundreds of plays presented at Athens between the time of the *Oresteia* and the time, presumably after 420, of the Euripidean *Elektra,* none except Sophokles' version had revived the myth of *Choephoroi.*[78] It is in fact probable that the tragic literary tradition of the Orestes saga was much more complex in the fifth century than it appears to be now. Second, even disregarding the possibilities for influence in the vast mass of lost plays, we are in possession of strong evidence for broad and detailed treatments of the myth in the work of poets such as Stesichoros. Many motifs shared by Sophokles and Euripides and disregarded by Aischylos must have had their origin, not in the invention of either, but in the nontragic versions of the story. Thus a complex web of literary interrelations, now lost, may be affecting the Euripidean treatment. Third, if Euripides is deviating from Sophokles in returning at some points to an Aeschylean treatment, there is no clear way to determine whether Euripides is unaware of other versions or has chosen to ignore them.

The assumption of complete independence between the two versions is rendered unlikely by the obvious parallels that cannot derive from Aischylos alone: the centrality of Elektra, the postponement of the recognition, and the offerings described by a third party.[79] Finally, it is occasionally possible to argue plausibly that one treatment of an inherited theme is secondary to another. Such a special case is the scene in which the recognition tokens from *Choephoroi* reappear in the Euripidean *Elektra.*[80]

78. See the figures in Seeck (1979, 156ff.): the overwhelming majority of playwrights and play titles are unknown to us. Euripides would have been well acquainted with plays produced during his own time; and, given the quality of the ancient memory, it would not have been necessary for him to have had them in manuscript in order for their influence to have been felt in his own work. All these playwrights had to find their topics somewhere in the range of Greek myth; and the degree of overlap in the work of three amazingly inventive dramatists should serve as a model for the practice of their presumably less gifted contemporaries. For further discussion, see App. D.

79. See W. H. Friedrich (1953, 83–84); Vögler (1967, 114–15); and analyses of Fritz (1962, 144–45) and Schwinge (1968.1, 301–3).

80. The analysis is essentially complete in Vögler (1967, 45ff.); but it appears there as a part of a proof that mixes some good with some very doubtful evidence. There is of course an immense amount of bibliography on this scene. The first wave was associated with attempts to determine priority—see U. v. Wilamowitz (1883, 236 n.2); Bruhn (1912, 20–48); Elisei (1931, 148–49); and the dissertations of Flessa (1882, 69–75) and Wolterstorff (1891, 29–35). The second wave was provoked by the radical attempt of E. Fraenkel to purge the second token from *Choephoroi,* with the concomitant suggestion that the scene from *Elektra* was an interpolation based on an interpolation (1950, 3.815–26). Support for the excision of *El* 518–44, first suggested by Mau (1877), has come from Böhme (1938; and his book [1956]) and Bain (1977); refutation and defense of both scenes, from Lloyd-Jones (1961), who points to the importance of the footprints as indicating Orestes' actual presence (177) and to the tendency of writers to criticize their predecessors (180); and in detail from Martina (1975). See also Matthiessen (1964, 86),

↗ Soph False news of
Orestes' death.
DIFFERENCE Between plays

+ are
↓ fo[...]w

    In Sophokles' version of the revenge of Orestes, the trick that catches
Klytaimestra and Aigisthos is the same as in Aischylos, a false report of
Orestes' death. But in Aischylos Elektra is privy to the conspiracy, while in
Sophokles' version she is deceived by the false news. Her exclusion from
the plot postpones the recognition until quite late in the play and produces a
remarkable concentration of audience attention and sympathy on Elektra.[81] In
the Euripidean version, there is no false announcement of death at all; and the
postponement of the recognition has the allusive quality of any plot element
that is without internal motivation. In this case the motivation is to be found
in the literary background, which apparently includes the Sophoclean version, since there we find both the postponement and the reuse of the
Aeschylean tokens proceeding directly out of the dramatic structure.[82] The
treatment of the tokens in Sophokles is an example of the deprecatory, or
depreciative, reuse first pointed out by T. Zielinski.[83] Chrysothemis proposes
something found at the grave, a lock of hair that Elektra has not seen but only
heard of, as evidence of Orestes' presence. But, by a strong irony, Elektra
has just heard the announcement of her brother's death; and she therefore has
reason to be certain that this circumstantial evidence has been misinterpreted.
The ease with which the Sophoclean Elektra, possessed of false "facts"
about her brother, pushes aside the doubtful evidence of Chrysothemis, and
the plausibility of Elektra's alternative explanation, imply a criticism of the
elaborate and slightly improbable series of tokens that Aischylos had manipulated with such suspenseful power.
    To understand the relationship between this kind of alteration of *Choe-
phoroi* and what we find in Euripides, it may be useful to attempt a reversed
explanation, namely that the particularly exaggerated and frontal critique of
Aischylos by Euripides inspired in Sophokles an attempt, presumably typical
of Sophoclean literary piety, to reuse Aischylos properly.[84] Sophokles would
have taken two unrelated oddities of the Euripidean version, a recognition
that is delayed without any motivation for this delay, and the proposal (and
rejection) of tokens proceeding from a grave visit that had been in no way

Vögler (1967, 168–75; with extensive bibliography), Bond (1974), Donelli (1980, a direct reply
to Bain), West (1980, 17–21).
    81. For this effect, see Kaibel ([1896] 1967, 47–48: Elektra is the mirror in which we see
the action reflected); Bruhn (1912, 43–48); Vögler (1967, 122–26). This type of plot device
may have originated in other Euripidean plays of intrigue and is at any rate unlikely to be original
to *Elektra* (2); see App. D.
    82. See Vögler (1967, 123–25, 137–41, 168–71).
    83. 1925; see discussion in Michelini (1982, 21ff., 33ff.). See Matthiessen (1964, 86) on the
grave scene as a repeated motif. For discussion of the uses made of these concepts by
Matthiessen and Vögler, see App. D.
    84. Solmsen (1967, 23) and Segal (Review [1968, 139] of Vögler [1967]) make this sugges-
tion.

expected or explained in the plot, and he would have linked them together so that the delay of the recognition (strongly motivated in his new version) now also logically entails the rejection of the tokens (also prepared by an elaborate treatment of the grave-visiting motif). And both these elements would now be arranged in the plot so as to show their direct derivation from *Choephoroi*, in which grave offerings, tokens, and recognition appear in a united sequence. Remarkable as the heuristic powers of Sophokles as a dramatist may have been, the assumption that he used them in this way seems at the least uneconomical and improbable. The model created has a resemblance to reversed-motion films in which the particles of an exploded object leap neatly back into their places in the disrupted structure.

It is of course unnecessary to assume that other reworkings of *Choephoroi* by other tragic authors may not also have contributed something to the motif in which delayed recognition correlates with rejected tokens; but the direct and primary way, demonstrated by Vögler, in which the Sophoclean version relates to the Aeschylean model makes it seem possible that the motif may originate with Sophokles. The stronger and more circumstantial criticism in the Euripidean version reflects the earlier presence of the motif of revision in Sophokles; and this line of literary descent makes explicable the exaggeration and stylization in the Euripidean treatment of the token scene, as well as the omission of a direct connection between this scene and major plot lines. While in Sophokles' version the rejection of the tokens marks the nadir of Elektra's hopes and the peak of her courage, the version of Euripides serves only as an accent or flourish introducing the true scene of recognition and suggesting the theme of tokens for further embellishment.

Also indicative of the inorganic quality of the token dialogue in Euripides' version is the lack of psychological support for Elektra's point of view. Critics who have attempted to motivate her rejection of the tokens in a cynicism somehow connected with a "neurosis" have overlooked the fact that they had traced Elektra's unrealistic heroic fantasies earlier in the play to the same psychic insufficiency.[85] In fact Elektra's character, with its traits of disappointment and social maladjustment, does not imply the sharp intelligence with which she skewers the suggestions of the Paidagogos.[86] For this scene, the particular character of Elektra fades a bit, as other considerations come to the fore. ⌐► Soph or Eurip.?

The character of the Paidagogos is slightly more relevant to the interchange: his antic senility makes him the ideal straight man to Elektra, as he proposes more and more absurd and remote possibilities for effecting a

85. E.g., Adams (1935, 120); Solmsen (1967, 16): Elektra shows "pride and misapplied intelligence"; Ronnet (1975, 67–69); Arnott (1981.1, 185–86).

86. See Vögler (1967, 50).

recognition through tokens.[87] But the dominating force in this dialogue, over-riding any considerations of psychology and dramatic situation, is the literary allusiveness in the recapitulation of an Aeschylean scene.[88] As R. Harriott has shown, tragic drama was for fifth-century Athens the material of discussion, daily banter, and endless conversation.[89] Euripides' allusions should not be associated with any particular revival of Aischylos, since such a use of the tokens implies a greater familiarity with the famous scene in *Choephoroi* than a single revival could provide.[90] Like the sleep-walking scene in *Macbeth,* the token scene was a byword, even with parts of the audience that had never seen a manuscript of the play. This becomes evident, when Aristophanes uses the scene in a very natural and unmarked way as the scaffolding for a complicated joke.[91] Just as famous Euripidean lines became the stuff of everyday slang and conversational parody, so that they could raise a laugh

87. Note that the whole possibility of a psychological interpretation of a given dramatic action depends upon the appearance of some dissonance between a given action and the plot structure. Otherwise, an action requires no explanation based on individual traits. See the masterly analysis by W. H. Friedrich (1953, 83) of the interpenetration of psychological motivation and form. I would argue that Elektra's rejection of the absurd suggestions of the Old Man needs little explanation; our psychological filling-in will tend to concentrate on the proposer of such notions. To this extent, there was some truth in suggestions that the characterization of the Old Man is a hit at Aischylos: see Kaibel ([1896] 1967, 60).

88. See Lloyd-Jones (1961, 180); Paduano (1970, 393); Donelli (1980, 114). I disagree with the assumption of Murray (1905, 90) and others (e.g., Ronnet [1975, 1970, 320]) that the obvious parallelism with the Aeschylean tokens can somehow be canceled out by certain psychological assumptions about Elektra. An alternate explanation, that Euripides here intends only to indicate the vanity of human rationalism, has been employed to the same purpose by Diller (1962, 97 – 98); Matthiessen (1964, 122 – 23); Vögler (1967, 50 – 51); and Pucci (1967, 369 – 71). (See also the odd theory of Klimpe [1970, 140 – 49].) But in neither case is it right to confuse the significance of Elektra's acts, in her own terms or in terms of the story, with the significance *for the audience* of this familiar sequence.

89. 1962, 1 – 2. Harriott points to the importance of the highly developed memories of an audience that had not yet learned to rely entirely on written texts.

90. I would oppose the assumptions of Newiger (1961) and Bain (1977, 109) that the audience could not have understood without the aid of some recent revival. This assumption permits Newiger to make yet another argument for dating *Elektra;* Bain refutes by denying the existence of revivals and attempting to excise the scene. See the reply of Donelli (1980, 115 – 16), which stresses the important position of Aischylos in Athenian culture.

91. *Clouds* 534 – 36. See the discussion of the lines by Newiger (1961). I do not accept his interpretation of a satiric aim at *Elektra* rather than *Choephoroi;* but his analysis does show clearly that the reference to Aischylos is not a strong or pointed joke. See the ambiguity pointed out by Böhme (1938, 205 – 6): is the *anagnôrisis* to be carried through by the (personified) play, or is it really the spectators who must recognize the play? The ambiguity is not resolvable and is the source of the problem in understanding the joke. The passage also indicates the association of the famous scene with the notion of family resemblances and inherited noble traits (see Pucci [1967, 365ff.]; Martina [1975, 15 – 19]), as well as with other stock features of comic or family drama (see line 530ff., just preceding).

for Aristophanes even in a glancing allusion, so Niobe's silence or Elektra's tokens were common coin.[92]

The debunking of the Aeschylean tokens accords perfectly with the rigorous circumstantiality of this *Elektra:* the whole first part of the play is a preparation for and a complement to this scene, where a famous dramatic moment is ruthlessly compared to a sternly factual reality.[93] That the criticisms are unfair and that the Aeschylean tokens permit a gentler interpretation is of little significance,[94] since Euripides' version is dealing precisely with a public memory of a traditional and very well loved scene. If quizzed on the subject, the audience might well agree that Orestes is unlikely to be wearing the same garment in which he left Argos;[95] but in a dramatic presentation the immediacy of the action overrides such concerns. If Aischylos had devised some dramatically effective yet circumstantially appropriate way to present the weaving sample, it is still unlikely that the posthumous productions or the public stereotypical memory of the scene worried about anything of the sort.[96] The distortion of the Aeschylean recognition is itself a reflection of the familiarity of this beloved stock piece.

In real life nobody recognizes an absent and unfamiliar relation by footprints or a lock of hair; and when such persons do appear in the flesh, they are unlikely to have brought along a supply of appropriate tokens. Sophokles managed his own version of the recognition with a seal ring, a token that a traveler would naturally bring with him; though, indeed, in the powerful emotionalism of the encounter, the token itself passes by almost without notice (1222–24).[97] The Euripidean version carefully saves and reutilizes a number of Aeschylean elements including the rush from concealment, which becomes a part of the first meeting, and the controversy over tokens, which receives an elaboration that is almost baroque. It has been pointed out that

92. See Chap. 4, above, on famous quotations from Euripides. U. v. Wilamowitz (1883, 224 n.1) argues that the Aristophanes citation shows that the saga form used in *Choephoroi* had become traditional ("die unbestritten Volksthümliche").

93. See Gellie (1981, 4–5), although G. does not interpret the reference to tokens as literary in intent.

94. For a defense of the logicality of *Choephoroi,* see Martina (1975, 164ff.); he analyzes various problems raised about verisimilitude in *Choephoroi* (65–69 and passim).

95. Mau (1877, 298) argued that the weaving was probably a sampler, and did not have to be a garment (but cf. the skeptical observations of West [1980, 20]). In pursuit of this, see Fitton Brown (1961, 368–69), who argues for a time scheme that would have permitted Orestes to wear the same clothing; and Denniston (1939, 114–15), who is perplexed. See also Dingel (1967, 128–31).

96. Cf. the distortion of famous lines from Shakespeare or popular moving pictures: the way in which a scene goes into the public memory is not necessarily the same as the way it appears in context.

97. See the comments of U. v. Wilamowitz (1883, 238–39) and Solmsen (1967, 32).

the actual token used by this play is, in typical Euripidean style, hallowed in literary tradition, as well as being rich in verisimilitude, since a scar is part of the body and does not require any external apparatus.[98]

This scene in *Elektra* must be confronted for what it is, an overt piece of literary allusion, the ultimate exaggeration of the Zielinskian principle of the rejected alternative. Nor can the tone be evaded: with the doddering Old Man for her interlocutor, Elektra builds through a series of increasingly far-fetched suggestions that, as critics have pointed out, become increasingly detached from the dramatic reality of the tomb offerings.[99] Elektra may be shown the first token, since the Old Man could have carried the lock of hair away from the grave.[100] But the suggestion that Elektra might compare her footprints with those at the grave is more remote. The Old Man does not say that he has seen such prints, and he certainly could not bring them with him. Elektra suggests that there can be none, while she also argues that the comparison would not work since men and women have different sized feet. The third token—a sample of Elektra's weaving that Orestes might produce— is purely hypothetical, since Orestes is not present and the Old Man does not seem to be sure that any such weaving exists. Elektra again rejects on grounds of possibility—she was too young to be weaving at that time— before she disproves on grounds of logic. This is a type of argument that Solmsen has identified as common in the period:[101] the reality of the evidence is disproved, before the argument itself is attacked on grounds of insufficient persuasive value and failure to conform to probability (*eikos*).

The comic undercurrent builds through the series, as Elektra first discusses the difference between male and female hair, a subtle difference based on custom, and next turns to the natural disparity between male and female feet. The reference to "low" physical detail helps the comic effect, as we are forced to picture the big feet of the Aeschylean Elektra.[102] The ludicrous image that Elektra makes of the third token, with Orestes still wearing his baby clothes, is the most telling of the three. Topped by the pert following line (Orestes cannot be wearing what she wove, "unless his clothes have

98. Tarkow (1981, 145–47); see *Od.* 19.390–466.

99. Bond (1974, 5–6).

100. I am less impressed by the suggestion that the removal of an offering from a tomb was sacrilege (Mau [1877, 297]—cf. discussion in Denniston [1939, 115]), than by the lack of a demonstrative (Denniston [ibid.]). The putative lock to be displayed would have been a very small object, so that proper cueing of the audience would have been important.

101. 1975, 10ff. See also Paduano (1970, 390).

102. Note that the actors of all stage Elektras were males, who could wear masks and wigs but could not disguise the size of their feet. On a more serious note, see the traditional association of hands and feet with recognition of identity and parentage, Paduano (1970, 400); Martina (1975, 72–73).

grown along with his body"),[103] the series of witticisms seems almost inevitably to lead to a laugh, and it is hard to see how the audience could restrain themselves.

But, if the audience laughs, can the tragic play maintain its tenor? We have seen that in Euripidean drama irony often strains the dramatic fabric; but here we seem to have a moment of rupture, when the comic rudely injects itself into the tragic mode. This scene comes at an important structural hinge in the play, the moment in which the pastoral domestic drama that has imposed itself on the Oresteia story is to be set aside, in favor of a return to the traditional line of the story's development. Soon Elektra and Orestes will complete their recognition and proceed along the well-worn lines of the oldest intrigue story in tragedy. If Elektra so far has not been what we have expected, and if Orestes has not been what Elektra expected, now they must both assume the roles already laid out for them, she to assist and he to manage the action. But Elektra's original identification with ordinary life and with a painful gulf between self-image and station is not effaced but remains as a force that continually deflects the story of revenge into new and unaccustomed channels. This scene brings into clear focus the alternate treatments of the Elektra story to which this play is opposed and through which it defines its own treatment. An explosive moment of humor marks the most violent collision between the "small" and the "great," the genre of real life and that of heroic achievement, while it also serves notice that the attitude toward the tradition will remain a critical one.

II. Elektra and Orestes

The second part of this essay will deal with the core of the traditional dramatic model that originated in *Choephoroi,* the recognition and intrigue that bring Elektra into relation with her brother Orestes. The parallelism with previous versions will continue to remain important; but the sequential relation to the Sophoclean *Elektra* and the question of chronology will be less relevant. In its treatment of the relation between the siblings, the Euripidean *Elektra* takes an approach that, at bottom, could be described as elementary rather than sophisticated and derivative. Other versions stress the relation between the siblings, while in fact substituting one for the other.[104] In Aischylos, Elektra disappears after the recognition; in Sophokles, Orestes is kept in the background until very late in the play. While emphasis in the Eu-

---

103. 544: εἰ μὴ ξυναύξοινθ' οἱ πέπλοι τῷ σώματι. Denniston (1939) refers to it as a "quip." Again, the power of the joke is in direct proportion to our fond and accepting memory of the parent scene in *Choephoroi.*

104. See the article by Tarkow (1979), on Elektra's role in *Choephoroi.*

Use in essay

ripidean version is also fixed on Elektra rather than her brother, the play succeeds in keeping both before our eyes and in tying them closely together so that the relation between the two is central.

II.A. THE MEETING

The first meeting between the siblings begins as a reworking, in the diminished modes of the Euripidean version, of the Aeschylean situation, in which Orestes burst upon Elektra, after observing her from concealment. This Elektra expands the momentary hesitation of the Aeschylean Elektra (*Cho.* 220) into a full panic. She takes Orestes for a criminal,[105] and her terror is not alleviated until she hears that he brings "word of your brother" (228). Orestes does not reveal his identity immediately; but, since he has no motivation for prolonged concealment, it is natural to assume that, after a period of ironic toying, he will complete the reunion. The model, which had probably already been used in other recognition dramas, is the scene in which Odysseus encourages his father to give a detailed account of his suffering, until emotion overcomes the son and he is unable to continue with the imposture.[106] But Orestes does not break down, and the promise of recognition offered by the dialogue is not fulfilled until much later.

E.-R. Schwinge has shown how the dialogue between the two proceeds through a series of little snags.[107] Though none is serious enough to create an impression that recognition is impossible, the combined effect of these moments is to inhibit movement toward and expectation of the recognition, while the psychological overtones illuminate the relation between the siblings, as Orestes seeks confirmation and reassurance, only to be threatened with a shameful failure to live up to heroic standards. But it is unnecessary to substitute psychological explanation completely for analysis of formal arrangements. For a traditional feature to be presented in exaggerated form and at the same time to be buttressed with a particular psychological motivation is itself a familiar procedure.[108] This encounter weakens audience confidence in Orestes: each time that we are encouraged to think of his real

105. *Kakourgos* (219) was the ordinary term for a malefactor. (See a recent discussion by Hansen [1981, 21–30]). Delays in the accomplishment of recognitions are frequently occasioned by hostile involvement of the parties (Bond [1974, 9]), so that we could say that Euripides' own style is as much model here as *Choephoroi* itself; see App. D.

106. *Od.* 24.318ff. See Matthiessen (1964, 107–8), who shows the importance of recognitions, not only to that epic, but to the cyclic *Nostoi.* As M. points out (96), the "test" Odysseus imposes on his father backfires and finally causes the tester's own emotions to break through. This parallel was developed especially strongly by Dingel (1969), who saw a close relationship between *Od.* 24 and *Elektra.*

107. 1968.1, in two very detailed discussions: pp. 252–61 and 295–317.

108. See W. H. Friedrich (1953, 83).

identity as brother hidden behind the false identity as messenger,[109] we are also forced to realize that there is something awkward and unsatisfying in his position. Elektra stresses his absence, with an implied rebuke: "He is an absent, not a present friend [ἀπὼν ἐκεῖνος, οὐ παρὼν ἡμῖν φίλος]" (245).[110] The same effect is created at lines 274–75, where Elektra directly rebukes the "messenger" for imagining that Orestes might hesitate to act, once he comes.[111] Elektra's assurance that she would not know Orestes, even if she did see him, also diminishes expectations,[112] while her statement that only the Old Man will know Orestes prepares the audience for a further postponement of the awaited moment.

Meanwhile, Orestes' emotion continues to rise and to be suppressed. He encourages Elektra to tell him about Agamemnon's tomb, attempting to excuse his obvious emotion by remarking that pity at the sufferings of others and the resulting pain are a necessary penalty of intelligence.[113] The chorus chimes in with its own motivation of what is plainly being marked as an otiose recital: they would love to hear what Elektra will tell, since, living in the country, they know little of what goes on in town.[114] Thus is inaugurated the

---

109. Schwinge (1968.1, 254) points to the exclamation *pheu* (something like "Ah!") as a sign that Orestes' thoughts turn to himself (lines 244, 262).

110. See also line 263: Orestes promises a reward for the Autourgos, but Elektra replies, "Yes, if indeed [εἰ δὴ ποθ'] the absent [*apôn*] should come home." See Schwinge (1968.1, 311ff.).

111. 275:

ἤρου τόδ' αἰσχρόν γ' εἶπας· οὐ γὰρ νῦν ἀκμή

On the meaning of the line, see Denniston (1939), Kamerbeek (1958, 20), Schwinge (1968.1, 313), Stoessl (1956.1, 56). For another and, in my opinion, less likely interpretation, see Solmsen (1967, 12). *Akmê* represents the last possible time for action; see the agricultural usages in Thukydides, which refer to grain ready for harvest (4.2.2, 2.19.1 [*akmazein*], 2.79.1, 3.1.1, etc.).

112. It does not, however, make it impossible for Orestes to speak out, as Schwinge (1968.1, 255) seems to imply.

113. 294–96. Neither Orestes nor Elektra is making any particular display of cleverness in this scene, and the *gnômê* therefore hangs a bit detached from its setting. (For a contrasting interpretation, see Schwinge [1968.1, 256ff.]). For parallel references, see Pucci (1980, 28, 78, 174). The theme of pity and intelligence is particularly apt for this play, since the close surely implies both the inadequacy of human intelligence to reach judgments and the necessity for pity.

114. Denniston remarks that there is "not much that is new" in the speech (1939, on line 292ff.); and it is true that Elektra recapitulates in the first half. The parallel is *Prom.* 631–34 or 783–84 (see Elisei [1931, 105–6]). But in the dramaturgically naive *Prometheus* the chorus' display of improbable curiosity is simply a signal to the audience that a tedious sequence of narratives is not yet over, while the remark of the Euripidean chorus is precisely calculated to mark Elektra's speech as a formal and slightly overdone excursus.

long narrative that has been so severely judged by a number of critics.[115] Elektra's speech is not solely a narrative of events "in the city" that are unknown to the chorus; it covers both her own humiliation in the country and the outrageous acts of the royal couple as they profane the memory of Agamemnon. Both parts of the recital are designed for a single effect: they must sting with shame the absent Orestes and inspire him to action. To Elektra's domestic humiliation is counterpoised the obscene splendor of Klytaimestra, rejoicing in the wealth of her first husband and living with the man who murdered him (314–22). The narrative of Aigisthos' behavior toward Agamemnon's tomb has a similar motivation, since it climaxes in a reported insult to Orestes, who if present (*parôn*) could defend his father's tomb, but who remains shamefully absent (*apôn,* 331).[116] In this version of the story there is no blasphemous offering by the murderers to their victim's ghost; instead, they proceed with a direct hostility to defame Agamemnon's memory.[117]

While her account cannot reasonably be treated as a tissue of lies, it is clear that Elektra states her cause in terms more of social humiliation than of moral outrage.[118] In part this is a result of situation, since she is remote from Aigisthos and Klytaimestra. She does speak in powerful terms of the pollution of murder in the palace: "The black blood still lies rotten [*sesêpen*] beneath the house" (318–19). Her description of her own suffering, too, shows a feeling not just for the outer trappings but for the inner meaning of her humiliating and anomalous status.[119] Yet the effect of the complaint is to support and enhance the antitragic and nonheroic materials in the play. The emphasis on household tasks and the detailed contrast between Elektra's ugly and dirty garments, woven by her own hand, and the elaborate costume of the queen's Phrygian attendants extend the domestic atmosphere of the play even

115. Besides those who have disliked the tone of Elektra's remarks and Elektra for making them, e.g., Tarkow (1981, 151: Elektra "whines about her predicament"), others have argued that, since Elektra is generally a liar, the accusations that she makes about Aigisthos are not to be believed (Kitto [(1939) 1961, 334 n.1]; Arnott [1981.1, 183–84]).

116. Note also that without this mention of the tomb of Agamemnon the theme of the crossing of two sets of offerings at the grave would be even more isolated than it is, since the grave would not have been mentioned between Orestes' first speech and the entrance of the Old Man.

117. There is also a parallel to this procedure in *Elektra* (2) 277–81: Klytaimestra actually celebrates with dances and sacrifices the anniversary of her husband's murder.

118. This was the primary basis for U. v. Wilamowitz' charge of "Frivolität" (1883, 230ff.); see Tarkow (1981, 151–52).

119. 311–13. On Elektra's virgin-wife status, which makes her a "social misfit," see Zeitlin (1970, 650). On the text, see Denniston (1939, 87–88) and U. v. Wilamowitz (1875, 63–64), who reject the reading of the manuscripts, γύμνας. It is defended by Schiassi (1956, 245–46) and more recently by Kovacs (1985, 306–10).

to this highly emotional and rhetorical moment.[120] The account of Aigisthos drunkenly[121] stoning Agamemnon's grave is similar in effect; while his actions are a source of pain and anger to Orestes, they also make the tyrant look loutish rather than terrible.

II.B. MORAL AMBIGUITY

Elektra's complaint is followed by Orestes' moralizing speech, in which he exclaims over the virtue of her farmer husband and proposes new ethical standards that will judge human beings, not by the trappings of status, but by conduct and association. If Orestes is right—and Elektra's later indictments of Klytaimestra and Aigisthos seem to indicate that, in terms of the play's ethic, he is—then the grounding for Elektra's complaints about her own lot is considerably weaker than it had seemed. Again, there is no simple Verrallian reversal to be understood: Elektra's sufferings are real, and so are the crimes of those who inflicted them upon her. We sense the ineptitude in Elektra's complaints, even as we sympathize with her; but her impatience and desire to shame Orestes into returning are also shared by the audience, as they observe the brother making no move to assume his identity.

Euripides has pulled Elektra and Orestes closer together by involving both siblings in responsibility for the killing of their mother and by making Elektra's personal experience the basis for the revenge. Matching the structural balance between the siblings is the balance between Klytaimestra and Aigisthos, whose deaths are kept separate, while the plot against each is governed by the sibling of the same sex as the victim. In this way, the moral effect of the two killings can be kept distinct, and the social and generic unsuitability of Elektra can affect our perception of the revenge against Klytaimestra.

The revenge story follows as in all Elektra dramas fast upon the recognition, and indeed this sequence has become paradigmatic for most Euripidean intrigues.[122] Most critics have been struck by the sympathetic circumstances

120. Note that, as Kubo (1967, 23) and Zeitlin (1970, 647ff.) point out, the contrast of costume becomes a part of the play's visual aspect at Klytaimestra's actual entrance.

121. The word βρεχθείς, "soused" (see Stevens [1976, 12]) has a prosaic and colloquial ring; and drunkenness itself is a touchy subject for the lofty atmosphere of tragedy, as witness Herakles in *Alkestis;* see Dale (1954, xx-xxi) and Stumpo (1960, 118–19).

122. On the structures of the intrigue or *mêchanêma* in Euripidean drama, see Solmsen (1934.1, 1932) and Diller (1962), and the varied explorations of the theme by other scholars, notably Ludwig (1957), Strohm (1957), and Burnett (1971). Most of the surviving dramas of intrigue are plays of rescue rather than revenge, like *Elektra*; see discussion in App. D. Note that all plays of intrigue are by definition bipartite, since a situation set up in the early part of the play is reversed in the second, usually through the peripety of the recognition (Solmsen [1932, 2–3]). Cf. the interesting, though wrongly applied, model of Frey (1947, 39–42).

in which the two villains come to die,[123] Aigisthos while acting as a polite host, and Klytaimestra, while performing a maternal duty. But each is still guilty of adultery and murder.[124] There is no exchange of apparent moral values for hidden and unexpected ones; instead, the play alters and contaminates what at first might seem simple and homogeneous.

The moral framework set up by Orestes' praise of the Autourgos seems to imply that Orestes' *eugeneia* too might be called into question; and indeed the Paidagogos remarks that one never can tell by high birth whether someone is truly noble (550 – 51).[125] Yet Orestes has said that habits and association are the only true mark of the *eugenês*; and for the second at least he cannot be faulted on his own terms, since Orestes has chosen the virtuous Autourgos as his associate. Elektra's unrealistic idealization of her brother reflects the same gap between expectation and reality that marks her character throughout; yet Elektra, with her shabby rags and her dedication to revenge, is no representative of the empty and complacent wealth denounced by Orestes.[126] In fact, Klytaimestra and Aigisthos play that part. The worst indictment of either brother or sister is simply their association through Klytaimestra with a doomed and evil house, a further proof that *eugeneia* is no guarantee of moral decency.[127] In what sense can someone with a heritage of such misery be said to be *eugenês*? If we view Elektra's family with the eye of the everyday, there is little to admire, but much to pity.[128]

The intrigue closes with a second ode in the grand style, this time a story closer to home, but still remote in the legendary and fabulous past, the tale of Thyestes and the golden lamb.[129] The sweeping opening, with its collection of decorative detail, purling phrase on phrase, leads down, as often in this style, from Pan, his pipes, and the mountains of Mykenai to the golden lamb. The festival to celebrate the lamb's arrival is given a familiar lyric

123. See, e.g., U. v. Wilamowitz (1883, 219, 222); Steiger (1912, 24); Elisei (1931, 137). There is a similar effect in *Herakleidai,* where Eurystheus creates an ambiguous impression. See Burian (1977, 3 – 4, 20): the end leads to a "disquieting revision of the play's guiding assumptions." This effect has led to attempts to make Eurystheus sympathetic (Stoessl [1956.2, 220 – 21]) or utterly unappealing (Burnett [1976, 24 – 25]).

124. For this point, see Fresco (1976, 103); Whitehorne (1978, 8 – 9 n.9).

125. See O'Brien (1964, 37). In fact this may be seen as a rather untactful remark, though, because delineating a bad nature for the Old Man has not occurred to anybody, it has not received the same attention as similar remarks by Orestes and Elektra.

126. Again, psychological overinterpretation can make of Elektra the same thing as the ones she accuses; see Tarkow (1981, 152): we can "document Electra's own obsessive fascination" with "physical beauty and exquisite clothing."

127. See the discussion of this theme by O'Brien (1964, 32 – 37), although O'B. does not mention the connection to the house of Atreus.

128. On this theme in *Elektra,* see Whitehorne (1978, 8). In late Euripides in general, see Strohm ([1949] 1968, 389 – 90); Solmsen (1934.1, 407).

129. On this saga, see Kubo (1967, 19ff.) and Zeitlin (1970, 654).

development, with references to sacrifices, flutes, and dances. All this gives us less the atmosphere of a remote mythical event than the decor of a particular kind of lyric expression, an impression that is strengthened by the repeated and rather extraneous introduction of music.[130] The actual events that build the story—the announcement of the herald and the successful intrigue of Thyestes—are tucked into the close of each verse.[131] The second strophe is an elaborate and elegant description of the effects of the sun's reversal of its path, a heavenly reaction to Thyestes' treachery.[132]

The story of the golden lamb is, of all the tales associated with Mykenai, the most fabulous and miraculous. It mixes the familiar theme of adultery with material—the "wonder" (teras) of the fleece and the reversal of the sun—that is wholly fantastic. The latter is a particularly naive element, if we take it to mean that one piece of sexual treachery occasioned a major astronomical disturbance; and in the antistrophe the chorus rejects the story as unbelievable. Their remarks bear some resemblance to Pindaric transitions, where for example the story of Perseus' killing of the Gorgon is broken off by a pious avowal of belief that admits the intrinsic implausibility of the tale.[133] But this instance more closely resembles the caveats we find in Herodotos.[134] The chorus are skeptical of the theological implications: how likely is it that the heavens will respond to violations of human justice (θνατᾶς ἕνεκεν δίκας, 741)? The ode ends with a reflection that sounds a number of significant chords in contemporary and Sophistic thought: this sort of story, incredible as it is, is designed to inject a salutary fear and to impel us to revere the gods.[135] But Klytaimestra has failed to take her warning.

What the first stasimon accomplished by simple juxtaposition of the fabulous past with the squalid dramatic present, this ode performs overtly,

130. 702ff., 716ff. in responding sections of the verse. See in Pindaros references to music accompanying the odes (Ol. 3.8, 7.12, 10.94; Ne. 9.8) and at the celebrations of the Hyperboreans (Py. 10.39).

131. See Panagl (1967, 60).

132. The word hedra seems to be used, or misused, with a play on its technical astronomical meaning of "quarter of the sky"; see Denniston (1939, on lines 739–40). U. v. Wilamowitz (1907, 31ff., 33) claimed that Euripides was without interest in such matters; but allusions to such matters may be limited more by the nature of tragic material than by any aversion of the author. For astronomical themes in Elektra see Albini (1962, 94–95).

133. Py. 10.48–50.

134. Lines 737–38: λέγεται · τὰν δὲ πίστιν σμικρὰν παρ' ἔμοιγ' ἔχει. For parallel phrases in Herodotos, see Powell's Lexicon under pistos.3: Herodotos commonly signals his criticism of material transmitted by the tradition with such phrases as ἐμοὶ μὲν οὐ πιστὰ λέγοντες.

135. The moral position is reversed to orthodoxy, but the argument is the same as that in Sisyphos (DK 2:88 fr. 25B.27–36), as is the astronomical context: tales of heavenly displeasure are untrue and designed with the purpose of enforcing moral norms among human beings. Of course we might wonder at the instructive value of a moral tale that is admittedly false.

proposing another fantastic tale and then subjecting that tale to criticism, and interpretive exegesis. The high standard of circumstantiality established for the current dramatic action acts as an inevitable elenchus and correction to the extravagances of lyricized legend. In particular, the question of punishment for adultery and the place of "human justice" in the cosmic scheme will continue to be raised in the lineverse scenes.[136] These are the only major odes, and after this the chorus will sing only brief songs that are closely involved in the action of the play. The strong division between genres that at first set off the low-life scenes with the Autourgos from the past of legend is replaced by a more unitary treatment, as the mythical events themselves take over, only to be presented in a way that constantly forces upon them the analogy of real life.

II.C. AIGISTHOS

The account of Aigisthos' death takes place in the same atmosphere of slightly tainted festivity as did the celebration of the golden lamb.[137] Orestes is assimilated to the role of victor in the games,[138] someone whose triumph is benign and is shared by the whole society.[139] Yet the narration of the death is, as has often been noted, ambiguous and emotionally confusing. We should expect nothing less; as William Arrowsmith remarked, "a note of firm tonality" in Euripides is always suspect.[140] The myrtles that Aigisthos never picked to adorn Agamemnon's grave (324) he picks now in festival to the nymphs, goddesses of fertility and childbirth.[141] The family of Klytaimestra and Aigisthos usurps the place of the legitimate family, but we are given every opportunity to picture the usurping family as real. There is even a faint hint of another horrible complication to the matricide. We know that Klytaimestra's marriage to Aigisthos has not been infertile (62ff.); and, when

136. See Sheppard (1918, 140).

137. For the motif of blasphemous or corrupted sacrifice in the play, see Zeitlin (1970); Z. shows that the theme of festivity, linked with that of victory, is the dominating motif of the play in lyric and in the dramatic situation.

138. For this theme in the play, see O'Brien (1964, 36); Zeitlin (1970, 652); Arnott (1981.1, 187–88). The theme has a traditional look, to judge by the long narrative of Orestes' "death" in *Elektra* (2); and we should again be reminded of the vast literary background that has been lost to us.

139. See Pindaros' use of the word "common," *xynon* (*Py.* 11.54, *Is.* 6.69), to indicate the community's participation in the victor's glory.

140. 1963, 37.

141. See Zeitlin (1970, 664–65 and n.56), who points out the link between these goddesses and Hera, whose festival is mentioned in the parodos. The connection of these goddesses with fertility has been pointed out earlier (at line 626) and is thus in active play in the scene.

Elektra lures her mother to the hut by claiming to have given birth, the queen may herself be pregnant.[142]

W. G. Arnott has shown the theatrical trick with which Euripides keeps us in suspense, not knowing when the blow will come, during Orestes' long narration of the plot against Aigisthos.[143] The invitation to skin the sacrificial victim places a knife in Orestes' hands; but he waits, as Aigisthos anxiously inspects the evil signs, until the host calls for a cleaver (*kopis,* 837) with which to lay open the chest cavity. Then, as Aigisthos bends over the entrails, our hero draws himself up and cleaves open his victim along the spine. "His whole body, above and below, gasped and shuddered in his death agony [ἤσπαιρεν, ἠλέλιζε δυσθνῄσκων φόνῳ]'' (843). The repellent detail of the narrative[144] blends with the ambiguous nature of sacrificial ritual, which combines holiness with butchery, to create a peculiar thrill of horror. The revulsion is not accurately directed at Orestes' impiety, however, but radiates from the whole scene.[145] Aigisthos is killed at an appropriate moment, just as he bends over the ominous entrails that themselves signify, predict, and in part justify his death. By postponing the death, Orestes allows the sacrifice to proceed to completion, a completion that may be said to include the murder itself. Is this piety, or blasphemy?

The same ambiguity marks the appearance of Orestes with the head of Aigisthos. The sight is a barbarous one, but the provocation has been great; and the jubilation of Elektra and the chorus is justified, in that Argos has indeed been freed from tyranny. Orestes' modest response to his sister's joy prudently places the gods first: they created the chance (*tychê*) by which he benefited, and he was only the servant of them and of *tychê*.[146] His suggestion that Elektra may decide on appropriate disposition of the corpse does seem to offer analogies with the Sophoclean version, where there are hints of

142. See lines 626–27: it is left uncertain whether Aigisthos is sacrificing for the health of his children, or for a coming birth.

143. Arnott on "Red Herrings" (1978, 3–4); see also 1977. For *Kresphontes* as a model, see App. D.

144. On the meaning, see Denniston (1939, on lines 842–43). Note that Aigisthos' body, not Aigisthos himself, seems to utter his death cry, a grotesque touch that reminds us of the kinship between the victim and the dead animal body he is inspecting. Orestes' posture, on his tiptoes to give greater force to the blow, also emphasizes the dehumanizing violence of the killing. See Arnott (1981.1, 187).

145. See O'Brien (1964, 28) on the "tainted justice" of the act. Arnott (1981.1, 186–87) sees the killing as ambiguous, both impure (*miaron*) and heroic at once.

146. Note this mildly modernized piety, in which *tychê* and the gods, usually rather provocatively juxtaposed as alternatives in Euripides, here share the honors. Compare *Hek* 799ff., where a similar formulation is given a later ironic development. In a Euripidean context such passages are meant to make a relatively colorless or "normal" impression. Such are the complexities of antitraditionalist drama: see further discussion in Chap. 8, Section III.A, below, on *Herakles*.

a dishonorable treatment for Aigisthos' body.[147] Orestes here openly suggests denial of burial, although no disposition of Aigisthos' body will in fact be made until the arrival of the Dioskouroi at the end. It is typical of Sophokles to leave such disquieting references vague, as it is of Euripides to make the reference explicit—and then reverse it.

Elektra now proceeds to denounce Aigisthos, or rather Aigisthos' head, saying to him in death what she was not able to in his life.[148] This is the formal equivalent to a verbal *agôn* between Elektra and her stepfather, a debate that is germane to Euripidean style and that will actually occur in the case of Klytaimestra. The grotesque effect of the "confrontation" should not be overlooked. There is both a painful appropriateness in the address of a long speech to Aigisthos' head—a final indignity for this rather undignified figure[149]—and a painful inappropriateness, since Elektra's speech is in fact analogous to what Aigisthos did in stoning the stone-dead grave of his predecessor.[150] Both show themselves weak in attacking a stronger enemy after death; but, since Elektra is a woman, her open admission of weakness does her less harm. The speech revives a major theme from the first segment of the play. The transformation of Elektra into a quasi matron, instead of being merely an anomaly in the mythic situation, is central to the Euripidean version, which repeatedly stresses the theme of marriage. The chorus celebrate in honor of Hera, Aigisthos sacrifices to goddesses of childbirth and rearing, and Klytaimestra is lured to Elektra's hut for a ceremony of purification following childbirth. Now, when Elektra comes to denounce Aigisthos and his life, her attack is an attack upon his marriage and upon him as a husband.

Elektra accuses Aigisthos of profaning and destroying a good family, in order to enter into a shameful marriage (916) with her mother. Since his marriage is founded on adultery, he may expect his wife to betray him, as she did her first mate; and thus he is assumed to be a cuckold from the start (918–24).[151] Aigisthos and Klytaimestra each know the other to be evil; by uniting themselves, both take upon themselves the fortunes (*tychai*) of both, a double dose of misfortune (925–29). Further, in this marriage, Aigisthos' role is the passive one, appropriate to the wife. This charge is familiar from

147. 896–97. Given the extensive literary background, no significant reference to *Elektra* (2) need be assumed.

148. 909–13, an elaborate formal *prooimion,* in which Elektra remembers how in secret she used to wail forth her resentment against Aigisthos.

149. We may compare the treatment of Pentheus' head in *Bakchai,* though there the initial effect is one of extreme pathos. On the effect of the already dead and detachable mask (or "face" [*prosôpon*]), see Segal (1982, 248ff.).

150. πέτροις τε λεύει μνῆμα λάινον πατρός (328).

151. This does not imply that Elektra actually accuses Klytaimestra of adultery against Aigisthos, nor yet that this may be another of Elektra's "lies."

Agamemnon, where it is supported by the fact that Klytaimestra, not Aigisthos, is the actual murderer.[152] Euripides substitutes a more conventional factor: since Klytaimestra, as the original queen and wife of Agamemnon, surpasses her second mate in status and wealth, their children are said to belong to her, not to her consort.[153] This charge blends with the underlying adultery, which disrupts paternal control over bloodlines and inheritance.[154] Aigisthos was a fool, who did not know or understand his own shame and his own misfortune.[155] But his peak of foolishness ("what deceived you the most in your ignorance," 938) was his assumption that the great wealth of Agamemnon's house would bring status. Inner, not outer, qualities—*physis* not *chrêmata*—alone are dependable. The moral is as old as Solon and as familiar, but it also echoes the moralizing of Orestes earlier, as do the references to Aigisthos' association with Klytaimestra's bad *tychê*.

Finally, Aigisthos is condemned for the seductive charm that led Klytaimestra into his power. Just as Aigisthos sires children who are their mother's and not his, so his reliance on sexual appeal rather than valor marks him as less than a true man. Elektra, a maiden (*parthenos*) herself, wants to have in marriage, not a "maiden-faced" male beauty, but a husband and father "of the masculine sort [τἀνδρείου τρόπου]" distinguished in war and battle, whose children will be like him (948–50). Aigisthos has won the rewards of the true man Agamemnon, through sexual prowess. Elektra's condemnation is strongly supported by Hellenic attitudes toward adulterers, and by the traditional punishment for this offense.[156] If Orestes' brilliant victory is tarnished both by the sacrilegious circumstances in which it takes place and by the low status of the opponent, Aigisthos has still deserved his death; and the manliness of Orestes and Pylades has been proven by their

152. The chorus reproaches Aigisthos (1633–35); and see the delineation by Jones (1962, 115–21) of Klytaimestra's aberrant role. In this play, Klytaimestra is not so monstrously masterful: the Autourgos imputes the *dolos* to her, the hand to Aigisthos (9–10), though at other times Klytaimestra's full complicity or even active participation is implied (e.g., line 279, a reference to her axe); see Hunger (1936, 12 n.29). The lack of vividness associated with the crime matches the tendency, noted by Whitehorne (1978, 7), for this play to stress the distorting effects of the passage of time between the actual murder and the vengeance.

153. Cf. the parallel passage in *Elektra* (2) 365–67; see Steiger (1897, 577 n.30).

154. As Lysias remarks, the adulterer makes it impossible to say whose the children are (1.33). See Erdmann, on the contrast in treatment between legitimate children, who always belong with the paternal line, and *nothoi,* who are the responsibility of the mother's family (1934, 400–1).

155. References to his foolishness: ἐς τοῦτο δ' ἦλθες ἀμαθίας (918); οὐ δοκῶν οἰκεῖν κακῶς (925). References to knowledge: ἴστω (921); δύστηνός ἐστιν, εἰ δοκεῖ (923); ᾔδησθα (926); οὐδὲν εἰδὼς (952–53).

156. See Dover (1978, 105–6): the purpose of anal rape was to feminize and thus to humiliate the adulterer, reversing the humiliation that he had inflicted on the husband.

"battle" against him.[157] Elektra's denunciation uses the moral values derived from the Autourgos' role to condemn Aigisthos. While the latter seemed to be a handsome, elegant, courtly, and wealthy man, possessed of sexual appeal and married to a complaisant and fruitful wife, he was in fact a wretch who comes off much the worse in comparison with the Autourgos, a poor, simple man, living in squalid circumstances, with a wife both bad-tempered and virginal.[158] We may expect that the comparison will be harmful to Klytaimestra as well, when she confronts her counterpart, Elektra.

II.D. KLYTAIMESTRA

Throughout the play, Orestes has assumed that his mother would be punished, but has never taken the lead in proposing her death.[159] Now he suddenly expresses doubt, even as Klytaimestra's carriage approaches the hut.[160] Earlier, Orestes had hung back, querying Elektra (278, 650) and the Paidagogos (612) as if to provoke their assertion that Klytaimestra should and must be killed. Now the same device recalls Orestes' last-minute question to Pylades in *Choephoroi,* as Orestes asks, "What shall we do? Shall we then kill our mother?" (967)[161] In the earlier scenes the absence of references to Apollon has had the effect of shunting aside the whole moral dilemma posed by the god's injunction to commit matricide. Now it breaks out in extreme form, Orestes referring over and over again to Klytaimestra's maternal

157. See line 884ff., for this imagery, and Zeitlin (1970, 655–59); Arnott (1981.1, 187–88). Here, Euripides has his motif both ways, using the parallel of athletics (the festive and harmless victory) and war (the truly valuable victory) to get the best parts of each. Martina (1975, 161–62) points out the ambiguity of such themes in Euripides; and the athletic metaphor is reused with ironic undertones at lines 954–56: one does not win the race with *Dikê* until one ends the course of one's life.

158. The paradox that personal beauty and pride do not assure real courage or effectiveness is as old as Archilochos (114W). Yet the extension of these ideas to undermine the traditional concept of *eugeneia* is new.

159. Again, estimates of his reluctance have varied; see Schwinge (1968.1, 88–89).

160. The assignment of individual lines is somewhat in doubt at this point. Some editors would assign to Elektra lines 959–61, the order to take Aigisthos' body into the hut; Orestes then interrupts, saying that he sees approaching "the mother who bore me [τὴν τεκοῦσαν ἥ μ' ἐγείνατο]" (964). See Denniston (1939, 166–67). Others prefer to follow the manuscripts in giving the initial command to Orestes, with Elektra interrupting and uttering line 964 in a spirit of bitter irony; see Schwinge (1968.1, 85ff. and 88–89). Line 964 seems to make its impression effectively, whichever sibling utters it; but at line 962 it is hard to see why Elektra in merely drawing attention to Klytaimestra's arrival should say "Stop! Let's talk of something else." If Orestes says this, the "something else" would be his doubts about the killing. Schwinge (1968.1, 88), who tends to rely heavily on psychological explanations (see Chap. 1, above), argues that Elektra is so excited that she forgets to note that she is not changing the subject.

161. τί δῆτα δρῶμεν μητέρ' ἢ φονεύσομεν two of Orestes' crucial questions include the particle *dêta* ("what then"—see Denniston [1954, 269ff.]), perhaps naively indicative of his reluctance to draw the obvious conclusion.

role.[162] Elektra strongly stresses the traditional Aeschylean answer: Orestes has been ordered by Apollon to fulfill completely binding obligations to his father. There is no reason to doubt the significance of this theme, when it is so stressed at such a crucial point.[163] One reason that it could be ignored earlier has been the concentration on Elektra's situation, since to her the mandate of Apollon is of less importance.

As Orestes hurries inside, Klytaimestra's arrival is accompanied by an honorific introduction from the chorus, who congratulate her on her wealth and good fortune.[164] Her first words sound the same note, as she boasts of the Trojan slaves who are to assist her down from the carriage, remarking that they are a small compensation (*smikron geras*) for her lost Iphigeneia. This Klytaimestra is no dominating, powerful virago derived from misogynist fantasy. Instead, like Hermione in the *Andromache,* she represents something familiar in contemporary Attica, the well-dowered bride, proud of her wealth and capable of asserting power in the household.[165] Elektra picks up her mother's arrogant opening, and sarcastically offers her hand too in assistance. The sarcasm is spoiled, however, when the complacent queen fails to notice it; and Elektra is forced to make her point again: she and these slaves, both dispossessed and orphaned, are of equivalent status.[166] The pettiness of Elektra's attack is a match for her mother's values: a person who can be consoled for the loss of a child by pecuniary compensations—and that while leaving a living child in poverty—falls outside moral norms in most

162. *Mêtêr* or corresponding terms appear seven times in seventeen lines: lines 961, 964, 968, 969, 973, 975, 977. But note that Elektra has periodically referred to Klytaimestra as "mother," something that the Sophoclean Elektra never does; see Vahlen (1885, 361).

163. Note the opposing view of Steiger (1897, 593ff.) and Conacher (1967, 203 and 210), who would attempt to ignore references to Apollon.

164. 988–97. Zeitlin (1970, 661) compares the laudatory language to that of cult hymns; but the echoes closer at hand may simply be other pompous entrances in tragedy—see Aischylos *Pe.* 150ff. The reference to the Dioskouroi is extended and significant: like Thetis in the *Andromache,* they are divine figures who have a direct link to the family.

165. See *Andr* 152–53 (Hermione's large dowry gives her "freedom of speech [ὥστ' ἐλευθεροστομεῖν]"); lines 209–14 (Andromache's accusation that Hermione thinks more of her family of birth than of her husband's family); lines 871–73. For the social reality of this, see Schaps (1979, 76): "The wife who contributed more than her husband [to the family treasury] had a good claim to be considered the senior partner."

166. 1008–10. See Zeitlin (1970, 647) on the visual effect of the attendants, carefully set up earlier in Elektra's complaint to Orestes (314–18). Elektra no doubt looks more like a common slave than the Trojan women do. The theme is already strongly laid down in *Choephoroi;* see lines 132–35, 915. The repetition of the sarcasm has been the occasion for proposed excision; see U. v. Wilamowitz (1883, 222 n.1). For a defense of the passage, however, see Vahlen (1891, 357–58).

societies.[167] This Klytaimestra is a living example of the triviality and emptiness with which Orestes had charged the standard representatives of
eugeneia. The terms of Orestes' homily would appear inadequate or
irrelevant beside the Klytaimestra of Aischylos; but, for this Klytaimestra,
they are appropriate.

Elektra's mention of her lost father (*patros orphanoi,* 1010) stings the
queen enough to provoke a reply. She begins with the death of Iphigeneia.
"My father did not give me in marriage to die, nor for the death of my children."[168] Such an act would have been justified if Agamemnon had been
sacrificing his daughter on behalf of the city.[169] But he did it for Helene's
folly, and because his brother did not know how to punish a betraying wife
(1027–28). The applications of this argument to Klytaimestra herself are
obvious, but she sweeps on. She would not have killed Agamemnon for that
alone, however; it was the offense of introducing two wives into the same
house that made her wild (*êgriômên,* 1031). Granted that women are vicious
(*môron*), still, when husbands err, wives are prone to mimic them.[170] Then
women are blamed, but those responsible (*aitioi*) are not.[171] This excuse
would be less plausible for the ancient audience, who conceived of adultery
as a sin against the family bloodlines, occurring only through the seduction of
a married woman.[172] Klytaimestra's rationalizations are not enough to push
aside the conventional basis of Greek marriage, especially since these con-

167. See Zeitlin (1970, 663 n.52) and Lesky ([1956] 1972.1, 400), "welcher Ersatz!" In
Greek terms, Klytaimestra's values place the *timê* derived from the family (which comes to
parents from children, as well as the reverse) behind that derived from wealth, a source traditionally low on the scale of Hellenic values.

168. 1019: οὐχ ὥστε θνῄσκειν, οὐδ᾽ ἃ γειναίμην ἐγώ. Denniston (1939, on line 1019)
points out the rhetorical effectiveness of Klytaimestra's implying that Agamemnon might as well
have the right to kill her as to kill her children. This jumps over the awkward question of paternal rights, since according to Hellenic usage the children belonged more to father than to mother.

169. One is reminded, of course, of the *Erechtheus,* the *Herakleidai,* and other Euripidean
plays in which a member of the family is sacrificed for such public goals.

170. For the meaning of *môron,* see *Tro.* 989, 1059, where the term is applied to Helene's
looseness. This special meaning of "folly" can be applied to males only in terms of a different
and personal sexual morality (see the new moral in the *Diktys* 331.2 N2—discussed in App. D—
and Theseus' comment, *Hipp* 966ff.). Paley (1874, on line 1027) glosses the word with *margos.*
The claim that she was imitating Agamemnon's misdeeds (*mimeisthai,* 1037) would seem to
imply that the queen had taken no missteps until the arrival of Kassandra, though the admission
of women's weakness (1035) rather implies the opposite. For a more favorable analysis of the
logic of Klytaimestra's arguments, see Vahlen (1891, 360).

171. See the somewhat similar argument of Pasiphaë in the *Cretan Men*; she also labels her
husband the *aitios,* not herself.

172. See the discussion in Pomeroy (1975, 86–87).

ventions have already been strongly emphasized in Elektra's indictment of
Aigisthos.

What conviction Klytaimestra's argument might have is destroyed by the
devices with which she makes her peroration. She first creates an imaginary
and absurd inversion of the real situation in which, Menelaos having been
"carried off secretly from the house" (1041), Klytaimestra would have to
sacrifice Orestes to get her sister's husband back. The argument resembles
and exaggerates the elaborate hypothetical constructs of the new rhetoric;[173]
but in this case the perfect reversal of sexual roles only reveals the flaws in
Klytaimestra's attempt to equate husbands and wives. The audience will
understand that wives do not have property rights in husbands, as husbands
do in wives. Finally, ignoring her earlier admission that the sacrifice was not
really the occasion of the murder, Klytaimestra claims that her need for
revenge forced an alliance with Agamemnon's enemy, Aigisthos (1046 ff.).
Elektra, in her reply, will cut through both arguments, claiming that
Klytaimestra's predilection for *to môron* antedated even the sacrifice itself.

Elektra's indictment again contrasts specious attractiveness with the
absence of decent moral *physis*. Klytaimestra, like Helene, is fine-looking,
and morally bad. Even before her daughter's death, she primped in her mirror, a sure sign of readiness for dalliance, when the man is away.[174] We may
compare the golden curls (1071) of the pampered temptress with Elektra's
own shorn locks and ugly dress. Klytaimestra preferred the image in her mirror, showing her an outward beauty resembling that of her sister; but she
should instead have used the actions of Helene as a soul mirror for her own
moral ugliness.[175] Elektra ends with a sentiment (*gnômê*) that has been
expunged by many editors for its inconsequence:

173. There were of course suggestions for the excision of these odd lines; see U. v.
Wilamowitz (1883, 223 n.1), opposed by Vahlen (1891, 358–59), who points out their
correspondence to Elektra's speech. On the frigidity of the passage, see Albini (1962, 106), "di
una bizzarria sconcertante."

174. 1069–71. Klytaimestra's defenders, who are often detractors of Elektra, see this as
another lie, or as the distortion of Elektra's warped mind. See U. v. Wilamowitz (1883, 230);
Arnott (1981.1, 184). It is true that the sententious tone and the trivial evidence offered create a
familiar effect in our perception of Elektra: she is "right" but she is not appealing.

175. 1085: παράδειγμα τοῖς ἐσθλοῖσιν εἰσοψίν τ' ἔχει. *Eisopsis* (insight) is a hapax; it
resembles and is meant to make us think of the *es-* or *katoptron*, the mirror, which Klytaimestra
used earlier in the speech. The theme of appearance is stressed by the language; see φαίνειν
πρόσωπον (1075), συννέφουσαν ὄμματα (1078). Cf. lines 372 and 387–89; as well as
948–49, 951.

Anyone who, with an eye on wealth or birth,
marries a bad woman is a fool. Small connections,
if they are decent [*sôphrona*],
make better marriages in the house than great.[176]

Those who excise must then also remove the closing comment of the chorus,
since they continue the theme by remarking that women's luck in marriage is
variable.[177] Almost no Euripidean long speeches (*rheseis*) end without closing summary remark or choral comment; and, if our received text looked like
the excised one, we would have been rightly suspicious of a lacuna.[178] In fact
the reference to marriage is tied to a dominating theme of the play, the
incompatibility of decency (*sôphrosynê*) with wealth. The contrast between
"small" (*mikra*) and "great" (*megala*) comes to us directly from the last
scene with the Autourgos. To the heroic image of a marriage of brilliance
and glory, are opposed the moral prescriptions of the new ethic, which
redefines *eugeneia* and scoffs at wealth.

Klytaimestra passes off Elektra's denunciation with a piece of domestic
wisdom: some children naturally love their fathers more; some, their mothers. Thematically, what she says correlates with Elektra's stricture about the
new family of Aigisthos: there, the children belong to the mother, not to the
male line (934 – 35). Klytaimestra sees this not as a moral issue, but as one
of the concrete realities of domestic life, necessitating a balancing of claims.
Later, she will place emphasis on the dual responsibilities of a mother, to
husband and to children (1133 – 34, 1138). Klytaimestra is struck with pity as

176. 1097 – 99:

ὅστις δὲ πλοῦτον ἢ εὐγένειαν εἰσιδὼν
γαμεῖ πονηρὰν μῶρός ἐστι · μικρὰ γὰρ
μεγάλων ἀμείνω σώφρον' ἐν δόμοις λέχῃ.

Suggestions for excision have been many—see Vahlen (1891, 362); Page (1934, 76); Denniston
(1939). C. Friedrich (1955, 222, 233 – 39) points to a number of other passages also dealing
with marriage and thought to be interpolated. But on, e.g., *Andr* 1279 – 83, see Steidle (1968,
125 – 26): the theme of marriage is central to that play as well.

177. 1100 – 1; see their earlier comment, lines 1052 – 54. Vahlen (1891, 363) pointed this
out. Denniston (1939, 185), evidently bothered by the problem, argues that "it does not perhaps
after all seem absolutely certain" that the choral comment cannot be kept, even if the end of
Elektra's speech is excised. But the chorus' remark is of a singular blandness and inconsequence; it must have a lead-in. A laconic first formulation, "That is the luck of women in regard
to marriage [τύχη γυναικῶν εἰς γάμους]" (for a divergent interpretation, see Denniston [1939,
on line 1100]), is clarified by the second—some marriages turn out well, some ill.

178. For examples of the Euripidean *agôn* ending with choral comment, see *Andr* 727, 232;
Hik 564; *Tro* 1033; *Phoin* 586; *Hel* 1030; *Or* 605. For omission, see *Andr* 384 and *Ion* 668. The
commands and suggestions in the speeches of this second type pass directly into dialogue,
without any intervening closing remarks or choral summation. By contrast, Elektra's speech
ended on a generalizing, sententious, and argumentative note, in classic Euripidean fashion.

222   Part II: Four Plays

she realizes Elektra's humiliation, "unwashed, ill-dressed, just after you have given birth." Her feelings of responsibility must be increased by the fact that it would normally have been her duty as parent to be with her daughter at this time, "when nothing is more comforting than one's mother [ἵν' οὐδὲν μητρὸς εὐμενέστερον]" (Alk 319). But when Elektra explains her need for help with birth ritual, Klytaimestra points out that such rites would normally be the office of one who assisted at the birth. The touch is typical of the play's rigid approach to circumstantial detail; but we also note the cold reluctance of the queen, and Elektra's explanation—that she was alone at the birth—emphasizes the fact of her abandonment. Klytaimestra has begun by expressing regret;[179] but the dialogue that follows suggests the awkwardness and pain of even a temporary rapprochement between mother and daughter. In this dark atmosphere, Klytaimestra's hopes to reconcile Elektra and Aigisthos (1119, 1121) seem shallow. Her repeated opposition between duties to daughter and duties to husband only stresses the gulf between the two very unequal poles of her loyalty.

The extreme moment of contrast between what is still queenly and heroic in Klytaimestra—that is, the outward show of her rank—and the irreducible reality of Elektra's life comes at the end of the scene, when Elektra, with more bitter sarcasm, invites her mother to "Come into this poor house, but watch out that the smoky place does not get your robe sooty."[180] The average Attic house was like Elektra's,[181] and the touch is exquisitely timed. Part of the reality of life, something ordinarily not "noticed" in literature, collides with the idealized wealth of the legendary era, with a strong effect of dissonance. Klytaimestra cannot even enter the house of her daughter without becoming contaminated by the brand of ordinary life. The cramped setting diminishes both protagonists even as it denounces the hypocrisy of Klytaimestra's pomp. It is in this setting that she will die; and, when the

179. The proposal of Denniston (1939, 186–87) to transfer lines 1107–8 to 1131 (followed by Diggle [1981.2]) will not do. The rhetoric of line 1006ff. is incoherent without the lines, which provide a transition from an ironic litotes to a more straightforward and emotional expression of regret. At line 1131 the transposed lines are thoroughly unconnected with grammar or context.

180. 1139–40:

χώρει πένητας εἰς δόμους· φρούρει δέ μοι
μή σ' αἰθαλώσῃ πολύκαπνον στέγος πέπλους.

This moment's obvious analogy is the "carpet scene" in the Agamemnon. Zeitlin (1970, 657 and n.37) has pointed out the parallels.

181. See D. M. Robinson's analysis of domestic architecture in the remains of Olynthos, dating from the late fifth and early fourth centuries. The usual arrangement was a hole in the ceiling, "a simple opening in the roof" (1946, 380–81), covered in bad weather by a tile (Robinson [49]; see Aristoph. Wasps 143–47). (I owe the reference to my colleague V. J. Harward.)

trappings of her rank have been thoroughly stripped away, the whole central action of the play, the revenge itself, will have changed.

II.E. THE EXODOS

The song with which the chorus fills the gap between Klytaimestra's entrance into the hut and her death cry from within does not absolve the victim. Instead it presents the death of Agamemnon as a betrayal between husband and wife, repeating the dying question of the husband, as he is slain "in the bath" (*loutrois,* 1148). The death cry of Agamemnon, thus remembered, overlaps with Klytaimestra's own death cry and points up the rightness of the vengeance. Yet, at the same time, the terms "wife" (*gynê*) and "husband" (*posis*), and the emphasis on the domestic setting, suggest the pathos of the corrupted family. As the chorus concludes, when the bloodied murderers appear, "no house is or ever was more pitiable [*athliôteros*] than that of Tantalos and his descendants" (1175–76).

The amoibaic lyric that follows the reentrance of the murderers must convey the whole shock of their reversal, since there is no dialogue development.[182] The scenic effect of the blood and the corpses on the eccyclema would presumably help to extend the impact of the lyric; and the scene of death should appear differently, when it is impossible to idealize the killers and view the victims as evil incarnate. The attempt to elevate the everyday, even the laughable, to high moral status, and the resulting portrayal of human motivation in its sentimental or comic, yet not inhuman, ineptitude, make the act of matricide something incomprehensible and dreadful. The pity that her children now feel for Klytaimestra is accessible to the audience through the pity that they have learnt to feel for Elektra and her brother. If we can understand the suffering that drove Elektra to kill her mother, and if we can understand the unheroic reluctance of Orestes to accept his destiny and act,[183] then we can also feel the pathos of the moment in which they cover their mother's body.[184]

But the moment is not prolonged. Kastor and Polydeukes appear over the plowman's hut, to assign the bloody and weeping protagonists to their place

182. The effect and purport of the lyric are partially obscured by textual problems: at least five lines seem to be missing between lines 1154 and 1182. For the state of the text, see Keene (1893, 111).

183. Note that the moral critiques of some commentators have extended to blaming Orestes for cowardice, either because he is reluctant to commit the crime (Ronnet [1975, 69]), or because he allows Elektra to shame him into it by appeals to his manhood (Adams [1935, 121]).

184. This act is the opposite to that of Orestes in the *Choephoroi,* who reveals the bodies of Klytaimestra and Aigisthos and who displays and apostrophizes what he calls the "winding sheet" (νεκροῦ ποδένδυτον, 998) of his father. This act of covering the body is one that should be performed for a parent by a child, as part of the burial rite. In the Sophoclean version, Klytaimestra's body is also uncovered (1469ff.), as a part of the final undeceiving of Aigisthos.

in the extended saga. The speech of Kastor is more than usually brisk and circumstantial, as it disposes of each in detail, adding on the whole story of Orestes' reception in Athens. The close packing of the information resembles the style of Euripidean prologues. Every loose end is disposed of at once, including the burial of Aigisthos—who will *not* be thrown to the dogs—while Klytaimestra will be interred by the returned Menelaos and her sister Helene, who, we are parenthetically informed, did not go to Troy. Even the Autourgos is remembered and settled comfortably. The eventual residences of Orestes and of Elektra as the wife of Pylades are made plain: they cannot live in Argos.

• The myth as heroic and genealogical chronicle is strongly contrasted here to the myth as enacted event. The Dioskouroi do not reinstate heroic values entirely, however, since they criticize the mysterious act of Apollon (1245–46) and since they show that the revenge did not and could not establish Elektra and her brother as heirs to their father's house. Yet the gods tie all knots neatly, assuring the protagonists of their future good fortune (1292). The human viewpoint is reasserted, however, as the chorus and Elektra muster the courage to question these divine disposers. The Dioskouroi are willing at first to speak to the chorus and then even to Elektra.[185] Their logic is weak, since they first state that it is right (*themis*) for them to speak only to those unpolluted by the murder.[186] This surely ought to exclude Elektra, who

185. Winnington-Ingram (1937) proposed transposing lines 1295–97 after 1302. The transposition removes the awkwardness of an opening in which Kastor successively grants the privilege of speech to two persons in series, after which each replies in series. The oddity of having the chorus speak to the *deus* has been pointed out (by Steidle [1968, 86]). But the etiquette of noncommunication between murderer and potential avenger is in operation here; and, in asking whether they may address the gods, the chorus point up the abnormality of the arrangement and in part excuse it. The assignment of line 1295 to Orestes does not seem likely either. (This is done by Denniston [1939, 208] and Keene [1893, 121].) In the arrangement I prefer, the chorus speak first; and the god points up the appropriateness of their unaccustomed role. Next, Elektra ventures to speak. The contradictory responses of the god then provoke a series of questions designed to elucidate their meaning. Kovacs (1985, 310ff.) gives lines 1292–93 to Orestes, 1295 to Elektra, and 1299–1300 to Orestes again. But the question, a natural one for outsiders like the chorus, as to why the Dioskouroi, "as gods and brothers to this dead woman here," did not prevent the murder becomes both cold and impudent in the mouth of Klytaimestra's son.

186. 1294: θέμις οὐ μυσαροῖς τοῖσδε σφαγίοις. The emendation of Orelli (μυσαραῖς) has been generally accepted: see Keene (1893, 121), Diggle (1981.2). The text as it stands is just suited to the odd treatment of the question of pollution here. The chorus asks, "Is it right for you to come to speech with us?" Kastor replies, "It is right for those who are not polluted by these deaths." See the remarks of Denniston (1939, 208). But note that the line is susceptible of a number of other interpretations. The *sphagioi* could be the murderers, if we interpret the word as an adjective; and the line could mean "It is right for these unpolluted slayers," or alternatively "It is not right for these polluted slayers." The ambiguity of this reply both raises the question of responsibility and encourages the intervention of Elektra.

had laid hold of the sword (1225 – 26). Yet, when she also asks to speak, the Dioskouroi permit it, laying the whole crime at Apollon's door, just as Apollon himself will accept this responsibility at Orestes' trial. The exemption for Elektra fits with her role in the saga, since it is Orestes and not she who must escape the Furies. Yet, as Elektra herself realizes, the excuse of divine impulsion also applies more to Orestes than to her: "What Apollon, what oracles made me become deadly to my mother?" (1303 – 4) The gods reply with an oracular ambiguity: "Common the deeds, common the fates; one inherited doom destroyed you both."[187] Elektra seems to have got off scot-free, in mythic terms, since she does not have to be involved in the process of trial and purification.

But just as human motivations, such as Elektra's anger at her humiliation, had more to do with Klytaimestra's death than any distant divine commands, so the punishment for that crime is situated more in the hearts of the criminals than in their roles in saga. Orestes, who does not address the Dioskouroi directly, speaks to Elektra, commiserating with her on their exile and separation.[188] The gods break in, pointing out that "she has suffered nothing pitiful; she has a house and a husband." Since Elektra is a woman, she is simply disposed of correctly, in marriage to a suitable husband.[189] Her role from that point on will be as part of the dynasty of Phokis. The disruption in marriage caused by Klytaimestra's murder of Agamemnon, her new alliance with Aigisthos, and the misalliance that Aigisthos had forced on Elektra is resolved; and presumably Elektra with her true husband, Pylades, and her quasi husband, the Autourgos, will live prosperously in Phokis, although she has missed out on the projected Argive marriage with her ideal and now divinized husband, Kastor.

But Elektra retains her feeling for the state and the family that she is losing; and she rejects the supposition of the Dioskouroi that, once married, she

187. 1305 – 8:

κοιναὶ πράξεις, κοινοὶ δὲ πότμοι,
μία δ' ἀμφοτέρους ἄτη πατέρων διέκναισεν.

188. Steidle (1968, 78 – 79) points to the symmetry of the embraces deferred at lines 596 – 97, which return at the end as a farewell instead of a greeting. Note the setting: the motif of the fear of discovery could not exist in Elektra's remote area. Abandonment of the suppression motif seems to be connected with the—for a Euripidean recognition drama—quite anomalous omission of a lyric of joy and greeting for the protagonists; see Solmsen (1967, 18) and Strohm (1957, 80 – 81). I would see this change as indicating the dominance of the specific model, the *Choephoroi,* over the general model of the recognition drama in this play.

189. 1311, πόσις ἔστ' αὐτῇ καὶ δόμος. A. W. Schlegel's fury at this play drove him to a truly inspired jibe, when he remarked that he could not imagine "wozu es Euripides überhaupt geschrieben, wenn es nicht war, um die Elektra *an den Mann zu bringen*" (1884, 371). His remark that it should have ended with a marriage ceremony (372) is justified by the play's extensive use of this typically comic theme.

can have no other concerns. "What sorrows are more agonizing than to leave the border of one's fatherland?" (1314–15). She and Orestes embrace, aware that their punishment is separation and exile, and an eternal share in their mother's curse (1321–24). When Orestes asks his sister to mourn as though he were dead,[190] even Kastor is touched. "What you have said is terrible, even for gods to hear. There is pity for suffering mortals in me and in the heavenly gods." Kastor, a dead human who shares immortality through special dispensation, may have retained a sensitivity to human woes greater than that of the true immortals;[191] but his original assumption that there is no sorrow in his resolution shows him already thinking more as god than as mortal.

As often in Euripides, the involvement of gods in human fate solves little, since gods do not understand the nature of mortal life. Apollon is especially prone to these errors of judgment, in the early *Alkestis* as in the late *Ion*; but Artemis in the *Hippolytos* is no different.[192] Since the Dioskouroi could not stop the crime and have difficulty understanding the experience of the criminals, their resolution has meaning only on the broad, heroic level; it cannot touch the realities of human existence that have been so much in the foreground in this play. Their cheerful and moralistic warning at the end that "We do not help the polluted [*mysaroi*]" (1350) jibes very poorly with their role in this scene; and it is hard to tell what their firm injunctions against wrongdoing can mean,[193] after watching the confused and destructive working out of a family doom in this play.[194] The chorus sadly concludes,

190. 1325–26: θανόντος δ' ὡς ἐπὶ τύμβῳ καταθρήνησον. The relation to *Elektra* (2) is an obvious one; there the mourning of Elektra, though real, is annulled by the resolution. Here, Orestes' death is only metaphorical; but the exile itself is real and permanent.

191. At lines 1329–30 Kastor slightly separates himself from the gods: ἔνι γὰρ κἀμοὶ τοῖς τ' οὐρανίδαις οἶκτος θνητῶν πολυμόχθων. In *Hel* 1643–45 the speaking member of the Dioskouroi is not differentiated by name; the speaker says, "We the twin [δισσοί] Dioskouroi call you." In this play, Kastor has a special role, since he is the link that ties Elektra to the divine and heroic part of her inheritance. He introduces himself by name (1240), referring to his brother as Πολυδεύκης ὅδε.

192. See the comments of Matthiessen (1979, 134 and 148 n.43), one of the most sophisticated treatments to date of divine figures in Euripides. On this quality of inconcinnity between divine and human in *Elektra*, see Matthiessen (1979, 150); Whitehorne (1978, 12); W. Schmidt (1963, 163). Line 1281 on the futility of the Trojan war points to the meaninglessness of divinely supervised events. (This interpretation of the line does not eliminate other significance, as an advertisement for the *Helene* of the following year. The reference is just remote and loosely connected enough to be serving such a purpose.)

193. See the advice of Kastor (1354): ἀδικεῖν μηδεὶς θελέτω.

194. I see no particular gain for interpretation of the *Elektra* in tying its date precisely to 413. But, in spite of Zuntz's arguments against contemporary references here (1955.1, 64–71), the coincidence of the *Helene* reference with this gratuitous hailing in of the *Pontos Sikelos* strongly hints at an external allusion. As usual, commentators want to use such references as simple signs indicating factual connections to historical reality. Within the intentional frame of the play, and in this atmosphere of moral contamination and confusion, a reference to the fleet of Demosthenes

"Farewell [*chairete*]; any mortal who can rejoice [*chairein*] and does not suffer under some mischance, is fortunate."[195]

This *Elektra* has not very deeply involved itself in the complex question of bloodguilt and fate.[196] Instead, centering on the experience of a figure from the heroic world who must live in the ordinary, it has shown the death of Klytaimestra and the life of Elektra as the product of a radical discontinuity between real and ideal. Unlike other Euripidean figures who courageously attempt to project the ideal of self in a hostile environment, Elektra is revealed almost from the start as self-betraying and self-deceiving. Hopelessly alienated from the heroic world by the wrong she has suffered, Elektra has been translated into a world where her heroic posture is meaningless. The new ethical world, in which the everyday man comes off better than the empty and pompous heroic ideal, is appealing, and provides an effective denunciation of Klytaimestra and Aigisthos, as it rehabilitates Elektra and Orestes from their humiliation. But, seen through the new ethical lens, the matricide toward which Elektra and Orestes are driven by their roles in heroic saga is a pitiful triumph, representing not the saving of the house of Atreus, but its collapse.

II.F. MALE AND FEMALE

The double focus in this play,[197] and the symmetricality in the pairs of antagonists, each containing a male and a female who share guilt and agency, corresponds to the play's emphasis on interaction between male and female in marriage and in other social institutions.[198] In urging Orestes on to his

takes on an ominous color that, from our perspective, appears prophetic indeed. Note the analogy with the *Troiades,* a play that pictures the ambiguities involved in *successful* invasions.

195. 1357–59:

χαίρετε· χαίρειν δ' ὅστις δύναται
καὶ συντυχίᾳ μή τινι κάμνει
θνητῶν εὐδαίμονα πράσσει.

See the optimistic interpretation of Kastor (1291). This view has been subjected to a reinterpretation, in human terms.

196. Steidle (1968, 86–89, 91).

197. Again, this alteration has been treated as a sequence of development from *Choephoroi* through *Elektra* (2) (Steiger [1897, 587]), with scholars on the other side proposing a reversed sequence. But, given the pairing of the siblings, which seems to have been in the tradition before Aischylos, only a limited number of treatments are open.

198. The equivalency of the male-female sibling relation to that of marriage is explicitly stated in *Or* 1045, a passage that has struck critics as either abnormal or touching, depending on their viewpoints. See Conacher (1967, 214–15); O. Longo (1975, 276–78); Erbse (1975, 439). The strict segregation of the sexes meant that the sibling relation was the only one existing between young men and women. Note the tendency, here exemplified by Pylades, for a brother to arrange marriage between his sister and a best friend.

deeds, Elektra performs a traditional female role. The warnings and wails of
the threatened women followed the men into battle, and victors in war or in
the games were received with female jubilation.[199] The contradictions built
into this role operate broadly within the play. Elektra puts immense pressure
on Orestes to perform well.[200] But at the same time she undermines his
heroic stature, since a man who must take his pattern from a woman is by
definition a failure in the male role. The role of shamer, helper, or inspirer is
an ambiguous one, with comic and negative overtones. Women who give
advice are typically seen—both in our own culture and in the Greek—as
assertive; but this role originates in female passivity and is in fact indicative
of two aims that are to a degree incompatible, a desire to control events, and
a desire to act through others.[201] The comic parallel, again, appears in the
earlier part of the play, when Elektra gives advice to her farmer husband.
That scene inevitably colors our view of her activities afterward, and it
becomes impossible not to see Elektra's supportive role as also insubordinate
and manipulative. The theme is closed by the reproach of the chorus: "You
have done a terrible thing, my friend, to your brother, who was unwill-
ing."[202] This evaluation is important, less because it labels the matricide as
wrong—since that was already clear—than because it establishes Elektra's
responsibility as inciter.

The paradox is most evident just before the murder of Klytaimestra, when
Elektra must spur her brother on with a warning not to "be a coward and fall

199. See Zeitlin (1970, 655–56): Elektra's behavior correlates with her reproach to her
mother (οὐκ ἐπὶ στεφάνοις, 163–65). See the role delineated by Dümmler ([1894] 1901,
406–10): in times of public emergency women may act as a focus of public opinion, pressuring
males to perform and threatening them with shame if they do not.

200. The text of lines 682ff. has been much discussed and many lines have been suspected:
Page (1934, 75–76) would cut lines 689–93. Broadhead (1968, 130–35) wants to excise lines
685–92. He keeps line 693, which he places immediately after line 684. Denniston (1939,
136–37) defends the manuscript arrangement. In line 693 (". . . And therefore you must be a
man.") the signs of dittography are most apparent: the line repeats πάντ' οἶδα and πρὸς τάδε
from lines 684–85. (But see Diggle [1981.1, 38–39]; and Broadhead [1968, 131] on πρὸς τάδ'.
Both feel that its usage in line 685 is more abnormal.) The interpolator of line 693—if there was
one—had an excellent grasp of what was needed, since this line anticipates line 982 very effectively.

201. As Aithra remarks, wise women must achieve what they hope to accomplish by working through men (*Suppl* 40–41). For the social reality corresponding to this remark, see Schaps
(1979, 48–52) on the legal necessity for women's economic activity to be mediated through a
male *kurios,* who was alone recognized as the responsible party.

202. 1203–5:

φρονεῖς γὰρ ὅσια νῦν, τότ' οὐ
φρονοῦσα, δεινὰ δ' εἰργάσω,
φίλα, κασίγνητον οὐ θέλοντα.

See Murray (1905, 96): this is the chorus' only explicit moral judgment.

into unmanliness [οὐ μὴ κακισθεὶς εἰς ἀνανδρίαν πέσῃ]'' (982). At that critical moment, the quality in Orestes that his sister reproaches is also the humanizing factor that unites him to the ethic he expounded earlier, in which *euandria* (manliness, 367) received a new definition not based on courage in battle or victory in games. That Orestes requires and submits to such goading thus threatens both the new ethic that supported his quest for revenge and the old ethic of manliness that had imposed it in the first place. Klytaimestra's suggestion that women like to imitate (*mimeisthai*) the male partner seems to have a further application in this light. When men and women are united in partnership, heroic autonomy is excluded. The failure of Klytaimestra and Aigisthos to be satisfyingly villainous corresponds to the web of relations in which they are embedded, their marriage, their new family, and their new and old social roles. Even Elektra's sham marriage is real enough to compromise her heroic status and her enmity with her mother. Klytaimestra's rather shallow notions about balancing off the claims of family members may seem in the end to have as much general validity as Elektra's dream of an ideal and dominant male partner.

R. Schottländer, in analyzing the ethical system of *Elektra* (1982), was struck by a contradiction. If it is true that the farmer is a good man, why is he not worthy of Elektra and why is his marriage to her a "deadly marriage [*thanasimos gamos*]"? In fact, he is praised precisely for not thinking himself worthy of his wife and for refusing to make their marriage a real one.[203] But this ethic, contradictory as it is, is not unique to *Elektra*. It has been noted that slaves in Euripidean plays show themselves ethically advanced by their selfless concern for their masters.[204] Women also fit this pattern: the good wife, as the chorus points out, subordinates herself in every respect to her husband (1052).

The passive or cooperative virtues in the dual system of Greek morality are commended especially to those for whom self-aggrandizement would be inappropriate, to young people, to poor people, to women, and to slaves.[205] The ethical change that we generally associate with Sokrates as a source

203. See O'Brien (1964, 33–34) and Schottländer (1982, 491ff.). Both scholars make a somewhat Verrallian use of this contradiction, assuming that it represents a more valid truth than the surface praise of the Autourgos. But I am arguing that this view is traditional and natural, so that its contradictions could not be immediately apparent to a Greek audience.

204. See Brandt (1973, 137–38). "Die Diener freilich zeigen sich nicht um sich selbst, sondern um ihre bedrohten Herren besorgt." Slaves argue with their masters and express strong opinions, which gives them a new importance in the plays. But in fact they are more, not less, subordinated to their masters and are concerned only with them: the plays show "eine spezielle Diener-Moral auf, nach der vor allem die Rettung des Herrn wichtig ist . . ."

205. Adkins (1960, 36–37): women's *aretê* is found, in contradiction to the masculine standard, among the quiet virtues. This happens, as A. points out, because "it is men who determine the nature of *arete*—both for men and for women."

reverses these values, so that the poor or women or even slaves turn out to be in some sense "better" than those traditionally placed above them in the social scale. But, since real social rankings do not change, hypocrisy and sentimentality are built into the new system, through the gulf between social reality and ethical standards. The aesthetic problem presented by the Autourgos—how to insert such a figure into a "serious" setting—is one with the social and moral problems of the new ethic. If *eugeneia* means what the Autourgos thinks it does, and what Orestes thinks it should, then the former's support of his patrons and their pretensions may be wrong. Worse, there are moments when the new moral hero looks silly rather than serious. The problem we have in assessing him is pointed up in his opening speech: is he a noble (*gennaios*) man, or a fool? If his wife is insubordinate, has the Autourgos anyone to blame but himself?[206] Orestes' despairing suggestion at line 379 was truer than he meant it to be: "it is better to let those things go at random."[207]

The schemes imposed on reality by the historical or theological viewpoint do not clear up the paradox of human suffering, any more than the disposition of a woman in marriage reduces her neatly to an instrument of genealogy. In the interstices of these arrangements life still continues. It is this irreducible relativity and impurity of human life, this dependency on environment, that is the focus of the comic viewpoint. The *Elektra* is a tragic play that includes and assimilates the comic universe; and by forcing us to feel sorrow for people who at other times—or at the same time—inspire repulsion or laughter, it becomes one of Euripides' most sustained and intensive responses to the problems of tragic form. In watching the play, it becomes difficult to keep life and death, horror and sympathy, laughter and tears separate; and we cannot ever achieve a satisfactory perspective from which to accommodate ourselves to these divisions. I would agree with Gellie in seeing the play as a remarkably bold innovation, with an "experimental" quality. The sweet aura of festival and celebration that faintly haloes the grisly story, melded with the awkward charm of the bucolic setting, creates a consistently maintained degree of dissonance with the action. When this dissonance breaks, at the end of the play, the tension between comic and tragic is resolved into an exquisitely balanced pity that is—in its lesser amplitude—analogous to the sublime bitterness at the end of the *Trachiniai* or the bitter sublimity at the close of the *Oidipous at Kolonos*.

206. We may compare the comic persona of Sokrates, with his shrewish wife (see Xenophon *Symp.* 2.10 and *Mem.* 2.7–9; and H. Dörrie in *RE* s.v. Xanthippe); or Euripides, with his adulterous one (Satyros xii, xiii [pp. 66–67 Arrighetti]).

207. κράτιστον εἰκῇ ταῦτ' ἐᾶν ἀφειμένα. Note the discussion above of the famous tag lines from Euripides, Chap. 3. This one, at any rate, while its meaning in the context is innocuous, has a hidden sting, a sting that is built into the play itself.

8

Herakles: Tragedy in Paradox

I. Some Critical Problems

Herakles of all the extant plays raises with greatest urgency the perennial Euripidean questions about the nature of dramatic unity, the role of the gods, and the uses of cult and legend; and it has been impossible for interpreters to proceed, while leaving these central issues unresolved. Yet the very directness with which this play approaches problems that elsewhere are masked in an irony of indirection makes the elements of its structure almost impossible to miss. As a result, the image of the play in critical literature is clear in general outline, although central areas remain severely distorted or out of focus.

Herakles raises problems of "unity" that are considerably more severe than those in other tragic plays that are thought to fall into two parts.[1] In the case of the Sophoclean "diptych" plays, or plays like *Hekabe* that combine two actions, or plays like *Hippolytos* that center on two protagonists, we note primarily a change of focus from one part of the play to another. But in *Herakles* the two dramatic actions are not causally related, do not move in the same direction, and in fact reverse and contradict each other radically.

---

1. Division of the play has been a subject of controversy, with some scholars arguing for *three* parts, counting the divine epiphany in the middle as a separate part. See Kamerbeek (1966, 2–4), Burnett (1971, 157–58). Gregory (1977, 259 n.2) summarizes groups of scholars in each camp; Strohm (1957, 108) argues against strong divisions, pointing to the close interrelation of the parts. For practical purposes—and such "divisions" have no other significance than convenience—it makes sense to treat the epiphany as a quasi prologue, setting off even more abruptly the second part from the first—see U. v. Wilamowitz (1895, 2:180); Bond (1981, 281).

The first half builds to a happy ending, with Herakles triumphantly returning to rescue his family from the usurper Lykos, while the second half shows the savior as the murderer of his family.[2] While in the other cases it is possible to trace the ways in which two actions have been interlaced, in this case we can only point to parallels and analogies between the actions. The central feature of the structure must remain the abrupt break that severs the play into two halves.

The emergence of the second action violates a familiar and long-lived stylistic criterion that requires a work of art to possess "organic unity", as if it were an independent ecology or system, an organism, rather than an intentional construct.[3] Since all art is in fact made for human purposes, this critical norm imposes yet another layer of artificiality upon the work: *ars est celare artem*. The "organically" designed play presents us with a series of dramatic events that appear to fit together causally as, from certain human viewpoints, some series of real events do. But the unity of a dramatic reality does not depend upon any editing or analysis by our consciousness, since all the elements in a work of art should be a part of the same system of significance. *Herakles* presents us with a part of reality usually left out of drama, a sequence of events that, like many sequences in life, is arbitrary, senseless, and contradictory. Because the events of the second half render the events of the first irrelevant and without meaning, the dramatic structure does not "make sense" and cannot be deciphered in the normal way. It is designed to be unintelligible.

The first part of *Herakles* is as W. G. Arnott has said (1978) a "red herring," a decoy that betrays the audience's understanding of what they are to expect from a play, even a play by Euripides. This is an extreme example of the ways in which Euripidean plays manipulate their audiences. We have seen that sympathy and identification, once developed, are often undercut, or may be put in question from the start, as when in *Elektra* or *Wise Melanippe* the audience is teased with an alternation between pathos and ludicrous overtones. In this case we are misled by an elaborate false front or dummy play, from which the real dramatic action emerges startlingly, like a jack from its

2. See Kröker (in his dissertation of 1938, the best single work published on *Herakles* in this century; pp. 110–13): the play creates a unit, "die zwei Gegensätze in unauflöslicher Problematik einander zuordnet." See also Zürcher (1947, 90) and Lesky ([1956] 1972.1, 379): in no other drama "ist die Bindung der Teile zur Einheit durch die Antithese so stark wie bei diesem." Conacher (1967, 58): "The action of the play is arrested and redirected by a series of three reversals, none of which is *caused* by something which has gone before . . ." And see Galinsky (1972, 57–58).

3. On the genesis of this analogy, see the important article by Pohlenz, ([1920] 1965, 438–39): P. points to the *Clouds* of Aristophanes, in which stylistic demands for unity (*systasis*) can be traced at line 1367, where Aischylos is called *axystatos* by a detractor.

box. The "unorganic" quality of this play corresponds to the artful or artificial way in which Euripidean drama reveals its manipulation of the dramatic event, inviting the audience to question how and why the action has been put into its present form.[4]

If the dramatic structure of *Herakles* is an extreme example of Euripidean shock tactics, the play also provides an extreme example of the critical and unsympathetic portrayal of divine agents. While in other plays the role of divinities is restricted to prologue and epilogue areas, where these problematic figures can appear to frame off the dramatic event and where we may even feel that the mimesis of reality has become less vivid, in *Herakles* they emerge in the play's center, breaking in upon the action and violently rearranging its course. Since it is these figures that precipitate the swerve into dramatic unintelligibility, we are forced to ask ourselves what sort of divine power, and therefore what sort of universal order, confronts human beings.[5]

Critical approaches to this difficult play have centered on the question of "unity."[6] This focus has enriched our understanding of the play in detail, even as it has predictably tended to falsification and denial of the play's central structures. U. von Wilamowitz in his pioneering study pointed out that *Herakles* centers on conflicting concepts of heroic *aretê,* opposing a new, modernized heroism, adopted by Herakles at Theseus' urging, to the traditional model of violence and force.[7] This emphasis on heroism also suggests an odd position of centrality for this play in the notoriously centrifugal work of Euripides. While other plays mark the Euripidean rejection of the *spoudaion* by selecting obviously ineligible protagonists, this play begins with the most renowned hero, working out its revisionist view through what would seem the most unlikely of subjects.

Wilamowitz' other major contribution to the debate on *Herakles* was his

4. See *Hekabe* as a kind of dramatic experiment in extreme misery, Chap. 6, above. On the artful and arbitrary structures of Euripidean drama, see the perceptive comments of Kitto ([1939] 1961, 268, on *Medeia*: "the whole play is conceived intellectually"; see also pp. 274–76).

5. Conacher (1967, 89): the plot of *Herakles* reveals "the arbitrary intrusion of the 'gods of myth' into the lives of men" and thus cannot "proceed in accordance with dramatic probability." "Dramatic probability" is a phrase that rather fudges the fact that what is likely to happen in dramas has little to do with probability in ordinary life.

6. See the complaints of Murray (1946, 112; the play is "broken-backed"); Kitto ([1939] 1961, 237). Note also discussions of previous views by Chalk (1962, 7–8); Gregory (1977, 259); Shelton (1979, 101).

7. 1895, 1.127–28. This notion is modified by Chalk (1962), who suggests that *aretê* and *bia* are shown as inevitably connected. See Kröker (1938, 90–91); Galinsky (1972, 65–66). Adkins, who attacked Chalk's interpretation (1966.1, 209ff.), used a rigid definition of *aretê* to explain away the evidence for the restructuring of traditional values in Euripidean plays. Cf. Adkins' discussion of Polyxene in the same article, and Chap. 6, Section IV, above. Dover (1983, 40–41) argued against Adkins for a more flexible interpretation of moral concepts.

attempt to remedy the disjunction between the two halves of the play by transforming the theme of heroism to mend the cleavage. Rather than an irrational incursion from outside, the madness of Herakles became an expression of the violence from which the hero would be purged by the play's end.[8] The parallel with critical approaches to *Oidipous Tyrannos* is interesting. In both cases a benevolent and heroic male in the prime of life is destroyed by a crisis that, through no apparent fault of his own, makes him responsible for the violent deaths of close family members and that shatters his relation to his own children.[9] In the case of Oidipous, attempts to make the hero himself responsible for his fate have largely been repudiated;[10] but in fact the Sophoclean play gives far more encouragement to such an exegesis than does *Herakles*. Herakles' behavior is less strikingly irascible and violent than that of Oidipous; and the offenses of Iokaste are considerably more serious and receive much more notice in the play than do any trivial errors ascribable to Megara.[11] In contrast to the doomed union of Oidipous and Iokaste, the marriage of Herakles is normal, and even exemplary. While in *Oidipous Tyrannos* the flaws and faults of the hero and his wife seem to run along in the same current with the surge of fate that overwhelms them, in this play there is no coherent movement that leads to the final catastrophe.[12] Attempts to link Herakles' character with his downfall aim at creating an aesthetic structure through which the events of the play will hang together and explicate each other, suggesting a significant universe. But that would not be the universe of this play.

Herakles like the hero of *Aias* goes mad because of the influence of a

8. 1895, 1:128: "Die Tat aber ist eine Folge der herakleischen eignen Natur geworden." This view was expanded and developed by Verrall in his usual colorful style (1905, 156ff.); he argues that Herakles is mad as a hatter from his first entrance. See also the odd theory of Blaiklock about Herakles' epileptic mania (1952, 124ff.) and Kamerbeek (1966, 10–13).

9. It will be pointed out that Herakles' children are, after all, dead; but burial provides a prolongation and reaffirmation of family ties, and this final relation is cut off for Herakles, because he is his children's murderer. For the comparison with *OT*, see Sheppard (1916, 78), Müffelmann (1965, 120–21).

10. Moralizing interpretations: Bowra (1944, 210–11): Oidipous "has been taught modesty through suffering"; Kitto ([1939] 1961, 180–81): Oidipous is hybristic. Cf. the valuable dissertation of Müffelmann (1965, 120ff.), who draws a parallel between the problems of guilt in the two plays. For rejection of Oidipous' guilt, see Whitman (1951, 124–28); and the trenchant discussion of Dodds, "On Misunderstanding *Oedipus Rex*" (1966), on the prevailing critical agreement on this point (38).

11. The views of Rohdich and Burnett, who blame Megara for excessive rationalism or a lack of faith in divine protection, are discussed above, Chap. 1, Section III.C.

12. Müffelmann (1965, 121) suggests that Euripides, in structuring *Herakles* as he did, may have been attempting to avoid the "mistake" by which Sophokles permits us to confuse Oidipous' fate with Oidipous' trivial errors; but the Sophoclean structure is not a mistake. (The problem of "tragic error" is discussed in the following chapter.)

goddess.[13] By treating Aias' madness, which was probably traditionally associated with his anger at the loss of Achilleus' arms,[14] as an external accession, unmotivated by any psychological experience, Sophokles builds sympathy for the hero, who betrays himself against his will. Aias sees himself as horribly shamed by his insane outburst, while at the same time the behavior of the Greek army confirms that Aias and his family have become social outcasts, subject to public scorn and mob attack.[15] But, because everyone in the play, including Aias' bitterest enemies, treats his madness as a divine punishment, Aias' humiliation is both his and not his; it is significant that, while Agamemnon and Menelaos indict the hero as a *hybristês* and a would-be murderer, they do not scorn him as a senseless madman.[16] The treatment of Herakles' madness is not dissimilar, and the effect is stronger in that there is no discernible psychological source for Herakles' acts. They do not even result from the deflection of an original sanely conceived intention, as those of Aias do.[17] The device of divine intervention permits us to see Herakles awakened on the stage as a totally separate person from "Herakles Mad" behind the scenes.[18] Like Aias, Herakles is not a madman, but a sane man who has suffered an isolated episode of madness, so that in the second half of

13. Hera sends madness to those she hates, usually because of her jealousy of Zeus' sons by mortals, e.g., Athamas (Apollod. 1.9.2, cf. 1:76 n.1 Frazer). Herakles and Dionysos offend Hera by their very existence; mortals such as Pelias or the Proitides (see Bakchylides 11.43ff.) may have offended by some impiety.

14. In the *Iliou Persis* (5:139 Allen) the physician Podaleirion recognizes the symptoms of Aias' incipient madness, which proceeds from his anger: ὅς ῥα καὶ Αἴαντος πρῶτος μάθε χωομένοιο / ὄμματα τ' ἀστράπτοντα βαρυνόμενον τε νόημα. This is a sufficient disproof of the argument of Drexler (1943, 314) that the Greeks always had treated madness as an external visitation.

15. Aias' shame: lines 367, 383, 454 (laughter of enemies); 408–9 (hostility of the Greek camp). Teukros' reception in the camp: εἴτ' ὀνείδεσιν ἤρασσον ἔνθεν κἄνθεν οὐδεὶς ἔσθ' ὃς οὔ (721–28). On the laughter of enemies as the greatest fear of the heroic personality, see Maddalena (1963, 138), who compares Medeia and Aias.

16. See Menelaos' indictment, lines 1057ff., 1126 (Aias as a virtual murderer); 1081–82, 1087–88 (Aias as *hybristês*). Note that this view of Aias' offense conflicts to some extent with the normal Hellenic "results-oriented" morality (see Adkins [1960, 51–57]) according to which Aias' actual humiliation rather than Aias' intended crime would be a more potent weapon in the hands of his enemies.

17. See Kröker (1938, 119; comparison with *Aias* 90–91), Müffelmann (1965, 119). The most diabolic quality of Athena's revenge is its potential as a source for the laughter most feared by the heroic figure: Aias' mistake in killing cattle in place of his enemies is a "joke" of which he finds himself the butt. This accounts for the different treatment of madness in the two plays. See Müffelmann ibid.: Aias' madness is trivial and humiliating, and therefore totally unassimilable to the hero's view of himself. By contrast, Herakles' murder of his children forces the hero to reassess his whole career.

18. But see Pucci (1980, 182–85). For parallel effects in Homeros, see Gundert (1940, 225–29).

the play, as in *Aias,* we see Herakles coming to terms with misfortune, shame, and guilt that are, in some significant sense, not really his.[19]

II. The Design of the First Half

II.A. ARCHAIZING STYLE IN DIALOGUE AND LYRIC

Euripidean language is quite consistently smooth, elegant, and limpid, pared of the exuberant Aeschylean vocabulary and avoiding the tense and elaborate (*katatechnon*) mannerism of Sophokles.[20] *Herakles,* however, makes a different stylistic impression. U. von Wilamowitz noted the elaborate diction of the lyrics and ascribed it to the evocation of an archaic ideal of heroism.[21] But even the language of the trimeter speeches presents some remarkable anomalies, particularly in the opening scenes.[22] The play begins typically enough with a precise and clear narrative prologue by Amphitryon, followed by dialogue between the old man and Megara; and the tone of instruction gives way to a greater depth of mimesis and pathos, as the woman tells of the lonely waiting for Herakles to return. The second part of Megara's speech is full of domestic atmosphere;[23] but the language of the first part is extremely formal. She begins with a tortuous honorific address to Amphitryon as the man who conquered the Taphians.[24] Her language reaches greater heights a few lines further on, as she remarks that her father held a tyranny "for whose sake the long spears leap with desire into fortunate

19. See discussion of Phaidra's moral responsibility for her erotic feelings, in the following chapter.

20. *Katatechnon* is the term used by Sophokles himself to characterize his middle period; see Plut. *Moral.* 79b (1:157 Paton & Wegehaupt). For modern assessments of Euripidean style, see Masqueray (1908, 31): "uni, fluide, d'une extraordinaire agilité"; and Kitto ([1939] 1961, 272): "simple and limpid." Pohlenz attempted to trace fifth-century estimates of Euripides' style, as suggested by *Frogs,* directly back to Gorgias ([1920] 1965, 456–57). Pohlenz (458 n.3) points to a reference in Quintilian (2.10.6) that may derive from the same unknown source in fifth-century critical prose as do Aristophanes' jokes about the "dieting" down of Aischylos' swollen style (*Frogs* 939–44). See also Wehrli (1946), who traces the genesis of the "low" or "thin" style (*ischnon, lepton*) back to the fifth-century criticism of tragedy (24–25).

21. 1895, 1:127.

22. See Paley's edition (1860, 3): Euripides seems to have aimed "at the grandiloquent and Aeschylean style of diction more than was his wont."

23. See U. v. Wilamowitz (1895, 1:119): "Der Kündiger des weiblichen Herzens hat sich in den wenigen Reden, die er Megara geliehen hat, nicht verleugnet." He saw Megara's *Leidenschaft* even in her anacolutha (2:20), a conclusion rightly denied by Bond (1981, 77).

24. 61: στρατηλατήσας κλεινὰ Καδμείων δορός. Taken piece by piece, the phrase is barely explicable; but as a unit the combination of an internal accusative with two genitives, along with the metonymic use of "spear" for "army," create a curiously unintelligible line.

bodies.''[25] This burst of elaborate language dissipates quickly: as Megara passes to her theme, the longing of the children for their father's return, the homely subject matter evokes appropriately simple language; and she ends with a request for counsel that is unaffected and natural.[26]

The elevated language that Megara uses in her first speech does not find many parallels later on. The most striking examples occur in Amphitryon's defense of Herakles, when he recounts his son's legendary and fabulous deeds.[27] But the chorus enters at line 107, and from then on they are the

25. 65–66:

ἧς μακραὶ λόγχαι πέρι
πηδῶσ' ἔρωτι σώματ' εἰς εὐδαίμονα

Bond (1981, 79–80) explicates well, but attempts to argue away the obvious link between *sômata* and *erôs*. The basis for this astonishing metaphor is in old epic, where the thwarted spear quivers in the dust, "longing to sate itself with flesh [λιλαιομένη χροὸς ἆσαι]" (*Il.* 21.168, etc.). This combines with the notion of tyranny as the ultimate object of human desire; see *Phoin.* 504–6. But these connections do not obviate the difficulty of the language. Particularly perverse is the use of *eudaimona*: it is into "fortunate" bodies that the spears, in their erotic longing, plunge, because the fortunate possess tyranny. Those impaled are, by definition, not "fortunate"; but the erotic metaphor fights against the meaning. The effect is much like that of line 61: the parts can be made to fit severally, but the effect of the whole cannot be got into focus. Cf. also line 63, where again it is the combination of οὔτ' ἐς πατέρ' (a "remarkable" usage in itself, according to Paley [1860, 13]) with the rather contorted ἀπηλάθην τυχῆς that creates difficulty. In line 71 a strong hyperbaton delays the triggering of the simile and creates another slight difficulty.

26. 85–86: ἥντιν' οὖν γνώμην ἔχεις / λέγ' ἐς τὸ κοινόν, μὴ θανεῖν ἕτοιμον ᾖ; The last clause does not make much sense as a dependent clause of fearing: "Speak out your opinion/plan, lest death be present for us." It reads better as an independent subjunctive of doubtful assertion, a "feinere Form der Behauptung" (2:1:224 Kühner-Gerth); Megara is saying, "May it not be true that death is at hand?" This is a colloquial usage found only in Platon; but that would make it especially appealing here. Cf. the proposal of Stevens (1946, 101) to inject this idiom elsewhere in Euripides, i.e., *El* 567–68.

27. Examples would include lines 177–80:

Διὸς κεραυνὸν ἠρόμην τέθριππά τε
ἐν οἷς βεβηκὼς τοῖσι γῆς βλαστήμασιν
Γίγασι πλευροῖς πτήν' ἐναρμόσας βέλη
τὸν καλλίνικον μετὰ θεῶν ἐκώμασεν·

Here, the extended *schema Ionikon* (in τοῖσι ... πλευροῖς, see U. v. Wilamowitz [1895, 2:44]) and the metaphor in *enarmosas* and *ekômasen* create a tense and elaborate impression. The theme, that of the *kômos* for the victor's (*kallinikos*) chariot procession, is significant; see discussion of epinician motifs below. τετρασκελὲς ὕβρισμα (four-legged outrage, 181) is an elaborate gloss; Bond remarks on the Aeschylean, riddling quality and compares a number of passages, all of which are in lyric. In line 199, "wounding the seeing with his unseen/blind shots [τυφλοῖς ὁρῶντας οὐτάσας τοξεύμασιν]," the metaphorical meaning of *typhlos* (unseen) is displaced jarringly by the real meaning (blind) in the vicinity of *horôntas* (seeing). Finally, in line 218, λόγους ὀνειδιστῆρας ἐνδατούμενος, *oneidistêr* is a hapax legomenon, and *endatoumenos* appears nowhere else in Euripides (cf. Aischylos 284M). Bond points to the three-word trimeter as possibly a deliberate archaism (1981, 122).

primary source of heroic and elevated diction. Their references to their extreme age and their boasts that they are singers strongly recall for modern readers the *Agamemnon* of Aischylos, a play in which the prophetic powers claimed by the chorus indicate the structural importance of a series of lengthy and dazzling choral odes.[28] In a style familiar from Aeschylean tragedy, the first two stasima are lengthy and elaborate songs that project themes related to the action into a wider circle of reference that illuminates and is independent of the stage events.

The first stasimon presents a kind of hybrid between dirge and victory ode, as it praises Herakles and mourns his loss; allusions to the tropes of Pindaric poetry are frequent.[29] But the orderly fashion in which the song deals with the twelve labors of Herakles has little in common with the contorted sophistication of Pindaric style. The meter, a simple series of glyconics and pherecratics in repetitive sequence, reinforces the effect of naiveté.[30] The effect of an almost primitive archaism lends the ode some of the authority of tradition. After a scene in which Herakles' achievements have been first denied and then rationalized, the ode reasserts the validity of the wonderful and legendary sequence of labors, much as does the ode following Tiresias' speech in the *Bakchai*.[31] Unlike the *Bakchai* lyrics, however, the first stasimon is not intense or vivid in poetic effect. The flourishes of high style, instead of supporting a coherent system of meaning, serve to embellish the orderly narration of all the twelve labors.[32] In the later strophes more

28. For the theme of the "aged singer" (*gerôn aoidos*), see line 110ff. (and comments by Bond, 1981; Parry [1965, 374 n.12]). In the long and elaborate first stasimon, the connection between praise and the aged singer is not drawn out, although both themes appear. In the second stasimon, the themes are at last united and brought to full development. For arguments against the tendency long prevalent (see U. v. Wilamowitz [1895, 1:114–15 and 2:149]; Kröker [1938, 53]; Pohlenz [(1930) 1954, 304]) to treat that piece as a personal statement of the poet, see Parry (1965, 363ff.), who points out the many parallels with Pindaric epinician odes.

29. For the interweaving of these themes, see U. v. Wilamowitz (1895, 2:84). W. remarks, "Das ganze Lied ist in der Form von aischyleischer Fülle und Erhabenheit, wie sie Euripides nicht oft anstrebt, selten erreicht, Sophokles auch nicht einmal anstrebt." See Bond (1981, 146): the ode is "unparalleled in length and formality among the plays of Euripides." When the chorus describes their song as a "garland of/for toils [στεφάνωμα μόχθων]," Bond remarks (ibid.), "a Pindaric phrase for a Pindaric poem."

30. Cf. the Epidaurian hymn to the Magna Mater (*PMG* 935), which has a similar meter. On the hieratic quality of this ode, see U. v. Wilamowitz (1921, 243).

31. See Roux's commentary (1970, 2:374–75).

32. For examples of decorative language, see U. v. Wilamowitz (1895, 2:88–89) on the play on words that creates the picture of Herakles' blond head engulfed in the muzzle of the blond lion (δεινοῦ χάσματι θηρός, 363). Elaborate figurative language adorns the grisly story of Diomedes' horses (381ff.; see Bond [1981, ad loc.]). Bond comments (166) on the "allusive, riddling style" of the ode. At line 431ff., he points to "emphatic and startling" hyperbata, as the ode comes to a close.

complex chains of dactyls alternate with briefer mesodes, which still repeat the stereotyped aeolic meters of the beginning. A simple schema of arrangement groups the most geographically remote feats at the end, closing appropriately with the trip farthest afield, the journey to Hades from which the hero has not returned. Because it is a dirge as well as a song of praise, the first stasimon treats Herakles' labors as an event of the past, cut off from the sad present. The primitive meter, naive subject matter, and accretive structure enhance this effect.[33]

The second stasimon has been analyzed by H. Parry (1965), who documents the recurrence of the encomiastic motifs of the first stasimon. In this song, which follows Herakles' triumphal exit into the house accompanied by his family, the praise of the hero no longer appears as posthumous. Parry argues that the chorus elevates Herakles to almost divine heights, and he notes the absence of the traditional epinician warnings about human limitations.[34] The primary theme of the ode, however, is the praise of youth and dispraise of old age. This theme derives from the actual weakness of the chorus and of Amphitryon, which has been continually emphasized during the scenes of threat and altercation with Lykos.[35] The chorus makes a quixotic suggestion for the reform of existence. Such visionary proposals are a fifth-century modification of the *topos,* familiar from archaic reflective poetry, that evils predominate over good in human life, where the best things are also the greatest source of sorrow.[36] The chorus propose that the good should be rewarded with a second youth, as a clear stamp of virtue (*phaneron charaktêr aretas,* 657) that would affirm the worth of their moral choices, as well as confirm that the gods notice human actions.

Such a proof would enable humans to direct their lives rightly, just as sailors plot their course by the stars.[37] Human life, as it now is, has no sure marks to steer by: "a winding-turning life [εἱλισσόμενός τις αἰών] magnifies only wealth" (671–72). To this uncertainty there is in Hellenic tradition only one antidote, the power of Memory as exercised by the Muses; and it is

33. Barlow (1971, 37): the ode presents an "idealized world of popular imagination" regarding the hero.

34. 1965, 364 and 371.

35. See discussion of this theme below; and Sheppard (1916, 74), Kröker (1938, 28).

36. These fantasized or utopian suggestions appear in lineverse more often than in lyric; see *Med* 573ff., *Hipp* 619ff., *Suppl* 1080, and discussion of this type of argument by Solmsen (1975, Chap. 3, 66ff.). As Bond points out (1981, 231), the utopian demand for a double youth in the antistrophe is an "intellectual corollary" to the traditional denunciation of old age and its defects in the strophe.

37. On the language of lines 667–68, see Bond (1981, 235).

to this that the old men turn in the second part of the ode.[38] Here their character as aged singers (*gerontes aoidoi*) is realized, as they rise above their own temporality and weakness in hymning the glories of Herakles, as the Delian maidens praise Apollon, who is a god.

Recent critics have rightly pointed out that the statements about poetry following line 673 are adequately grounded by the characterization of the chorus, who never cease to define themselves as aged and as singers. L. Kretz, however, saw farther when he argued that, whenever references to poetry or the task of the poet come up, we are to hear and must hear overtones of authorial intention.[39] In this case, the effect—to make us think of the author and his agency in producing the fiction—is more important than the content, a very traditional formulation of the poet's role. Along with the other references to song, and the reminiscences of encomiastic poetry and traditional lyric, this passage draws our attention to the function of poetry within the play and within the culture. The self-consciousness and solipsism are deliberate, since themes of self-reference will become strikingly and paradoxically exaggerated in the last scene of the play.

II.B. PLOT STRUCTURE

To the archaism of the choruses corresponds the simplicity of the plot structure in the first half,[40] which is notably lacking in tension and suspense.[41] The sympathetic characters have no resources with which to repel the threats against them; and Lykos has often been pointed out as a flat and uninteresting villain, without a single trait to relieve his characterization.[42] In *Helene* and *Iphigeneia Among the Taurians* the oppressors are violent and unjust; but, according to their barbarian lights, they behave in kingly fashion. The focus, in any case, is not on them, but on the Hellenic protagonists, whose rather unprincipled tricks win our sympathy against such unappealing adversaries. The closest analogue to Lykos is the despicable Menelaos in *Andromache,* who is also defied by—and this time actually worsted by—a plucky old hero. But Menelaos' willingness to act wrongly in support of his daughter is significant of family corruption, a major theme of

38. For Pindaric parallels, see Parry (1965, 371). The complex of attitudes that links nostalgia for *hêbê* with the role of memory in preserving deeds of youthful valor is well analyzed by Vernant (1982, esp. pp. 53–54).

39. Kretz was still somewhat understandably confused by this complex problem of intentionality, but he argued strongly that *no* utterance in the plays is ''a genuine, intended, personal utterance'' (*"wirklich, gewollte,* persönliche *Äusserung* [1934, 8]).

40. Strohm calls it "hocharchaisch" (1949–50, 147).

41. See Kitto ([1939] 1961, 239): "Is there in the whole of Greek drama a set of scenes that can rival these in debility?"; Arnott (1978, 6): the first half is "incomparably feeble."

42. See U. v. Wilamowitz (1895, 1:118): a typical "Bühnenbösewicht." Also Sheppard (1916, 75); Kitto ([1939] 1961, 239–40); Gregory (1977, 263); Arnott (1978, 7).

the play. Lykos, an invented figure without a background in saga,[43] combines the vileness of Menelaos with the flatness of the barbarian villains; and
this makes him a singularly limited figure.

Corresponding to Lykos' failure to be an interesting villain is the weakness of the sympathetic characters who oppose him. Megara and Amphitryon are not as resourceful and active, or as lucky, as Helene and Menelaos
or Iphigeneia and Orestes. A revolution in Thebes has given the outsider
Lykos powerful support, while the protagonists are seconded only by the
aged and feeble chorus. Their debates concern, not any active course, but a
choice between ungrounded hope and capitulation to fate, or between a
shameful death and a marginally more honorable one. Nor are their attempts
at persuasion likely to succeed, since, given Lykos' lack of a legitimate claim
to the throne, his attack on the family of Herakles makes sense in terms both
of traditional Hellenic morality and of dynastic opportunism.[44] The theme of
human weakness is very dominant in this part of the play; and, as E. Kröker
has shown,[45] it will later be of major significance. But in the first half, taken
by itself, the theme of weakness guarantees an unsatisfying and flaccid
dramatic structure. As we realize that the sympathetic characters have no
resources and no plans, it becomes evident that they cannot effect any resolution of the dramatic conflict. The continual references to the divinized and
legendary Herakles, on the other hand, make clear that only he can save his
family.

The more the "suspense" is drawn out, the more predictable is the shape
of the necessary resolution. Every moment of delay increases suspense only
at the cost of closing off other avenues for the plot, until at the last the play
has no alternative left open but to save the suppliants in their last extremity,
or let them die. But, since the device of suppliancy presupposes some sort of
rescue, the choice of letting the suppliants die is no real choice at all.[46] Such
dramatic structure as we have here matches the choral odes in its archaism;
but in this case the archaism and naiveté create effects that are unsatisfying
and below the level of sophistication and mastery that fifth-century audiences
had a right to expect from Euripides. As in the case of the prologue/epilogue
frame, Euripides seems to utilize for special purposes elements that are

---

43. On Lykos' lack of roots, see Chalk (1962, 8: the whole first part of the play is a free
invention on an unusually large scale); Kamerbeek (1966, 3); Bond (1981, xxviii). For an
interesting connection between Lykos' name and his nature as scoffer and blasphemer, see Foley
(1985, 180–81).

44. See U. v. Wilamowitz (1895, 2:55).

45. 1938, 11, 49–50, 105.

46. Kröker did not see this, and so credited the first part of the play with more suspense and
excitement than it has (1938, 41ff.).

dramaturgically archaic and inept.[47] Here, the effect, as Arnott has suggested, is to mark the first half of the play as disposable and to whet audience appetite for the missing reversal that does not appear in the first half. When that reversal does emerge, it will be one of the most devastating in literature.

III. Herakles as Modern Hero

III.A. HERAKLES THE BOWMAN

Herakles has a unique status as a Euripidean male protagonist who does not make an unheroic impression. This does not mean that this Euripidean hero replicates such Sophoclean or Aeschylean figures as Eteokles or Oidipous. Instead the atypical mythical persona of Herakles makes him an appropriate choice for a nontraditional exploration of heroism. Herakles is the greatest of all heroes, the only one to bridge the enormous gulf between human and divine; but he does not really fit into any of the great war sagas of Greek mythology, and he has comic overtones that give him a plebeian aura.[48] His feats are associated not with battle, but with the older and less Hellenic occupation of hunting; and his weapons are not those of the traditional armored warrior, but the bow and club.[49] Herakles' deviancy may be explicable to moderns as a sign of his original function in an older stratum of legend; but, in the eyes of Euripides' contemporaries, for whom myth was the inheritance of the "real" and historical past, Herakles' archaism may have looked more like modernity.[50] Because Herakles' saga—unlike that of other heroes—could be seen as one of service rather than self-aggrandizement, he alone was suitable as a model for the new prescriptive morality. Such a figure reforms the concept of heroic achievement, just as a figure such as Prometheus reforms the concept of divinity. And like

47. See Kitto on the play ([1939] 1961, 241): "This absence of the dramatic is clearly the result of deliberate choice."

48. The ultimate source of Herakles' identification with people of low status is likely to be his role as hunter and bringer of food, a less highly ranked role than that of the warrior; see Dumézil's analysis of the three functions (1968, 65ff. on the Pandava is particularly suggestive; Herakles has obvious correlations with the club-bearing and gluttonous Bhima.) See Burkert (1979, 93ff.): Herakles is "founder of altars and lord of feasts."

49. Burkert (1979, 94): Herakles, a savage clad and armed primitively, reflects very old and almost universal shamanistic cults of hunting. "His main job is to tame and bring back animals which are eaten by man." Herakles the Victor (*kallinikos*) marks also a human victory over wildness, since he permanently transfers ownership of animals to human beings (97).

50. Herakles represents the union of the primitive with the civilized, destruction with hope, the animal with the human (Burkert [1979, 97–98]). Galinsky (1972, 27ff.) tries to trace a gradual reform of Herakles' image from Pindaros and Bakchylides; but the two sides of the hero, joined quite logically in the myth, are severely bifurcated in the fifth century. Herakles the comic glutton has little in common with Prodikos' hero of self-denying *aretê*. For Herakles' evolution from most primitive to most modern hero, see Murray (1946, 108).

Prometheus, a benevolent Herakles suggests an implicit criticism of the Olympians, whose relation to human beings is not altruistic and benign.

Throughout the first section of *Herakles,* the hero's labors are conceived in terms of their value for humankind; and G. W. Bond has shown that the first stasimon emphasizes this theme even at the cost of slight distortions in the saga.[51] Herakles is the bringer of civilization, who favors the growth of crops and maps the wild reaches of the seas, to the benefit of mortals.[52] This characterization fits in with the contemporary interest in the development of civilization. It was one of the primary contributions of the Sophists to introduce a picture of early human life as brutal and miserable, rather than golden and abundant; in doing this, they weakened the authority of the past by introducing the destabilizing notion of progress.[53] Although Herakles is not directly associated as is Prometheus with the technological improvement of human existence in general, these hints persistently and from the earliest point of the drama suggest the possibility of new standards and a new definition for heroic *aretê.*

Herakles' odd armament, substituting club, lionskin, and bow for the usual helmet, shield, and spear is the visual symbol of his deviancy from traditional heroic models. But of his armaments only the bow is suitable to serve as a symbol of the modern hero, since from a contemporary point of view the bow was an innovative weapon, currently coming more into favor.[54] If a playwright dealing with Herakles wanted to assimilate this figure as closely as possible to heroic norms, he would downplay the bow as much as possible.[55]

---

51. See Bond (1981, 157–58), on line 368ff., where the centaurs are pictured as rendering the land unfruitful. See also line 376, on the Hind of Artemis, which is described as συλήτειραν ἀγρωστᾶν, "plunderer of farmers."

52. See lines 401–2 on the western travels of Herakles, and Amphitryon's indictment of Greece for failing to succor the Herakleidai (225–26), in recompense for the "cleansing of the seas and land." The closing summary of the second stasimon repeats essentially the same claims (698–99); and, most tellingly of all, Lyssa herself confirms them: ἄβατον δὲ χώραν καὶ θάλασσαν ἀγρίαν ἐξημερώσας (851–52).

53. On this theme, see Dodds (1951, 183–84; and his 1969 lecture, published in 1973, 1–25) as well as Edelstein (1967, 21–56). The latter makes clear the intellectual importance of the concept of a human race developing away from bestiality toward a fuller humanity (23ff.). See also discussion of this theme in Collard's edition of *Suppliants* (1975.2, 160–61).

54. For the attempts of the scholars of the historicist school to tie the references to the bow in this play to contemporary warfare, see Parmentier & Grégoire (1923, 12); Delebecque (1951, 33); Goossens (1962, 350–51). They were wrong only in their assumption that the bow, because it had contemporary correlatives, was without correlatives in the meaning system of the play. For an early example of this treatment in *Herakles,* see Fix's edition of 1842, xi.

55. In *Trachiniai,* for instance, references to the bow concentrate only on the death of the centaur. Meeting the Achelous, Herakles (513) is pictured by the chorus as brandishing "bow, spears, and club." And, when he summarizes his labors at line 1090ff., Herakles addresses his mighty hands and body; the bow is not mentioned.

Conversely, emphasis on the bow differentiates the Euripidean Herakles from the standard model of the hero. G. W. Bond has noted that in the first stasimon the bow is imported even into labors where it seems less than appropriate.[56] But the most emphatic treatment of the bow occurs in the *agôn* between Amphitryon and Lykos; the latter attacks Herakles as a bowman, while the former defends him on the same grounds. This debate has been treated as an egregious example of Euripidean inconsequence, but it is in fact an important part of the portrait of Herakles as a modern and revisionist hero.[57] As we found in the case of *Hekabe,* anachronism is by no means a sign of irrelevance in Euripidean theater.

Lykos attacks the desperate hopes and the pathetic indignation of the Herakleid family by attacking the pretensions of Herakles to be *aristos phôs,* the "best of men." He proceeds to denounce the famous labors in rationalist terms, even explaining the miracle of the strangling of the Nemean lion by the same sort of etymological rationalization that Tiresias uses to explain the birth of Dionysos in *Bakchai.*[58] The major point of Lykos' indictment, however, is the contrast between Herakles' struggle against beasts and the more traditional achievements of the warrior. This is a time-honored trope, going back to Tyrtaios (12W.3 – 8), who contrasts a variety of heroic qualities possessed by mythological figures with the single important ability of the fighting man. Like the Spartan poet, Lykos is convinced that coming to close quarters with the enemy is the only test of valor: a bowman can always flee, so that his is a cowardly weapon (*kakiston hoplon*).[59]

56. 1981, 165 on line 392. Cf. Chalk (1962, 14 n.33); Kamerbeek (1966, 6 – 7).

57. Kröker (1938, 25) saw this and pointed out that it hardly matched the standard Dorian hero that U. v. Wilamowitz saw in Herakles (1895, 1:127ff.). In agreement with Kröker, see Kamerbeek (1966, 11).

58. *Ba* 291ff. *Her* 153 – 54: Herakles throttled the Nemean lion in a noose (*brochos*), which was misinterpreted as being his arms (*brachiôn*). See U. v. Wilamowitz (1895, 2.41); Bond (1981, 69 [on line 23]; 107 [on line 153]), who remarks that "such rationalizing of mythology was common enough in the fifth century." Galinsky (1972, 59).

This technique of assimilating the old poetic texts to an enlightened understanding was already well-worn; see the allegorizing interpretations of Theagenes, Anaxagoras, Metrodoros, and Demokritos, discussed in Konrad Müller's *RE* article "Allegorische Dichtererklärung" (*Supplbnd.* 4.17) and Pépin's survey (1976, 97 – 102).

59. 158 – 61:

ὁ δ᾽ ἔσχε δόξαν οὐδὲν ὢν εὐψυχίας
θηρῶν ἐν αἰχμῇ, τἄλλα δ᾽ οὐδὲν ἄλκιμος,
ὃς οὔποτ᾽ ἀσπίδ᾽ ἔσχε πρὸς λαιᾷ χερὶ
οὐδ᾽ ἦλθε λόγχης ἐγγὺς ἀλλὰ τόξ᾽ ἔχων,
κάκιστον ὅπλον, τῇ φυγῇ πρόχειρος ἦν.

Cf. Tyrtaios 12W.10 – 12: only battle strength (*alkê*) makes the *anêr agathos.* Such a man displays his *aretê* by daring to confront death and coming to close quarters with the enemy (ἐγγύθεν ἱστάμενος).

While Lykos' indictment is built on traditional ground, it is, like his etymologizing debunking of Herakles' feats, contemporary and Sophistic in tone. A variation of the same technique appears in *Clouds,* when modern habits are excused on the grounds that Herakles used hot baths or Nestor frequented the marketplace (*Clouds* 1048ff.). In both cases the modernist strips legend of its authority by pointing out the incongruity between traditional beliefs and current customs. Amphitryon's reply, after a generalized and passionate defense of the labors, proceeds to a well-marked and quite separate defense of the bow. The naively instructive tone of line 189— "Now hear what I have to say and become wise"—sets off the excursus as an intellectual exercise, typical of the new thought.[60]

A defense of Herakles' bow on traditional grounds would presumably situate the bow in its mythological context, perhaps adducing its place in the hands of Artemis and Apollon. Instead, Amphitryon defends the bow as a clever invention, *pansophon heurêma*.[61] The bowman is a free individualist, who depends for his safety neither on a single weapon nor on his fellow soldiers.[62] This independence contrasts with the social rewards and sanctions that supported the traditional method of warfare.[63] The bowman is able to hurt his enemies, without placing his body at risk; and this represents the best kind of wisdom (*to sophon*) in battle (201 – 2). But, since wisdom is not really the province of the warrior, a preference for cleverness in fighting suggests the Odyssean side of Hellenic culture, which was adopted by the Sophists as their own. It is typical of the methods of Euripidean drama, first to create a slightly modified but still idealized hero who can be acceptable on

60. Bond (1981, 117) cites three parallels that just catch the rather pompous tone of this kind of introduction. Apollon (*Eum.* 657) and Sokrates (*Clouds* 822) use it to introduce paradoxical and incredible doctrines, while, in an amusing reversal, the tipsy Herakles in *Alk* 779 makes it a preface to the commonest sort of truisms. Amphitryon ends with a two-line tag (204 – 5) that marks his speech as a rhetorical *logos* set up in opposition to that of Lykos.

61. 188. See the comment of Bond (1981, 117) on *pansophos*. He compares Aischylos 303M, πρῶτα μὲν τὸν πάνσοφον ἀριθμὸν εὕρηκ' ἔξοχον σοφισμάτων, a reference (probably by Palamedes) to the invention of number, and Platon *Prot.* 315e7, where it is used of Prodikos. Cf. Aischylos *Suppl.* 320, used of Danaos.

62. The transposition of lines 193 – 94 to follow line 190 (U. v. Wilamowitz [1895, 2:52]) has the usual effects of these proposals. It clears up the logic at line 191, at the cost of destroying the rhetorical opposition in lines 194 – 95, where "one defense" (μίαν ... ἀλκήν) is opposed to "the one best thing" (ἓν μὲν τὸ λῷστον), namely the myriad of arrows available to the bowman. The arrangement in the manuscripts emphasizes without stating it the dependency of the hoplite on his weapons and on his fellow soldiers. Note also the parallelism of τῶι σώματι / θάνατον ἀμῦναι (193 – 94) and τὸ σῶμα ῥύεται μὴ κατθανεῖν (196).

63. For the penalties, see Tyrtaios 11W.15 – 18; 10W.11ff. Rewards are summarized in 12W.23 – 44. Foley (1985, 172 – 74) suggests that Herakles the bowman is later assimilated to the role of the hoplite, through the transfer of his activities to Athens.

modernist terms, and next to confront this figure with annihilation by an irrational and repellent evil.[64]

III.B. MASCULINE FOCUS AND THE ROLE OF MEGARA

I argued above, in the chapter on *Hekabe,* that the structure chosen for a play must be analyzed on its own terms, rather than in terms of other structures judged more "regular" or appropriate.[65] But the choice of such a specialized structure as that of *Herakles* does impose its conditions upon the play. The break in the middle involves a general changeover in the protagonists, since Herakles must be absent during most of the first part, while Lykos, Megara, and the children are dead in the second. Although the character of Amphitryon provides a link between both halves, the domestic drama must center on a complementary relation of absence and presence between husband and wife.

By coincidence this relation was one already given in the social arrangements of Hellenic marriage, which marked out different areas as suitable for each gender. Places set aside for either sex within the house reflect a broader distinction that located men for preference outside the house,[66] or even outside the community, while women were limited to an interior existence,[67] and absent from the public environment. Herakles, always roaming to the ends of the earth on his quests, exaggerates this distinction and creates a paradoxical result: the presence of the wife outside is caused by and justified by Herakles' absence. At the return of Herakles, Megara would disappear in any case, even if she had not been killed.[68]

A complementarity between married partners who are kept apart is one of many similarities that link this play to the other major drama about Herakles, Sophokles' *Trachiniai.*[69] But in the latter play Deianeira's selflessness,

64. See Kröker (1938, 19 n.1): only through a confrontation with the myth (e.g., a critical treatment of Herakles' traditional feats) "ist der Dichter fähig, nunmehr den Her. in den Mittelpunkt seiner Dichtung zu stellen."

65. See Friedländer (1926, 85): to blame Euripides for choosing such a structure as that of *Herakles* is like condemning Raphael for painting his *Transfiguration* in two sections.

66. Xenophon (*Oik.* 7.30–31) makes this clear: being inside too much is as shameful for men as the reverse is for a woman.

67. Note that Herakles' praise of Megara centers precisely on her long and patient endurance (*diantlousa*) of house watching (*oikouria*): μακρὰς διαντλοῦσ᾽ ἐν δόμοις οἰκουρίας (1371–73).

68. Note that Herakles is shocked to see her outside "in a crowd of males" when he returns (527: ὄχλῳ τ᾽ ἐν ἀνδρῶν τὴν ἐμὴν ξυνάορον). See Chap. 6, above, on the use of the term *ochlos* in *Hekabe.*

69. U. v. Wilamowitz was convinced, on the basis of little evidence, that no one had treated the Herakles story before Euripides (1895, 1:100); see Seeck (1979, discussed in Chap. 7) on the overwhelming mass of lost tragedies. Parmentier & Grégoire supposed that Euripides' play made it impossible ever again to treat Herakles in conventional terms (1923, 18–19): "Au lendemain du jour où Euripide avait créé une telle figure d'Héraclès, il etait trop tard pour la

characterized as "humane" (*anthrôpinon*), contrasts with the brutish—and divine—egotism of her mate.[70] Megara's more colorless role is to perform as a surrogate for the absent Herakles. In her debate with Amphitryon over the choice between hope and despair, as she attempts to "imitate" her husand in *eugeneia* (294), Megara anticipates and gives a preliminary formulation of Herakles' final dilemma. This substitution of wife for husband is one of the devices of analogy that link the severed halves of the play together. The role of Megara marks the first half of the play as provisional and destined for replacement. But it also marks a relation of female to male roles unique in extant Euripidean plays.

Only in *Herakles* are female dramatic roles subordinated to male ones in this manner. Admetos is weakened and even humiliated by the heroic action of Alkestis, and Iason in contrast with Medeia seems less than active and daring. *Andromache* and *Herakleidai* are plays notable for their omission of the heroic male: Hyllos and Neoptolemos, although important to the plots, take no part in the dramatic action. Theseus in *Suppliants* is indeed heroic, but— as he does in *Herakles* itself—he stands for a wholly new and different standard of behavior; and he harshly corrects the representative of the old heroism, Adrastos.[71] The continual prominence given to female figures is a necessary correlative to the revision of heroic standards in Euripidean drama. By their very presence and through their injection into the plays of concerns labeled as female, Euripidean women disrupt the rhythms of Hellenic culture, continually compromising the standards of male heroism and leaving their male counterparts diminished. Both *Elektra* and *Hekabe* are in different ways instances of this process. When Elektra warns her brother not to be a coward, he is diminished, however he decides; and both Polyxene and Hekabe at separate moments express, in almost the same words, a generous and heroic contempt for their male counterparts, Odysseus and Agamemnon.[72]

The complementary structure of *Herakles* guarantees that this compromising of the male by a female focus cannot occur. Megara's interaction is with children and old men, males whose infirmity places them almost on a level

---

représenter encore dans son âpreté héroïque." Schwinge's first work (1962) was an attempt to establish the chronological relation of *Trachiniai* and *Herakles* through typical *Prioritätsfrage* methods. See App. D for a critique of these methods and the presuppositions on which they depend.

70. For the graded scale between subhuman and superhuman and its application in *Trachiniai*, see Dubois (1979) and Segal (1977).

71. See Collard's conclusion that Adrastos is not fit to pronounce the funeral oration over the Seven, until his own standards of heroism and honor have been reformed by the influence of Theseus (1972, 48).

72. Both say *tharsei* as they note the embarrassed hesitation of the Greek lord, who is in each case prevented by state policy from acting in accordance with traditional standards (345, 875); cf. line 869ff.

with women;[73] and she herself is an unfamiliar Euripidean figure, a woman
who neither much exceeds nor falls short of cultural norms for her sex. The
masculine line that extends from Amphitryon to Herakles and to Herakles'
sons is the dominant theme of this play, supplemented at the end by the addition of Herakles' comrade Theseus,[74] while Megara serves in the traditional
female role of linking the male generations together.

Aside from her injection of a strong note of sentiment and pity (*oiktos*)
through her description of the children's behavior, Megara's other notable
contribution to the play is her urging that the Herakleidai not hold out longer
but accept the death that is being forced on them by Lykos. In making this
suggestion, she is led to confront Amphitryon with an assertiveness that
dismayed some nineteenth-century commentators.[75] But their first dialogue
on this theme is desultory and quickly resolved when Amphitryon reasserts
his hopes and instructs Megara to busy herself with the children (98–100).
She injects herself into the action only later, in a manner that bears strong
structural resemblances to the way in which Euripidean self-sacrificers rather
suddenly proclaim their intentions. After negotiations between contending
parties have reached an impasse, the self-sacrificer speaks up, offering to
resolve the conflict without violence by an act of self-abnegation.[76] Megara's
decision is not of the same exotic moral stamp, but the structure serves a
similar purpose in clarifying the motivation for the decision. Had she broken
in upon the debate between Lykos and Amphitryon, she might well have
seemed to usurp a male prerogative and to push her father-in-law aside. The
intervention of the aged and infirm chorus, whose similarity to Amphitryon
makes them suitable surrogates at this point, adds a new and altruistic
motivation to Megara's intervention: by offering to die freely, she will
preserve not only the dignity of the family but also the lives of her friends.[77]

73. Note Amphitryon's depreciating reference to himself (45) as *trophos* and *oikouros*; as
Bond points out (1981, 73), these are terms of contempt because they are female terms applied to
a male.

74. On the (rare) prominence of males here, see Howald (1914, 53).

75. See Patin ([1841–43] 1873, 2:7). Characters in Euripidean plays suggest a standard of
female behavior resembling that prevailing in Patin's era, which expected from women a complete and sensitive compliance to male needs. But the finer details had not been worked out in
the fifth century: Euripidean women often express themselves with a bluntness appropriate to a
culture in which women were policed by men instead of being expected to police themselves.

76. See J. Schmitt (1921, 15–16). Examples are Iphigeneia in *Iphigeneia at Aulis* 1368ff.
and Polyxene. "Makaria" in *Herakleidai* enters at the crucial moment, while Menoikeus in
Phoinissai waits until Kreon's exit before expressing his resolve (991ff.).

77. We may compare the apparent effect on Iphigeneia, when she realizes that Achilleus is
likely to die for her and to die in vain; see Lesky (1972.2, 213–14). In *Herakles* the chorus
intervenes in a long trimeter speech. I have argued elsewhere that the occasional long trimeter
speeches of Euripidean choruses may be conscious reminiscences of older technique (1982, 39
n.40, 56). In the context of highly accented archaism set up for the first part of *Herakles*, such a

Thus prefaced, Megara's remarks seem both appropriate and justified. Her argument centers on the necessity for Herakles' family to follow his example of courage. That abandonment of hope is the path of courage might well be questioned, and Amphitryon had earlier defined the brave man (*anêr aristos,* 105) as one who never loses hope. But those arguments do not emerge in this changed situation. Lykos is threatening to turn the altar into a pyre, and Megara's point, that such a grisly death would allow enemies to mock, is unanswerable in traditional terms. She supports this view with a traditional sentiment: honor consists in being able to define dishonor as worse than death.[78] Put in this way, Megara's courage looks like what she claims it to be, the reflection of Herakles' own heroic image.[79] While it is quite true that Herakles' final decision about what his honor demands will be different from Megara's here, that does not lessen the presumption that she does, at this moment and in this instance, conform to traditional moral norms of what is "noble" (*kalon, eugenes*).

In urging a dignified acquiescence to the inevitable, Megara does display a courage out of the ordinary; but she is the wife of Herakles and owes back to the household tradition the honor it has given her.[80] She wins Amphitryon's agreement by recalling his own heroic youth and the standards of breeding that are undeniably his.[81] Far from proposing to do things unexampled or singular or to set up a new and higher standard of personal duty for women, Megara places her choice firmly inside a traditional framework, which she explicitly derives from her husband's example as a man of unquestioned *aretê.*[82] Amphitryon has little to oppose to her reasoning, except hope (*elpis*),

---

feature seems particularly appropriate; it accompanies the use of the chorus in an interventionist role that can often be paralleled in Aischylos but that is extremely rare in Euripides.

78. 284–94. On the choice of dishonor before death, see the words of Polyxene (*Hek* 378), with their echo of *Aias.* I would agree with Adkins that such concepts have the power to override most other formulations in moral discourse (1960, 186).

79. After pointing out the claims to honor of the children and Iolaos, she modestly adds, "And I must not thrust aside the imitation of my husband [ἐμοί τε μίμημ' ἀνδρὸς οὐκ ἀπωστέον]" 294. Unlike Klytaimestra in *Elektra,* who imitates (*mimeisthai,* 1037) the vices of her lord, Megara, the exemplary wife, uses Herakles' honor as a model for her own reduced version. For Megara's complementary relation to Herakles, see Galinsky (1972, 61), who points to her use of *ekmochthein* (work/toil out, 309) and compares lines 22 and 1369. But a better parallel yet is the crucial *ekponein* (581), and cf. Megara at line 281.

80. 287: ὀφείλομεν γὰρ πολλὰ δώμασιν καλά. See Adkins (1966.1, 211).

81. Once she appeals to Amphitryon's memories of his own glory (288, 308), he responds with vigor and enthusiastically offers to die (319ff.)

82. Herakles' *eukleia* requires no witnesses (290). This may be a hinted correction of Amphitryon's defense, which involved an elaborate figure of summoning witnesses to his son's valor (176ff.).

a principle notoriously uncertain in Greek tradition, and one that will be
crushingly repudiated by the action of this play.[83]

III.C. DOMESTIC DRAMA

Herakles is not only a military innovator; he is also a hero deeply
immersed in domesticity. This theme of family implies an obvious dramatic
irony, in that Herakles displays love for his family just before he slaughters
them. But the family relation among males is a major theme of this play,[84]
since it links Herakles and Amphitryon, Herakles and Zeus, Herakles and his
children, and even echoes through the final encounter with Theseus. Just as
the serviceable Megara raises the issues of death or endurance before Herakles grapples with them in the last scene, so her reminiscences of family life
reveal the domestic Herakles and his children's longing for their father. This
is appropriately her office, since "pity" is the province of women,[85] a province, however, that in this play will eventually be usurped by males.

The elaborate rhetoric in Megara's first speech coexists with very strongly
contrasting notes of domestic life. The second part of the speech evokes a
tone of domestic pathos equaled only by the deathbed scene in *Alkestis*. This
is the mode that Frye called the low mimetic, an attempt to assimilate the
strong audience sympathy and deep emotional involvement of the heroic—or
spoudaion or high mimetic—to less remote and less socially elevated
objects.[86] When Admetos mourns Alkestis, and his little son joins in the
dirge, we seem to be present at the deathbed of any mater-familias, although
of course Alkestis is specially to be loved, missed, and honored.[87] So, here,
the homely descriptive touches, familiar to everybody—because, as Herakles
later says, parental love is common to all human beings—will remind the
audience that Megara faces the same touching and familiar problems as
other, more ordinary and more contemporary, mothers of children. The split
in language (noted in Section II.A., above) in Megara's first speech is
thematic for her role. Megara as mythical and dynastic figure, daughter of a
tyrant and wife of the noble Herakles, and Megara as ordinary and domestic
figure define for this play two stylistic and tonal poles, the heroic and the sentimental, between which it will continue to vibrate to the last. Unlike *Hekabe*

83. See discussion of *elpis* in Bond (1981, 89–91).
84. See Gregory (1977).
85. At 536 Megara excuses her intervention by remarking that "the female is somehow more
pitiful than males [τὸ θῆλυ γάρ πως μᾶλλον οἰκτρὸν ἀρσένων]."
86. For Frye's theories, see Chap. 2. In the case of *Herakles* the first two modes do express
just the particular kind of artistic change that takes place when artists try to transfer the mode of
the heroic *spoudaion* to the sphere of ordinary life.
87. For ironic overtones, see discussion in App. B. For the parallel with Theseus' scene with
Hippolytos and his mourning for Phaidra—another spot of low mimetic—see Rivier (1972, 139).

and *Elektra, Herakles* generally does not fall below the upper two levels of Frye's stylistic hierarchy. The play's irony is generated out of clashes between these two modes, as we contemplate Herakles the killer of monsters and Herakles as mourning father, or the dual genealogies of Herakles, connected to the aged and mortal Amphitryon on the one side and to the supreme divinity on the other.

The element of bathos or bad taste that played such a powerful role in *Hekabe* is largely absent, as is the overt use of comic themes that can be traced in *Elektra*. The higher tone entails the absence both of "low" or sordid elements and of the idealized prettiness that often appears as a counterbalance. After the usual Euripidean palette, with its frequent juxtaposition of lurid fire with the pastel and idyllic,[88] *Herakles* makes a more somber and conventional impression. The touches of archaic style reinforce the elevated tone; and we are concomitantly encouraged to accept that, in the vibration between high and low mimetic, no severe jars will occur. Megara, Amphitryon, and Herakles will continue to be honorable and admirable figures; and we will not, in the usual Euripidean way, suddenly find ourselves contemplating with distaste their failure to maintain the standard of the *spoudaion*. The domestic pathos generated by Megara's speeches about her children, and by the later narration of their deaths, is allowed to stand without qualification or irony, because the role of irony in *Herakles* is not to undermine our faith in the protagonists, but to undermine our faith in the play itself.

The contrast between *Herakles* and other plays featuring children or groups of children is illuminating. The suppliants in *Herakleidai* never acquire individuality, and even single figures like Molossos in *Andromache* serve only as undifferentiated objects of pathos. But Megara recreates for us scenes that convey in unequaled detail and vividness the domestic life of parents and children. Following line 70, after an elaborate reworking of the familiar Euripidean image of the chick beneath the mother bird's wing,[89] Megara's language becomes limpid, as she quotes the exact words of her children. They question her about their father, while Megara tries to distract them by telling them stories (*logoisi mytheuousa*) to pass the time (76–77).[90] Yet whenever they hear a sound at the door, the little boys will start up, ready to embrace their father. The theme is a commonplace in Greek literature: the inexperience of the very young makes them miss the dangers that adults

88. See App. C, on lyric in *Hekabe*.
89. A frequently repeated and endlessly varied trope; see Delulle (1911, 3ff.).
90. Cf. the pathetic quotation of Astyanax by Hekabe (*Tro* 1182–83); this is another domestic scene, as the child climbs into his grandmother's bed (ἐσπίπτων λέχος. For couches or beds as the natural resting place for the infirm aged, see Bond [1981, 94] on *Her* 108 and 555). Bond (82–83) compares lines 99–100, where Amphitryon advises Megara to "charm them with stories, a pitiful deceit [κλέπτουσα μύθοις ἀθλίους κλοπὰς ὅμως]."

know to fear, while they are alarmed by things that have no significance.[91] The fullest development of this trope is *Ilias* 6, where the domestic Hektor puts aside his great helmet because it frightens the baby. The child's howl makes the adults smile, while correspondingly they are aware of real and terrible fears that an infant cannot know. The emotional effect of such scenes is precisely the smiling tearfulness of the Homeric Andromache.[92] It is hard to think of any places in classical Greek literature except these two where such vivid and concrete descriptions of domestic behavior appear.[93]

The companion piece to this first domestic scene is the last speech of Megara, in which we are given a lengthy narration, this time recalling directly the children's love for and intimacy with their father. Megara opens her speech as she enters in the center of a pathetic group, composed of her father-in-law and the children, dressed for the grave, "old men, children, and mothers together" (455). She is presumably holding the hands of and supporting the children, since she refers to the group as a "yoking," *zeugos,* and since she left the scene in the same manner, guiding the steps of the boys (336–37). Her speech begins with a standard theme of rhetorical pathos, as she compares the high hopes of the past with the sad results of the present. But she moves on to a remarkable sketch of past scenes in which Herakles played with his children, promising them their future kingdoms. The children are individualized: there are only three of them, and each is to receive a different realm from Herakles' inheritance. Later, in the grisly narration of their deaths at the hand of this same father, the death of each little boy receives a separate treatment, as one runs around a pillar, while another cowers by the altar, and the last is shot through in his mother's arms (973ff.).

The games that accompany Herakles' distribution of his estate again reflect the sort of pathetic humor that we have seen above. The father plays with his children, letting one wear the lionskin (465), and allowing the other to "hold" the club, as a "pretend gift,"[94] a piquant juxtaposition of Herakles, sacker of cities, and Herakles, father of children. Megara continues

91. Cf., on the blissful ignorance of the infant, Simonides, *PMG* 543, 18–20, εἰ δέ τοι δεινὸν τό γε δεινὸν ἦν, καί κεν ἐμῶν ῥημάτων λεπτὸν ὑπεῖχες οὖας, and *Aias* 552–59.

92. *Il* 6.484: δακρύοεν γελάσασα.

93. See Vahlen (1908, 255); and Kröker (1938): "Auf der attischen Bühne ist solch ein Stimmungsbild neuartig" (47); Megara's feelings show themselves in "intimen Zügen der häuslichen Welt" (13).

94. The club would be impossible for a child to hold, so Herakles "lets it down" into the child's hand (*kathiei*). For the interpretation of *pseudê dosin* see Bond (1981, 186–87); the grimmer and more ironic interpretation of U. v. Wilamowitz (1895, 2:116) is not necessarily excluded by this primary meaning.

with the more conventional maternal anticipation of marriage[95] and the familiar topos of the marriage with Hades. Her peroration is a device familiar from *Hekabe* and *Elektra* as a final appeal to pity (*eleos*). As Hekabe pictured various parts of her anatomy joining in a grotesque supplication, and Elektra spoke for an artificial group, composed of her "hand, tongue, suffering mind and shaven head" (334–35), so Megara will embrace her children in turn, gathering up from each their tears and groans, to combine them into her own, as the bee gathers honey.[96]

The climax of the theme of domesticity is the famous exit scene that follows, when the returned Herakles enters the house, with his children desperately clinging to him. Herakles genially asks his children to cheer up and come inside; but they and Megara cling to Herakles in abject dependency. Herakles urges his wife to let go, adding teasingly, "I have no wings and am not trying to fly off from my friends."[97] As Bond remarks, this is "a joke for the children."[98] It gives us the same Herakles as we saw in Megara's speech, except that now Megara too is as dependent as a child, as she clings to Herakles' robe.[99] But the children will not let go: their infant fear, in its irrationality, provides a pathetic reminder of their past danger. Now Herakles must awkwardly move into the house, repeating the gesture of Megara and taking over her task, as he drags and shepherds the three little boys inside.

The metaphor Herakles uses fits with other jocular language in the scene: he is like a tow barge, pulling little ships in his wake. The vivid language recreates the atmosphere of games between parents and children,[100] and it

95. See *Alk* 165–66, 314–16.

96. 487–89. Bond (1981, 190–91) seems to find the style inappropriate here; but I see the passage as an almost perfect blend of elaborate and forced rhetoric (we have reached the peak of "suspense" and the reversal cannot be longer delayed) and genuine pathos. The comparison of Megara to the bee is very fitting for this best of housewives (see Semonides 7W.83ff.).

97. οὐ γὰρ πτερωτὸς οὐδὲ φευξείω φίλους, 628. Desiderative verbs (*pheuxeiô*) are rare in tragedy. Pearson on fr. 991 of Sophokles (1917, 3:131) cites a list of these verbs; but all are examples of *draseiô* or *ergaseiô*, used with ominous significance, e.g., *Med* 93. This example falls outside the range and probably gives the passage a playful or colloquial tone.

98. 1981, 222. See Kitto ([1939] 1961, 244), "homely pleasantries designed to banish acute terror." (For the jocular tone, compare discussion below of Theseus' gentle taunting of the despondent Herakles.)

99. See Bond (1981, 221), who sees the children as the object of the last urgings, since Megara has already let go. Note that Megara's last line was at line 561. She had apologized for breaking in before Amphitryon at line 533; but, once the emotional freight of her relief has been unloaded, she has no more to say.

100. The metaphor reappears in a serious context later (1424); see Grube (1941, 260). A difference between the two occurrences is that at line 632 the metaphor is glossed ("I'll tow you as a ship does [ναῦς δ' ὣς ἐφέλξω]"), presumably a touch aimed at the children, who will like the image and who will also need to have it explained. This literary moment corresponds to a plate in Galinsky's book, illustrating a vase by the Siren Painter (*ARV*, 2d edn., 1:289), in which Herakles, still holding his club, stretches out his arms to receive his child from his wife. Galin-

also suggests some visual awkwardness in the exit. Herakles, in order to care for his children, must put his heroic dignity aside and even look a bit absurd. He acknowledges the apparent inappropriateness as he protests, "And indeed I do not reject the care of my children [οὐκ ἀναίνομαι / θεράπευμα τέκνων]" (632–33). If Herakles is extraordinary in his benevolence and in his modern mode of warfare, he is more singular in his willingness to compromise his heroic dignity out of love and care for his children.

All human beings, both the better sort, and those who are of no account, are equal in love for their children. "We differ in wealth, but the whole human race is child-loving [πᾶν δὲ φιλότεκνον γένος]" (633–36). With these words, Herakles leaves the scene. The theme of domestic love between parents and children has found its culmination in this moment, as the greatest of heroes acknowledges a trait that unites him with all mankind, men and women, rich and poor.[101] The moment is a perfect expression of low-mimetic tone, which with its blend of tears and laughter, awkwardness and charm, enobles the ordinary and raises the *geloion* almost to the level of the *spoudaion*. In this moment of harmony at the end of the first half of the play, the clash between the legendary Herakles and Herakles as mortal, along with the clash between the concern and love shown by Herakles' mortal father and the apparent indifference of his divine father, seems to have been resolved. It would seem that humanity and heroic strength are congruent; and Zeus, in bringing Herakles to save his family, seems to observe something like the standards of loyalty and faith that have been established for mortals.[102] But the violent dissolution of this fragile harmony will re-pose the questions in ever more extreme antinomies.

IV. Human Strength and Human Weakness

IV.A. HERAKLES' DUAL PARENTAGE

The theme of human weakness pointed to by Kröker comprehends both the extreme old age of the chorus and Amphitryon, and the helplessness of Megara and the children. But if "weakness" is one way to isolate the system of ideas that runs through the play, another means might be through the concept of care and service that is expressed by the Greek words *therapeia* and *trophê*. Both signify the human aid that supplements and relieves human

---

sky argues (1972, 62) that the Euripidean Herakles "sets his arms aside"; but neither the vase nor the text suggests this. Herakles must enter doubly burdened, with children and with arms; note his later references to the *hopla*.

101. See Croiset & Croiset (1913, 348–49): in Sophokles the "rare" sentiments dominate, whereas Euripides uses feelings that unite all humankind.

102. See Kröker (1938, 57–58).

deficiencies.[103] The play presents the inevitable cycle of human life, a journey between the weakness of childhood and the feebleness of old age. Herakles as son and as parent stands between his father and children as a representative of mature and youthful strength, *hêbê*.

But Herakles bears an ambiguous relation to this cycle, since his apparent immunity to old age and human weakness makes him unique among human beings. In the second stasimon's apostrophe of old age some faint echoes of Herakles' apotheosis resound, in the emphasis given to *hêbê*, in the suggestion of a renewal of youth, and in the high praise given an almost divinized Herakles. We are likely to remember that Herakles, according to most stories, vanquished old age, married Hera's daughter Hebe, and joined the circle of the immortals.[104] In his infancy Herakles himself was never feeble and helpless, as his sons are: his toils (*ponoi*) began in the cradle, when he strangled the snakes sent by Hera.[105] But in the moment when the hero seems invulnerable, the sudden and brutal intervention of the gods assures that Herakles will indeed experience the reality of human infirmity.[106]

The question of Herakles' parentage implies the contradiction between his human and his divine identities.[107] In a common trope of encomiastic poetry, the chorus in the first stasimon are undecided whether to praise the absent Herakles as son of Amphitryon or son of Zeus.[108] Later, when Lykos has been killed, they assert the truth of Herakles' divine parentage.[109] After the disaster this theme receives its strongest and most paradoxical expression:

103. See Garzya (1962, 30–31) and Conacher (1967, 83ff.) on the theme of *philia* in the play. The theme of friendship and *therapeia* is presented in *Iphigeneia Among the Taurians* and *Orestes*. At *IT* 314 Pylades cares for (θεραπείαισιν εὐεργετῶν) Orestes during the latter's fit, while also warding off attacks from the Taurians. He wipes off foam from his friend's mouth, as does Elektra in *Orestes* (221ff.), who remarks "See! this office [*douleuma*] is pleasant, and I do not repine [*ouk anainomai*, cf. *Her* 632], tending [*therapeuein*] my brother with a sister's hand." While *therapeuma* at line 633 is the only instance of these words in *Herakles;* see the use of *trophê* cognates in lines 45 (Amphitryon's description of himself) and 902 (of Megara).

104. See also the iconographic evidence for legends about Herakles' conflict with a hateful figure called Old Age (*Gêras*), referred to by Burnett (1971, 42–43; 1965, 249) and Bond (1981, 230). For the iconography see Hartwig (1891).

105. This miracle is alluded to after the disaster (1266ff.).

106. See the comment of Iris, the only justification given for her actions (841–42).

107. See Conacher (1967, 89) and the article of Gregory (1977).

108. 353–55:

εἴτε Διός νιν εἴπω
εἴτ' Ἀμφιτρύωνος ἶνιν . . .

For this question about divine names, see Fraenkel (1950, 2:99–100).

109. 798ff. Past doubts are now resolved: ὡς πιστόν μοι τὸ παλαιὸν ἤδη λέχος, ὦ Ζεῦ, τὸ σὸν οὐκ εὐέλπιδι φάνθη (801–2). (The reading of Bond seems better [1981, 277].)

eloquently denouncing his life as a cycle of miseries,[110] Herakles traces the misfortune inherent in both his parentages, the human and the divine. A recitation of Amphitryon's troubles with his wife's family is followed by a proverb (*gnômê*) that can apply to both alternative lines of descent: when the foundation of a family is awry, the descendants must be unlucky (1261–62). Herakles then begins again with his divine family: "Zeus, whoever Zeus is, bore me as an enemy to Hera." The expression is an ideal one for Euripides, since it is both pious and traditional, and potentially blasphemous.[111] The hero seems to be reciting from rote something essentially incomprehensible: we almost expect him to add after Hera's name, "whoever *she* is." He then turns immediately to Amphitryon and interjects, "Do not be offended, old man; I consider you my father in place of Zeus."[112] The effect is to leave open the factual reality of Zeus' parenthood, and in a common Euripidean fashion to draw attention to a paradox: Herakles' achievements and misfortunes are best explained as deriving from his divine parentage, but the father who shows active concern for Herakles throughout is not Zeus but Amphitryon.

Herakles' words do imply that Amphitryon rather than Zeus deserves to be considered his true father. The contrasting treatment of this theme in *Trachiniai* is illuminating: in that play Herakles and Zeus exercise paternal authority with equal harshness and incomprehensibility, so that patriarchal power beomes virtually identical with the order of the universe: "those who

110. The tone is highly rhetorical; note the self-referential mention of argumentation: "Hear now, how I oppose in argument your advice." 1255–56:

ἄκουε δή νυν, ὡς ἁμιλληθῶ λόγοις
πρὸς νουθετήσεις σάς·

Note the resemblance to Amphitryon's close at lines 204–5: like his, Herakles' remarks will be controversial and will not follow conventional views. For the *hamilla logôn* see the introduction to the debate at *Suppl* 428, ἄμιλλαν γὰρ σὺ προύθηκας λόγων.

111. 1263–64:

Ζεὺς, δ' ὅστις ὁ Ζεύς, πολέμιόν μ' ἐγείνατο
Ἥρᾳ

For the traditionality, see *Ag.* 160. See the stories concerning scandal about—and the alternate version of—the similar opening line of *Wise Melanippe* N2 480–81.

112. 1264–65:

σὺ μέντοι μηδὲν ἀχθεσθῇς, γέρον·
πατέρα γὰρ ἀντὶ Ζηνὸς ἡγοῦμαι σ' ἐγώ.

The phrase *anti Zênos*, "in place of Zeus," is particularly rich in meaning, since it could mean that Amphitryon is Herakles' real father in fact; or that he is equivalent in value to Zeus, the real father (see LSJ s.v. *anti*, III.2); or that he serves as father adoptively, in lieu of Zeus.

bore us and are called fathers oversee such suffering.''[113] In *Herakles* another standard of fatherhood, based on *therapeia* and mutual concern, throws Amphitryon into harsh contrast with the divine parent, even as it throws the achievements of Herakles, *ponoi* undertaken in the service of humankind, into contrast with the actions of the ungrateful gods.

When Herakles awakens from his madness, Theseus, by offering his ungrudging support, persuades him to endure life. Their final exit, with the victim leaning on his protector, parallels the end of the first part, binding together the two separate halves by the usual process of analogy. The striking visual image, repeated now for the fourth time, of a group moving in a concert of mutual support and weakness cannot be missed. The parallel is strengthened by the repetition of the odd metaphor of the tow barge and its dependent vessels (*epholkides*).[114] Herakles, who was the tow barge at the end of the first part, now is in need of a tow himself. He tells Theseus (1401) that, having lost his children, he considers Theseus his child in their place (παῖδ᾽ ὅπως ἔχω σ᾽ ἐμόν). But, since Theseus is the stronger of the two and must support his "father," the relation more closely resembles that between Herakles and his father Amphitryon. Herakles is so diminished from his former stature that he needs Theseus' assistance to get Kerberos to Mykenai (1386ff.). It has been suggested that his difficulties with the completion of the last labor are of no significance because they are purely psychological;[115] but the reality of Herakles' physical incapacity is not removed by its mental cause. Indeed, when Herakles comes to the moment of leaving, his feeble-

---

113. 1268–69: οἱ φύσαντες καὶ κληζόμενοι πατέρες τοιαῦτ᾽ ἐφορῶσι πάθη. On Herakles' behavior as father, see Winnington-Ingram (1980, 84); Segal (1981, 102–4). Sorum (1978) shows the importance of the theme of family in *Trachiniai*; but she sees Herakles as more enlightened at the end of the play, a view I do not share. Herakles remains monstrous, demonic, and self-absorbed throughout. Cf. Murray (1946, 113): *Trachiniai* presents the relation between male and female largely from the female viewpoint. In *Herakles*, where the males incorporate a female and nurturant function, the opposition disappears.

114. See *Andr* 200. The more common usage may have been *epholkion*—see Plut. *Pompeius* 73.5, Strabon 2.3.4; but neither word appears elsewhere in fifth-century literature. To judge by the entries in Stephanos, the word may well have been known to literature in the later period largely through the lexica and metaphorical usages derivable from Euripides.

115. Bond (1981, 408) argues against Kröker that the passage "is an antiquarian's footnote," i.e., has no significance and has been included as an irrelevance. Pohlenz ([1930] 1954, 2:125) argues that Herakles fears he may be driven to suicide. The line is designed to be ambiguous, so that it may suggest suicide, or simply danger from the monster, depending on whether we take *paidôn* with *lypêi* ("lest I suffer something in my loneliness, through grief for my children") or with *monoumenos* ("lest I suffer something [untoward] through grief, when I have been deprived of my children").

ness is such that he cannot stand without help,[116] and he can walk only with the support of his friend.

IV.B. THESEUS AS COMFORTER

The effect of Theseus' entry has been compared to that of the *deus ex machina*,[117] although in fact Theseus is much more involved with the action and with the ideas of the play than these presiding divinities can be. He does, however, enter late and somewhat unexpectedly; and his entrance sharply redefines the reaction to the catastrophe, opening up new possibilities. Although Theseus is a familiar Euripidean type, he is a new sort of character for *Herakles,* which has been notably lacking in ideologues and reformers. Amphitryon's modernist statements seemed to reflect more a desire to defend Herakles than a reformist tendency; and, while the views of Amphitryon and Megara on *aretê* and *eugeneia* are just different enough to permit some mild disagreement, on neither side do these positions harden into sharply defined ideological stances. Theseus, however, especially in his rejection of the dangers of pollution,[118] resembles the sententious hero of *Suppliants.* Such affinities between characters in different plays reflect the essentially schematic use of character traits by Euripides, whose protagonists are as much representatives of certain moral or intellectual positions as they are individuals. When Herakles warns Theseus away because of the extraordinary degree of pollution (*miasma*) attending the infanticide, the latter responds with two countering theories: Herakles cannot spread pollution in being revealed to the light, because mortals cannot pollute what belongs to the gods (1232);[119] and Herakles offers no danger to Theseus, because no spirit of doom (*alastôr*) can come to friends from friends.[120]

Theseus, like Andromache, or Orestes in *Elektra,* or Hekabe in *Troiades,* has enlightened views that lead him to criticize traditional attitudes and practices. He has picked a particularly weak spot. Traditional attitudes toward pollution were among the most persistent and the least rational elements in the Hellenic moral system, and the problem of assigning penalties for

116. In his grief, Herakles' "joints have frozen" (1395). Theseus draws the appropriate conclusion: "[Yes], for *tychai* bring low even the strong" (1396).

117. Rohdich (1968, 101).

118. *Suppl.* 767–68; see also 939–40. Note that Adrastos calls touching such corpses *aischron,* a strong term of condemnation. See also Theseus' correlative refusal to let the mothers handle the bodies (941–46). (That this is convenient to the dramaturgy does not mean that it lacks other significance.)

119. See Bond (1981, 376). Parker (1983, 316–17) remarks that these ideas also seem to express the feelings of social exclusion experienced by the polluted person.

120. 1234. For the meaning of *alastôr,* a kind of personified spirit of pollution, see Bond (1981, 377), who cites for comparison another exemplary friend, Pylades in *Or* 792ff.

unintentional offenses was still a matter for controversy in the fifth century.[121] Theseus takes another element of the old system, loyalty to friends (*philoi*), and elevates it to a principle that will override inhibitions deeply rooted in Greek culture. The contrary case is powerfully stated in Herakles' rebuttal, which describes the customary shunning of homicides in its concrete social aspect. With great rhetorical power, the hero demonstrates the impossibility of an existence in which every avenue is closed by his crime and the dreadful reputation that will follow it.[122] To these arguments the most effective answers are Theseus' promises of social acceptance and honor for Herakles in Athens. These human *timai* will replace those taken by the gods, for that is the office of a friend.[123]

Once Herakles has accepted and agreed to live, Theseus presses his rejection of ritual pollution even further. It is easy even for modern readers to grasp the sensational effect of line 1400, where Theseus embracing the bloody Herakles, who shrinks from him, says, "Wipe it off on me. Do not hesitate. I do not shrink from it."[124] For Theseus, even the instinctive

121. See the extended discussion in Adkins (1960, 86ff.). I would disagree with Adkins' historicist assumption that these beliefs were a product of the turmoil of the archaic period. (Cf. now the contrary arguments of Parker [1983, 66 – 70 and 130 – 38].)

122. For the form "Where shall I turn?" cf. the complaint of Medeia (499ff.), where the rhetorical nature of the questions is made explicit. I would read Hermann's *kêlidoumenoi* at line 1288. The word connects the theory of pollution to the concrete realities of human social practice. Cf. Parker's comments on this scene (1983, 317ff.) and his remark that pollution is "a vehicle through which social disruption is expressed" (121). I would accept the U. v. Wilamowitz' excision of lines 1291 – 93 and 1299 – 1300, which seem in hopeless conflict with the rhetoric of the passage. Without them, the speech moves vividly and powerfully from the quoted insult of the stranger (1290; on the vulgarity of *apophtharêsetai,* see Bond [1981, 388]; and Stevens [1976, 17 – 18]) to the rejection by earth, sea, and rivers, making Herakles a veritable Ixion (1298). The suggestion that Hera will dance in triumph (1303ff.) follows perfectly, since Ixion, like Herakles, was an enemy of Hera. The twist at the end, in which Herakles' misery becomes an indictment of Hera herself, is the more effective at the close of this breakneck peroration.

123. Lines 1338 – 39 are to be retained: Euripidean speeches do not end without closing summaries, and in this case the mention of the gods redirects attention to the question of divine nature that is raised by Herakles at the opening of his speech. Bond repeatedly states (1981, 397) that the couplet is "irrelevant," but that seems merely to mean that its connection to the preceding lines is left unexpressed. Clearly the honors offered by Theseus are to replace what the gods have taken away. The couplet is an apt reply to Herakles' speech, which paints a horrific picture of the life of one hated by the gods (note the phrase *theois echthros,* not used by Herakles, but underlying his negative view of his future).

124. 1400: ἔκμασσε, φείδου μηδέν· οὐκ ἀναίνομαι. *Ekmattein* is used for the removal of any dirt or pollution. *Pheidou meden* implies that Herakles should wipe off the blood freely, without any squeamishness. *Ouk anainomai* is an important phrase for this play (cf. *Or* 221ff.). Herakles used it to signify his acceptance of (potentially demeaning) care for his children (632), and he also used it for his acceptance of his relation to Theseus (1235). Theseus, on the other hand, had argued that the *eugenês* endures divine reversals, *oud' anainetai* (1228). (Herakles made the only positive use at line 1124, to express his dismay and humiliation at being tied to the pillar.) Now Theseus uses it to express acceptance of Herakles, even bloodied and polluted. Cf.

revulsion that blood inspires can be swept aside, because, by the standards of the new prescriptive morality, such merely external concerns are irrelevant.

It is probable that Theseus' opposition to suicide is in line with other reformist and modernist positions that he takes. Traditional Greek attitudes toward suicide display an ambivalence that is expressed in Platon's dictum that suicide is excusable only for those who suffer an intolerable shame.[125] In terms of the *aretê* morality, those who kill themselves occupy an uncertain and therefore an interesting position: their death is both a proof of dishonor and a proof that they, like the soldier in battle, preferred death to shame. Clearly, Hellenic audiences were fascinated with and moved by such dilemmas, as they were by the other paradoxes of the *aretê* standard; and suicide is familiar to us as an aesthetic device of Sophoclean drama.[126] In Euripidean plays, however, voluntary death is not an escape from shame but is treated as positive heroism, and may even serve the public interest;[127] and in *Herakles* the rejection of suicide as an escape from shame implies a new standard of human conduct and value.

In spite of all Theseus' logic and his facility with moral questions, he is not allowed to replace Herakles as tragic protagonist. It is not he but Herakles who best states the case against suicide, arguing that it displays not courage but cowardice.[128] Like other characters of this opinionated stamp, Theseus is ironized, while Herakles is not. His sympathetic kindness is qualified by a faintly teasing and harassing tone, both at his entry, when he forces Herakles to face life,[129] and at the end of the play when Herakles

---

Amphitryon at line 1113. The notion conveyed by this phrase, that of a humble and ungrudging acceptance of limitations and obligations, is a miniature reflection of the play's major themes.

125. *Laws* 9.873c: suicide victims are to be buried, with due regard for traditional rites, but without a memorial stele. These sanctions, however, apply only to those who choose suicide out of cowardice or laziness (*argia*), and not to those forced into suicide by some unavoidable and painful suffering, or those who suffer "inescapable and unendurable shame [αἰσχύνης τινὸς ἀπόρου καὶ ἀβίου μεταλαχών]."

126. For the prevalence of suicide in Sophokles, see Katsouris (1975, esp. p. 231) and Valgiglio (1966, 44–45).

127. See the vainglorious attitude of Euadne, *Suppl* 1055–61. It is notable that the one self-sacrificer who dies largely for her own honor and to escape disgrace rather than for others receives the most public death and the most general honor; this is Polyxene in *Hekabe*. See Valgiglio on the public and altruistic nature of such Euripidean deaths (1966, 61 and 114ff. [on Polyxene]).

128. This notion is admittedly implied by much that Theseus has said; see line 1250ff., where Theseus argues that the choice of suicide does not fit Herakles the Enduring.

129. Note the brusque and unceremonious commands with which he rouses Herakles at lines 1214–15:

εἶέν· σὲ τὸν θάσσοντα δυστήνους ἕδρας
αὐδῶ φίλοισιν ὄμμα δεικνύναι τὸ σόν.

See lines 1226–27 and 1244. Such a brisk manner is therapeutic, but carries a touch of the patronizing. See also the rather teasing question at line 1246, unnecessary since Theseus, who

seems to weaken, longing to embrace his dead children and his father.[130] We
do not have to range as far as the Book of Job to trace the psychology of
Theseus' role; it appears in vignette form in *Prometheus*. Herakles is a more
patient sufferer than the Titan, and Theseus a better friend than Okeanos; but
a familiar admonitory rhetoric appears in both scenes.[131] Parallels of other
sufferers are adduced to persuade the subject that what he experiences is
nothing unexampled; and he may be reminded that death and sorrow are
inevitable parts of human existence.[132] This sort of consolation tends to provoke resentment and irony, for the reason Herakles gives at line 1249: "You
are giving me advice [*noutheteis*], while you are outside misfortune yourself."[133] By taking the role of parent to child, and by pronouncing on what he
has not himself experienced, the comforter denies the victim the authority
that the latter has earned through a direct experience of pain. Theseus' brisk
and vigorous tone shows him superior in emotional control to Herakles, who
is completely immured in his misery; but at the same time it suggests that
Theseus has only a superficial understanding of the tragic situation.[134]

The little stings of inappropriateness in Theseus' behavior build up, until
consciousness of their significance can be triggered just at the play's end,
when Herakles turns on his well-meaning tormentor.[135] He reminds Theseus
that not too long ago, when places were reversed and Theseus was a helpless

---

already knows that Herakles intends to kill himself, merely wants to make him state it more
plainly. (There are textual problems probably caused by a lacuna at line 1241; see Broadhead
[1968, 145 – 46].) See also the rhetorical questions at lines 1250 ("The much-enduring Herakles
says *that*?") and 1252.

130. 1410 (when Herakles embraces his father): "Have you so [completely] forgotten your
labors?" 1412: "If anyone sees you acting effeminate, he will not approve." Herakles
responds, "I live now in a low mode [ζῶ σοι ταπεινός]. But before I do not think [I did]." The
essential meaning must be "I am lowly [humiliated] in your eyes." I see no reason to translate it
as a question. "I live" (*zô*) here (as Bond points out [413]), if indicative, is functionally
equivalent to "I seem" (*phainomai*), given the ethical dative *soi*.

131. See Mullens (1939, 166), who simply cites parallel language in *Her* 1249 and *Prom.*
265 – 67.

132. Note the words of the chorus in *Alk* 930ff. (Wives have died before, "What is new
about that? [τί νέον τόδε]"; cf. *Hipp* 834 – 35) and *Alk* 903ff. (the example of an aged father
who lost his only son).

133. Cf. line 1256, with the emendation of Pierson. The word *nouthetein* is an invidious
one; see the sarcastic usages in Sophokles: *Aias* 1156; *Phil.* 1284; *El.* 343, 1025; *OC* 593. When
used in a nonsarcastic context, it usually implies that the advice giver has parental authority; see
Tro 1015, *Suppl* 337, *IA* 692. For a sarcastic use in Euripides, see the rather closely parallel passage in *Hipp* 395 – 96: the tongue cannot be trusted, for it knows how to advise outsiders
(θυραῖα μὲν / φρονήματ' ἀνδρῶν νουθετεῖν ἐπίσταται) but only hurts itself.

134. See Kitto ([1939] 1961, 247): "The fine and intelligent Theseus is intelligent only to a
certain point."

135. These rebukes disturbed Bond so much that he argued for transposition of the entire
passage at lines 1410 – 17 to lines 1253 – 54 (1981, 417).

prisoner in the underworld, he too seemed not to be himself. His friend admits, "in spirit (*lêma*) I was a man weaker than any" (1416). Herakles' experience of parenthood was one that he shared with all human beings; and his grief, too, is something common to all. Theseus' earlier rebuke, "You have spoken the words of an ordinary (*epitychôn*) person," was both justified and unjustified. It is true that Herakles is no ordinary person; and he does later reject suicide as inappropriate to his pride. But still he has been weakened, spiritually and even physically, by his grief; and this weakness puts him, as it did Theseus in Hades, on a level with ordinary people.

IV.C. Heroism in Paradox

When Herakles turns the tables on Theseus, this may jar the sense of etiquette of some in the audience; but the event is a common one in tragedy and finds many parallels in Sophokles' work. The sharpness and bitterness of such a moment are part of its value, as the tragic sufferer himself takes mental control of his experience and interprets it to those outside. Instead of blandly "understanding" the sufferer's experience externally, we are projected into the center of it. Herakles' tragic knowledge, the fruition of the theme of human weakness, now leads, as H. Chalk has seen, to the construction of an ethic that inverts and corrects the traditional standard of heroism.[136] The fact that Theseus and Herakles work cooperatively in constructing this tragic revelation, each correcting the limitations of the other, supports the thesis that human beings require *philia* and *therapeia* from each other. In his enlightened way, Theseus treats the necessity for Herakles to leave Thebes as purely a matter of customary observance, *nomos*;[137] but he fails to understand the reality behind this observance. Herakles' unwilled guilt has cut him off from his children, as we see, when he asks Amphitryon to bury them and weep for them, "For the law (*nomos*) does not permit me" (1361). At the last moment, when he irritates Theseus by being dilatory, Herakles attempts to turn back to look at the dead children (1406)—because he still longs for them (*pothô*)—and to embrace his father one last time. The tears of Herakles acknowledge an irreducible evil that cannot be expunged by right thinking or good advice.

Like *Antigone, Aias,* or *Oidipous Tyrannos,* this play presents the impact of fate on an individual whose fortune, stature, and courage place him beyond the ordinary. Herakles, because he, unlike his friend Theseus, is not a reformist ideologue, can retain the unqualified allegiance and sympathy of the audience. His insight into his own predicament produces a satisfying sensation of tragic illumination, as we identify with one who has proceeded to

136. Chalk (1962, 12ff.); see also Garzya (1962, 39–40).
137. See line 1322, Θήβας μὲν οὖν ἔκλειπε τοῦ νόμου χάριν.

the very edge of human experience.[138] But that is only a part of *Herakles.* In permitting Herakles to retain his legendary stature, Euripides has created an almost impossible and paradoxical tension between that stature and Herakles' experience. The greatest of heroes is being transformed before our eyes into something very like other Euripidean tragic protagonists, helpless and humiliated, perhaps even awkward and ludicrous figures, whose endurance and suffering capture audience sympathy in spite of these negative characteristics.

Herakles' speech in which he plots his revenge on Thebes sets up the antinomies whose play will govern the reassessment of the labors. The bloodthirsty tone of the speech has been seized upon as a sign of early mental imbalance, or as a token of an excessive violence in the hero. But, for all the humane motivation for his actions, Herakles is a warrior; and it is his business to kill. His point in the speech is that such powers and such violence do indeed become senseless, if they cannot be used in the service of *philoi.* "Whom should I defend more than my wife and children and old father?" Herakles demands; he goes on to say, "Farewell my labors! For it was in vain that I accomplished them instead of this. . . . Or shall we say it's noble to go to battle with Hydra and with lion at Eurystheus' behest—and shall I not labor out my children's death?"[139]

Herakles' anticipation of his revenge on the Thebans is indeed sanguinary. While there is no reason to see this tone as a sign of mental imbalance per se, it stands out a bit awkwardly in the context of a modernized and benevolent heroism. Lykos' head is to be cut off and thrown to the dogs, a revenge that fits the vileness (*kakia*) of the adversary, while doing no great credit to the

---

138. See Segal (1981, 10) on the "terrible coherence" of patterns of conflict that impress on the hero's life "its hallmark of loneliness, suffering, death." Eventually, however, the hero in some way learns to "discover and accept" (8) this larger social pattern, of which his life is a part and for which it provides a focus.

139. 575 – 81:

. . . χαιρόντων πόνοι·
μάτην γὰρ αὐτοὺς τῶνδε μᾶλλον ἤνυσα.
καὶ δεῖ μ' ὑπὲρ τῶνδ', εἴπερ οἵδ' ὑπὲρ πατρός,
θνῄσκειν ἀμύνοντ'· ἢ τί φήσομεν καλὸν
ὕδρᾳ μὲν ἐλθεῖν ἐς μάχην λέοντί τε
Εὐρυσθέως πομπαῖσι, τῶν δ' ἐμῶν τέκνων
οὐκ ἐκπονήσω θάνατον;

The final phrase is remarkable. *Ekponêsô thanaton* is an evident play upon *ponos,* "labor"; see Herakles' later speech, in which (1279) he identifies the death of his children as his last *ponos,* which has capped his house with evils.

hero.[140] Next, any Thebans who have betrayed Herakles' kindness will be slaughtered with the club,[141] while the mass of offenders will be "torn apart" with bow shots.[142] Their bodies will fill the Ismene and the Dirke with blood, much as once the blood of Achilleus' foes polluted the Xanthos.[143] A touch of restraining criticism is offered by Amphitryon. He notes the link between Herakles' lust for revenge and the traditional Hellenic ethic: "It is like you to be kind to those you love and to hate what is inimical"; but he urges his son not to "press too hard [μὴ πείγου λίαν]" (586). Amphitryon advises Herakles to wait in the house for Lykos and not to "disturb your city" until after he is dead.[144]

Herakles' abortive plan of vengeance helps to obviate the implied clash between the hero's straightforward nature and the secrecy of the plot against Lykos.[145] But the way the plan is framed also attracts attention to the dangers of violence. We may compare Amphitryon's lyric description of Herakles' initial reaction to the catastrophe: he begs his son to "restrain the spirit (*thymon*) of the fierce lion, through which you are led into a bloody, impious race, wishing to link evils to evils."[146] The comparison of a hero to a lion is again time-honored and Homeric, but there is an implied criticism, at least of the efficacy of Herakles' usual temperament in these new circumstances. Even before the disaster, Herakles was led to question the value of his powers, when he rejected the title of Herakles the Victorious for the future, if

140. See the remark of Dodds (1960, 99–100, on *Ba* 241) on the Hellenic repugnance for the cutting off of heads.

141. While the bow, the symbol of Herakles' revisionist heroism, dominates the first scenes of the play, the club later comes back into its own. One of the little boys is allowed to hold it in play (and the bow does not appear, 470ff.); a child (presumably the same child) is killed by this club (991ff.) later. At the end, when Herakles resumes his weapons, he must pick up both the club and the bow. The bow is a better symbol for modernism; but the club better indicates primitive violence, the other side of Herakles. See Bond (1981, 208) on the opposition, expressed in line 570 only through the δέ, between the two modes of punishment.

142. 571. See Bond (1981, 208–9): Herakles "is very angry; he dwells lovingly on the bloody details . . ."

143. 571–73. The parallel is appropriate, since Achilleus' valor at this moment in the *Ilias* (21.214ff.) is both super- and subhuman.

144. 605: πόλιν δὲ σὴν / μὴ πρὶν ταράξῃς πρὶν τόδ᾽ εὖ θέσθαι, τέκνον. *Tarassô* is a strong word, and it faintly hints a criticism of Herakles' plan.

145. See Matthiessen (1964, 161–63) on the many parallel instances of this device.

146. 1211ff.:

κατάσχεθε λέοντος ἀγρίου θυμόν, ᾧ
δρόμον ἐπὶ φόνιον ἀνόσιον ἐξάγῃ
κακὰ θέλων κακοῖς συνάψαι, τέκνον.

The text is uncertain, and Bond wishes to retain *bromon*, "roar," instead of emending to get *dromon*, "run" (1981, 372–73). But it is hard to see why a mere roar should be "bloody and impious."

he should not be able to help his threatened family.[147] Now the hero's power has been turned against his family, to destroy them.

Herakles' former violence is not so much wrong or excessive as it is irrelevant to the human experience of Herakles the man. Megara, in her role as surrogate for Herakles, had argued against the preservation of life at any cost, adducing the standard of *eugeneia*. But this familiar warrior ethic is altered when Herakles compares his decision to dare life with the prototypical decision of the *agathos* not to run in battle.[148] Throughout the play Herakles is presented as the tamer, the civilizer, who renders the wild places of the earth gentle; and this gentling of his own fierce *aretê* is in a sense the last of his conquests.[149] In spite of the nurturing love with which he serves his friend, Theseus cannot understand or accept the feminizing effect of Herakles' grief and he is driven to remark, "If someone sees you being a woman, he will not approve."[150] But, just as Herakles was not ashamed to take over his wife's role in caring for his children, just as he learns to ask for help to accomplish what he has always done alone,[151] so the hero, in giving over his struggle to maintain his honor, shows himself more yielding than Megara herself. She attempted to imitate his pride; but in the end he imitates her female humility.

Like much else in the play, Herakles' bow is prominent in the first half but displays its real significance in the second. I have argued that the bow is used to characterize Herakles as a faintly enlightened and modernized hero; but this idealized figure, which blends—sometimes harmoniously and sometimes clashingly—archaic traits with modern ones, is still destined for a radical revision in the passage following line 1377, where Herakles debates whether to take his traditional weaponry with him into exile. After the killing it is natural that Herakles should view with horror the bow and club, now

147. He had referred to his club as his "victorious (*kallinikos*) weapon" shortly before (570).

148. 1350ff. He ends with a formula that has spawned endless controversy. The manuscript has the strange phrase *enkartêresô thanaton,* which ought to mean "I will resolutely face death" (1351). Wecklein's emendation changes this to *enkartêresô bioton,* "I will endure life." But are we right in accepting this radical revision? Attempts to justify the received text (see Kranz [1927]; Ebener [1981, 179]) seem still to leave us with a puzzling and opaque expression (see Bond [1981, 403]; B. suggests Heimsoeth's emendation of "fate" [*potmon*]). If we retain the text, it can be understood only as a kind of riddle, in which "facing death" means *not* choosing death but awaiting its natural coming.

149. This point is made by Galinsky (1972, 58, 65–66); see *exêmerôsas* in Lyssa's defense of Herakles (852).

150. 1412, εἴ σ' ὄψεταί τις θῆλυν ὄντ' οὐκ αἰνέσει. Note that earlier it was Herakles who feared to be seen in his shame.

151. Note that in the bow speech, Amphitryon emphasized the independence and lack of reliance on others of the bow fighter (190–93).

symbols of murder rather than of heroism. Bond has pointed out the odd association of children and weapons following line 1376:[152] Herakles' realization that the past delights of family love are poisoned is immediately paralleled by a reference to the weapons, "And baneful is my association with these arms [λυγραὶ δὲ τῶνδ' ὅπλων κοινωνίαι]. I cannot decide (amêchanô) whether to keep them or let them go."[153] He goes on with strikingly metaphorical language to say that the weapons "embracing my ribs will say this, 'With us you destroyed children and wife. You keep us as your infanticides [παιδοκτόνους σούς].'[154] Then shall I lift them in my arms?"[155] It is as though the weapons themselves, which had killed the children, had also replaced them. While one set of baneful embraces are forbidden Herakles forever, the even more baneful embraces of his murderous weapons cannot be escaped, once the hero has decided to live. Without weapons, Herakles' decision to show courage by endurance would be meaningless, since in his weakened state his arms are all that stand between him and humiliation.[156] "They must not be left; they must wretchedly be kept [ἀθλίως δὲ σωστέον]" (1385). Just as Herakles recognizes the paradoxical coexistence in himself of weakling and hero, so he recognizes the necessity for retaining his heroic office, even though his understanding of its pointlessness makes him inadequate to complete it.[157]

152. 1981, 407.
153. Note the exact grammatical parallelism of the two passages, and the repetition of lygros.
154. The weapons "fall upon" or embrace Herakles' ribs (πλευρὰ τἀμὰ προσπίτνοντ') just as his children did on his return. See Bond (1981, 407), who cites lines 79 and 986. Grube points out (1941, 260) that the weapons were polluted in terms of Attic law (Latte's RE article [1968, 385] mentions this transfer of guilt to inanimate objects, which can literally be treated as "murderers"; cf. Parker [1983, 117]).
155. 1381: εἶτ' ἐγὼ τάδ' ὠλέναις / οἴσω; Bond (1981, 408) points out that it is a peculiarly Euripidean usage to substitute "arm" (ôlenê) for "hand" (cheir). But here there is also a real significance in the substitution, which suggests an embrace.
156. 1382–84:

ἀλλὰ γυμνωθεὶς ὅπλων
ξὺν οἷς τὰ κάλλιστ' ἐξέπραξ' ἐν Ἑλλάδι
ἐχθροῖς ἐμαυτὸν ὑποβαλὼν αἰσχρῶς θάνω;

If all Herakles' kala are not to become aischra, he must keep the arms.
157. See Müffelmann's perceptive analysis of the role of introspection (synesis) in Euripidean drama (1965, 109ff., 134, 156).

V. The Gods

V.A. THE PROBLEM OF DIVINE AGENCY

No play of Euripides gives more prominence to divinities and to questions of religion than does *Herakles*. In other plays divine figures in prologue and epilogue interpret the action through genealogy and cult rather than in terms of the human interactions that compose the play "proper," thus forcing upon the audience questions about truth and reality that the dramatic illusion represses. In *Herakles,* where the gap between myth and reality is central, the appearance of the *deus ex machina* is centralized as well, invading the play at its core.

The clash in *Herakles* between low and high mimetic, heroic and domestic tragedy, is reflected in the clash between Herakles in his human associations, as a member of a chain of loving relationships stretching between fathers and children (as well as between Herakles and his other *philoi,* Theseus and Megara), and Herakles as the hero, specially marked out by his parentage from Zeus and his enmity with Hera, for a life of achievement. When the triumphant and victorious Herakles is praised with echoes of epinician tradition, he is assimilated to those divine beings who are also praised in *hymnoi.* But later, when Herakles in his suffering reinterprets the whole course of his life as a progress in misery, he radically differentiates himself from the gods, whose actions become incomprehensible and who are subjected to severe criticism. Amphitryon, at his peak of misery in the first half, also turns against Zeus and judges him in human terms, claiming that "I, a mortal, surpass you, a great god, in *aretê*" (342)—because Amphitryon is loyal and does not betray his *philoi,* as Zeus does.[158] This indictment hangs in the air and is reactivated by the intervention of Hera and Iris and the example of Theseus. The theme of human weakness that forces a revision of the *aretê* standard also forces a revised view of the gods.

Zeus in this play is pulled down to the level of the humans who judge him, and the leverage for this suppression of divine dignity comes from Zeus' relation to Hera. The mortal actors in *Herakles* differ from those in other

158. 342. Adkins' strict definition of *aretê* (1966.1, 213; cf. comment by Bond [1981, 91]) breaks down here. Amphitryon, in his ineffectiveness and feebleness, has not displayed *aretê* as a *philos* in Adkins' terms; but he claims it nonetheless. This, along with Amphitryon's paradoxical definition of the *anêr aristos* as one who never gives up hope, is a striking and argumentative statement that helps to direct the dialogue in the play about the nature of *aretê;* see Chalk (1962; but C.'s work could have benefited from Adkins' stricter terminology. The "*arete* of . . . impotent endurance" is a rather paradoxical formulation [12]). See Strohm (1949–50, 150–51) and Galinsky (1972, 63) on the play as a redefinition of *eugeneia.* This latter concept can readily coexist with misfortune (cf. Pindaros, *Py* 3.83: the *agathoi* bear evils well, "turning the good [part] to the outside [τὰ καλὰ τρέψαντες ἔξω]").

plays in their conformity to social norms: far from diminishing or embarrassing her husband's heroic pretensions, Megara enhances them; and Herakles'
corresponding acceptance of his domestic responsibilities presents us with a
hero who is both modern and admirable. The ironic treatment of male-
female complementarity is displaced into the divine sphere, for the king and
queen of the gods resemble nothing so much as unreconstructed Euripidean
erotic protagonists, embroiled in intrigues and jealous plots.

The traditional treatment of Hellenic divinities allows a slightly different
etiquette for lesser gods, who display strong jealousies and violent enmities,
while Zeus holds aloof from such things. In the *Ilias* he is a neutral and
appreciative observer of the conflict, while Hera is the most violent of parti-
sans.[159] This corresponds to an ethical split in which Zeus, as supreme divinity, is charged with the maintenance of sanctions for what A. W. H. Adkins
calls the "cooperative virtues,"[160] while the lesser gods hold firmly to the
aretê standard. Another way of putting this would be to say that Zeus ceases
to be "anthropomorphic" when he becomes the enforcer of *dikê,* or alternatively, that anthropomorphism directly correlates with the application of the
aretê morality to divinities. In this play, Zeus' relation to Alkmene and to
Hera severely compromises his divine dignity and brings his allegiance to
dikê much into question: Amphitryon gives the supreme divinity a choice of
being labeled *adikos* (unjust) or *amathês* (ignorant).[161]

That the latter may, in some sense, really be the case is suggested by the
language of the second stasimon, in which the gods are said not to possess
intelligence (*synesis* and *sophia*) in human terms, *kat' andras.* L. Kretz[162]
argued that such carefully moderated statements carry an implied tone of
authorial approval. His point was that extreme statements in the mouths of
dramatic characters (e.g., "all women are treacherous and vile") are polemical and thus imply an opposite viewpoint, while qualified statements (e.g.,
"some—or many—women are treacherous and vile") tend to obviate
controversy (54–55). Here, the chorus says something that may inspire
some agreement both from the pious and the impious: human virtues may
be irrelevant in a divine context.[163] This of course does not mean that we
have isolated "Euripidean ideas" about the gods. These expressions create

159. For the negative and anti-Olympian associations and qualities of Hera, see the article of
Eitrem in *RE,* s.v. Hera, p. 399.
160. *Dikê* in Hesiodos is said to be the daughter of Zeus and to report directly to him.
Again, the contrast with the Homeric Zeus is due not so much to historical development as to a
different context, in which prescriptive morality is more important; see Dover (1983, 48 n.32).
161. For the effect of Hera's intervention, see Kröker (1938, 95).
162. 1934, 2–3; see also p. 20 (a dissertation written under Howald).
163. See Bond (1981, 233): such words "could be used by a pious theist."

a specific rhetorical effect, as more controversial pronouncements do elsewhere.

Amphitryon begins the play by referring to himself as "the bed partner of Zeus," an ambiguous reference that just grazes the edge of the ludicrous, but may pass by safely in the heavily genealogical context of the speech's opening.[164] Following line 339, however, when Amphitryon has finally resigned his hopes, he turns again to Zeus and pictures the relationship in dangerously everyday terms. After making his claim to superior *aretê,* the old man charges, "You knew how to make your way to bed in secret, taking someone else's place without permission; but you do not know how to preserve your friends."[165] The charge of abandonment and neglect here is based on a tacit original charge of adultery. The implication is that Amphitryon, in spite of the fact that he did not consent to Zeus' act, would condone it retroactively, if Zeus had kept his share of the bargain by supporting the family of Herakles. Also implicit is the suggestion that, by failing to act in a way proper to a *grand seigneur,* Zeus falls to the level of a common adulterer.[166]

The charges against Zeus fade away at the false happy ending of the first half, when he seems to defend the Herakleidai and enforce *dikê.* But confidence is suddenly disrupted, when Hera's messenger Iris, and Lyssa, the personification of (insane) Rage, appear above the chorus. Iris, who gives no reason for the extreme hatred of Herakles that she shares with Hera (831 – 32), refers with neutral irony to Herakles as one "who, they claim, is from Zeus and Alkmene."[167] Herakles' punishment is not justified by Iris at all, except as a necessity for maintaining the primacy of gods over mortals. Lyssa is one of those lesser divinities who personify the unappealing but necessary supports for Olympian power. Like Kratos and Bia in *Prometheus* or the Eumenides in Aischylos, her obvious predecessors,[168] Lyssa, precisely

---

164. See Bond's comment (1981, 63) on the potential ambiguity; on the ludicrous overtones, see Grube (1941, 244 – 45).

165. 344 – 46:

σὺ δ᾽ ἐς μὲν εὐνὰς κρύφιος ἠπίστω μολεῖν,
τἀλλότρια λέκτρα δόντος οὐδενὸς λαβών,
σῴζειν δὲ τοὺς σοὺς οὐκ ἐπίστασαι φίλους.

166. The charge of rape against Apollon in *Ion* is handled in just the same way: the explicit charge brought against the god is not rape, but nonsupport. Burnett (1962, 95 – 96) as usual attempts to get Apollon completely exonerated by making oversharp distinctions on this point. As usual, this is not persuasive. The implications of sexual misconduct for divine dignity are not erased simply because the accusation is not worked out in juridical detail.

167. 826. Herakles' mere claim, whether grounded or not, to direct descent from Zeus is sufficient to provoke enmity from Hera, while at the same time his divine enemies do not admit the relation.

168. That is, the resemblance to *Eumenides* will occur to us. There may have been an original Lyssa in *Xantrides,* after whom this was copied; see Duchemin (1967, 133ff.). For parallels between the Lyssa scene and *Prometheus,* see Burnett (1971, 169).

because of her frightening and repellent qualities, is a necessary agent for Hera's anger. But Euripides' Lyssa belies her nature in true Euripidean form.[169] While Iris sees only a contest of prestige between a god and a mortal, Lyssa phrases Herakles' claim upon the gods in terms of the "cooperative virtues": through his benevolence he has aided not only the human race but also the gods, whose cults had fallen into disuse.[170] The irony of Lyssa's attempting to advise Hera and Iris to avoid rash actions is explicitly marked by Iris' final response, which has a very sharp and witty ring: "Zeus' wife did not send you here to be sober."[171] This witticism seems to be aimed as much by the play at itself as by Iris at Lyssa, since it points up the perversity of the characterization. If even Rage herself sees the inappropriateness of Hera's rage against a mortal, then the audience is strongly encouraged to see it too.[172]

After the disaster, references to Zeus naturally again return to the theme of neglect.[173] The most striking may be Amphitryon's apostrophe at line 1127, "O Zeus, from beside Hera's throne, do you see this?"[174] The picture of Zeus as sharing his rule with his queen, who is enthroned beside him, well expresses the essentially compromising effect of Hera on Zeus' status as supreme god. Hera is called "the bed partner of Zeus," the same phrase with which Amphitryon described himself at the opening of the play.[175] Herakles' cynical account of his birth also links the two gods: "Zeus,

169. U. v. Wilamowitz (1895, 1:124) points out that Lyssa's traditionality is indicated precisely by Euripides' perverse use of her.

170. 853: τιμὰς πιτνούσας ἀνοσίων ἀνδρῶν ὕπο. The connection to Herakles' actual Labors is loose, since, unlike Theseus, he practiced his skill less on wicked men than on beasts. But U. v. Wilamowitz cites a few human opponents—Kyknos, Diomedes, Busiris—who might be characterized as "impious" (1895, 2:185). See Galinsky (1972, 17–18) on Kyknos in the Hesiodic *Shield of Herakles* as a "personification of sacrilegious impiety and evil."

171. 857: οὐχὶ σωφρονεῖν γ' ἔπεμψε δεῦρό σ' ἡ Διὸς δάμαρ.

172. See Kröker (1938, 60–61); Müffelmann (1965, 120).

173. Note the chorus' remark (1087–88): "O Zeus, why do you so violently hate [ἤχθηρας ὧδ' ὑπερκότως] your own child?" See τὸν σόν, in enjambment, which emphasizes the relation. The contrast with Amphitryon's touching remark at line 1113, "Though faring ill, you are still my child," is obvious.

174. ὦ Ζεῦ, παρ' Ἥρας ἆρ' ὁρᾷς θρόνων τάδε; There is no need to see, as Bond does (1981, 353), an "offensive" sexual allusion to Zeus, who is presumed to be sitting on Hera.

175. At line 1268, where Herakles tells of her first attack, in his cradle. The structure of the lines ironically and scornfully juxtaposes Hera's rank as Zeus' mate with her attempt to destroy a baby: "when I was yet a nursling, snakes / she let in upon my cradle / she, the mate of Zeus, that I might be destroyed."

ἔτ' ἐν γάλακτί τ' ὄντι γοργωποὺς ὄφεις
ἐπεισέφρησε σπαργάνοισι τοῖς ἐμοῖς
ἡ τοῦ Διὸς σύλλεκτρος, ὡς ὀλοίμεθα.

whoever Zeus is, bore me as an enemy to Hera" (1263–64). Zeus' mystery is stripped of its awe, when he is linked with his wife.

After a powerful summary of the miseries that are before him, a social outcast and like Ixion hated by Hera and Zeus, the hero concludes with a bitter picture of Hera's triumph. "Let the famous consort of Zeus dance, striking the plain of Olympos with her sandal, for she has accomplished what she wished, in overturning from the very foundation the first man of Greece. Who would pray to such a god, who, for a woman and out of jealousy for Zeus' bed, destroyed the benefactor of Hellas, who was without guilt?"[176] A traditional image of divine dancing is nicely poised here against the rather grotesque image of the queen of the gods in an ecstasy of satisfied rage.[177] On balance, the effect is not enobling for the goddess. The anthropomorphic standard of divine behavior is here driven to a violent extreme, and the result is a violent rejection of the divinity. If Olympian gods are like that, why should human beings, who are morally superior after all, give them worship? But we must not lose sight of the fact that the consequences for Zeus himself are equally damning: he is at the center of the sordid sexual jealousy that has ruined Herakles; and it was his dalliance that provoked Hera's rage.

At this point Herakles' view of himself as hero and of his relation to his divine father reaches its nadir. The emotional power of the speech contributes to its impact, while at the same time it suggests the possibility that this may be a one-sided view. Herakles seems to have brought us full circle, so that we approach from the opposite direction the negative and rationalistic view of Lykos. To Lykos, Herakles' accomplishments were trivial feats, distorted into myth by misunderstanding. To Herakles, his *ponoi* were indeed real as reported; but, seen from the perspective of his final fate, they are

176. 1303–10:

> χορευέτω δὴ Ζηνὸς ἡ κλεινὴ δάμαρ
> †κρόουσ᾽ Ὀλυμπίου Ζηνὸς ἀρβύλῃ πόδα.†
> ἔπραξε γὰρ βούλησιν ἣν ἐβούλετο
> ἄνδρ᾽ Ἑλλάδος τὸν πρῶτον αὐτοῖσιν βάθροις
> ἄνω κάτω στρέψασα. τοιαύτῃ θεῷ
> τίς ἂν προσεύχοιθ᾽; ἢ γυναικὸς οὕνεκα
> λέκτρων φθονοῦσα Ζηνὶ τοὺς εὐεργέτας
> Ἑλλάδος ἀπώλεσ᾽ οὐδὲν ὄντας αἰτίους.

The text of line 1304 is quite uncertain, but its gist is obvious: Hera's sandled foot strikes Olympos, as she dances for joy at Herakles' destruction. "For a woman [*gynaikos houneka*]" (1308) is almost a reflex of the many denunciations of the Trojan war. Here the implication may be that Hera, who is herself a female with typically female concerns, is a morally unworthy adversary for the noble and benevolent Herakles.

177. Hera's dance corresponds to the dance of madness that she inflicted on Herakles (877ff., 888).

revealed to be merely a series of sufferings and humiliations.[178] From whatever side the myth is inspected, whether it is believed or disbelieved, it seems equally unsatisfactory. The puzzle-box structure of the plot is thus replicated in the kaleidoscopic fragmentation of Herakles' image, as we are continually presented with different and contradictory versions of the hero and of the gods. It is not entirely surprising to find that, in his next speech, Herakles appears to repudiate the basis for his indictment of the gods and to reestablish his heroism on a new basis as well.

V.B. THE FICTION ERASES ITSELF

Theseus responds to Herakles' denunciation of the gods in a rather unexpected way that picks up his friend's argument and turns it in a different direction.[179] We have just heard that no one should pray to a god as vile as Hera. Theseus, by contrast, accepts the frailty of the gods and uses it to argue for Herakles' survival.[180] The mythological instances used to prove divine liability to chance (*tychê*, 1314, 1321) make their appearance normally in two sorts of rationalizing and reformist arguments. In an earlier period they support the repudiation of the gods of myth and their replacement by a figure or figures better suited to enforce and to exemplify *dikê* in accordance with the demands of a prescriptive ethic.[181] In the fifth century, however, instances of divine frailty are more likely to be used to excuse and justify the abandonment of traditional moral standards.

The examples that Theseus uses were familiar sources of scandal about mythology.[182] The gods, "if the poet's stories are not false," have contracted improper sexual liaisons among themselves and have "stained [*ekêlidôsan*]

178. This paradox too is built into the tradition and undoubtedly explains in part Herakles' association with plebeian matters: his relation of servitude to Eurystheus (and Omphale) makes it natural for slaves and poor laborers to identify with him. Kröker (1938, 113) cites the phrase from Hesiodos *ponêrotaton kai ariston* (fr. 248 – 49 Merkelbach/West); we cannot know for certain that *ponêros* had already acquired its social meaning of "wretched, low," at this early date, but it nowhere appears as an honorific or neutral term.

179. Theseus' argument may be in large part lost to us. There is evidently a lacuna before line 1313, when he is adducing the analogy of the gods.

180. What Theseus seems to be saying has the potential to be an interesting argument, since it is a kind of reversal of the famous rationale for heroism offered by Sarpedon in *Il.* 12.322ff.: if mortals were immortals, we should not fight but enjoy life. But, since death awaits us in any case, we must seek glory. (Therefore, death before dishonor.) Here Theseus seems to say that, if existence were potentially happy, we would be right in choosing suicide over a bad life. But, since not only mortals but gods suffer humiliation, we should accept our lot without complaint. (Therefore, endure dishonor.) Note that the idea of a *similarity* between gods and humans is the basis of Theseus' argument.

181. See Xenophanes DK 1:126 fr. B1.21 – 23 as well as B11, 12, 23 – 26. Herakleitos DK 1.149 fr. A22, 23; 1.160 fr. B42.

182. See Xenophanes 11B: κλέπτειν μοιχεύειν τε καὶ ἀλλήλους ἀπατεύειν; *Eum.* 641.

their fathers with chains for the sake of tyranny.''[183] Both these examples apply best directly to Zeus, whose sexual proclivities have just been mentioned by Herakles, and who is the only Olympian god to have bound his own father.[184] In both cases we have a very strong contrast readily available on the mortal side in Herakles, whose marriage with Megara is harmonious, and who is loyal to his father. If Herakles in his insane rage almost murdered his father, that was not done, as Zeus' action was, "for the sake of tyranny." But, in Theseus' bland formulation, such degrading crimes are assimilated to *tychê,* which all must equally endure.[185]

The similarity of Theseus' argument to that employed by the Nurse in *Hippolytos* is obvious, as are the connections in both cases to the Sophistic. But the Nurse's theory was rejected by Phaidra, and indeed such arguments transparently invite repudiation.[186] Theseus' arguments against pollution, although extreme, are plausible and conform to cultural changes that were already on foot; and the traditionalist might have had little to offer in opposition except instinctive feelings of propriety.[187] But the argument of divine frailty is, at bottom, paradoxical; and Herakles has already undermined it by his polemic: if the gods are such morally vile creatures, on what basis can they be used as models for human behavior at all? Theseus' examples raise more questions than they settle; and, if taken to a logical extreme, they would devalue all moral standards—since any crime could be labeled a vicissitude of *tychê.*

Theseus' argument is not really the one that we would expect him to make at this point. He has been a purist whose high standards of conduct led to a

183. 1316–17. For the usage of *ekêlidôsan,* see Bond (1981, 394): it refers to the pollution associated with insults to parental prerogatives, even those falling short of murder. Cf. Herakles at line 1288.

184. Of course, as some have pointed out (Giube [1941, 57–59]; Gregory [1977, 273]), the sexual problems of Zeus in this play are not precisely those of irregular unions with *other gods.* But this is quibbling (on the sophistry of these arguments, see Brown [1978, 23]). As we have seen, here and in *Ion* this question is finessed by presenting the divinity's sexual misbehavior, while covering it with the question of support for the humans subjected to rape or adulterous seduction. Here, where the general moral problem of gods who behave like common adulterers needs to be kept to the fore, the injection of the human question would be distracting and over-complex. See also the Xenophanes passage, DK 1.132 fr. B11–12, where the behavior of the gods toward each other (*allêlous*) was explicitly cited.

185. Müffelmann (1965, 124–25) points to the turning of attention to *tychê* as beginning at lines 1236–37, when Herakles first expresses pity for himself. This is an important step in his persuasion: he begins to acknowledge his relation to Theseus and to share his suffering with another human being.

186. See Bond (1981, 393). In *Hippolytos,* the argument is used to characterize the Nurse; but that does not seem to be the point of it here.

187. Parker (1983, 126–28) points to the obsolescence of these beliefs in a society where legal remedies to the disruptions introduced by violence were readily available.

ruthless disregard for traditional taboos, while now he seems to make a rather disingenuous appeal to tradition.[188] But the course of the argument has been distorted by Herakles' violent repudiation of his own legend. It is rhetorically awkward for the opposing speaker to picture suicide as cowardice, once Herakles has dismissed honor and reputation as a chimera. In responding as he does, Theseus redirects the argument by utilizing Herakles' position in a new way: it is true that the gods are frail creatures; but, since we are frail creatures too, we had better follow their example and live. To maintain other standards would be a sign of arrogance (1320–21) in a human being.

Taken together, the two views of the gods just analyzed are complementary as well as opposed. Both agree that the gods are prone to morally deplorable behavior and that human life may be wretched as a result. But Herakles does not accept what has happened to him, and it is his indignation against such divinities that spurs him to suicide. Theseus argues that we can and must accept the gods as they are, even continuing to use them as models for our own lives, although this would make moral judgment in human affairs impossible. Taken together, these arguments present us with an impasse. To retain the right to moral judgment is to repudiate the gods, while to accept the gods as they appear to be is to abandon moral judgment. It is at this point that Herakles returns to the question, offering a sudden revision of his previous views that caps all the reverses of this paradoxical drama.

Herakles begins his speech with a disclaimer familiar to us from the notorious excursus in *Hekabe*. "Alas," he cries, "this is irrelevant to my own troubles."[189] The marker of irrelevance to present plot concerns is also a marker of significance to broader concerns of the play, as well as of a thinning of characterization. Like Hekabe's, Herakles' words have a significance that goes beyond what his character can intend;[190] and in his case they contradict his own recent words as well as the events of the play. He explicitly rejects the idea that one god can be master (*despotês*) of another, although both the gods that we have seen on stage are divine inferiors.[191] His final

188. In saying this, I do not intend to raise the question of Theseus' psychology, apart from the kind of psychology of plausibility that is inherent in his rhetoric. See Gould (1978). His functions as comforter and as rationalist largely exhaust the psychology of his role.

189. 1340, οἴμοι πάρεργα ⟨μὲν⟩ τάδ' ἔστ' ἐμῶν κακῶν. Bond (1981, 398) assumes that "this" (τάδ') refers to the previous offers of honors by Theseus. But such an explanation leaves the following lines totally without connection to the opening. (Τάδ') should here refer, as it usually does, to what follows, namely the remarks about the gods that Herakles is about to make.

190. The suggestion of Grube (1941, 60) that Herakles is simply "wrong" about the gods, and a recent similar explanation by Stinton (1976.2, 83; refuted by Brown [1978]) assume that what characters know or think is the limit of what their words can mean.

191. Iris introduced herself as "the lackey of the gods [ἡ θεῶν λάτρις]" (823); and Lyssa was clearly forced by Hera's superior authority to act against her better judgment. Bond argues learnedly (1981, 281) that Iris' reference to herself as a *latris* or flunky is not invidious; but it is not without significance either.

generalization seems to wipe out the whole anthropomorphic concept of divinity: "God, if he is truly a god, needs nothing. These are the wretched tales of the poets."[192] Theseus had rightly cited the poets as a source for his legends about divine misbehavior and humiliation, a reference that virtually demanded such a rebuttal as this. Herakles' new standard of the perfect god, who lacks nothing, goes to the same Eleatic sources that were the origin of Theseus' examples.[193] But, if this view of divinity is right, the whole story of Herakles' life can make no sense.

In the plane of the play's mimesis of reality, what Herakles says is patently untrue. Gods do commit crimes; they do rule over one another; and they are not perfect beings, in need of no addition. But no play, and especially no play by Euripides, exists solely on the plane of its mimetic "reality." At every point this play, of all Euripidean plays, has raised the question of the trustworthiness of poetic fiction. The major odes with their emphasis on the poet's function, and their evocation of encomiastic poetry, have encouraged us to see the gulf between different treatments of mythic tradition, or between fiction and reality. The betrayal of our expectations in the dissonant and mocking plot reversal, which gives us threatened disaster, salvation, and a new disaster in the space of three hundred lines, has encouraged us to question not only the apparent wrong done by the gods to Herakles but also the poet himself, who, in wronging his hero in an inappropriate and unexpected manner, has wronged the audience as well. With the overt reference to the possibility that the *logoi* of the poets may be false, we are forced to consider that *Herakles* itself, the play we are watching, is also a mere fiction, a tale told by a poet who may be lying. It has been said that the play here "crosses itself out" or destroys its own supporting structure.[194] The mention of lying poets projects outside the frame of the drama, as a self-referential suggestion that our interpretation of this play should not confine itself within the boundary of the fictional "reality."

By "crossing itself out" in this way, the play invites our consideration of the problem of human suffering, taken aside from the apparatus of divine

192. 1345–46:

δεῖται γὰρ ὁ θεός, εἴπερ ἔστ' ὀρθῶς θεός,
οὐδενός· ἀοιδῶν οἵδε δύστηνοι λόγοι.

193. The idea of a divinity as needing nothing was a powerful concept that spawned the whole later ideal of philosophic *autarkeia*. See Chromik (1967, 121).

194. Lesky (1956, 210): we must ask "ob wir nicht vom Dichter seine eigene Schöpfung wieder durchgestrichen sehen." See Kröker (1938, 100): "Hebt denn der Dichter am Schluss des tragischen Spieles seine eigene Gestaltung auf?" Conacher remarks on *Herakles* that (1967, 89–90, 43) Euripides here dispenses with the scaffolding on which his play was erected and that such a reversal is "an impudent and typically Euripidean device." See the similar remark of Reinhardt (1957, 622) on *Orestes*: "Die Dichtung kehrt sich gegen sich selbst."

causation that until this point has been so laboriously attached to it. This view is encouraged by Herakles' reference to theological speculation as a side issue (*parergon*) to his sufferings. While Hera's malevolence articulates and defines Herakles' tragedy, there is a sense in which Hera and her intrigues are as negligible to the human truth of this play as is Herakles' special status as god-related and supremely gifted hero. The superstructure of heroic relations to divinity, used to set off the problem of human suffering from complicating or trivializing factors, is later "kicked away," leaving behind only the universals shared by all human beings in the world of ordinary existence.[195]

Herakles, a specially gifted and divinely related human being who serves as our link to immortality, ideally expresses both the aspirations and dangers of humanity. Euripides' play forces to breaking point the contradictions inherent in this traditional Hellenic archetype, and it does this by attempting to formulate the archetype in Euripidean terms. The attempt breaks down, not once, but over and over again, each time generating more violent contradictions. The play uses the pathos and grandeur of a lowered and modernized *spoudaion,* the equivalent of Frye's low mimetic, to gain our acquiescence to a radical revision of heroic myth and of the tragic experience as a celebration of human identity. Yet at the very moment when Herakles' tragic experience reaches its moment of climax, the tensions between the human and the heroic views also reach a peak. Whomever we can believe Herakles to be at various stages in the play, the tragic insight of the ending reveals the untenability of his heroic identity: as Theseus says, "In your sickness, you are not the famous Herakles."[196] When the case of the hero receives its most extreme formulation, the paradoxical presence of godlike powers in a human being becomes identical with the traditional tragic paradox of divine purpose and human suffering.

195. See Chromik (1967, 122): the gods cease to be mentioned in the very end (except at line 1393) of the play. But cf. also Pucci (1980, 175–87), who points out that the repudiation of divine responsibility creates an even more irrational universe, in which doubt of Herakles himself must replace our anger at the gods.

196. 1414, accepting the persuasive emendation of U. v. Wilamowitz: ὁ κλεινὸς Ἡρακλῆς οὐκ εἶ νοσῶν.

9

Hippolytos: An Exceptional Play

The negative critical response to Euripides' work has produced the alternating postures of defense, apology, and attack that ran in a repetitive pattern through the first chapter of this book. But most critics have been willing to exempt a select minority of plays that seemed to lack the faults of the rest. The list has fluctuated. H. Patin, representing the orthodox French critical position for the nineteenth century, favored *Iphigeneia at Aulis,* evidently largely because of its associations with the Racinian version.[1] The prominent and fascinating personality of the heroine of the *Medeia* has often caused that play to be seen as a heroic drama of character and has thus prompted its inclusion in the canon of select Euripidean plays.[2] And those who study tragic form sometimes include *Herakles* among the plays answering the essential demands of the genre as established by Euripides' predecessors.[3]

But time and again two plays, *Hippolytos* and *Bakchai,* are chosen as the

1. See Patin ([1841 – 43] 1873, 1:42): *Iphigeneia at Aulis* and *Hippolytos* are, unlike other Euripidean plays, "parfaitement conformes à l'esprit de la tragédie antique," i.e., that of Sophokles and Aischylos.

2. See Kitto ([1939] 1961): *Medeia* and *Hippolytos* are contrasted with "war plays and social tragedies" (250) and both are later put into a group with *Bakchai* (372 – 73). Rivier ([1944] 1975, 30) selects five plays as "les plus achevés sous le rapport de l'unité dramatique," *Alkestis, Medeia, Hippolytos, Iphigeneia at Aulis, and Bakchai.* This selection is cited by Lesky (1956, 156).

3. Dawe (1968, 94) includes *Herakles* in a group of plays that match the formula of a noble person going to his doom; the other two are *Hippolytos* and *Bakchai.* See also Conacher (1967, 13 – 14), who places *Herakles* third, after the exceptional *Hippolytos* and *Bakchai,* but recognizes its differing approach to myth.

exemplars. Once installed in this special category they are separated from the other fifteen plays, while at the same time they are rather paradoxically allowed to represent Euripidean work as a whole.[4] Some critics have been frank about the basis for their selection: of all the Euripidean plays, these two seem to fit the general rule of tragedy best, to be, as Kitto puts it, "more regular."[5] It will be the purpose of this chapter to determine what in *Hippolytos* creates the impression of "regularity" and what this work's relation is to the general artistic stance that I have already established for Euripides. In taking this approach, I do not intend to diminish the artistic stature of what some feel to be the best Euripidean play. But understanding of the other plays and of *Hippolytos* has often been impeded by the imposition on this play of the role of archetype: an archetype that is also an exception is a dangerous critical tool.[6] The result has often been merely another attempt to fit Euripidean drama to the Sophoclean model.

Although *Hippolytos* and *Bakchai* do seem to belong together in their ability to "satisfy" some demands that we are accustomed to make of serious dramas, the plays are quite dissimilar, in structure and in technique.[7] *Bakchai*, it has often been pointed out, makes an archaic impression, first, because it features a very dominant chorus whose lyrics are closely connected with stage events,[8] and second, because the plot develops in a spare

4. See Conacher (1967, 14); Kitto ([1939] 1961, 370–71) lists the two along with *Medeia* as being "best constructed"; Lesky (1956, 201), on *Bakchai;* Pohlenz ([1930] 1954, 269) on *Hippolytos.* Verrall (1905, 167 n.2) suggests that these two plays may form an exception to his ironic rule, in that the appearances of the gods may not be intended to be shams; cf. Norwood (1908, 157). For parallels between the two plays, see Bellinger (1939, 26); Dodds (1944, xli); Merklin (1964, 12). A. W. Schlegel (1846, 171) praised *Hippolytos* and *Bakchai* for their unity and judged them the best of the plays.

5. (1939) 1961, 203, on *Hippolytos.* See Spranger (1927.1, 19): in contrast to other plays, in *Hippolytos* events follow "in correct dramatic order." Martin (1958, 276): *Hippolytos* is more perfect than the other plays and is "un tout achevé." Hooker (1960, 45): of all the Euripidean plays this play conforms most closely to Aristoteles' ideal of drama. Pohlenz ([1930] 1954, 269) remarks that "der äussere Aufbau" of *Hippolytos* resembles Sophoclean technique. See Kitto ([1939] 1961, 207): Euripides has reconciled his own form of composition "more nearly with the Sophoclean form of drama." The reasons why "more regular" should be synonymous with "more like Sophokles" have been laid out in the first two chapters of this book.

6. For an example of this tendency, see Merklin's dissertation (1964), a discussion of the role of the gods in Euripidean tragedy that essentially limited itself to *Hippolytos* and *Bakchai.* M. remarks that the great majority of interpreters have pointed to *Hippolytos* as the natural correlative to *Bakchai* (12), but he fails to see that two such similar plays are not likely to represent adequately the general Euripidean approach to divinities.

7. Their similarities, however, are sufficiently striking and will be discussed later in this chapter, Section IV.B.

8. Manning (1916, 21); Winnington-Ingram (1948, 2); Dodds' edition ([1944] 1960, xxxvi); Kitto ([1939] 1961, 380–81).

and linear fashion.[9] It seems plausible that Euripides is exaggerating in this
play the archaizing tendencies that have always been a part of his style; and
there are hints of very old models lost to us, perhaps of Aeschylean
Dionysiac plays such as *Edonoi*.[10] *Hippolytos,* by contrast is dramatically
complex, transferring interest between the plights of two protagonists who
are kept separate; it features a female chorus of passive observers similar to
that in other Euripidean plays;[11] and it deals with a theme, erotic love, that
has been notoriously familiar as Euripidean. In what, then, does the "regularity" of *Hippolytos* consist?

Hippolytos has impressed critics as being "richer" in language play than
other work by Euripides and thus as being more receptive to a literary analysis based on imagery.[12] The theme of speech, silence, and oath has received
several treatments, the best being the earliest, an article by B. M. W. Knox.[13]
The chains of imagery in the play, associated with nets and hunting,
meadows and water, and the themes of the golden age, were traced by
Charles Segal and others.[14] Certain passages were sensed as particularly significant, either because of richness of language, as in the case of Hippolytos'
prayer to Artemis (73–87), or because of intellectual allusiveness and complexity, as in the case of Phaidra's formulations about virtue (373ff.); and
these have been subjected to a variety of close examinations in recent critical
literature.[15] The study of language has generally led to a better understanding

9. Murray (1913.1, 181–82); Kitto ([1939] 1961, 371–72).

10. See Krausse (1905, 160ff.); Lesky ([1956] 1972.1, 485); Dodds ([1944] 1960, xxviii-ix).
See also a recent treatment by Aëlion (1983, 1:251ff.).

11. The chorus is passive, and—to a degree—more a hindrance than a help to the plot (see
the discussion of the oath problem by Heldmann [1968, 93]).

12. For its greater linguistic complexity, see Rivier ([1944] 1975, 53): the play has "un des-
sin d'une grande richesse." Delebecque (1951, 95): it is "très travaillée." Winnington-Ingram
(1958, 171): "The play is rich, complex, subtly-patterned (as are few of Euripides) . . ." Segal
(1969, 297): Euripides is "attentive and skilful . . . in the handling of small details in this carefully structured work."

13. 1952, 12–16. See also Avery (1968); Segal (1972.1).

14. Segal (1965, 1979); Parry (1966); Frischer (1970, 88–89); Berns (1973, 165–69); Bremer (1975); Turato (1974); Pigeaud (1976, 3–7); Fowler (1978); Orban (1981.2, 194–97).
(F. I. Zeitlin's article, "The Power of Aphrodite" [in Burian (1985, 52–111)] reached me too
late to be incorporated in this chapter.) Segal's first article, a long and comprehensive study, was
marred by the attempt to associate a sea theme with the "waters of ocean" referred to by the
chorus as their washing place (1965, 122). (For the association of this spring with a real place on
Troizen, see Barrett [1964, 184–85].) Segal's treatment of the themes of the golden age has
been further developed by Turato (see also Pigeaud [4–7]), who shows the connection of this
imagery with an aristocratic ideology in this play.

15. For Hippolytos' speech, see the references listed in the previous note, Frischer through
Orban. For Phaidra's speech, see Snell (1948); Hathorn (1957); Merklin (1964, 82ff.); Willink
(1968, 10–26); Claus (1972); Solmsen (1973); Turato (1974, 140 n.30); Pigeaud (1976, 7–24);
A. Schmitt (1977, 31–39); Manuwald (1979); Orban (1981.1, 9–16); Irwin (1983, 183–91).

of Hippolytos' prayer than of Phaidra's philosophizing. In the case of the latter, the persistent tendency to interpret parts of the plays as authorial manifestos without aesthetic significance has led to predictable and familiar confusions.[16]

This chapter, to a greater extent than previous ones, will be able to build on considerable achievements in current criticism, an advantage that makes it possible to focus more concentratedly on the place of Euripidean work in its literary tradition. I will be arguing that the impression of "regularity" created by *Hippolytos* derives from the attitude that it takes toward its protagonists. *Hippolytos,* alone among the works of Euripides, maintains a high and fairly consistent level of identification with its major figures. The techniques used are in a sense the inversion of those in *Elektra:* both Phaidra and Hippolytos are permitted to be *spoudaioi. Hippolytos* marks a unique degree of relaxation in the Euripidean opposition to Sophoclean style, and in the ironic tensions that sustain the Euripidean antithesis. Techniques that manipulate our view of the characters and of the moral significance of their acts can be traced in this play, with the help of the principle of K. von Fritz that moral relations and moral judgments are basic to tragedy and to the persistent questions about "tragic guilt."

I. Tragic Morality

I.A. THE MANIPULATION OF "DRAMATIC EFFECT"

Tycho von Wilamowitz' examination of Sophoclean dramatic technique first revealed the extent to which dramatic reality is a formed or distorted reality, designed like a pedimental sculpture or the columns at the corners of a Doric building, to be apprehended from a certain aesthetically preconditioned viewpoint. If Wilamowitz could demonstrate these techniques in the work of Sophokles, whose plays have most powerfully impressed centuries of readers and audiences as an authentic mimesis of human nature, it should be no surprise to find Euripides, notoriously a facile master of stage technique, making use of them too. In *Orestes,* for instance, the almost unbearable tension of the closing scene is heightened by the convergence of a number of threats and challenges whose logical interrelation has proven very difficult to sort out.[17] At the end of the play everything seems to happen at

16. The most striking example is the work of Snell (1948; see also 1971, 60ff.); but cf. Irwin (1983, 195–97). For correction of this tendency, see Pigeaud (1976, 11) who remarks, "Bien autre chose qu'une thèse, il y a une démonstration"; and Turato (1974, 140 n.30), who argues as I would that the ethical problem discussed by Phaidra cannot be treated as extraneous to her dramatic character and situation. See also the valuable discussion of Segal (1970.1).

17. The plot develops out of a suicide plan that includes an attack on Helene (1098–99). Pylades a little later proposes that, if they fail, they should fire the house, ending with the bold motto of "dying nobly or being saved nobly" (1152). But in fact the plan for survival comes at

once: Hermione is threatened, Menelaos capitulates, Orestes triumphs, Pylades begins to torch the house, and Menelaos angrily summons the Argive population in arms to punish the matricide.[18] A similar area of vagueness in *Iphigeneia Among the Taurians* makes it impossible to reconstruct the sacrificial practices that the heroine has supervised.[19] In order for the audience to have the requisite feelings about the encounter between Orestes and his sister, they must be in some apprehension that Orestes may indeed become a sacrificial victim; but they must not be able to picture Iphigeneia as inured to the slaughter of Greeks. All these incongruities pass by without notice, because the interest of the audience has been firmly attached to Iphigeneia's feelings and to Orestes' peril, rather than to the sacrificial practices of the Taurians.

The point to be made here is not that dramatists are careless of verisimilitude but that the dramatic event, although mimetic, is not of the same order as the real event. When we watch the last scene of *Orestes,* our conviction that events have proceeded to an absolute impasse is much stronger and more vivid than it could be if the event that we are witnessing had been designed to be coherent in motivation. Maintenance of a powerful impression of tension or sympathy takes precedence over the imitation of real events and over the logic of human motivation. If this principle of dramatic construction is accepted in its broadest sense, it can reveal the dependency of the peculiar moral structure common to many tragedies upon the requirements of dramatic form in the mode of the *spoudaion.* In making this point, I follow the path laid out by K. von Fritz and T. C. W. Stinton, who have argued that the Aristotelian analysis of tragic responsibility must be understood in terms that are primarily literary and aesthetic.[20] Examination of the moral structure of *Hippolytos* will confirm the former's conclusion that, precisely because serious theater deals so intimately with moral problems and relations, it leaves behind no moral residue.

In a passage of the *Poetics* in which the tone of "advice for the

---

line 1177, when Elektra proposes that Hermione should be taken hostage. In Orestes' threats to Menelaos the theme of house burning reemerges, illogically juxtaposed with threats to the hostage's life (1594).

18. At the moment of Menelaos' capitulation ("You've got me [ἔχεις με]," 1617), Orestes both triumphs over his enemy and suddenly gives the command to set the house on fire. Menelaos promptly summons the Argives, in spite of the obvious danger to his daughter. Seeck (1969) tries to solve the inconcinnities by excising offending lines; while Steidle (1968, 115–16) and Erbse (1975, 451ff.) attempt a psychological exegesis. Cf. the discussion of Burkert (1974, 102 n.25).

19. Sansone (1978) details the meanderings of this motif through the play and draws appropriate dramaturgical conclusions. See also Brown (1978, 30 n.8).

20. See discussion of Fritz in Chap. 1, above. Stinton's article (1975) is particularly valuable.

professional'' is particularly notable,[21] Aristoteles remarks that certain kinds of dramatic action will fail to produce in the audience the required effect, which he has already defined as a blend of pity and fear.[22] The downfall of the wicked will satisfy ''human feeling'' (*to philanthrôpon*) but will be unlikely to arouse the requisite emotional involvement, while the misfortune of the truly good protagonist will produce, not pity, but indignation at the injustice of such an ''abominable'' (*miaron*) event.[23] This indignation is as likely to be directed against the author of the fiction as against the powers of fate. The tragic protagonist therefore, although he must be ''better rather than worse'' (1453a16), cannot be perfect; the source of his misfortune, which should come through a fault or error (*hamartia*) and not through vice (*kakia*), may or may not be traceable to this imperfect character.[24] The formula of the *Poetics* reflects, in the fertile imprecision of its language, especially the term *hamartia,* a complex interaction of ethical and artistic standards.[25] In tragedy the ''guilt'' of the protagonists, as critics have long recognized, is and apparently must be disproportionately small in relation to the

21. 1452b28–30: ''What one should aim at and what one should avoid in composing and the source of the effect proper to tragedy [καὶ πόθεν ἔσται τὸ τῆς τραγῳδίας ἔργον] are the topics that must follow what has preceded.'' See the commentary of Dupont-Roc and Lallot (1980, 238): ''L'analyse descriptive du *muthos* et de ses formes s'ordonne ici à une perspective nettement normative.''

22. On *eleos* and *phobos,* see the articles of Schadewaldt (1955) and Pohlenz (1956); the latter, while agreeing with Schadewaldt that *eleos* does not mean ''Mitleid,'' points out that it does posit a somewhat greater degree of personal involvement than other terms, e.g., *oiktos* (51–52). For the origins of this concept before Aristoteles, see Pohlenz (1920, 168–70).

23. See Stinton (1975, 238ff.).

24. It was the great service of Fritz to have made this point ([1955] 1962, 3–4); see also Stinton (1975, 238).

25. Much has recently been written on *hamartia,* but most of it has been impaired by the tendency to impose philosophical concepts on juridical ones and then to force poetry into conformity with the resulting mixture. (See the discussion of Vernant [1972, 23], who argues that tragic vocabulary must be analyzed internally.) H. Funke's dissertation (1963), which began by giving a precise and modern juridical definition to ''tragic guilt'' (*Schuld*), reached the conclusion that tragic figures possessed no such guilt, but only completely innocent errors (*hamartiai*). Cf. J. Bremer, who also defined *hamartia* as (entirely unconscious) error and was then forced to reimport the concept of guilt (1969, 139): *hamartia* ''does not contribute much to the understanding of the play unless it is integrated in the more comprehensive notion of *ate*'' (a concept B. had derived from Dawe [1968]). Saïd (1978) also tends to impose juridical distinctions where they have little relevance, e.g., in a discussion of human reaction to disaster in *Trachiniai,* a situation for which Antiphon's speeches provide little illumination (208–9). (Cf. the analysis of Stinton [1975, 245–46].) None of these three authors takes account of the well-known fact that distinguishing between conscious responsibility and accidental agency was difficult for early Greek ethic and that the term *hamartia* is useful precisely because it covers both areas (see the analysis of Latte [(1920) 1968, 17–21].) This being the case, it makes as much sense to ask whether *hamartia* refers to ''guilt'' or ''accidental error'' as it does to question whether a given phoneme in Japanese is an *L* or an *R*.

disaster that befalls them. This has nothing to do with "poetic justice," and is in fact a recipe for poetic injustice.[26] This odd and illogical causal sequence, in which consequences must have causes, but the causes *must not fit,* is not a moral theory, but an aesthetic recipe for producing the desired effect from serious drama.

I.B. THE *SPOUDAION* AND HUMAN FEELING (*TO PHILANTHROPON*)

If we ask what factors would be most likely to produce the minimum of detachment in the spectators of a drama, we can list a series of elements that are most unlikely to appear together in real life. Some of these factors even work at cross-purposes: for instance, guiltless sufferers provoke more pity; but the events that produce their suffering may appear pointless, or even revolting (*miaron*), unless they occur in a causal and logical sequence. But, just as a contradictory treatment of events and motivations can heighten tension or sympathy, so tragic poets can manipulate potentially contradictory sources of audience involvement and sympathy for the protagonists.

The characteristic traits of leading figures in serious drama have been thoroughly analyzed by critics, who have often been puzzled by the paradoxical results. Tragic protagonists, we are told, must suffer something that seems special to themselves, whether or not what happens has a direct connection with the personality of the sufferer.[27] This suffering, although it may not end in death, inflicts irretrievable damage upon the protagonists and their prospects for the future.[28] Such sufferings must not fall upon figures that are resigned or helpless: tragic protagonists must struggle desperately, but of course vainly, against the tragic events.[29] When the catastrophe arrives,

26. See Dawe (1968, 95): tragic error must produce "disastrous, and above all disproportionate, consequences." Among general books on tragedy, see Henn (1956, 62ff.); Raphael (1960, 65–66); Brereton (1968, 278–79). Segal (1970.2) cites Max Scheler (1923, 257) on the concept of "unlocalized guilt," and applies this concept to *Hippolytos;* see also Crocker (1957, 239).

27. See Brereton (1968, 46) who suggests that there should be "a cause connected in some way with the personality of the participants," or that there should at least be a *hamartia* that will ward off the sensation of predetermination, which is "inimical to tragedy," an art form which "requires a degree of uncertainty" (269). See W. V. O'Connor's dismissal of a modern tragic protagonist (1943, 153): "His problem was answerable, and therefore hardly tragic," and Henn (1956, 35ff.), on the "illusion of liberty" (40) that must accompany "our sense of inevitability" (34).

28. See Orr (1981, xii), "irreparable loss"; Watts ([1955] 1963, 93–104): whereas comedy is cyclic, tragedy is linear and is concerned with the (irreversible) fate of an individual.

29. See Scheler (1923, 254): it is typical that "das Übel ... zu denen gehört, gegen die überhaupt ein Kampf aufzubieten ist, und dass ein solcher Kampf auch tatsächlich aufgeboten wird." Cf. the complaints that modern tragic figures are too passive (Heilman [1968, 249]); and Heilman's approving reference to the "rasping or even quarrelsome tone" of the hero in *Samson Agonistes* (252). This is the same tone that Knox has traced in Sophoclean protagonists (1964, 19–21). See also Kuhn (1942, 60–63).

however, it should find the protagonists neither able nor willing to slough off responsibility for the disaster. Finally, the tragic victim should somehow be aware of the significance of what has happened to him and should be able to articulate some response that indicates assimilation of the event.[30]

That these desiderata include a number of contradictory elements should be obvious. The potential for contradiction is perhaps best demonstrated by the play that Aristoteles and the critical tradition which he founded have used as a model for tragedy, *Oidipous Tyrannos*. What has happened to Oidipous is an arbitrary and unlikely concatenation of accidents; and there is manifestly no real connection between this terrible destiny and the protagonist's somewhat irascible and unreasonable behavior during the course of the play. But Oidipous' manner not only obviates any incongruity that would be apparent in the assignment of such a dreadful fate to a perfectly virtuous man; it also creates a sensation of energy and activity that prevents our seeing Oidipous as what in stern reality he is, a passive victim of outside forces.

The characteristics of tragic protagonists are designed to maximize audience involvement and sympathy. Disasters that are general and not peculiar to the individual dissipate the focus on a single fate; misfortunes that are retrievable cannot evoke the same concern as those that are not. The self-knowledge desired of tragic figures is a further contributor to the significance of the event that involves them, and to their own stature as participants. Resigned victims or manifest criminals cannot make us anxious over the outcome, since we might detach ourselves from the tragic sufferers by blaming them for their suffering, or by seeing them as mere hapless unfortunates, with whom we would rather not identify at all. The paradoxical conjunction of struggle and moral responsibility with an inevitable and extraneous disaster intensifies emotional attachment to the dramatic event: the plight of the protagonists, illogically but obviously, will involve us the most deeply, if it is *both* entailed by their actions *and* undeserved. And, while this odd situation may not match any actual human experience, it has a considerable correspondence to our confused perception of moral responsibility. The question of free will and predetermination was not yet isolated in Sophokles' day, but the problems of human responsibility and agency were perhaps better understood in their complexity before these unhelpful paradoxes came to be formulated.[31]

---

30. See W. V. O'Connor & M. A. O'Connor (1943, 124–25). Discussion of this tragic element occurs in the previous chapter on *Herakles*, Section IV.C.

31. Thomas Gould has discussed the question of "free will" in the context of the ancient term *aitios*, suggesting that it means something like "he acted in accordance with his own character" (1966, 482). See also Agard (1933), and the interesting discussion in Vernant & Vidal-Naquet (1972, 43ff.: "Ébauches de la volonté"). Gundert (1940) has shown similar mechanisms in the treatment of Homeric heroes; and see also the recent article of Rutherford (1982), on the parallelism between Sophoclean heroes and the Homeric Achilleus (146).

If we consider the way moral problems are presented in the dramatic work on which modern conceptions of tragic heroism are based, that of Sophokles, we find that the dramatic situation is manipulated in analogous ways in several plays. Euripidean alteration of traditional mythical material has often been noticed,[32] while less has been made of the mythic form of Sophoclean plays. But the difficulties of adapting myth to the conventions of the new high mimetic did not escape Aristoteles. In the *Poetics* he discusses the way to use traditional myths "well,"[33] and cites two modern methods of handling the myth, opposing these to the "old-fashioned" method (ὥσπερ οἱ παλαιοὶ ἐποίουν) of making the protagonists act in full knowledge (εἰδότας καὶ γιγνώσκοντας).[34] It was this older method that Euripides revived in *Medeia,* where the heroine explicitly tells us that she knows the magnitude of what she intends to do.[35] The modern method, however, comes in two forms, both of which depend on ignorance (*agnooüntas,* 1453b30) and a recognition that may either follow the irretrievable error (*hamartia*) or forestall it altogether. Dreadful acts (*deina*) are the subject matter of tragedy; but, in the more modern treatment, these *deina* are divorced from the will of the agents. Aristoteles suggests that the second of these forms, the forestalling of the *deina* by a recognition (*anagnôrisis*), may be the best (1454a4 – 5). It is notable that Euripides appears in two places in this analysis, both as the archaizer who uses the unreconstructed method of the self-aware protagonist, and as the innovator who devises the (presumably latest) method, threatening but not performing the act of violence.

Sophokles' *Oidipous* is mentioned as an example of the first improvement, the recognition that comes too late. In fact, several Sophoclean plays make a striking use of *agnoia* or ignorance to dissipate the responsibility of the tragic protagonist and maintain a stronger bond of audience identification. *Trachiniai* is the best extant example. The story of Deianeira, as the heroine's name suggests, is the tale of a revengeful woman who brought an end to

32. See G. Hermann (1837, 24 – 25): Euripides' radical alteration of the plot of the Oidipous myth is due to an attempt to differentiate his work from previous treatments. U. v. Wilamowitz (1875, 177ff.); Will (1959); Reckford (1968, 332).

33. 1453b22 – 26: τοὺς μὲν οὖν παρειλημμένους μύθους λύειν οὐκ ἔστιν . . . , αὐτὸν δὲ εὑρίσκειν δεῖ καὶ τοῖς παραδεδομένοις χρῆσθαι καλῶς. See the analysis of the different interpretations in Dupont-Roc & Lallot (1980, 255ff.). But I do not accept their reading of *chrêsthai* as dependent on *heuriskein:* the technique involves both invention and a "proper" utilization of traditional material. That is, it is the addition of the invented material that rescues the tradition.

34. Rostagni (1945, 78 – 79) suggests that the "old" dramatists are Sophokles and Aischylos; but Sophokles follows the "new" method.

35. 1453b29. For self-awareness in *Medeia,* see line 1078ff.

Herakles through her treachery.[36] But in Sophokles' version of this myth, Deianeira is explicitly deprived of any motivation deriving from jealousy or rage, and in fact she becomes a virtual paragon of marital tolerance and forgiveness.[37] In the Sophoclean version of the Hippolytos myth, Phaidra's culpability was lessened by her belief that Theseus, long absent in the underworld, was dead.[38] This twist could transform the traditional "Potiphar's wife" story of the older woman who attempts to use sexual coercion against a dependent male[39] into an instance of tragic "guiltless guilt." Phaidra's erotic susceptibility would be only mildly culpable, if she thought herself a widow; yet on the sudden return of her husband she would find herself caught in a painful and compromising situation that could plausibly lead to tragic consequences.

In both of these cases Sophokles has altered the myths in the direction pointed out by Aristoteles. As a result, instead of violent and sexually aggressive female protagonists, we have modest and decent women, betrayed by forgivable weaknesses into actions that they did not intend.[40] This is both a demonstration of the means by which sympathy can be purchased, and a confirmation of the suggestion in *Frogs* that it is the poet's job to censor myths that are indecent or improper.[41] In these cases it might seem that the whole point of the old myth has been sacrificed in adapting it to tragic form. In most Euripidean plays, however, particularly in the early period, the "real story"[42] is preferred to the modified and modernized one. But, as Aristoteles points out, it was also he who took the modification one step farther with plays like *Kresphontes,* in which the threatened mistake of identity, instead of leading to disaster, is forestalled by a timely recognition.[43] Only in *Hippolytos* does Euripides choose the middle or Sophoclean path.

36. See Errandonea (1927) on her mythic role as "man killer"; Schwinge (1962, 25 n.3).

37. For her explicit disavowal of jealousy, see lines 543, 552, 582ff. Solmsen (1932, 10–13) saw this as an allusive rejection of the Euripidean intrigue. At any rate, these denials underline in a marked fashion the emotions natural to Deianeira's role and the signal absence of these motivations in this version. On Deianeira as an example of female perfection, see Whitman (1958, 115, 118–19).

38. See the analysis in Barrett's edition (1964, 32); the fragments of the *Phaidra* are collected on pp. 22–26 of Barrett. Discussion of the Sophoclean version in Herter (1940, 283–86). The crucial fragment is 624 N2 in which an interlocutor expresses surprise to see Theseus return, when he had been thought to be dead.

39. For the widespread correlatives of this tale in foreign and in Greek myth, see Tschiedel (1969, 9–21).

40. See Webster's analysis (1968, 37).

41. 1053, ἀλλ' ἀποκρύπτειν χρὴ τὸ πονηρὸν τόν γε ποιητήν.

42. See Euripides' defense: was not the story of Phaidra "real" (ὄντα λόγον)? (*Frogs* 1052).

43. On *Kresphontes,* an early example of Euripidean inventiveness, see App. D. This sort of forestalled mistake is typical of the Menandrian comedy. The blameless and humane protagonists of New Comedy often seem to spend the first half of the play leaping to false conclusions and the second half in being happily disabused of them. On "uplift" in Menandros, see Post

II. The Second *Hippolytos*

II.A. REVISION

The Euripidean *Hippolytos* is the only play known to have been presented at the City Dionysia as a reworking of an earlier version, known as *Hippolytos Veiled.*[44] Evidence seems to indicate that tragic poets were little given to presenting alternate versions of the same story; and in view of the many productions they put on and the length of their creative careers, this suggests the workings of some unspoken etiquette. If the second *Hippolytos* broke with such a custom and was still awarded a first prize, that may indeed indicate that the play had, as the ancient editor's comment suggests, a palinodic function and was offered to the audience as a replacement for the first *Hippolytos.*[45] The reception of *Hippolytos Veiled* (*Kalyptomenos*) may have marked a point at which the touchy relationship between artist and audience (traced in Chapter Three) suffered a rupture. The danger was certainly not that the play would come in last in the competition, probably not an uncommon event for Euripidean work, but that the production would be interrupted by a public uproar (*thorybos*) that would spoil its effect or even prevent its completion. If anything could justify a second production, presumably, it would be the failure of the first to come off at all.[46] But this is speculation. Clearly the first *Hippolytos* presented a Phaidra who shocked and repelled the audience by her sexual aggressiveness, as we can tell both from Aristophanes' use of the play as a landmark and from the extant fragments, in which Phaidra boasts of her boldness (*thrasos* and *tolma*).[47]

The supposition that the first play included a scene in which Phaidra approached Hippolytos directly, prompting him to veil himself from shame, is a tempting one and is likely enough to be true. But, since it is virtually

---

(1964, 100); there is a good discussion of the aesthetic role of moral values in Menandros in Arnott (1981.2, 215–16). See also Xanthakis-Karamanos (1979) on the decorous modifications introduced in fifth-century material by the versions of the fourth-century tragedians.

44. The closest correlative would be *Clouds,* but there the second version may never have been put on in its present form; see Dover (1968, lxxxxff.), and A. Masaracchia (1972).

45. The shorter of the hypotheses probably is a fragment of Aristophanes of Byzantion's work. The author suggests that this play is likely to be later than *Hippolytos Veiled,* τὸ γὰρ ἀπρεπὲς καὶ κατηγορίας ἄξιον ἐν τούτῳ διώρθωται τῷ δράματι.

46. Pickard-Cambridge (1968, 99) suggests that only unsuccessful plays may have been so revised and points out that other double versions may reflect a revision for production outside Athens.

47. *Frogs* 1043. Fr. 430N2 = Barrett (1964, 18) fr. C.; as Barrett points out, the only eligible speaker of these lines is Phaidra herself, although we cannot be sure that they were directed at Hippolytos. They may have been spoken to another interlocutor, in this case probably a Nurse who would behave more like the Old Man in the first scene with Hippolytos; see Kalkmann (1881, 27).

unsupported by reliable evidence,[48] it must remain a supposition. A scene of open sexual confrontation might well have provoked an uproar, in spite of the attempt to mitigate the scandal through Hippolytos' modest and withdrawn attitude.[49] The behavior and manner that the first Phaidra would have displayed are easily supplied from the Helene of *Troiades,* or the Pasiphaë in the amazing fragment from *Cretan Men,* both glib and eloquent apologists for sexual deviation. Such a Phaidra would balance well with a Hippolytos not far removed from the extant one, giving us the kind of violent juxtaposition of male and female types that we find in *Medeia,* composed at about the same time.[50] As in other Euripidean plays, sympathy for either antagonist would be qualified by distaste for the repellent behavior of each.[51] A priggish and nonconformist Hippolytos would show at his worst in contrast with such a Phaidra, while he could effectively expose the unchastity and impudence of the queen.

In the extant version of *Hippolytos* Phaidra has been altered radically, and in a manner familiar from Sophoclean drama.[52] She surprises us as does the Sophoclean Deianeira by sternly rejecting what in the original story must have been the keystone of her character, in Phaidra's case the indulgence of sexual impulse. She displays a concern for modesty (*aidôs*) and reputation (*kleos*) that is quite in conformity with Hellenic moral norms for females;[53] but, unlike most other Euripidean "good" women, Phaidra speaks for conventional moral norms, presenting them in terms that are neither reformist nor modern. Her role as representative of social values is calculated to inspire sympathy and even respect, in spite of the improper nature of her dilemma. Confusions in evaluating Phaidra's moral level have derived from

48. Various scholars present this account of *Kalyptomenos* without any supporting evidence at all, e.g., Barrett (1964, 37 and n.1); Fauth (1958, 548). For other suppositions, none of which are persuasive, see Paratore (1972, 303ff.; 1952). For the use of veiling gestures in tragedy, see Shisler (1945, 385).

49. The reconstruction of *Kalyptomenos* has been marred by very careless assumptions about the usefulness of Seneca's *Phaedra* as a model for the first play; see the confident statements of W. H. Friedrich (1953, 112), a scholar ordinarily quite sophisticated in his study of influences. Barrett points out (1964, 16–17) that Seneca's plays often differ radically from Greek models, and Kalkmann long ago (1881, pt. II) made an interesting study of the modifications in the Alexandrian period of motifs from *Hippolytos.*

50. Zürcher (1947, 85) points out the presumable similarity of the first Phaidra to Medeia. On the alteration in Phaidra, see Winnington-Ingram (1958, 172); Kitto ([1939] 1961, 205–6).

51. See Fauth (1958, 560): in the case of the first *Hippolytos,* "Die äusserste Schamlosigkeit forderte die äusserste Tugendhaftigkeit als notwendiges Korrelat."

52. See discussion of the change between the two versions in Linforth (1914, 7); Herter (1940, 289ff.).

53. See Tschiedel (1969, 203 n.98). Kretz (1934, 58) remarks that the whole presentation of Phaidra's character seems designed to block accusations of shamelessness; and see Lattimore (1962, 7): Phaidra is "rehabilitated."

a modern value system in which concern for appearances and reputation ranks very low, whereas in traditional Hellenic terms this kind of *aidôs* was the prime guarantor of moral integrity.[54] As usual in Euripides the moral norms will not pass without question; but as usual in Euripides we must be able to make out where the norms lie, in order to understand the game at all.

Just as Phaidra's moral views are the reverse of what we would have expected, so her role in the slanderous destruction of Hippolytos is surrounded with qualifiers that are typical of the catastrophe brought about through ignorant error. Aphrodite herself informs us that Phaidra's passion has been forced on her, though she remains a woman of "good reputation" (*eukleês*).[55] The line's ambivalence expresses just the paradox of "tragic responsibility." Is Phaidra called *eukleês* because she has not yet yielded to her passion, or because she was formerly a woman of good reputation; or does the god really mean to imply that Phaidra's reputation should receive no stain from what is to follow?[56] Her action in slandering Hippolytos is extenuated by a number of factors: the ferocity with which he denounces her to the Nurse arouses fears that he intends to reveal the truth to Theseus, as does his impulsive repudiation of the oath of silence that the Nurse had extracted.[57] It is natural too that Phaidra's concern for reputation should lead her to attempt to achieve a death that will bequeath honor to her family.

Most suggestive in this connection is the moment at which Phaidra permits the Nurse to go in the house to find the medicine (*pharmakon*) that will cure her longing. As Barrett has shown, the language is exquisitely balanced to assure that the audience will suspect that the Nurse means to approach

54. See Willink (1968, 20) who believes that the audience will be shocked by the evidence that Phaidra is deterred from adultery only by the fear of discovery; similar views in Köhnken (1972, 187). For the coincidence of *aidôs* with female virtue, see Adkins (1960, 36–37 and 161–62): "No woman . . . must be found, however innocently, in a compromising situation, for it is reputation which counts above all."

55. 47: ἡ δ' εὐκλεὴς μὲν, ἀλλ' ὅμως ἀπόλλυται.

56. The last is Barrett's interpretation (1964, 166).

57. Line 612, "My tongue swore, but my mind is unsworn." The arguments of W. D. Smith (1960.2) and Østerud (1970) that Phaidra does not overhear the speech and that the Nurse sings the lament at line 668 overlook the important structural necessity that the misunderstanding arise from Phaidra's misinterpretation of this speech. (There is also the awkwardness and bathos of having Phaidra, who has gone inside, presumably to commit suicide, pop out again unexpectedly to denounce the Nurse.) For the psychological significance of Phaidra's revengeful desire to bring Hippolytos down to her level, see Bonnard (1944, 9), who points out that it must be particularly galling for Phaidra to hear herself accused of all the traits she has so rigorously suppressed. W. H. Friedrich (1953, 146) found the disappearance of her love inexplicable; but of course it has not disappeared—see Lesky (1960, 21): it makes human sense "dass sie im Hasse und im Tod vereinen will, was ihre Liebe und das Leben nicht zusammenzufügen vermochten." See the similar view of Valgiglio (1957.1, 19 and n.23).

Hippolytos, while they also understand that Phaidra is being misled.[58] Yet the voicing of her suspicions by Phaidra shows that she too is not far from seeing through the Nurse. Arguments about her complicity or innocence have long raged.[59] In fact just this indeterminacy is the hinge upon which "tragic guilt" must turn. In order for Phaidra to be both involved in the proposal to Hippolytos and innocent of vile intent, both betrayed by the Nurse and shamed by the hideous results of her betrayal, we must remain unsure of her awareness. The question of what Deianeira could have been thinking about when she decided that the blood of Nessos would be the right charm for Herakles' love is exactly analogous to the question of what Phaidra thought the Nurse was planning.

II.B. ÊTHOS

An essential technique of Euripidean theater is the use of incongruous elements to force a reevaluation of apparently admirable and sympathetic protagonists. The second *Hippolytos,* by contrast, introduces each of its major protagonists in scenes of leisurely beauty and emotive power that encourage sympathy, while making it possible for the audience to take a perspective on the inner state of the protagonists and to grasp their motivation in detail.[60] Euripidean prologues conventionally close with a scene in dialogue, usually marking the first movements of a vigorous and complex plot. In *Medeia* we hear that Kreon is exiling the already afflicted heroine; in *Herakleidai* the Theban herald assaults the suppliants; in *Andromache* the protagonist lays plans for her rescue. The dialogue portion of *Hippolytos* differs from all others in that it contributes nothing toward the forward motion of the drama. The hero's refusal to honor Aphrodite is without plot significance, since the god has already stated her determination to repay earlier slights by destroying Hippolytos. Because the activities and attitudes displayed in the scene are evidently habitual, what we see confirms Aphrodite's account of Hippolytos, while her statement that this day is his last (57) gives an intense

58. 1964, 252–53.

59. Extreme distrust by U. v. Wilamowitz ([1898] 1926.2, 112): the second Phaidra is barely an improvement over the first, although the former is more in conformity with tragic style. See also Grene (1939, 56–57); Fauth (1958, 536); Orban (1981.1, 5, 8–9, 16–17). She is defended by Kalkmann (1881, 15ff.) and in Barrett's commentary (1964). See also the refutation by Claus (1972, 224ff.) and others discussed below of the psychological interpretation that would make of Phaidra's references to leisure a confession of her own weaknesses.

60. W. H. Friedrich (1953, 117) remarks on the "Tendenz zum Schönen, zur Verschönung des Mythos." Norwood (1954, 94) imagines Euripides saying to his audience, "'Very well: you shall have an edifying and beautiful play.'"

pathos to the tranquillity and beauty of the scene, and to his prayer that he may end the course of his life as he began it.[61]

The scene functions primarily as a device to reveal Hippolytos to us.[62] He enters with a subchorus singing a hymn to Artemis; and the language of his prayer breathes the hypnotic charm of the best of Sappho, as he brings to Artemis a crown from the "uncut meadow" where no shepherds go and which the spring bee haunts.[63] The effect reaches a peak at line 78, where, in a metaphor that is strangely powerful in the matter-of-fact atmosphere of the trimeter, Hippolytos speaks of a personified Modesty (*Aidôs*) as the gardener of Artemis' meadow (ποταμίαισι κηπεύει δρόσοις). Recent detailed analyses have revealed many complex patterns of imagery in this single, concentrated passage.[64] The very decorativeness and lack of plot attachment contribute to the effect of special significance. We are being enthralled in this scene in a way that we seldom are in Euripidean theater; and the sympathy invested by the audience in the exclusive world of this eccentric figure[65] in turn increases the effect of pathos when Hippolytos rejects the old servant's warnings. It is not possible to stand aside and judge Hippolytos' behavior as folly, once we have been pulled into his world and have seen in it the moral and aesthetic beauty that he sees.

At the entry of the main chorus, with the charmingly low-life reference to gossip about Phaidra at the washing rocks, we seem to be on more familiar Euripidean ground. But the full and leisurely exposition of Phaidra's feelings that follows is unlike anything else in Euripides and strongly evokes Sophoclean models. The chorus begins by querying what may be going on in

61. 87: τέλος δὲ κάμψαιμ' ὥσπερ ἠρξάμην βίου. See Bonnard (1944, 17–18), who points to Hippolytos' rejection of the natural cycles of life. This notion was sidetracked for a time by arguments as to whether Hippolytos was an "Orphic" (refutation by D. W. Lucas [1946]); see the comments of Barrett (1964) on *Hipp* 952ff. For recent development of the theme, as a flight from reality into ideal and paradisal retreats, see Turato (1974, 142).

62. See Merklin (1964, 65), who points out that such scenes are more typical of Sophokles; and Fauth (1958, 522–23); Tschiedel (1969, 234).

63. On the language and its relation to lyric poetry, see Merklin (1964, 63), "poetischer Zauber"; Bremer (1975, 271), parallels to Sappho.

64. Pigeaud (1976, 3ff.) points to the lore about gardens, citing Detienne (1972), and their association with rootless and fruitless cultivation, a possible metaphor for Hippolytos' life, but also reminiscent paradoxically of the world of sexuality that Hippolytos rejects (see Rankin [1974, 84]). But the associations of the "meadow" are complex; see Bremer (1975, 275ff.). Turato (1974, 137) points to elements in the tradition that connect the meadow (*leimôn*) with the remote paradise of the blessed and with the age of gold.

65. For the eccentricity of Hippolytos' religious notions, particularly his emphasis on exclusivity, which emerges clearly in 79–81, lines strongly marked by exaggerated hyperbata, see Turato (1974, 150ff.); Barrett (1964, 172–73); Segal (1970.1, 279); Orban (1981.2, 198).

Phaidra's mind and body to create these disturbances.[66] As in *Aias*, there is
an alternation among lyric outbursts by the agonized protagonist, lyric speculation about the protagonist by the chorus, and dialogue between the chorus
and a sympathetic but baffled associate of the protagonist. But the progression from these modes to the actual self-expository speech of the protagonist
is here greatly prolonged and is complicated by Phaidra's persistent refusal to
reveal her real meaning.[67] The result of this suspense is a heightening of
interest, but also a deeper involvement in Phaidra's subjective state. Unlike
the Nurse and the chorus, the audience already knows what is wrong with
Phaidra; but what they do not know is Phaidra's own response to her malady.
Phaidra's reluctance even to speak of her passion makes it more likely that,
when she does come to speak of modesty (*aidôs*), we will believe her and
will not mistake her concern for a mere hypocritical show.

Euripidean plays ordinarily do not much explore the psychological roots
of the characters' actions. *Medeia* is the play most often compared to *Hippolytos* for its exposition of the psychology of a woman; but the contrast is
striking. Medeia's agonizing is limited to her offstage singing. When she
does emerge from the house, she immediately begins her persuasive
approach to the chorus. Even in the major opening speeches of the two
women, similar as they are in their elaborate and somewhat opaque introductions, there is a strong contrast between the polished and disingenuous *captatio benevolentiae* of Medeia and the broodings of Phaidra, which, in spite of
the formality of the trimeter rhesis, circle repetitively around the heroine's
subjective reaction to her dilemma. It is true that later in the play we witness
a debate between one part of Medeia's self and another. But there is no gradual exposition of her repinings; and, in the dreadful apotheosis at the end, her
subjectivity disappears as suddenly as it had emerged.[68] This is another

66. Particularly interesting is the relation between the clothing (*pharea*) that the chorus were
washing and the cloths (*pharê*, 132) that shade Phaidra's head as she keeps to her sickbed. When
Phaidra enters, she casts off her head covering, and then, ashamed (243), "hides" it again: μαῖα,
πάλιν μου κρύψον κεφαλήν, / αἰδούμεθα γὰρ τὰ λελεγμένα μοι / κρύπτε . . . ; cf. line 139.
The theme of concealment and veiling is restated from the first play, but this time it is appropriately connected with the special world of women; see Ortkemper (1969, 79). The epode (161ff.),
often dismissed as a simple reference to pregnancy (see Barrett [1964, 192]), evokes the secret
troubles of women (cf. line 293ff.); Pigeaud (1976, 7–9) compares a section from a Hippocratic
text on female diseases (8:126 Littré). For other themes in the parodos, see Segal (1965,
122–24).

67. For the complexity of the long scene (it extends over four hundred lines), see Barrett
(1964, 210), who points out how the philosophizing of the Nurse at line 250ff. closes off the first,
lyric part of the scene.

68. See Reinhardt (1957, 626).

dramatic style, less delicately shaded, less naturalistic, and much more in tune with that of other Euripidean plays.[69]

Elsewhere, we are not encouraged to penetrate much to the inner life of Euripidean characters, who usually appear not in a meditative and private mood[70] but at the last extremity, ready to confront verbal or physical threats that demand instant response. Such figures as Andromache and Hermione seem to start forth into action, fully formed and ready to oppose each other. It is most unlikely that *Cretan Men* featured much exploration of the subjective state of Pasiphaë; but whatever may have preceded must have been flattened by the polished polemic of her defensive speech.[71] Admetos' subjectivity is finely suggested by his response to a number of tests and trials; but that subjectivity is of little significance in comparison with the impossible, embarrassing, and contradictory situation in which Admetos finds himself. It is not necessary to divide this lack of introspection from other complementary aspects of Euripidean style: the rejection of the *spoudaion* mode of character implies a greater emphasis on event and situation.

Hippolytos is Sophoclean in its emphasis on *êthos* as a wellspring of action; but it remains Euripidean in its choice of material, thus providing us with a valuable test case for examining the contributions of the ironic mode to this dramatic style. The play is Euripidean in its preference for dividing attention among a number of protagonists, who arrange themselves in a familiar relation of balance and opposition. Audience sympathy is similarly divided. Because of Phaidra's association with a shameful kind of sexuality, it is easier to motivate the misunderstanding between the protagonists from Hippolytos' side than from hers. Her hostile counterreaction to his misogyny is in fact extenuated at the price of some sympathy for Hippolytos.[72]

Misogyny is a device very useful to the tragic poet in his manipulation of moral attitudes. The weakness in such a prejudice did not escape notice in a

69. Early analyses of *Hippolytos* saw Phaidra, like Medeia, as a passionate and culpable woman. (The rationalizing interpretation that dismisses the agency of the gods as unimportant supports this treatment of Phaidra—see Pohlenz [(1930) 1954, 269–73]; Winnington-Ingram [1958, 182–83].) But Phaidra is not really representative of demonic *Leidenschaft;* and Medeia's peculiar psychological style is reproduced in no other Euripidean play (see Schadewaldt [1926, 206]; Lesky [1960, 21]).

70. See Masqueray's remark on this scene: we seem to breathe the intimate atmosphere of the women's quarters, where no man comes (1908, 51).

71. See Strohm (1957, 28): it is one of the functions of the *agôn* to place the action on a more general and typical basis. For a parallel, consider *Orestes,* where touches of subjectivity are quickly submerged, as Orestes enters into conflict, first with Tyndareos and Menelaos, and then with the whole Argive populace—see Lanza (1961, 58–59); W. D. Smith (1967.2, 301).

72. Fauth (1958, 540–42) and Lattimore (1962, 15) see this change in Hippolytos as an error on the poet's part.

society that was increasingly fascinated by variations in local custom.[73] Yet the condemnation of women and female behavior played an important role in Greek society, enhancing male solidarity and helping to enforce the value system centering on *aretê*. Aischylos had used these contradictions most effectively in *Seven Against Thebes* to convey Eteokles' role as leader and as representative of the male warrior class of his community, while at the same time suggesting a potential distortion in his relation to religious and family tradition.[74] When Hippolytos denounces women, he is more in harmony with community values than at any other time in the play;[75] but there is a stylistic break between Hippolytos' character in the rest of the play and the impression that he makes in this scene.[76] As the rhetorical and polemical atmosphere of the first *Hippolytos* seems to move through the play, sympathy for Phaidra is increased, and the sympathetic Hippolytos moves somewhat out of focus. His speech is a gross distortion of what Phaidra has so carefully and thoughtfully examined; and, in saying what he does, Hippolytos frightens Phaidra into despair and guarantees his own fate. His *hamartia* is thus the complement to her own, based like hers in his inability to comprehend and appreciate his opposite. The shock that he has received and the conventionality of his views excuse what he says; but the slight effect of alienation makes us see him as Phaidra does for a chilling moment.

When Hippolytos appears again in the play, he is the dominant protagonist, since Phaidra is dead; and his posture in his encounter with Theseus is very different from that in his scene with the Nurse. Now it is Hippolytos who is misjudged and condemned without a hearing, while Theseus listens only to the self-serving rhythms of his own rhetoric.[77] The speech of Hippolytos himself is delivered with a tactlessness—or an honesty—that dooms it from the start. The conventional arguments given him serve only to reveal Hippolytos' fatal distance from others and to alienate him from his father.[78]

73. Early Amazon myths, such as that in the *Aithiopis,* indicate very early interest in the question of gender roles. On the interest in foreign cultures in the late fifth century, see Baldry (1965, 33ff.).

74. See Winnington-Ingram (1983, 27). Sophokles used the same device, less subtly and equivocally, in Kreon's rhetoric in *Antigone*. Vernant & Vidal-Naquet (1972, 33–34) point out the parallel.

75. For the assumption that the audience will see misogyny as a mark of deviance, see Tschiedel (1969, 237).

76. On his unsympathetic behavior, see Conacher (1967, 30, 33); Sale (1977, 35ff.)

77. Note his "rhetorical" questions, which take the place of a real answer to Hippolytos' queries, while the latter remarks on the inappropriateness of this play with words (923, 935). See Hippolytos' reply to the long speech, "There is matter for fine speeches [τὸ μέντοι πρᾶγμ᾽ ἔχον καλοὺς λόγους]; yet, if one opens it up, it is not fine" (985).

78. The argument—an intelligent man like me would have no reason to aim at rebellion—is traditionally assigned to the unjustly accused, the basic model being the *Palamedes* of Gorgias (DK 2:294–303 fr. 11B). On the conventionality of the piece, see J. Gould (1978, 57–58); Rivier (1958, 57). Antiphon defends himself by this means in Fr. 1a (Thalheim), his greatest

In the course of his appeal, Hippolytos depreciates monarchy to a monarch and the charms of Phaidra to her widower.[79] The warning of the servant in the prologue is confirmed, and we can see that Hippolytos' alienation from Aphrodite derives from the same trait of awkward honesty, or arrogance. He is unable to pay the lip service that piety or tact demands.[80]

The play's three main figures are joined in a perfectly balanced mating of error, misjudgment, and misunderstanding that derives in part from the character of each, but for which no one of them can be assigned an unequivocal responsibility. The combined anger and sympathy that we are made to feel for Phaidra and Hippolytos vary in measure, but never fall entirely out of proportion. Theseus is arbitrary and unfair, but we are unlikely to judge him as harshly as Artemis does.[81] In terms of the effect on the audience, however, her severity may be necessary to redirect Theseus' previously expressed rage and to put the king into a mood that will permit him to beg Hippolytos' forgiveness in the last scene. The resolution between father and son wipes out Theseus' culpability, while at the same time Hippolytos' ability to forgive puts the best light on his moral pretensions and obliterates the alienating note of rigidity in some earlier scenes.[82] Phaidra is exculpated by both goddesses: Aphrodite calls her *euklees,* and Artemis terms her revenge on Hippolytos "lust—or a kind of nobility."[83] The equivalency between Phaidra at the play's opening and Hippolytos at its close[84] helps to divide our sympathies evenly, as we see that both are worthy of respect and understanding, even from Theseus, the representative of power and established authority.

---

speech (Plut. *Vit. Ant.,* 11.20 [833d]). Sophokles gave this same argument to another innocent, Kreon (*OT* 587 – 89). In the Sophoclean version the accused is less important to the play, nor is he characterized as an intellectual. Newton (1980) argues for the priority of this version; but searches for the "originators" of such commonplaces are unrewarding, since examples depend on an understood norm that may be constituted in full by no single member of the group.

79. See the analysis of Sale (1977, 48ff.).

80. Mensch (1976, 83).

81. See her extremely severe assessment: Theseus is shamed (*aischyntheis,* 1291) and no longer has a place among the noble (*en agathois andrasin* [1294]), a devastating rebuke in terms of Adkins' scale of values (1960).

82. As Stinton points out (1975, 240) tragic poets have other means besides the *hamartia* by which they can diminish "outrage" at the protagonist's downfall. In this case, Hippolytos' death seems less harsh because of Theseus' changed attitude. For the effect, see Knox (1952, 29 – 30).

83. 1300 – 1, οἶστρον ἢ τρόπον τινὰ / γενναιότητα. Barrett (1964, 399) points out the oxymoronic quality of the expression, which both defines and attempts to bridge over the gulf between the two possible views of Phaidra's conduct.

84. For this equivalency, see discussions by Segal (1965, 151 – 52; 1969, 300 – 4; and 1970.2, 137), who stresses the complementary reversals in their fates and behavior; see also Bremer (1975, 278). Strohm (1957, 69 and n.1) notes the "garland-like" structure that interweaves their appearances, while keeping them separate; note the similar effect of the dramatic arrangements of *Herakles.*

Hippolytos is as rigid and as idealistic as the youthful self-sacrificers that appear in many of the plays; but he is given a much more complex and subjectively oriented moral development. The treatment of his oath and his decision to keep it is typical of the play's complex and nonlogical balancing of audience sympathies. Hippolytos decides to keep to his oath partly because he is certain that he will not be believed anyway, and the effect of his last-minute wavering is to enhance audience identification in a crucial moment.[85] When a dramatic character retains moral norms where most of us would jettison them, his downfall begins to look like a result of his own perversity. Most of us, like most fifth-century Athenians, tend to place self-preservation before moral scruples; and the confusions in moral systems delineated by A. W. H. Adkins (1960) must have led to increased flexibility, or untrustworthiness, in adherence to norms of behavior. Hippolytos' momentary reconsideration of his oath naturalizes him; and Hippolytos the chaste, who sets rules for himself that have no meaning for other men, is a character particularly in need of humanizing and softening touches.

At the moment when he considers abandoning his oath, Hippolytos makes the kind of calculation that most of us would make at such a moment, and he comes to what is manifestly a wise decision. To break his oath would offend the gods, without convincing Theseus; and that would be the worst of bad bargains, especially for a man with such pride in his integrity.[86] Similarly, Hippolytos' first instinct to ignore the oath, in his earlier speech to the Nurse, has many extenuating circumstances in his feelings and in his shock at her immoral proposition. His distinction between the swearing of the "tongue" and that of the mind expresses Hippolytos' scorn for the mere surface of virtue; and the pride with which he boasts of his "unsworn mind" matches other refusals to be trammeled by the conditions of ordinary existence. The oath is presented throughout so that we can apprehend it in its human meaning to Hippolytos and so that it never becomes a mere abstraction. In the last scene Artemis naturally mentions none of these waverings and overtones:

> He, as was right, did not agree with [the Nurse's] words,
> nor, when he was maligned by you,

---

85. 1060ff. Against Hippolytos' morality, Orban (1981.2, 201–2). Valgiglio (1957.1, 7ff.) argues, as I do, that this touch humanizes Hippolytos and makes him a more eligible tragic hero. Crocker (1957, 246) formulates it thus: Hippolytos has "tragic guilt," but lacks "ethical guilt."

86. Orban (1981.2, 201–2) points out that the following tag by the chorus, which commends the reliability of Hippolytos' oath to Theseus, may also serve to underline for Hippolytos the importance of not breaking faith.

> did he take the seal of trust from his oaths,
> for he was pious (*eusebês*).[87]

The management of the oath makes it possible for the audience to appreciate Artemis' praise as the appropriate moral validation for Hippolytos, while still retaining their fellow feeling (*to philanthrôpon*) for this character.

III. Socratic Ideology

III.A. PHAIDRA'S SPEECH

Hippolytos presents a most Euripidean pair of protagonists, a lovesick matron and a fanatic boy; but it expends the whole arsenal of Sophoclean dramatic devices to purchase approval and sympathy for these characters. Of all the plays, *Hippolytos* offers the least challenge to the generic norms of tragedy and of society. Two incompatible value systems are allowed to flourish in an ideal form, with a corresponding blurring of the ironic vision that reveals each side *as it appears to the other.* Phaidra and Hippolytos appear to us more nearly as they would see themselves; and the only irony is in the incompleteness and complementarity of their clashing life views.

Surely the greatest evidence of confusion in the traditional view of Euripidean poetry has been the persistent misinterpretation of the opening lines of Phaidra's long speech as a bald anti-Socratic polemic. It should always have been evident that, for this of all Euripidean plays, what is said by the speakers is made to correspond to a carefully developed *êthos.* Phaidra's values are traditional; and her speech, taken as a whole and without severing its introduction from its body, constitutes a masterly exposition of what we might call the fifth-century moral status quo. She arrives at no clear formulation, but since it is the contradictions in the convention that are being explored, clarity is not necessarily an asset. Because the speech reflects the limitations of Phaidra's personality and experience more than Euripides' speeches usually do, the values it presents are not so much analyzed as laid open to the *elenchos* of the play's action.

Hippolytos is not distant enough in time from *Erechtheus* or *Suppliants* or *Hekabe* for us to speak of an evolution in Euripides' rhetorical skills: the artist was certainly capable of his typically clear and logical style at this

---

87. 1307 – 9:

ὃ δ᾽, ὥσπερ οὖν δίκαιον, οὐκ ἐφέσπετο
λόγοισιν, οὐδ᾽ αὖ πρὸς σέθεν κακούμενος
ὅρκων ἀφεῖλε πίστιν, εὐσεβὴς γεγώς.

For the text of line 1307, see Barrett (1964, 399).

period. Since the introduction to Phaidra's speech is a piece whose logical structure does not work, it makes sense to assume that the confusion is part of the discourse, rather than an "error" extraneous to it. Down to the middle of line 381, Phaidra's thought is limpid and perspicuous:[88] many people possess good sense enough (*eu phronein*); but, although having sufficient knowledge and experience to choose well, we choose badly from lack of effort, and from laziness.[89] Phaidra's points are even underlined neatly by touches of rhetorical didacticism;[90] but, as she begins to describe the nature and causes of the laziness (*argia*) that spoils human moral endeavors, her thought seems to become cloudy and to drift.

> We do not work it out, some through laziness,
> and some putting before the good
> some other pleasure.[91]

The passage seems to imply either that *argia* is some sort of pleasure, or, more likely, that some other sort of pleasure than that which normally accompanies the "good" (*kalon*) will prevent the completion of moral impulses.[92] Phaidra goes on to say that

---

88. The controversy over the "exact meaning" of *prassein kakion* in line 378 is meaningless: there is no distinction between "doing well" and "behaving well" at this point. (See Snell [1971, 67], who argues that it must be ethical in the strictest sense; and Claus [1972, 226].) Some of the parallel Platonic passages that illustrate this ambivalency are analyzed by Pigeaud (1976, 12–13).

89. 380–81:

τὰ χρήστ᾽ ἐπιστάμεσθα καὶ γιγνώσκομεν
οὐκ ἐκπονοῦμεν δ᾽, οἱ μὲν ἀργίας ὕπο ...

See the interesting uses of *ekponein* in *Herakles*. Here, the strenuous approach, condemned by Megara as lacking in dignity and good sense, is commended by Phaidra as the only means of making actions match our knowledge of what is right. Both uses contain the same notion of an extra, will-directed effort, which may prove to be vain. Moline (1975, 54) argues with some plausibility that the double use of *epistamai* and *gignôskô* indicates a degree of philosophical precision for this speech. See also Irwin (1983, 190).

90. See the phrase in line 379, "But this is the way one should consider it [ἀλλὰ τῇδ᾽ ἀρθρητέον τόδε.]." See Chap. 8, on the use of such instructive and pedantic tag lines in the rhetoric of Herakles and Amphitryon.

91. 382: οἱ δ᾽ ἡδονὴν προθέντες ἀντὶ τοῦ καλοῦ / ἄλλην τιν᾽ ...

92. Barrett (1964, 229) interprets *allên tin'* to mean "something else [besides laziness], namely some pleasure." But Willinck (1968, 14) has shown that an emphatic *allos* such as this cannot take that interpretation; see also Claus (1972, 227).

There are many pleasures in life,
long talks and leisure, a baneful delight,
and shame.[93]

There is no apparent source in Hellenic tradition for labeling "long talks and leisure"—an evident hendiadys—as evil. We would expect Phaidra to refer to the temptations of sexuality, not those of conversation. The phrase "baneful delight" (or "delightful evil," *terpnon kakon*) underlines this oddness, since it virtually forces a reference to *erôs*.[94] The most readily available gloss to this passage is Phaidra's reference to her own nightly ponderings,[95] but that seems illogical: how can a meditation on, or a conversation about moral failure itself lead to moral failure? Further ambiguity is contributed by the fact that the program of line 383 very clearly leads us to expect a catalogue of pleasures, and it is as puzzling to find "shame" ending the catalogue as it was to find leisurely conversations beginning it.[96] She continues:

There are two; the one is not bad,
the other is a burden to houses. If the mark (*kairos*)
          were clear,
they would not be two things spelled with the
          same letters.[97]

93. 383–85:

> . . . εἰσὶ δ' ἡδοναὶ πολλαὶ βίου
> μακραί τε λέσχαι καὶ σχολή, τερπνὸν κακόν,
> αἰδώς τε . . .

94. See Claus (1972, 233 n.16). We might attempt to make a connection through Semonides' fear of sexual conversations (ἀφροδισίους λόγους, 7W.91) among married women. Interpretation in the direction of naturalistic psychology (Phaidra and women like her have too much time on their hands; see U. Wilamowitz [(1898) 1926.2, 112]; and Winnington-Ingram [1958, 176–77]) is certainly possible, but is not encouraged by the schematic and rhetorical form of the passage.

95. Note the repetition of "lengthy" (*makros*) in 375 and 384.

96. The doubled *te* that links *aidôs* and the other "pleasures" is a very strong indication of pairing. Barrett (1964, 230) is certainly not right to assume that the appending of *aidôs* is any ordinary sort of anacoluthon, since our intuitive interpretation of the passage will follow its logical form, not diverge from it. The problem is that the logical form does not seem to make any sense.

97. On *kairos,* see the discussion of Barrett (1964, 231); and Pigeaud (1976, 18–19). Willinck's interpretation (1968, 15ff.: that the "two" are not shames but pleasures) is supported by an attempt to make fine distinctions that have no basis in Greek ethics or in poetic style. Further, it is rhetorically unlikely that *dyo* could refer back to *hêdonai,* which are originally mentioned as being many (*pollai*), and would now have to be reformed into a single abstraction, and then split in half. For a long note on the bibliography of this controversy, see Orban (1981.1, 12–13 n.26). Early discussion in Dodds (1925, 103).

Phaidra drifts from her apparent theme—effort as a solution to moral failure—into musings on *aidôs,* ending this long *prooimion* on a note of inconsequence, since there is no resumption of the central topic to end the digression. What has happened to the main thought? Or rather, where is the main thought to be found? Since the passage is logically incoherent, it seems best to look for other sources of coherence. *Aidôs* (shame or modesty) is traditionally opposed to pleasure, rather than linked with it; but it does have many associations with inactivity, a theme which runs throughout the passage.[98] The general point is hard to miss: there is here a strong opposition between Phaidra's resolution to struggle with her inclinations and some principle of inertia, which may or may not be pleasurable. But the result is paradox, since the passage seems to undermine the prime support of morality in conventional Hellenic thought. We, from our perspective within the new ethic, can fill in the reasons why *aidôs* might be a seductive principle of inertia tending to moral collapse; but this perspective was not available to Euripides' audience. For them, in particular, this passage is a riddle without a solution.[99]

However unclear the connection of *aidôs* to pleasure (*hêdonê*) and inactivity (*argia*) may be, the trailing close has ended the introduction precisely upon the central topic of the rest of the rhesis. As Phaidra begins to apply her principle—and such an incoherent principle will prove predictably awkward to apply—and to move from generalizations to her own particular case, the problem of *aidôs* will be laid bare, not through an orderly analysis, but through the repetitive and spiraling desperation of her thoughts. It has rightly been pointed out that Phaidra does not intend her strictures against long conversations and other forms of *argia* to apply to herself, since she is embracing the tonic and active side and will "work out" (*ekponein*) her trou-

98. See Barrett (1964, 230) and the tag from *Ion* 337. Müffelmann (1965, 28 and 51–52) discusses the link between *aidôs* and *argia* at some length, linking both to the inaction imposed by intellectual analysis (hence, the long conversations).

99. I have not raised the question of the two *aidôi* and what they might mean, because I have throughout tried to avoid over-precision in a passage that is designed to be imprecise and puzzling. However, a number of traditional passages, particularly in Hesiodos, do offer divisions between "good" and "bad" sides of moral principles, such as *aidôs* and conflict (*eris, WD* 17–19). See Barrett (1964, 230). One of the best discussions of the ethical values around *aidôs* is that of Segal (1970.1), although it is marred by the assumption that an "outer" and an "inner" *aidôs* can be distinguished here (293). That they cannot be distinguished is precisely the problem. But see Winnington-Ingram (1958, 183–84), who points to the fact that Phaidra's *aidôs* and *sôphrosynê* are maintained by custom (*nomôi*), while those of Hippolytos are rooted in nature (*physei*). On the confusions see Hathorn (1957, 214): "As long as words refer to natural objects . . . they are relatively manageable, but when we cross the border into the realm of human conduct, we find that they may slip, expand, and turn into their opposites."

bles.[100] But the very vagueness of her formulation leaves open the suggestion that there is more in her discourse than she can consciously embrace.[101]

She begins with a restatement of the resolute rhetoric of moral determination: she will not be corrupted by any poison so as to let her thought "fall backward" and reverse itself (τοὔμπαλιν πεσεῖν φρενῶν, 390). Like all will-power rhetoric, this contains the ominous germ of its own dissolution: to "fall" one need only relax, while to resist implies a continual struggle. Her first expedient was that normal to *aidôs,* silence and concealment of the "disease." In a movement of familiar Euripidean "inconsequence" Phaidra adds that speech, which knows how to advise others on their troubles, most often harms itself. A faint echo of the delightful evil (τερπνὸν κακόν) of leisurely speech can be heard. Can this speech that Phaidra is making be itself a self-harming discourse? Except for this single digression, the sequence of Phaidra's remedies for her passion is coldly and logically set forth: first, silence; second, self-control (*to sôphronein*); and finally, death, "strongest of plans—no one will deny it."[102]

But, when she begins to draw the moral from her three resolutions, Phaidra's thought flows into contradictory and self-revelatory patterns. She begins with a *gnômê* or maxim that sounds fairly conventional:

I would not escape notice when doing good things (*kala*)
nor, doing shameful (*aischra*) ones, have many witnesses.

On the surface this can be taken as a somewhat elaborate statement of the obvious, that shameful things must be concealed. Taken farther, it could explain Phaidra's decision to gain some honor by revealing her struggle before she ends her life, although in her predicament Phaidra can gain honor only by revealing her shame. The paradox is an illustration of the Thucydidean maxim that the woman with the best reputation (*doxa*) is the most unknown.[103] Pressed further yet, of course, this tag reveals the weakest point of the shame ethic: it is not what one really does that matters, but what one is seen or known to have done. Phaidra goes on to say that she knows that the "act" and the "disease" are a source of bad fame (*dysklea*): thus, as W. Barrett points out, not only the actual performance of adultery, but even

100. See Willinck (1968, 17); Claus (1972, 225ff.); Solmsen (1973). This confusion, however, persists in Irwin's discussion of Phaedra's "incontinence" (1983).
101. See Manuwald (1979).
102. Note *kratein* above (401); and see Turato (1974, 158) on this term and its use in Antiphon (58B).
103. She says to the Nurse, "You will destroy me. Yet the matter brings me honor [ὀλῇ. τὸ μέντοι πρᾶγμ' ἐμοὶ τιμὴν φέρει]" (328). Cf. line 331, "Out of shameful matters [*aischrôn*] I am contriving noble ones [*esthla*]." Knox (1952, 9) partially anticipated this point.

the malady of *erôs* itself, brings shame to women.[104] This, of course, makes a mockery of Phaidra's earlier hope that revelation of her struggle would bring honor. For, as she goes on to say, only to be a woman is to incur loathing on all sides.[105] The mechanism of misogyny is such that any woman can bring shame to the rest, while the good woman, regarded as a rare exception, has no effect on the general fame of the sex.[106] The woman who first devised adultery thus indelibly blackened the reputation of the sex.

Adulterous women shame the secret marriage bed before outsiders (*thyraioi*, 409), exposing the household to ignominy. Yet it must have been from noble houses that this practice first derived, for when the noble (*esthloi*) decide upon shameful deeds, then such actions will certainly' seem good (*kala*) to the low (*kakoi*). A major problem for ancient ethics is packed into Phaidra's words: since the terms for high social status in many cases are identical with those for moral goodness, there is a complete confusion of values when the "shameful" is condoned by those who are "noble."[107] Where is the sanction on which Phaidra can base her desperate resolution to master (*kratein*) her desires? The women that Phaidra hates, those who are decent (*sôphronas*) only in word, destroy the system of virtue based on *aidôs*. For if shame derives from what is known, the successful adulteress is not shamed; and what should be *aischron* can appear unchallenged as *kalon*. In desperation, Phaidra is thrown back upon a fantasy in which the house itself, the entity whose honor and secrets have been betrayed to the outsiders, cries out and denounces the offender. While this may seem to be the beginning of a sense of "guilt,"[108] the parable of the speaking house also expresses the impossibility of converting shame into guilt. Unless the woman can find some reason within herself to reject deceit, she is frightening herself with a meaningless imagination. "That is just what is killing me, my

104. 1964, 233–34.
105. Barrett's analysis of the phrase "an object of loathing to all [*misêma pasin*]" (1964, 234) makes distinctions where none will hold. The bad fame of women has its primary and—in such a context as this—its determining source in women's sexuality; *misêma*, "object of scorn/hatred" or "sexual deviant", therefore can hold its several meanings together and there is no need to eliminate any of them from the passage.
106. See the discussion between Agamemnon and Odysseus in the underworld: the evil deed of Klytaimestra brings bad fame and suspicion of evil doing to all women, even those as fine as Penelopeia (*Od.* 11.433–34). See Euripidean comments fr. 657 N2 (*Protesilaos*) and especially 493 (*Melanippe*): ἄλγιστόν ἐστι θῆλυ μισηθὲν γένος, which could serve as a gloss on our passage.
107. See Adkins (1960, 76ff.) on Theognis and the confusion introduced by disjunction between class standards and moral standards.
108. But see *Agamemnon* (37–38, cf. 1091ff.), where this same image also appears in a context of concealed adultery.

friends,'' Phaidra cries, ''may I never be caught shaming my husband and children.''

The most maddening feature of the shame ethic is the tremendous rewards available to successful hypocrisy, matched with the immense penalties ready for any failure, indeed for any suspicion of failure, since women, ''objects of loathing,'' are assumed—as Hippolytos assumes—to have a natural bent to lewdness. Knowledge of their sexuality brings to women shame and self-hatred, leaving them with no inner principle to oppose to the temptations of secrecy. Women and their doings must simply be hidden, that is the only rule. When Phaidra tries to picture positively the values of a good reputation (421ff.), she moves in imagination out of the close atmosphere of the women's quarters into the open air of the public *polis,* where reputatons are acquired by activity and where the individual's view of himself (γνώμη δικαία κἀγαθή) can provide support for the maintenance of honor. But, in Phaidra's world, where can such supports be found?[109]

We do not have long to wait before the contradictions in Phaidra's speech become overt. The rebuttal of the Nurse offers the perfect contemporary refutation for this tangle of moral confusions, revealing the folly of Phaidra's efforts to be ''strong'': ''human beings should not struggle overmuch with life.''[110] Phaidra's sense of a menace in the appeal of *logoi* was well founded: all the Nurse really has to do is place Phaidra's own arguments in a new context. Wise people, she reasons, keep hidden (or ignore, *lanthanein*) what is not honorable (*ta mê kala,* 465–66). Phaidra's own view, that virtue requires the exertion of tremendous moral effort, makes her vulnerable to the Nurse's ridicule of those who would set excessively high standards for themselves.[111] On the other hand, if one takes the shame standard in the ''easy'' way, as the Nurse does, it is no standard at all, but simply an etiquette for concealing what is better not seen.

Phaidra's response is to blame all mortal troubles on ''excessively fine speeches'' (*kaloi lian logoi*). The double meaning of *kalos,* aesthetically pleasing, and morally fine or noble, is in play throughout this dialogue. A moment later (499) she will call the Nurse's talk (*logous*), ''most shameful/ugly'' (*aischistous*), and then again at line 503 she will admit that the Nurse speaks ugly/shameful things (*aischra*) beautifully (*kalôs*).[112] Phaidra's ''exhaustion'' that leads her to accede to the half-disguised plan of

109. See H. Parry's fine dissection of the imagery of concealment and openness, indoor (female) pollution and outdoor (male and asexual) purity (1966, 324ff.).

110. 467: οὐδ' ἐκπονεῖν τοι χρὴ βίον λίαν βροτούς.

111. Note her use of *perissos* at lines 237 and 445; at line 473ff. she even argues that it is mere *hybris* to attempt to surpass the gods in virtue.

112. Note that this riddle appears twice in four lines: εὖ λέγεις γὰρ, αἰσχρὰ δέ (503) and τὰσχρὰ δ' ἦν λέγῃς καλῶς (505) .

the Nurse proceeds as much from the torment of these unresolved and unresolvable confusions as from her mental and physical weakness.[113] Her fear and suspicion of discourse seem justified by the verbal morass into which she has strayed.[114]

While in one sense Phaidra's failure is a demonstration that people who "know better" can still be weak, in another sense it reveals the seductiveness of the Socratic argument that nobody willingly commits a moral error,[115] since the collapse of her resistance evidently proceeds from the contradictions in her *logos*. Any attempt to suggest the relation of this speech to a positive Socratic "doctrine" would carry the implication that such a doctrine existed and that it can, in the absence of any writings by Sokrates, be recaptured from traces in Platon and elsewhere. But, like Antisthenes' denial of refutation and other paradoxical arguments attributed to Socratics and other Sophists, the argument that all moral errors are involuntary works better as a tool to expose contradictions than as the foundation for any sort of coherent theory.[116] In this passage, and in the passage of *Medeia* that recalls Socratic terms,[117] Euripides is giving free play to some of the problems that made this argument so interesting and so fertile for fifth-century thinkers.[118] Seen in that light, Phaidra's speech looks more like a tribute to Socratic influence than a "polemic" against the philosopher.

III.B. HIPPOLYTOS AS SOCRATIC HERO

The analysis of Phaidra's speech does not exhaust the Socratic associations of *Hippolytos*. The tendency of philosophers to study their field in terms of arguments and doctrines makes it difficult for them to approach most of the figures of the Sophistic movement, since these thinkers seem not to present systems so much as to play, often in a quite self-conscious and

113. Barrett (1964, 256) draws heavily on psychological extrapolation: Phaidra is weakened by her fast and is "too exhausted and bemused" to follow up the Nurse's ambiguous discourse.

114. See Pigeaud on the relation between the theme of disease and medicine and that of *logos* and rhetoric (1976, 17–18), a favorite metaphor of Gorgias.

115. Οὐδεὶς ἑκὼν ἁμαρτάνει, see *Prot.* 345e1, *Apol.* 37a5.

116. I disagree with Irwin (1977) about the existence of solid and fixed Socratic *dogmata* (hypostatized by I. under a set of acronyms, xv-xvii).

117. See Snell (1971, 55ff.).

118. Irwin (1983, 191–92) is certainly right in pointing out that the phrasing of the dilemmas in *Hippolytos* and especially in *Medeia* is designed to bring the problem of "incontinence" to the fore, in much the same form in which it would present itself to an abstract thinker, a philosopher. But distinctions that Irwin attempts to make, between an emotion that will "prevent someone from thinking straight" and one that "overwhelms someone with desire, even when he does think straight" (188), are psychologically unreal. "Incontinence" is a peculiarly philosophical way of dissecting a psychological phenomenon: *Medeia* opts for this mode of discourse, and much of the fascinating "absurdity" of that play derives from its presentation of Medeia as completely aware of two conflicting drives and sets of motivations at once.

ironic fashion, with words and concepts.[119] Although we know little of Sokrates' positive teachings, his impact on those who found in him a model for human conduct must have derived in part from his practice in philosophy and argument. If we limit our study of Sokrates to what we know about this social impact and if we take account of some of the stories about him, as I tried earlier to take account of some of the stories about Sophokles and Euripides, we can make out the outline of a human figure that has strong affinities with the reformist characters in Euripidean plays, and particularly with the hero of *Hippolytos.*[120]

As in the case of many legendary figures, the most important feature of the legend about Sokrates seems to have been the way he came to his death.[121] A number of versions of his defense speech were produced; and these, along with accounts of his courage in death, were important as proofs of Sokrates' special nature.[122] Although encouraged to go into exile, Sokrates insisted on remaining in Athens and, by refusing to propose his own penalty at the trial, virtually forced a sentence of death upon his jurors.[123] I have mentioned (in Chapter Three, above) the close parallels between the reasoning of such self-sacrificers as Polyxene, Makaria, and Menoikeus, and the Platonic Sokrates' explanation of his decision not to evade death. Like facing battle, a voluntary submission to death requires courage; but, unlike the warrior's death, the end of the self-sacrificer is marked by passivity. This new standard of *aretê* is directly entailed by the resolution of the conflict between "cooperative" and "competitive" virtues in the favor of the former. We can now admire the courage and public spirit of the sufferer, without having to admire aggression and self-aggrandizement. The tranquillity with which the Euripidean figures meet their end, and their refusal to

119. Magalhães-Vilhena's book *Le problème de Socrate* (1952, 113) contains a good discussion of the tendency to interpret the work of individuals from the inside, as a self-consistent system, and the results for intellectual history.

For the playful and ironic mode, see the work of Zenon of Elea, of whom H. Fränkel remarked ([1924] 1960, 236) that it is almost impossible to separate the lighter side of his art from the important ideas he presented. On the controversy over whether Zenon could be allowed these "Sophistic" traits and still be considered a philosopher, see Kerferd (1981, 61ff.)

120. The conventional methods of isolating historical "fact" and "truth" have entered into a paradoxical circle in the case of Sokrates, since nothing remains except the reception, elaboration, and interpretation of the Socratic thought and personality in the work of others. The most sophisticated discussion of this problem is that of Magalhães-Vilhena (1952, 110ff.).

121. See the legends surrounding the deaths of poets, discussed by G. Nagy (1979, 301ff.).

122. The range of writers on Sokrates moves from untalented but devoted disciples like Aischines of Sphettos through figures like Platon and Antisthenes who were thinkers in their own right to rhetors like Polykrates and Lysias, who picked up the theme of the defense or accusation of Sokrates, probably when it was already celebrated, as a likely subject for a display piece—see Gigon (1947, 23); Hirzel (1887).

123. For the extraordinary nature of Sokrates' trial and death sentence, see Dover (1976, 47).

repine against what they have accepted as the right course of action, are another mark of similarity to the Socratic myth.

In his idealism and his willingness to sacrifice life for principle, Hippolytos resembles the self-sacrificers. Most of them are girls or young women, who assimilate their death to a traditional model of courage. Like them, Hippolytos displays moral concerns that are somewhat inappropriate to his sex. Sexual continence was praised without being clearly prescribed for Greek males, except in the period of adolescence when boys were vulnerable to homosexual approaches.[124] In abstaining from heterosexual activity, Hippolytos brings male "modesty" (*aidôs*) into a role never envisaged by the culture; but the peculiar ideas of Hippolytos about sexuality have a considerable affinity to those of at least one member of the Socratic school. Antisthenes was famous for his hostility to all forms of *hêdonê* (pleasure), particularly the sexual.[125] Platon's account of Sokrates' views on sexuality appears to be strongly opposed to that of Antisthenes;[126] but, as in the case of Phaidra's remarks on responsibility and will power, it is more useful, at least for the purpose of understanding Euripidean drama, to note the common concerns of Socratic thinkers with certain key topics than to attempt to make fine distinctions between their doctrines. Just as we can detect, without being able to localize it, a pervasive concern with female roles and potential in the Socratic school,[127] so we can point to an intense involvement with the problems centering on self-control (*egkrateia*), pleasure, and *erôs*.[128] In spite of their disagreements, both Platon and Antisthenes deprecated the hedonic or appetitive element in human psychology.[129] Hippolytos, who despises the sexual act, is frequently surrounded by his age mates (*hêlikes*), who show their devotion by escorting him into exile;[130] and his association with Artemis also

124. See Dover (1978, 81ff.).

125. See the fragments in Caizzi (1966, 53–55) fr. 108a-109b: "I had rather be mad than have pleasure [μανείην μᾶλλον ἢ ἡσθείην]." Fr. 108e-f: "One should never move a finger for the sake of pleasure [μηδέποτε χάριν ἡδονῆς δάκτυλον ἐκτείνειν]." He described *erôs* as *kakia tês physeôs* and asserted that he would (like Diomedes, *Il*.5.348ff.) take a shot at Aphrodite, if he saw her (fr. 109 a-b).

126. Antisthenes himself thought so: see the notorious sexual slur in the title of his antiplatonic tract, Caizzi (1966, fr. 18.32).

127. This is another obvious connection with the Euripidean plays. Note that Antisthenes apparently wrote about Aspasia to denounce her as a sexual creature, while Aischines, Xenophon (*Oec.* 3.14; *Mem.* 2.6.36), and Platon (*Menexenos*) mention her favorably, combining this with arguments in favor of female intellectual potential. For Aischines, see Humbert (1967, 226–27).

128. See Antisthenes' discussion of various *hêdonai* in Xenophon *Symp.* 4.39–41.

129. The latter apparently argued for a limited and utilitarian heterosexuality; see Xenophon *Symp.* 4.38.

130. 1102ff. Hippolytos is asexual, not homosexual; but these positions are not mutually exclusive. As Dover has shown (1978, 103 and n.88), Athenian society had an ambivalent view of the physical side of homosexual *erôs*.

Barrett's careful analysis of the evidence for a double chorus here (1964, 366–69), leads to

suggests close and intimate comradeship accompanied by a denial of sexuality.[131] There is strong evidence that a similar ideal of intimacy without physical sexuality emanated from the Socratic circle.

Sokrates' surface persona, his fabled ugliness, his primitive garb, and his comic behavior are the markers of a new morality, in which *to kalon* is located inside the individual, in his *psychê*, rather than in his outward attributes.[132] The fascination with Sokrates among young men of the most distinguished class, who were themselves the natural inheritors of traditional *aretê*, was an indication that, in some Athenian circles in the late fifth century, the definition of the *spoudaios* was undergoing radical change. Like the young aristocrats who were attracted to Sokrates, Hippolytos is devoted to the traditional standards and activities, in his case hunting and gymnastics,[133] of the gentleman (*kalos k' agathos*).[134] Like them, he is exclusive and snobbish, on both moral and political grounds.[135] As an audience for his oratory,

---

something of a *non liquet*. But Barrett may be too hasty in concluding that the escort cannot be doing the singing, since they must leave with the hero. It seems easiest to assume that the youths form two groups, one to accompany the chorus and the other to leave with Hippolytos, corresponding to the two commands to "address us [προσείπαθ' ἡμᾶς]" (1099) and "escort us [προπέμψατε]." See also later references to the huge throng following him (1179−80): μυρία δ' ὀπισθόπους / φίλων ἄμ' ἔστειχ' ἡλίκων ⟨θ'⟩ ὁμήγυρις

131. See the ambivalent use of ξυνεῖναι, a word that can also refer to sexual intercourse, to describe Hippolytos' comradeship with Artemis, "forever in intercourse with a virgin [παρθένῳ ξυνὼν ἀεὶ]" (17), a contradiction in terms (cf. lines 85, 949).

132. See *Symposion* 215b. Aristophanes, Xenophon (*Symp.* 4.19, see 5.6), and Platon are agreed on one trait of Sokrates, namely his personal oddity and singular ugliness. Sokrates cannot be the normal *spoudaios* because he has all the markers of the *geloios*, even down to the face of the ultimate *geloios*, the satyr. An obvious parallel in Euripides to this concern with inner worth would be the treatment of the role of the Autourgos in *Elektra*.

133. The hunting was obviously part of the story; but see his orders for the horses, which he intends to exercise after he has eaten (112), and his reference to the games as the arena in which he would wish to excel. Theseus taunts him that "You have trained yourself to worship yourself much more than to be just and pious toward your parents" (1080−81):

πολλῷ γε μᾶλλον σαυτὸν ἤσκησας σέβειν
ἢ τοὺς τεκόντας ὅσια δρᾶν δίκαιος ὤν.

The reference to training (*êskêsas*) ties together Hippolytos' special regimen of abstinence from sex with his references to games and athletic exercises.

134. Note that it is necessary, and quite appropriate, to distinguish Sokrates himself—a comic and plebeian figure—from the brilliant and aristocratic associates that he acquired and to the best of whom I would assimilate Hippolytos.

135. For the exclusivity of Hippolytos' religiosity, see discussion above, Section II.B. The picture given by Montuori (1974, 286f.) of Sokrates' political position, though exaggerated, seems valid. For Hippolytos, see Turato (1974, 151ff.), Blomqvist (1982, 414). Knox (1952, 21) remarks that "most of the commonplaces of the aristocratic attitude are put into his mouth in the course of the play. But he is also an intellectual and a religious mystic." Turato (150ff.) sees him as a conformist aristocrat and a reproach to contemporary Sophistic youth; but Knox is closer to the truth.

he rejects the democratic mob (*ochlos*) and prefers the few (*oligoi*), who are wise (986–89). Hippolytos' rejection of tyranny is couched in the same political terms: one should wish to be first in the games, but second in the city, "and always to do well, with the best people as friends."[136]

Hippolytos' adherence to aristocratic standards is not in itself striking. His world is the heroic one; and the relative dearth of irony and of its concomitant anachronism in this play does not encourage the audience to look for contemporary social significance in his tastes. But the conjunction of non-conformist habits and attitudes with these aristocratic tastes is suggestive, as is the relationship between Hippolytos and his father. We do not see the two together before the breach between them, but the kind of abuse that Theseus gives Hippolytos implies that the supposed crime of his son has actualized a potential alienation of some long standing. Hippolytos' boasts (*kompoi*) of association with a god are now revealed as the vauntings of a quack.[137] Pretensions to divine favor, as well as to a special moral purity, bring upon the devotee of nonstandard ethics the accusation of being excessive or overnice (*perissos*), hence Theseus' unfair gibes about Orphic cults and vegetarianism.[138]

Hippolytos at times is treated as the sole and lonely devotee of Artemis, and indeed he is the only one who hears her voice. But he claims to have a circle of intimates who understand better what he means, when he speaks of *sôphrosynê*, than his father and the rest of the uninitiated are likely to. This split between the generations again has its parallel in the accusations by Sokrates' enemies that sons were alienated from fathers by his teachings.[139]

136. 1018, σὺν τοῖς ἀρίστοις εὐτυχεῖν ἀεὶ φίλοις. See Pindaros *Py*. 11.50ff.

137. See line 952, *auchei*, "boast away." Hippolytos is also called *semnos*, 957; and see lines 93 (and commentary by Köhnken [1972, 184–85]) and 1080–81. See the studies on *semnos* in this play by Segal (1965, 128) and Köhnken (185–86); the word exactly defines the difference between divine and human prerogatives: for a human being to be *semnos* is wrong (as Hippolytos admits [94]), while it is highly appropriate to a god.

138. 952–53. In spite of textual disturbance it is easy to make out what Theseus is saying: he tells his son, "Now go all the way and become a full-fledged cultist, since you've been caught out [ἐπεί ἐλήφθης, 955)] as a fraud." Cf. Kassandra's bitter account of the neglect of her prophetic powers at Troy (*Ag*. 1273–74): she was treated like any starveling oraclemonger. Note that Theseus also addresses Hippolytos with associated insulting terms at line 1038, "wizard" and "magician" (*epôidos, goês*). It is unnecessary to associate Hippolytos directly with any such cult; see Barrett (1964, 342–43). Yet there is an analogy between Hippolytos and others who have eccentric definitions of virtue. People who avoid eating meat are, in Hellenic terms, comparable to a male who practices a sexual continence demanded by no normal moral code. Cf. Tschiedel (1969, 240): there is a kernel of truth in Theseus' remarks.

139. Note the reflection of this in the accusation of the *katêgoros* (possibly the rhetorician Polykrates—see above) in Xenophon *Mem*. 1.2.49: τοὺς πατέρας προπηλακίζειν ἐδίδασκε. The best evidence is Aristophanes' *Clouds*, which captures the trauma of generational dislocation under the influence of the new education. For this "generation gap" see Mensch (1976); but M. associates the gap with the differences that separate Hippolytos from Phaidra as well, which somewhat diffuses his treatment.

While any training in the Sophistic could cause disruption between the trained and the untrained, training that had a positive ethical content may have been potentially more unsettling. Immoral youth is the oldest of saws, but young people who follow a code that is more strict and exacting than the one in which they were brought up seem to reverse the traditional relations between generations. Theseus' rage at his son implies some stored-up resentment at Hippolytos' past failure to defer appropriately to parental authority.

Theseus' treatment of Hippolytos has certain interesting parallels with the maligning of Sokrates in *Clouds;* there too we hear that Sokrates is a charlatan and a trickster.[140] He too is *semnos* and gives himself airs.[141] The danger of appearing to be overfine, to claim special dispensations, to have a private truth is the same for both. It has been noted that the strictures of the Nurse against those who have the arrogance to set special conditions for their lives apply best to Hippolytos,[142] since he has a morality based on interior rather than community standards. Hippolytos' special truth gives him the certainty that Phaidra lacks; but it exposes him to being misunderstood and misjudged. The element of narcissism and arrogance in the boy's words is instantly perceived by Theseus (1080); but the more sympathetic audience, knowing that Hippolytos is not a liar, will also sense pathos, when in a remarkable figure of speech he imagines standing opposite himself to weep for himself (1078–79).

Since he has been judged a *kakos* by his own father, Hippolytos has fallen outside the community standards of the shame culture. He is utterly alone.[143] Phaidra, who fears that the mirror of time will reveal to others what must be concealed, can find no inner principle to stiffen her resolve, while Hippolytos is shut up inside his integrity, unable to share this inner view with any other

140. Gelzer (1956, 76–77) points out that Aristophanes makes the same kind of jokes about Sokrates and uses the same kind of language as he does in lampoons of those traditional religious *alazones,* the begging priests. *Clouds* 102: S. and Chairephon are *alazones;* and note Sokrates' trick at line 178. See also Eupolis 9M (2:553, Sokrates as a trickster and thief) and 10M (S. is a beggar, *ptôchos*). For the prophetic or oracular quality of the *daimonion,* see Rist (1963, 15–20).

141. For his arrogant demeanor, see *Clouds* 362–63: *semnoprosôpeis.* See lines 226, 1400. See also the reproach to Euripides in *Frogs* (1491ff.): τὸ δ' ἐπὶ σεμνοῖσιν λόγοισι . . . διατριβὴν ἀργὸν ποιεῖσθαι. Kallias in *Pedetai* (12K) has someone ask an interlocutor (a poet?), "What do you give yourself such airs about? [τί δὴ σὺ σεμνοῖ]." The other replies, "Sokrates is responsible (αἴτιος)."

142. See Merklin (1964, 123–24); Segal (1965, 128); A. Schmitt (1977, 32 n.64).

143. See Merklin (1964, 123): his wish to observe himself is an indication of his total lack of social support. See also J. Gould (1978, 57).

person, since there is no witness to his nature, "such as I am myself."[144]
Whereas Phaidra imagines herself denounced by the very rafters of her
house, Hippolytos wishes that he could call this house to witness, for it alone
could defend him.[145] Through these two moral strategies, the play explores
the problem of Platon's *Republic;* how can we find a ground for virtue in the
interior of the soul, rather than in the eyes of others?[146] Hippolytos' experience is that of the just man who learns what it truly means to be, and yet not
to seem, *sôphrôn* and *agathos.* "Never having done wrong, let him have a
reputation of the greatest wrongdoing, that he may be put to the test in regard
to justice . . ."[147]

IV. The *Spoudaion* in *Hippolytos*

IV.A. ARISTOCRATIC NORMS

The role of the Nurse in the second *Hippolytos* differs from those of servants in other plays, reflecting the changes that have been introduced into the
usual Euripidean dramatic forms. Euripidean slaves almost always act "seriously," showing a grasp of moral issues and an authority that seems somewhat unlikely, given their low status in Hellenic society.[148] For relatively
clear cases of "comic relief" in Greek tragedy we must usually look to
Sophokles or Aischylos.[149] This Nurse, however, while she too can be a subtle as well as an unscrupulous moralizer, also has some comic traits, which
are the more striking in the virtual absence of the ironic or ludicrous from the
treatment of Phaidra. The long opening to the scene, during which Phaidra
resists speaking, gives ample scope for us to observe the Nurse as well; and
she, like other characters in the play, develops a fuller and more detailed
êthos than is common in Euripidean drama.

144. See Pigeaud (1976, 14 – 15), who points out the necessity of mediation in getting a picture of the self. P. illuminates the curious metaphor of the mirror that closes Phaidra's speech at
lines 428 – 30, connecting it with the "connaissance de soi" and the complexities of *aidôs.*
While Pigeaud believes (23) that the mirror may reveal the approach of old age, surely what it
reveals to the "young maid" (παρθένῳ νέᾳ) is her maturity, and thus the approach of that
overwhelming and oppressive atmosphere of *aidôs* that conditions the lives of women.

145. 418, 1074 – 75.

146. See Winnington-Ingram (1958, 185); Segal (1970.1, 294); L. Bergson (1971, 78ff.).

147. Platon, *Rep.* 361c4: μηδὲν γὰρ ἀδικῶν, δόξαν ἐχέτω τὴν μεγίστην ἀδικίας, ἵνα ᾖ
βεβασανισμένος εἰς δικαιοσύνην . . .

148. A mild example, suitable to the greater naturalism of this play, is the old servant who
reproaches Hippolytos in the first scene.

149. Examples would be the Guard in *Antigone,* or the naive charm of the Watchman in
Agamemnon and the Nurse in *Choephoroi.* See Petersen (1915, 12), who pointed out that in
Sophokles and Aischylos realism is unsuitable for highborn characters, but suitable for lower
ones.

The *êthos* of the Nurse is that suitable to her social role, which combines servile attentions with parental moralizing and advice.[150] Her officious bustling manner provides an amusing counterpoint to the feverish passion of Phaidra's opening lyric, as in her first anapaestic passage she complains of her hard life and the tedium of nursing an invalid who cannot make up her mind.[151] Such remarks serve to show the Nurse as operating on a different level of seriousness from that of her mistress: we sympathize with Phaidra, but we smile at her attendant. Immediately after these homely reflections, however, the Nurse shifts gears and moves into another aspect of her role, musing quite subtly on the persistence of human dreams and hopes.[152]

Similarly, at the close of the anapaestic interchange, the Nurse again moralizes, this time about the necessity for loose rather than tense attachments in life.[153] But in this passage the Nurse's function as moralizer merges with her *êthos* as comic figure; and she closes her generalizations by remarking, "Thus I approve excess less than moderation, and the wise will agree with me [καὶ ξυμφήσουσι σοφοί μοι]." [154] This oldest of Delphic commonplaces is presented with a naive self-satisfaction that renews the humorous impression of her first remarks. The Nurse's social function is prominent in the following trimeters, as she cajoles and threatens Phaidra into revealing the cause of her illness. Once she learns the truth, however, she displays enormous emotionality, closing off the dialogue with a violent outburst. Her lines are a virtual parody of tragic despair, as she indulges, all in trimeters, in the emotional repetitions usually found in the lyric dirge form, wishing and threatening to die and ending with "Farewell, I am no more!"[155] The Nurse utters here just one or two notes of pathos in excess of what our sympathies

150. See Knox (1952, 11): the Nurse treats Phaidra like a child.
151. The mode of course is that of Phoinix in *Il.* 9.490–95 and the reminiscences of Kilissa (*Cho.* 748ff.). These two are recalling the *ponoi* of nursing a (now grown) infant, and illness makes Phaidra a kind of infant. The Nurse grumbles that it is better to be sick than to do the nursing (186), since she gets both pain (*lypê*) and toil (*ponos*).
152. 191ff. "But whatever might be better than life / darkness hides and involves in mists / and we are revealed as unlucky lovers / of whatever this is that gleams here upon the earth."

ἀλλ' ὅτι τοῦ ζῆν φίλτερον ἄλλο
σκότος ἀμπίσχων κρύπτει νεφέλαις.
δυσέρωτες δὴ φαινόμεθ' ὄντες
τοῦδ' ὅτι τοῦτο στίλβει κατὰ γῆν ...

153. 266. For this theme, see Knox (1952, 26), on images centering on tripping and nooses (*sphallein*), and Fowler (1978, 17ff.)
154. Or, "less than the [good old] 'nothing too much' [τοῦ μηδὲν ἄγαν]." Barrett (1964, 210) points out that the old proverb is treated grammatically in the Nurse's phrase as "a kind of indeclinable noun," such is its familiarity.
155. 354–55: οὐκ ἀνασχέτ'· οὐκ ἀνέξομαι / ζῶσ', ἐχθρὸν ἦμαρ, ἐχθρὸν εἰσορῶ φάος. / ῥίψω μεθήσω σῶμα. On repetition in the *thrénos,* see Kranz (1933, 188–89).

will bear. The bathetic effect is a caricature of Phaidra's earlier lyric; and indeed the Nurse is as quick to recover from her passion as Phaidra was retentive of hers.

The characterization of the Nurse is a blend of two potentially disparate elements. She is at one and the same time a comic servant and a parody Sophist. In attacking Phaidra's determination to die, the Nurse employs a celebrated argument in which the gods of traditional myth are used as a model for human behavior.[156] She derides the seriousness of Phaidra and her malady: love would indeed be a terrible thing, if all who experienced lust should have to die for it (441–42). Aphrodite, on the other hand, is great and powerful, a goddess who commands even the gods.[157] It is those who struggle against Kypris who are treated violently, not those who yield. If gods can endure *erôs,* so must mortals, "Unless your father sired you under special agreement!"[158] The joshing, hectoring tone suits the Nurse's vulgarity, while at the same time her arguments are plainly marked as deriving, not from her, but from certain learned iconoclasts, such as Euripides himself. "Those who have writings of the ancients and are themselves always among the Muses,"[159] claims the Nurse, know that gods like Zeus and Eos were subject to erotic vagaries. Euripides may mean the audience to understand himself by those who have libraries, but he must be understood to refer to

156. For this argument, see the discussion above, in Chap. 8, on *Herakles,* where Theseus uses it. It is less perfectly adapted to that locus, since Theseus' point is that we, like the gods, must accept suffering; the original purpose of this argument, as in *Clouds* 1080–82, is to provide a rationale for sexual license. See Knox (1952, 18–21) esp. p. 19: "The powerful speech . . . is easily recognizable as contemporary sophistic rhetoric at its cleverest and worst." See Turato (1974, 158–59); A. Schmitt (1977, 32 n.64).

157. Turato points out that a respect for Aphrodite is another mark of the Nurse's plebeian status (1974, 156–57; see also 159–60); see line 13.

158. 459ff.:

σὺ δ' οὐκ ἀνέξῃ χρῆν σ' ἐπὶ ῥητοῖς ἄρα
πατέρα φυτεύειν . . .

The phrase *epi rhêtois,* "under (special) conditions," caps the joke with a prosaic phrase. Though not very common (cf. Hdt. 5.57.2; Platon *Symp.* 213a.2; Thuc. 1.122.1; Andokides 3.22) the phrase always seems to imply a truce or treaty that contains concrete specifications about the behavior of the parties; for its tendency to acquire an ironic tone, see the Thukydides reference: it is rare for war to be conducted *epi rhêtois.*

159. 451–52:

ὅσοι μὲν οὖν γραφάς τε τῶν παλαιτέρων
ἔχουσιν αὐτοί τ' εἰσὶν ἐν μούσαις ἀεὶ . . .

The *graphai* may be pictures but are more likely to be texts (see Barrett [1964, 242]).

himself when the Muses come into it.[160] The passage invites us to treat the Nurse as a mouthpiece for, or a caricature of, these deviant intellectuals.

In a play where the protagonists are given such a sympathetic quality, the Nurse stands out in sharp contrast. There are obvious parallels with the role of Theseus in *Herakles.* Both characters are ironized more than the protagonists, to whom they form a foil. Both use the same argument to administer bracing therapy in a rather heavy-handed way to a friend who despairs of life.[161] Like the heroine of *Hekabe* or the Autourgos in *Elektra,* the Nurse appears both in her own character and as the mouthpiece of certain kinds of rhetoric and argumentation. Unlike Phaidra, she gives a well-organized and pointed speech, directed to a clearly defined rhetorical aim. Her pert and facile reasoning, along with the note of the ludicrous that she injects, recalls the ironic tone of *Andromache* or *Alkestis,* or the arguments of Iason in *Medeia.* But the Nurse is not posing as a heroic character,[162] so that in *Hippolytos* there is a contrast between parodic and idealized elements of the Sophistic, the thought of Phaidra and Hippolytos representing the aspects, later associated with Sokrates, that offer a more "serious" and less ironic approach to philosophical problems.

The devotion of the Nurse to Phaidra, though exaggerated and rendered amusing, is the central pillar of her motivation;[163] and, judged by this standard, the Nurse is a failure, since she loses both Phaidra's life and Phaidra's love. The harsh words with which the queen repudiates her servant (706–9), permit the audience to get as clear a moral bearing on the Nurse as they do on the other characters. In her eagerness for survival, both for herself and for her charge, the Nurse resembles many other Euripidean protagonists;[164] but she differs signally from Hippolytos, who may be said to choose death over dishonor, and from Phaidra, whose longing for death undergoes only a brief and disastrous remission under the Nurse's influence.[165] In this play the ironizing features that elsewhere thwart the development of an unqualified sympathy for the major protagonists are given to a figure that we would never mistake for a *spoudaios.* The morally questionable and undignified aspects

160. See Kretz (1934, 30ff.).

161. Unlike the Nurse, Theseus is admirable; he is also less deeply characterized, so that his use of an amoralist argument does less to affect our perception of him.

162. Knox (1952, 18): "The Nurse has no aristocratic code of conduct." See Merklin (1964, 72): she seems to represent an ordinary and common way of thinking, presented with pejorative overtones.

163. See her opening comments (186): the mental pain that she mentions (*lypê phrenôn*) can derive only from sympathy and concern for Phaidra. This theme appears again at lines 253–61 and 285–87.

164. Note the import of her beautiful anapaestic lines (191ff.), in which the attachment of mortals to life is called a vain *erôs* (δυσέρωτες δὴ φαινόμεθ' ὄντες).

165. Turato (1974, 161 n.44) emphasizes the Nurse's aim to save Phaidra's life.

of Phaidra's dilemma are purged by being visited on a lowborn scapegoat, whose dismissal leaves Phaidra alone in her sad and elevated status.

The function of social status in creating audience identification was discussed above in the chapter on *Elektra*. As F. Turato has pointed out, both protagonists in *Hippolytos* are alike in their dedication to the standards of the aristocracy.[166] Phaidra, a woman, embodies traditional concerns about the reputation and honor of the family for whose male inheritors she is the (endangered and polluted) source. Hippolytos, however, is a representative not of old standards, but of new and more demanding ones that create a new image of the *spoudaios*. Both come into conflict with the Nurse, and her speech of rebuttal is a polemic against both of these seekers after moral precision. But since neither protagonist can fit the traditional pattern of the *agathos*, the contrast with the Nurse seems to be necessary to stiffen the social distinctions that are inseparable from the effect of the *spoudaion*.[167]

In their use of class and social rank, the other plays analyzed above make a strong contrast to *Hippolytos*. In *Hekabe* the old queen is forced into the world of slavery, there to learn the trade of rhetor and the analogous trade of bawd; Polyxene, with her stern loyalty to aristocratic status and standards, remains a sentimentalized and somewhat unreal figure. In *Elektra* the lowborn Autourgos is the moral point of reference for all others in the play, with the result that heroic values are profoundly distorted. In *Herakles* the most aristocratic and most powerful of heroes is shown to be akin to the lowest common denominator of humanity, first in his love for family, and second in his weakness. These social configurations are reproduced in many other Euripidean plays.[168] The different effect of *Hippolytos* is caused by the conjunction of strong audience sympathy with class lines and class ideology. Combined with the dramaturgical mechanism of "guiltless guilt" analyzed above, the social factor gives a powerful momentum to audience sympathy and identification, directing them toward and focusing them upon the two protagonists.

In *Hippolytos* the strong flavors and dissonant charms of other Euripidean work are modified and rearranged into patterns that do not disrupt emotional

166. 1974, 150ff.

167. Knox (1952, 19) associates the Nurse with democratic styles and methods, characterized by relativism, expediency, flexibility. But note that these contrasts in political style are always paralleled and elaborated in literary and generic terms as well, e.g., in the contrast between Odysseus and Achilleus. Segal (1970.2) has discussed lines 1465–66, where Hippolytos is referred to as being one of the "great" (τῶν μεγάλων). Cf. the close of *Hippolytos Veiled,* in which Hippolytos is referred to as a *hêrôs* (446 N2).

168. There is a wide variety of tactics available. Plays in which women confront men (*Medeia*), slaves confront masters (*Andromache, Hypsipyle, Alexandros, Troiades, Hekabe*), or heroes are humiliated and lowered in the world (*Helene, Telephos* and *Bellerophon*) all contribute to the same effect.

participation. The play's indulgence in poetic richness and beautiful writing enhances identification, as it permits more unalloyed enjoyments; and the literary hedonist in each of us may regret that Euripides did not produce more plays of this sort.[169] That is a matter of taste; even those who have—as I do—a preference for the abrasive style of ironic drama may be moved by the appealing pathos of this play. But, if *Hippolytos* represents a Euripidean high mimetic, we can still note differences that sever it from Sophoclean art. The Sophoclean protagonists, in their lonely suffering, embody still the best values of the threatened community. But Hippolytos is too eccentric and Phaidra too closely enmeshed in community standards to have such paradigmatic or representative value; and in the end the touching death of Hippolytos lacks some of the heavier reverberations of the Sophoclean catastrophes. Instead, the play finds its best resolution, as most Euripidean plays do, in the interplay between the contrasting moralities exemplified by each of the dual protagonists.[170] Phaidra, who dies to change shame to honor, and Hippolytos, who endures shame for the sake of his personal conception of virtue, define between them a single human tragedy, just as the play is divided between two goddesses whose action and significance are really united.[171] The opposing value systems of Euripidean dualism have not been purged from *Hippolytos.* Instead they appear in balance, each with its representative, each with "a sort of nobility." The aetiological ritual founded by Artemis at the end merges them and their tragedies, assuring that Phaidra's love will not be kept silent[172] and that Hippolytos, his name forever linked with Phaidra's, will be honored by girls who are leaving the precinct of Artemis, in which he will remain.

IV.B. THE ROLE OF THE GODS: *HIPPOLYTOS* AND OTHER PLAYS

While it is true that *Bakchai* and *Hippolytos* are different in many ways, there are evident similarities that have led critics to associate the two in a

169. F. Schlegel well expressed the voluptuous satisfactions of art that gives us what we want (1979, 217): modern poetry leaves a sting in the heart and takes more than it gives. "*Befriedigung* findet sich nur in dem vollständigen Genuss, wo jede erregte Erwartung erfüllt, auch die kleinste Unruhe aufgelös't wird; wo alle Sehnsucht schweigt." (See also p. 219.) Schlegel also suggests the reasons why artists have difficulties satisfying these demands: the new becomes old; the rare, common; "und die Stachel des Reizenden werden stumpf" (223).

170. Turato has a long note on the controversy over which protagonist is the dominant one, and he notes that many psychological interpretations give Phaidra the place of importance (1974, 150 n.83). Interpretations that favor Hippolytos over Phaidra may tend to be oriented in the direction of the concept of (Sophoclean) tragic heroism; cf. Crocker (1957, 246).

171. See Knox (1952, 28–29), who points to similarity in the behavior of each goddess, as well as in the imagery related to each; see also Frischer (1970, 88ff.), on "imagistic confluence."

172. 1429–30: κ'οὐκ ἀνώνυμος πεσὼν / ἐρὼς ὁ Φαίδρας εἰς σὲ σιγηθήσεται. Note that Phaidra's whole aim throughout was to conceal this same *erôs.*

special category of the Euripidean oeuvre. The final step in assessing *Hippolytos* is to discuss what it shares with *Bakchai,* namely a particular treatment of divine roles. Aside from *Ion,* no other plays both begin and end with divine appearances. Both plays focus to some extent on the full relation between humans and gods, including the aspect of religious devotion or worship. The plays also share two other traits. In no other Euripidean plays but these do the central figures of the play end the drama in death. And, although it is difficult to get final agreement on general impressions, both these plays appear to be richer in sensuous imagery than the other works of this poet.[173] In *Hippolytos,* however, these traits are associated with the generation of strong audience involvement, while *Bakchai* makes a more typically Euripidean use of ironic or ludicrous elements.[174]

In all the plays except *Hippolytos, Bakchai,* and *Herakles,*[175] the divinities who appear on stage are benevolent ones, who intend to help, direct, exonerate, and comfort the human protagonists.[176] But only in *Orestes* does a divine protector come on stage to face human protagonists whose lives he has affected. When Athena alludes to Apollon's absence in *Ion,* the effect is to play upon this, evidently conventional, extenuation of divine responsibility. The reason for the taboo is evident when we see it broken. K. Reinhardt (1957) has shown the effect of absurdity and unreason created by the epiphany of *Orestes:* the resolution is unequal in weight to the dreadful events that preceded it, and the question of the god's responsibility intrudes too powerfully. In *Hippolytos, Bakchai,* and *Herakles,* by contrast, far from being benevolent and propitious, the gods behave in the style of old myth, as destroyers and tormentors of the protagonists.[177] In *Herakles* these powerful and malevolent deities work as in other plays through subordinate divine agents, but the absurdity introduced into the play by divine responsibility is

173. For *Bakchai* the very detailed analysis of Segal (1981, and see also the fine earlier book of Winnington-Ingram [1948]) is sufficient evidence, along with the extensive bibliography listed there.

174. For humor in the notorious scene between Kadmos and Tiresias, see Deichgräber (1935, 327). The strongest piece of irony, however, comes in the last scene, where indirect evidence indicates a grotesque reassemblage of Pentheus' body by his mother—see Kirchoff (1853, 83ff.); and Dodds ([1944] 1960, 57, 232). The centerpiece of the play, of course, the travesty of Pentheus, is itself a hideous piece of humor; see Boer (1967).

175. These plays were associated by Dawe (1968) with tragic catastrophes in the Aeschylean or Sophoclean manner. *Troiades* also is a special case: as O'Neill (1941, 289ff.) pointed out, the gods do not directly affect the fates of the protagonists, and their plans serve only as a foil to the main action (see also Albini [1970, 313]; and C. Friedrich [1955, 39]).

176. See Strohm (1949–50, 153) on the good intentions of the gods. I would not agree, however, with his supposition that things go wrong only because of human mistakes.

177. See Conacher's reference (1967, 28) to the "neo-Homeric primitivism" of the gods in *Hippolytos.*

driven to violent extremes. In *Hippolytos* and *Bakchai*, while the gods inspire anger with their cruelty and unfairness to human beings, there are compensating factors that prevent the absurdity of *Orestes* or *Herakles*.

Along with a vivid portrayal of divine malevolence, we also receive strong intimations of the possibility of religious connection with the gods. These intimations come in *Bakchai* from the magnificent choral odes and in *Hippolytos* from the opening scene and the hero's prayer to the goddess, a passage notable for its beauty of language and its hints of deeper significance. The absence of this kind of poetic style in other Euripidean dramas is explained by its effect in these plays, where our surrender to poetic beauty serves a precise dramatic purpose. In *Hippolytos* divine evil and divine beauty are divided between the "bad" Aphrodite and the "good" goddess, Artemis, with whom Hippolytos maintains a kind of mystical communion. But Aphrodite too is projected through the language and imagery of the play as powerful, mysterious, and *semnê*.[178] In *Bakchai* this paradox is more frontally presented, in that the beauty of Dionysiac worship coexists and is coextensive with the horror of Dionysiac violence.[179] Although the divine persona, as it directs human dooms without morality or understanding,[180] appears as empty and absurd as elsewhere in Euripides, we also feel the mystery of divine power that inspires worship. Since Greek divinities, at this deeper level, do seem to represent central aspects of human experience,[181] it is tempting to interpret the plays in a rationalizing or euhemerizing way.[182] But these gods also continue to represent with remarkable fidelity the motivations and behavior of Homeric divinities. The result is a dual focus, never entirely resolved, on divinity as the mysterious object of cult and worship, and divinity as anthropomorphic agent. This dual picture of the gods makes them seem at the same time both awesome and despicable.

The gods are problematic and have overtones of the absurd, not just in the plays where they appear as avengers, but even, or especially, in the plays where they are saviors. As we have seen in *Elektra,* their attempts to reassure and comfort human beings go awry, because of a hopeless discrepancy

178. See the analysis of Segal (1965).

179. See Segal (1982, 53, 232 – 40); Winnington-Ingram (1948, 11, 39, and 174ff.: the temptations in communal religious unity).

180. See Chromik (1967, 289 – 90): *dikê* may rule human affairs, but the gods have nothing to do with it.

181. See Chromik (1967, 76).

182. For an early example, see Dodds (1929, 102); cf. Conacher (1967, 29). More recently Blomqvist (1982, 410 – 11) has stated as an assumption that will be generally accepted that the Euripidean gods are only metaphors for something else.

between human and divine nature.[183] It is inevitable that the plays which show benevolent gods arranging everything for their favorites may make us feel most uneasy and uncertain, or that this careful providence coincides with an increasingly insistent emphasis on the randomness and meaninglessness of human life.[184] We are even more likely to be thrust back upon the baffling mystery of human experience, when the presiding deities themselves are seen to be of no help. Euripides found the use of divine actors such a wellspring of irony that, even with all the ethical safeguards that usually cushion the divine honor of the benevolent *dei ex machina,* the paradoxes of human suffering and divine responsibility still reverberate through the plays. When the device of divine impulsion is carried to its logical extreme, as it is in *Herakles,* the result is the oxymoronic combination of a powerful and moving human tragedy with a concentration of irony that seems to dissolve even the poetic fiction itself.

Perversely, but predictably, the relation between human and divinity in the exceptional plays, *Hippolytos* and *Bakchai,* is ameliorated by the final nature of the catastrophes. These are the only extant plays in which the central protagonists do not survive. In all the other plays, whether or not gods are involved, the necessity for survival and continued coping pulls the protagonists back down to everyday level and keeps them hopelessly involved in the compromises of life. *Herakles* is again the most extreme case: if life must be lived on, then the agency of the gods becomes less significant, and the help and comfort of other human beings become more important. But in their deaths, Hippolytos, Phaidra, and even Pentheus become timeless figures, in a permanent relationship to the gods who destroyed them.

In choosing to involve divine actors with dramatic events directly, Euripides returned, although with signal differences, to the model of Aeschylean drama. In *Hippolytos,* although he employs some Sophoclean devices to mitigate the responsibility of the protagonists, the use of Aphrodite as motivator leaves it possible to explore erotic passion directly. The Sophoclean method of exoneration goes a step farther: his Phaidra, thinking her husband dead, cannot experience the mental struggles of the Euripidean heroine; and in *Trachiniai* the experience of jealousy never really touches Deianeira at all. This difference between two forms of drama has been confused by the identification of the Euripidean model with specifically female and sexual passion (*Leidenschaft*). But other emotions can provoke violent deeds, as in the rage of Aias. In Sophokles' treatment the hero's passion is thrust outside the frame of the play, so that we concern ourselves, not with

183. See Fuqua (1976, 78): Euripides has separated gods and humans into "distinct entities, each with their own criteria of existence and normative standards." See also Hathorn (1957, 211): these are "two ill-yoked teams," providing a dual view of human experience.

184. See Strohm (1949–50, 152–53).

the motivation for Aias' attack on the Atreidai, but with the aftermath, his attempt to maintain his integrity in the face of overwhelming threats. For most Sophoclean plays the mechanism of exoneration and extenuation, through the ambivalent *hamartia* or through other devices, guarantees that it will *not* be the passions of the protagonists that motivate the action.[185] While in *Trachiniai* Herakles' passion for Iole does bring about his downfall, the focus of the action and the immediate cause of the catastrophe is not what Herakles does but the mistake that Deianeira makes. The Sophoclean Elektra and Philoktetes hate their enemies; but in the end it is the lonely defense of integrity that is the focus of their stories. Kreon in *Antigone* is one exception to this group,[186] in that he does commit an intentional act that leads to his doom. But Kreon is a foil for the protagonist; and his punishment is the final vindication of her integrity.[187] In *Hippolytos,* by contrast, a combined use of divine actors and the techniques of exoneration permits us to explore motivation and culpability, without a loss of sympathy.

J.-P. Vernant has argued that tragedy in the hands of Aischylos and Sophokles dealt with a crucial and intractable problem in the division between human and divine responsibility.[188] If Euripides does not make much use of the device of innocent error that we quite often find in Sophoclean plays, he also seldom employs the Aeschylean device in which a protagonist is presented with a hard choice, offering pain and guilt on both sides of the balance.[189] In both cases, the problems that tragedy chooses to emphasize are exotic ones, specially selected to present the dilemma of responsibility and fate in an intelligible way. Euripides' method, as usual, is both straightforward and subversive. In most of the plays his protagonists, faced with concrete and unambiguous threats, move into action with vigor and decision.[190] But this very obvious and natural way of building a plot does not "work" in terms of producing the effects proper to the tragic genre. As they attempt to act, Euripidean protagonists reveal the weakness of human integrity, instead of celebrating its power. Involved in the meshes of life by their sufferings and by their deeds, these figures are dissipated and used up by experience, eventually finding a place in wider landscapes that, without

185. Müffelmann (1965, 1) remarks that motivation is more important in Aischylos and Euripides than in Sophokles. On moral issues, see Stoessl (1966, 100): the Euripidean Palamedes drama reintroduces questions of guilt and responsibility that had been muted by Sophokles; and Matthaei (1918, 124), "misguided by Aristotelian tradition, the literary world has been a little inclined to gloss over . . . wickedness"; but Euripides is "profoundly courageous" in confronting this problem.

186. As Saïd has shown (1978, 398, 410).

187. See Stinton (1975, 240).

188. Vernant & Vidal-Naquet (1972, 35 – 40). See also the following article "Ébauches de la volonté," and discussion of the issue of "free will" above, Section I.B.

189. See Vernant & Vidal-Naquet (1972, 44ff.); Saïd (1978, 163 – 66).

190. See the schema delineated by Jaekel ("ΠΑΘΟΝΤΙ ΑΝΤΙΔΡΑΝ"; 1973, 28ff.).

transcending or erasing it, include human suffering as a lesser element. As exemplary figures Euripidean protagonists fail again and again, forcing us to confront the deep flaw, or paradox, or mystery for which tragedy exists. In *Hippolytos* and *Bakchai,* even though the tone is less ironic, the prominent intervention of the gods serves to keep this paradox in focus. At every moment in every play this various and shifting, yet constantly maintained, balance between reason and unreason threatens to collapse into absurdity. But, in its bold challenge to the enigma of tragedy, this "dance above the abyss" is as central and as germane to the tradition of the art form as is the work of Euripides' great predecessors and rivals.

Appendix A
Melodrama

The use of the critical term "melodrama" is a long-standing one. An early association with Euripidean drama was made by A. W. Verrall (1905, x), who remarks that *Helene,* an unserious play (47ff.), is commonly regarded as a "melodrama." The term developed out of popular French plays combining pantomime, music, ballet, and other excitements; and it was next associated with British popular drama of the nineteenth century. (See the historical analysis of J. L. Smith [1973, 1 – 6].)

The most extended treatment of a theme that runs through most modern treatments of tragedy is to be found in R. B. Heilman's *Tragedy and Melodrama* (1968), a book that makes a determined attempt to develop the concept of separate genres, only to fall continually into a severely normative and prescriptive stance. See particularly the ingenuous admission: "To take *melodrama,* which is usually a derogatory term that means popular, machine-made entertainments, and to apply it to a wide range of literature that includes much serious work ... may seem capricious to the point of scandal" (75). (See the confirming analysis of J. L. Smith [1973, 7], who follows Heilman's categories, even while admitting that melodrama is used generally as "a blanket term of abuse and contempt.") Heilman points out that what recommends the distinction to him is the fact that "to most people melodrama and tragedy will seem mutually exclusive" (75 n.). While Heilman argues that the prescriptive and evaluative approach to melodrama is wrong (75, 228), in fact he severely faults plays that become "melodramatic'' when tragic tone is called for. While he admits that the reverse would also be a fault, he argues that offenses against the rules of melodrama need not be considered, since "melodrama can generally be counted on to take care of itself'' (101). In fact, plays that are faulty in any way turn out to be melodramas, e.g., *Richard II* (187ff.).

Melodrama is "a world of shock and thrill and sensationalism''; it may traffic in ideas, but these tend to be treated in "a hackneyed or easily acceptable way'' (76). It presents the "simple pleasures of conventional or straightforward conflict, decked out in the various excitement of threats, surprises . . . all this against a background of ideas and emotions widely accepted at the time'' (78). (Cf. J. L. Smith [1973, 6]: "vulgar extravagance, implausible motivation, meretricious sensation and spurious pathos.'') In Heilman's view the plays of Ibsen are melodramas and use the "same conception of character'' as do cowboy adventure novels (80). Severe indictments of O'Neill (49ff.) and Arthur Miller (233ff.) follow. (For an attempt to apply the categories of Heilman to late Sophokles, see Craik [1979, 1980]).

Originally used to refer to the combination of elegance and effectiveness   .
in style and construction with a relatively flat or unsatisfying aesthetic content, the term suggests the stylistic effect of an outworn convention of the "high mimetic.'' (For this term, see Frye [1957] and discussion in Chapters 2 and 7, above, on *Elektra*.) Because of its hackneyed nature, or because it is used inappropriately, the language or stage behavior that would ordinarily produce a strong emotional reaction from the audience is judged not to work. This judgment may reflect one of two things: either the "melodramatic'' bit fails and falls flat, leaving the audience cold; or, although the audience is thrilled, the critic feels that they—and perhaps the critic too—were moved by something meretricious which ought to have left them cold. This latter, evaluative meaning is of course basic to Heilman's theory. Clearly there could be two views of the second type of melodrama, and the subimplication is that there are certain sorts of dramatic enjoyment that are inferior and that will be depreciated by people of taste. (For the sizable element of class snobbery involved, see J. L. Smith [1973, 15ff.], who makes plain that "melodrama'' took over the London theater when a "vast workforce of uneducated country people'' were brought into town by the industrial revolution.)

Another recent analysis of tragic and nontragic drama (Styan [1968, 64]) employs the term in a way that seems more useful, to refer to the familiar or overly familiar dramatic conventions of emotional expression and plot situation prevalent in nineteenth-century European drama. Once the term has been divested of its prescriptive content and is recognized as indicating a style of formal rigidity and mannerism, it also becomes susceptible of valid critical use. If a dramatic situation can become hackneyed or "melodramatic'' by the exaggeration or mechanical manipulation of certain conventions, then—while the standards for determining such an effect would manifestly be very different for Euripidean theater and for the nineteenth-century authors—the effect itself could be present in any well-developed dramatic tradition. A clumsy author would betray his lack of art by unintentional mannerism; an effective author could presumably use mannerism as powerfully as he would use other dramatic techniques. (Heilman [24 – 25], followed by J. L. Smith [1973, 62 – 63] attempts to make a the distinction between tragedy and melodrama, according to whether the hero is "responsible" for his downfall or not. For this problem, that of "tragic guilt," see discussion in Chapters 8 and 9 above, on *Herakles* and *Hippolytos*.)

Mannerism was one of the primary indictments brought against Euripides by the Schlegels; see Schwinge (1968.1, 15 – 19) on the frequent references in early scholarship and criticism to "hässliche Manier." A discussion of formalism and mannerism in Euripides appears in Chapter 4, above. For the mechanism by which a convention becomes perceived as "dead," "rigid," or "empty," see the analyses of the Russian formalist or structuralist critics, e.g., Shklovskij ([1916] 1969).

Appendix B
Albin Lesky and *Alkestis*

Alkestis has been a touchstone of Euripidean criticism for many years. The work of one of the most prominent figures in German scholarship on tragedy, Albin Lesky, was almost wholly dominated by this play. While Lesky produced valuable articles, particularly on the psychology of Euripidean drama, he wrote little criticism of individual plays, limiting himself largely to the play with which he had begun his scholarly career in Euripidean studies, *Alkestis* (*Alkestis, der Mythos und das Drama* [1925]; see reviews by Morel [1926], Ebeling [1927], and Drexler [1927]).

Alkestis seems peculiarly suited to force the antinomies of Euripidean critical positions into sharp definition, as Lesky was aware (1957–58, 345; cf. 1976, 217): "An den Schwierigkeiten, die hier für uns gegeben sind, scheiden sich nach wie vor die Interpreten in einer Weise, in der Entscheidendes für die gesamte Euripidesdeutung enthalten ist." By the strong emotion it provokes, Alkestis' death scene makes a particularly marked contrast with succeeding scenes, an anomaly that earlier criticism had attempted to explain by the anomalous generic position of the "prosatyric" play (see Bloch [1901, II.114–18]). But later critics, who felt that they had detected rationalism and irony or "satire" in Euripidean drama, were quick to point out that such traits were not limited to *Alkestis*. And, in their turn, critics concerned to interpret *Alkestis* as a portrait of Alkestis' love and sacrifice refused to allow the tragic content to be dismissed, as it would be if the play were to be understood as essentially comic. (This was basically

Lesky's position [1925, 80, 85]. For an earlier anticipation, see Bloch [1901, II.113]: Euripides wrote the play wholly for the sake of the charming portrait of Alkestis that it afforded.)

The major obstacle to the straightforward interpretation of the play as a romantic drama is the role of Admetos. When he repudiates his father in acrimonious language over the body of his wife, it is hard to overlook the painful inappropriateness of such unfilial behavior at such an occasion. A further exacerbation is the fact that funerals in Greek culture were important precisely as solemn reminders of the solidarity of the family and of the bond between parents and children, which Admetos here tries to forswear (662–65). (See the telling point made by Lennep [1949, 112] that severe provocation, such as selling a child for prostitution, removed the obligation for support but did not remove the obligation of the son to provide burial for the father.) Further, the retorts of his father seem to place Admetos in an even worse light.

Lesky argued that the scene at the funeral should simply be overlooked as a rhetorical exercise without further meaning (1925, 82. See later repetitions: 1938, 143; 1956, 160.). As Verrall had used religious arguments to excuse the omission of certain parts of the plays from his interpretation, Lesky used structural studies to argue that the independence of separable parts in Euripidean style permitted his interpretation (1938, 143). Similarly, he later suggested that the work of T. v. Wilamowitz and W. Zürcher invalidated the attempts of psychologically oriented critics to interpret Alkestis' behavior in a cynical light (1956, 159–60; cf. 1957–58, 345–46). Lesky's own articles on the psychology of Euripidean plays, while they were valuable in themselves, also provided a support for this continuing polemic, since it was on the *Labilität* (1958, 45) of the Euripidean psyche that Lesky had built his interpretation of Admetos (1956, 160; for psychology in Euripides, see Lesky [1958, 127ff.; 1960; 1972.2]).

While Lesky's views on the play underwent some modification, he remained convinced that the dissonant elements in Admetos' role were a minor flaw that must be overlooked in a correct interpretation of the play. (See [1956] 1972.1, 298; "Der angeklagte Admet," 1964, 210–13; 1976, 216–17). The dissonance, Lesky believed, stemmed from an "Antinomie" that lay deep in the personality and work of Euripides, in fact in the traditional split between "poet" and "thinker" (1956, 207. In the third edition of *Tragische Dichtung* the term reappears [(1956) 1972.1, 512]; as does the heading "Dichter und Denker.") In a real sense one might say that such an interpretation, while designed to save the play as a work of art worthy of serious attention, does so in a paradoxical way by impugning the artistic quality and coherence of the piece. (This point was made by an anonymous reviewer of Lesky [1925] in *JHS* 1926.)

Lesky's role as a historian of scholarship and a summarizer of "progress" in research to date left him largely at the mercy of the recurring paradoxes in Euripidean studies, and his espousal of the anti-ironist viewpoint on the *Alkestis* had a profound influence on a generation of scholars, especially in Germany. I have not chosen to devote a chapter in this book to this play simply because it seems to me that most of the work has already been done by others; a valid and effective interpretation can be stitched together from the many articles written by scholars whose critical perspectives were less narrowly focused on the romantic aspect of Alkestis' role.

One aspect of the ironist interpretation of *Alkestis* that was rightly attacked by Lesky was the attempt to derive from the dissonances in the play a psychological view of Alkestis that was in a limited sense Verrallian, since the attitudes assigned to her are nowhere present in the surface of the play. An early example is U. v. Wilamowitz (1906.1, 25ff.), who assumes that Alkestis' less than romantic behavior reflects her disillusionment with her husband. (See also Fritz [1956, 39ff.]; Schwinge [1970].) In fact Alkestis' behavior makes sense in terms of Hellenic cultural norms for women, once we have allowed for the special and awkward situation in which she and her husband find themselves.

A major problem in interpreting *Alkestis* has been the deep confusion between *erôs* and *philia* in the European terms for "love." The use of the term "amore" by C. Diano and H. Paratore (in a discussion following the paper of Sicking [1967, 166ff.]) was attacked by R. Cantarella (171ff.), who pointed out the "romantic and Christian" basis of their interpretation (see also Paduano [1968] and criticism by Garvie [Review of P. (1973, 86)]). A. M. Dale's truism that Alkestis "of course . . . loves Admetos—what else made her die for him?" (1954, xxvi, quoted with approval by Lesky [(1956) 1972.1, 298]) rests on the same misapprehension. (Erbse [1972, 39] seems to suggest that we should translate "I, putting you first [ἐγώ σε πρεσβεύουσα]," as "Ich liebe dich"!) The Hellenic marriage necessarily implied *philia* (see Scodel [1979]) and did not exclude *erôs*; but it would be fair to say that erotic attachment was optional and not obligatory. Since Alkestis in dying is showing *aretê* in doing what—in the highest possible sense—social obligation might demand of her, the erotic aspect of her action is necessarily secondary. On the other hand, in the case of Admetos, who is attempting to compensate for this immeasurable gift, erotic motifs are a most appropriate decoration, even if their baroque extravagance does suggest the inner falsity of his position.

Myres (1917, 200–4) pointed out the motivation for Alkestis' heroism: she shows her deep bond with Admetos by sacrificing herself to the preservation of that bond, namely their children and the family unit which those children constitute. (See also W. D. Smith [1960.1, 137]; for an opposing view, see Paduano [1968, 45 – 47].) Euripides did not have to explain to the audience what was part of their background knowledge about life: young women, once widowed, would ordinarily return to their fathers' houses, leaving behind the children of the first marriage, and enter a new marriage (see Erdmann [1934, 408]; Schaps [1979, 81 – 82]). Only Admetos, who being male was responsible for himself, could keep the household together after his mate's death. (Erdmann [1934, 403 – 4] also points out that there were numerous proverbs urging men not to contract a second marriage: a widower had the power to make such a decision, as a widow did not.)

The interpretations of Sheppard (1919) and Scodel (1979)—see also W. D. Smith (1960.1), Kullmann (1967, 145), Fritz (1956), Musurillo (1972), Bradley (1980)—reveal the ironic twist at the heart of the play. Admetos has accepted a gift that he can never repay and can therefore never enjoy. The submotif of the host-guest relation with Herakles turns on exactly similar problems of embarrassing and inappropriate gifts. Admetos' courtesy, quixotic and self-willed as it is, is of a piece with the odd interpretation he has of the duties of parents and spouses. He thoroughly humiliates Herakles by his extravagant hospitality, which puts his friend in the position of one who, as we might say, "presumes." In such a position, just as in the position of Admetos vis-à-vis Alkestis, the giver gains prestige at the expense of the recipient, who must scramble desperately to repay, in order to regain his position as a good and equal *philos* (see Scodel [1979, 52 – 54]). Admetos promises social isolation and total celibacy in an attempt to equal Alkestis in generosity; but his extravagant vows are contradicted almost immediately by his reception of Herakles (see W. D. Smith [1960.1, 143]), as well as later, by his acceptance of Herakles' "gift" of a veiled woman. Herakles, however, is a man of remarkable power, who is able to settle his own social account and save Admetos as well, with a single gesture.

The deathbed scene, taken quite by itself, is an exquisite and touching moment, pushed just a trace below the heroic into what Frye would call the "low mimetic." But there are dissonances, which for the time pass unnoticed in a flood of genuine emotion. Alkestis cannot respond adequately to Admetos' protestations (Bloch [1901, I.37 – 39]; Stumpo [1960, 115 – 16]), because she has more serious concerns than the feelings of her husband. Admetos, as has often been noticed, uses conventional mourning formulas (pointed out by Rivier [1973, 135]) in a manner that is just slightly wrong, since he ignores what is unique about this deathbed scene. (See Fritz [1956, 37]; W. D. Smith [1960.1, 131]; Conacher [1967, 337]; Kullmann [1967, 132, 133]; Musurillo [1972, 278]; Bradley [1980, 117].) The ordinary mourner does not benefit so signally by the decease of his beloved.

The trigger to unleash audience awareness of the repressed dissonances is the remarkable scene with Pheres, when all the bad aspects of Admetos' position emerge with a vengeance. (See Fritz [1956, 60]; Müffelmann [1965, 10–11], who remarks that Pheres reveals to Admetos what Alkestis' gift implies about its recipient; Kullmann [1967, 141]. An analogous effect in miniature, the treatment of Polyxene's death scene, is discussed in Chapter 6 on *Hekabe*.) The argument that we may ignore what Pheres says because Pheres is unlikable (See Lesky [1925, 82; 1964, 213; 1972.1, 295]; Dale [1954, xxv]; Vicenzi [1960, 530–31]; Albini [1961, 25–26]; Burnett [1965, 249]; Steidle [1968, 143–44].) goes against the basic given of dramatic performance, namely the cogency and power of whatever is presented through mimesis. Unpleasant truths are usually spoken by unpleasant people, and Pheres' nasty characteristics make him more rather than less likely to stick in the memories of the audience. Nor does he by any means have the worst of the argument; and—as winners in the *agôn* do elsewhere—he speaks last. (See A. C. Schlesinger [1937, 69–70].)

The last scene, rather perversely interpreted by some critics as a proof of Admetos' constancy (See Myres [1917, 214–18]; Sheppard [1919, 46]; Kumaniecki [1930, 10]; Chromik [1967, 18]; Rivier [1973, 142]; Hübner [1981]; Erbse [1972, 49–50]. For disagreement, see W. D. Smith [1960.1, 145]; Bradley [1980, 125].), runs up against the same brutal realities of stage production. The whole scene is summed up in the significant gesture in which Admetos capitulates to Herakles and accepts the stranger woman, an act that Admetos himself has labeled a betrayal of Alkestis' memory. (For the importance of gesture in the scene, see Ortkemper [1969, 35ff.].) The fact that we know the stranger woman to be Alkestis herself makes no difference, since Admetos *believes* that he is betraying his promise. Admetos is embarrassed here doubly, since he is forced to choose between his two contradictory pretensions and ends by failing both as perfect host and as ever-faithful widower. (See Beye [1959, 117]; Bradley [1980, 122, 125].) This scene is an exact requital for Herakles, who by gaining the upper hand in the contest of gift giving, revenges himself for Admetos' embarrassing favor and—as he boasts—proves himself a proper guest (*gennaios xenos,* see Scodel [1979, 59, 61]). No gift can top that of a human life—ψυχῆς γὰρ οὐδέν ἐστι τιμιώτερον (301).

When Admetos promises a "better life than the one before," (1157–58) he must mean more than merely that he will be happy now that Alkestis is back; and he therefore must be implying some improvement on his way of life before Alkestis' death. The question as to whether this and the phrase with which Admetos acknowledges his late learning (*arti manthanô,* 940) refer to a "change of heart" is largely predicated on the odd standards of "character" and "change" developed by scholars like Zürcher. If we ask whether Admetos would now accept the gift of Apollon and once again permit Alkestis to die in his place, the answer ought to be obvious. (See Lesky [1958, 145]; Gregory [1979, 266–69].) Admetos has to some extent reversed himself, but this hardly necessitates a change in his nature. Admetos seems to have the character appropriate to his actions, as Alkestis does to hers. We are told he is admirable; and, if he appears ridiculous at times, that need not call his basic quality into question. As K. von Fritz has shown, Admetos has been placed in a hopelessly false position (1956, 68); that position is what ought to engage our interest. (See also Strohm [1957, 6]: what is significant is the inextricability—*Ausweglosigkeit*—of the situation.)

Finally, the question of the relation to comedy cannot entirely be pushed aside: tragedy seems to deal with incurable evil (ἀνήκεστον πάθος.) (Cf. Watts [(1955) 1963, 93–104]: tragic actions, unlike comic ones, are irreversible.) This definition seems to apply well to every Euripidean play: there is always an undissolved bitter residue, even in the relatively bland "tragicomedies." In this play, however, the worst *pathos* of all does prove curable. (Suggestions of Alkestis' disaffection are based on the assumption of her—disappointed—erotic motivations; but Admetos has betrayed only his own, exaggerated vows of eternal chastity. Alkestis had not expected perpetual mourning: see line 381.) To that extent, *Alkestis* does seem to stand apart from the tragic genre; it features protagonists who, instead of striving desperately against evil, learn that even divine favor and all the largesse of fortune cannot reverse the conditions of human life.

Appendix C
Lyrics in *Hekabe*

The lyrics in *Hekabe* are not closely related to the events on stage. After the emotional scene in which Polyxene is led off to her death, Hekabe collapses in despair and lays a curse on Helene for the misery she brought Troy; but the chorus has no direct comment on what they have witnessed. (See C. Müller [1933, 21−24]). Instead they sing a song of escape, imagining their sea voyage to a future life of servitude in Hellas. The scene in which Polyxene's death is narrated is followed by a brief song about Alexandros and Helene, the judgment of Paris, and the sorrow of Trojan and Greek women at the war. After the discovery of Polydoros' corpse their song returns to this theme in a more ambitious structure. The thematic similarity of the three odes is striking: all contain references to sea voyages, all refer to the misery of women in war, and all center upon the experience of the chorus without ever making any direct return to the signal and obvious miseries of Hekabe, which are being enacted on stage (on the interrelation, see Hofmann [1916, 71ff.]).

These songs also have in common a remote and fantasied quality that could not contrast more severely with the lurid atmosphere, grotesque style, and hurried pace of the play that they adorn. The first chorus derives its theme from Polyxene's denunciation of slavery in the preceding scene; but the treatment in lyric is completely inverted. Polyxene pictures the life of a slave in accurate and even anachronistic colors: she thinks she may be forced to prepare food, sweep the house, work at the loom, and share the bed of a

330

slave (362–66)—whereas in epic the Trojan princesses had a more elevated role as concubines of the Greek heroes. The chorus, by contrast, imagine themselves taking part in several picturesque and famous Hellenic religious ceremonies, in a prettified travelogue of slavery.

The chorus' fantasy of their future is more than idealized; it is full of blatant errors. Rosivach (1975, 354–57) has shown that they seem to imagine a virginal service to Artemis and Athena, although they themselves are matrons and the sexual slaves of Greek victors. In addition to this, the chorus imagine themselves as participating in religious ceremonies, such as weaving the robe for Athena at the Panathenaia, that were certainly closed to slaves and noncitizens. The response of the audience to this sort of lyric will not be one of rejection (à la Verrall) but one of (repressed) confusion: lyric, especially escapist lyric of this sort, is meant to present us with a glorified or beautified reality. But it is nowhere laid down how far this glorification can go; and in this case the inaccuracy of the chorus' expectations is extreme. While Polyxene sees death as the only escape from reality, the chorus simply transform reality into an altered, more picturesque version. Clearly, after having begun their lyric with a parodos that was not really a lyric interlude at all, the chorus are turning abruptly away from the mimesis of reality in the stage events.

The second ode is marginally more closely tied to stage action. Hekabe ends the scene (620ff.) with an address to the house of Priamos and its lost glory, and the chorus also sing of Troy's destruction. But their theme is generalized and, like the first ode, this song centers on the chorus rather than on the actors. (Note the repeated "for me, for me pain was fated" in the opening lines [629–30].) The role of Alexandros and Helene is emphasized, as well as the beauty of the latter and the contest between the three goddesses. The epode, again lightly paralleling the previous scene, refers to the sorrow of Greek women, mentioning a "Spartan girl" as well as an old mother, the Greek counterparts of Polyxene and Hekabe, who have been so sharply juxtaposed in the previous scene. The sympathetic reference to Greece, like the fantasy of inclusion in Greek society in the first stasimon, parallels the sentimental identification between Greek and Trojan in Polyxene's death. The theme of female beauty plays fitfully over the ode, without acquiring any central focus; and this theme also recalls the spectacular description of Polyxene's lovely body in the previous scene.

The last stasimon pulls together, concentrates, and expands the themes of the other two. It is a full-scale ode, marking both with its length and with its superior poetic beauty, the high point of the play's lyric. It has appropriately been called a miniature *Iliou Persis* (see Kranz [1933, 216]; C. Müller [1933, 22]; Heitsch [1955, 91]). The remoteness of the ode from the action is particularly striking, since it follows the climactic scene of Hekabe's degradation, in which the sexual theme, glorified at Polyxene's death, is modulated into a harsh dissonance (Hofmann [1916, 73]), as Hekabe becomes an accomplished rhetor and pimp before our eyes. In the first ode, the chorus looked into the future; the second explained present misery by the events of the past. The third proceeds less directly out of the chorus' situation; instead, the events of the city's capture, a favorite theme of epic, are vividly recreated. The link to the chorus' present situation comes only at the end, when the narrative moves up to the present, as the chorus embark on ships, cursing Helene and Paris. (Note these themes in the other odes as well.)

The style is elaborate and is a slightly muted anticipation of the "dithy-rambic" extravagance of late Euripidean lyric. (Note the repetition of δορὶ δὴ δορὶ πέρσαν [Kranz (1933, 231)], as well as the direct address to Ilion [Kranz (239); Panagl (1971, 7–9 and 1972)].) The most extraordinary part of the ode is the remarkable picture of the chorus, metamorphosed into a sin-gle female figure, gazing at her own beauty in a hand mirror, as she lets down her hair for the night. (See Matthaei [1918, 143]: the scene has a mood of "dreamlike, pensive melancholy.") This image pulls together a number of themes from the play, notably those of feminine beauty and the pictorial or artistic representation—either of beauty, or of misery. In this case, the vivid pictures suggest *ekphrasis* of contemporary paintings as much as they do recollection of epic, although both sources are dark to us. (The mirror as an image of feminine vanity and sexuality is paralleled in the *Elektra,* where Klytaimestra primps in her mirror after Agamemnon has left: see discussion in Chapter 7.) The theme of sexual slavery in war is glamorized by the initial picture of the young matron's complacent beauty, at the same time as the image of her serenity generates strong pathos. Surprised by the Greeks, she runs out, "in a single garment, like a Dorian girl." Here the parallel with Greek women seems to be less important than the sexual image of the bare thighs and the associations of Spartan girls—such as Helene—with beauty and loose sexuality (see *Andr* 595–600). The Trojan woman wished to sup-plicate Artemis, goddess of asexuality, but she did not reach the shrine, and she curses Helene and Paris: because of them, she has been exiled from her home by a "marriage that is no marriage, but a curse." (Note that the ambi-guous phrase could refer both to the union of Helene and Paris, and to the rape of the speaker, who was "married" [ἄγομαι, 936] to the Greek victor at the moment of her first husband's death.)

The sexual themes moving through *Hekabe* vibrate between the grim and sordid images of slavery and the glamorous and sentimental picture of Polyxene's death. In this lyric, both sides are for once blended together, with an effect of delicate pathos. The greater freedom of the lyric to deal with such themes is used to the full. The chorus, as at all times when they are immersed in lyric (as opposed to their anapaestic parodos, when they were involved with Hekabe's situation), are self-absorbed and form a striking antithesis with the heroine. She is old, while they are young and beautiful, sexually appealing, yet with virginal aspirations (see Cataudella [1939, 131]).

While the chorus like Hekabe are matrons, these qualities link them to Polyxene; and the delicate and affected beauty of their songs seems to keep her influence in the play alive long after she has disappeared. The emphasis on Helene and Paris, two figures renowned for their beauty and their love, also sounds, in a fainter way, notes of glamour and sexuality that fall just near enough to the harsh tone of the dramatic action to create a powerful dissonance.

Appendix D
Dating, Influence, and Literary Analysis

The attempt to derive methods of literary analysis from what often appears to be the only "fact" attachable to the maddeningly oblique literary work, namely its date of production, has resulted in many scholarly sand castles. And, when stylistic criteria are used to provide dates for the many undated plays, the results are generally even less satisfactory. The use of Zielinski's metrical criteria (1925; see extension by Ceadel [1941]) gives us a broad, general picture of where plays fit in the fifty-year career of the poet; but the striking variation between *Hippolytos* and *Andromache,* or between *Phoinissai* and *Orestes,* suggests the inadequacy of such criteria as a means of precise dating. In any case, I would agree with H. D. F. Kitto ([1939] 1961, 314 n.1) that dating is not a particularly useful tool in the analysis of Euripidean plays, even when the date is determined by outside evidence. For all its tumultuous formal variety, Euripides' art as far back as we can trace it has an amazingly homogeneous and mature quality. Parallels between *Elektra* and two earlier plays make clear the general irrelevance of precise dating for this play.

The figure of the Autourgos seems a peculiar feature of Elektra, and we might be tempted to trace the introduction of this radically untragic figure to the vagaries of a Euripidean "late period." But he seems to have a close relation in the hero of *Diktys,* which was put on with *Medeia* in 431. In that play a noble and impoverished fisherman saved Danaë and Perseus from the machinations of the evil king, his brother. (See fr. 332 N2 and Nauck's citations above [pp. 459–60]; Mette [1982, 115, fr. 442]. On the plot see Webster [1967, 61–64] and Lesky [(1956) 1972.1, 313].) Diktys was in part a more conventional model, since he was really a mythological figure and a king; but in another sense, his status was even lower than that of the Autourgos, since fishermen were among the poorest of social classes. (See the fondness of Hellenistic writers for these figures: the letters of Philostratos, which rework comic motifs, feature fishermen as well as farmers. For such themes in comedy, see Gow [1952, 2:369]; and Webster [1967, 83–84].) Diktys has left behind a number of sententious fragments on eugeneia (331, 333, 334, 341, and especially 336 [ὁ μὲν γὰρ ἐσθλὸς εὐγενὴς ἔμοιγ' ἀνήρ], a close relation to Elektra 367ff.). Also striking is fr. 331, probably spoken by the hero himself, in which erôs for a friend (philos) is spoken of as having seized the speaker, but without "turning me toward folly [τὸ μῶρον] or toward Aphrodite [Κύπριν]." The speaker refers to a passion that is erotic without being physical (See Mette [1982, 112, on fr. 427]: "ein 'platonischer' Eros." See also fr. 388 N2.), a notion that has strong Socratic and Antisthenic overtones (see Chapter 9, Section III.B). Diktys, like the Autourgos, was a figure designed to present the themes of revisionist morality— eight years before the first production of Clouds.

Another striking parallel is that between Elektra and Kresphontes, a play that is firmly dated to before 424 by a reference in Aristophanes (453 N2; cf. Mette [1982, 160, fr. 613]) and that made a new use of the Aeschylean false message of the hero's death. The villains in both plays seem to have met similar ends: see Hyginus 137 (N2, p. 497): "rex laetus cum rem divinam faceret, hospes falso simulavit se hostiam percussisse eumque interfecit" (Austin [1968, 41]. See Schmid Stählin [3:395–6]; and Webster [1967, 137–43]). The obvious conclusion was drawn by T. v. Wilamowitz, only to be ignored by subsequent generations of scholars (1917, 251–52): Kresphontes makes clear that already in the 420s Euripides was exploiting the form of Choephoroi to create his own recognition dramas, and that he was already sophisticated enough at that early period to build an elaborate variation on the theme. If proof other than that of common logic were needed to refute the assumption that complex form is an indication of late date and late development, the case of Kresphontes would provide it.

Kresphontes uses the theme of the false message to produce, not mere despair or elation in various characters, but an intrigue that nearly leads to the murder of the hero by his mother. It is of course salutary to note the close parallelism with the plot of Ion, usually supposed to be a late play. Whatever the actual dates of Ion and Elektra, it is clear that Euripides continued to rework these familiar themes in various ways and in various moods, some naive (Iphigeneia Among the Taurians, and to an extent Ion) and some ironic. In this light it becomes apparent how unnecessary it is to see the reference to the "false message" motif in Helene ("The plan is somewhat

outworn [παλαιότης γὰρ τῷ λόγῳ ἔνεστί τις]'' [1056]) purely as an allusion
to Sophokles (Kannicht's commentary [1969, 2:268–69] repeats this suggestion of U. v. Wilamowitz [1883, 241 n.1].). T. v. Wilamowitz points out
(1917, 255–56) that *Kresphontes* very likely antedates the Sophoclean *Elektra* and therefore provides a model for its use of the false message to deceive
the friends of the avenger; he also remarks that the role of the Old Man in
Elektra and the role of the *paidagôgos* in the Sophoclean version both are
likely to have an antecedent in *Kresphontes,* as well as in the role given
Talthybios in pre-tragic versions (1917, 255; he cites Robert [1881, 164, cf.
155, 157]). Again we see evidence of the fertility and variety of Euripidean
dramaturgy, and of the richness and complexity of the lost tradition behind it.

If *Elektra* cannot be much illuminated by its presumptive date in the middle or late teens, attempts to use the fine points of dramatic structure to position the play before or after *Iphigeneia Among the Taurians* or the Sophoclean *Elektra* are even less plausible. (The attempt of Theiler [1966, 109] to
make use of *Kresphontes* to date *Elektra* deserves no reply beyond that given
it by Schwinge [1969, 2ff.].) The most important factor in determining the
shape of *Elektra* is its relation to *Choephoroi,* which for this play is not
merely the abstract dramaturgical paradigm of the recognition play, but a
direct literary antecedent. Matthiessen, like some other scholars who saw
structure as a key to the *Prioritätsfrage,* sometimes seems to overlook the
position of *Choephoroi* as primary literary model in attempting to derive the
Elektra of Euripides from that of Sophokles (1964, 82–88); cf. earlier criticism of Steiger (1912) by Elisei (1931, 113). The use of Zielinski's principle
of the *locus rudimentalis* (1925) as a tool of dating similarly results in the
imposition of rigid simplifications on what is a fluid and elusive expressive
system (see Vögler's attempt to use Zielinski [1967, 116]). It is true that, in
the progressive elaboration of inherited forms, elements of previous structures become ornamental additions to new structures, although they bear little
weight in the new design (see Michelini [1982, 22]). It is also true that this
often leads to a quality of vagueness or dissonance. But poets are not obliged
to proceed in this way, and it is wrong to assume that a version using a traditional motif is always older than the one using a *variatio.* (See Segal's criticism [review (1968, 138) of Vögler (1967)]: V. ''seems to assume that one
can trace literary influences in the same way as one would solve a problem in
geometry.'')

Finally, while I have argued that the Sophoclean *Elektra* is very likely to
be one of the major literary antecedents to this play, I have tried to show
throughout the analysis in Chapter 7 that there are only a very few places
where parallels between the plays are likely to be significant. As in the case
of *Hekabe* and *Polyxene, Herakles* and *Trachiniai, Hippolytos Crowned* or
Hippolytos Veiled and *Phaidra,* relations between individual plays, where
they have been preserved for us, illuminate a general opposition between Eu-

ripidean tragedy and Sophoclean tragedy, or a general allusiveness of one artist to the other, rather than rigidly defined and temporally fixed relations between pairs of matched dramas. The response of the Euripidean *Elektra* to Sophoclean drama as a whole remains always more significant than its response to the *Elektra* of Sophokles.

Reference List

Abrahamson, E. L. 1952. "Euripides' Tragedy of Hecuba." *TAPA* 83: 120–29.

Adams, S. M. 1935. "Two Plays of Euripides." *CR* 49: 118–22.

Adkins, A. W. H. 1978. "Problems in Greek Popular Morality." *CPh* 73: 143–58.

Adkins, A. W. H. 1966.1. "Basic Greek Values in Euripides' *Hecuba* and *Hercules Furens*." *CQ* n.s. 16: 193–219.

Adkins, A. W. H. 1966.2. "Aristotle and the Best Kind of Tragedy." *CQ* n.s. 16: 78–102.

Adkins, A. W. H. 1960. *Merit and Responsibility: A Study in Greek Values*. Oxford: Clarendon Pr.

Adrados, F. Rodriguez. 1959. "El amor en Euripides." In *El descubrimento del amor en Grecia*, ed. M. F. Galiano et al., pp. 181–200. Madrid: Univ. of Madrid.

Aélion, Rachel. 1983. *Euripide: Héritier d' Eschyle*. 2 vols. Collections d'Études Mythologiques. Paris: Les Belles Lettres.

Agard, W. R. 1933. "Fate and Freedom in Greek Tragedy." *CJ* 29: 117–26.

Albini, Umberto. 1976. *Interpretazioni teatrali: Da Eschilo ad Aristofane*. Vol. 2. Florence: Le Monnier.

Albini, Umberto. 1972. *Interpretazioni teatrali: Da Eschilo ad Aristofane*. Vol. 1. Florence: Le Monnier.

Albini, Umberto. 1970. "Linee compositive delle *Troiane*." *PP* 25: 312–22.

Albini, Umberto. 1962. "L'*Elettra* di Euripide." *Maia* 14: 85–108.

Albini, Umberto. 1961. "L'*Alcesti* di Euripide." *Maia* 13: 3–29.

Alexiou, Margaret. 1974. *The Ritual Lament in Greek Tradition*. Cambridge: Univ. Pr.

Alt, Karin. 1962. "Zur *Anagnorisis* in der *Helena*." *Hermes* 90: 6–24.

Aly, Wolf. 1929. *Formprobleme der frühen griechischen Prosa*. Philologus Supplbnd. 21.

Arnott, W. G. 1981.1. "Double the Vision: A Reading of Euripides' *Electra*." *G&R*
    Ser. 2, 28: 179–92.
Arnott, W. G. 1981.2. "Moral Values in Menander." *Philologus* 125: 215–27.
Arnott, W. G. 1978. "Red Herrings and Other Baits: A Study in Euripidean Tech-
    nique." *MPhL* 3: 1–24.
Arnott, W. G. 1977. " Ἡ διατήρηση τοῦ ἐνδιαφέροντος τῶν θεατῶν: Μερικὰ
    τεχνάσματα τοῦ Εὐριπίδου." *Dodone* 6: 41–53.
Arrowsmith, William. 1963. "A Greek Theater of Ideas." *Arion* 2 no.3: 32–56.
Auerbach, Erich. 1946. *Mimesis: Dargestellte Wirklichkeit in der abendländischen
    Literatur*. Bern: Francke.
Austin, Colin. 1968. *Nova Fragmenta Euripidea in Papyris Reperta*. Kleine Texte
    187. Berlin: de Gruyter.
Austin, Colin. 1967. "Des nouveaux fragments de l'*Érechthée* d'Euripide." *RecPap*
    4: 11–67.
Avery, H. C. 1982. "One Antiphon or Two?" *Hermes* 110: 145–58.
Avery, H. C. 1973. "Sophocles' Political Career." *Historia* 22: 509–14.
Avery, H. C. 1968. "'My Tongue Swore, but My Mind Is Unsworn.'" *TAPA* 99:
    19–35.
Bain, David. 1977. "[Euripides,] *Electra* 518–544." *BICS* 24: 104–16.
Baldry, H. C. 1965. *The Unity of Mankind in Greek Thought*. Cambridge: Univ. Pr.
Barlow, S. A. 1971. *The Imagery of Euripides: A Study in the Dramatic Use of Pic-
    torial Language*. London: Methuen.
Barrett, W. S., ed. 1964. *Euripides: Hippolytus*. Oxford: Clarendon Pr.
Bates, W. N. 1930. *Euripides: A Student of Human Nature*. Philadelphia: Univ. of
    Pennsylvania Pr.
B.[ayfield], M. A. 1912. "Obituary: Dr. A. W. Verrall." *CR* 26: 172–73.
Behler, Ernst. 1983. "The Brothers Schlegel and the Nineteenth Century's *Damnatio
    Euripidis*." Unpublished paper delivered at *APA* annual meeting.
Bellinger, A. R. 1939. "The *Bacchae* and *Hippolytus*." *YClS* 6: 17–27.
Ben, N. van der. 1978. "Empedocles, Fragments 8, 9, 10DK." *Phronesis* 23:
    197–215.
Benedetto, Vincenzo di. 1971.1. *Euripide: Teatro e societa*. Turin: Einaudi.
Benedetto, Vincenzo di. 1971.2. "Il rinnovamento stilistico della lirica dell' ultimo
    Euripide e la contemporanea arte figurativa." *Dioniso* 45: 326–33.
Benedetto, Vincenzo di, ed. 1965. *Euripides: Orestes*. Florence: La Nuova Italia.
    Review: K. Reckford, *AJPh* 89 (1968) 231–33.
Bergson, Henri. 1912. *Le rire: Essai sur la signification du comique*. 8th edn. Paris:
    Alcan & Guillaumin.
Bergson, Leif. 1971. *Die Relativität der Werte im Frühwerk des Euripides*. Stock-
    holm: Almqvist & Wiksell.
Berlage, Johannes. 1888. *Commentatio de Euripide Philosopho*. Leiden: Brill.
Bernhardy, G. 1872. *Grundriss der griechischen Litteratur*. Part 2.2. 3d edn. Halle:
    Anton.
Berns, Gisela. 1973. "*Nomos* and *Physis* (An Interpretation of Euripides' *Hippo-
    lytus*)." *Hermes* 101: 165–87.

Besenbeck, Alfred. 1930. *Kunstanschauung und Kunstlehre August Wilhelm Schlegels*. Berlin: Ebering.

Beye, C. R. 1959. "Alcestis and her Critics." *GRBS* 2: 112–27.

Biehl, Werner. 1966. "Das Kompositionsprinzip der Parodos in Euripides' *Hekabe* (98–153)." *Helikon* 6: 411–24.

Biehl, Werner. 1957. "Die Interpolationen in Euripides' *Hekabe*, V. 59–215." *Philologus* 101: 55–69.

Biffi, Lydia. 1961. "Elementi comici nella tragedia greca." *Dioniso* 35: 89–102.

Bjørck, Gudmund. 1950. *Das Alpha Impurum und die tragische Kunstsprache: Attische Wort- und Stilstudien*. Acta Societatis Litterarum Humaniorum. 39. Uppsala.

Bjørck, Gudmund. 1952. "Das Tragikomische und das Wort νεανικός (Euripides *Hippolytus* 1204)." In EPMHNEIA, Festschr. Otto Regenbogen, pp. 66–70. Heidelberg: Winter.

Blaiklock, E. M. 1952. *The Male Characters in Euripides: A Study in Realism*. Wellington: New Zealand Univ. Pr.

Bloch, Leo. 1901. "Alkestisstudien," I & II. *NJA* 4: 23–50, 113–24.

Blomqvist, Jerker. 1982. "Human and Divine Action in Euripides' *Hippolytus*." *Hermes* 110: 398–414.

Bloom, Harold. 1973. *The Anxiety of Influence: A Theory of Poetry*. London: Oxford Univ. Pr.

Boella, Umberto, ed. 1964. *Euripide Ecuba*. Turin: Loescher.

Boer, C. W. 1967. "The Language of Tragic Humor." Diss. SUNY Buffalo.

Böhme, Robert. 1956. *Bühnenbearbeitung äschyleischer Tragödien* I. Basel: Schwabe.

Böhme, Robert. 1938. "Aischylos und der Anagnorismos." *Hermes* 73: 195–212.

Bond, G. W., ed. 1981. *Euripides: Heracles*. Oxford: Clarendon Pr.

Bond, G. W. 1974. "Euripides' Parody of Aeschylus." *Hermathena* 118: 1–14.

Bond, G. W., ed. 1963. *Euripides: Hypsipyle*. Oxford: Clarendon Pr.

Bongie, E. B. 1977. "Heroic Elements in the *Medea* of Euripides." *TAPA* 107: 27–56.

Bonnard, André. 1944. "L'*Hippolyte* d' Euripide et le drame de la passion refoulée." *Bulletin* (Soc. des Ét. des Lettres) 18 no.1: 1–18.

Borecký, Borsivoj. 1955. "La tragédie *Alopé* d' Euripide." In *Studia Antiqua*, Festschr. Antonio Salač, pp. 82–89. Prague: Czech Akad.

Bowra, C. M. 1944. *Sophoclean Tragedy*. Oxford: Clarendon Pr.

Bradley, E. M. 1980. "Admetus and the Triumph of Failure in Euripides' *Alcestis*." *Ramus* 9: 112–27.

Brandt, Herwig. 1973. *Die Sklaven in den Rollen von Dienern und Vertrauten bei Euripides*. Hildesheim: Olms.

Breitenbach, Wilhelm. 1934. *Untersuchungen zur Sprache der euripideischen Lyrik*. Tübinger Beiträge 20. Stuttgart: Kohlhammer.

Bremer, J. M. 1975. "The Meadow of Love and Two Passages in Euripides' *Hippolytus*." *Mnemosyne* ser. 4, 28: 268–80.

Bremer, J. M. 1971. "Euripides *Hecuba* 59–215: A Reconsideration." *Mnemosyne* ser.4, 24: 232–50.

Bremer, J. M. 1969. *Hamartia: Tragic Error in the Poetics of Aristotle and in Greek Tragedy.* Amsterdam: Hakkert.

Brereton, Geoffrey. 1968. *Principles of Tragedy: A Rational Examination of the Tragic Concept in Life and Literature.* Coral Gables: Univ. of Miami Pr.

Broadhead, H. D. 1968. *Tragica: Elucidations of Passages in Greek Tragedy.* Christchurch, N.Z.: Univ. of Canterbury Pr.

Brooks, Cleanth. 1947. *The Well Wrought Urn: Studies in the Structure of Poetry.* New York: Harcourt, Brace, & World.

Brown, A. L. 1978. "Wretched Tales of the Poets." *PCPhS* n.s. 24: 22 – 30.

Bruhn, Ewald, ed. 1912. *Elektra.* Vol. 5 of *Sophokles,* ed. F. W. Schneidewin & A. Nauck. Berlin: Weidmann.

Bundy, E. L. 1962. *Studia Pindarica I.* Berkeley: Univ. of California Pr.

Burian, Peter 1985. *Directions in Euripidean Criticism: A Collection of Essays.* Durham: Duke Univ. Pr.

Burian, Peter. 1976. "Euripides the Contortionist." *Arion* 3: 96 – 113.

Burian, Peter. 1977. "Euripides' *Heraclidae*: An Interpretation." *CPh* 72: 1 – 21.

Burkert, Walter. 1979. *Structure and History in Greek Mythology and Ritual.* Berkeley: Univ. of California Pr.

Burkert, Walter. 1974. "Die Absurdität der Gewalt und das Ende der Tragödie: Euripides' *Orestes.*" *A&A* 20: 97 – 109.

Burnett, Anne Pippin. 1977. "*Trojan Women* and the Ganymede Ode." *YClS* 25: 291 – 316.

Burnett, Anne Pippin. 1976. "Tribe and City, Custom and Decree in *Children of Heracles.*" *CPh* 71: 4 – 26.

Burnett, Anne Pippin. 1973. "*Medea* and the Tragedy of Revenge." *CPh* 68: 1 – 24.

Burnett, Anne Pippin. 1971. *Catastrophe Survived: Euripides' Plays of Mixed Reversal.* Oxford: Clarendon Pr. Reviews: B. M. W. Knox (under Knox 1972.1); C. Segal, *CW* 65 (1972) 275; H. Strohm, *Gnomon* 46 (1974) 341 – 46.

Burnett, Anne Pippin. 1965. "The Virtues of Admetus." *CPh* 60: 240 – 55.

Burnett, Anne Pippin. 1962. "Human Resistance and Divine Persuasion in Euripides' *Ion.*" *CPh* 57: 89 – 103.

Burnett, Anne Pippin. 1960. "Euripides' *Helen,* A Comedy of Ideas." *CPh* 55: 151 – 63.

Busch, Gerda. 1937. *Untersuchungen zum Wesen der* τυχή *in den Tragödien des Euripides.* Heidelberg: Winter.

Busolt, Georg. 1893 – 95. *Griechische Geschichte bis zur Schlacht bei Chaeronea.* Vol. 1. 2d edn. Gotha: Perthes.

Butaye, D. 1980. "Sagesse et bonheur dans les tragédies de Sophocle." *LEC* 48: 289 – 308.

Buttrey, T. V. 1976. "Tragedy as Form in Euripides." *Mich. Quart. Rev.* 15: 155 – 72.

Buxton, R. G. A. 1982. *Persuasion in Greek Tragedy: A Study of Peitho.* Cambridge: Univ. Pr.

Byl, S. 1975. "Lamentations sur la vieillesse dans la tragédie grecque." In *Le monde grec,* Festschr. Claire Préaux, ed. J. Bingen et al, pp. 130 – 39. Brussels: Ed. de l'Univ. de Bruxelles.

Bywater, Ingram. 1909. *Aristotle on the Art of Poetry.* Oxford: Clarendon Pr.

Caizzi, F. D., ed. 1966. *Antisthenis Fragmenta.* Milan: Ist. Editoriale Cisalpino.

Calder, W. M., III. 1972. "A Note on the Dating of Euripides' *Phaethon.*" *CPh* 67: 291–93.

Calder, W. M., III. 1971. "Sophoclean Apologia: *Philoctetes.*" *GRBS* 12: 153–74.

Calder, W. M., III. 1966. "A Reconstruction of Sophocles' *Polyxena.*" *GRBS* 7: 31–56.

Canevet, M. 1971. "Aspects baroques du théâtre d'Euripide." *BAGB* 4: 203–10.

Cantarella, Raffaele. 1965. "Atene: La polis e il teatro." *Dioniso* 39: 39–55.

Cantarella, Raffaele, ed. 1964. *Euripide, I Cretesi.* Milan: Ist. Editoriale Italiano.

Carpenter, Reeves. 1941. "Observations on Familiar Statuary in Rome." *MAAR* 18.

Carrière, Jean. "Sur l'essence et l'évolution du tragique chez les grecs." *REG* 79: 6–37.

Casa, Adriana della. 1962. "Ennio di fronte all' *Ecuba* di Euripide." *Dioniso* 36: 63–76.

Cataudella, Quintino. 1972. *Studi classici.* Vol.1. Festschr. ed. Salvatore Costanza et al. Univ. di Catania: Facoltà di lett. e filos.

Cataudella, Quintino. 1969. *Saggi sulla tragedia greca.* Florence: D'Anna.

Cataudella, Quintino. 1939. "L'*Ecuba* di Euripide." *Dioniso* 7: 118–34. Repr. in 1969, 263–89.

Ceadel, E. B. 1941. "Resolved Feet in the Trimeters of Euripides and the Chronology of the Plays." *CQ* 35: 66–89.

Chalk, H. H. O. 1962. "'Αρετή and Βία in Euripides' *Herakles.*" *JHS* 82: 7–18.

Chapouthier, Fernand. 1952. "Euripide et l'accueil du divin." In *Entretiens* 1952, pp. 205–25.

Chromik, Christian. 1967. "Göttlicher Anspruch und menschliche Verantwortung bei Euripides." Diss. Kiel.

Chroust, A.-H. 1957. *Socrates, Man and Myth: The Two Socratic Apologies of Xenophon.* London: Routledge & Kegan Paul.

Claus, David. 1972. "Phaedra and the Socratic Paradox." *YClS* 22: 223–38.

Coles, R. A. 1968. "A New Fragment of Post-classical Tragedy from Oxyrynchus." *BICS* 15: 110–18.

Collard, Christopher. 1975.1. "Formal Debates in Euripides' Drama." *G&R* ser. 2 no.22.1: 58–71.

Collard, Christopher, ed. 1975.2. *Euripides: Supplices.* 2 vols. Groningen: Bouma's Boekhuis.

Collard, Christopher. 1972. "The Funeral Oration in Euripides' *Supplices.*" *BICS* 19: 39–53.

Collard, Christopher. 1970. "On the Tragedian Chaeremon." *JHS* 90: 22–34.

Conacher, D. J. 1981. "Rhetoric and Relevance in Euripidean Drama." *AJPh* 102: 3–25.

Conacher, D. J. 1972. "Some Questions of Probability and Relevance in Euripidean Drama." *Maia* 24: 199–207.

Conacher, D. J. 1967. *Euripidean Drama: Myth, Theme and Structure.* Toronto: Univ. of Toronto Pr. Reviews: J. Petroff, *CW* 62 (1968) 30; C. A. Seeck, *Gnomon* 41 (1969) 16–29; W. D. Smith, *Phoenix* 23 (1969) 394–95; J. R. Wilson, *CJ* 64 (1968–69) 80–81.

Conacher, D. J. 1961. "Euripides' *Hecuba*." *AJPh* 82: 1–26.

Conacher, D. J. 1959. "The Paradox of Euripides' *Ion*." *TAPA* 90: 20–39.

Conacher, D. J. 1956. "Religious and Ethical Attitudes in Euripides' *Suppliants*." *TAPA* 87: 8–26.

Conacher, D. J. 1955. "Theme, Plot, and Technique in the *Heracles* of Euripides." *Phoenix* 9: 139–52.

Corte, Francesco della. 1962. "Il Polidoro euripideo." *Dioniso* 36: 5–14.

Crocker, L. G. 1957. "On Interpreting *Hippolytus*." *Philologus* 101: 238–46.

Craik, E. M. 1980. "Sophokles and the Sophists." *AC* 49: 247–54.

Craik, E. M. 1979. "*Philoctetes*: Sophoklean Melodrama." *AC* 48: 15–29.

Croiset, Alfred, & Maurice Croiset. 1913. *Histoire de la littérature grecque.* Vol. 3. 3d edn. Paris: Fontemoing. First published 1891.

Croiset, Maurice. 1910. "Ce que nous savons d'Euripide." Paris: Éditions de la Rev. Politique. Lecture, first printed in *Revue Bleue*, Jan. 1910.

Cunningham, M. P. 1954. "Medea ἀπὸ μηχανῆς." *CPh* 49: 151–60.

Daitz, S. G., ed. 1973. *Euripides: Hecuba.* Leipzig: Teubner.

Daitz, S. G. 1971. "Concepts of Freedom and Slavery in Euripides' *Hecuba*." *Hermes* 99: 217–26.

Dale, A. M. 1956. "Seen and Unseen on the Greek Stage: A Study in Scenic Conventions." *WS* 69: 96–106.

Dale, A. M., ed. 1954. *Euripides: Alcestis.* Oxford: Clarendon Pr.

Dalfen, Joachim. 1974. *Polis und Poiesis: Die Auseinandersetzung mit der Dichtung bei Platon und seinen Zeitgenossen.* Munich: Fink.

Dawe, R. D. 1968. "Some Reflections on *Ate* and *Hamartia*." *HSCPh* 72: 89–123.

Decharme, Paul. 1966. *Euripide et l'esprit de son théâtre.* Brussels: Culture & Civilisation, 1966. First published Paris: Garnier, 1893. English trans. James Loeb. *Euripides and the Spirit of his Dramas.* London: MacMillan, 1906.

Decharme, Paul. 1889. "Euripide et Anaxagore." *REG* 2: 234–44.

Deichgräber, Karl. 1935. "Die Kadmos-Teiresiasszene in Euripides' *Bakchen*." *Hermes* 70: 322–49.

Delebecque, Edouard. 1951. *Euripide et la guerre du Péloponnèse.* Paris: Klincksieck.

Delulle, H. 1911. "Les répétitions d'images chez Euripide: Contributions à l'étude de l'imagination d'Euripide." Diss. Louvain. Bureaux du Recueil.

Denniston, J. D., ed. 1939. *Euripides: Electra.* Oxford: Clarendon Pr.

Denniston, J. D. & Denys Page, ed. 1957. *Aeschylus: Agamemnon.* Oxford, Clarendon Pr.

Denniston, J. D. 1954. *The Greek Particles.* 2d edn. Oxford: Clarendon Pr.

Detienne, Marcel. 1977. *Dionysos mis à mort.* Paris: Gallimard.

Detienne, Marcel. 1972. *Les jardins d' Adonis.* Paris: Gallimard.

Detienne, Marcel, & J.-P. Vernant. 1974. *Les ruses de l'intelligence: La mètis des grecs.* Paris: Flammarion.

Diggle, James. 1981.1. *Studies on the Text of Euripides.* Oxford: Clarendon Pr.

Diggle, James, ed. 1981.2. *Euripidis Fabulae.* Vol. 2. Oxford: Clarendon Pr.

Diggle, James, ed. 1970. *Euripides: Phaethon.* Cambridge: Univ. Pr.

Dihle, Albrecht. 1977. "Das Satyrspiel *Sisyphos*." *Hermes* 105: 28–42.

Diller, Hans. 1968. "Die *Bakchen* und ihre Stellung im Spätwerk des Euripides." In Schwinge 1968.2, pp. 469–92. First published in *AAWM* 5 (1955) 453–71.

Diller, Hans. 1962. "Erwartung, Enttäuschung und Erfüllung in der griechischen Tragödie." *Serta philol. Aenipontana* 7–8: 93–115.

Diller, Hans. 1958. "Umwelt und Masse als dramatische Faktoren bei Euripides." In *Entretiens* 1958, pp. 89–105.

Diller, Hans. 1939. "Der griechische Naturbegriff." *NJAB* 114: 241–57.

Dingel, Joachim. 1970. "Der Sohn des Polybos und die Sphinx: Zu den Ödipustragödien des Euripides und des Seneca." *MH*: 90–96.

Dingel, Joachim. 1969. "Der 24. Gesang der *Odyssee* und die *Elektra* des Euripides." *RhM* 112: 103–9.

Dingel, Joachim. 1967. "Das Requisit in der griechischen Tragödie." Diss. Tübingen.

Dirat, Maurice. 1976. "Le personnage de Ménélas dans *Hélène*." *Pallas* 23: 3–17.

Dittmar, Heinrich. 1912. *Aischines von Sphettos: Studien zur Literaturgeschichte der Sokratiker.* Philologische Unters. 21. Berlin: Weidmann.

Dobson, J. F. 1908. "Euripides Unbound." *CR* 22: 211–13.

Dodds, E. R. 1973. *The Ancient Concept of Progress and Other Essays on Greek Literature and Belief.* Oxford: Clarendon Pr.

Dodds, E. R. 1966. "On Misunderstanding the *Oedipus Rex*." *G&R* 13: 37–49. Repr. in 1973, pp. 64–77.

Dodds, E. R., ed. 1960. *Euripides' Bacchae.* 2d edn. Oxford: Clarendon Pr. First published 1944.

Dodds, E. R. 1951. *The Greeks and the Irrational.* Berkeley: Univ. of Calif. Pr.

Dodds, E. R. 1929. "Euripides the Irrationalist." *CR* 43: 97–104. Repr. in 1973, pp. 78–91.

Dodds, E. R. 1925. "The ΑΙΔΩΣ of Phaedra and the Meaning of the *Hippolytus*." *CR* 39: 102–4.

Dohrn, Tobias. 1957. *Attische Plastik: Vom Tode des Phidias bis zum Wirken der grossen Meister des IV. Jahrhunderts v. Chr..* Krefeld: Scherpe.

Donelli, G. B. 1980. "Euripide, *Elettra* 518–544." *BICS* 27: 109–19.

Dörrie, Heinrich. 1966. "Der Mythos im Verständnis der Antike, II: Von Euripides bis Seneca." *Gymnasium* 73: 44–62.

Dover, K. J. 1983. "The Portrayal of Moral Evaluation in Greek Poetry." *JHS* 103: 35–48.

Dover, K. J. 1978. *Greek Homosexuality.* Cambridge, Mass.: Harvard Univ. Pr.

Dover, K. J. 1976. "The Freedom of the Intellectual in Greek Society." ΤΑΛΑΝΤΑ 7: 24–54.

Dover, K. J. 1973. "Classical Greek Attitudes to Sexual Behavior." *Arethusa* 6: 59–73.

Dover, K. J., ed. 1968. *Aristophanes: Clouds.* Oxford: Clarendon Pr.

Dreizehnter, Alois. 1981. "Zur Entstehung der Lohnarbeit und deren Terminologie im Altgriechischen." In Welskopf 1981, 3:269–81.

Drexler, Hans. 1943. "Zum *Herakles* des Euripides." *NAWG* 9: 311–43.

duBois, Page. 1979. "On Horse/Men, Amazons, and Endogamy." *Arethusa* 12: 35–49.

Duchemin, Jacqueline. 1967. "Le personnage de Lyssa dans l'Héraclès Furieux d'Euripide." *REG* 88: 130–39.

Dumézil, Georges. 1968. *Mythe et épopée: L'idéologie des trois functions dans les épopées des peuples indo-européens.* Vol. 1. Paris: Gallimard.

Dümmler, Ferdinand. 1901. "Der Ursprung der Elegie." In *Kleine Schriften,* 2:405–516. Leipzig: Hirzel. First published *Philologus* 53 (1894) 280–86.

Dupont-Roc, Roselyne & Jean Lallot, eds. 1980. *Aristote: La poétique.* Paris: Seuil.

Dupréel, Eugène. 1948. *Les sophistes: Protagoras, Gorgias, Prodicus, Hippias.* Neuchâtel: Éd. du Griffon.

Dupréel, Eugène. 1922. *La légende socratique et les sources de Platon.* Brussels: Sand.

Earp, F. R. 1944. *The Style of Sophocles.* Cambridge: Univ. Pr.

Ebener, Dietrich. 1981. "Selbstverwirklichung des Menschen im euripideischen *Herakles.*" *Philologus* 125: 176–80.

Edelstein, Ludwig. 1967. *The Idea of Progress in Classical Antiquity.* Baltimore: Johns Hopkins Univ. Pr.

Ehrenberg, Victor. 1954. *Sophocles and Pericles.* Oxford: Clarendon Pr.

Eichner, Hans. 1970. *Friedrich Schlegel.* New York: Twayne.

Eisner, Robert. 1980. "Echoes of the *Odyssey* in Euripides' *Helen.*" *Maia* 32: 31–37.

Eisner, Robert. 1979. "Euripides' Use of Myth." *Arethusa* 12: 153–74.

Elisei, Anna. 1931. "Le due *Elettre*: La questione della priorità fra l'*Elettra* di Sofocle e quella di Euripide." *RAL* 7: 93–169.

Else, G. F. 1957. *Aristotle's Poetics: The Argument.* Cambridge, Mass.: Harvard Univ. Pr.

Elsperger, Wilhelm. 1907. *Reste und Spuren antiker Kritik gegen Euripides.* Philologus Supplbnd. 11.1–176.

England, E. T. 1926. "The *Electra* of Euripides." *CR* 40: 97–104.

Entretiens sur l'antiquité classique. 1958. Vol.6. *Euripide.* Fondation Hardt. Geneva: Vandoeuvres. Published 1960.

Entretiens sur l'antiquité classique. 1952. Vol.1. *La notion du divin depuis Homère jusqu'à Platon.* Fondation Hardt. Geneva: Vandoeuvres. Published 1954.

Erbse, Harmut. 1975. "Zum *Orestes* des Euripides." *Hermes* 103: 434–59.

Erbse, Harmut. 1972. "Euripides' *Alkestis.*" *Philologus* 116: 32–52.

Erdmann, Gerd. 1964. "Der Botenbericht bei Euripides: Struktur und dramatische Funktion." Diss. Kiel.

Erdmann, Walter. 1934. *Die Ehe im alten Griechenland.* Munich: Beck.

Errandonea, Ignacio. 1927. "Deianira vere ΔHI-ANEIPA." *Mnemosyne* 55: 145–64.

Fairweather, J. A. 1974. "Fiction in the Biographies of Ancient Writers." *AncSoc* 5: 231–75.

Falco, Vittorio de. 1928. *La tecnica corale di Sofocle.* Naples: Sangiovanni.

Fauth, Wolfgang. 1958. *Hippolytos und Phaidra: Bemerkungen zum religiösen Hintergrund eines tragischen Konflikts,* I. AAWM 9: 517–88.

Festugière, A. J. 1965. *Euripide le contemplatif.* Cuadernos de la fundación Pastor 11. Madrid: Taurus.

Festugière, A. J. 1957. "Euripide dans les *Bacchantes.*" *Eranos* 55: 127–44.

Finley, J. H. 1967. *Three Essays on Thucydides.* Cambridge, Mass.: Harvard Univ. Pr.

Fitton, J. W. & F. D. Harvey. 1977. "Menander and Euripides: Theme and Treatment (1956)." *Pegasus* 20: 9–15.

Fitton, J. W. 1961. "The *Suppliant Women* and the *Herakleidai* of Euripides." *Hermes* 89: 430–61.

Fitton Brown, A. D. 1961. "The Recognition Scene in *Choephori.*" *REG* 74: 363–70.

Fix, Theobald, ed. 1843. *Euripidis Fabulae.* Paris: Firmin-Didot.

Flessa, Ferdinand. 1882. *Die Prioritätsfrage der sophokleischen und euripideischen Elektra und ihr Verhältnis zu einander, sovie zu den Choephoren des Aischylos.* Bamberg: Gärtner.

Foley, H. B. 1985. *Ritual Irony: Poetry and Sacrifice in Euripides.* Ithaca: Cornell Univ. Pr.

Foley, H. B. 1982. "Marriage and Sacrifice in Euripides' *Iphigeneia in Aulis.*" *Arethusa* 15: 159–80.

Ford, J. E. 1981. "Rationalist Criticism of Greek Tragedy: A Critical History". Dissertation, Univ. of Chicago.

Forehand, W. E. 1979. "Truth and Reality in Euripides' *Ion.*" *Ramus* 8: 174–87.

Förs, Helmut. 1964. "Dionysos und die Stärke der Schwachen im Werk des Euripides." Diss. Tübingen.

Förster, Richard. 1883. "Zu Achilleus und Polyxena." *Hermes* 18: 475–78.

Fortenbaugh, W. W. 1981. "Theophrast über den komischen Charakter." *RhM* 124: 245–60.

Fowler, Barbara Hughes. 1978. "Lyric Structures in Three Euripidean Plays." *Dioniso* 49: 15–51.

Fraenkel, Eduard. 1963. *Zu den Phoenissen des Euripides.* SBAW 1. Munich.

Fraenkel, Eduard, ed. 1950. *Aeschylus: Agamemnon.* 3 vols. Oxford: Clarendon Pr.

Franke, Olga. 1929. *Euripides bei den deutschen Dramatikern des achtzehnten Jahrhunderts.* Das Erbe der Alten. 16. Leipzig: Dieterich.

Fränkel, Hermann. 1960. "Zenon von Elea im Kampf gegen die Idee der Vielheit." In *Wege und Formen frühgriechischen Denkens: Literarische und philosophiegeschichtliche Studien,* pp. 198–236. 2d edn. Munich: Beck. First published *Am. Journ. Philos.* (1924).

Frei, Peter. 1981. "*Isonomia*: Politik im Spiegel griechischer Wortbildungslehre." *MH* 38: 205–19.

Fresco, M. F. 1976. "Zur Schuld des Orestes." In Kamerbeek 1976: pp. 85–123.

Frey, Viktor. 1947. "Betrachtungen zu Euripides' *Aulischer Iphigenie.*" *MH* ser. 4, no.4: 39–51.

Friedländer, Paul. 1926. "Die griechische Tragödie und das Tragische." *Antike* 2: 79–112.

Friedrich, Claus. 1955. "Die dramatische Funktion der euripideischen Gnomen mit Hinweisen auf das Interpolationenproblem." Diss. Freiburg.

Friedrich, W. H. 1968. "Medeas Rache." In Schwinge 1968.2, pp. 177–237. First published *NAWG* 4 (1960) 67–111. Repr. in 1967, pp. 7–56.

Friedrich, W. H. 1967. *Vorbild und Neugestaltung: Sechs Kapitel zur Geschichte der Tragödie.* Göttingen: Vandenhoeck & Rupprecht.

Friedrich, W. H. 1966. "Medea in Kolchis." *A&A* 12: 3–28.

Friedrich, W. H. 1953. *Euripides und Diphilos: Zur Dramaturgie der Spätformen.* Zetemata 5. Munich: Beck. Review: T. B. L. Webster, *Gnomon* 26 (1954) 128–30.

Friedrich, W. H. 1935. "Zur *Aulischen Iphigenie.*" *Hermes* 70: 73–100.

Frischer, B. D. 1970. "*Concordia Discors* and Characterization in Euripides' *Hippolytus.*" *GRBS* 11: 85–100.

Fritz, Kurt von. 1962. *Antike und moderne Tragödie: Neun Abhandlungen.* Berlin: De Gruyter. Review: H. Lloyd-Jones, *Gnomon* 34 (1962) 737–47.

Fritz, Kurt von. 1959. "Die Entwicklung der Iason-Medeasage und die *Medea* des Euripides." *A&A* 8: 33–106. Repr. in 1962, pp. 322–429.

Fritz, Kurt von. 1956. "Euripides' *Alkestis* und ihre modernen Nachahmer und Kritiker." *A&A* 5: 27–70. Repr. in 1962, pp. 256–321.

Fritz, Kurt von. 1955. "Tragische Schuld und poetische Gerechtigkeit." *Studium Generale* 8: 195–232. Repr. in 1962, pp. 1–112.

Fritz, Kurt von. 1936. "Danaidentrilogie des Aeschylus." *Philologus* 91: 121–36/249–69. Repr. in 1962, pp. 160–92.

Fritz, Kurt von. 1934.1. "Haimons Liebe zu Antigone." *Philologus* 89: 19–34. Repr. in 1962, pp. 227–240.

Fritz, Kurt von. 1934.2. "Zur Interpretation des Aias." *RhM* n.F. 83: 113–28. Repr. in 1962, pp. 241–255.

Frye, Northrop. 1970. *The Stubborn Structure: Essays on Criticism and Society.* Ithaca, N.Y.: Cornell Univ. Pr.

Frye, Northrop. 1957. *The Anatomy of Criticism: Four Essays.* Princeton: Princeton Univ. Pr.

Funke, Hermann. 1963. "Die sogenannte tragische Schuld: Studie zur Rechtsidee in der griechischen Tragödie." Diss. Cologne.

Fuqua, Charles. 1978. "The World of Myth in Euripides' *Orestes.*" *Traditio* 34: 1–28.

Fuqua, Charles. 1976. "Studies in the Use of Myth in Sophocles' *Philoctetes* and the *Orestes* of Euripides." *Traditio* 32: 29–95.

Gagarin, Michael. 1976. *Aeschylean Drama.* Berkeley: Univ. of California Pr.

Galinsky, G. K. 1972. *The Herakles Theme: The Adaptations of the Hero in Literature from Homer to the Twentieth Century.* Totowa, N.J.: Rowman & Littlefield.

Gamble, R. B. 1970. "Euripides' *Suppliant Women*: Decision and Ambivalence." *Hermes* 98: 385–405.

Gantz, Timothy. 1981. "Divine Guilt in Aischylos." *CQ* 31: 18–32.

Garton, Charles. 1972. "The 'Chameleon Trail' in the Criticism of Greek Tragedy." *Stud. Philol.* 69: 389–413.

Garton, Charles. 1957. "Characterisation in Greek Tragedy." *JHS* 77: 247–54.

Garzya, Antonio. 1967. "Technische Neuerung und moralisches Anliegen im Theaterwerk des Euripides." *Altertum* 13: 195–205.

Garzya, Antonio. 1962. *Pensiero e tecnica drammatica in Euripide: Saggio sul motivo della salvazione nei suoi drammi.* Collana di stud. greci 36. Naples: Libreria Scientifica.

Garzya, Antonio. 1954. "Intorno all' *Ecuba* di Euripide." *GIF* 7: 206 – 12.

Garzya, Antonio. 1951. "Interpretazione dell' *Andromaca* di Euripide." *Dioniso* 14: 109 – 38.

Gellie, G. H. 1981. "Tragedy and Euripides' *Electra*." *BICS* 28: 1 – 12.

Gellie, G. H. 1972. *Sophocles: A Reading.* Netley: Melbourne Univ. Pr.

Gellie, G. H. 1963. "Character in Greek Tragedy." *AUMLA* 20: 241 – 55.

Gelzer, Thomas. 1956. "Aristophanes und sein Sokrates." *MH* 13: 65 – 93.

Gerhard, Melitta. 1919. *Schiller und die griechische Tragödie.* Weimar: Duncker.

Gernet, Louis. 1917. *Recherches sur le développement de la pensée juridique et morale en Grèce.* Paris: Leroux.

Ghiron-Bistagne, Paulette. 1976. *Recherches sur les acteurs dans la Grèce ântique.* Paris: Les Belles Lettres.

Gigon, Olof. 1981. "Σπουδαῖος." In Welskopf 1981, 4:7 – 10.

Gigon, Olof. 1968. "Jugend und Alter in der Ethik des Aristoteles." In *Antiquitas Graec-Romana ac Tempora Nostra.* Acta Congr. Int., ed. J. Burian & L. Widman, pp. 188 – 92. Prague: Academia.

Gigon, Olof. 1947. *Sokrates: Sein Bild in Dichtung und Geschichte.* Bern: Francke.

Girard, René. 1972. *La violence et le sacré.* Paris: Grasset.

Glanville, I. M. 1949. "Tragic Error." *CQ* 43: 47 – 56.

Göbel, J. A. 1849. *Euripides de vita privata ac domestica quid senserit.* Munich: Theissing.

Gollwitzer, Ingeborg. 1937. *Die Prolog- und Expositionstechnik der griechischen Tragödie, mit besonderer Berücksichtigung des Euripides.* Munich: Tussentka-mer.

Gomperz, Heinrich. 1912. *Sophistik und Rhetorik: Das Bildungsideal des* εὖ λέγειν *in seinem Verhältnis zur Philosophie des V. Jahrhunderts.* Leipzig: Teubner.

Goossens, Roger. 1962. *Euripide et Athènes.* Acad. Royale de Belgique. Mémoires 55, no.4. Brussels.

Gotoff, H. C. 1980. "Thrasymachus of Calchedon and Ciceronian Style." *CPh* 75: 297 – 311.

Gould, J. P. 1980. "Law, Custom and Myth: Aspects of the Social Position of Women in Classical Athens." *JHS* 100: 38 – 59.

Gould, J. P. 1978. "Dramatic Character and 'Human Intelligibility' in Greek Tragedy." *PCPhS* n.s. 24: 43 – 67.

Gould, J. P. 1973. "*Hiketeia*." *JHS* 93: 74 – 103.

Gould, T. F. & C. J. Herington, eds. 1977. *Greek Tragedy.* YClS 25.

Gould, Thomas. 1966. "The Innocence of Oedipus: The Philosophers on *Oedipus the King*." Part 3, *Arion* 5: 478 – 525.

Gould, Thomas. 1965. "The Innocence of Oedipus: The Philosophers on *Oedipus the King*." Part 1, *Arion* 4: 363 – 86. Part 2, ibid., 582 – 611.

Gouldner, A. W. 1965. *Enter Plato: Classical Greece and the Origins of Social Theory.* NY: Basic Books.

Gow, A. S. F., ed. 1950. *Theocritus: Edited with a Translation and Commentary.* 2 vols. Cambridge: Univ. Pr.

Grande, Carlo Del. 1964. "*Nomos, physis,* e qualche riflesso tragico." *Vichiana* 1: 357 – 75.

Grande, Carlo Del. 1962. "Euripide, *nomos* e *physis.*" *Dioniso* 36: 46 – 49.

Gredley, B. 1973. "Choruses in Euripides." *BICS* 20: 164 – 65.

Greenwood, L. H. G. 1953. *Aspects of Euripidean Tragedy.* Cambridge: Univ. Pr. Reviews: J. G. Griffith, *JHS* 74 (1954) 198 – 99; G. Norwood, *Phoenix* 8 (1954) 34 – 35.

Greenwood, L. H. G. 1930. "The Gods in Euripides: A Suggestion." Resumé in *PCPhS* 153: 5.

Grégoire, Henri & M. R. Goossens. 1940. "Les allusions politiques dans l'Hélène d'Euripide: L'épisode de Teucros et les débuts du Teucride Évagoras." *CRAI,* pp. 206 – 27.

Gregory, Justina. "Euripides' *Heracles.*" In Gould & Herington 1977, pp. 259 – 75.

Grene, David. 1939. "The Interpretation of the *Hippolytus* of Euripides." *CPh* 34: 45 – 58.

Gresseth, G. K. 1958. "The System of Aristotle's *Poetics.*" *TAPA* 89: 312 – 35.

Griessmair, Ewald. 1966. *Das Motiv der Mors immatura in den griechischen metrischen Grabinschriften.* Comm. Aenipontanae 17. Innsbruck: Wagner.

Griffin, Jasper. 1977. "The Epic Cycle and the Uniqueness of Homer." *JHS* 97: 39 – 53.

Griffith, J. G. 1953. "Some Thoughts on the *Helena* of Euripides." *JHS* 73: 36 – 41.

Griffith, Mark. 1977. *The Authenticity of Prometheus Bound.* Cambridge: Univ. Pr.

Groningen, B. A. van. 1977. *Euphorion.* Amsterdam: Hakkert.

Gross, Adolphus. 1905. *Die Stichomythie in der griechischen Tragödie und Komödie: Ihre Anwendung und ihr Ursprung.* Berlin: Weidmann.

Grube, G. M. A. 1941. *The Drama of Euripides.* London: Methuen.

Guépin, J. P. 1959. "Euripides, rationalist of gelovige? Het raadsel van de *Iphigeneia in Aulis.*" *Hermeneus* 31: 150 – 58.

Gundert, Hermann. 1940. "Charakter und Schicksal homerischer Helden." *NJAB* 1 – 2: 225 – 37.

Guthrie, W. K. C. 1971. *Socrates.* Cambridge: Univ. Pr. First published in *History of Greek Philosophy.* Pt.2, vol.3. 1969.

Hadley, W. S., ed. 1894. *The Hecuba of Euripides.* Cambridge: Univ. Pr.

Haigh, A. E. 1896. *The Tragic Drama of the Greeks.* Oxford: Clarendon Pr.

Hajistephanou, C. E. 1975. *The Use of ΦΥΣΙΣ and Its Cognates in Greek Tragedy with Special Reference to Character Drawing.* Diss. Univ. of London 1968. Nicosia: Zavallis.

Hamilton, Richard. 1978. "Prologues, Prophecy and Plot in Four Plays of Euripides." *AJPh* 99: 277 – 302.

Hamilton, Richard. 1974. "Objective Evidence for Actors' Interpolations in Greek Tragedy." *GRBS* 15: 387 – 402.

Hanne, 1914. "Euripides und Ibsen." Resumé in *Gymnasium* 25: 123 – 24.

Hansen, M. H. 1981. "The Prosecution of Homicide in Athens: A Reply." *GRBS* 22: 11 – 30.

Harbsmeier, D. G. 1968. *Die alten Menschen bei Euripides.* Göttingen: Funke.

Harries, Hermann. 1891. *Tragici graeci quo arte usi sint in describenda insania.* Kiel: H. Fiencke.

Harriott, Rosemary. 1962. "Aristophanes' Audience and the Plays of Euripides." *BICS* 9: 1–8.

Harsh, P. W. 1945. "Ἁμαρτία Again." *TAPA* 76: 47–58.

Hartung, J. A. 1843. *Euripides restitutus, sive scriptorum Euripidis ingeniique censura.* Hamburg: Perthes.

Hartwig, P. 1891. "Herakles und *Geras.*" *Philologus* 50: 185–90.

Hathorn, R. Y. 1957. "Rationalism and Irrationalism in Euripides' *Hippolytus.*" *CJ* 52: 211–18.

Hawkes, Terence. 1977. *Structuralism and Semiotics.* Berkeley: Univ. of California Pr.

Heberden, C. B., ed. 1901. *Euripides: Hecuba.* Oxford: Clarendon Pr.

Heilman, R. B. 1968. *Tragedy and Melodrama: Versions of Experience.* Seattle: Univ. of Washington Pr.

Heinemann, Karl. 1920. *Die tragischen Gestalten der Griechen in der Weltliteratur.* Das Erbe der Alten. 3–4. Leipzig: Dieterich.

Heinimann, Felix. 1945. *Nomos und Physis: Herkunft und Bedeutung einer Antithese im griechischen Denken des 5. Jahrhunderts.* Basel: Reinhardt.

Heitsch, Ernst. 1980. "Der Anfang unserer *Ilias* und Homer." *Gymnasium* 87: 38–56.

Heitsch, Ernst. 1955. "Zur lyrischen Sprache des Euripides." Diss. Göttingen.

Heldmann, Konrad. 1968. "Senecas Phaidra und ihre griechischen Vorbilder." *Hermes* 96: 88–117.

Henn, T. R. 1956. *The Harvest of Tragedy.* London: Methuen.

Herington, C. J. 1963. "The Influence of Old Comedy on Aeschylus' Later Trilogies." *TAPA* 94: 113–25.

Hermann, G. F. 1837. *Quaestionum oedipodearum libri.* Marburg: Garthe.

Herter, Hans. 1940. "Theseus und Hippolytus." *RhM* 89: 273–92.

Hinks, D. A. G. 1940. "Tisias and Corax and the Invention of Rhetoric." *CQ* 34: 61–69.

Hirzel, Rudolf. 1887. "Polykrates' Anklage und Lysias' Vertheidigung des Sokrates." *RhM* 42: 239–50.

Hofmann, W. & H. Kuch. 1973. *Die gesellschaftliche Bedeutung des antiken Dramas für seine und für unsere Zeit.* Schriften zum Gesch. & Kultur der Antike 6. Berlin: Akademie-Verl.

Hofmann, H. H. 1916. *Über den Zusammenhang zwischen Chorliedern und Handlung in den erhaltenen Dramen des Euripides.* Diss. Leipzig. Weida in Thür: Thomas & Hubert.

Hogan, J. T. 1980. "The ἀξίωσις of Words at Thucydides 3.82.4." *GRBS* 21: 139–49.

Hooker, E. M. 1960. "Changing Fashions in Ancient Drama I." *G&R* 7: 36–53.

Houben, J. A. 1850. "Euripidis *Iphigenia in Aulide* Tragoedia cum Racinii comparata." Trier: Lintz.

Howald, Ernst. 1930. *Die griechische Tragödie.* Munich: Oldenbourg. Reviews: A. Lesky, *DLZ* 3, no.2 (1931) 346 – 54; W. Schadewaldt, *Gnomon* 8 (1932) 1 – 13.

Howald, Ernst. 1923. "Ionische Geschichtsschreibung." *Hermes* 58: 113 – 46.

Howald, Ernst. 1914. *Untersuchungen zur Technik der euripideischen Tragödien.* Habilitationsschrift Zürich. Tübingen: Laupp.

Hübner, Ulrich. 1981. "Text und Bühnenspiel in der Anagnorisisszene der *Alkestis.*" *Hermes* 109: 156 – 66.

Huemer, Kamillo. 1930. *Das tragische Dreigestirn und seine modernen Beurteiler: Randbemerkungen zu griechischen Tragödien.* Vienna: Fromme.

Humbert, Jean. 1967. *Socrate et les petits socratiques.* Paris: Univ. de France.

Hunger, H. 1936. "Realistische Charakterdarstellung in den Spätwerken des Euripides." *Comm. Vind.* 2: 5 – 28.

Huxley, G. L. 1969. *Greek Epic Poetry: From Eumelos to Panyassis.* Cambridge, Mass.: Harvard Univ. Pr.

Imhof, Max. 1966. *Euripides' Ion: Eine literarische Studie.* Bern: Francke. Review: S. Radt, *Gymnasium* 75 (1968) 393 – 94.

Imhof, Max. 1957. *Bemerkungen zu den Prologen der sophokleischen und euripideischen Tragödien.* Winterthur: Keller.

Irwin, T. H. 1983. "Euripides and Socrates." *CPh* 78: 183 – 97.

Irwin, T. H. 1977. *Plato's Moral Theory: The Early and Middle Dialogues.* Oxford: Clarendon Pr.

Jaekel, Siegfried. 1979. "The *Aiolos* of Euripides." *GB* 8: 101 – 18.

Jaekel, Siegfried. 1977. "Wahrheit und Trug in den Dramen des Euripides." *Arktos* 11: 15 – 40.

Jaekel, Siegfried. 1973. "ΠΑΘΟΝΤΙ ΑΝΤΙΔΡΑΝ : Ein Kompositionsprinzip der griechischen Tragödie bei Sophokles und Euripides." In Festschr. Gerhard Storz, *Über Literatur und Geschichte,* pp. 21 – 46. Frankfurt am Main: Athenaeum.

Jahn, Otto, ed. 1882. *Sophoklis Elektra.* 3d edn. rev. A. Michaelis. Bonn: Marcus.

Jakob, D. J. 1976. "Zu Euripides *Hippolytos* 1 Fr. 443 N2." *Hermes* 104: 379 – 82.

Janske, Jos. 1866. "De Euripidis Philosophia." *Jahresbericht.* Königl. kathol. Gymnasium Breslau.

Jaruzelska, H. B. 1973. "Der Elektra-Stoff von Sophokles bis Hauptmann." In Hofmann & Kuch 1973, pp. 79 – 90.

Jens, Walter, ed. 1971. *Die Bauformen der griechischen Tragödie.* Munich: Fink.

Jens, Walter. 1964. *Euripides/Büchner.* Stuttgart: Neske.

Johansen, H. F. 1959. *General Reflection in Tragic Rhesis: A Study of Form.* Copenhagen: Munksgaard.

Johnson, R[alph]. 1959. "The Poet and the Orator." *CPh* 54: 173 – 76.

Jones, John. 1962. *On Aristotle and Greek Tragedy.* London: Chatto & Windus.

Jouan, François. 1970. "Le Prométhée d'Eschyle et l'Héraclès d'Euripide." *REA* 72: 317 – 31.

Jouan, François. 1966. *Euripide et les légendes des chants cypriens.* Paris: Les Belles Lettres.

Kaibel, Georg, ed. 1967. *Sophokles: Elektra.* Stuttgart: Teubner. First published 1896.

Kaimio, Maarit. 1970. *The Chorus of Greek Drama Within the Light of the Person and Number Used.* Commentat. Hum. Litt. 46. Helsinki.

Kahn, C. H. 1960. *Anaximander and the Origins of Greek Cosmology.* New York: Columbia Univ. Pr.

Kakridis, J. T. 1949. "The Motif of Intaphernes' Wife and the Ascending Scale of Affection." App. 3 in *Homeric Researches.* Lund: Gleerup.

Kalkmann, August. 1881. "De Hippolytis Euripideis quaestiones novae." Diss. Bonn.

Kamerbeek, J. C. 1976. *Miscellanea Tragica.* Festschr. ed. J. M. Bremer et al. Amsterdam: Hakkert.

Kamerbeek, J. C. 1966. "The Unity and Meaning of Euripides' *Heracles.*" *Mnemosyne* ser. 4, 19: 1–16.

Kamerbeek, J. C. 1963. "Individualiteit bij Euripides." *FL* 4: 191–206.

Kamerbeek, J. C. 1958. "Mythe et réalité dans l'oeuvre d'Euripide." In *Entretiens* 1958, pp. 3–41. (includes discussion following)

Kannicht, Richard, ed. 1969. *Euripides: Helena.* 2 vols. Heidelberg: Winter.

Karsai, Gyorgy. 1979. "Electra or Clytemnestra?" *Homonoia* 1: 9–36.

Katsouris, A. G. 1975. "τὸ μοτίβο τῆς αὐτοκτονίας στὸ ἀρχαῖο δράμα." *Dodone* 4: 203–34.

Keene, C. H., ed. 1893. *The Electra of Euripides.* London: Bell.

Kennedy, G. A. 1959. "The Earliest Rhetorical Handbooks." *AJPh* 80: 169–78.

Kerferd, G. B. 1981. *The Sophistic Movement.* Cambridge: Univ. Pr.

Keyes, C. W. 1940. "Half-sister Marriage in new Comedy and the *Epidicus.*" *TAPA* 71: 217–29.

King, F. W., ed. 1938. *Euripides' Hecuba.* London: Bell & Sons.

Kirchoff, A. 1853. "Ein Supplement zu Euripides' *Bacchen.*" *Philologus* 8: 78–93.

Kirkwood, G. M. 1965. "Homer and Sophocles' *Ajax.*" In *Classical Drama and Its Influence.* Festschr. H. D. F. Kitto, ed. M. J. Anderson, pp. 51–70. London: Methuen.

Kirkwood, G. M. 1947. "Hecuba and *nomos.*" *TAPA* 78: 61–68.

Kirkwood, G. M. 1942. "Two Structural Features of Sophocles' *Electra.*" *TAPA* 73: 86–95.

Kirsch, Wolfgang. 1982. "Probleme der Gattungsentwicklung am Beispiel des Epos." *Philologus* 126: 265–88.

Kitto, H. D. F. 1961. *Greek Tragedy: A Literary Study.* 3d edn. London: Methuen. First published 1939.

Kitto, H. D. F. 1950. *Greek Tragedy: A Literary Study.* 2d edn. London: Methuen. First published 1939.

Kitto, H. D. F. 1952. "The Idea of God in Aeschylus and Sophocles." In *Entretiens* 1952, pp. 169–89.

Kitto, H. D. F. 1950. *Greek Tragedy: A Literary Study.* 2d edn. London: Methuen. First published 1939.

Klimpe, Peter. 1970. *Die Elektra des Sophokles und Euripides' Iphigenie bei den Taurern: Ein Beitrag zur Diskussion über das Aufführungsjahr von Sophokles' Elektra.* Diss. Tübingen. Göppingen: Kümmerle.

Klinkenberg, J. 1881. *De Euripideorum prologorum arte et interpolatione.* Bonn: Marcus.

Knox, B. M. W. 1979.1. *Arktouros: Hellenic Studies Presented to Bernard M. W. Knox on the Occasion of his Sixty-fifth Birthday.* Ed. G. W. Bowersock et al. Berlin: De Gruyter.

Knox, B. M. W. 1979.2. *Word and Action: Essays on the Ancient Theater.* Baltimore: Johns Hopkins Univ. Pr.

Knox, B. M. W. 1979.3. "Euripidean Comedy." In 1979.2, pp. 250–74. First published in *The Rarer Action,* Festschr. F. Ferguson, A. Chase & R. Koffler eds., pp. 68–96. New Brunswick, N.J.: Rutgers Univ. Pr., 1970.

Knox, B. M. W. 1972.1. "New Perspectives in Euripidean Criticism." Review of Burnett 1971. *CPh* 67: 270–79.

Knox, B. M. W. 1972.2. "Euripides *Iphigenia in Aulide* 1–163 (in that order)." *YClS* 22: 239–61. Repr. in 1979.2, pp. 275–94.

Knox, B. M. W. 1966. "Second Thoughts in Greek Tragedy." *GRBS* 7: 213–32. Repr. in 1979.2, pp. 231–49.

Knox, B. M. W. 1964. *The Heroic Temper; Studies in Sophoclean Tragedy.* Berkeley: Univ. of California Pr.

Knox, B. M. W. 1952. "The *Hippolytus* of Euripides." *YClS* 13: 3–31. Repr. in 1979.2, pp. 205–30.

Koestler, Arthur. 1964. *The Act of Creation.* N.Y.: Macmillan.

Köhnken, Adolf. 1972. "Götterrahmen und menschliches Handeln in Euripides' *Hippolytos.*" *Hermes* 100: 179–90.

Kolb, Frank. 1979. "Polis und Theater." In Seeck 1979, pp. 504–46.

Kovacs, P. D. 1985. "Castor in Euripides' *Electra* (*El.* 307–13 and 1292–1307)." *CQ* 35: 306–314.

Kovacs, P. D. 1980.1. *The Andromache of Euripides: An Interpretation.* American Class. Studies 6. Chico, Calif.: Scholars Pr.

Kovacs, P. D. 1980.2. "Euripides *Hippolytus* 100 and the Meaning of the Prologue." *CPh* 75: 130–37.

Kovacs, P. D. 1976. "Euripides' *Hecabe* and *Andromache.*" Diss. Harvard Univ.

Kranz, Walther. 1933. *Stasimon: Untersuchungen zu Form und Gehalt der griechischen Tragödie.* Berlin: Weidmann.

Kranz, Walther. 1927. "ΕΓΚΑΡΤΕΡΗΣΩ ΘΑΝΑΤΟΝ." *PhW* 47: 138–39.

Kraus, Friedrich. 1889–90. "Utrum Sophoclis an Euripidis *Electra* aetate prior sit quaeritur." *Programm.* Gymnas. Passau.

Krausse, Otto. 1905. *De Euripide Aeschyli instauratore.* Diss. Jena. Neuenholm: Hahn.

Kretz, Louis. 1934. *Persönliches bei Euripides.* Zürich: Leeman.

Krischer, Tilman. 1982. "Die Stellung der Biographie in der griechischen Literatur." *Hermes* 110: 51–64.

Kröker, Ernst. 1938. "Der Herakles des Euripides: Analyse des Dramas." Diss. Leipzig.

Kubo, Masaaki. 1967. "The Norm of Myth: Euripides' *Electra.*" *HSCPh* 71: 15–31.

Kuch, Heinrich. 1973. "Die troische Dramengruppe des Euripides und ihre historischen Grundlagen." In Hofmann & Kuch 1973, pp. 105–23.

Kuch, Heinrich. 1968. "Kriegsgefangenschaft und Arbeit in der *Hekabe* des Euripides." In *Eirene,* Acta Conventus XI, pp. 47–53. Warsaw.

Kuhn, Helmut. 1942. "The True Tragedy: On the Relationship Between Greek Tragedy and Plato, II." *HSCPh* 53: 37–88.

Kuiper, E. J. 1959. "*Iphigeneia in Aulis.*" *Hermeneus* 31: 134–38.

Kullmann, Wolfgang. 1967. "Zum Sinngehalt der euripideischen *Alkestis.*" *A&A* 13: 127–49.

Kullmann, Wolfgang. 1960. *Die Quellen der Ilias.* Hermes Einzelschr. 14. Wiesbaden: Steiner.

Kumaniecki, C. F. 1930. *De consiliis personarum apud Euripidem agentium.* Cracow: Gebettner & Wolff.

Lane, Michael, ed. 1970. *Introduction to Structuralism.* N.Y.: Basic Books.

Lanza, Diego. 1963. "Νόμος e Ἴσον in Euripide." *RIFC* 91: 416–39.

Lanza, Diego. 1961. "Unità e significato dell' *Oreste* euripideo." *Dioniso* 35, no.1: 58–72.

Latacz, Joachim. 1966. *Zum Wortfeld "Freude" in der Sprache Homers.* Heidelberg: Winter.

Latte, Kurt. 1968. *Kleine Schriften zu Religion, Recht, Literatur und Sprache der Griechen und Römer.* Ed. O. Gigon et al. Munich: Beck.

Lattimore, Richmond. 1962. "Phaedra and Hippolytus." *Arion* 1 no.3: 5–18.

Leaf, Walter. 1912. "The Late Professor Verrall." *Cambr. Rev.,* Oct. 17, p. 13.

Lee, K. H. 1955. "Euripides' *Andromache*: Observations on Form and Meaning." *Antichthon* 9: 4–16.

Leeuwen, Johannes van. 1876. *De Aristophane Euripidis censore.* Amsterdam: Spin.

Lefkowitz, M. R. 1981. *The Lives of the Greek Poets.* Baltimore: Johns Hopkins Univ. Pr.

Lefkowitz, M. R. 1979. "The Euripides *Vita.*" *GRBS* 20: 187–210.

Lennep, D. F. W. van. 1949. *Euripides, Selected Plays: I. Alkestis.* Leiden: Brill.

Lesky, Albin. 1976. "Alcestis und Deianeira." In Kamerbeek 1976, pp. 213–23.

Lesky, Albin. 1973. "Γιὰ τὴν ἑνότητα τοῦ ἔργου τοῦ Εὐριπίδη." *EEThess* 12: 97–108.

Lesky, Albin. 1972.1. *Die tragische Dichtung der Hellenen.* 3d edn. Göttingen: Vandenhoeck and Ruprecht. First published 1956.

Lesky, Albin. 1972.2. "Zur Darstellung seelischer Abläufe in der griechischen Tragödie." In Festschr. W. Kraus. *Antidosis,* ed. R. Hanslik et al. Wiener Studien Beiheft 5, pp. 209–26.

Lesky, Albin. 1968.1. "Recht und Staat bei Protagoras." In *Antiquitas Graeco-Romana ac Tempora Nostra.* Acta Congr. Int., ed. J. Burian & L. Widman, pp. 67–72. Prague: Academia.

Lesky, Albin. 1968.2. "Euripides und die Pädagogik." *WHB* 11: 16–19.

Lesky, Albin. 1966.1. "Der Mythos im Verständnis der Antike I: Von der Frühzeit bis Sophokles." *Gymnasium* 73: 27–44.

Lesky, Albin. 1966.2. *Gesammelte Schriften: Aufsätze und Reden zur antiken und deutschen Dichtung und Kultur.* Ed. Walther Kraus. Bern: Francke.

Lesky, Albin. 1966.3. "Zum Problem des Tragischen." In 1966.2, pp. 213–19. First published *Gymn. Helv.* 7 (1953) 2–10.

Lesky, Albin. 1964. "Der angeklagte Admet." *Maske und Kothurn* 10: 203–16.

Lesky, Albin. 1961. "Göttliche und menschliche Motivation im homerischen Epos." *SHAW* 4.

Lesky, Albin. 1960. "Zur Problematik des Psychologischen in der Tragödie des Euripides." *Gymnasium* 67: 10–26. Repr. in 1966.2, pp. 247–63.

Lesky, Albin. 1958. "Psychologie bei Euripides." In *Entretiens* 1958, pp. 125–80 (includes discussion following).

Lesky, Albin. 1957–58. *Geschichte der griechischen Literatur.* Bern: Francke. 2d edn. 1963.

Lesky, Albin. 1956. *Die tragische Dichtung der Hellenen.* Göttingen: Vandenhoeck and Ruprecht.

Lesky, Albin. 1948–67. "Forschungsbericht: Die griechische Tragödie." In 1–7 "Fortsetzungen." *AAHG.*

Lesky, Albin. 1938. *Die griechische Tragödie.* Stuttgart: Kröner Taschenausgabe. 143. 2d edn. 1958.

Lesky, Albin. 1931. "Die griechische Tragödie in ihren jüngsten Darstellungen." *NJW* 7: 343–55.

Lesky, Albin. 1925. *Alkestis, der Mythos und das Drama.* SAWW 203.2: pp. 1–86. Reviews: Anon., *JHS* 46 (1926) 124; H. Drexler, *Gnomon* 3 (1927) 441–55; H. Ebeling, *AJPh* 48 (1927) 89–92; W. Morel, *BphW* 46 (1926) 705–8.

Linforth, I. M. 1914. "Hippolytus and Humanism." *TAPA* 45: 5–16.

Lloyd-Jones, Hugh. 1983. *The Justice of Zeus.* 2d edn. Berkeley: Univ. of California Pr. First published 1971.

Lloyd-Jones, Hugh. 1980. "Euripides, *Medea* 1056–80." *WJA* 6: 51–59.

Lloyd-Jones, Hugh. 1972. "Tycho von Wilamowitz-Möllendorff on the Dramatic Technique of Sophocles." *CQ* 22: 214–28.

Lloyd-Jones, Hugh. 1961. "Some Alleged Interpolations in Aeschylus' *Choephori* and Euripides' *Electra*." *CQ* n.s. 11: 171–84.

Lloyd-Jones, Hugh. 1952. "The Robes of Iphigenia." *CR* 66: 132–35.

Longo, Oddone. 1975. "Proposte di lettura per l'*Oreste* di Euripide." *Maia* 27: 265–87.

Longo, Vincenzo. 1963. "'Deus ex Machina' e religione in Euripide." In *Lanx Satura,* Festschr. N. Terzaghi, pp. 237–48. Ist. d. fil. class. et med. 16. Genoa.

Looy, Herman van. 1964. *Zes verloren tragedies van Euripides.* Vlaamse Akad. Brussels, Kl. Lett. 25, no.51.

Looy, Herman van. 1963. "Les Fragments d'Euripide." *AC* 32: 162–99, 607–8.

Lotman, Jurij. 1977. *The Structure of the Artistic Text.* Trans. R. Vroom. Michigan Slavic Contributions 7. Ann Arbor.

Lucas, D. W., ed. 1968. *Aristotle Poetics.* Oxford: Clarendon Pr.

Lucas, D. W. 1962. "Pity, Terror, and *Peripeteia*." *CQ* 12: 52–60.

Lucas, F. L. 1923. *Euripides and His Influence.* Our Debt to Greece and Rome Series. Boston: Marshall Jones.

Ludwig, Walther. 1957. *Sapheneia: Ein Beitrag zur Formkunst im Spätwerk des Euripides.* Diss. Tübingen. Bonn: Habelt.

Luschnig, C. A. E. 1975–76. "Euripides' *Hecabe*: The Time Is Out of Joint." *CJ* 71: 227–34.

Luther, Wilhelm. 1966. *Wahrheit, Licht und Erkenntnis in der griechischen Philosophie bis Demokrit.* ABG 10: pp. 1–240.

MacCary, W. T. 1982. *Childlike Achilles: Ontogeny and Phylogeny in the Iliad.* N.Y.: Columbia Univ. Pr.

MacKay, L. A. 1962. "Antigone, Coriolanus, and Hegel." *TAPA* 93: 166–74.

Macleod, C. W. 1982. "Politics and the *Oresteia*." *JHS* 102: 124–44.

Maddalena, A. 1963. "La *Medea* di Euripide." *RIFC* ser. 3, 91: 129–52.

Magalhães-Vilhena, V. de. 1952. *Le problème de Socrate: Le Socrate historique et le Socrate de Platon.* Paris: Univ. de France.

Mahaffy, J. P. 1879. *Euripides.* London: Macmillan.

Maniet, A. 1947. "Hélène, 'comédie' d'Euripide." *LEC* 15: 305–22.

Manning, C. A. 1916. *A Study of Archaism in Euripides.* New York: Columbia Univ. Pr.

Manuwald, Bernd. 1979. "'Phaidras' tragischer Irrtum: Zur Rede Phaidras' in Euripides' *Hippolytos* (vv. 373–430)." *RhM* 122: 134–48.

Marrou, H. I. 1948. *Histoire de l'éducation dans l'antiquité.* Paris: Seuil.

Martin, Victor. 1958. "Euripide et Ménandre face à leur public." In *Entretiens* 1958, pp. 245–72.

Martina, Antonio. 1975. *Il riconoscimento di Oreste nelle Coefore e nelle due Elettre.* Rome: Ediz. dell' Ateneo.

Martinazzoli, Folco. 1946. *Euripide.* Rome: Editrice Faro.

Masaracchia, Agostino. 1972. "Una polemica di Euripide con il suo pubblico: *Hipp.* 373–402." In Cataudella 1972, pp. 289–302.

Masaracchia, Emanuela. 1977. "Interpretazioni Euripidee." *Helikon* 17: 155–77.

Masqueray, Paul. 1908. *Euripide et ses idées.* Paris: Hachette. Review: S. Mekler, *BphW* 30 (1910) 289–96.

Massimi, Alghiero. 1960. "Introduzione all' ellenismo: La cultura sofistica e la letteratura della sua età." *GIF* 13: 42–58.

Mastronarde, D. J. 1979. *Contact and Discontinuity: Some Conventions of Speech and Action on the Greek Tragic Stage.* Univ. of California Pub. in Classical Studies. 21. Berkeley.

Mastronarde, D. J. 1978. "Are Euripides *Phoinissai* 1104–1140 Interpolated?" *Phoenix* 32: 105–28.

Matejka, L. & K. Pomorska. 1971. *Readings in Russian Poetics: Formalist and Structuralist Views.* Cambridge, Mass.: M.I.T. Pr.

Matthaei, L. E. 1918. *Studies in Greek Tragedy.* Cambridge: Univ. Pr.

Matthiessen, Kjeld. 1979. "Euripides: Die Tragödien." In Seeck 1979, pp. 105–54.

Matthiessen, Kjeld. 1968. "Zur Theonoeszene der euripideischen *Helena*." *Hermes* 96: 685–704.

Matthiessen, Kjeld. 1964. *Elektra, Taurische Iphigenie und Helena: Untersuchungen zur Chronologie und zur dramatischen Form im Spätwerk des Euripides.* Hypomnemata 5. Göttingen: Vandenhoeck & Rupprecht. Reviews:

J. Gould, *JHS* 86 (1966) 178–79; D. W. Lucas, *CR* 79 (1965) 161–63; E. Schlesinger, *Gnomon* 37 (1965) 338–44.

Mau, August. 1877. "Zu Euripides' *Elektra.*" In *Commentationes Philologae, Festschr. T. Mommsen,* pp. 291–301. Berlin: Weidmann.

Maxwell-Stuart, P. G. 1971. "Gilden Euripides." *PP* 26: 5–13.

Mayer, Maximilian. 1885. "Der *Protesilaus* des Euripides." *Hermes* 20: 101–43.

Mellert-Hoffmann, Gudrun. 1969. *Untersuchungen zur Iphigenie in Aulis des Euripides.* Heidelberg: Winter.

Mensch, Fred. 1976. "The Conflict of Codes in Euripides' *Hippolytus.*" In *The Conflict of Generations in Ancient Greece and Rome,* ed. S. Bertman, pp. 75–88. Amsterdam: Grüner.

Mensching, Eckart. 1964. "Zur Produktivität der alten Komödie." *MH* 21: 15–49.

Méridier, Louis. 1911. *Le prologue dans la tragédie d'Euripide.* Bordeaux: Feret et Fils.

Meridor, Ra'anana. 1978. "Hecuba's Revenge: Some Observations on Euripides' *Hecuba.*" *AJPh* 99: 28–35.

Merklin, Harald. 1964. "Gott und Mensch im *Hippolytos* und den *Bakchen* des Euripides." Diss. Freiburg.

Mesk, Josef. 1931. "Die *Antigone* des Euripides." *WS* 49: 1–12.

Mette, H. J. 1982. *Euripides (inbesondere für die Jahre 1968–1981), Erster Hauptteil: Die Bruckstücke.* Lustrum 23–24. Göttingen: Vandenhoeck & Ruprecht.

Michel, Laurence & R. B. Sewall. 1963. *Tragedy: Modern Essays in Criticism.* Englewood Cliffs, N.J.: Prentice-Hall.

Michelini, A. N. 1985. "Aeschylean Stagecraft and the Third Actor." *Eranos* 82 (1984) 135–47.

Michelini, A. N. 1982. *Tradition and Dramatic Form in the Persians of Aeschylus.* Leiden: Brill.

Michelini, A. N. 1979. "Characters and Character Change in Aeschylus: Klytaimestra and the Furies." *Ramus* 8: 153–64.

Michelini, A. N. 1974. "ΜΑΚΡΑΝ ΓΑΡ ΕΞΕΤΕΙΝΑΣ." *Hermes* 101: 524–39.

Miller, Arthur. 1957. *Collected Plays: With an Introduction.* N.Y.: Viking.

Miller, J. B. 1976. *Toward a New Psychology of Women.* Boston: Beacon.

Moline, Jon. 1975. "Euripides, Socrates and Virtue." *Hermes* 103: 45–67.

Montuori, Mario. 1974. *Socrate: Fisiologia di un Mito.* Florence: Sansoni.

Moss, Howard. 1982. "Good Poems, Sad Lives." Rev. of Eileen Simpson, *Poets in Their Youth. N.Y. Review of Books,* July 15.

Muecke, D. C. 1970. *Irony.* The Critical Idiom. 3. London: Methuen.

Müffelmann, Günther. 1965. "Interpretationen zur Motivation des Handelns im Drama des Euripides." Diss. Hamburg.

Mukařovský, Jan. 1978. *Structure, Sign, and Function: Selected Essays.* Ed. and trans. J. Burbank & P. Steiner. New Haven: Yale Univ. Pr.

Mullens, H. G. 1939. "*Hercules Furens* and *Prometheus Vinctus.*" *CR* 53: 165–66.

Müller, Clemens. 1933. *Vom Chorlied bei Euripides.* Göttingen: W. Postberg.

Müller, Eduard. 1826. *Euripides, deorum popularium contemptor.* Bratislava: Kupfer.

Müller, K. O. 1857. *Geschichte der griechischen Literatur bis auf das Zeitalter Alexanders.* Vol. 2. 2d edn. rev. E. Müller. Breslau: Max. First published 1841.

Müller, Reimar, ed. 1976. *Der Mensch als Mass der Dinge: Studien zum griechischen Menschenbild in der Zeit der Blüte und Krise der Polis.* Berlin: Akademie-Verl.

Müller, W. A. 1906. *Nacktheit und Entblössung in der altorientalischen und älteren griechischen Kunst.* Leipzig: Teubner.

Murray, Gilbert. 1954. "Memories of Wilamowitz." *A&A* 4: 9–14.

Murray, Gilbert. 1946. *Greek Studies.* Oxford: Clarendon Pr.

Murray, Gilbert. 1917. *A History of Ancient Greek Literature.* London: Heinemann. First published 1897.

Murray, Gilbert. 1913.1. *Euripides and His Age.* London: Williams and Norgate. 2d edn. 1946.

Murray, Gilbert. 1913.2. "A. W. Verrall: 1851–1912." Bursians *Biogr. Jhb.* 35: 118–20.

Murray, Gilbert. 1912. "Euripides." In *Encycl. of Religion and Ethics,* ed. James Hastings. N.Y.: Scribners.

Murray, Gilbert, trans. 1905. *The Electra of Euripides.* London: Allen & Unwin.

Musurillo, Herbert. 1972. "Alcestis: The Pageant of Life and Death." In Cataudella 1972, pp. 275–88.

Myers, H. A. 1956. *Tragedy: A View of Life.* Ithaca: Cornell Univ. Pr.

Myres, J. L. 1917. "The Plot of the *Alcestis.*" *JHS* 37: 195–218.

Nagavajara, Chetana. 1966. *August Wilhelm Schlegel in Frankreich: Sein Anteil an der französischen Literaturkritik.* Tübingen: Niemayer.

Nagy, Gregory. 1979. *The Best of the Achaeans: Concepts of the Hero in Archaic Greek Poetry.* Baltimore: Johns Hopkins Univ. Pr.

Nauck, August, ed. 1913. *Euripidis Tragoediae.* Vol. 1. Leipzig: Teubner. First published 1871.

Nestle, Walter. 1930. *Die Struktur des Eingangs in der attischen Tragödie.* Tübinger Beiträge 10. Stuttgart: Kohlhammer.

Nestle, Wilhelm. 1901. *Euripides: Der Dichter der griechischen Aufklärung.* Stuttgart: Kohlhammer. Review: M. Schneidewin, *WklPh* 18 (1901) 1310–18.

Neuberger-Donath, Ruth. 1970. "Die Rolle des Sklaven in der griechischen Tragödie." *C&M* 31: 72–83.

Newiger, H.-J. 1961. "Elektra in Aristophanes' *Wolken.*" *Hermes* 89: 422–30.

Newton, R. M. 1980. "*Hippolytus* and the Dating of *Oedipus Tyrannus.*" *GRBS* 21: 5–22.

Nicolai, Rudolf. 1873. *Griechische Literaturgeschichte.* Vol. 1. Magdeburg: Heinrichshofensche Buchhandl.

Nietzsche, Friedrich. 1968. *Die Geburt der Tragödie aus dem Geiste der Musik.* In *Studien Ausgabe* 1, ed. H. A. Holz. Frankfurt am Main: Fischer. First published 1872.

Norris, Christopher. 1982. *Deconstruction: Theory and Practice.* London: Methuen.

North, H. F. 1981. "Inutilis Sibi, Perniciosus Patriae: A Platonic Argument Against Sophistic Rhetoric." *ICS* 6: 242–71.

Norwood, Gilbert. 1954. *Essays on Euripidean Drama.* Berkeley: Univ. of California Pr.

Norwood, Gilbert. 1921. *Euripides and Shaw, With Other Essays.* Boston: Luce.

Norwood, Gilbert. 1920. *Greek Tragedy.* Boston: Luce.

Norwood, Gilbert. 1908. *The Riddle of the Bacchae: The Last Stage of Euripides' Religious Views.* Manchester: Univ. Pr.

Nussbaum, M. C. 1980. "Aristophanes and Socrates on Learning Practical Wisdom." *YClS* 26: 43–97.

O'Brien, M. J. 1967. *The Socratic Paradoxes and the Greek Mind.* Chapel Hill: Univ. of North Carolina Pr.

O'Brien, M. J. 1964. "Orestes and the Gorgon: Euripides' *Electra.*" *AJPh* 85: 13–39.

O'Connor, J. B. 1908. *Chapters in the History of Actors and Acting in Ancient Greece: Together with a Prosopographia Histrionum Graecorum.* Diss. Princeton. Chicago.

O'Connor, W. V. & M. A. O'Connor. 1943. *Climates of Tragedy.* Baton Rouge: Louisiana State Univ. Pr.

Oeri, Jakob. 1905. *Euripides unter dem Drucke des sicilischen und des dekeleischen Krieges.* Basel: Kreis.

Olson, Elder. 1961. *Tragedy and the Theory of Drama.* Detroit: Wayne State Univ. Pr.

Olvieri, A. 1897. "Appunti critici: I. Il mito di Oreste nel poema di Agia di Trezene; II. Le due *Elettre.*" *RIFC* 25: 570–99.

O'Neill Jr., E. G. 1941. "The Prologue of the *Troades* of Euripides." *TAPA* 72: 228–320.

Orban, Marcel. 1981.1. "*Hippolyte*: Palinodie ou revanche?" *LEC* 49: 3–17.

Orban, Marcel. 1981.2. "*Hippolyte*: 'Souffrir pour comprendre'." *LEC* 49: 193–212.

Orban, Marcel. 1970. "*Hécube,* drame humain." *EC* 38: 316–30.

Orr, John. 1981. *Tragic Drama and Modern Society: Studies in the Social and Literary Theory of Drama from 1870 to the Present.* Totowa, N.J.: Barnes & Noble.

Ortkemper, Hubert. 1969. "Szenische Techniken des Euripides: Untersuchungen zur Gebärdensprache im antiken Theater." Diss. Berlin.

Østerud, Svein. 1976. "*Hamartia* in Aristotle and Greek Tragedy." *SO* 51: 65–80.

Østerud, Svein. 1970. "Who Sings the Monody 669–79 in Euripides' *Hippolytus*?" *GRBS* 11: 307–20.

Ostwald, Martin. 1958. "Aristotle on AMAPTIA and Sophocles' *Oedipus Tyrannus.*" In Festschr. E. Kapp, pp. 93–108. Hamburg: Schröder.

Owen, A. S., ed. 1939. *Euripides: Ion.* Oxford: Clarendon Pr. Review: G. Norwood, *AJPh* 63 (1942) 109–13.

Padel, Ruth. 1974. "'Imagery of the Elsewhere': Two Choral Odes of Euripides." *CQ* n.s. 24: 227–41.

Paduano, Guido. 1970. "La scena del reconoscimento nell' *Elettra* di Euripide e la critica razionalistica alle *Coefore.*" *RIFC* 98: 385–405.

Paduano, Guido, ed. 1969. *Euripide: Alcesti.* Florence: La Nuova Italia.
Paduano, Guido. 1968. *La formazione del mondo ideologico e poetico di Euripide.* Pisa: Nistri-Lischi. Review: A. F. Garvie, *CR* 23 (1973) 86.
Paduano, Guido. 1967. "Il motivo del re mendicante e lo scandalo del *Telefo.*" *SCO* 16: 330–42.
Pagani, Giacomo. 1970. "Il dramma di Polissena nell' *Ecuba* di Euripide." *Dioniso* 44: 46–63.
Page, D. L. 1973. "Stesichorus: The *Geryoneis.*" JHS 93: 138–54.
Page, D. L. 1940. *Literary Papyri: Poetry.* Select Papyri III. Loeb Class. Libr. Cambridge, Mass.: Harvard Univ. Pr.
Page, D. L., ed. 1938. *Euripides: Medea.* Oxford: Clarendon Pr.
Page, D. L. 1934. *Actors' Interpolations in Greek Tragedy: Studied with Special Reference to Euripides' Iphigeneia in Aulis.* Oxford: Clarendon Pr. Reviews: R. Hölzle, *Gnomon* 13 (1937) 591–94; W. Morel, *PhW* 55 (1935) 401–7; A. Schlesinger, *AJPh* 56 (1935) 271–73; F. Solmsen, *CR* 49 (1935) 131–32.
Paley, F. A., ed. 1874. *Euripides with an English Commentary.* 2d edn. Vol. 2. London: Whittaker.
Paley, F. A., ed. 1860. *Euripides with an English Commentary.* Vol. 3. London: Whittaker.
Panagl, Oswald. 1972. "Zur Funktion der direkten Reden in den 'dithyrambischen Stasima' des Euripides." *WS* n.F. 6: 5–18.
Panagl, Oswald. 1971. *Die "dithyrambischen Stasima" des Euripides: Untersuchungen zur Komposition und Erzähltechnik.* Vienna: Notring.
Pandiri, Thalia. 1974–75. "*Alcestis* 1052 and the Yielding of Admetus." *CJ* 70 no.2: 50–52.
Paratore, Ettore. 1972. "Lo Ἱππόλυτος καλυπτόμενος di Euripide e la *Phaedra* di Seneca." In Cataudella 1972, pp. 303–46.
Paratore, Ettore. 1952. "Sulla *Phaedra* di Seneca." *Dioniso* 15: 199–234.
Parker, Robert. 1983. *Miasma: Pollution and Purification in Early Greek Religion.* Oxford: Clarendon Pr.
Parmentier, Léon & Henri Grégoire, eds. 1923. *Euripides.* Vol. 3. Assn. G. Budé. Paris: Les Belles Lettres.
Parmentier, Léon. 1893. *Euripide et Anaxagore.* Paris: Bouillon.
Parry, Hugh. 1969. "Euripides' *Orestes*: The Quest for Salvation." *TAPA* 100: 337–53.
Parry, Hugh. 1966. "The Second Stasimon of Euripides' *Hippolytus* (732–775)." *TAPA* 97: 317–26.
Parry, Hugh. 1965. "The Second Stasimon of Euripides' *Heracles* (637–700)." *AJPh* 86: 363–74.
Patin, H. 1873. *Études sur les tragiques grecs: Euripide.* 2 vols. 4th ed. Paris: Hachette. First published 1841–43.
Patin, H. 1871. *Études sur les tragiques grecs: Aeschyle.* Vol. 1. 4th ed. Paris: Hachette. First published 1841–43.
Paton, J. M. 1901. "The *Antigone* of Euripides." *HSCPh* 12: 267–76.
Pearson, A. C. 1917. *The Fragments of Sophocles.* Cambridge: Univ. Pr.

Pépin, Jean. 1976. *Mythe et allégorie: Les origines grecques et les contestations judéo-chrétiennes.* 2d edn. Paris: Études Augustiniennes.

Perrotta, Gennaro. 1963. *Sofocle.* Stud. Philol. 2. Rome: Bretschneider.

Petersen, Eugen. 1915. *Attische Tragödie als Bild- und Bühnenkunst.* Bonn: Cohen.

Petruzzelis, Nicola. 1965. "Euripide e la sofistica." *Dioniso* 39: 356 – 79.

Piatkowski, Adelina. 1981. "La description de la figure humaine dans le drame grec du IV-ème siècle av. n. ère." *Philologus* 125: 201 – 10.

Pickard-Cambridge, Arthur. 1968. *The Dramatic Festivals of Athens.* 2d edn., rev. John Gould & D. M. Lewis. London: Oxford Univ. Pr.

Pigeaud, J. 1976. "Euripide et la connaissance de soi: Quelques réflexions sur *Hippolyte* 73 à 82 et 373 à 430." *LEC* 44: 3 – 24.

Podlecki, A. J. 1980. "Festivals and Flattery: The Early Greek Tyrants as Patrons of Poetry." *Athenaeum* 58: 371 – 95.

Poggioli, Renato. 1968. *The Theory of the Avant-Garde.* Trans. Gerald Fitzgerald. Cambridge, Mass.: Harvard Univ. Pr.

Pohlenz, Max. 1956. "Furcht und Mitleid? Ein Nachwort." *Hermes* 84: 49 – 74.

Pohlenz, Max. 1954. *Die griechische Tragödie.* 2 Vols. 2d edn. Göttingen: Vandenhoeck & Ruprecht. First published Leipzig: Teubner, 1930. Reviews: A. Körte, *PhW* 52 (1932) 35 – 42; I. Linforth, *CPh* 26 (1931) 207 – 9; A. Pickard-Cambridge, *CR* 45 (1931) 61 – 62. 2d edn.: R. Lattimore, *AJPh* 77 (1956) 197 – 202; A. Lesky, *Gnomon* 28 (1956) 22 – 30.

Pohlenz, Max. 1920. "Die Anfänge der griechischen Poetik." *NAWG* 42: 142 – 78. Repr. in *Kl. Schr.* 2, ed. H. Dörrie. Hildesheim: Olms, 1965.

Pomeroy, Sara. 1975. *Goddesses, Whores, Wives, and Slaves: Women in Classical Antiquity.* New York: Shocken.

Porson, Richard, ed. 1851. *Euripidis Tragoediae.* 3d edn. rev. J. Scholefield. Cambridge: Univ. Pr.

Porterfield, Amanda. 1980. *Feminine Spirituality in America: From Sarah Edwards to Martha Graham.* Philadelphia: Temple Univ. Pr.

Post, L. A. 1964. "Menander and the *Helen* of Euripides." *HSCPh* 68: 99 – 118.

Post, L. A. 1951. *From Homer to Menander: Forces in Greek Poetic Fiction.* Berkeley: Univ. of California Pr.

Prader, Florian. 1954. *Schiller und Sophokles.* Zürich: Atlantis.

Prato, Carlo. 1964. "Il contributo dei papiri al testo dei tragici greci." *SIFC* 36: 5 – 79.

Prato, Carlo. 1955. *Euripide nella critica di Aristofane.* Amici del libro 13. Galatina: Colonna.

Pucci, Pietro. 1980. *The Violence of Pity in Euripides' Medea.* Ithaca: Cornell Univ. Pr.

Pucci, Pietro. 1977. *Hesiod and the Language of Poetry.* Baltimore: Johns Hopkins Univ. Pr.

Pucci, Pietro. 1967. "Euripides *Heautontimoroumenos.*" *TAPA* 98: 365 – 71.

Pucci, Pietro. 1962. *Aristofane ed Euripide: Ricerche metriche e stilistiche. MAL* ser. 8a, 10:359, pp. 277 – 416.

Queck, G. A. 1844. "De Euripidis Electra." Diss. Jena.

Radt, S. L. 1973. "Zu Aischylos' *Agamemnon.*" *Mnemosyne* ser. 4, 26: 113–26.

Ramage, E. S. 1961. "An Early Trace of Socratic Dialogue." *AJPh* 82: 418–24.

Rankin, A. V. 1974. "Euripides' *Hippolytus*: A Psychopathological Hero." *Arethusa* 7: 71–94.

Raphael, D. D. 1960. *The Paradox of Tragedy.* Bloomington: Indiana Univ. Pr.

Rawson, Elizabeth. 1970. "Family and Fatherland in Euripides' *Phoenissae.*" *GRBS* 11: 109–27.

Reckford, K. J. 1974. "Phaedra and Pasiphae: The Pull Backward." *TAPA* 104: 307–28.

Reckford, K. J. 1968. "Medea's First Exit." *TAPA* 99: 329–59.

Reinhardt, Karl. 1957. "Die Sinneskrise bei Euripides." *Eranos* Jb. 26: 279–317. Repr. in *Tradition und Geist* (Ges. Schriften, 1960); and in Schwinge 1968.2, pp. 507–42.

Reinhardt, Karl. 1933. *Sophokles.* Frankfurt am Main: V. Klostermann. Eng. translation, by H. Harvey & D. Harvey, with intro. by H. Lloyd-Jones. New York: Barnes & Noble, 1979.

Reiss, T. J. 1980. *Tragedy and Truth: Studies in the Development of a Renaissance and Neoclassical Discourse.* New Haven: Yale Univ. Pr.

Ribbeck, Otto. 1885. "Zu Sophokles' und Euripides' *Elektra.*" *Leipziger Stud.* 8: 382–86.

Ridgway, B. S. 1981. *Fifth Century Styles in Greek Sculpture.* Princeton: Princeton Univ. Pr.

Rist, J. M. 1963. "Plotinus and the *Daimonion* of Socrates." *Phoenix* 17: 13–24.

Ritoók, Zigismond. 1973. "Politische und humanistische Elemente im *Philoktet* des Sophokles." In Hofmann & Kuch 1973, pp. 65–78.

Rivier, André. 1975. *Essai sur le tragique d'Euripide.* 2d edn. Paris: Boccard. First published Lausanne: Rouge, 1944.

Rivier, André. 1973. "En marge d'*Alceste* et de quelques interprétations récentes, II." *MH* 30: 130–43.

Rivier, André. 1972. "En marge d'*Alceste* et de quelques interprétations récentes, I." *MH* 29: 124–40.

Rivier, André. 1958. "Euripide et Pasiphaé." In *Lettres d' Occident,* Festschr. A. Bonnard. Ed. G. Anex & A. Bonnard, pp. 51–74. Neuchâtel: Ed. de la Baconnière.

Robert, Carl. 1915. *Oidipous: Geschichte eines poetischen Stoffs im griechischen Altertum.* Berlin: Weidmann.

Robert, Carl. 1881. *Bild und Lied: Archäologische Beiträge zur Geschichte der griechischen Heldensage.* Philol. Unters. 5. Berlin: Weidmann.

Robertson, Martin. 1970. "Ibycus: Polycrates, Troilus, Polyxena." *BICS* 17: 11–15.

Robinson, D. M. 1946. *Excavations at Olynthus XII: Domestic and Public Architecture.* Baltimore: Johns Hopkins Univ. Pr.

Rohde, Erwin. 1903. *Psyche: Seelenkult und Unsterblichkeitsglaube der Griechen.* 2 vols. 3d edn. Tübingen: Mohr.

Rohdich, Hermann. 1968. *Die euripideische Tragödie: Untersuchungen zu ihrer Tragik.* Heidelberg: Winter. Reviews: K. Matthiessen, *Gymnasium* 77 (1970)

237–40; G. Müller, *Gnomon* 46 (1974) 328–41; K. J. Reckford, *CW* 62 (1968) 279; J. R. Wilson, *CJ* 65 (1969–70) 327–28.

Romilly, Jacqueline de. 1976. "L'excuse de l'invincible amour dans la tragédie grecque." In Kamerbeek 1976, pp. 309–21.

Romilly, Jacqueline de. 1972. "L'assemblée du peuple dans l'*Oreste* d'Euripide." In Cataudella 1972, pp. 237–51.

Romilly, Jacqueline de. 1967. "The *Phoenician Women* of Euripides: Topicality in Greek Tragedy." *Bucknell Rev.* 15: 108–32.

Romilly, Jacqueline de. 1965. "Les *Phéniciennes* d'Euripide: Ou l'actualité dans la tragédie grecque." *RPh* 39: 28–47.

Romilly, Jacqueline de. 1963. "Le thème du bonheur dans les *Bacchantes*." *REG* 76: 361–80.

Romilly, Jacqueline de. 1961. *L'évolution du pathétique d'Eschyle à Euripide*. Paris: Les Belles Lettres.

Ronnet, Gilberte. 1975. "L'ironie d'Euripide dans *Électre* (vers 513 à 546)." *REG* 88: 63–70.

Ronnet, Gilberte. 1970. "Réflexions sur la date des deux *Électres*." *REG* 83: 309–32.

Rorty, Richard. 1979. *Philosophy and the Mirror of Nature*. Princeton: Princeton Univ. Pr.

Rosen, Charles & Henri Zurner. 1982. "What Is, and Is Not, Realism?" *New York Rev. of Books*, Feb. 18, pp. 21–26.

Rosivach, V. J. 1975. "The First Stasimon of the *Hecuba*, 444ff." *AJPh* 96: 349–62.

Rosler, Wolfgang. 1980. *Dichter und Gruppe: Eine Untersuchung zu den Bedingungen und zur historischen Funktion früher griechischer Lyrik am Beispiel Alkaios*. Munich: Fink.

Rössler, Detlev. 1981. "Handwerker." In Welskopf 1981, 3:193–268.

Rostagni, Augusto, ed. 1945. *Aristotle: Poetica*. 2d edn. Turin: Chiantore.

Roux, Jeanne. 1970. *Euripide: Les Bacchantes*. Vol. 2. Paris: Les Belles Lettres.

Russell, A. G. 1936. "Euripides and the New Comedy." *G&R* 6: 103–10.

Russo, C. F. 1960. "Euripide e i concorsi tragici lenaici." *MH* 17: 165–70.

Rutherford, R. B. 1982. "Tragic Form and Feeling in the *Iliad*." *JHS* 102: 145–60.

Saïd, Suzanne. 1978. *La faute tragique*. Paris: Maspero.

Sale, William. 1977. *Existentialism and Euripides: Sickness, Tragedy, and Divinity in the Medea, the Hippolytus, and the Bacchae*. Berwick, Austr.: Aureal.

Sansone, David. 1978. "A Problem in Euripides' *Iphigenia in Tauris*." *RhM* 121: 35–47.

Savage, C. A. 1907. "The Attic Family: A Sociological and Legal Study, Based Chiefly on the Works of the Attic Orators." Diss. Johns Hopkins.

Schachermeyr, Fritz. 1972. "Zur Familie des Euripides." *WS* Beiheft. 5: 306–26.

Schadewaldt, Wolfgang. 1970. "Sophokles und Athen." In *Hellas und Hesperien: Gesammelte Schriften zur antike und zur neueren Literatur*. 2d edn. Vol. 1, pp. 370–85. Zürich: Artemis Verl. First published 1935.

Schadewaldt, Wolfgang. 1955. "Furcht und Mitleid? Zur Deutung des aristotelischen Tragödiensatzes." *Hermes* 83: 129–71.

Schadewaldt, Wolfgang. 1952. "Zu einem florentiner Papyrusbruchstück aus dem *Alkmeon in Psophis* des Euripides." *Hermes* 80: 46–66. Repr. in Schwinge 1968.2, pp. 156–78; and *Hellas und Hesperien* (Ges. Schriften, 2d edn., 1960) vol. 1, pp. 516–34.

Schadewaldt, Wolfgang. 1926. *Monolog und Selbstgespräch; Untersuchungen zur Formgeschichte der griechischen Tragödie.* Neue Philol. Unters. 2. Berlin: Weidmann. Reviews: A. Körte, *PhW* 47 (1927) 1–7; J. T. Sheppard, *CR* 41 (1927) 177–78; U. v. Wilamowitz, *DLZ* 47 (1926) 851, cited in 1935, pp. 464–66.

Schaps, David. 1979. *The Economic Rights of Women in Ancient Greece.* Edinburgh: Edinburgh Univ. Pr.

Schaps, David. 1977. "The Woman Least Mentioned: Etiquette and Women's Names." *CQ* 27: 323–30.

Schein, S. L. 1975. "Mythical Illusion and Historical Reality in Euripides' *Orestes.*" *WS* n.F. 9: 49–66.

Scheler, Max. 1923. *Vom Umsturz der Werte: Schriften zur Soziologie und Weltanschauungslehre.* Vol. 1. Leipzig: Neue Geist.

Schiassi, Giuseppe. 1956. "Note critiche ed esegetiche all' *Elettra* di Euripide." *RIFC* n.s. 34: 244–65.

Schiller, Friedrich. 1962. "Über naive und sentimentalische Dichtung." In *Werke,* ed. H. Koopman & B. v. Wiese. Nationalausgabe, Vol. 20. Philosophische Schr., T. 1, pp. 413–503. Weimar: Bölhaus. First published 1795–96.

Schlegel, A. W. 1884. *Vorlesungen über schöne Literatur und Kunst.* 2d edn. Teil 1. Deutsche Litteraturdenkmale des 18. und 19. Jahrhunderts. Vol.18. Heilbronn: Henninger.

Schlegel, A. W. 1846. *Vorlesungen über schöne Literatur und Kunst.* In *Sämtliche Werke,* ed. E. Bocking. Vol. 5. Leipzig: Weidmann. Translations: Anon., *Cours de littérature dramatique,* 2 vols. (Paris: Paschoud, 1814). John Black, *A Course of Lectures on Dramatic Art and Literature.* (Philadelphia: Hogan & Thompson, 1833).

Schlegel, A. W. 1807. *Comparaison entre la Phèdre de Racine et celle d' Euripide.* Paris: Tourneisen.

Schlegel, Friedrich. 1979. *Studien des klassischen Altertums.* Kritische Friedrich-Schlegel-Ausgabe 1.1, ed. Ernst Behler. Paderborn: Schöningh.

Schlegel, Friedrich. 1958. *Wissenschaft der europäischen Literatur: Vorlesungen, Aufsätze und Fragmente aus der Zeit von 1795–1804.* Kritische Friedrich-Schlegel-Ausgabe 11.2, ed. Ernst Behler. Paderborn: Schöningh.

Schlesinger, A. C. 1963. *Boundaries of Dionysus: Athenian Foundations for the Theory of Tragedy.* Martin Classical Lectures 17. Cambridge, Mass.: Harvard Univ. Pr.

Schlesinger, A. C. 1937. "Two Notes on Euripides." *CPh* 32: 67–70.

Schlesinger, Eilhard. 1966. "Zu Euripides' *Medea.*" *Hermes* 94: 26–53. Trans. in *Twentieth Century Views of Euripides,* ed. E. Segal, pp. 70–89. Englewood Cliffs, N.J.: Prentice Hall, 1968.

Schmidt, E. G. 1976. "Das Menschenbild bei Aischylos und Sophokles." In R. Müller 1976, pp. 93–135.

Schmidt, Margot. 1967. "*Herakliden*: Illustrationen zu Tragödien des Euripides und Sophokles." In *Gestalt und Geschichte, Festschr.* K. Schefold, ed. P. von der Mühll et al., pp. 174–85. Bern: Francke.

Schmidt, Wieland. 1963. "Der Deus ex Machina bei Euripides." Diss. Tübingen.

Schmitt, Arbogast. 1977. "Zur Charakterdarstellung des Hippolytos im *Hippolytos* von Euripides." *WJA* 3: 17–42.

Schmitt, Johanna. 1921. *Freiwilliger Opfertod bei Euripides: Ein Beitrag zu seiner dramatischen Technik.* Giessen: Töpelmann.

Schoell, M. 1824. *Histoire de la littérature grecque profane.* Vol. 2. 2d edn. Paris: Libr. de Gide Fils.

Schottländer, Rudolf. 1982. "Fortschrittsverkündung oder Adelsrhetorik? Zu einer euripideischen Maxime." *Hermes* 110: 490–94.

Schuster, Heinrich. 1954. "Interpretationen der Hekabe des Euripides." Diss. Tübingen.

Schwartz, Edw., ed. 1887. *Scholia in Euripidem.* Vol. 1 (incl. *Genos Euripidou*). Berlin: G. Reimer.

Schwarz, Alfred. 1978. *From Büchner to Beckett: Dramatic Theory and the Modes of Tragic Drama.* Athens: Ohio Univ. Pr.

Schwinge, E.-R. 1981. "Griechische Poesie und die Lehre von der Gattungstrinität in der Moderne: Zur gattungstheoretischen Problematik antiker Literatur." *A&A* 27: 130–62.

Schwinge, E.-R. 1970. "Zwei sprachliche Bemerkungen zu Euripides' *Alkestis.*" *Glotta* 47: 36–39.

Schwinge, E.-R. 1969. "Abermals: Die *Elektren.*" *RhM* 112: 1–13.

Schwinge, E.-R. 1968.1. *Die Verwendung der Stichomythie in den Dramen des Euripides.* Heidelberg: Winter. Review: W. Calder, *CW* 63 (1969) 19–20.

Schwinge, E.-R., ed. 1968.2 *Euripides.* Wege der Forschung 89. Darmstadt: Wissenschaftliche Buchgesellschaft.

Schwinge, E.-R. 1962. *Die Stellung der Trachinierinnen im Werk des Sophokles.* Hypomnemata 1. Göttingen: Vandenhoeck & Rupprecht.

Scodel, Ruth. 1979. "ΑΔΜΗΤΟΥ ΛΟΓΟΣ and the *Alcestis.*" *HSCPh* 83: 51–62.

Scodel, Ruth. 1977. "Apollo's Perfidy: *Iliad* Ω 59–63." *HSCPh* 81: 55–57.

Seaford, Richard. 1982. "The Date of Euripides' *Cyclops.*" *JHS* 102: 161–72.

Seaford, Richard. 1981. "Dionysiac Drama and the Dionysiac Mysteries." *CQ* 31: 252–75.

Seeck, G. A., ed. 1979. *Das griechische Drama.* Darmstadt: Wissenschaftliche Buchgesellschaft.

Seeck, G. A. 1969. "Rauch im *Orestes* des Euripides." *Hermes* 97: 9–22.

Segal, C. P. 1982. *Dionysiac Poetics and Euripides' Bacchae.* Princeton: Princeton Univ. Pr.

Segal, C. P. 1981. *Tragedy and Civilization: An Interpretation of Sophocles.* Martin Class. Lectures 26. Cambridge, Mass.: Harvard Univ. Pr.

Segal, C. P. 1979. "Solar Imagery and Tragic Heroism in Euripides' *Hippolytus.*" In Knox 1979.1, pp. 151–61.

Segal, C. P. 1978. "The Magic of Orpheus and the Ambiguities of Language." *Ramus* 7: 106–42.

Segal, C. P. 1977. "Sophocles' *Trachiniae* : Myth, Poetry, and Heroic Values." In Gould & Herington 1977: pp. 99 – 158.

Segal, C. P. 1972.1. "Curse and Oath in Euripides' *Hippolytus*." *Ramus* 1: 165 – 80.

Segal, C. P. 1972.2. "Les deux mondes de l'*Hélène* d'Euripide." *REG* 85: 293 – 311.

Segal, C. P. 1971. "The Two Worlds of Euripides' *Helen*." *TAPA* 102: 553 – 614.

Segal, C. P. 1970.1. "Shame and Purity in Euripides' *Hippolytus*." *Hermes* 98: 278 – 99.

Segal, C. P. 1970.2. "Euripides' *Hippolytus* and Scheler's 'Phenomenon of the Tragic.'" *Arethusa* 3: 129 – 46.

Segal, C. P. 1970.3. "Hippolytus 'The Great': *Hipp.* 1465 – 66." *AC* 39: 519 – 21.

Segal, C. P. 1969. "Euripides, *Hippolytus* 108 – 112: Tragic Irony and Tragic Justice." *Hermes* 97: 297 – 305.

Segal, C. P. 1966. "The *Electra* of Sophocles." *TAPA* 97: 473 – 545.

Segal, C. P. 1965. "The Tragedy of the *Hippolytus* : The Waters of Ocean and the Untouched Meadow." *HSCPh* 70: 117 – 69.

Segal, C. P. 1962. "Gorgias and the Psychology of the *Logos*." *HSCPh* 66: 99 – 155.

Seidensticker, Bernd. 1978. "Comic Elements in Euripides' *Bacchae*." *AJPh* 99: 303 – 20.

Seta, Alessandro Della. 1930. *Il nudo nell' arte: I, Arte antica*. Milan: Bestetti & Tumminelli.

Sewall, R. B. 1980. *The Vision of Tragedy*. 2d edn. New Haven: Yale Univ. Pr.

Sharpe, R. B. 1959. *Irony in the Drama: An Essay on Impersonation, Shock, and Catharsis*. Chapel Hill: Univ. of North Carolina Pr.

Shelton, Jo-Ann. 1979. "Structural Unity and the Meaning of Euripides' *Herakles*." *Eranos* 77: 101 – 10.

Sheppard, J. T., ed. 1924. *Euripides' Hecuba: Partly in the Original and Partly in Translation*. Oxford: Clarendon Pr.

Sheppard, J. T. 1919. "Admetus, Verrall, and Professor Myres." *JHS* 39: 37 – 47.

Sheppard, J. T. 1918. "The *Electra* of Euripides." *CR* 32: 137 – 41.

Sheppard, J. T. 1917. "ΤΥΡΑΝΝΟΣ, ΚΕΡΔΟΣ, and the Modest Measure in Three Plays of Euripides." *CQ* 11: 3 – 10.

Sheppard, J. T. 1916. "The Formal Beauty of the *Hercules Furens*." *CQ* 10: 72 – 79.

Shey, H. J. 1976. "Tyrtaeus and the Art of Propaganda." *Arethusa* 9: 5 – 28.

Shipp, G. P. 1978. *Nomos "Law"*. Austral. Acad. of the Humanities, Monogr. 4. Sydney: Sydney Univ. Pr.

Shisler, F. L. 1945. "The Use of Stage Business to Portray Emotion in Greek Tragedy." *AJPh* 66: 377 – 97.

Shklovskij, Viktor. 1969. "Die Kunst als Verfahren." In Striedter 1969, pp. 3 – 35. First published 1916.

Sicking, C. M. J. 1967. "*Alceste* : tragédie d'amour ou tragédie du devoir?" *Dioniso* 41: 155 – 74 (includes discussion following).

Silk M. S., & J. P. Stern. 1981. *Nietzsche on Tragedy*. Cambridge: Univ. Pr.

Sisti, F. 1979. "Su due hypotheseis papiracee." *BollClass* 27: 105–11.

Smith, J. L. 1973. *Melodrama*. The Critical Idiom. 28. London: Methuen.

Smith, W. D. 1979. "Iphigeneia in Love." In Knox 1979.1, pp. 173–80.

Smith, W. D. 1967.1. "Expressive Form in Euripides' *Suppliants*." *HSCPh* 71: 151–70.

Smith, W. D. 1967.2. "Disease in Euripides' *Orestes*." *Hermes* 95: 291–307.

Smith, W. D. 1960.1. "The Ironic Structure in *Alcestis*." *Phoenix* 14: 127–45.

Smith, W. D. 1960.2. "Staging in the Central Scene of the *Hippolytus*." *TAPA* 91: 162–77.

Smith, W. D. 1957. "Dramatic Structure and Technique in Euripides' *Suppliants*." Diss. Summary. *HSCPh* 62: 152–54.

Snell, Bruno. 1971. *Szenen aus griechischen Dramen*. Berlin: De Gruyter.

Snell, Bruno. 1968.1. "Euripides' *Aulische Iphigenie*." In Schwinge 1968.2, pp. 493–506. First published in *Aischylos und das Handeln im Drama, Philologus Supplbnd*. 20.1, pp. 148–60 (1928).

Snell, Bruno. 1968.2. "Aristophanes und die Aesthetik." In Schwinge 1968.2: pp. 36–59. Repr. in *Entdeckung des Geistes,* 3d edn. 1955, pp. 161–83. First published *Antike* 13 (1937) 249–71.

Snell, Bruno. 1948. "Das frühste Zeugnis über Sokrates." *Philologus* 97: 125–34.

Solmsen, Friedrich. 1975. *Intellectual Experiments of the Greek Enlightenment*. Princeton: Princeton Univ. Pr.

Solmsen, Friedrich. 1973. "'Bad Shame' and Related Problems in Phaedra's Speech (Eur. *Hipp*. 380–388)." *Hermes* 101: 420–25.

Solmsen, Friedrich. 1967. "Electra and Orestes: Three Recognitions in Greek Tragedy." *Mededelingen* (K. Akad. van Wetensch., Amsterdam) n.s. 30: 31–62.

Solmsen, Friedrich. 1934.1. "Euripides' *Ion* im Vergleich mit anderen Tragödien." *Hermes* 69: 390–419. Repr. in Schwinge 1968.2, pp. 428–68.

Solmsen, Friedrich. 1934.2. "Ὄνομα and Πρᾶγμα in Euripides' *Helen*." *CR* 48: 119–21.

Solmsen, Friedrich. 1932. "Zur Gestaltung des Intriguenmotivs in den Tragödien des Sophokles und Euripides." *Philologus* 87: 1–17. Repr. in Schwinge 1968.2, pp. 326–44.

Sorum, C. E. 1978. "Monsters and the Family: The Exodos of Sophocles' *Trachiniae*." *GRBS* 19: 59–73.

Sourvinou, Christiane. 1971. "Aristophanes, *Lysistrata* 641–647." *CQ* n.s. 21: 339–42.

Soury, Guy. 1943. "Euripide rationaliste et mystique, d'après *Hippolyte*." *REG* 56: 29–52.

Spira, Andreas. 1960. *Untersuchungen zum Deus ex Machina bei Sophokles und Euripides*. Kallmünz: Lassleben. Reviews: A. P. Burnett, *CPh* 57 (1962) 64–67; W. Fauth, *Gymnasium* 68 (1961) 164–66; H. van Looy, *AC* 30 (1961) 553–55; H. Strohm, *Gnomon* 34 (1962) 344–48.

Spranger, J. A. 1927.1. "The Meaning of the *Hippolytus* of Euripides." *CQ* 21: 18–29.

Spranger, J. A. 1927.2. "The Problem of the *Hecuba*." *CQ* 21: 155–58.

Spranger, J. A. 1925. "The Political Element in the *Heracleidae* of Euripides." *CQ* 19: 117–28.

Stanley-Porter, D. P. 1973. "Mute Actors in the Tragedies of Euripides." *BICS* 20: 68–93.

States, B. O. 1971. *Irony and Drama: A Poetics*. Ithaca: Cornell Univ. Pr.

Steidle, Wolf. 1968. *Studien zum antiken Drama: Unter besonderer Berücksichtigung des Bühnenspiels*. Munich: Fink.

Steidle, Wolf. 1966. "Zur *Hekabe* des Euripides." *WS* 79: 133–42.

Steiger, Hugo. 1925. "Euripides, ein antiker Ibsen?" *Philologus* 80: 113–35.

Steiger, Hugo. 1912. *Euripides: Seine Dichtung und seine Persönlichkeit*. Das Erbe der Alten 5. Leipzig: Dieterich. Review: W. Kranz, *DLZ* 34 (1913) 477–79.

Steiger, Hugo. 1900. "Warum schrieb Euripides seine *Troerinnen*?" *Philologus* 13: 362–99.

Steiger, Hugo. 1898. "Wie entstand der *Orestes* des Euripides?" *Programm* k. h. Gymnasium. Augsburg: Pfeiffer.

Steiger, Hugo. 1897. "Warum schrieb Euripides seine *Elektra?*" *Philologus* n.F. 10: 561–600.

Stevens, P. T. 1976. *Colloquial Expressions in Euripides*. Hermes Einzelschr. 38.

Stevens, P. T. 1956. "Euripides and the Athenians." *JHS* 76: 87–94.

Stevens, P. T. 1946. "Euripides, *Electra* 567–8 and *Alkestis* 1126–7." *CR* 60: 101–2.

Stinton, T. C. W. 1976.1. "Iphigenia and the Bears of Brauron." *CQ* n.s. 26: 11–13.

Stinton, T. C. W. 1976.2. "'Si Credere Dignum Est': Some Expressions of Disbelief in Euripides and Others." *PCPhS* n.s. 22: 60–89.

Stinton, T. C. W. 1975. "*Hamartia* in Aristotle and Greek Tragedy." *CQ* n.s. 25: 221–54.

Stoessl, Franz. 1966. "Die Palamedestragödien der drei grossen Tragiker." *WS* 79: 93–101.

Stoessl, Franz. 1962. "Zur Iris-Lyssa-Szene in Euripides' *Herakles*." *Serta Philol. Aenipontana* 7–8: 117–18.

Stoessl, Franz. 1956.1. "Die *Elektra* des Euripides." *RhM* n.F. 99: 47–92.

Stoessl, Franz. 1956.2. "Die *Herakliden* des Euripides." *Philologus* 100: 207–34.

Straat, E. 1959. "Dupliek." *Hermeneus* 31: 138–42.

Striedter, Jurij, ed. 1969. *Texte der russischen Formalisten*. Bd. 1. Theorie und Gesch. der Literatur und der schönen Kunst, Texte und Abhandl., Bd. 6. Munich: Fink.

Strohm, Hans. 1981. "Zum Problem der Einheit des euripideischen Bühnenwerks." *WS* 15: 135–55.

Strohm, Hans. 1977. "Zur Gestaltung euripideischer Prologreden." *GB* 6: 113–32.

Strohm, Hans. 1968–77. "Forschungsbericht: Die griechische Tragödie." Fortsetzungen 8–12. *AAHG*. See Lesky 1948–67.

Strohm, Hans. 1968. "Euripides' *Iphigenie im Taurerland*." In Schwinge 1968.2: pp. 373–91. First published as preface to edn. 1949. Munich: Oldenbourg.

Strohm, Hans. 1959. "Beobachtungen zum *Rhesos*." *Hermes* 87: 257–74.

Strohm, Hans. 1957. *Euripides: Interpretationen zur dramatischen Form.* Zetemata 15. Munich: Beck. Reviews: P. N. Boulter, *AJPh* 79 (1958) 435 – 37; A. M. Dale, *JHS* 79 (1959) 165 – 66; G. Zuntz, *Gnomon* 31 (1959) 404 – 11.

Strohm, Hans. 1949 – 50. "Trug und Täuschung in der euripideischen Dramatik." *WJA* 4: 140 – 56.

Strycker, E. de. 1950. "Les témoignages historiques sur Socrate." Festschr. H. Grégoire. *Annuaire* (Ist. Philol. de Bruxelles) 10: 199 – 230.

Stuart, D. C. 1918. "Foreshadowing and Suspense in the Euripidean Prologue." *Stud. Philol.* 15: 295 – 306.

Stumpo, Beniamino. 1960. "L'*Alcesti* di Euripide." *Dioniso* 34: 105 – 23.

Styan, J. L. 1968. *The Dark Comedy: The Development of Modern Comic Tragedy.* 2d edn. Cambridge: Univ. Pr.

Swinburne, A. C. 1926. "Recollections of Professor Jowett." In *The Complete Works,* ed. E. Gosse & T. J. Wise. Vol. 5, Prose Works, pp. 243 – 59. London: Heinemann. First published 1893.

Szlezák, T. A. 1981.1. "Bemerkungen zur Diskussion um Sophokles, *Antigone* 904 – 920." *RhM* 124: 108 – 42.

Szlezák, T. A. 1981.2. "Sophokles' *Elektra* und das Problem des ironischen Dramas." *MH* 38: 1 – 21.

Szondi, Peter. 1977. "Theorie des modernen Dramas." In *Schriften* I., ed. W. Fiektau. Frankfurt am Main: Suhrkamp. First published 1956.

Taplin, Oliver. 1978. *Greek Tragedy in Action.* Berkeley: Univ. of California Pr.

Taplin, Oliver. 1977. *The Stagecraft of Aeschylus.* Oxford: Clarendon Pr.

Taplin, Oliver. 1972. "Aeschylean Silences and Silences in Aeschylus." *HSCPh* 76: 57 – 98.

Tarkow, T. A. 1981. "The Scar of Orestes: Observations on a Euripidean Innovation." *RhM* n.F. 124: 143 – 53.

Tarkow, T. A. 1979. "Electra's Role in the Opening Scene of the *Choephoroi.*" *Eranos* 77: 11 – 21.

Tedeschi, Gennaro. 1978. "Euripide nemico del popolo?" *QFC* 1: 27 – 48.

Terzaghi, Nicola. 1937. "Finali e prologhi Euripidei." *Dioniso* 6: 304 – 13.

Theiler, Willy. 1966. "Die ewigen *Elektren.*" *WS* 79: 102 – 12.

Thompson, A. R. 1946. *The Anatomy of Drama.* 2d edn. Berkeley: Univ. of California Pr.

Thompson, A. R. 1948. *The Dry Mock: A Study of Irony in Drama.* Berkeley: Univ. of California Pr.

Tierney, Michael, ed. 1946. *Euripides: Hecuba.* Dublin: Browne & Nolan.

Todorov, Tzvetan. 1978. *Les genres du discours.* Paris: Seuil.

Treves, Piero. 1930. "Interpretazioni dell'arte e del pensiero di Euripide." *RIFC* n.s. 8: 306 – 10.

Tschiedel, H. J. 1969. *Phaidra und Hippolytos: Variationen eines tragischen Konfliktes.* Erlangen: Nürnberg.

Tuilier, André. 1968. *Recherches critiques sur la tradition du texte d' Euripide.* Paris: Klincksieck.

Turato, Fabio. 1974. "L'*Ippolyto* di Euripide tra realtà e suggestioni di fuga." *BIFG* 1: 136 – 63.

Turner, E. G., et al. 1962. *Oxyrynchus Papyri 27*. Edinburgh: Clark. Review: H. Lloyd-Jones, *Gnomon* 35 (1963) 433 – 54.

Tynjanov, Jurij. 1969.1. "Über die literarische Evolution." In Striedter 1969, pp. 432 – 61. First published 1927. Eng. Trans. in Matejka & Pomorska 1971, pp. 66 – 78.

Tynjanov, Jurij. 1969.2. "Das literarische Faktum." In Striedter 1969, pp. 392 – 431. First published 1924.

Tynjanov, Jurij. 1969.3. "Dostoevskij und Gogol." In Striedter 1969: pp. 301 – 71. First published 1921.

Vahlen, Johannes. 1908. *Opuscula Academica*. Vol. 1. Leipzig: Teubner.

Vahlen, Johannes. 1891. "Zu Sophokles' und Euripides' *Elektra*." *Hermes* 26: 351 – 65.

Vaio, John. 1964. "The New Fragments of Euripides' Oedipus." *GRBS* 5: 43 – 55.

Valckenaer, L. C. 1767. *Diatribe in Euripidis Perditorum Dramatum Reliquias*. Leipzig: Luzac & Le Mair.

Valgiglio, Ernesto. 1966. *Il tema della morte in Euripide*. Turin: Bibl. d. Riv. d. stud. class.

Valgiglio, Ernesto, ed. 1957.1. *L'Ippolito di Euripide*. Turin: Ruata.

Valgiglio, Ernesto. 1957.2. "L'*Iphigenia in Aulide* di Euripide." *RSC* 5: 47 – 72.

Vellacott, Philip. 1975. *Ironic Drama: A Study of Euripides' Method and Meaning*. Cambridge: Univ. Pr.

Vermeule, E. & S. Chapman. 1971. "A Protoattic Human Sacrifice?" *AJA* 75: 285 – 93.

Vernant, J.-P. 1982. "La belle mort et le cadavre outragé." In *La mort, les morts, dans les sociétés anciennes*, ed. G. Gnoli & J.-P. Vernant, pp. 45 – 76. Cambridge & Paris: Cambridge Univ. Pr. & Edn. de la Maison des Sciences de l'Homme.

Vernant, J.-P. 1968. "Le moment historique de la tragédie en Grèce: Quelques conditions sociales et psychologiques." In *Antiquitas Graeco-Romana ac Tempora Nostra*. Acta Congr. Int., ed. J. Burian and L. Widman, pp. 246 – 250. Prague: Academia. Repr. in 1972, pp. 1 – 17.

Vernant, J.-P. & Pierre Vidal-Naquet. 1972. *Mythe et tragédie en Grèce ancienne*. Paris: Maspero.

Verrall, A. W. 1913. *Collected Literary Essays, Classical and Modern*, ed. M. A. Bayfield & J. D. Duff (includes "Memoir" by Bayfield). Cambridge: Univ. Pr.

Verrall, A. W. 1905. *Essays on Four Plays of Euripides: Andromache, Helen, Heracles, Orestes*. Cambridge: Univ. Pr. Review: Wilhelm Nestle, *WklPh* 23 (1906) 617 – 23.

Verrall, A. W. 1895. *Euripides the Rationalist: A Study in the History of Art and Religion*. Cambridge: Univ. Pr.

Verrall, A. W. 1890. *The Ion of Euripides*. Cambridge: Univ. Pr.

Veyne, Paul. 1983. *Les grecs, ont-ils cru à leur mythes? Essai sur l'imagination constituante*. Paris: Seuil.

Vicenzi, Otto. 1960. "Alkestis und Admetos: Versuch einer Euripides-Interpretation." *Gymnasium* 67: 517 – 33.

Vickers, Brian. 1973. *Toward Greek Tragedy: Drama, Myth, Society*. London: Longman.

Vögler, Armin. 1967. *Vergleichende Studien zur sophokleischen und euripideischen Elektra.* Heidelberg: Winter. Reviews: H. Lloyd-Jones, *CR* 19 (1969) 36–38; K. Matthiessen, *Gymnasium* 77 (1970) 236–37; R. Sprague, *CW* 61 (1967–68) 182–83; C. Segal, *CJ* 64 (1968) 137–40.

Walcot, Peter. 1976. *Greek Drama in Its Theatrical and Social Context.* Cardiff: Univ. of Wales Pr.

Waldock, A. J. A. 1951. *Sophocles the Dramatist.* Cambridge: Univ. Pr.

Walsh, G. B. 1977. "The First Stasimon in Euripides' *Electra.*" In Gould & Herington 1977, pp. 277–89.

Walters, H. B. 1898. "On Some Black-Figured Vases Recently Acquired by the British Museum, I." *JHS* 18: 281–301.

Wankel, Hermann, ed. 1976. *Demosthenes: Rede für Ktesiphon über den Kranz.* 2 Vols. Heidelberg: Winter.

Watts, H. H. 1963. "Myth and Drama." In Michel & Sewall 1963, pp. 83–105. First published *Cross Currents* 5 (1955) 154–70.

Webster, T. B. L. 1969. *An Introduction to Sophocles.* 2d edn. London: Methuen.

Webster, T. B. L. 1968. "Euripides, Traditionalist and Innovator." In *The Poetic Tradition,* ed. D. C. Allen & H. T. Rowell, pp. 27–45. Baltimore: Johns Hopkins Univ. Pr.

Webster, T. B. L. 1967. *The Tragedies of Euripides.* London: Methuen.

Webster, T. B. L. 1965. "The *Andromeda* of Euripides." *BICS* 12: 29–33.

Webster, T. B. L. 1954. "Fourth Century Tragedy and the *Poetics.*" *Hermes* 82: 294–308.

Wehrli, Fritz. 1946. "Der erhabene und der schlichte Stil in der poetisch-rhetorischen Theorie der Antike." In *Phyllobolia,* Festschr. P. Von der Mühll, ed. O. Gigon et al., pp. 9–34. Basel: Schwabe.

Weil, Henri. 1879. *Sept tragédies d'Euripide.* 2d edn. Paris: Hachette.

Weil, Simone. 1953. *La source grecque.* Paris: Gallimard.

Welskopf, E. C. 1981. *Soziale Typenbegriffe im alten Griechenland.* Vols. 3 & 4. Berlin: Akademie-Verl.

West, M. L. 1980. "Tragica 4." *BICS* 27: 9–22.

West, M. L. 1967. "Alkman and Pythagoras." *CQ* n.s. 17: 1–15.

Whiston, Robert, ed. 1859. *Demosthenes* Vol. 1. London: Bell.

Whitehorne, J. E. G. 1978. "The Ending of Euripides' *Electra.*" *RBPh* 56: 5–14.

Whitman, C. H. 1974. *Euripides and the Full Circle of Myth.* Cambridge, Mass.: Harvard Univ. Pr.

Whitman, C. H. 1958. *Homer and the Heroic Tradition.* Cambridge, Mass.: Harvard Univ. Pr.

Whitman, C. H. 1951. *Sophocles: A Study of Heroic Humanism.* Cambridge, Mass.: Harvard Univ. Pr.

Wilamowitz-Möllendorff, Tycho von. 1917. *Die dramatische Technik des Sophokles.* Philol. Unters. 22. Berlin: Weidmann.

Wilamowitz-Möllendorff, Ulrich von. 1935. *Kleine Schriften.* Vol. 1. Berlin: Weidmann.

Wilamowitz-Möllendorff, Ulrich von, ed. 1926.1. *Ion des Euripides.* Berlin: Weidmann.

Wilamowitz-Möllendorff, Ulrich von, trans. 1926.2. *Die griechischen Tragödien.* Vol. 1. Berlin: Weidmann. First published 1898.

Wilamowitz-Möllendorff, Ulrich von. 1922. "Die griechische Tragödie und ihre Dichter." *Die griechischen Tragödien.* Vol. 4.XIV, pp. 233–394. Berlin: Weidmann.

Wilamowitz-Möllendorff, Ulrich von. 1921. *Griechische Verskunst.* Berlin: Weidmann.

Wilamowitz-Möllendorff, Ulrich von. 1909. "Lesefrüchte, CXXIV." *Hermes* 44: 446–51.

Wilamowitz-Möllendorff, Ulrich von. 1907. *Einleitung in die griechische Tragödie.* Berlin: Weidmann.

Wilamowitz-Möllendorff, Ulrich von, trans. 1906.1. *Euripides: Alkestis. Die griechischen Tragödien.* Vol. IX. Berlin: Weidmann.

Wilamowitz-Möllendorff, Ulrich von, trans. 1906.2. *Euripides: Medea. Die griechischen Tragödien.* Vol. X. Berlin: Weidmann.

Wilamowitz-Möllendorff, Ulrich von, trans. 1906.3. *Euripides: Troerinnen. Die griechischen Tragödien.* Vol. XI. Berlin: Weidmann.

Wilamowitz-Möllendorff, Ulrich von et al. 1905. "Die griechische Literatur des Altertums." In *Die griechische und lateinische Literatur und Sprache,* ed. U. von Wilamowitz-Möllendorff et al. Kultur der Gegenwart I.8. Berlin: Teubner.

Wilamowitz-Möllendorff, Ulrich von. 1899. "Exkurse zum *Oedipus* des Sophokles." *Hermes* 34: 55–80.

Wilamowitz-Möllendorff, Ulrich von. 1895. *Euripides: Herakles.* 2 vols. 2d edn. Berlin: Weidmann. Repr. 3 vols. Bad Homburg: Gentner, 1959.

Wilamowitz-Möllendorff, Ulrich von. 1883. "Die beiden *Elektren.*" *Hermes* 18: 214–63.

Wilamowitz-Möllendorff, Ulrich von. 1875. *Analecta Euripidea.* Berlin: Bornträger.

Will, Frederic. 1959. "Remarks on Counterpoint Characterization in Euripides." *CJ* 55: 338–44.

Willem, A., ed. 1929. *Hécube.* 2d edn. Liége: Dessain.

Willink, C. W. 1971. "The Prologue of *Iphigenia at Aulis.*" *CQ* n.s. 21: 343–64.

Willink, C. W. 1968. "Some Problems of Text and Interpretation in the *Hippolytus.*" *CQ* 18: 11–43.

Winckelmann, J. J. 1925. *Kleine Schriften zur Geschichte der Kunst des Altertums.* Ed. H. Uhde-Bernays. Leipzig: Insel.

Winiarczyk, Marek. 1980. "Diagoras von Melos—Wahrheit und Legende, II." *Eos* 68: 51–75.

Winiarczyk, Marek. 1979. "Diagoras von Melos—Wahrheit und Legende, I." *Eos* 67: 191–213.

Winnington-Ingram, R. P. 1983. *Studies in Aeschylus.* Cambridge: Univ. Pr.

Winnington-Ingram, R. P. 1980. *Sophocles: An Interpretation.* Cambridge: Univ. Pr.

Winnington-Ingram, R. P. 1969. "Euripides: *Poiêtês Sophos.*" *Arethusa* 2: 127–42.

Winnington-Ingram, R. P. 1958. "*Hippolytus*: A Study in Causation." In *Entretiens* 1958, pp. 171–91.

Winnington-Ingram, R. P. 1948. *Euripides and Dionysus: An Interpretation of the Bacchae.* Cambridge: Univ. Pr. Reviews: J. A. Davison, *JHS* 67 (1947) 139; G. M. A. Grube, *Phoenix* 4 (1950) 115–17; G. Norwood, *AJPh* 70 (1949) 317–20.

Winnington-Ingram, R. P. 1937. "Euripides, *Electra* 1292–1307." *CR* 51: 51–52.

Wolff, Christian. 1965. "The Design and Myth in Euripides' *Ion.*" *HSCPh* 69: 169–94.

Wolterstorff, Rikard. 1891. *Sophoklis et Euripidis Electrae: Quo ordine sint compositae.* Jena: Pohl.

Woodbury, Leonard. 1970. "Sophocles Among the Generals." *Phoenix* 24: 209–24.

Woodbury, Leonard. 1968. "Pindar and the Mercenary Muse: *Isth.* 2. 1–13." *TAPA* 99: 527–42.

Xanthakis-Karamanos, Georgia. 1981. "The *Hector* of Astydamas: Reconstruction and Motifs." *MPhL* 4: 213–23.

Xanthakis-Karamanos, Georgia. 1979. "Deviations from Classical Treatments in Fourth-Century Tragedy." *BICS* 26: 99–103.

Zeitlin, F. I. 1980. "The Closet of Masks: Role-playing and Myth-making in the *Orestes* of Euripides." *Ramus* 9: 51–77.

Zeitlin, F. I. 1978. "The Dynamics of Misogyny: Myth and Myth-making in the *Oresteia.*" *Arethusa* 11: 149–84.

Zeitlin, F. I. 1970. "The Argive Festival of Hera and Euripides' *Electra.*" *TAPA* 101: 645–69.

Zielinski, Thaddeus. 1925. *Tragodumenon: Libri Tres.* Cracow: Pol. Acad.

Zielinski, Thaddeus. 1902. "Antike Humanität: Zweiter Aufsatz." *NJA* 5: 635–51.

Zimmern, A. E. 1931. *The Greek Commonwealth: Politics and Economics in Fifth-Century Athens.* 5th edn. Oxford: Clarendon Pr.

Zuntz, Günther. 1965. *An Inquiry into the Transmission of the Plays of Euripides.* Cambridge: Univ. Pr.

Zuntz, Günther. 1958.1. "Contemporary Politics in the Plays of Euripides." *Acta Congr. Madvigiani* 2, no.1: 155–68.

Zuntz, Günther. 1958.2. "On Euripides' *Helena*: Theology and Irony." In *Entretiens* 1958, pp. 201–27.

Zuntz, Günther. 1955.1. *The Political Plays of Euripides.* Manchester: Manchester Univ. Pr. Reviews: P. N. Boulter, *AJPh* 77 (1956) 425–28; H. Diller, *Gnomon* 32 (1960) 229–34; E. Delebecque *RPh* 30 (1956) 95–96; G. Italie, *Mnemosyne* ser. 4, 9 (1956) 162–63.

Zuntz, Günther. 1955.2. "Über Euripides' *Hiketiden.*" *MH* 12: 20–34. Repr. in Schwinge 1968.2, pp. 305–25.

Zuntz, Günther. 1933. "Die taurische Iphigenie des Euripides." *Antike* 9: 245–54.

Zürcher, Walter. 1947. Die Darstellung des Menschen im Drama des Euripides. Basel: Reinhardt. Reviews: G. Müller, *Gnomon* 21 (1949) 167–69; R. P. Winnington-Ingram, *CR* 63 (1949) 15–16.

Index

absurdity. *See* Reinhardt, K.

Achilleus, 168

actor, use of third, 58 *and n28*, 97, 98–99

Adkins, A., 169 *and n145*, 268, 296. *See also aretê; agathos anêr*

adultery: of divinities, 269 *and n166*, 273 *and n184*, 312 *and n156*

agalma (decoration/votive offering/statue), 160, 167–68 *and n41*, 198 *n73*

agathos anêr or agathos (good/capable man), 91, 140, 141, 183 *n6*, 265, 307, 314. *See also* Adkins, A.; *aretê*

agôn (struggle/contest/debate), 33 *n142*, 97 *and n11*, 142, 144 *and n56*, 148, 155, 157, 215, 221 *n178*, 328

aidôs (shame/modesty), 291, 292, 297–304 *passim*, 306

aischron (shameful/ugly), 131–80 *passim* (*see esp.* 138–41, 168–70), 195 *n59*, 301–3 *passim*

AISCHYLOS (AESCHYLUS)

Topics

choice or decision, 319; choral role in, 138, 238 *and n28*, 248–49 *n77*; Euripides, contrasts with, 60, 97; Euripides, parallels with, 21, 63, 90, 96, 97, 100–103 *passim*, 138, 238, 279, 318; female roles, 63, 75, 78, 81; position in canon, 59, 62–63, 125–26; rivalry with Sophokles, 58–59; revival of plays, 59; Sophokles, mentioned with, as representative of pre-Euripidean tragedy, 23, 42, 122, 236, 310, 319

Works

Agamemnon, 88, 160 *and n111*, 216 *and n152*, 238, 308 *n138*; *Choephoroi*, 37, 199–206 *passim*, 207, 217, 335, 336; *Danaides*, 86, 102; *Edonoi*, 279; *Eumenides*, 109 *and n63*, 155, 269; *Niobe*, 204; *Oresteia*, 59, 63, 102, 171 *and n154*; *Persians*, 102, 134–35; *Prometheus* (attributed to Aischylos), 117, 208 *n114*, 261 *and n131*, 269; *Seven Against Thebes*, 242, 294; *Xantrides*, 269 *n168*; Frag. 145M, 109 *n62*; Frag. 284M, 109 *and n62*

Aithiopis, 168 *and nn143–44*

aition (myth used to explain a current practice), 107

ambiguity in art, 118 *and nn4–5*

amoibaion (lyric duet or interchange), 123, 135, 223

anagnôrisis (scene of recognition), 22, 33,

374